McDOUGAL, LITTELL

LITERATURE
AND LANGUAGE

• GREEN LEVEL •

PORTRAIT OF NITO   Peter Hurd   Phoenix Art Museum,
museum purchase.

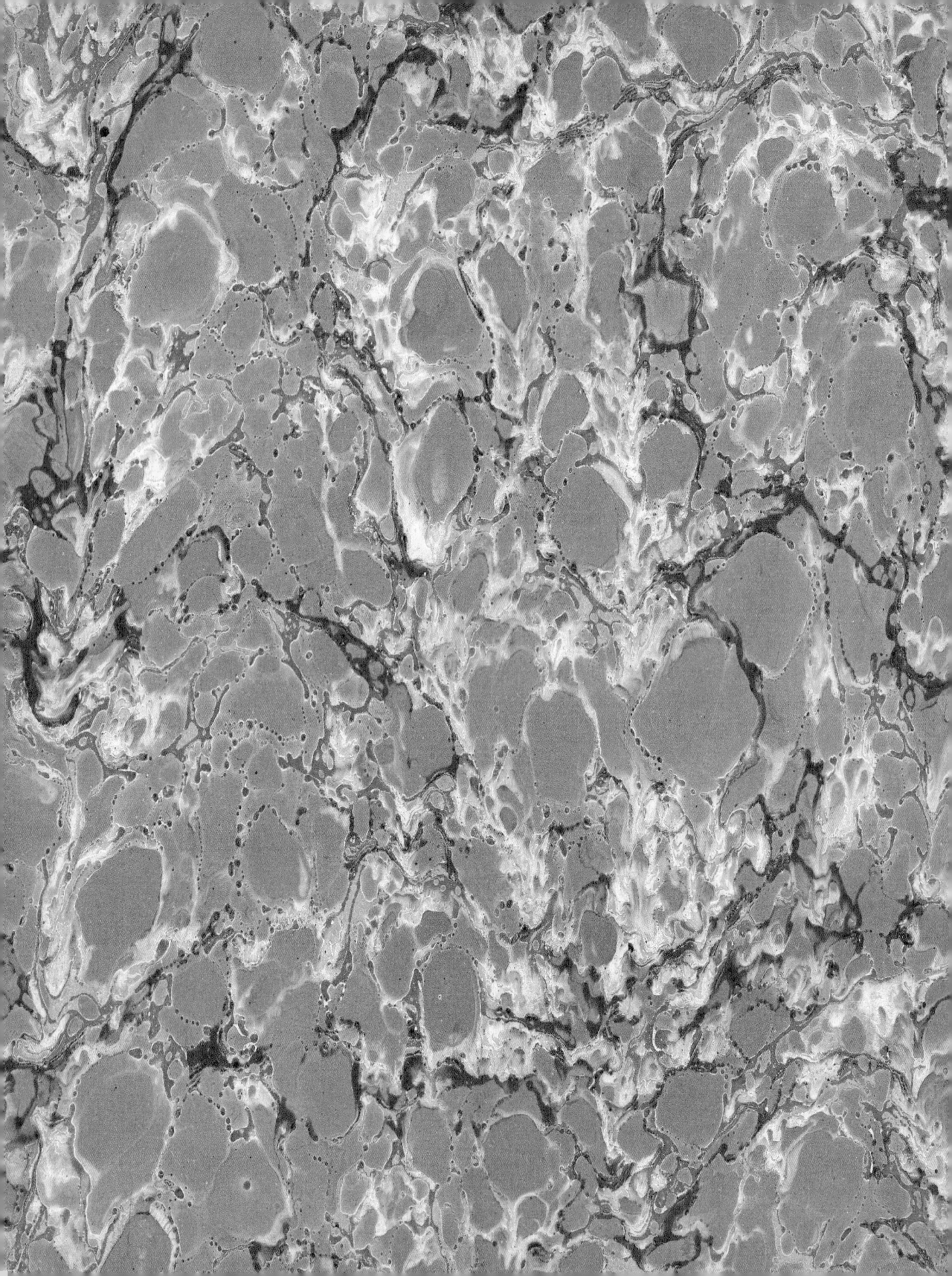

McDOUGAL, LITTELL

LITERATURE AND LANGUAGE

Green Level

Senior Consultants

Arthur N. Applebee
State University of New York at Albany

Andrea B. Bermúdez
University of Houston–Clear Lake

Susan Hynds
Syracuse University, Syracuse, New York

Judith A. Langer
State University of New York at Albany

James Marshall
University of Iowa, Iowa City

Donna E. Norton
Texas A&M University, College Station

McDOUGAL, LITTELL & COMPANY

Evanston, Illinois
New York · Dallas · Columbia, SC

Acknowledgments

Hazel Shelton Abernethy and Nacogdoches County Chamber of Commerce Convention and Visitors Bureau: "The Home Front: 1941-1945" by Hazel Shelton Abernethy, originally appeared in *The Nacogdoches Sampler,* Volume 99, No. 1, Spring 1992. Reprinted by permission of the author and Nacogdoches County Chamber of Commerce Convention and Visitors Bureau.

F. E. Albi: "Moco Limping" by David Nava Monreal, from *Sighs and Songs of Aztlan.* Reprinted by permission of Dr. F. E. Albi, Editor.

Guadalupe Baca-Vaughn: "The Souls in Purgatory" by Guadalupe Baca-Vaughn, from *Voces: An Anthology of Nuevo Mexicano Writers,* edited by Rudolfo Anaya, copyright © 1987. Reprinted by permission of the author.

Bill Berger Associates, Inc.: "The Dinner Party" by Mona Gardner, originally appeared in *Saturday Review,* January 31, 1942. Copyright 1942,© 1970 by Mona Gardner. Reprinted by permission of Bill Berger Associates, Inc.

Susan Bergholz Literary Services: "Dusting" by Julia Alvarez. Copyright © 1984 by Julia Alvarez. Originally published in *Homecoming,* Grove Press, Inc., copyright © 1984. Reprinted by permission of Susan Bergholz Literary Services, New York.

The Estate of Morley Callaghan: "A Cap for Steve" by Morley Callaghan, copyright 1952, © 1980. Reprinted by permission of the Estate of Morley Callaghan.

Judith Ortiz Cofer: "Aunty Misery" by Judith Ortiz Cofer. Originally appeared in *Third World,* Pig Iron Press, copyright © 1988. Reprinted by permission of the author.

Ruth Cohen, Inc., and Lensey Namioka: "The Inn of Lost Time" by Lensey Namioka from *Connections: Short Stories by Outstanding Writers for Young Adults,* edited by Donald R. Gallo, Delacorte Press, copyright © 1989. Permission granted by Lensey Namioka, Author, and Ruth Cohen, Agent.

Council Oak Books: "The Ice Man," from *Once Upon a Time When We Were Colored* by Clifton L. Taulbert. Copyright © 1989 by Clifton L. Taulbert. Reprinted by permission of Council Oak Books, Tulsa.

Doubleday: "The Tale of the Gentle Folk," from *Tales from Silver Lands* by Charles J. Finger. Copyright 1924 by Doubleday, a division of Bantam Doubleday Dell Publishing Group, Inc. Used by permission of Doubleday, a division of Bantam Doubleday Dell Publishing Group, Inc.

Continued on page 841

Cover Art
PORTRAIT OF NITO (detail)   Peter Hurd   Phoenix Art Museum, museum purchase.
Background photograph © David Muench.

ISBN: 0-8123-8045-2

Copyright © 1994 by McDougal, Littell & Company
Box 1667, Evanston, Illinois 60204

2 3 4 5 6 7 8 9 - DWO - 97 96 95 94 93

Senior Consultants

The senior consultants guided conceptual development for the *Literature and Language* series. They participated actively in shaping prototype materials for major components, and they reviewed completed prototypes and/or completed units to ensure consistency with current research and the philosophy of the series.

Arthur N. Applebee
Professor of Education, State University of New York at Albany; Director, Center for the Learning and Teaching of Literature; Senior Fellow, Center for Writing and Literacy

Andrea B. Bermúdez
Professor of Multicultural Education; Director, Research Center for Language and Culture, University of Houston–Clear Lake

Susan Hynds
Associate Professor and Director of English Education, Syracuse University, Syracuse, New York

Judith A. Langer
Professor of Education, State University of New York at Albany; Co-director, Center for the Learning and Teaching of Literature; Senior Fellow, Center for Writing and Literacy

James Marshall
Associate Professor of English and Education, University of Iowa, Iowa City; Executive Secretary, High School Task Force, National Standards Project for English Language Arts K-12.

Donna E. Norton
Professor of Children's Literature, Texas A & M University, College Station

Senior Writer

The senior writer participated in the conceptual development of the series and wrote all the lessons for the literature selections in this text.

Adrienne B. Lieberman
Educational Materials Specialist; formerly middle school teacher, Skokie School, Winnetka, Illinois.

Writers

Audrey Simon (Workshops)
Educational Materials Consultant, Essex, Connecticut

Wordworks (Language Handbook)
Educational Publishing Services, Gloucester, Massachusetts

Multicultural Advisory Board

The multicultural advisors reviewed literature selections for appropriate content and made suggestions for teaching lessons in a multicultural classroom.

Andrea B. Bermúdez, Professor of Multicultural Education; Director, Research Center for Language and Culture, University of Houston–Clear Lake
Alice A. Kawazoe, Director of Curriculum and Staff Development, Oakland Unified School District, Oakland, California
Sandra Mehojah, Project Coordinator, Office of Indian Education, Omaha Public Schools, Omaha, Nebraska
Alexs D. Pate, Writer and columnist on multiculturalism, literature, and teaching; Adjunct faculty member, University of Minnesota and Macalester College

Manuscript Reviewers

The following educators reviewed prototype lessons and tables of contents during the development of the *Literature and Language* program.

Marlane Anish, Syracuse City Schools, Syracuse, New York

Cheryl S. Archiable, Teacher, Shroder Paideia Middle School, Cincinnati Public Schools, Cincinnati, Ohio

William A. Battaglia, Teacher/Chairperson, Herman Intermediate School, Oak Grove School District, San Jose, California

Joanne Robertson Bizarro, Literature Teacher, St. Kevin's School, Catholic Diocese of Brooklyn, Flushing, New York

Martha W. Christian, Secondary English Department, Curriculum Specialist, Consultant, Southwestern Middle School, Southwestern Central School District, Jamestown, New York

Margaret J. Cummings, Language Arts Department Chairperson, William Chrisman High School, Independence Schools, Independence, Missouri

Charleen Delfino, Director San Jose Area Writing Project; English Coordinator, East Side Union High School District, San Jose, California

Kathleen Forslund, Principal, Aquinas Middle School, La Crosse, Wisconsin

Lorraine Gerhart, Reading Teacher, Chairperson and Team Leader, Elmbrook Middle School, Elmbrook Schools, Elm Grove, Wisconsin

Deborah Lynn Moeller, Teacher and Language Arts Department Chairperson, Attucks Middle School, Broward County Schools, Hollywood, Florida

Josephine Scott, Supervisor of Multicultural Education, Northgate Center, Columbus Public Schools, Columbus, Ohio

Elaine G. Sherman, Administrative Specialist, Secondary English and Reading, Division of Curriculum and Instruction, Clark County School District, Las Vegas, Nevada

Martha T. Stewart, Teacher and Chairperson of Language Arts, Turrentine Middle School, Burlington City Schools, Burlington, North Carolina

Sandra Childress Stringer, Principal, Lincoln Elementary School, Evanston District 65, Evanston, Illinois

Joel A. Turetzky, Ed.D., Teacher and Chairperson, Department of English, Raleigh Egypt Junior High School, Memphis City Schools, Memphis, Tennessee

Richard Wagner, Language Arts Curriculum Coordinator, Paradise Valley School District, Phoenix, Arizona

Virginia L. Woodley, English Department Chairperson, Brixner Junior High School, Klamath County School District, Klamath Falls, Oregon

Student Board

The student board members read and evaluated selections to assess their appeal for eighth-grade students.

Hasan J. Artharee, Beaumont Middle School, Portland, Oregon **Austin Barger,** Litchfield Middle School, Akron, Ohio **Heather Anne Culbertson,** Chambersburg Area Middle School, Chambersburg, Pennsylvania **Kenya Shawnese Ervin,** Orchard Knob Middle School, Chattanooga, Tennessee **Wesley Hicks,** Hartman Middle School, Houston, Texas **Evan Krozy,** Pollard Middle School, Needham, Massachusetts **Alison Locke,** Pat Neff Middle School, San Antonio, Texas **Chip McKee,** Owen Goodnight Junior High School, San Marcos, Texas **Timothy Milam,** Chute Middle School, Evanston, Illinois **Tyrone Olds,** McKnight Middle School, Renton, Washington **Monika Parrish,** Chute Middle School, Evanston, Illinois **Allison Pupkin,** Castillero Middle School, San Jose, California **Christina Stawiarski,** Chute Middle School, Evanston, Illinois **Serena Tang,** Shea Middle School, Phoenix, Arizona **Jason Artis Thompson,** Grandview East Junior High School, Grandview, Missouri

Contents

Unit Three

NOTHING STAYS THE SAME 238

Unit Four

MATTERS OF THE HEART

Literature-based
Workshops

Unit Six

THEMES IN FOLKLORE FROM THE AMERICAS 644

xvii

Handbook Section

CONTENTS OVERVIEW

FOLKLORE

WRITER'S WORKSHOPS

LANGUAGE WORKSHOPS

RELATED SKILLS WORKSHOPS

Reader's Workshops

Vocabulary Workshops

Speaking and Listening Workshops

INTRODUCING

*L*ITERATURE AND LANGUAGE

Literature and Language is different from other books you have used in two important ways. First, it is organized to help you tie together your study of the language arts–literature, writing, and language. The literature, chosen for its appeal to your life, serves as the starting point for all your learning. Students like you helped to select the stories, plays, articles, and poems that appear in this book (see their names on page vi). You'll find stories that have been favorites for many generations, as well as works by current writers.

Second, as you use this book, you will find that it does not present a "right" way to understand a story or to write a paper. Instead, it requires you to think for yourself. It asks you to form your own opinions and make your own decisions.

Unit Organization

All the parts of this book fit closely together. If you look at the Table of Contents, on pages vii–xviii, you will see that the book is divided into six units. Each unit is organized around a theme, such as "Personal Codes" or "Nothing Stays the Same," that connects to your life and the world around you. To narrow the focus of these broad themes, each unit is further divided into two subunits. For example, "Personal Codes" is divided into "Moments of Truth" and "Defining Yourself."

After the literature selections in each subunit, you will find a Writer's Workshop, a Language Workshop, and a third workshop that varies in content. These workshops are based upon the literature selections, so that all the parts of the subunit work together.

Organization of the Literature Lessons

Each literature lesson follows a carefully designed pattern, described below.

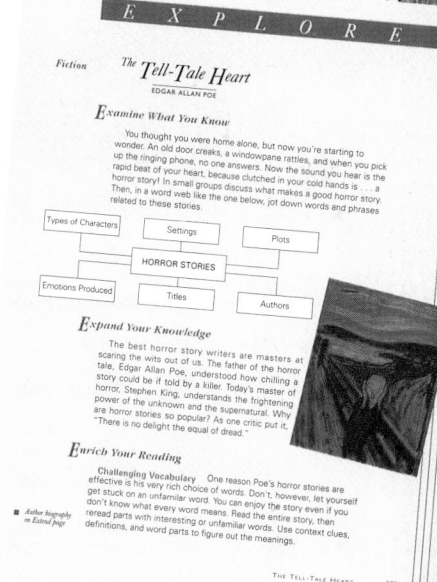

EXPLORE: Before You Read An **Explore** page, marked by a green band at the top, appears before each selection. Its three parts prepare you for reading.

• **Examine What You Know** provides an activity or discussion question based on your own experiences to help you get into the selection.

• **Expand Your Knowledge** gives you useful background information about the selection.

• **Enrich Your Reading** or **Write Before You Read** provides a specific reading or writing activity to help you better understand the literature you are about to read.

3

Reading the Selection   Useful words that you should add to your vocabulary are underlined in the selection. These words are defined in a blue box at the bottom of the page where they first appear. Other difficult words and phrases are defined in footnotes, which appear beneath a black line at the bottom of the page.

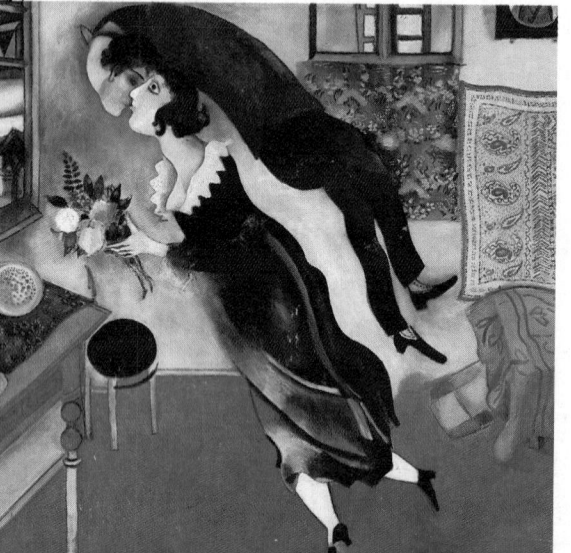

EXPLAIN: After You Read
You'll find one or two **Explain** pages at the end of the selection, marked by a red band at the top. This section starts with discussion questions about the literature. The questions, which have no "right" or "wrong" answers, help you develop your own ideas and interpretations.

After the discussion questions, a literary concept is presented to help you become aware of literary techniques and their importance. In addition, writing activities give you another way of thinking about the literature. Finally, a vocabulary practice is provided if the selection includes vocabulary words.

EXTEND: Beyond the Reading   This page, marked by a purple band at the top, gives you creative ways to display your understanding. These **Options for Learning** allow you to show what you have learned in many different ways such as group projects, dramatics, art, storytelling, and debates. An author biography also appears here.

Literature-based Workshops

Three workshops appear at the end of each subunit.

Writer's Workshop Each Writer's Workshop guides you through an entire writing assignment closely related to the literature and theme of the subunit. Clear instructions, helpful hints, optional suggestions, examples from literature, and models of student writing will help you write your own compositions.

Language Workshop Each Language Workshop focuses on skills that are related to your work in the Writer's Workshop as well as other writing that you do.

Related Skills Workshop The third workshop gives you additional tips in reading, vocabulary, or speaking and listening.

Reading on Your Own

Two pages at the end of each unit suggest novels that tie in with the unit theme. The plot summaries of these novels will help you choose books to read on your own.

Handbook Section

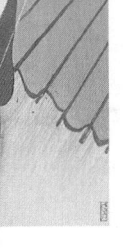

At the back of the book, you'll find three reference handbooks to round out your language-arts studies—a **Reader's Handbook,** a **Writer's Handbook,** and a **Language Handbook.**

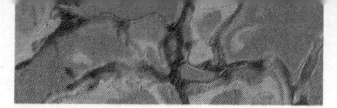

Strategies for
READING

Have you ever been so involved in reading that you didn't pay attention to anything happening around you? When you are that excited about what you are reading, you are an active reader. Active readers not only step into the actions, times, and places of stories and poems but also become more involved in the issues and events they read about in magazines, newspapers, and textbooks. Try the strategies below. They describe the kinds of thinking good readers engage in as they read.

- **Questioning** Ask questions about what is happening. Exploring possible reasons for what is going on in the selection and how characters feel can help you "get into" the selection. Also, make mental notes about words or statements that confuse you, but don't get sidetracked. Things may get clearer as you read further in the selection.

- **Connecting** Think of similarities between what is described in the selection you are reading and what you have experienced, heard about, or read about.

- **Predicting** Try to figure out what will happen next and how the selection might end.

- **Reviewing** Stop occasionally for a quick review of what you understand so far. Be prepared, however, to have your understanding change as you read on and get more information and ideas.

- **Evaluating** Form opinions about what you read, both during and after reading. Develop your own images of and ideas about characters and events.

The model that begins on the next page shows how one reader used these strategies while reading the story "On Hope." Since you think in your own way, you might have different questions and make different connections. However, the idea is the same. When you think while you read, you're an active reader.

On Hope
SPENCER HOLST

▶ I wonder what the title means. *(Questioning)*

The monkey leaped on the man's shoulder. The man shuddered, for he knew who it was. He knew exactly which monkey of the ten thousand that roam about on the Rock of Gibraltar,[1] tame and free as pigeons, walking around in the parks and streets.

It was a demon monkey.

▶ What's a demon monkey? *(Questioning)*

▶ This might explain what he means. *(Reviewing)*

▶ "Sunk in snoring" is a good way to describe the women. *(Evaluating)*

It was the one he'd trained to bring him necklaces, who brought him pearls, garnets, and amber from moonlit bedrooms in the big hotels–stolen from women sunk in snoring.

The monkey dangled before his eyes the largest diamond in the world.

The whole thing began several days previously, when all on Gibraltar went into an uproar. The Rock of Gibraltar was visited by royalty, by the queen mother and the princess. A battleship brought them and their entourage,[2] and with them the famous necklace, the largest stone of which was the Diamond of Hope,[3] which the princess was to wear at some great state occasion. (There's a curse on the necklace, you know, and misfortune had followed it and come to whoever possessed it until it became part of the British crown jewels in the middle of the nineteenth century.)

▶ I've heard about the Hope diamond. This story must have something to do with it. *(Connecting, Reviewing)*

On the very first night the royal party was in, the monkey returned to his gypsy master with the necklace. The necklace, of course, was valueless. It couldn't possibly be sold. Gibraltar would be swarming with police searching for it.

---

1. Rock of Gibraltar: a massive hill at the southern tip of Spain; Gibraltar is a small (2 1/2-square-mile) British colony with Spanish and British residents.

2. entourage (än´ tσσ räzh´): a group of attendants or associates.

3. Diamond of Hope: The Hope diamond, a famous large gemstone.

The gypsy was annoyed with the monkey, irritated at its genius, and terrified of being caught by the police with the gems; and besides, although he had no particular regard for the government (being a gypsy), he liked the idea of "the princess" and wouldn't dream of stealing her necklace. So he quickly wrapped it up and addressed the package to her and dropped it in an ordinary mailbox. He enclosed a note to her saying something like, "You really ought to guard this more carefully."

The next night the monkey returned again with the necklace.

This time his note implored her to have the police guard the necklace more carefully, and he even gave them advice. He advised them to place the necklace in the center of a cage.

(For a monkey, of course, couldn't get into a locked cage.)

Then the third night, when this story begins, the monkey again brought the gypsy the necklace and fell at the gypsy's feet, dead. Shot. Very probably the monkey had been fatally wounded by a guard as he was escaping.

The gypsy shuddered[4] at the diamond and was not surprised at the death of his friend.

The first two times it had been like some freak occurrence, like a weird accident—to unexpectedly discover oneself in possession of part of the British crown jewels! But now . . .

When he received the gems for the third time, the whole thing was plunged into meaning. It no longer seemed like an accident. He had been given the necklace. Fate was at work. Now, the necklace was his.

He put it in his pocket.

It never occurred to him (being a gypsy) to doubt the reality of the curse which accompanied the diamond, and he accepted his fate with the stone. Quietly and secretly he buried the animal.

▶ The gypsy seems worried. *(Evaluating)*

▶ Why does the monkey keep bringing back the same necklace? Something's going to happen to the gypsy. *(Questioning, Predicting)*

▶ The gypsy was worried; now the monkey's dead. *(Reviewing)*

---

4. shuddered: trembled in fear.

Illustration by Gary Kelley.

And as he thought about it, he was actually a little pleased that he, a gypsy, had been singled out by fate to take the curse off the princess and the English throne.

He walked down to the shore of the Mediterranean and took off his clothes and—having nothing in which to put the necklace, he put it on—dove in and swam.

There was a full moon, and the sea was perfectly calm.

Just off Gibraltar there's a very deep place in the Mediterranean. It's called the Gibraltar Trench. Only a mile from shore the sea is a mile deep.

The gypsy was a very good swimmer.

He swam out a mile, over this spot, took the necklace off and dropped it.

▶ Is this why the monkey kept bringing back the necklace? I think something bad's going to happen to the gypsy.
(Questioning, Predicting)

▶ It seems dangerous for the gypsy to wear the necklace.
(Evaluating)

At that moment a smile lit his face as he imagined the thousands of Sherlock Holmeses searching for it for the next fifty years.

The man lazily began to swim back toward shore, and the necklace fell down into the depths.

They each had a mile to go—the man had a mile to swim, and the gems had a mile to fall.

The necklace fell much faster than the gypsy swam.

It fell straight down until it got about a hundred feet from the bottom, where it came to rest on the dorsal fin[5] of a shark.

The shark had been sleeping, but the necklace woke it, and it turned around and around, wondering what was happening. It decided to go up to investigate.

▶ Is the shark going to get him? (Questioning)

The shark swam upward even faster than the necklace had fallen.

Meanwhile, the man still lazily swam toward the huge "rock," now ablaze as never before with the royal festivities, with a million electric light bulbs—and he thought of the curse. The stone would never bring its misfortune to anyone ever again; it was finished forever, its power over man extinguished for good, buried beneath a mile of water.

Then he looked over his shoulder and saw the necklace floating a foot above the water, moving slowly past him.

(The gypsy did not see the shark's fin, he only saw the necklace glittering in the moonlight, as if floating in the air, not coming toward him, but moving past him, now receding into the distance.)

▶ That would look weird—the necklace floating around. (Evaluating)

The man immediately realized that one of two things was true. Obviously, either he was witnessing a miracle (and the whole thing smacked of the miraculous), or he was having a hallucination.[6]

He decided to find out.

Was it a miracle, or was it a delusion?

He began to shout and wave his arms and splash, and he began to swim after the necklace.

▶ He shouldn't be splashing! Sharks are attracted by splashing water. (Connecting)

---

5. **dorsal fin:** a fin on the back of a fish.
6. **hallucination:** the seeing of unreal things.

And sure enough, the necklace stopped and after a moment began to move toward the man.

The man is swimming toward the necklace. The necklace is moving toward the man.

That is where the story ends.

However, I can't help noticing, at this moment, that at first glance it seems inevitable—you know, that the shark will devour the man.

But I do not believe that result is as inevitable as it seems at first glance; that is, I believe there are several reasons, so to speak, for hope.

1. I do not think a shark has ever been approached like this before, that is, by a man wondering whether the shark is a miraculous manifestation[7] or whether it is merely a figment of his own imagination. Such a man would smell different.

2. The man is a gypsy animal trainer.

3. The shark is now in possession of the necklace.

▶ Good story. A little odd, but good. . . . You wonder if the gypsy got eaten or what. It's like another story I read where you have to decide the ending yourself. Anyway, I think the gypsy got away, because the curse is on the shark now.
(Evaluating, Connecting, Predicting)

---

7. **manifestation:** an appearance of a spirit; a vision.

PERSONAL CODES

*W*ithout knowing

what I am and

why I am here,

life is impossible.

Leo Tolstoy

MORNING TIDE (detail)
1983   Ken Danby
Courtesy, Gallery Moos, Toronto.

Moments of Truth

Have you ever been a scout? or an athlete? Are there certain rules that scouts and athletes must follow? Scouts must be honest and trustworthy. Athletes must be physically fit and mentally alert. This is all part of their personal code of living. The title of Unit One, "Personal Codes," refers to a way of living, the code by which a person lives.

Sometimes people come to realize their personal code—who they are and what they believe in—during a moment of truth. "Moments of Truth" refers to crucial moments or times in a person's life. A moment of truth can be as dramatic as a matador's confrontation with a raging bull, or as ordinary as a decision to join a swimming team.

In the following selections, you will read about many moments of truth and see how characters are tested. The personalities and experiences of each of these characters contribute to the final outcome.

Elements of
FICTION

When you read a story, you are reading a work of fiction. **Fiction** is writing that comes from an author's imagination. Although the author makes the story up, he or she might base it on real events.

Fiction writers write either short stories or novels. A **short story** usually revolves around a single idea and is short enough to be read at one sitting. A **novel** is much longer and more complex. In this book, the fiction selections that you will read are short stories. However, at the end of each unit you will find recommendations for novels that you can read on your own.

Understanding Fiction

Character　**Characters** are the people, animals, or imaginary creatures that take part in the action of the story. Usually, a short story centers on events in the life of one person or animal. He or she is the **main character.** Generally, there are also one or more **minor characters** in the story. Minor characters sometimes provide part of the background of the story. More often, however, minor characters interact with the main character and with one another. Their words and actions help to move the plot along.

Setting　The **setting** is the time and place at which the events of the story happen. The time may be the past, the present, or the future; day or night; and any season. A story may be set in a small town or a large city, in a jungle or an ocean.

Plot　The sequence of events in a story is called the **plot.** The plot is the writer's blueprint for what happens in the story, when it happens, and to whom it happens. One event causes another, which causes another, and so on until the end of the story.

Generally, plots are built around a **conflict**—a problem or a struggle between two or more opposing forces. Conflicts can be as serious as a boy's attempt to cope with his father's illness or as humorous as a teacher's struggle with a foreign language.

Although the development of each plot is different, traditional fiction generally follows a pattern that includes the following stages:

• **Exposition**　Exposition sets the stage for the story. Characters are introduced, the setting is described, and the conflict begins to unfold.

• **Complications**　As the story continues, the plot gets more complex. While the characters struggle to find solutions to the conflict, suspense and a feeling of excitement and energy build.

• **Climax**　The climax is the point of highest interest or suspense in the story. It is the turning point, when the action reaches a peak and the outcome of the conflict is decided. The climax may occur because of a decision the characters reach or because of a discovery or an event that changes the situation. The climax usually results in a change in the characters or a solution to the conflict.

• **Resolution**　The resolution occurs at the conclusion of the story. Loose ends are tied up and the story comes to a close.

Theme The **theme** of a story is the main message the writer wishes to share with the reader. This message might be a lesson about life or a belief about people and their actions. A theme is usually not stated directly. It is like a hidden message that the reader must decode. As you discuss literature, however, you will find that different readers can discover different themes in the same story. The following suggestions will help you unlock themes.

• Review what happened to the main character. Did he or she change during the story? What did he or she learn about life?

• Skim the selection for key phrases and sentences—statements that move beyond the action of the story to say something important about life or people.

• Think about the title of the selection. Does it have a special meaning that could lead you to the main idea of the piece?

*S*trategies for Reading Fiction

To really "get inside" a story, try the following strategies:

1. **Preview** a story before you read it by looking at the title and the pictures, or even skimming through the pages, reading some words here and there.

2. Try to **visualize** the setting and the characters. Can you picture a similar place in your mind? Can you "see" the action and the characters?

3. As you read, **make connections.** Do any of the characters have thoughts or experiences that you have had? Does the story remind you of an event or person you've heard of or read about?

4. While you read, **question** events, characters, and ideas. "Why isn't he able to talk about what happened?" "Why is he so angry?" Asking good questions is at the heart of good reading.

5. During your reading, stop occasionally and **predict** what might happen next and how the story will end.

6. As you read, **build** on what you're learning about the characters and events in the story. Let your thoughts change and grow as you learn more.

7. Continually **evaluate** the story as you read. Think about your feelings toward the characters and their actions. Also consider how well the author is telling his or her story.

Remember, a story never tells you everything. It leaves room for you to build your own ideas. When you read, you gather first impressions, but you need to be able to elaborate and explain them by referring to the story, your own experiences, and other stories you have read.

Fiction

Stop the Sun

GARY PAULSEN

Examine What You Know

How much do you know about the Vietnam War or about what happened to Vietnam veterans after the war? Either in a small group or as a class discuss what you already know about the Vietnam War and the veterans of the war. Use a chart like the one started below.

Information About the Vietnam War
—happened in 1960s and 1970s —caused lots of protests

Expand Your Knowledge

In Vietnam, the United States fought its longest and most unpopular war. The United States tried, unsuccessfully, to prevent North Vietnam from invading South Vietnam and creating a single communist country. Many people came to believe that the United States had no business getting involved in this conflict. When U.S. soldiers returned home, many were ignored or even criticized. In addition, some had to deal with painful memories of the jungle warfare they experienced in Vietnam.

Some Vietnam veterans still suffer from psychological problems stemming from their war experiences. Sometimes referred to as the "Vietnam syndrome," the symptoms include nervousness, anger, nightmares, and flashbacks to war experiences. Frequently, these veterans find it hard to talk about their war memories, even with their own families.

Enrich Your Reading

Predicting   Trying to figure out what will happen next in a story—**predicting**—is one of the natural mental tasks you do as you read. In the following story a war veteran suffers from "Vietnam syndrome." As you begin reading, predict how this problem might affect him, as well as his wife and his son.

■ *Author biography on Extend page*

Stop the Sun

GARY PAULSEN

Terry Erickson was a tall boy, 13, starting to fill out with muscle but still a little awkward. He was on the edge of being a good athlete, which meant a lot to him. He felt it coming too slowly, though, and that bothered him.

But what bothered him even more was when his father's eyes went away.

Usually it happened when it didn't cause any particular trouble. Sometimes during a meal his father's fork would stop halfway to his mouth, just stop, and there would be a long pause while the eyes went away, far away.

After several minutes his mother would reach over and take the fork and put it gently down on his plate, and they would go back to eating—or try to go back to eating—normally.

They knew what caused it. When it first started, Terry had asked his mother in private what it was, what was causing the strange behavior.

"It's from the war," his mother had said. "The doctors at the veterans' hospital call it the Vietnam syndrome."[1]

"Will it go away?"

"They don't know. Sometimes it goes away. Sometimes it doesn't. They are trying to help him."

"But what happened? What actually caused it?"

"I told you. Vietnam."

"But there had to be something," Terry persisted. "Something made him like that. Not just Vietnam. Billy's father was there, and he doesn't act that way."

"That's enough questions," his mother said sternly. "He doesn't talk about it, and I don't ask. Neither will you. Do you understand?"

"But, Mom."

"That's enough."

And he stopped pushing it. But it bothered him whenever it happened. When something bothered him, he liked to stay with it until he understood it, and he understood no part of this.

Words. His father had trouble, and they gave him words like Vietnam syndrome. He knew almost nothing of the war, and when he tried to find out about it, he kept hitting walls. Once he went to the school library and asked for anything they might have that could help him understand the war and how it affected his father. They gave him a dry

---

1. **Vietnam syndrome:** a group of mental disorders experienced by some Vietnam War veterans.

Words
to Know
and Use
| **persist** (pər sist′) v. to continue stubbornly

JOSEPH 1984 Joseph Raffael Courtesy, Nancy Hoffman Gallery, New York.

history that described French involvement, Communist involvement, American involvement. But it told him nothing of the war. It was all numbers, cold numbers, and nothing of what had *happened*. There just didn't seem to be anything that could help him.

Another time he stayed after class and tried to talk to Mr. Carlson, who taught history. But some part of Terry was embarrassed. He didn't want to say why he wanted to know about Vietnam, so he couldn't be specific.

"What do you want to know about Vietnam, Terry?" Mr. Carlson had asked. "It was a big war."

Terry had looked at him, and something had started up in his mind, but he didn't let it out. He shrugged. "I just want to know what it was like. I know somebody who was in it."

"A friend?"

"Yessir. A good friend."

Mr. Carlson had studied him, looking into his eyes, but didn't ask any other questions. Instead he mentioned a couple of books Terry had not seen. They turned out to be pretty good. They told about how it felt to be in combat. Still, he couldn't make his father be one of the men he read about.

And it may have gone on and on like that,

with Terry never really knowing any more about it, except that his father's eyes started going away more and more often. It might have just gone the rest of his life that way except for the shopping mall.

It was easily the most embarrassing thing that ever happened to him.

It started as a normal shopping trip. His father had to go to the hardware store, and he asked Terry to go along.

When they got to the mall, they split up. His father went to the hardware store, Terry to a record store to look at albums.

Terry browsed so long that he was late meeting his father at the mall's front door. But his father wasn't there, and Terry looked out to the car to make sure it was still in the parking lot. It was, and he supposed his father had just gotten busy, so he waited.

Still his father didn't come, and he was about to go to the hardware store to find him when he noticed the commotion. Or not a commotion so much as a sudden movement of people.

Later, he thought of it and couldn't remember when the feeling first came to him that there was something wrong. The people were moving toward the hardware store, and that might have been what made Terry suspicious.

There was a crowd blocking the entry to the store, and he couldn't see what they were looking at. Some of them were laughing small, nervous laughs that made no sense.

Terry squeezed through the crowd until he got near the front. At first he saw nothing unusual. There were still some people in front of him, so he pushed a crack between them. Then he saw it: His father was squirming along the floor on his stomach. He was crying, looking terrified, his breath coming in short, hot pants like some kind of hurt animal.

It burned into Terry's mind, the picture of his father down on the floor. It burned in and in, and he wanted to walk away, but something made his feet move forward. He knelt next to his father and helped the owner of the store get him up on his feet. His father didn't speak at all but continued to make little whimpering sounds, and they led him back into the owner's office and put him in a chair. Then Terry called his mother, and she came in a taxi to take them home. Waiting, Terry sat in a chair next to his father, looking at the floor, wanting only for the earth to open and let him drop in a deep hole. He wanted to disappear.

Words. They gave him words like Vietnam syndrome, and his father was crawling through a hardware store on his stomach.

When the embarrassment became so bad that he would cross the street when he saw his father coming, when it ate into him as he went to sleep, Terry realized he had to do something. He had to know this thing, had to understand what was wrong with his father.

What happened to Terry's father? *review*

When it came, it was simple enough at the start. It had taken some courage, more than Terry thought he could find. His father was sitting in the kitchen at the table, and his mother had gone shopping. Terry wanted it that way; he wanted his father alone. His mother seemed to try to protect him, as if his father could break.

Terry got a soda out of the refrigerator and popped it open. As an afterthought, he handed it to his father and got another for himself. Then he sat at the table.

His father smiled. "You look serious."

"Well . . ."

It went nowhere for a moment, and Terry was just about to drop it altogether. It may be the wrong time, he thought, but there might never be a better one. He tightened his back, took a sip of pop.

"I was wondering if we could talk about something, Dad," Terry said.

His father shrugged. "We already did the bit about girls. Some time ago, as I remember it."

"No. Not that." It was a standing joke between them. When his father finally got around to explaining things to him, they'd already covered it in school. "It's something else."

"Something pretty heavy, judging by your face."

"Yes."

"Well?"

I still can't do it, Terry thought. Things are bad, but maybe not as bad as they could get. I can still drop this thing.

"Vietnam," Terry blurted out. And he thought, there, it's out. It's out and gone.

"No!" his father said sharply. It was as if he had been struck a blow. A body blow.

"But, Dad."

"No. That's another part of my life. A bad part. A rotten part. It was before I met your mother, long before you. It has nothing to do with this family, nothing. No."

So, Terry thought, so I tried. But it wasn't over yet. It wasn't started yet.

"It just seems to bother you so much," Terry said, "and I thought if I could help or maybe understand it better . . ." His words ran until he foundered, until he could say no more. He looked at the table, then out the window. It was all wrong to bring it up, he thought. I blew it. I blew it all up. "I'm sorry."

But now his father didn't hear him. Now his father's eyes were gone again, and a shaft of something horrible went through Terry's heart as he thought he had done this thing to his father, caused his eyes to go away.

"You can't know," his father said after a time. "You can't know this thing."

Terry said nothing. He felt he had said too much.

"This thing that you want to know—there is so much of it that you cannot know it all, and to know only a part is . . . is too awful. I can't tell you. I can't tell anybody what it was really like."

It was more than he'd ever said about Vietnam, and his voice was breaking. Terry hated himself and felt he would hate himself until he was an old man. In one second he had caused such ruin. And all because he had been embarrassed. What difference did it make? Now he had done this, and he wanted to hide, to leave. But he sat, waiting, knowing that it wasn't done.

His father looked to him, through him,

21

somewhere into and out of Terry. He wasn't in the kitchen anymore. He wasn't in the house. He was back in the green places, back in the hot places, the wet-hot places.

review If Terry's father is not "in the kitchen anymore," where is he?

"You think that because I act strange, we can talk and it will be all right," his father said. "That we can talk and it will just go away. That's what you think, isn't it?"

Terry started to shake his head, but he knew it wasn't expected.

"That's what the shrinks say," his father continued. "The psychiatrists tell me that if I talk about it, the whole thing will go away. But they don't know. They weren't there. You weren't there. Nobody was there but me and some other dead people, and they can't talk because they couldn't stop the morning."

Terry pushed his soda can back and forth, looking down, frightened at what was happening. *The other dead people,* he'd said, as if he were dead as well. *Couldn't stop the morning.*

"I don't understand, Dad."

"No. You don't." His voice hardened, then softened again and broke at the edges. "But see, see how it was . . ." He trailed off, and Terry thought he was done. His father looked back down to the table, at the can of soda he hadn't touched, at the tablecloth, at his hands, which were folded, <u>inert</u> on the table.

"We were crossing a rice paddy in the dark," he said, and suddenly his voice flowed like a river breaking loose. "We were crossing the paddy, and it was dark, still dark, so black you couldn't see the end of your nose. There was a light rain, a mist, and I was thinking that during the next break I would whisper and tell Petey Kressler how nice the rain felt, but of course I didn't know there wouldn't be a Petey Kressler."

He took a deep, ragged breath. At that moment Terry felt his brain swirl, a kind of whirlpool pulling, and he felt the darkness and the light rain because it was in his father's eyes, in his voice.

You think that because I act strange, we can talk and it will be all right.

"So we were crossing the paddy, and it was a straight sweep, and then we caught it. We began taking fire from three sides, automatic weapons, and everybody went down and tried to get low, but we couldn't. We couldn't get low enough. We could never get low enough, and you could hear the rounds hitting people. It was just a short time before they brought in the mortars,[2] and we should have moved, should have run, but nobody got up, and after a time nobody *could* get up. The fire just kept coming and coming, and then incoming mortars, and I heard screams as they hit, but there

---

2. **mortars:** small cannons that fire shells at a high angle.

Words to Know and Use | **inert** (in ʉrt') *adj.* not active; motionless

MINE ON PATROL 1966 John Steel Courtesy, Navy Art Collection, Naval Historical Center, Washington, D.C.

was nothing to do. Nothing to do."

"Dad?" Terry said. He thought, maybe I can stop him. Maybe I can stop him before . . . before it gets to be too much. Before he breaks.

"Mortars," his father went on, "I hated mortars. You just heard them *wump* as they fired, and you didn't know where they would hit, and you always felt like they would hit your back. They swept back and forth with the mortars, and the automatic weapons kept coming in, and there was no radio, no way to call for artillery. Just the dark to hide in. So I crawled to the side and found Jackson, only he wasn't there, just

part of his body, the top part, and I hid under it and waited, and waited, and waited.

"Finally the firing quit. But see, see how it was in the dark with nobody alive but me? I yelled once, but that brought fire again, so I shut up, and there was nothing, not even the screams."

His father cried, and Terry tried to understand, and he thought he could feel part of it. But it was so much, so much and so strange to him.

"You cannot know this," his father repeated. It was almost a chant. "You cannot know the fear. It was dark, and I was the only one left alive out of fifty-four men, all dead but

23

me, and I knew that the Vietcong[3] were just waiting for light. When the dawn came, 'Charley'[4] would come out and finish everybody off, the way they always did. And I thought if I could stop the dawn, just stop the sun from coming up, I could make it."

Terry felt the fear, and he also felt the tears coming down his cheeks. His hand went out across the table, and he took his father's hand and held it. It was shaking.

"I mean I actually thought that if I could stop the sun from coming up, I could live. I made my brain work on that because it was all I had. Through the rest of the night in the rain in the paddy, I thought I could do it. I could stop the dawn." He took a deep breath. "But you can't, you know. You can't stop it from coming, and when I saw the gray light, I knew I was dead. It would just be minutes, and the light would be full, and I just settled under Jackson's body and hid."

He stopped, and his face came down into his hands. Terry stood and went around the table to stand in back of him, his hands on his shoulders, rubbing gently.

"They didn't shoot me. They came, one of them poked Jackson's body and went on, and they left me. But I was dead. I'm still dead, don't you see? I died because I couldn't stop the sun. I died. Inside where I am—I died."

What does Terry's father mean by saying he died?

review

Terry was still in back of him, and he nodded, but he didn't see. Not that. He understood only that he didn't understand and that he would probably never know what it was really like, would probably never understand what had truly happened. And maybe his father would never be truly normal.

But Terry also knew that it didn't matter. He would try to understand, and the trying would have to be enough. He would try hard from now on, and he would not be embarrassed when his father's eyes went away. He would not be embarrassed no matter what his father did. Terry had knowledge now. Maybe not enough and maybe not all that he would need.

But it was a start. ✷

---

3. **Vietcong:** Communist rebels who fought to overthrow the South Vietnamese government.
4. **'Charley':** a version of *Victor Charlie,* a slang term for the Vietcong.

Responding to Reading

First Impressions

1. Which **character** do you have the strongest feeling about, Terry or his father? Explain.

Second Thoughts

2. If you were Terry, how would you handle his dilemma—his desire to help and understand his father versus the need not to upset him?

3. Do you think Terry and his father have changed now that they have had their moment of truth?

    Think about
    - when Terry said "It was all wrong to bring it up . . . I blew it."
    - when Terry's father asked "I'm still dead, don't you see?"
    - when Terry said "He understood only that he didn't understand."
    - your experience with family discussions of difficult issues

4. Imagine Terry, his father, and his mother ten years later. What lasting effects on each of them do you think the war will have?

Broader Connections

5. Some Vietnam veterans feel they have not received the benefits that returning soldiers from other wars have received. Many Vietnam veterans feel that because they fought in an unpopular war, the public has ignored their needs. Some, like Terry's father, have been treated at hospitals, yet remain deeply troubled. What kinds of recognition or help do you think the United States owes its veterans?

Literary Concept: Internal Conflict

The struggle between two opposing forces is called **conflict.** Every story has it. The conflict makes you keep reading the story to learn the outcome of the struggle. When one character fights another character or battles nature, the conflict is referred to as **external conflict.** When the struggle takes place within a character, it is an **internal conflict.** In "Stop the Sun" the main conflict is internal: Terry struggles to bring himself to ask his father a painful question. Explain the father's internal conflict in this story. How are these two conflicts resolved at the end—or are they?

Writing Options

1. Imagine that you are Gary Paulsen's editor. Paulsen has sent you his story "Stop the Sun" and has asked for your opinion. Write a **letter** back to him commenting on the good (and perhaps the not-so-good) aspects of the story. Among other things, comment on the title. Is it the best title or can you think of a better one?

2. Imagine you are starting a support group that will bring Vietnam veterans together to talk about their problems. Write an **advertisement** for this support group. Think of statements that would encourage troubled veterans like Terry's father to join the group.

3. How does "Stop the Sun" compare to other war stories or films you have encountered? Write a **comparison paper,** discussing some of the similarities and differences in characters, battle scenes, and effects of the war.

4. Terry was terribly embarrassed when his father broke down in the hardware store. Imagine that you are Terry and keep a personal journal. In a **journal entry,** tell what happened and how you felt about it.

Vocabulary Practice

Exercise   On your paper, write the word from the list that best completes each sentence below.

1. The patient at the veterans' hospital spent many days lying __?__ on his bed.

2. The soldier tried to tell his story, but when he remembered the tragic fate of his platoon, he would __?__ and then stop talking.

3. The soldier's doctor decided to __?__ and kept coaxing the soldier to talk.

4. Suddenly, without thinking, the soldier began to __?__ out the whole story.

5. The soldier told of a terrible ambush in which he was the sole survivor. At the end of his story, he repeated in a kind of __?__, "If you weren't there, you can't understand."

> *Words to Know and Use*
>
> **blurt**
> **chant**
> **founder**
> **inert**
> **persist**

E X T E N D

Options for Learning

1 • One Day in the Life of a War
The peak years of U.S. troop involvement in the Vietnam War were 1965 to 1969. Choose one particular day in this period, such as a day that matches your birthday. At your library, locate a newspaper published on the day you have chosen. Read what happened in the war on this day and report back to your class. You may want to show pictures from books or magazines to help your classmates visualize what you describe.

2 • Happy Father's Day Design a Father's Day card that Terry might send to his father. Include a meaningful picture or design on the front and a personal message on the inside. The card should reflect Terry's new understanding of his father.

3 • A Little Night Music If you were making a movie version of "Stop the Sun," what music would you use to capture the emotions of the story? Compose or find a piece of music that could serve as background for the father's memory of Vietnam. Play the music for your class.

4 • Go to the Source Call a local veterans' group to find a Vietnam veteran who is willing to be interviewed by you about his or her war experiences. Tape-record your interview and share highlights from it with your class.

 FACT FINDER HISTORY
How many Americans were killed in the Vietnam War?

Gary Paulsen
1939–

For their material, writers draw on their imaginations and their life experiences. What a wealth of experience Gary Paulsen has to draw on! He has worked as a teacher, engineer, actor, director, farmer, rancher, truck driver, trapper, professional archer, migrant farm worker, singer, and sailor. He also served in the U.S. Army between 1959 and 1962. Paulsen describes his main work by saying he has "taught at the University of Colorado and Bemidji State College; won various awards; done some acting; some living, but mostly writing. Just writing."

Paulsen's writing often reflects his keen interest in the outdoors. He twice competed in the grueling Iditarod trans-Alaskan dogsled race from Anchorage to Nome; he later used this experience as background for his novel *Dogsong.* Another Paulsen novel, *Hatchet,* tells the story of a young boy's ordeal in the Canadian wilderness. Both *Dogsong* and *Hatchet* are Newbery Honor Books.

Fiction

The Dinner Party

MONA GARDNER

Examine What You Know

On a chart like the one below, write a brief description of what you think most men would do in the situation and what you think most women would do.

Situation	Men	Women
1. Seeing a bleeding wound 2. Getting a flat tire 3. Seeing a mouse or a snake		

In a small group, compare your answers. Have males and females in your class responded differently? Discuss whether or not people still have stereotyped ideas about male-female behavior.

Expand Your Knowledge

For the two hundred years before India's independence in 1947, it was a British colony. "The Dinner Party" takes place in colonial India, when the British ruled by assigning governors to each of India's eleven provinces. Some of the attitudes held by the British people of that era would be considered backward today. Most British officials felt superior to their subjects and rarely socialized with the Indians. Similarly, the men had an attitude of superiority over women, an attitude that becomes an issue in the story.

Enrich Your Reading

Stereotype   Someone's oversimplified view of an entire group of people is known as a **stereotype.** Sweeping statements—such as "that's what all police officers are like" or "that's how all rich people act"—are stereotypes. As you read the following story, look for the stereotype expressed by a guest at the dinner party and see whether the stereotype holds true.

■ *Author biography in Reader's Handbook*

The Dinner Party

MONA GARDNER

The country is India. A colonial official[1] and his wife are giving a large dinner party. They are seated with their guests—army officers, and government attachés[2] with their wives, and a visiting American naturalist[3]—in their spacious dining room, which has a bare marble floor, open rafters, and wide glass doors opening onto a veranda.[4]

A spirited discussion springs up between a young girl who insists that women have outgrown the jumping-on-a-chair-at-the-sight-of-a-mouse era and a colonel who says that they haven't.

"A woman's unfailing reaction in any crisis," the colonel says, "is to scream. And while a man may feel like it, he has that ounce more of nerve control than a woman has. And that last ounce is what counts."

A woman's unfailing reaction in any crisis is to scream.

The American does not join in the argument but watches the other guests. As he looks, he sees a strange expression come over the face of the hostess. She is staring straight ahead, her muscles contracting slightly. With a slight gesture, she summons the native boy standing behind her chair and whispers to him. The boy's eyes widen, and he quickly leaves the room.

Of the guests, none except the American notices this or sees the boy place a bowl of milk on the veranda just outside the open doors.

The American comes to with a start. In India, milk in a bowl means only one thing—bait for a snake. He realizes there must be a cobra in the room. He looks up at the rafters—the likeliest place—but they are bare. Three corners of the room are empty, and in the fourth the servants are waiting to serve the next course. There is only one place left—under the table.

His first impulse is to jump back and warn the others, but he knows the commotion would frighten the cobra into striking. He speaks quickly, the tone of his voice so arresting that it sobers everyone.

"I want to know just what control everyone at this table has. I will count to three hundred—that's five minutes—and not one of

---

1. colonial official: in this story, a high-level employee of the British government serving in India, one of England's colonies.
2. attachés (at´ə shāz´): people who work for an ambassador to a foreign country.
3. naturalist: a person who studies living things.
4. veranda: a long, roofed porch along the side of a building.

DINNER AT HADDO HOUSE (detail)   1884   A.E. Emslie   National Portrait Gallery, London

you is to move a muscle. Those who move will forfeit fifty rupees.[5] Ready!"

The twenty people sit like stone images while he counts. He is saying "two hundred and eighty" when, out of the corner of his eye, he sees the cobra emerge and make for the bowl of milk. Screams ring out as he jumps to slam the veranda doors safely shut.

"You were right, Colonel!" the host exclaims. "A man has just shown us an example of perfect control."

"Just a minute," the American says, turning to his hostess. "Mrs. Wynnes, how did you know the cobra was in the room?"

A faint smile lights up the woman's face as she replies. "Because it was crawling across my foot." ❧

---

5. **rupees** (roo′ pēz): units of money in India.

E X P L A I N

Responding to Reading

First Impressions

1. What were your reactions to the story? Jot down your thoughts in your journal or on a sheet of paper.

Second Thoughts

2. In moments of truth, courage can take many different forms. In what ways do **characters** in this story show courage?

3. Consider the thoughts you had in the Examine What You Know activity. How does this story compare with your ideas about how men and women react to tense situations?

4. Do you think this incident will change the colonel's **stereotyped** opinion of women? Explain your answer, using story details and your own experience.

5. What might have happened if the naturalist hadn't noticed the servant with the milk?

Literary Concept: Suspense

A writer creates **suspense** by keeping the reader guessing about how the story will end. In "The Dinner Party" we learn something early on that most of the characters don't know—there is a deadly snake loose in the room. Suspense is created as we begin to imagine all the things that could go wrong. How does the naturalist's challenge to the guests add suspense?

Writing Options

1. What do you suppose Mrs. Wynnes is saying to herself as the cobra is crawling across her foot? Write Mrs. Wynnes's **interior monologue,** her train of thought during this tense moment.

2. Picture the look on the face of the colonel after Mrs. Wynnes tells the group about the cobra. What would this man—who has such a stereotyped view of women—say next? Add a final part to the story, the **dialogue** between the colonel and Mrs. Wynnes.

3. Write a **personal essay** about a time when someone showed great control in a moment of tension or danger.

Fiction   ## Dancer

VICKIE SEARS

Examine What You Know

Think about your ethnic background for a moment. What traits, beliefs, and customs do people of your background often share? Use a word web like the one below to give your impressions of your ethnic heritage.

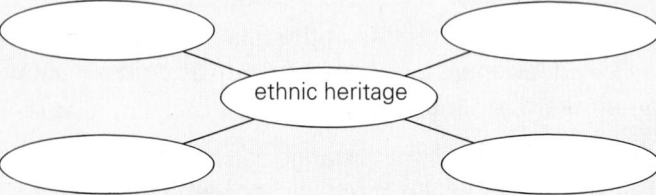

Then discuss how important your ethnic heritage is to your understanding of yourself.

Expand Your Knowledge

In the Native American culture, ceremonial dances traditionally were performed to bring sun or rain, to ensure good hunting, to prepare for battle, and to get closer to nature. In many Native American communities today, a monthly dance called a powwow remains a regular event. The powwow keeps the traditional culture alive, and for many Native Americans this reminder of their ethnic heritage is a way to develop and maintain self-esteem and self-knowledge. Dances such as the owl dance, the friendship dance, the circle dance, and the hoop dance are performed by Native Americans of all ages.

Enrich Your Reading

Voice   The first thing you may notice as you read this story is the writing style used for the narrator's voice. A Native American mother tells the story in her own, very distinctive way of speaking. She has an earthy, conversational style. It is often nonstandard, as when she says, "I don't know nothing from that." Her descriptions are colorful —her foster child's nightmares are "real screamer dreams." This plain-spoken, open-hearted foster mother tries to help her troubled foster child gain self-confidence through her ethnic identity. As you read, be aware of the narrator's voice and how it makes her come alive on the page.

■ *Author biography on Extend page*

Dancer

VICKIE SEARS

Tell you just how it was with her. Took her to a dance not long after she come to live with us. Smartest thing I ever done. Seems like some old Eaglespirit woman saw her living down here and came back just to be with Clarissa.

Five years old she was when she come to us. Some foster kids come with lots of stuff, but she came with everything she had in a paper bag. Some dresses that was too short. A pair of pants barely holding a crotch. A pile of ratty underwear and one new nightgown. Mine was her third foster home in as many months. The agency folks said she was *so-cio-path-ic*. I don't know nothing from that. She just seemed like she was all full up with anger and scaredness like lots of the kids who come to me. Only she was a real loner. Not trusting nobody. But she ran just like any other kid, was quiet when needed. Smiled at all the right times. If you could get her to smile, that is. Didn't talk much, though.

Had these ferocious dreams, too. Real screamer dreams they were. Shake the soul right out of you. She'd be screaming and crying with her little body wriggling on the bed, her hair all matted up on her woody-colored face. One time I got her to tell me what she was seeing, and she told me how she was being chased by a man with a long knife what he was going to kill her with and nobody could hear her calling out for help. She didn't talk too much about them, but they was all bad like that one. Seemed the most fierce dreams I ever remember anybody ever having outside of a vision seek.[1] They said her tribe was Assiniboine,[2] but they weren't for certain. What was for sure was that she was a fine dark-eyed girl just meant for someone to scoop up for loving.

Took her to her first dance in September, like I said, not long after she came. It wasn't like I thought it would be a good thing to do. It was just that we was all going. Me, my own kids, some nieces and nephews, and the other children who was living with us. The powwow was just part of what we done all the time. Every month. More often in the summer. But this was the regular first

---

1. **vision seek:** a Native American rite in which a person receives guidance or powers in a dream.
2. **Assiniboine** (ə sin′ ə bɔin): a Native American tribe of northeastern Montana and parts of Canada.

Friday night of the school year. We'd all gather up and go to the school. I was thinking on leaving her home with a sitter 'cause she'd tried to kill one of the cats a couple of days before. We'd had us a big talk and she was grounded, but, well, it seemed like she ought to be with us.

Harold, that's my oldest boy, he and the other kids was mad with her, but he decided to show her around anyhow. At the school he went through the gym telling people, "This here's my sister, Clarissa." Wasn't no fuss or anything. She was just another one of the kids. When they was done meeting folks, he put her on one of the bleachers near the drum and went to join the men. He was in that place where his voice cracks but was real proud to be drumming. Held his hand up to his ear even, some of the time. Anyhow, Clarissa was sitting there, not all that interested in the dance or drum, when Molly Graybull come out in her button dress. Her arms was all stretched out, and she was slipping around, preening on them spindles of legs that get skinnier with every year. She was well into her seventies, and I might as well admit, Molly had won herself a fair share of dance contests. So it wasn't no surprise how a little girl could get so fixated on Molly. Clarissa watched her move around-around-around. Then all the rest of the dancers after Molly. She sure took in a good eyeful. Fancy dance. Owl dance. Circle dance. Even a hoop dancer was visiting that night.[3] Everything weaving all slow, then fast. Around-around until that child

couldn't see nothing else. Seemed like she was struck silent in the night, too. Never had no dreams at all. Well, not the hollering kind anyways.

Next day she was more quiet than usual, only I could see she was looking at her picture book and tapping the old one-two, one-two. Tapping her toes on the rug with the inside of her head going around and around. As quiet as she could be, she was.

A few days went on before she asks me, "When's there gonna be another dance?"

I tell her in three weeks. She just smiles and goes on outside, waiting on the older kids to come home from school.

The very next day she asks if she can listen to some singing. I give her the tape recorder and some of Joe Washington from up to the Lummi reservation and the Kicking Woman Singers. Clarissa, she takes them tapes and runs out back behind the chicken shed, staying out all afternoon. I wasn't worried none, though, cause I could hear the music the whole time. Matter of fact, it like to make me sick of them same songs come the end of three weeks. But that kid, she didn't get into no kind of mischief. Almost abnormal how good she was. Worried me some to see her so caught up, but it seemed good too. The angry part of her slowed down so's she

---

3. **Fancy dance. Owl dance. Circle dance. Even a hoop dancer . . . that night:** refers to the performance of traditional Native American dances; respectively, a competitive dance for showing performers' best steps, an expressive dance imitating an owl, a social dance performed in a circle, and a novelty dance for a single performer using hoops.

Words to Know and Use | **preen** (prēn) *v.* to show pride and self-satisfaction
fixated (fiks' āt' id) *adj.* having one's attention absorbed; engrossed **fixate** *v.*

BASKET OF BEAUTY
Lisa Danielle
Private collection.

wasn't hitting the animals or chopping on herself with sticks like she was doing when she first come. She wasn't laughing much either, but she started playing with the other kids when they come home. Seemed like everybody was working hard to be better with each other.

Come March, Clarissa asks, "Can I dance?"

For sure, the best time for teaching is when a kid wants to listen, so we stood side to side with me doing some steps. She followed along fine. I put on a tape and started moving faster, and Clarissa just kept up all natural. I could tell she'd been practicing lots. She was doing real good.

Comes the next powwow, which was outside on the track field, I braided Clarissa's hair. Did her up with some ermine and bead ties, then give her a purse to carry. It was all beaded with a rose and leaves. Used to be my aunt's. She held it right next to her side with her chin real high. She joined in a circle dance. I could see she was watching her feet a little and looking how others do their steps, but mostly she was doing wonderful. When Molly Graybull showed up beside her, Clarissa took to a seat and stared. She didn't dance again that night, but I could see there was dreaming coming into her eyes. I saw that fire that said to practice. And she did. I heard her every day in her room. Finally bought her her very own tape recorder so's the rest of us could listen to music too.

Some months passed on. All the kids was getting bigger. Clarissa, she went into the first grade. Harvey went off to community college up in Seattle, and that left me with Ronnie being the oldest at home. Clarissa was keeping herself busy all the time going over to Molly Graybull's. She was coming home with Spider Woman stories and trickster tales.[4] One night she speaks up at supper and says, right clear and loud, "I'm an Assiniboine." Clear as it can be, she says it again. Don't nobody have to say nothing to something that proud said.

Next day I started working on a wing dress for Clarissa. She was going to be needing one for sure real soon.

Comes the first school-year powwow, and everyone was putting on their best. I called for Clarissa to come to my room. I told her, "I think it's time you have something special for yourself." Then I held up the green satin and saw her eyes full up with glitter. She didn't say nothing. Only kisses me and runs off to her room.

Just as we're all getting out of the car, Clarissa whispered to me, "I'm gonna dance with Molly Graybull." I put my hand on her shoulder to say, "You just listen to your spirit. That's where your music is."

We all danced an owl dance, a friendship dance, and a couple of circle dances. Things was feeling real warm and good, and then it was time for the women's traditional.[5] Clarissa joined the circle. She opened her arms to something nobody but her seemed to hear. That's when I saw that old Eagle woman come down and slide right inside of Clarissa, scooping up that child. There Clarissa was, full up with music. All full with that old, old spirit, letting herself dance through Clarissa's feet. Then Molly Graybull come dancing alongside Clarissa, and they was both the same age. ❧

---

4. **Spider Woman stories and trickster tales:** Indian legends about the sun god's wife and mischievous heroes with magical powers.

5. **women's traditional:** a slow Native American dance historically reserved for women.

Responding to Reading

First Impressions

1. What are you left wondering about as the story ends?

Second Thoughts

2. Reread the final paragraph of the story. What do you think the mother means by her description of Clarissa?

3. Consider the change in Clarissa from the beginning of the story to the end. Explain the influences that you think cause Clarissa to change.

4. Why do you think Clarissa becomes so interested in Molly Graybull and the powwow dances?

5. Which **character** in this story did you like the best? Explain why.

Broader Connections

6. Clarissa gains pride and confidence when she learns about her tribe, the Assiniboine, and takes part in the traditional dances. Some people say that learning about your ethnic heritage and practicing some of the ancient customs is important to your identity. Others say that "getting back to your roots" is unnecessary and irrelevant to life in the modern world. Which group of people do you agree with and why?

Literary Concept: Characterization

How does a writer make the characters in a story come alive? Writers use certain methods of **characterization** to help readers see and understand the characters. The writer may have the narrator give either a physical description of a character or an explanation of some trait. A character's personality can also be shown through his or her actions, statements, or thoughts. The things that other people in a story say about a character is another method of characterization. Which of these methods are used in "Dancer" to characterize Clarissa?

Writing Options

1. Some Native American tribes give each of their members a name that reflects the person's nature. For example, Molly's last name, Graybull, may suggest her importance in the tribe, her wisdom, and her leadership. Think of a tribal name for Clarissa or her foster mother that reflects some important quality of the character. Write an **explanation** telling why you chose the name.

2. Imagine that you are Clarissa. Write a **letter** nominating your foster mother for the Mother of the Year Award. Consider all the things she did to be worthy of this prize.

3. Write Molly Graybull's **will.** In the will, leave several special possessions to Clarissa. Have Molly explain why she is leaving these things to the child.

4. Write your own **story** about a tradition from your heritage. Let the story show how it feels to be a part of this tradition.

Vocabulary Practice

Exercise On your paper, write the letter of the situation that best demonstrates the meaning of the boldfaced word.

1. **sociopathic**
   a. The student misplaced the teacher's book.
   b. The boy was shockingly cruel in fights.
   c. A guide showed us the sociology office.

2. **preen**
   a. The boy spent an hour combing his hair.
   b. The twelve-year-old was not yet a teenager.
   c. The material looked just like velvet.

3. **fixated**
   a. How can we thank you for your generosity?
   b. For months Sue read books about dinosaurs.
   c. The plumber came to repair the sink.

4. **ferocious**
   a. The lioness growled angrily at the hunter.
   b. The monkey let its baby ride on its back.
   c. She practiced playing the piano twice a day.

5. **loner**
   a. Kathy let her brother use her car.
   b. The violent storm raged all night.
   c. Erik lives alone and rarely talks to anyone.

Words to Know and Use

ferocious
fixated
loner
preen
sociopathic

Options for Learning

1 • **Tell a Tale** Trickster tales and spider tales are just two of the kinds of stories that Native Americans like to tell. Look through several books until you find a Native American story that particularly appeals to you. Learn it well enough to tell it to your classmates.

2 • **The Right Dress** Clarissa gets a brand-new wing dress for the first powwow of the school year. Do some research on Native American costumes and then draw a detailed picture of Clarissa's special dress.

3 • **Dancing Music** On your own or with a small group, find music to accompany a particular type of Native American dance. Bring in the music and share it with your classmates. You might also wish to discuss the instruments used and the history of the dance.

4 • **Pick a Tribe** With a partner, research a particular Native American tribe. In words and pictures, relate some of the most important information about the tribe's people. Be sure to include their history, where they live now, and what traditional customs they still honor.

 FACT FINDER GEOGRAPHY

Where does the Assiniboine tribe live today?

*V*ickie Sears
1941–

A descendant of Cherokee, Spanish, and English ancestors, Vickie Sears lives in Seattle, Washington. There she works as a writer, therapist, and teacher.

Simple Songs, the collection of short stories in which "Dancer" appears, was published in 1990. Sears was thinking of children like Clarissa when she wrote this dedication for her book: "To all of the children who ever lived in an orphanage or foster home and had a dream."

Elements of
NONFICTION

While some readers enjoy getting lost in the imaginary world of fiction, others prefer the authenticity of stories from real life. **Nonfiction** is writing about real people, places, and events.

There are two broad categories of nonfiction. One category, called **informative nonfiction,** is mainly written to provide factual information. Nonfiction of this type includes science and history texts, informational books, encyclopedias, pamphlets, and most of the articles in magazines and newspapers. The main purpose of this material is to inform.

The other category of nonfiction is called **literary nonfiction** because it is written to be read and experienced in much the same way you experience fiction. However, literary nonfiction differs from fiction in that real people take the place of fictional characters, and the settings and plots are not imagined but are actual places and true events.

The following are the types of literary nonfiction you will read in this book.

*U*nderstanding Nonfiction

Autobiography An autobiography is the true story of a person's life, told by that person. It is almost always written using the first-person point of view. In this book you will read an excerpt from an autobiography by Clifton Taulbert. In it, Taulbert describes an influential person in his life.

An autobiography is usually book length because it covers a long period of the writer's life. However, there are shorter types of autobiographical writing such as **journals, diaries,** and **memoirs.**

Biography A biography is the true story of a person's life, told by someone else. The writer, or **biographer,** interviews the subject if possible and also researches the **subject's** life by reading letters, books, diaries, and any other information he or she can find. In this book, you will read an excerpt from a biography about Harriet Tubman, famous for her role in helping escaped slaves flee to Canada.

As you will see, biographies and autobiographies often seem like fiction because they contain many of the same elements, such as character, setting, and plot.

Essay An essay is a short piece of nonfiction writing that deals with one subject. Essays are often found in newspapers and magazines. The writer might share an opinion, try to entertain or persuade the reader, or simply describe an incident that has special significance. These essays that explain how the author feels about a subject are called **informal,** or **personal,** essays. In this book, the selection "Memories of Dating" is an example of an informal essay. Formal essays are serious and scholarly and are rarely found in literature textbooks.

*S*trategies for Reading Nonfiction

Nonfiction can be read as a piece of literature or as a source of information. The nonfiction you will read in this book has been included because of the interesting story it has to tell—because of its literary quality. As you read, try to step into and enjoy the true stories and opinions the authors have to share.

Use the following strategies when you read nonfiction.

1. **Preview** a selection before you read. Look at the title, pictures, diagrams, subtitles, and any terms in boldfaced or italic type. All of these will give you an idea of what the selection is about.

2. **Figure out the organization.** If the work is a biography or autobiography, the organization is probably chronological, that is, in the order that events happened. Other articles may be arranged around ideas the author wants to discuss.

3. **Separate facts and opinions. Facts** are statements that can be proved, such as "'Pompeii' is the longest nonfiction selection in this book." **Opinions** are statements that cannot be proved. They simply express the writer's beliefs, such as "'Pompeii' is the best nonfiction selection in this book." Writers of nonfiction sometimes present opinions as if they were facts. Be sure you recognize the difference.

4. **Question** as you read. Why did things happen the way they did? How did people feel? What is the writer's opinion? Do you share the writer's opinion, or do you have different ideas on the subject?

5. During your reading, stop now and then and try to **predict** what will come next. Sometimes you will be surprised by what happens or by what the author has to say about an issue.

6. As you read, **build** on your understanding. Add new information to what you have already learned and see if your ideas and opinions change.

7. Continually **evaluate** what you read. Evaluation should be an ongoing process, not just something that is done when you have finished reading. Remember that evaluation means more than saying a selection is good or bad. Form opinions about people, events, and ideas that are presented. Decide whether or not you like the way the piece was written.

Finally, it is important to recognize that your understanding of a selection does not end when you stop reading. As you think more about what you have read and discuss it with others, you will find that your understanding continues to grow.

Nonfiction   ## *M*emories of *D*ating

DAVE BARRY

*E*xamine What You Know

Has this ever happened to you? You have this great friend; the two of you are practically inseparable . . . until it happens. Your friend develops a crush on someone and becomes a different person. It is almost as if the friend you thought you knew has been replaced by someone who looks the same, but who doesn't act the same. You will just have to face it—your friend has entered THE WORLD OF DATING. With your classmates, compile a list of some dating advice that you could give your friend. You may want to organize the tips into categories such as Most Helpful, Most Humorous, and so on.

Dating Tips
1. wear clean socks
2. bring extra money
3. comb your hair
4. choose a funny movie

*E*xpand Your Knowledge

Dave Barry writes a weekly humor column for the *Miami Herald's Tropic Magazine*. Syndication, or sale to other newspapers, brings Barry's column to more than four hundred papers, including one in Thailand. Barry's humor depends on several ingredients: humorous references to current events, wild exaggerations of the truth, and irony—a method of expression in which an intended meaning is opposite of what is expected. In the column you are about to read, Barry combines all of these elements as he gives a boy named Eric some humorous advice on dating.

*E*nrich Your Reading

■ *Author biography in Reader's Handbook*

Hyperbole   In his column, Barry claims that if a girl had refused his invitation for a date, he would have had to leave junior high forever and become a bark-eating hermit. This extreme exaggeration, called **hyperbole,** helps make Barry's writing humorous. As you read, note other examples of hyperbole.

Memories of Dating

DAVE BARRY

As a mature adult, I feel an obligation to help the younger generation, just as the mother fish guards her unhatched eggs, keeping her lonely vigil day after day, never leaving her post, not even to go to the bathroom, until her tiny babies emerge and she is able, at last, to eat them. "She may be your mom, but she's still a fish" is a wisdom nugget that I would pass along to any fish eggs reading this column.

But today I want to talk about dating. This subject was raised in a letter to me from a young person named Eric Knott, who writes:

"I have got a big problem. There's this girl in my English class who is really good-looking. However, I don't think she knows I exist. I want to ask her out, but I'm afraid she will say no, and I will be the freak of the week. What should I do?"

Eric, you have sent your question to the right mature adult, because as a young person, I spent a lot of time thinking about this very problem. Starting in about eighth grade, my time was divided as follows:

Academic Pursuits: 2 percent
Zits: 16 percent
Trying to Figure Out How to Ask Girls
    Out: 82 percent

The most sensible way to ask a girl out is to walk directly up to her on foot and say, "So you want to go out or what?" I never did this. I knew, as Eric Knott knows, that there was always the possibility that the girl would say no, thereby leaving me with no viable option but to leave Harold C. Crittenden Junior High School forever and go into the woods and become a bark-eating hermit whose only companions would be the gentle and understanding woodland creatures.

"Hey, Zitface!" the woodland creatures would shriek in their cute little Chip 'n' Dale voices while raining acorns down upon my head. "You wanna *date?* Hahahahahaha."

So the first rule of dating is, Never risk direct contact with the girl in question. Your role model should be the nuclear submarine, gliding silently beneath the ocean surface, tracking an enemy target that does not even begin to suspect that the submarine would like to date it. I spent the vast majority of 1960 keeping a girl named Judy under surveillance, maintaining a minimum distance of fifty lockers to avoid the danger that I might somehow get into a conversation with her, which could have led to disaster.

Judy: Hi.
Me: Hi.
Judy: Just in case you have ever thought about having a date with me, the answer is no.
Woodland Creatures: Hahahahahaha.

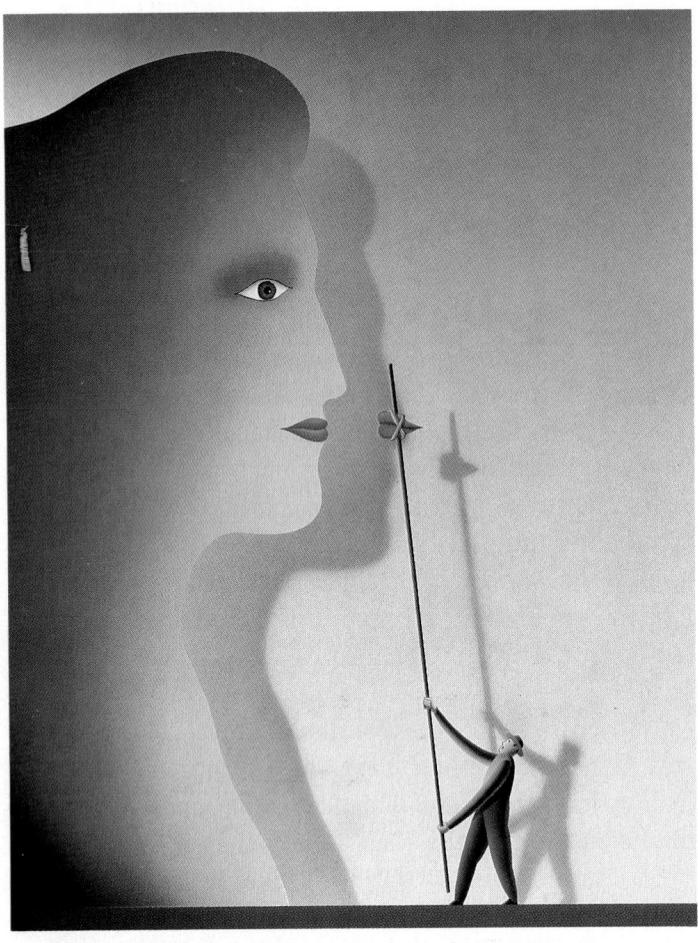

Illustration by Michael McGurl.

The only problem with the nuclear-sub-marine technique is that it's difficult to get a date with a girl who has never, technically, been asked. This is why you need Phil Grant. Phil was a friend of mine who had the ability to talk to girls. It was a mysterious superhuman power he had, comparable to X-ray vision. So, after several thousand hours of intense discussion and planning with me, Phil approached a girl he knew named Nancy, who approached a girl named Sandy, who was a direct personal

friend of Judy's and who passed the word back to Phil via Nancy that Judy would be willing to go on a date with me. This procedure protected me from direct humiliation, similar to the way President Reagan[1] was protected from direct involvement in the Iran-Contra scandal[2] by a complex White House chain of command that at one point, investigators now believe, included his horse.

Thus it was that, finally, Judy and I went on an actual date, to see a movie in White Plains, New York. If I were to sum up the romantic ambience[3] of this date in four words, those words would be, "My mother was driving." This made for an extremely quiet drive, because my mother, realizing that her presence was hideously embarrassing, had to pretend she wasn't there. If it had been legal, I think she would have got out and sprinted alongside the car, steering through the window. Judy and I, sitting in the back seat about seventy-five feet apart, were also silent, unable to communicate without the assistance of Phil, Nancy, and Sandy.

After what seemed like several years, we got to the movie theater, where my mother went off to sit in the Parents and Lepers Section. The movie was called *North to Alaska,* but I can tell you nothing else about it because I spent the whole time wondering whether it would be necessary to amputate my right arm, which was not getting any

---

1. **President Reagan:** Ronald Wilson Reagan, 1911- ; U.S. president 1981-89.
2. **Iran-Contra scandal:** a case in which U.S. government officials were suspected of improperly selling weapons to Iran to raise funds for Nicaraguan rebel forces.
3. **ambience** (am′ bē əns): an atmosphere or environment.

blood flow as a result of being perched for two hours like a petrified snake on the back of Judy's seat exactly one molecule away from physical contact.

So it was definitely a fun first date, featuring all the relaxed spontaneity of a real-estate closing,[4] and in later years I did regain some feeling in my arm. My point, Eric Knott, is that the key to successful dating is self-confidence. I bet that good-looking girl in your English class would *love* to go out with you. But *you* have to make the first move. So just do it! Pick up that phone! Call Phil Grant. ❧

---

4. **real-estate closing:** a meeting at which the rights to land or a building are officially transferred from seller to buyer.

INSIGHT

your little voice
E. E. CUMMINGS

your little voice
          Over the wires came leaping
and i felt suddenly
dizzy
     With the jostling and shouting of merry flowers
wee skipping high-heeled flames
courtesied before my eyes
               or twinkling over to my side
Looked up
with impertinently exquisite faces
floating hands were laid upon me
I was whirled and tossed into delicious dancing
up
Up
with the pale important
             stars and the Humorous
                  moon
dear girl
How i was crazy how i cried when i heard
            over time
and tide and death
leaping
Sweetly
     your voice

Illustration by Tatjana Krizmanic.

E X P L A I N

*R*esponding to Reading

First Impressions

1. What is your reaction to Barry's observations about young people and dating?

Second Thoughts

2. Do you agree with Barry's first rule of dating? Explain.

   Think about
   - the advantages and disadvantages of having a friend serve as a go-between
   - the advantages and disadvantages of asking the person yourself
   - the "moment of truth" when you finally must talk to each other on the date

3. From what you know or have heard about dating, which parts of Barry's description seem accurate? Which parts contain examples of **hyperbole**?

4. Look back at the list of dating advice that you created in the Examine What You Know activity. Turn your suggestions into ones that Barry might make using humor and exaggeration.

Broader Connections

5. Although Barry's recollection of dating is presented here in a humorous fashion, many young people can identify with his confusion about the rules of dating. At what age do students in your community start dating? Is this too young? too old? just right?

*W*riting Options

1. Write a **letter** to Phil Grant, asking him to set up a date for you.

2. Create your own **advice column,** responding as Dave Barry might to requests for advice about problems that students your age face.

3. Imagine you are Judy, the girl Barry talks about in his column. Write a **diary entry** describing your date with Dave.

Nonfiction

from **Once Upon a Time When We Were Colored**

CLIFTON TAULBERT

Examine What You Know

The autobiographical excerpt you are about to read tells about an incident that Clifton Taulbert experienced while growing up in Mississippi during the 1950s. Taulbert's moment of truth had to do with discrimination—being treated differently due to having a particular set of beliefs or belonging to a particular race, class, or gender group. Think about a time when you or someone you know or have read about experienced discrimination. Discuss the experience with your classmates.

Expand Your Knowledge

Tongs for delivering ice.

Many aspects of Taulbert's childhood in Mississippi no longer exist today. For example, a 1969 Supreme Court ruling helped end segregation (the forced separation of races) in Mississippi public schools. Uncle Cleve's occupation, delivering ice, also became obsolete as refrigerators became more affordable. Finally, minstrel shows—traveling variety shows featuring white performers with blackened faces—rarely, if ever, are performed today.

Enrich Your Reading

Sensory Details   Taulbert gives his readers a more vivid picture of his childhood in Mississippi by including many details that appeal to the senses. The description of the hot grits and sausages that he had for breakfast, for example, may make your mouth water as you read. After you finish reading, find other sensory details in this selection and add them to the chart below.

smell	hot grits and sausage
sight	
hearing	
touch	
taste	

■ *Author biography on Extend page*

from *Once Upon a Time When We Were Colored*

CLIFTON TAULBERT

Surely if my Uncle Cleve were alive today, he'd find a reason to be a black Republican. He was short, neatly dressed, and <u>conservative</u>. Uncle Cleve came from Cold- water, Mississippi. I know very little about his early life with my great-aunt Willie, but I do recall his strong personality and the <u>impact</u> he had on my life growing up in Glen Allan.

I never heard him raise his voice. When he talked, he always talked politics and demonstrated a real business sense. Independence and nonconversance[1] were his most notable characteristics. I called him Uncle Cleve, Ma Ponk called him Bro. Cleve, and every other colored person called him Mr. Cleve. The white community with which he had contact called him Mormon, his last name, their badge of respect.

Uncle Cleve, Mr. Cleve, Bro. Cleve, or Mormon—he was my first employer. From him, I learned a sense of responsibility that undergirds my approach today. He ran the only icehouse in town. Refrigerators were a rarity in the colored community and among the poor whites, and nearly all the small businesses used ice to keep their goods from spoiling. Only Mr. Cleve provided the ice needed in Glen Allan. Twice daily, we'd see him driving the red flatbed truck up and down the streets, announcing "The iceman is here." For years, I would run alongside the truck as Uncle Cleve stopped at each house and chipped his sales of fifteen or thirty pounds of ice. Occasionally someone would buy fifty pounds, but that was rare. He was always quick, <u>responsive</u>, and very polite—not given to extra conversation when waiting on his customer. His business made our lives better, and he was always received as a welcome sight.

Being an assistant to Mr. Cleve was viewed as a good job, and I couldn't wait until I was old enough to work with my cousin Joe, Uncle Cleve's son. Uncle Cleve had been training me by taking me with him to Hollandale, Mississippi, to buy ice from

---

1. **nonconversance:** a term used here to describe Uncle Cleve's habit of saying very little.

Words to Know and Use	**conservative** (kən sʉr′ və tiv) *adj.* traditional in style and manner **impact** (im′ pakt) *n.* a strong effect **responsive** (ri spän′ siv) *adj.* quick to react to another

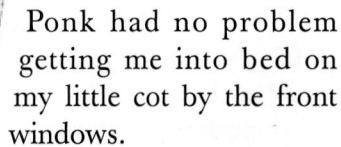

Clifton Taulbert as a child.
Courtesy, Council Oak Books.

the ice factory. We would ride to Hollandale together, just the two of us. I recall the trip taking hours, but really it was very short. We'd drive down the road eating salami and crackers, and every once in a while he would talk to me about life.

"Yes, git you a good pattern and follow it. Always be early for work, and save fifty cents out of every dollar you make."

I didn't try to answer. I just sat in the cab of the truck and listened as he continued talking. All I wanted was the chance to show him that I could handle the big three-hundred-pound blocks of ice. If I could prove my ability to handle the big blocks, he would let me work at his icehouse.

Finally one Saturday, he gave me the chance. I must have been about twelve years old. Child-labor laws weren't in vogue in Glen Allan, and when you were strong enough to handle the job, nobody worried about how old you were. I could hardly sleep the Friday night before, although Ma

Ponk had no problem getting me into bed on my little cot by the front windows.

"Boy, git to bed early, 'cause Bro. Cleve will leave you if you ain't ready to go when he comes by," Ma Ponk told me as she securely tucked me in bed.

Saturday morning didn't come soon enough. I found myself waking up nearly every hour, straining my eyes to see the hands on the clock. Finally I heard Ma Ponk's voice through the quilts. "Cliff, git up and git some food in you, 'cause you know Bro. Cleve ain't gonna stop."

No sooner had she spoken than I jumped from bed and ran to get the wash pan so I could wash up before eating my breakfast. The smell of hot oil sausages and grits[2] floated through the house, and I could hardly wait. How lucky could I be—a trip to Hollandale with Uncle Cleve, *and* my favorite breakfast. The food went fast, and I

---

2. **grits:** short for *hominy grits,* a popular Southern dish made of coarsely ground dry corn.

found myself ready and waiting when Uncle Cleve came by. True to form, he was a little early.

"'Bye, Ma Ponk!" I yelled as I jumped from the porch to the ground.

Our trip was not unusual, but this time I would have the chance to show my uncle that I was big enough to help him with the business.

"Cleve, pull your truck in next," a colored man yelled as we pulled up to the Hollandale Icehouse.

Uncle Cleve let me out of the cab and told me to take the steps to the dock; he'd meet me there. He never made suggestions. You simply did what he told you, and quickly. After parking the truck so the bed would be against the dock, Uncle Cleve came around to the side where I was standing.

"OK, Cliff, we'll see if you can handle the big one."

As we walked into the icehouse, all I could see was a cold vapor rising from hundreds of blocks of ice. Each block weighed three hundred pounds. Standing inside the door, I felt the chill as Uncle Cleve took the giant ice hook off the wall.

"Cliff, pay attention." Uncle Cleve proceeded to show me how to put the ice hook securely into the block while using my knee as an anchor.

I watched and I watched and I watched. Finally, it was my turn. I walked over to a huge block of ice and carefully repeated what I had been shown many times. I securely hooked my ice, carefully placed my knee, and began to gently pull the block to the floor. Before I could get fearful, I had

finished. The three-hundred-pound block of ice was on the floor, and I was pulling it out to the truck.

"New helper you got, Mormon?" one of the white men asked.

"Yes, sir," Uncle Cleve nodded as he watched me load the truck for the very first time.

My ride home could not have been sweeter. Uncle Cleve stopped by a local store and bought me a large grape soda and a moon pie[3]—my reward. We didn't say much on the way back, but we both knew it had been a good day.

Many months later, nearing the end of the summer, Uncle Cleve promised to take me with him to Jackson as a gift for having done a good job for him. The day of our trip finally arrived. It started out as one of the happiest days of my life. My uncle was taking me to Jackson to the biggest tent show that had ever come our way. Ma Ponk got me all dressed up in my Sunday church clothes, combed my hair until my scalp was sore, and had me ready at least two hours early. Uncle Cleve was a slow driver, so we were going to leave in plenty of time to get to the seven o'clock grand opening.

I was ready at three o'clock and sitting out on the front steps waiting for the familiar sound of Uncle's 1947 green International truck that purred like a kitten. Ma Ponk and I were waiting, and there was absolutely no way of missing Uncle Cleve. When the truck pulled up, I almost jumped

---

3. **moon pie:** a round chocolate-covered marshmallow candy.

Underwood Photo Archives.

out of my pants, but Uncle Cleve only smiled slightly as I ran around to the passenger's side and tucked myself firmly in, secure with the knowledge that tonight was going to be a really big night for me. Uncle Cleve was very confident, only telling me that he never messed with the small-town minstrel shows[4] that came to Glen Allan to rob you blind. If he was going to waste his time and spend his money, it would be at something like the big show that we were going to in Jackson.

I know I counted every tree and rock between Glen Allan and Jackson, because Uncle drove so slowly. He never hurried about anything. Moving meticulously, like a well-greased snail, he'd get the work of two men done in half the time. His driving was

the same perfect execution of the rules, never speeding, just fast enough to beat running.

It was almost 150 miles to Jackson. Ma Ponk didn't even pack me a lunch, because Uncle Cleve had promised to buy my lunch. Packed lunches in greasy brown paper bags were for old church ladies, not the two of us.

Finally we reached Jackson. There were more bright lights than I had ever seen. This was a large city, not like Glen Allan. Uncle Cleve took the city in stride. After all, he had been to Memphis, and Jackson was just another city to him. To me, however, Jackson was the biggest and the brightest. It

---

4. **minstrel shows:** variety shows featuring white performers with blackened faces.

51

even had uniformed policemen directing the traffic, and I saw my first traffic jam.

I was so excited about being in a city I didn't realize we had gotten near the show grounds. There seemed to be hundreds of cars and people. But my uncle knew where we were going. He parked the truck and held my hand tightly as we followed the crowd. Finally we got to the main gate, where a big curly-headed white man reached down and took our tickets. We were ushered in with the crowds of other people to a tent that seemed big enough to cover the whole world.

White people were everywhere, laughing and talking and eating popcorn and pulling their children behind them, as we all headed toward the big tent.

It was so crowded in the tent and we were so far back that I could hardly see, but I remember when those gigantic curtains opened and I saw all those beautiful ladies in sequined stockings.[5] I could hardly sit still. I know I was too small to fully appreciate that beauty, but the glitter I understood. The music was loud all around us, and sweaty men were yelling and whistling; but my uncle just smiled slightly, ate one piece of popcorn at a time, and watched.

We couldn't have been there any more than twenty minutes when the usher came over to us and said, "I am sorry, but this ain't the night for niggers."[6]

My uncle's smile dropped from his face, and his warm eyes became cold as steel as he jerked me up and we walked out. We hadn't even seen half the show.

The long trip back was completely silent. I sat in the car, miserable, trying not to cry. I was too young to understand why this had happened to us, and my uncle would not explain. ❧

---

5. **sequined stockings:** stockings decorated with small shiny disks.

6. **niggers:** *slang,* a derogatory name for African Americans. The word is considered to be extremely offensive.

*R*esponding to Reading

First Impressions

1. Did the selection end the way you expected it to? Explain your answer.

Second Thoughts

2. How would you describe Uncle Cleve's personal code?

3. Why do you think Uncle Cleve refused to explain the discrimination he and Cliff encountered in Jackson?

4. Although Cliff is twelve years old at the end of the selection, he seems unaware of racial prejudice. Do you think this is possible? Discuss, using examples from the selection and your own experience as evidence.

Broader Connections

5. The kind of discrimination that Cliff and his uncle encountered at the tent show does not exist today. What other kinds of discrimination *do* exist? What do you think are some of the major causes?

*L*iterary Concept: Autobiography

Clifton Taulbert's account of his relationship with his uncle is part of his autobiography, or story of his life. Written from a first-person point of view, an **autobiography** provides insight into the writer's personality and development. If you were to write your autobiography, which events would you be sure to include?

Concept Review: Characterization   You know that **characterization** refers to the ways a writer creates and develops a character. The way characters look, talk, and act, and the way other characters respond to them, all contribute to characterization. Find an example of one of these types of characterization that gives important information about Uncle Cleve.

Writing Options

1. Imagine you are a newspaper reporter who witnessed what happened to Cliff and Uncle Cleve in Jackson. Write an **article** to appear in the morning edition of your paper.

2. Uncle Cleve advises Cliff to "get you a good pattern and follow it. Always be early for work, and save fifty cents out of every dollar you make." Write an **essay** explaining the best or worst advice you've ever received.

3. Stories always take on a slightly different meaning when told from another person's perspective. Step into the shoes of Ma Ponk and write a **story** about Cleve and Cliff from her point of view.

4. If Uncle Cleve had talked to Cliff about the incident in Jackson, what might he have said? Consider his personality and manner and what Cliff might say in response. Write a **report** describing the dialogue between the two.

Vocabulary Practice

Exercise Decide if the following pairs of words are synonyms or antonyms. On your paper, write *S* for synonym or *A* for antonym.

1. vogue—fashion

2. meticulously—carelessly

3. conservative—liberal

4. impact—force

5. responsive—sympathetic

> *Words to Know and Use*
>
> ---
>
> **conservative**
> **impact**
> **meticulously**
> **responsive**
> **vogue**

EXTEND

Options for Learning

1 • Kids at Work Cliff was about twelve when he went to work for his uncle. Is it legal for twelve-year-olds to work today? Research the child labor laws in your state. Find out what age children must be to obtain certain jobs, how long they may work each day, and whether or not they must have a permit to work.

2 • Emotional Roller Coaster Cliff experiences a variety of emotions, ranging from extreme happiness to deep misery. Make an "emotions graph," plotting at least three events on the horizontal line, and Cliff's emotions, from low to high, on the vertical line.

3 • Fond Farewell Write a speech to deliver at Uncle Cleve's retirement party. You may want to award him a gift for his years of service to the community.

4 • All Over the Map Draw a map of Mississippi that highlights the towns and cities mentioned in this selection: Coldwater, Glen Allan, Hollandale, and Jackson.

FACT FINDER HISTORY
When were refrigerators first sold for home use in the United States?

Clifton Taulbert
1945–

The "colored child" who grew up in small-town Mississippi has become a leading businessman in Tulsa, Oklahoma. Today Clifton Taulbert heads the Freemount Corporation, a marketing and consulting firm, and is a partner in Fine Airport Parking, Inc., a multi-million dollar company.

Of his childhood in segregated Mississippi, he wrote, "I would never want to return to forced segregation, but I also have a deeply felt sense that important values were conveyed to me in my colored childhood, values we're in danger of losing in our integrated world."

Taulbert, who graduated first in his high school class, served in the U.S. Air Force and attended the Universities of Maine and Maryland before graduating from Oral Roberts University with a degree in sociology and history. He wrote his autobiography because he wanted his children "to know of the lifestyle that gave them their father and their mother."

WORKSHOP

PERSONAL WRITING

USE PERSONAL WRITING FOR
journals
logs
notes
letters
diaries
autobiographies
memoirs

Like the characters in this subunit, most of us have experienced "moments of truth." While many such moments are serious, some, as in Dave Barry's "Memories of Dating," help us look at ourselves through humor. These experiences—both the serious and the humorous—help define who we are and what we believe in. In this workshop you will write a humorous memoir. A **memoir** (related to the word *memory*) is a first-person recollection of an experience or event. You can write about an event that you witnessed or one in which you participated. Writing about these experiences can help you understand them. Finding the humor in a situation can help you face your moments of truth with a more positive attitude.

Here is one writer's PASSkey to this assignment.

GUIDED ASSIGNMENT: HUMOROUS MEMOIR

Use humor to describe a moment of truth. Explore what happened as a result of the experience.

PURPOSE: To tell about a humorous experience

AUDIENCE: Classmates, family, friends

SUBJECT: A moment of truth

STRUCTURE: A memoir

STUDENT MODEL

▶ Before you write, read how one student responded to the assignment.

▶ The writer tapped into his memory of a special trip to create an idea for a humorous memoir.

> A Night in the Country
> · by Franklin Lincoln
>
> Can you picture thirty city kids camping out in the woods overnight? Neither could I--until it happened. Mr. Rivera, our social studies teacher, had this crazy idea that camping in the woods overnight would help us city kids appreciate country living. Boy, was he wrong! This trip was doomed from the start. The farther we got from skyscrapers and pavement and bus fumes, the worse I felt.

You see, everything about the country makes me nervous—even grass. After all, it's ALIVE! Mr. Rivera kept telling us how great it would be to sleep under the stars. I looked at my pals Tomás and Lee; they looked at me. We guys all rolled our eyes.

The nightmare began the minute we arrived at Shady Dale Woods. Mr. Rivera told Tomás and me to build a fire. None of us wanted anything to do with wood-gathering duty. Tomás said he had allergies. Lee claimed he had a sore ankle. I just stalled. I was sure that hundreds of escaped convicts were lurking in the bushes near the edge of our campsite.

What followed was the longest night in recorded history. I lay shivering inside my sleeping bag wondering what would get me first. A hungry forest animal? A regiment of bat-sized mosquitoes? A slithering snake? All night long I heard sounds. I felt bugs. I saw beady little eyes. No doubt about it! I was scared to death.

I finally fell asleep, only to be jolted awake by a bird--or was it a BAT!!--divebombing past my head. I felt something bounce off my sleeping bag; I let out a bloodcurdling scream. I tried to get out of my sleeping bag, but my pajamas got caught in the zipper. Tomás and Lee jumped up and started stomping on whatever it was that tried to attack me. We looked at the vicious monster and then at one another. We had just killed . . . a twig! The three of us broke into laughter when we realized how silly we had been. This little incident taught us all something--we shouldn't fear the unknown as much we did. Maybe Mr. Rivera's crazy idea wasn't so crazy after all!

As you continue reading, pay particular attention to the descriptive words Franklin has chosen. How do these words add to the humor of his memoir?

References to "the longest night in recorded history" and "bat-sized mosquitoes" indicate the writer's use of **hyperbole,** or extreme exaggeration, to create humor.

In the final paragraph the writer brings his story back to the present and explains the results of his moment of truth.

Now that you've read Franklin's paper, it's time to begin your own.

Prewrite and Explore

WRITER'S CHOICE

If you can't think of an idea you like, try asking a parent, a sibling, or even a close friend if they can recall any humorous stories about you.

▶ **1** **Search your memory**   If you need some writing ideas, review your personal history. Think about places you've visited. Look through any mementos you have collected from these places, such as photographs, postcards, and souvenirs. Think about activities that you enjoyed, as well as interesting people you met. Keep a notebook nearby to jot down any ideas or images that come to mind.

2 **Choose your topic and gather information**   Be sure to choose a topic that you will enjoy writing about and that readers will find interesting. Make sure your topic is suitable for a humorous approach. After you've chosen a topic, start gathering details that will help you write.

GATHERING INFORMATION

Replay the memorable moment in your mind, looking for the humorous angles. What did you learn from the experience? Jot down the major images and feelings you want to portray, especially those that might be humorous. Look at the notes Franklin made. He jotted down several details about the camping trip and classified them according to the time they took place. Notice that Franklin is thinking "humor" even when he writes his notes.

STUDENT MODEL

Compare Franklin's list of details with those he actually included in his memoir. Which ones are most effective?

> **Beginning**
>
> Mr. Rivera's crazy idea
> Group of city kids on camping trip
> New experience to kids
> Activities planned for trip

▶

Middle	**Ending**
Bus ride to Shady Dale Woods	Tension felt by Tomás,
Telling jokes on bus	Lee, and me
Setting up camp	Lee wearing glasses to bed
Safety of bus	Mr. Rivera keeping
Isolated campsite	flashlight at his side
Dangers in woods	Strange sounds at night
Bat-sized mosquitoes	Attack by twig
Pajamas stuck in zipper	Learned a lesson about
Crazy Ivan, escaped convict	fear of the unknown

Draft and Discover

1 **Begin drafting**   As you write, think about the notes you gathered. Which ones do you want to include? Which ones will bring your memoir to life? Which ones might not be needed? Organize your final list of notes into groups that relate to some part of your experience. These groups of details may become separate paragraphs in your memoir.

2 **Decide on a starting point**   A memoir is often written in chronological order. However, you may wish to start your story by showing the final results first. You can then use the rest of the memoir to show how you achieved those results.

◀ COMPUTER TIP
. . . .
Try using the "move" function on your computer to compare the impact of putting the final results at either the beginning or the end of your story.

Revise Your Writing

1 **Fine-tune your draft**   Now that you have your basic story mapped out, you can shape your writing. For this assignment, focus on choosing just the right words to create the clearest, most humorous picture of what happened in your experience. Franklin reworked his draft many times before he was satisfied with the final version.

  Because you are writing a humorous memoir, you might experiment with using figurative language to achieve your goal. Look back at Franklin's model. He used **hyperbole** (extreme exaggeration) to create humorous images.

ASK FOR HELP
. . . .
Not sure where the humor is? Try telling your story to a classmate. As you talk, you may spot new aspects of the incident that are potentially funny.

2 **Try a peer reader**   You might ask a friend to respond to your draft. The following questions can help.

Revision Questions	
For You	**For a Peer Reader**
1. Did I clearly explain the sequence of events?	1. Did I place the results of my moment of truth for the most impact?
2. Did my choice of details and language add humor to my story?	2. What did you find funny? Did any jokes fall flat?
3. Did I explain the results of my moment of truth?	3. What was my moment of truth?

Proofread

When you have finished revising your paper, proofread for errors in grammar, spelling, punctuation, and capitalization. If possible, ask a friend to review your work. In this assignment, pay special attention to how you use personal pronouns.

NEED MORE HELP?

See the Language Workshop that follows (pages 61–63) and pages 781–782 of the Language Handbook.

THE EDITOR'S EYE: PERSONAL PRONOUNS

Use personal pronouns correctly in phrases like *we girls* and *us boys*.

When you use pronouns in phrases like *we girls* and *us boys*, you must be sure that you choose the correct form—the subject form or the object form. You can tell which form to choose by dropping the noun and saying the sentence without it.

Problem   (We, Us) guys all rolled our eyes.
Correct   We guys all rolled our eyes.
Also Correct We all rolled our eyes.

Publish and Present

Here is a suggestion for sharing your work with others.

Comedy Club   With your classmates, choose the best and most humorous memoirs to be used in a comedy-club revue. Each chosen memoir can be presented as a stand-up comedy routine.

Reflect on Your Writing

FOR YOUR PORTFOLIO ▶ Briefly answer the following questions. Put your answers with your paper, and add both to your portfolio.

1. Which parts of your memoir do you think are the most effective? the most humorous? Why?
2. How did you like writing humor? Did you find it easy or difficult? Explain.

LANGUAGE
WORKSHOP

USING PRONOUNS CORRECTLY

> Use **personal pronouns** correctly in your speaking and writing.

Most of the time you use pronouns correctly without even thinking about them. However, there are a few specific situations where some study is required.

Pronouns in Compound Constructions

> Use the same pronoun in a compound subject or a compound object that you would use if the pronoun stood alone.

Pronouns can be used as either subjects or objects. You may recall that the subject pronouns are *I, you, he, she, it, we,* and *they.* The object pronouns are *me, you, him, her, it, us,* and *them.*

When you use one of these pronouns by itself, you almost always use it correctly. Your ear tells you what is right. For example, you would never say, "*Me* am going to the store" or "Give the book to *I.*" Mistakes happen when a pronoun is paired with another noun or pronoun in a compound subject or object. Which pronouns would you choose in the following sentence?

> (Him, He) and (I, me) discussed how to ask Judy and (she, her) to the dance.

There's an easy way to get the right answers. Try each pronoun by itself. Which ones sound right?

Him discussed . . .   how to ask *she*
He discussed . . .   how to ask *her*

I discussed . . .
Me discussed . . .

He, I, and *her* are correct.

We and Us Used With Nouns

A problem similar to the use of compound constructions is the use of a pronoun and a noun together in phrases like *we girls* or *us boys*. Which pronoun would you choose for the following sentence?

(We, Us) girls wonder why the boys are so nervous.

You can tell which pronoun to use by dropping the noun *girls* and saying the sentence without it. Which sentence sounds right?

We wonder why the boys are so nervous.
Us wonder why the boys are so nervous.

If you chose the first sentence, you are correct.

Exercise 1   Concept Check   Write the correct pronoun.

1. Phil and (I, me) decided to meet Judy and Meg at the dance.
2. Don't tell anyone, but (we, us) guys spent an hour getting ready.
3. I wonder if it took Judy and (she, her) that long.
4. When the girls saw Phil and (I, me) they said we looked sharp.
5. (We, Us) four went into the gym.
6. The music was perfect for (we, us) students, but some teachers said it was too loud.
7. I asked Judy to dance, and (she, her) and (I, me) headed for the middle of the dance floor.
8. (We, Us) two had just begun when I tripped and fell.
9. I stumbled out the door, figuring it was the end for Judy and (I, me).
10. Guess what! (Us, We) two started laughing and Judy said that (she, her) and (I, me) should try a slow dance next time.

Possessive Pronouns and Contractions

A **possessive pronoun** never has an apostrophe; a **contraction** always has an apostrophe.

A **possessive pronoun** shows ownership: *your* jacket, *his* skateboard, *their* tickets. A **contraction** is a word formed by squeezing two words together into one. When this happens, some letters are dropped and the apostrophe shows where these letters used to be. A problem occurs because some possessive pronouns sound like contractions.

Possessive Pronouns	Contractions
its	it's (it + is or has)
your	you're (you + are)
their	they're (they + are)
whose	who's (who + is or has)

CAUTION

In formal types of writing, such as reports and business letters, you should not use contractions. Contractions are acceptable, however, in written dialogue and in informal writing such as friendly letters.

Since possessive pronouns and contractions have completely different meanings, be sure to use them correctly. Remember:

1. When you use one of two words that sound alike, ask yourself whether it stands for one word or two. If it stands for two words, it is a contraction and needs an apostrophe.

2. Never use an apostrophe in a possessive pronoun.

Exercise 2   Concept Check   Write the correct answer.

1. (Who's, Whose) read "The Dinner Party"?

2. (Its, It's) about a cobra that crawls under a table.

3. When cobras are excited, they flatten (they're, their) necks.

4. In case (you're, your) wondering, cobras are not that dangerous.

5. (They're, Their) size is frightening—up to eighteen feet long.

6. (Their, They're) slower than many other snakes.

7. A cobra is slow, and (its, it's) striking distance is very short.

8. A brave person (who's, whose) close can easily knock down a cobra.

9. A snake charmer (who's, whose) music seems to hypnotize a cobra is tricking you.

10. (You're, Your) ears can hear the music, but the snake is deaf.

Exercise 3   Proofreading   Correct the following paragraph.

On our class trip to Washington, D.C., us eighth graders visited the Vietnam Memorial. It's an unforgettable experience. Arnetta and me had been giggling and telling jokes, but as her and I got closer to that somber black wall, we two were suddenly quiet. People who's relatives had died in the war were looking for names on the wall. They ran their fingers over it's shiny, dark surface when they found the right inscription. If you're travel plans include Washington, see the wall.

Exercise 4   Revising Your Writing   Review the memoir you wrote for the Writer's Workshop on pages 56–60. Lightly underline any pronouns or contractions you used and correct any errors you find.

LANGUAGE HANDBOOK

For review and practice:
Section 4, Using Pronouns, pages 776–778, 781–782.

VOCABULARY
WORKSHOP

CONTEXT CLUES

As you read, you often come across unfamiliar words. Many times you can determine the meaning of these words by studying context clues—the words and sentences around a word. Sometimes, however, you will find that there is no single clue to a word's meaning. When this happens, you may be able to **infer,** or figure out, what a word means by piecing together several ideas in the context. These hints or suggestions about meaning are called **inference clues.** Look at the example below.

> Lee was angry and shouted <u>vehemently</u> during a quarrel with his best friend. The <u>adverse</u> weather conditions had forced them to stay indoors, and they were both on edge.

The paragraph gives some information to help you figure out the meaning of *vehemently.* You know what *angry* means, and you know how people feel when they quarrel. From this, you can figure out that *vehemently* has something to do with strong emotion or intense feeling. What does the context tell you about the meaning of *adverse?*

Exercise   Use context to infer the meaning of each underlined word. Write definitions for the words. Then check the accuracy of your definitions by looking in a dictionary. Finally, write sentences that show your understanding of the words.

1. Jerry was so <u>fixated</u> on getting a date with Victoria that he followed her every move during the school day.
2. Jerry practiced his speech for the fiftieth time, as he <u>meticulously</u> planned how he would ask Victoria for a date.
3. The sound of Victoria's voice had such a strong <u>impact</u> on Jerry, he was sure he would lose the ability to speak.
4. Instead of following his plan, Jerry suddenly <u>blurted</u> out "Movies Friday night?" in the middle of math class.
5. After Victoria answered, Jerry <u>chanted</u> to himself over and over again, "She said 'yes'! She said 'yes'! She said 'yes'!"

DEFINING YOURSELF

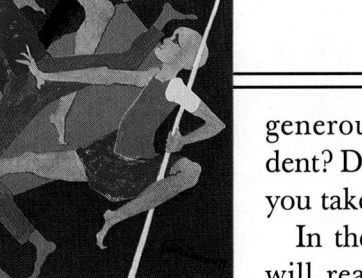

If you had to describe in a few words or phrases the kind of person you are, what would you say? Think about the things that help make you unique—your ethnic or racial background, your age, your gender. Think about your interests, your likes and dislikes—even the role you play in your family. Are you kind? Are you generous? Are you a good student? Do you excel at sports? Do you take part in school activities?

In the following selections you will read about characters who define themselves or get defined by someone else. Sometimes these characters are defined by actions they perform or by experiences they have.

Nonfiction

Von

"VON," *a Vietnamese youth*
as interviewed by JANET BODE

Examine What You Know

Look around your classroom. How many of the people in your class immigrated, or moved, to the United States from other countries? How many have parents or grandparents who did? In small groups discuss what you know or have experienced about immigration. Compile your notes into a web based on questions such as the following:

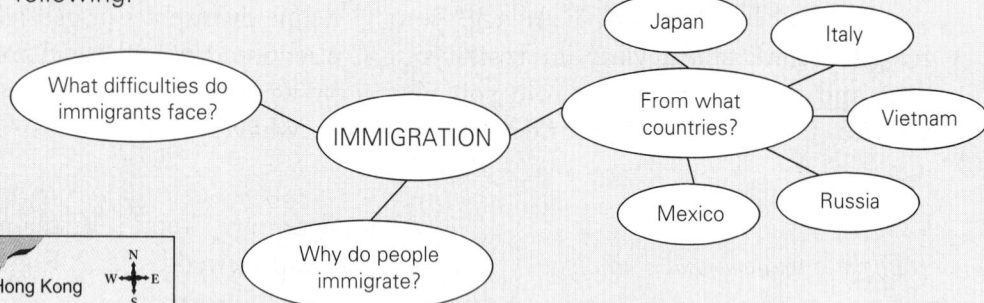

What difficulties do immigrants face?

IMMIGRATION

Why do people immigrate?

From what countries?

Japan

Italy

Vietnam

Mexico

Russia

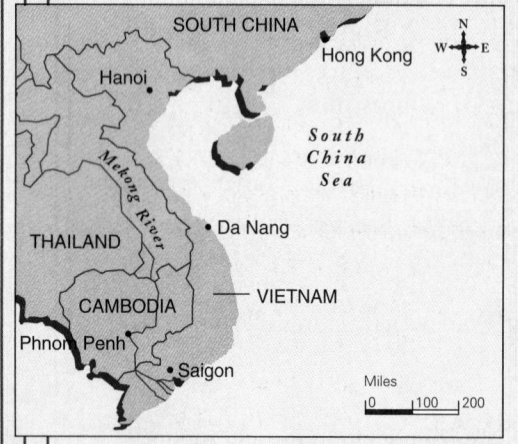

SOUTH CHINA

Hong Kong

Hanoi

South China Sea

Da Nang

THAILAND

Mekong River

VIETNAM

CAMBODIA

Phnom Penh

Saigon

Miles
0 100 200

Expand Your Knowledge

This selection is a true account of a boy's immigration to the United States from South Vietnam. Many Vietnamese people, including the boy's father, who had opposed the Communists during the Vietnam War, were forced to relocate to "re-education centers," where they were brutally treated as political prisoners. As soon as the boy (Von) and his father could, they—and at least a million others—fled Vietnam to escape these camps.

Enrich Your Reading

Chronological Order Like most narrators, Von tells his story in **chronological order,** the order in which things occurred. If you need help keeping track of the events in Von's life, try charting them on a time line. Copy this time line into your journal or onto a sheet of paper and write in Von's experiences:

■ *Author biographies on Extend page and in Reader's Handbook*

1968   1972   1975   1978   1980   1988

Von born

Von

"VON," *a Vietnamese youth*
as interviewed by JANET BODE

On April 30, 1975, Saigon, the capital of South Vietnam, fell, ending this stage of the tragedy that by then had cost 1.3 million Vietnamese and 56,000 American lives. Von is a survivor of that war and the devastating *years that followed. Today when you see him—slim, handsome, with an* optimistic *and ready grin—it's hard to imagine what his eyes have seen. Over a series of days, we met in hours sandwiched between his busy schedule of school and work. He begins at his beginning.*

I was born in Saigon. My father was a navy officer for South Vietnam. He worked for the United States government. I have three brothers and three sisters. I am number four. I'm the only one who came to America with my father. My mother and the rest of them are still in Vietnam. Sometimes on Sundays after church, my father and I talk about our past memories, what brought us here and of the future. I decided that someday I would like to write of my family, and of him and me together. You are the first person I ever told my family's story to. . . .

In 1972, when Von was four years old, the family moved to Da Nang in the central part of the country. Von's earliest memories of the war were of hiding and eating in bomb shelters while waiting for the daily bombing raids to end. When Saigon fell to the Communists in 1975, Von's father could have escaped to the United States, but he made his way back at great peril to rejoin his family. However, the Communists soon put Von's father in a "re-education center." At this center, actually a concentration camp, Von's father worked at hard labor from six in the morning until nine in the evening every day for three years, without breaks or vacations.

In the meantime, Von's family had to sell everything they owned in order to get enough money to buy food. For several years, Von could no longer go to school, but he continued to try to read on his own. When Von's father was finally released from the concentration camp in 1978, the government told him he must take only one child and work in the countryside. Von and his father were sent to a place near the border, where fierce battles raged between Cambodia and Vietnam. "We were caught," Von says, "in the middle again."

One day they told my father, "You, tomorrow, because you were an officer, you must go and clean out the grenades." The Cambodians put grenades under the trees. They put boobytraps everywhere. In the morning when we went to the farms and started working, sometimes people blew up. . . .

Of course my father didn't say "no" to them. He said, "When?" To me he said, "Oh, my God. I have to risk my life for this? NO! I can't take anymore." My father, he could not sleep. He thought, it's my life. All this time I work to become a good man. I come back and for this? I will die for nothing? Should I leave or should I stay? If I stay, I will get killed. He kept what he planned a secret. He just said to me, "You and me, we're leaving. We must go back to your mother."

At six o'clock in the morning, we were supposed to be in the mission at work. They didn't think he would leave. It was dark out and I was afraid. Even in the countryside they have security guards. We did not go on the road. We sneaked through the trees. Finally we got to a place where we could take a bus. We had little money left for the month, but I was so young, my father didn't have to pay for my bus ticket.

We got back to Saigon, but we could just see my mother for a few hours. It was too dangerous for everybody if we stayed. Too soon, he had to say to my mother, "I must leave you." To me he said, "I must take a younger son with me, you. I take you because you suffer so much. You have a feeling."

I always cared for my mother. I always helped her. My mother said to my father, "Von will be good." She was crying so much. She said, "This is right. This is the way we have to do it. You must leave me."

She said to me, "You take care of your father." And she told my father, "Take care of Von. Get him schooling." My brothers and sisters just looked at me. They were so sad. They knew we were leaving, even though my father didn't tell them. If he told them, they would say, "Why do you take Von? You don't love me?"

My mother said, "I love you." And we left.

At that time, many South Vietnamese people were trying to sneak out of the country. They were looking for navy men who knew how to row the boat, who knew how to get to Thailand. Do you know anything about the boat people?[1] They make a boat and they sail and they try to get to freedom. My father was on the sea for almost twenty-five years. Some people learned this, and they said to him, "We offer you a job. We make a fake ID for you and your son. We take care of a boat. We get food, and you two can go with us."

My father said, "OK." But somehow the Communists found out and took the boat and the money, too. He was afraid the government might be looking for him. "I must leave you," he told the people.

My father found another connection. This time poor, poor people came to him. They could pay him no money, but they had a boat. For three months, my father prepared. He mended the motor. He bought a map, a compass. Then with the boat, my father and I sneaked out to the river. We were picking

---

1. **boat people:** refugees who used small boats to escape from Southeast Asia.

Vietnamese boat people © Richard Tomkins / Gamma Liaison.

up people as we were going along. People here, people there, all poor country people who wanted to escape to a better life.

There were fifty-two people in a twelve-foot-long boat. We could not move. I sat with my knees in my face. I could not lie down. There were a lot of men and a few women. There were some kids, but most of the people were in their early twenties. I was maybe eleven or twelve.

We left on a rainy night. There were military police boats out in the sea looking for the escape boats, looking for the boat people. But with the rain, they went inside. We

go and go and go. One night and the next day in the evening, we went all the way down the river to the sea because my father rowed so fast. We go and go and go. We were going to Indonesia. My father knew we shouldn't go to Thailand, because there were a lot of pirates. Most of the people who went to Thailand got killed. After four days we saw a blinking light! Oh, we thought, that's an American ship! We first saw the light around two in the morning, and by six we could see the boat.

The boat was all black. It was so big, and it said "Thailand" on it. My father told me, "They are dangerous people." We were afraid they would attack us. They know the

Children at a refugee camp
© Richard Tomkins / Gamma Liaison.

boat people often have money and gold. They are pirates.

. . .We only had one gun, a shotgun. The people were saying, "What should we do? Shoot them?"

My father said, "No, we cannot. There are so many of them. If we shoot at them, they will definitely kill us. It is better to let them rob us."

They came on board our little boat. They had knives and hammers. My father said, "Try to act cool." I was so scared I was shaking. Even my feet were shaking. They ordered all the men to go onto their big ship. I was so small that one man took my hand, picked me up, and threw me to another man on their ship. It looked so far, and the ship was rocking, that I was afraid they would miss me and I would fall into the sea. They would not bother to save me.

The pirates went around our boat checking for gold. They asked for watches and rings and money and said, "If you lie, we'll throw you into the sea." Everybody gave them everything they had, all their savings for their new lives. But after that the pirates gave us food. We were all very hungry people. They took us back to our boat. We were lucky. They didn't kill us. I guess they felt sorry for us.

We were back alone on the sea, and then we saw some more big, big ships. One was from Holland, another from Italy. They saw us and didn't stop! We lay there. We were so hot. Every time we saw a big ship we got so happy. They came so close that then we got afraid that we could get caught in their waves. My father always put a white flash, a message, and it said, "If you want to pick us up, we come close. If no, we stay away."

Why didn't the ships stop?   *question*

Some of the ships said, "Yes, we take you," and then when we came close, they tried to hit us to make us drown and die in the sea. My father knew they used that trick a lot. They didn't want us there, and if we died, nobody knew. So many people were coming out of Vietnam. Other countries didn't want to take any more. It's even worse today.

We go and go and go. In two weeks we saw a ship from Germany with a red cross on it. My father rowed, rowed, rowed, and he came very nicely right next to the ship. The Germans took us on board their ship. They gave us food, a shower, blankets. They told us to sleep. And they asked to speak to the captain of the boat. My father, he doesn't know German but he knows French, he went and spoke French to them. They said, "Tomorrow we will take you and your people to an island, to a refugee camp."

My father said, "Oh, thank you very much."

A new land! A new life!

The first island they brought us to was one where nobody had lived. It was called Coocoo. The food was poison, the water polluted. And the mosquitoes! People had come there, cut down the trees, and built some houses. But it was dangerous for the people, and a lot of us were sick. Some of us died. They took us to the hospital at the refugee camp. They gave us injections.

After a month we had an interview from the United Nations. They called our names. My father said, "I worked for the United States government in South Vietnam." They took all the information down and then said, "OK, we will call Washington, D.C. You must wait while we do that."

While we waited, my father worked for the chief commander in the refugee camp in Indonesia. I worked, too. The United Nations had donated some money to build some more houses to make the camp bigger. I sought them out for a job. They said, "If you want to help the people, gather the wood so they can build the barracks."

I said, "Fine, fine, I volunteer."

Most of the people at the refugee camp were Vietnamese. Some of them had so sad stories, oh my. "In Thailand they stole my sister," one said. "My brother and my mother got killed because the boat sink," another

said. But on the island, we all lived together in barracks, and life at that time was beautiful. Each day the United Nations gave every person a half cup of rice and a half cup of another food. The American Peace Corps[2] came there, too. We people built a school, and they tried to teach a little English. We stayed there for eight months, until one afternoon we heard our name called again. They told us, "You have a sponsor from the United States."

I thought, Oh wow! A new land! A new life! The United Nations had a special boat to Singapore. They take the refugees that are leaving to that city, we stay a week, and from there we take an airplane to Hong Kong and on to Alaska.

I looked out the window of the airplane in Alaska, and I was so surprised. I tell my father, "Rice! Rice! Rice is falling from the sky!" He explained to me what snow is. From there we went to California, where we stayed in a shelter for a week. The people said, "Enjoy this; soon you will be in your new home, Detroit, and there the weather is very cold."

What would your reaction have been if you had never seen snow before?   *connect*

It was January when we came to Detroit. I said, "What a dirty city." There were a lot of newspapers flying in the air, and it was so cold. A lady met us at the airport and took us in a really strange and crazy hotel filled

---

2. **Peace Corps:** a volunteer organization set up by the U.S. government to help people in underdeveloped countries.

with new immigrants and mental people.[3] She said, "Here is fifty dollars. I'll see you in fifteen days." We never saw her again.

At night at the hotel, the people screamed loud. They banged on the walls. We had nothing to cook. We didn't know what to eat. We didn't know what is American food. My father went out to the corner store, and he got some coffee and a sandwich. Then he bought some soup and some rice to cook. He told me, "Stay inside." I said, "Why? American people very nice. They wouldn't hurt anybody." He told me, "Stay inside."

I think of South Vietnam. It is a beautiful country. I think of my mother and brothers and sisters and grandmother. I think new people to America are hungry for their countries. Governments can be so cruel.

After two, three weeks, we had a phone call, a Vietnamese voice. We were excited. There were no other Vietnamese in the hotel. He said, "You will meet your sponsor. It is a rabbi and his congregation. They have found a home for you. One of the ladies speaks French, so you can talk to them."

When we meet them, the lady asks me, "Von, do you drink milk?" I'm too big to drink milk. With Vietnamese, milk is only for a baby. It is too expensive to buy.

I think, this is strange. Why does she ask me this?

"How about soda?" she says.

"Oh, yes, I love soda."

"What kind of food do you eat? Hamburger?"

I tell her, "Oh, I love hamburger." I never eat hamburger, but I'd heard of it a lot.

So they took us to our home. It was in the basement, one bedroom and one living room. The Jewish people from the temple, everybody gave a little bit. We got a TV, two beds, some furniture, a table, cups and plates and cooking things. After that the lady and the rabbi took us to a supermarket. They said, "Von, take all the food you want."

I think of South Vietnam. It is a beautiful country.

I had never seen anything like this supermarket. The lady showed me the shopping cart and what to do. The first thing I grabbed was Coca-Cola. I knew that. And bread. Then I looked around, and I didn't see anything to eat. It was all frozen. I'd never seen that in Vietnam. There we had all fresh fruit and vegetables. I got some cans of food. At the refugee camp, I saw those for the first time.

The lady said, "Do you like potato chips?"

I said, "What are potato chips?"

She bought some chicken for us. My father said, "I feel so bad. They brought us here, and they had to take us shopping." That afternoon, three more Jewish ladies came to the house. They showed us how to cook, how to make chicken, how to use the stove, where to put the milk and soda. They were so nice. I didn't understand a word they said, but I always smiled.

The next day they took me and my father shopping for clothes. I was so skinny, and the pants were so big. They told my father

---

3. **mental people:** people suffering from mental illness.

Village in South Vietnam   © Cohen / Gamma Liaison.

and me, "You have to come to temple to meet the people." I got shoes, too. They said to my father, "Tomorrow, we will take Von to get a shot so you can put him in school."

They got my father a job as a typewriter repairman. He didn't know anything about that. He wanted to work on the ships, but they said to do that you must be a United States citizen. He said, "OK."

I was very scared to start school after six years. I had to skip a lot of grades. Most of the students looked at me because the way I was dressing was strange. It was so cold I wore everything I'd bought. I didn't know where anything was. I came late to every class. I was confused, and I could not ask

people. They told me in sign language, "Go to eat." I went into the cafeteria. There were hundreds of people.

A supervisor knew I was a new student. He took me to the head of the line to get a hamburger, and the other students got angry. "Why does that boy get to go first?" I told the supervisor, "I want to wait in the line. Please." He said, "Don't worry about it. Take the food."

On that day and on other days, when I had a hard problem to solve or when I felt sad or confused, I always look back on my past. I say, "Wow, what happened in the past is even harder. This is nothing." Let's face it, this is easy here.

There were no Vietnamese kids at the school and only one Chinese boy, but he became my best friend. After a while I got along with the other students. I met a very nice black boy. He thought I was Chinese and all Chinese know karate and kung fu. He said, "I like your country's movies." I told him, "I'm Vietnamese." But he didn't know what was Vietnamese. He took me home to meet his mother, and, wow, did they have a big TV. He said, "What do you want? Food?" "Yeah." He made food for me, and we ate and drank soda. I didn't understand what I was seeing. I couldn't answer his questions, but we understood each other.

question   What does he mean?

Later I invited him to my house. I was doing the laundry, but I didn't know how to do laundry here. In Vietnam we use a brush to scrub it, then take it outside and hang it in the wind. I washed it by hand in the bathtub and left it to dry. Two, three days, and it was not dry! The boy went, "Von, what is this? Why don't you bring it to a laundromat?" He didn't know my family never had even seen a washing machine.

Other kids did bring some trouble to me. They talked about the way my hair looked, my clothes. When they called me "Chinese," they did it to make fun of me. They didn't call me by name. They laughed because I could not speak well. I was really upset about it, but then again I thought, so what?

I took an art class, and the teacher said, "You draw whatever you like." I drew a map of Vietnam, the boat I escaped in, my family, and all the blood. One of my draw-

ings I put in my father's bedroom, and on it I wrote "NO MORE WAR!!!"

I got along well with my teachers. The English teacher gave me vocabulary to learn, like *breakfast, dinner, orange juice*. I'd take it home and translate and study it. The pronunciation was hard for me, words like *brother*. I'd practice my English by recording my voice on a tape recorder. I'd read from a book, then play it back. I watched TV news a lot, CNN.[4]

Even though my father was working, the rabbi paid the rent, the telephone bill, the food, everything for six months! They took us to the temple and made a party to introduce us. They gave us a hat to wear, a yarmulke.[5] We still have it today. They knew it was my birthday. I had never had a birthday party in my life. They made a big cake, and they told me to hold it and blow out the candles. They told me to give a speech. I was only here two, three months. I didn't know anything. My father said, "Whatever people give you, you have to say 'Thank you.'" I said, "Thank you, thank you."

It was wonderful. They gave me the whole cake to take home. I ate it for one month! Every day after school, I cut one piece and ate it. The rabbi always called to see how we were. He said, "If you have any problem, we are here to help."

After six months, I said to my father and the rabbi, "Let me go look for a job." We don't want the temple to pay for us anymore.

The rabbi said, "We wouldn't recommend that you work. You better concentrate on school."

---

4. **CNN:** Cable News Network.
5. **yarmulke** (yär′ məl kə): a small brimless cap worn by Jewish men and boys.

Without telling them, I looked. I saw a lot of students go to work, so I copied them. I started walking from my house. I went into a supermarket. I was interviewed by the manager, and he told me, "Sorry, you have an English problem. Study more and come back in six months." I went into many supermarkets that day, many small stores.

I love this country. This country is my country now.

They didn't understand what I was talking about. I didn't understand what I was talking about. But I already knew the words for juice, milk, fruit, so that's why I was interested in those stores. I went home. I was so sad. I didn't want to bother my father. He was very busy, too, learning a new job and studying English in night school.

The next day after school, I went to look again. My school had a work-study program, and a teacher told me about a job at Burger King. I was interviewed, and the boss knew that I had an English problem. I begged him, "I can do anything! I can take the cooking test, but I can't take the writing test. I don't know English." So he went check, check, check, like that, on the test, and I passed. So my first job in America was to cook hamburgers. I took the frozen hamburger and put it inside the fire. That's all he wanted me to do.

But then I saw customers who didn't throw their food in the trash. I came out, and I cleaned the tables. I saw someone had thrown sodas on the floor. I took a mop and cleaned it up. I wanted to show him that I could work. He gave me a uniform and said, "You start today."

I ran home and said to my father, "I must write a letter to the rabbi. I must say, 'Thank you for everything you've done for us. Someday when I have a good job, I will donate money to this temple to keep it forever. Now my father and I both work and won't need any more help.'"

My father said, "Oh, that is great."

The rabbi called my house. He said, "Von, we want to help you. We don't want anything from you. You've only been here a few months. Remember your schoolwork, but you do what you want." I sent my money to my mother.

My father and I have been here for a long time now, eight, nine years. For five years we have had all the papers in order to have my mother and my brothers and my sisters come here. We have sent a letter to the United States ambassador to Thailand. We have written to the United States representative at the United Nations. We contacted our congressman, and he wrote a letter. The congressman said, "Your family is qualified to come to the United States. They are at the top of the list." Still we wait and we wait and we wait. The Communist government doesn't want to give them visas.

This year on July 4, my father and I became citizens of the United States. I'm a free man! I read the Constitution. We the

Words to Know and Use	**ambassador** (am bas′ ə dər) *n.* a country's chief representative in a foreign land **qualified** (kwôl′ i fīd′) *adj.* having met the requirements **qualify** *v.* **visa** (vē′ zə) *n.* an official permission to leave or enter a country

people are all equal. Now no one can say, if the United States someday has a problem, "You have to go back to Vietnam." I love this country. This country is my country now. I never go back.

My brothers and sisters don't have the opportunities that I do. Today it is September, and I am starting university. I am a very lucky person. And when my family gets here and we are together again, we will make such a celebration! ❧

Illustration by Paola Piglia.

Foreign Student

BARBARA B. ROBINSON

In September she appeared
   row three, seat seven,
   heavy pleated skirt,
   plastic purse, tidy notepad,
there she sat,
silent,
straight from Tai Pei,
and she bowed
when I entered the room.
A model student
I noticed,
   though she walked
   alone through the halls,
every assignment neat,
on time, complete,
and she'd listen
when I talked.

But now it's May
and Si Lan
is called Lani.
She strides in
with Noriyo and Lynne
and Natavidad.
She wears slacks.
Her gear is crammed
into a macramé
shoulder sack.
And she chatters with Pete
during class
and
I'm glad.

Responding to Reading

First Impressions

1. What did you think about Von as you read this selection? Take a minute to describe your thoughts in your journal or on a sheet of paper.

Second Thoughts

2. Which of Von's experiences do you think were the most difficult for him? Why?

3. In what ways do you think Von's actual experiences in the United States might have differed from his expectations?

4. Compare the relationship between Von and his father with the relationship between Terry and his father in "Stop the Sun," on pages 17–27.

Broader Connections

5. In 1990 alone, over 1.5 million people immigrated to the United States. Like Von and his father, some of these immigrants were refugees—people who are fleeing persecution, war, and other misfortunes. Do you think the United States should admit more or fewer refugees? Explain your response.

Literary Concept: Genre

A **genre** is a particular type of literature. The main literary genres are fiction, nonfiction, poetry, and drama. Within the nonfiction category, Von's story is an oral history based on an interview. In this genre a writer interviews a person, usually with a tape recorder. Then the writer transcribes the tape and arranges the interview into a coherent story. In her introduction to the volume in which Von's story appears, Janet Bode wrote, "At times the sentence construction might seem a little awkward. The grammar might not always be perfect." Why do you think this writer chose not to correct her subject's grammatical errors?

Writing Options

1. Imagine that Von and Terry (from "Stop the Sun," on pages 17–27) have become pen pals. Take the role of either Von or Terry and write your pen pal a **letter.** Choose a scene from one of the selections and describe it in detail for your pen pal.

2. Write a **letter** from Von to the Vietnamese government, trying to persuade government officials to let the rest of your family leave the country and come to the United States.

3. You have just read about Von's adjustment to life in a new land. Now write a **journal entry** about a time when you or someone you know moved to a different place. Describe the difficulties you or that person encountered in adapting to the new place and a new group of people. How are these experiences similar to and different from Von's?

4. How do you think Von's life experiences helped define him now that he is an American citizen? Write an **account** of his life, using examples from the selection.

Vocabulary Practice

Exercise   On a sheet of paper, write the word from the list that best completes each sentence.

1. Von and his father remained __?__ despite all their misfortunes.
2. The U.S. __?__ was apologetic, but he could not help the family with their emigration problems.
3. To be __?__ for citizenship in a particular country, you may have to take a test on the constitution and laws of the country.
4. The immigration officer asked the man for his passport and __?__ as he entered the country.
5. The family left their homeland to escape the __?__ effects of the war.

Words to Know and Use

ambassador
devastating
optimistic
qualified
visa

*O*ptions for Learning

1 • **Coming to America** Everyone in the United States has an ancestor who emigrated from another land—even Native Americans, whose ancestors migrated across the Bering Strait to the Americas. Research your own family's arrival in this country. Prepare a written or oral report that includes relevant pictures, maps, and artifacts.

2 • **Tell Me About It** Using a tape recorder or a video camera, interview an immigrant to the United States. If you need help thinking of interview questions, you may want to look back at the "Immigration" web you made in Examine What You Know. Share highlights from your interview with classmates.

3 • **Map Maker** Just as Von did, draw a map of the country from which your ancestors emigrated to the United States. If you would like, illustrate your map with a picture that relates to your ancestral homeland or write a suitable motto or quotation at the bottom of your map.

4 • **New Kids' Survival Guide** Create a brochure that would help new students adjust to life at your school. Think about the most important things they would need to know. Keep your language simple and direct; use pictures if possible. Include a vocabulary list of essential terms, perhaps writing the meanings in several languages.

 FACT FINDER SOCIAL STUDIES

How does someone become a citizen of the United States?

"*V*on"
1968–

"Von," whose name was changed to protect his privacy and the safety of his family, was born in Saigon, South Vietnam, in 1968. His father, an officer in the South Vietnamese army, studied in the United States before Von was born. When Von looked at his father's pictures of California, he secretly hoped, "Maybe someday I be there." As the selection explains, Von and his father eventually came to the United States and became citizens. Many years later, the rest of Von's family finally got permission to emigrate.

Fiction

*D*ancing for *P*oppa

PAT MacENULTY

*E*xamine What You Know

"May I have the pleasure of this dance?" "Let's cut a rug!" "D'ya wanna dance?" The way we say it may change over time, but the sentiment is always the same: "Let's dance!"

How do you feel about dancing? Are you the first one on the dance floor the minute you hear music, or are you happier sitting and watching others? Take a few moments to discuss how you feel and what you know about dancing.

*E*xpand Your Knowledge

People dance for many reasons. Some people dance to entertain others; through dance they tell stories, set moods, or express feelings and emotions. Other people dance to have fun and to socialize. Still other people dance to express their religious beliefs.

Dance is probably the oldest of all the arts. One form of dance, ballet, began in Italy in the 1400s and spread throughout Europe during the next several hundred years. Today young girls all over the world practice and dream of becoming prima ballerinas, the lead dancers in ballet companies.

One ballet, *Swan Lake,* with music by the Russian composer Peter Ilich (il' yich) Tchaikovsky (chī kôf' skē), is mentioned in this story. *Swan Lake* has been a favorite with audiences for many years. It becomes a favorite of Connie's in this story as she dances it for "Poppa."

*W*rite Before You Read

Music and dance inspire many artists' works. Study the sculpture and the painting that illustrate this story and write about them in your journal or on a sheet of paper. What further impressions of dancing do they give you? What thoughts or feelings do they evoke? As you read, think about how your impressions compare to those of the characters in the story.

■ *Author biography in Reader's Handbook*

Dancing for Poppa

PAT MacENULTY

I stood at Poppa's graveside along with my parents, cousins, aunts, and uncles. Grandma leaned on my left arm as Uncle Henry threw a clod of dirt on Poppa's ivory-colored coffin. The cemetery was cooled by large oak trees shading the plots. Flower arrangements dotted the grass or lay upon the cool granite tombs. Poppa would be happy here, I hoped. But I didn't know if he would be happy with me, his only grand-daughter.

"Poppa" is what I called my grandfather; he was also my friend, the one who knew my dreams. He lived in the small town of Mandarin, Florida, with Grandma, in a big white house on the St. John's River. I used to love to visit him and pick oranges from his trees or play on the banks of the river, catching tiny brown fiddler crabs.

When I was seven years old, Poppa came to the house and handed me a big box.

"What's in it, what's in it?" I cried.

He looked down at me with his heavy-lidded brown eyes and said, "Open it up, Tinkerbell."[1] And I tore the flimsy gold elastic ribbon from the box. Inside, underneath the soft white paper, were pink tights, a black leotard, and a pair of pink ballet slippers. I looked back up at Poppa for some explanation.

"It's for your lessons," he said. "Ballet lessons."

I hadn't even known that I wanted to take ballet, but when he said "ballet lessons," I felt that I had been asking for nothing else my whole life. I screamed with excitement and ran into my room. After I donned my new outfit, I went prancing into the living room. My older brother, Randy, pretended to gag; Daddy said that it was very nice; and Momma asked who was going to pay for these ballet lessons. Poppa said he would as I hopped around him like a little bird.

"You're going to drive into town every week to take her?" my mother asked. We lived in Jacksonville, a half-hour away from his house.

"Twice a week," he said and kissed me. That night I slept in my new leotard and tights.

The next Monday Poppa took me to Ophelia Bell's School of Dance in San Marco, a quaint little shopping area with a

---

1. **Tinkerbell:** a nickname based on the name of a pixie in *Peter Pan,* a play by James M. Barrie.

Words to Know and Use | **don** (dän) *v.* to put on; dress in
quaint (kwānt) *adj.* pleasantly unusual or old-fashioned

81

movie theater, a community theater, a bakery, a five-and-dime, and several dress shops where my mother had charge accounts. The dance school was located in a big art-deco[2] building at the end of the block. We went inside.

Clasping his hand as if it were a large branch from which I dangled, I timidly looked around at the big girls, who seemed so self-assured in their outfits as they waited for their own classes to begin. They laughed among themselves and stretched their sleek muscles. It was a performance in itself.

"This is Connie," Poppa said to Miss Bell, and she smiled at me. As she bent down, her cologne engulfed me. Even now, whenever I smell Chantilly, I think of Miss Bell. She led me into an enormous room with wood floors and mirrors along the front wall. Standing along the other wall, about twenty little girls, all approximately my size, clung with one hand to a wooden rail, which I later learned was called the barre. I got in the back of the line.

"Just follow along," Miss Bell told me. Well, I followed along fine until suddenly everyone turned around and I was in the front of the line. I had to keep glancing over my shoulder to see what we were doing. I wanted to quit that very day. I would tell Poppa, I thought. He wouldn't make me come here again if I didn't want to. After the lesson I came out, holding my breath so that I wouldn't burst into sobs.

"You were fantastic," Poppa said. "A natural."

At the next lesson, which was on Thursday, I was smart and got a space in the middle of the barre so that I had someone to follow no matter what direction we faced. Miss Bell paced along the line with a long stick, counting the beats on the wood floorboards and sometimes using the stick to tap our tummies or our buttocks to make sure we were holding them in tight. "Tendu,"[3] she'd say, and we all pointed our toes to the side without having the vaguest idea what *tendu* meant.

After the funeral the family returned to our house to eat baked ham, potato salad, and freshly sliced tomatoes. There was also a red-velvet cake, Poppa's favorite. I helped mother serve everyone, about ten people in all. The others—friends and people who had worked with Poppa for Seaboard Coastline—had left after the service. Only the family went to the graveside and came to the house afterward.

"Here Grandma, let me pour your tea for you," I said and poured the hot orange-pekoe tea into a china cup. She took it, her hand shaking, the tea cup clattering on the saucer, and I held my breath as she brought it up to her trembling lips. Miraculously, not a drop spilled.

"Why couldn't Randy make it?" she asked querulously.

"He had a final exam, Grandma, and he just couldn't get out of it," I told her for the fourth time that day.

---

2. **art-deco:** in a style of the 1920s and 1930s that featured bold geometric forms.
3. **tendu** (tän dü´): a ballet movement in which a leg is stretched out stiffly.

Words to Know and Use | **engulf** (en gulf´) *v.* to flow over; overwhelm

"Pretty soon you'll be gone, too. Every-one will be gone," she said with a moan. I knew it was her way of missing Poppa, as tears slid down her cheeks.

"I'll be back for vacations, Grandma," I said, more to comfort myself than her.

"What are you going to major in, Connie?" Aunt Maryjane asked me.

"I don't know," I said.

"Pre-law," my father said. Yuck, I thought, but smiled. He knew I didn't want to be a lawyer.

"She should do something that makes a lot of money," Aunt Lynn advised and licked some red-velvet cake from her lips.

"Or marry someone who is going to make lots of money," Uncle Henry said, poking Aunt Lynn with his fork.

Grandma surprised them all by say-ing, "This isn't the fifties. She doesn't need to marry anybody. And she doesn't need to make a lot of money. All she needs to do is some-thing that makes her happy. That's what her Poppa would have wanted."

"Thanks, Grandma," I said and stroked her plump little pigeon of a hand. "More tea?"

She nodded, and I poured another cup for her.

"Just as long as you don't think you're going to be a ballerina," my mother said as she got up from the chair in the corner and cut herself another piece of cake. Poppa always thought I would be a ballerina. And I guess I did, too, until I was about fourteen and realized that even though I was quite

© Blaine Harrington / The Stock Market

good, I wasn't good enough to be a star for a major ballet company, and I didn't want to be in a company if I was just going to be a member of the corps. I had been a star in Miss Bell's senior class, and that had spoiled me for anything but the spotlight.

For the first five years, I had been a main-stay of the back row; but I started coming to the school and practicing by myself early in the mornings, and one day Miss Bell asked me to lead the class. In our eighth-grade recital I had my first solo. Poppa embarrassed me by standing up and clapping at the end of my performance, and he kept clapping long after it was time for the next girl to come on. He cried afterward, saying, "I am young again when I watch you up there dancing like a fairy princess. It makes me young."

I am young again when I watch you up there dancing like a fairy princess.

A week before his death I visited him in the hospital. He wanted to know what my plans were, whether I was going to New York to try out for the American Ballet Theatre.[4]

"No, Poppa," I told him. "I'm going to Florida State with Cathy and my other friends from school."

"But I thought you liked performing," he said, crossing his hands. An IV tube[5] was stuck in his arm, and he had lost at least thirty pounds, but his eyes had the same dark intensity as ever.

"I love it, but it's not enough for me. I want to do more with my life, maybe help people somehow." I couldn't explain, but I knew there was more to life for me than the stage, even if I had been good enough to be a star. He didn't say he was disappointed, but his smile seemed weak. Maybe that was just the illness.

"Come with us to your grandmother's, Connie," my mother said after I collected the plates from around the living room and took them into the kitchen.

"Would you mind if I didn't?" I leaned against the sink. I had not been able to cry for Poppa the way everyone else had. If I could have just cried, maybe my knees wouldn't have felt as though they would sink like sandbags to the floor.

"Yes, Connie, I would mind very much." But my father overheard us from the dining room and came into the kitchen.

"Let her stay here, honey. She's been so strong for everyone else," he said, and he gave my mother a long look. "They were very close," he added, in a voice so soft he must have thought I couldn't hear him.

"I'll stay with her," Aunt Lynn piped in as she followed my father into the kitchen. Oh no, I thought. She'll chatter my head off. But fortunately my father corralled her like a shepherd's dog herding the sheep.

"No," he said. "Then we'll have to make an extra trip to take you home. Besides, Connie will be busy cleaning up the house."

Aunt Lynn shrugged. My mother sighed and grimaced, the way she does when something is no longer important to her, as my father ushered them out.

Soon the house was quiet except for the running water as I rinsed off the dishes before loading them into the dishwasher. Every dish felt heavy in my hands, and I thought of the pallbearers carrying Poppa's big coffin. They kept their backs so straight,

---

4. **American Ballet Theatre:** a famous ballet company in New York City.
5. **IV tube:** abbreviation of *intravenous tube,* a device for injecting food or medicine directly into a person's veins.

Words to Know and Use | **intensity** (in ten′ sə tē) *n.* strength or energy
corral (kə ral′) *v.* to capture; round up
grimace (grim′ əs, or gri mās) *v.* to make a face

as if it didn't weigh a thing, but I knew by the way their knuckles turned red that it was heavy. I scraped the pieces of leftover velvet cake into the food disposal and placed the dishes just so in the dishwasher. Then all the dishes were loaded, and the dishwasher was making its churning sound, and the counters were wiped, and all the chairs were put back into their proper places. The house was back to normal, as if Poppa had never died, as if he would come in any moment and say, "How's my princess?"

I sat in the living room on the couch where earlier Aunt Lynn and Aunt Maryjane had been discussing Poppa's will. He had left enough to take care of Grandma and a few <u>tokens</u> for members of the family. He had left me a framed photograph of the Degas[6] statue the *Little Ballerina,* which sat on the coffee table next to the catalog from the college where I had been accepted.

I opened the catalog. There was a section for arts and sciences. I thumbed through the pages, perusing the courses. Some of them I would have to take: first-year composition and algebra. When I came to the page of dance classes, I stopped a moment to day-dream. I imagined being on stage, felt the warmth of the lights and the tightness of the costume with its sequins and straps. I looked back at the catalog and noticed something I hadn't seen before. Just below the list of dance courses was a section of dance-<u>therapy</u> classes. I had never even

LITTLE BALLERINA   1881   Edgar Degas
Shelburne Museum, Shelburne, Vermont   Photograph by Ken Burris.

---

6. Degas (də gä′): Edgar Degas, a nineteenth-century French painter and sculptor.

---

heard of dance therapy, but it made sense. I turned to the course descriptions and found that there was even a major for dance therapy.

"Dance makes people happy," Poppa had said one Christmas after a family dinner. "Even a little baby knows how to dance. Before she can walk or talk, she'll start bouncing when she hears music. Look at that little one there." Mirabella, my cousin's daughter, was only eleven months old, and she was swaying and banging her hands to the old swing music[7] that Poppa liked.

He was right. Dancing had always made me happy. And watching me dance had always made Poppa happy. It occurred to me that perhaps Poppa didn't want me to cry for him. Maybe he just wanted me to be happy, like Grandma had said.

I walked to my bedroom and found my toe shoes hanging by their laces in the closet. I stuffed some fresh lamb's wool in the toes, pulled on my tights and leotard, and went back into the living room. We had a recording of *Swan Lake,* and I lowered it onto the turntable. The music started, soft and sad. Instead of dancing the traditional version, I made up my own steps. My arm swung above my head, and I rose up on my toe and stretched my leg out in an arabesque.[8] My leg rose higher and straighter than it ever had before. Then I brought my foot to my knee. My body had a life of its own as I twirled. It seemed that I twirled in slow motion and that sitting on the couch, Poppa was clapping and shouting, "Bravo!" My torso stretched taller than ever, and I could pirouette[9] three times in one continuous spiral.[10] Every movement was perfect. I played side one and then side two, and then I started over again. I danced until, with bleeding toes, I landed in a lake of dreams.

Dancing had always made me happy.

The next morning my mother woke me up and said, "Hey, you slept in your ballet clothes. Might as well get up. You've only got a couple of weeks left until summer vacation is over. Better enjoy every minute of it."

She opened the window before she left. I rolled over in my bed and inhaled the last notes of my childhood. Outside a breeze danced through the leaves of a chinaberry tree, and it sounded like distant applause. ❧

---

7. swing music: dance music of the 1930s and 1940s.

8. arabesque (ar′ ə besk′): a ballet position in which a dancer stands on one leg and extends the other leg backward.

9. pirouette (pir′ ōō et′): a ballet movement in which a dancer whirls around on one foot.

10. spiral: a circling toward a fixed point.

Words to Know and Use | **torso** (tôr′ sō) *n.* the part of the body between the neck and legs, not including the arms

*R*esponding to Reading

First Impressions

1. What was the strongest emotion you felt as you read this story? Jot down some of your thoughts.

Second Thoughts

2. Why do you think Connie is unable to cry about her grandfather's death?

3. Describe the **characters** of Connie and Poppa as you understand them from your reading. What are some of their defining characteristics?

4. Why do you think dancing is important to Connie? Why was it important to Poppa?

5. What kind of childhood do you think Connie had?

   Think about
   - her relationship with her mother
   - her relationship with her father
   - her relationship with Poppa
   - her thoughts about herself

*L*iterary Concept: Flashback

A **flashback** interrupts the sequence of events in a story to present something that happened earlier. Authors use flashbacks to provide information that readers need to know in order to understand the present events of the story. For example, as Connie stands at Poppa's graveside, she thinks back to the time when she was seven and Poppa bought her her first ballet clothes. This information helps readers understand the special relationship that Connie and Poppa had and the way Poppa got Connie interested in ballet. Besides this flashback, "Dancing for Poppa" contains three others. Find at least one of them and explain what its use adds to the story.

*W*riting Options

1. Close your eyes as you listen to a recording of the music for *Swan Lake*. What thoughts and feelings do you have as you listen? Write your impressions in your **journal** or on a sheet of paper. Don't worry about writing in complete sentences or even making sense; simply respond to the music.

2. Imagine that you are Connie and write an **essay** for your college application. Tell why you have chosen dance therapy for your major.

3. Write a **letter** that Connie might send to Grandma from college. Tell Grandma what you are doing, try to console her, and share a favorite memory of Poppa.

4. In some ways, Connie has defined herself through dance. Think about something you do that you feel defines your personality. Write a **report** that describes how this activity makes you feel truly yourself.

*V*ocabulary Practice

Exercise   On a sheet of paper, write the letter of the word whose meaning is most unlike the meanings of the other words in the set.

1. (a) brace   (b) support   (c) mainstay   (d) ruin
2. (a) gather   (b) corral   (c) scatter   (d) collect
3. (a) grimace   (b) smile   (c) laugh   (d) grin
4. (a) gift   (b) token   (c) memento   (d) request
5. (a) body   (b) trunk   (c) legs   (d) torso
6. (a) strange   (b) quaint   (c) odd   (d) normal
7. (a) surround   (b) enclose   (c) omit   (d) engulf
8. (a) weakness   (b) strength   (c) power   (d) intensity
9. (a) illness   (b) therapy   (c) sickness   (d) disease
10. (a) disrobe   (b) don   (c) dress   (d) clothe

Words to Know and Use

corral
don
engulf
grimace
intensity
mainstay
quaint
therapy
token
torso

Elements of

POETRY

Poetry is the most compact form of literature. A poem packs all kinds of ideas, feelings, and sounds into a few carefully chosen words. The words, the sounds—even the form of a poem—all work together to create a total effect.

Understanding Poetry

Form   The way a poem looks—or its arrangement on the page—is its **form.** Poetry is written in **lines,** which may or may not be sentences. Sometimes the lines are separated into groups called **stanzas.** Remember that poets choose the arrangements of words and lines deliberately. The form of a poem can add to its meaning.

Sound   Poems are meant to be read aloud. Therefore, poets choose and arrange words to create the sounds they want the listener to hear. There are many techniques poets can use to achieve different sounds. Three of these are described below.

• Rhyme   Words that end with the same sounds rhyme. In Western cultures traditional poems, such as "Paul Revere's Ride" on page 91, often contain rhyming words at the ends of the lines:

> One, if by land, and two, if by *sea;*
> And I on the opposite shore will *be,*

• Rhythm   The rhythm is sometimes called the "beat" of the poem. It is the pattern of stressed (ˊ) and unstressed (˘) syllables, or those word parts that are read with more and less emphasis, in a line of poetry. In these lines from "Paul Revere's Ride," listen for the beat that makes them sound like the pounding of horses' hooves.

> ˘ ˊ ˘ ˘ ˊ ˘ ˘ ˘ ˘ ˊ
> The hurrying hoof-beats of that steed,

> ˘ ˘ ˊ ˘ ˊ ˘ ˘ ˊ ˘ ˊ
> And the midnight message of Paul Revere.

Poems which do not have a regular rhythm and sound more like conversation are called **free verse.** The poem "your little voice" on page 45 is written in free verse.

• Repetition   Poets often choose to repeat sounds, words, phrases, or whole lines in a poem. Repetition helps the poet emphasize an idea or give a certain feeling.

Imagery   Imagery involves words and phrases that appeal to the five senses. Poets use imagery to create a picture in the reader's mind or to remind the reader of a familiar sensation. Notice how these lines from "Paul Revere's Ride" give you a visual picture as well as a sound picture. They help bring the poem "inside" of you.

> Then he said, "Good night!"
>   and with muffled oar,
> Silently rowed to the Charlestown shore,
> Just as the moon rose over the bay,

Figurative Language   Poets use figurative language when they choose words and phrases that help the reader to picture ordinary things in new ways. These special descriptions, called **figures of speech,** are explained on the next page.

• **Simile**   A comparison that uses words such as *like, as, than,* or *resembles* is called a simile. This simile from "Pole Vault" on page 203 compares the speed of a pole vaulter to that of a wasp:

> He is running like a wasp,

• **Metaphor**   A comparison that does not use the words *like, as, than,* or *resembles* is called a metaphor. To what is the hurricane compared in these lines from "The Hurricane" on page 153?

> On the tip of its toes,
> Agile dancer, it sweeps whirling

• **Personification**   When a poet describes an animal or object as if it were human or had human qualities, he or she is using personification. In this line from "Dusting" on page 101, the poet gives human characteristics to the towel.

> My name was swallowed in the towel

Theme   All the poetic elements you have read about help the poet establish the theme. Just as in fiction, the message about life that the poem conveys is its theme.

Strategies for Reading Poetry

1. **Preview the poem.** Notice the poem's form: its shape, its length, the length of the lines, and whether or not it has stanzas.

2. **Read the poem aloud.** Pause at the ends of complete thoughts, not necessarily at the ends of lines. Look for end punctuation to help you find the end of a complete thought. As you read, see if there is rhyme and listen for rhythm as well as the overall sound of the words in the poem.

3. **Visualize the images.** In your mind's eye, picture the images and comparisons the poem makes. Do the images remind you of feelings or experiences you have had?

4. **Think about the words and phrases.** Allow yourself to wonder about any phrases or words that seem to stand out. Think about what that choice of words adds to the poem.

5. **Try to figure out the theme.** Ask yourself, What's the point of the poem? What message is the poet trying to send or help you create?

6. **Let your understanding grow.** When you finish reading, you are left with first impressions of the poem. Over time, you will add to your understanding based on the poem, your discussion in class, and other poetry you read.

7. **Allow yourself to enjoy poetry.** Remember that poetry is about feelings. You may connect with a particular poem because it expresses feelings that you yourself have felt.

Poetry

Paul Revere's Ride
HENRY WADSWORTH LONGFELLOW

Examine What You Know

How would you define a patriot? What thoughts does this word bring to mind? Use the sentence starters below to explore your notions of patriotism. Then write these ideas in your journal.

A patriot always ____.

A patriot never ____.

A patriot might ____.

Expand Your Knowledge

On the third Monday of each April, Boston celebrates Patriots' Day. The celebration commemorates the Battles of Lexington and Concord, which began the Revolutionary War. This poem relates the dramatic events that took place on the night before these battles. In 1775 many American colonists had grown rebellious toward their British rulers. The British decided to arrest the rebel leaders and march to Concord to seize a stockpile of colonial weapons. The rebels anticipated this attack but did not know the route the British would take as they left Boston. Would the troops sail across the Charles River and head west from Charlestown, or would they go by land to Cambridge and then head west (see map on page 93)? On the night of April 18, Paul Revere nervously awaited the answer from a spy. Revere had agreed to ride out and warn the colonists of the British advance, a ride that would make him famous.

Enrich Your Reading

Narrative Poetry   This selection is called a **narrative poem** because it tells a story, or narrative, in poetic form. It is the story of a patriot's heroic mission. Like a story, a narrative poem has a setting, a plot, and characters. Unlike stories, a narrative poem usually contains **rhyme** and **rhythm.** Rhyme is the repetition of sounds at the ends of words. Rhythm refers to a regular beat in a poem. Look for these elements as you read.

■ *Author biography on Extend page*

Paul Revere's Ride

HENRY WADSWORTH LONGFELLOW

Listen, my children, and you shall hear
Of the midnight ride of Paul Revere,
On the eighteenth of April, in Seventy-five;
Hardly a man is now alive
5 Who remembers that famous day and year.

He said to his friend, "If the British march
By land or sea from the town to-night,
Hang a lantern aloft in the belfry arch[1]
Of the North Church tower as a signal light,—
10 One, if by land, and two, if by sea;
And I on the opposite shore will be,
Ready to ride and spread the alarm
Through every Middlesex[2] village and farm,
For the country folk to be up and to arm."

15 Then he said, "Good night!" and with muffled oar
Silently rowed to the Charlestown shore,
Just as the moon rose over the bay,
Where swinging wide at her moorings[3] lay
The Somerset, British man-of-war;[4]
20 A phantom ship, with each mast and spar[5]
Across the moon like a prison bar,
And a huge black hulk, that was magnified
By its own reflection in the tide.

---

1. belfry (bel' frē) **arch:** a curved opening in a bell
tower.
2. Middlesex: an eastern Massachusetts county where
the first Revolutionary War battle was fought on April
19, 1775.
3. moorings: the place where a ship is docked.
4. man-of-war: a warship.
5. spar: a pole supporting a ship's sail.

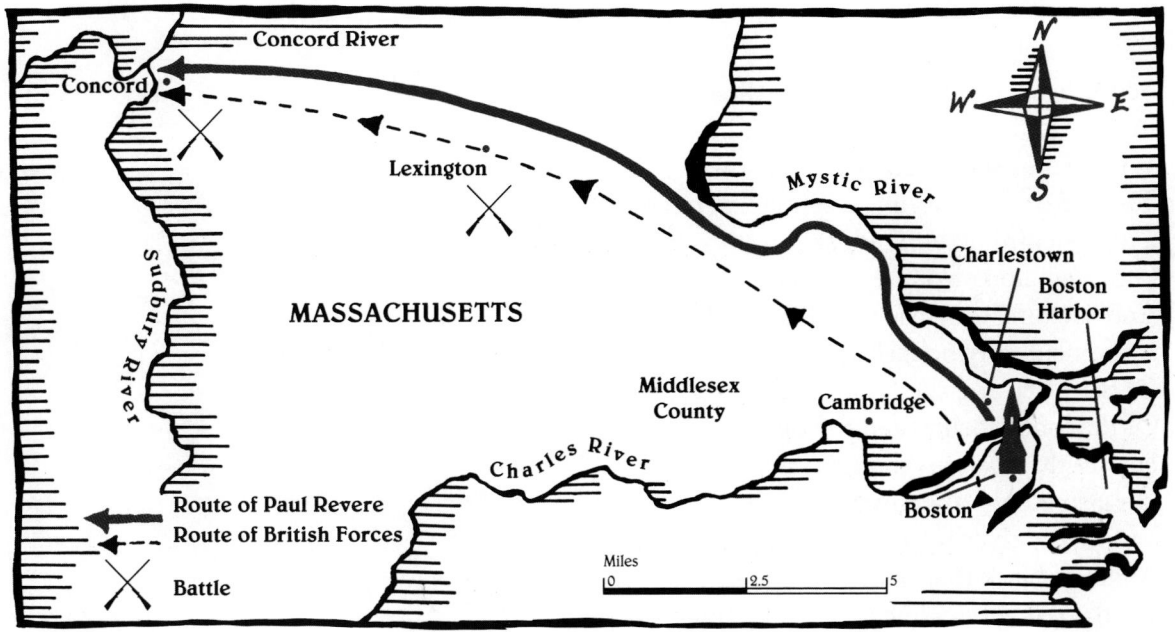

Meanwhile, his friend, through alley and street,
25 Wanders and watches with eager ears,
    Till in the silence around him he hears
    The muster of men at the barrack door,
    The sound of arms, and the tramp of feet,
    And the measured tread of the grenadiers,[6]
30 Marching down to their boats on the shore.

    Then he climbed the tower of the Old North Church,
    By the wooden stairs, with stealthy tread,[7]
    To the belfry-chamber overhead,
    And startled the pigeons from their perch
35 On the somber[8] rafters, that round him made
    Masses and moving shapes of shade,—
    By the trembling ladder, steep and tall,
    To the highest window in the wall,
    Where he paused to listen and look down
40 A moment on the roofs of the town,
    And the moonlight flowing over all.

---

6. **grenadiers** (gren' ə dirz'): foot soldiers.
7. **stealthy tread:** quiet footsteps.
8. **somber:** gloomy.

Beneath, in the churchyard, lay the dead,
In their night-encampment on the hill,
Wrapped in silence so deep and still
45 That he could hear, like a sentinel's[9] tread,
The watchful night-wind, as it went
Creeping along from tent to tent,
And seeming to whisper, "All is well!"
A moment only he feels the spell
50 Of the place and the hour, and the secret dread
Of the lonely belfry and the dead;
For suddenly all his thoughts are bent
On a shadowy something far away,
Where the river widens to meet the bay,—
55 A line of black that bends and floats
On the rising tide, like a bridge of boats.

Meanwhile, impatient to mount and ride,
Booted and spurred, with a heavy stride
On the opposite shore walked Paul Revere.
60 Now he patted his horse's side,
Now gazed at the landscape far and near,
Then, impetuous,[10] stamped the earth,
And turned and tightened his saddle-girth;[11]
But mostly he watched with eager search
65 The belfry-tower of the Old North Church,
As it rose above the graves on the hill,
Lonely and spectral[12] and somber and still.
And lo! as he looks, on the belfry's height
A glimmer, and then a gleam of light!
70 He springs to the saddle, the bridle he turns,
But lingers and gazes, till full on his sight
A second lamp in the belfry burns!

---

9. sentinel's: belonging to a guard or sentry.
10. impetuous (im pech′ o͞o əs): acting suddenly, on impulse.
11. saddle-girth: the strap attaching a saddle to a horse's body.
12. spectral: ghostly.

A hurry of hoofs in a village street,
A shape in the moonlight, a bulk in the dark,
75 And beneath, from the pebbles, in passing, a spark
Struck out by a steed flying fearless and fleet:
That was all! And yet, through the gloom and the light,
The fate of a nation was riding that night;
And the spark struck out by that steed, in his flight,
80 Kindled the land into flame with its heat.

He has left the village and mounted the steep,
And beneath him, tranquil and broad and deep,
Is the Mystic,[13] meeting the ocean tides;
And under the alders,[14] that skirt its edge,
85 Now soft on the sand, now loud on the ledge,
Is heard the tramp of his steed as he rides.

It was twelve by the village clock,
When he crossed the bridge into Medford town.
He heard the crowing of the cock,
90 And the barking of the farmer's dog,
And felt the damp of the river fog,
That rises after the sun goes down.

It was one by the village clock,
When he galloped into Lexington.
95 He saw the gilded weathercock
Swim in the moonlight as he passed,
And the meeting-house windows, blank and bare,
Gaze at him with a spectral glare,
As if they already stood aghast,[15]
100 At the bloody work they would look upon.

---

13. **Mystic:** a short river in Massachusetts, flowing into Boston Harbor.
14. **alders:** trees of the birch family.
15. **aghast** (ə gast′): terrified.

It was two by the village clock,
When he came to the bridge in Concord town.
He heard the bleating[16] of the flock,
And the twitter of birds among the trees,
105 And felt the breath of the morning breeze
Blowing over the meadows brown.
And one was safe and asleep in his bed
Who at the bridge would be first to fall,
Who that day would be lying dead,
110 Pierced by a British musket-ball.

You know the rest. In the books you have read,
How the British Regulars[17] fired and fled,—
How the farmers gave them ball for ball,
From behind each fence and farm-yard wall,
115 Chasing the red-coats down the lane,
Then crossing the fields to emerge again
Under the trees at the turn of the road,
And only pausing to fire and load.

So through the night rode Paul Revere;
120 And so through the night went his cry of alarm
To every Middlesex village and farm,—
A cry of defiance and not of fear,
A voice in the darkness, a knock at the door,
And a word that shall echo forevermore!

125 For, borne on the night-wind of the Past,
Through all our history, to the last,
In the hour of darkness and peril[18] and need,
The people will waken and listen to hear
The hurrying hoof-beats of that steed,
130 And the midnight message of Paul Revere.

---

16. bleating: crying of sheep.
17. British Regulars: members of Great Britain's standing army.
18. peril: danger.

*R*esponding to Reading

First Impressions

1. What feelings about the midnight ride of Paul Revere are you left with? Jot some ideas in your journal or on a sheet of paper.

Second Thoughts

2. Think about your notes from Examine What You Know. To what extent does Paul Revere fit or not fit your idea of a patriot?

3. "Paul Revere's Ride" was written more than 130 years ago. In what ways do you think this poem is relevant or not relevant today?

4. The emotional effect a poem or story has on its reader is called **mood.** Choose and reread one stanza from "Paul Revere's Ride." Think about the emotional effect the words have on you, then describe the mood that is created.

5. How would the impact of "Paul Revere's Ride" differ if it were told as a narrative story instead of a narrative verse?

*L*iterary Concept: Sound Devices

Poets use certain **sound devices** to give their poems a musical quality. **Rhyme** is one of the most common sound devices. **Alliteration,** the repetition of consonant sounds at the beginnings of words, is another such device. "Paul Revere's Ride" contains examples of alliteration, as in line 44: "Wrapped in <u>s</u>ilence <u>s</u>o deep and <u>s</u>till." The repetition of the *s* sound adds to the ghostly mood in the stanza. Can you find other examples of alliteration?

*W*riting Options

1. Think about your answer to question 5 above. Then turn the story of Paul Revere's ride into a **news article.** Your report should answer these important journalistic questions: *who, what, when, where,* and *why.* Include a headline that conveys the drama and importance of this event.

2. Longfellow says that in times of peril Americans will always "listen to hear . . . the midnight message of Paul Revere." Write a **personal response** to this statement, explaining why you agree or disagree with it.

*O*ptions for Learning

1 • **Listen My Children**   Practice a dramatic reading of "Paul Revere's Ride." You may wish to work with a partner and read alternate stanzas. After rehearsing, tape-record your performance. Add appropriate sound effects or background music. If possible, play the tape for a history class studying the Revolutionary War.

2 • **Picture the Ride**   Illustrate one scene from "Paul Revere's Ride." The children's section of your library may have illustrated versions of this poem, which can give you art ideas. In your picture, capture the mood of the scene.

3 • **This Magic Moment**   "Paul Revere's Ride" describes a famous moment in U.S. history. With a partner think of another famous moment in U.S. history. Research the event and then write a narrative poem about it. Study "Paul Revere's Ride," and try to match its style.

4 • **Get the Facts**   Henry Wadsworth Longfellow changed or left out several key facts about Paul Revere's ride. Research what really happened that night and then report your findings to the class in a talk or a written narrative.

 FACT FINDER GEOGRAPHY
How far is it from Boston to Concord?

*H*enry Wadsworth Longfellow
1807–1882

Henry Wadsworth Longfellow was the most famous poet of the United States in the 1800s. He was the foremost of a group of writers known as the Fireside Poets. These poets wrote verse that was morally uplifting, historical or humorous, and easy to understand. The poems were suitable for a family to read aloud while sitting by a fireplace, a common form of entertainment in those days. His narrative poems, such as *Evangeline* and *The Song of Hiawatha,* were household favorites.

Longfellow traveled widely, knew ten languages, and was one of the first teachers of modern languages in a U.S. university. As a young professor, he had to create his own textbooks because the study of modern languages was such a new field.

Longfellow's reputation as the greatest U.S. poet declined after he died, yet some of his poems remain among the most famous works of American literature.

Poetry

I'm Nobody! Who are you?

EMILY DICKINSON

Dusting

JULIA ALVAREZ

Examine What You Know

You have probably heard the statement, "I want to be somebody someday." Being somebody means different things to different people; it may mean having fame, fortune, or happiness, for example. Jot some notes in your journal or on a sheet of paper about what being somebody means to you.

Expand Your Knowledge

These two poems express opposing views on being somebody. The poems "I'm Nobody! Who are you?" and "Dusting" are **lyric poems**—short poems that express the thoughts or feelings of a single speaker. Many popular songs, and even greeting-card messages, are written as lyric poems.

Enrich Your Reading

Reading Aloud   Since poetry is usually written to be read aloud, poets often choose words for the way they sound as well as for what they mean. Reading a poem aloud may help you discover something you might not notice if you read it silently.

After you read these two poems to yourself, practice reading each of them aloud. Experiment with different ways of speaking, noticing how changes in your voice affect the poem's meaning. See whether a slow, a medium, or a fast pace seems to work best. Follow the punctuation, pausing at commas and periods instead of stopping at the end of each line in a singsong manner.

■ *Author biographies in Reader's Handbook*

I'm Nobody! Who are you?

EMILY DICKINSON

GIRL LOOKING AT LANDSCAPE
1957   Richard Diebenkorn
Collection of Whitney Museum of American Art, New York.
Photography by Geoffrey Clements, New York.

I'm Nobody! Who are you?
Are you–Nobody–Too?
Then there's a pair of us?
Don't tell! they'd banish us–you know!

5   How dreary–to be–Somebody!
How public–like a Frog–

To tell one's name–the livelong June–
To an admiring Bog!

*R*esponding to Reading

First Impressions of "I'm Nobody! Who are you?"

1. What is your reaction to the speaker's message? Jot down your thoughts in your journal or on a sheet of paper.

Second Thoughts on "I'm Nobody! Who are you?"

2. What kind of person do you imagine the speaker of this poem to be?

3. Why do you think the speaker compares being somebody to being a frog in a bog?

4. Do you share Emily Dickinson's view of what it means to be Somebody? Why or why not?

Dusting

JULIA ALVAREZ

Each morning I wrote my name
on the dusty cabinet, then crossed
the dining table in script, scrawled
in capitals on the backs of chairs,
5 practising signatures like scales
while Mother followed, squirting
linseed from a burping can[1]
into a crumpled-up flannel.

She erased my fingerprints
10 from the bookshelf and rocker,
polished mirrors on the desk
scribbled with my alphabets.
My name was swallowed in the towel
with which she jeweled the table tops.
15 The grain surfaced in the oak
and the pine grew luminous.
But I refused with every mark
to be like her, anonymous.

---

1. **squirting linseed from a burping can:** squeezing
wood-cleaning oil from a metal container.

Responding to Reading

First Impressions of "Dusting"

1. What is your reaction to this poem? Discuss.

2. Which character do you have stronger feelings about, the mother or the daughter? Explain your answer.

Second Thoughts on "Dusting"

3. Why do you think the speaker keeps writing her name on the furniture?

Comparing the Poems

4. How do you think the two speakers would define themselves?

5. Which poem expresses ideas closer to your own ideas about being Somebody?

Literary Concept: Simile

A **simile** is a comparison of two things that includes words such as *like, as, than,* or *resembles*. Poets often use similes to give their readers a clearer picture of what they are describing. "Jack's face got as red as a beet when he was embarrassed" contains an example of a simile. Find one simile in "I'm Nobody! Who are you?" and one in "Dusting."

Writing Options

1. Think about a major characteristic that defines you or someone you know. Using either of the two poems you just read as a model, write a **poem** in a way that highlights that characteristic.

2. What if the speakers of the two poems both appeared at the same party? How might each one act? Do you think the two would interact? Write a **society column** for a newspaper or magazine. Describe what both people said and did, as well as what they wore.

Fiction

Raymond's Run
TONI CADE BAMBARA

Examine What You Know

This story deals with a young girl and her mentally handicapped brother. For a moment imagine yourself in the shoes of the sister. How do you think you would deal with having a handicapped brother? How would you handle the responsibility of taking care of him? What feelings would you have if you were with your brother and you met friends or rivals? Explore these feelings by writing about them in your journal or on a sheet of paper. Can you think of any circumstances that might cause these feelings to change?

Expand Your Knowledge

In this story, the main character's brother has a medical condition known as hydrocephalus (hī′ drō sef′ ə ləs). In this condition an abnormal amount of fluid collects in the skull and makes the head swell. Hydrocephalus may be caused by an infection, a tumor, or a malformation of the brain. If detected early enough, hydrocephalus can sometimes be treated successfully with surgery. In more severe cases the excess fluid presses on the brain and causes mental retardation, which is the condition of the brother in this story.

Enrich Your Reading

Dynamic and Static Characters   In a short story the main character is usually the only one who develops and grows in the course of the story. Such a character is said to be **dynamic.** The minor characters in a story are often **static,** or unchanging. In "Raymond's Run" the main character, Squeaky, is a dynamic character. After you have read the story, use a chart like the one below to note how her feelings change across time.

Feelings	Squeaky at beginning	Squeaky at end
How She Defines Herself		
How She Feels About Raymond		
How She Sees Her Rival		

■ *Author biography on Extend page*

Raymond's Run

TONI CADE BAMBARA

I don't have much work to do around the house like some girls. My mother does that. And I don't have to earn my pocket money by hustling; George runs errands for the big boys and sells Christmas cards. And anything else that's got to get done, my father does. All I have to do in life is mind my brother Raymond, which is enough.

Sometimes I slip and say "my little brother Raymond." But as any fool can see, he's much bigger and he's older too. But a lot of people call him my little brother 'cause he needs looking after 'cause he's not quite right. And a lot of smart mouths got lots to say about that too, especially when George was minding him. But now, if anybody has anything to say to Raymond, anything to say about his big head,[1] they have to come by me. And I don't play the dozens[2] or believe in standing around with somebody in my face doing a lot of talking. I much rather just knock you down and take my chances, even if I am a little girl with skinny arms and a squeaky voice, which is how I got the name Squeaky. And if things get too rough, I run. And as anybody can tell you, I'm the fastest thing on two feet.

There is no track meet that I don't win the first-place medal. I use to win the twenty-yard dash when I was a little kid in kindergarten.

Nowadays it's the fifty-yard dash. And tomorrow I'm subject to run the quarter-meter relay all by myself and come in first, second, and third. The big kids call me Mercury[3] 'cause I'm the swiftest thing in the neighborhood. Everybody knows that—except two people who know better, my father and me.

I'm the fastest thing on two feet.

He can beat me to Amsterdam Avenue with me having a two fire-hydrant head start and him running with his hands in his pockets and whistling. But that's private information. 'Cause can you imagine some thirty-five-year-old man stuffing himself into PAL shorts to race little kids? So as far as everyone's concerned, I'm the fastest, and that goes for Gretchen, too, who has put out the tale that she is going to win the first-place medal this year. Ridiculous. In the second

---

1. **big head:** enlarged skull, the result of a condition called *hydrocephalus,* in which an unusual amount of fluid collects around the brain.

2. **play the dozens:** a slang term referring to an exchange of rhyming insults.

3. **Mercury:** in Roman mythology, the swift messenger of the gods.

place, she's got short legs. In the third place, she's got freckles. In the first place, no one can beat me, and that's all there is to it.

I'm standing on the corner admiring the weather and about to take a stroll down Broadway so I can practice my breathing exercises, and I've got Raymond walking on the inside, close to the buildings, 'cause he's subject to fits of fantasy and starts thinking he's a circus performer and that the curb is a tightrope strung high in the air. And sometimes after a rain, he likes to step down off his tightrope right into the gutter and slosh around, getting his shoes and cuffs wet. Then I get hit when I get home. Or sometimes if you don't watch him, he'll dash across traffic to the island in the middle of Broadway and give the pigeons a fit. Then I have to go behind him apologizing to all the old people sitting around trying to get some sun and getting all upset with the pigeons fluttering around them, scattering their newspapers and upsetting the wax-paper lunches in their laps. So I keep Raymond on the inside of me, and he plays like he's driving a stagecoach, which is OK by me so long as he doesn't run me over or interrupt my breathing exercises, which I have to do on account of I'm serious about my running and don't care who knows it.

Now some people like to act like things come easy to them, won't let on that they practice. Not me. I'll high-prance down 34th Street like a rodeo pony to keep my knees strong even if it does get my mother uptight so that she walks ahead like she's not with me, don't know me, is all by herself on a shopping trip, and I am somebody else's crazy child.

Now you take Cynthia Procter for instance. She's just the opposite. If there's a test tomorrow, she'll say something like, "Oh, I guess I'll play handball this afternoon and watch television tonight," just to let you know she ain't thinking about the test. Or like last week, when she won the spelling bee for the millionth time, "A good thing you got *receive*, Squeaky, 'cause I would have got it wrong. I completely forgot about the spelling bee." And she'll clutch the lace on her blouse like it was a narrow escape. Oh, brother.

I'm serious about my running and don't care who knows it.

But of course when I pass her house on my early morning trots around the block, she is practicing the scales on the piano over and over and over and over. Then in music class, she always lets herself get bumped around so she falls accidently on purpose onto the piano stool and is so surprised to find herself sitting there, and so decides just for fun to try out the ole keys and what do you know—Chopin's waltzes just spring out of her fingertips, and she's the most surprised thing in the world. A regular prodigy. I could kill people like that.

I stay up all night studying the words for the spelling bee. And you can see me any time of day practicing running. I never walk if I can trot, and shame on Raymond if he can't keep up. But of course he does, 'cause if he hangs back, someone's liable to walk up to him and get smart, or take his allowance from him, or ask him where he got that great big pumpkin head. People are so stupid sometimes.

I always win 'cause I'm the best.

So I'm strolling down Broadway breathing out and breathing in on counts of seven, which is my lucky number, and here comes Gretchen and her sidekicks—Mary Louise, who used to be a friend of mine when she first moved to Harlem from Baltimore and got beat up by everybody till I took up for her on account of her mother and my mother used to sing in the same choir when they were young girls, but people ain't grateful, so now she hangs out with the new girl, Gretchen, and talks about me like a dog; and Rosie, who is as fat as I am skinny and has a big mouth where Raymond is concerned and is too stupid to know that there is not a big deal of difference between herself and Raymond and that she can't afford to throw stones. So they are steady coming up Broadway, and I see right away that it's going to be one of those Dodge City scenes 'cause the street ain't that big and they're close to the buildings just as we are. First I think I'll step into the candy store and look over the new comics and let them pass. But that's chicken, and I've got a reputation to consider. So then I think I'll just walk straight on through them or over them if necessary. But as they get to me, they slow down. I'm ready to fight, 'cause like I said, I don't feature a whole lot of chitchat; I much prefer to just knock you down right from the jump and save everybody a lotta precious time.

"You signing up for the May Day races?" smiles Mary Louise, only it's not a smile at all.

A dumb question like that doesn't deserve an answer. Besides, there's just me and Gretchen standing there really, so no use wasting my breath talking to shadows.

"I don't think you're going to win this time," says Rosie, trying to signify with her hands on her hips all salty, completely forgetting that I have whupped her behind many times for less salt than that.

"I always win 'cause I'm the best," I say straight at Gretchen, who is, as far as I'm concerned, the only one talking in this ventriloquist-dummy routine.[4]

Gretchen smiles, but it's not a smile, and I'm thinking that girls never really smile at each other because they don't know how and don't want to know how and there's probably no one to teach us how 'cause grown-up girls don't know either. Then they all look at Raymond, who has just brought his mule team to a standstill. And they're about to see what trouble they can get into through him.

"What grade you in now, Raymond?"

"You got anything to say to my brother, you say it to me, Mary Louise Williams of Raggedy Town, Baltimore."

"What are you, his mother?" sasses Rosie.

"That's right, Fatso. And the next word out of anybody and I'll be their mother too." So they just stand there, and Gretchen shifts from one leg to the other and so do they. Then Gretchen puts her hands on her hips

---

4. **ventriloquist-dummy routine:** a situation in which a person speaks the thoughts of another.

BUILDERS (GREEN AND RED BALL) 1979 Jacob Lawrence Gouache on paper.
New Jersey State Museum Collection, Purchase FA 1987.28.

and is about to say something with her freckle-face self but doesn't. Then she walks around me looking me up and down but keeps walking up Broadway, and her side-kicks follow her. So me and Raymond smile at each other, and he says, "Gidyap" to his team, and I continue with my breathing exercises, strolling down Broadway toward the icey man on 145th with not a care in the world 'cause I am Miss Quicksilver herself.

I take my time getting to the park on May Day because the track meet is the last thing on the program. The biggest thing on the program is the May Pole dancing, which I can do without, thank you, even if my mother thinks it's a shame I don't take part and act like a girl for a change. You'd think my mother'd be grateful not to have to make me a white organdy dress with a big satin sash and buy me new white baby-doll shoes that can't be taken out of the box till the big day. You'd think she'd be glad her daughter ain't out there prancing around a May Pole getting the new clothes all dirty and sweaty and trying to act like a fairy or a flower or whatever you're supposed to be when you should be trying to be yourself, whatever that is, which is, as far as I am concerned, a poor black girl who really can't afford to buy shoes and a new dress you only wear once a lifetime 'cause it won't fit next year.

I was once a strawberry in a Hansel and Gretel pageant when I was in nursery school and didn't have no better sense than to dance on tiptoe with my arms in a circle over my head doing umbrella steps and being a perfect fool just so my mother and father could come dressed up and clap. You'd think they'd know better than to encourage that kind of nonsense. I am not a strawberry. I do not dance on my toes. I run. That is what I am all about. So I always come late to the May Day program, just in time to get my number pinned on and lay in the grass till they announce the fifty-yard dash.

I put Raymond in the little swings, which is a tight squeeze this year and will be impossible next year. Then I look around for Mr. Pearson, who pins the numbers on. I'm really looking for Gretchen, if you want to know the truth, but she's not around. The park is jam-packed. Parents in hats and corsages and breast-pocket handkerchiefs peeking up. Kids in white dresses and light blue suits. The parkees unfolding chairs and chasing the rowdy kids from Lenox[5] as if they had no right to be there. The big guys with their caps on backwards, leaning against the fence swirling the basketballs on the tips of their fingers waiting for all these crazy people to clear out the park so they can play. Most of the kids in my class are carrying bass drums and glockenspiels[6] and flutes. You'd think they'd put in a few bongos or something for real like that.

Then here comes Mr. Pearson with his clipboard and his cards and pencils and whistles and safety pins and 50 million other things he's always dropping all over the place with his clumsy self. He sticks out in a crowd 'cause he's on stilts. We used to call him Jack and the Beanstalk to get him mad. But I'm the only one that can outrun

---

5. **Lenox:** an avenue in the Harlem section of New York City.

6. **glockenspiels** (gläk′ ən spēlz): marching-band instruments consisting of metal bars that are tapped with light hammers.

him and get away, and I'm too grown for that silliness now.

"Well, Squeaky," he says, checking my name off the list and handing me number seven and two pins. And I'm thinking he's got no right to call me Squeaky if I can't call him Beanstalk.

"Hazel Elizabeth Deborah Parker," I correct him and tell him to write it down on his board.

"Well, Hazel Elizabeth Deborah Parker, going to give someone else a break this year?" I squint at him real hard to see if he is seriously thinking I should lose the race on purpose just to give someone else a break.

*J*ust before I take off in a race, I always feel like I'm in a dream.

"Only six girls running this time," he continues, shaking his head sadly like it's my fault all of New York didn't turn out in sneakers. "That new girl should give you a run for your money." He looks around the park for Gretchen like a periscope in a submarine movie. "Wouldn't it be a nice gesture if you were . . . to ahhh . . ."

I give him such a look he couldn't finish putting that idea into words. Grown-ups got a lot of nerve sometimes. I pin number seven to myself and stomp away—I'm so burnt. And I go straight for the track and stretch out on the grass while the band winds up with "Oh the Monkey Wrapped His Tail Around the Flag Pole," which my teacher calls by some other name. The man

on the loudspeaker is calling everyone over to the track, and I'm on my back looking at the sky trying to pretend I'm in the country, but I can't, because even grass in the city feels hard as sidewalk and there's just no pretending you are anywhere but in a "concrete jungle," as my grandfather says.

The twenty-yard dash takes all of the two minutes 'cause most of the little kids don't know no better than to run off the track or run the wrong way or run smack into the fence and fall down and cry. One little kid, though, has got the good sense to run straight for the white ribbon up ahead, so he wins. Then the second graders line up for the thirty-yard dash, and I don't even bother to turn my head to watch 'cause Raphael Perez always wins. He wins before he even begins by psyching the runners, telling them they're going to trip on their shoelaces and fall on their faces or lose their shorts or something, which he doesn't really have to do since he is very fast, almost as fast as I am. After that is the forty-yard dash, which I use to run when I was in first grade. Raymond is hollering from the swings 'cause he knows I'm about to do my thing 'cause the man on the loudspeaker has just announced the fifty-yard dash, although he might just as well be giving a recipe for angel food cake 'cause you can hardly make out what he's saying for the static. I get up and slip off my sweat pants, and then I see Gretchen standing at the starting line kicking her legs out like a pro. Then as I get into place, I see that ole Raymond is in line on the other side of the fence, bending down with his fingers on the ground just like he knew what he was doing. I was going to yell at him, but then I didn't. It burns up your energy to holler.

Every time, just before I take off in a race, I always feel like I'm in a dream, the kind of dream you have when you're sick with fever and feel all hot and weightless. I dream I'm flying over a sandy beach in the early morning sun, kissing the leaves of the trees as I fly by. And there's always the smell of apples, just like in the country when I was little and use to think I was a choo-choo train, running through the fields of corn and chugging up the hill to the orchard. And all the time I'm dreaming this, I get lighter and lighter until I'm flying over the beach again, getting blown through the sky like a feather that weighs nothing at all. But once I spread my fingers in the dirt and crouch over for the Get on Your Mark, the dream goes, and I am solid again and am telling myself, Squeaky you must win, you must win, you are the fastest thing in the world, you can even beat your father up Amsterdam if you really try. And then I feel my weight coming back just behind my knees, then down to my feet, then into the earth, and the pistol shot explodes in my blood and I am off and weightless again, flying past the other runners, my arms pumping up and down, and the whole world is quiet except for the crunch as I zoom over the gravel in the track. I glance to my left and there is no one. To the right a blurred Gretchen, who's got her chin jutting out as if it would win the race all by itself. And on the other side of the fence is Raymond, with his arms down to his side and the palms tucked up behind him, running in his very own style and the first time I ever saw that, and I almost stop to watch my brother Raymond on his first run. But the white ribbon is bouncing toward me, and I tear past it racing into the distance till my feet with a mind

of their own start digging up footfuls of dirt and brake me short. Then all the kids standing on the side pile on me, banging me on the back and slapping my head with their May Day programs, for I have won again, and everybody on 151st Street can walk tall for another year.

I am off and weightless again, flying past the other runners.

"In first place . . ." the man on the loudspeaker is clear as a bell now. But then he pauses, and the loudspeaker starts to whine. Then static. And I lean down to catch my breath, and here comes Gretchen walking back, for she's overshot the finish line too, huffing and puffing with her hands on her hips taking it slow, breathing in steady time like a real pro, and I sort of like her a little for the first time. "In first place . . ." and then three or four voices get all mixed up on the loudspeaker, and I dig my sneaker into the grass and stare at Gretchen, who's staring back, we both wondering just who did win. I can hear old Beanstalk arguing with the man on the loudspeaker and then a few others running their mouths about what the stopwatches say.

Then I hear Raymond yanking at the fence to call me, and I wave to shush him, but he keeps rattling the fence like a gorilla in a cage like in them gorilla movies, but then like a dancer or something he starts climbing up nice and easy but very fast. And it occurs to me, watching how smoothly he climbs hand over hand and remembering how he looked running with his arms

Illustration by Andy Dearwater.

down to his side and with the wind pulling his mouth back and his teeth showing and all, it occurred to me that Raymond would make a very fine runner. Doesn't he always keep up with me on my trots? And he surely knows how to breathe in counts of seven 'cause he's always doing it at the dinner table, which drives my brother George up the wall. And I'm smiling to beat the band, 'cause if I've lost this race, or if me and Gretchen tied, or even if I've won, I can always retire as a runner and begin a whole new career as a coach with Raymond as my champion. After all, with a little more study I can beat Cynthia and her phony self at the spelling bee. And if I bugged my mother, I could get piano lessons and become a star. And I have a big rep as the baddest thing around. And I've got a roomful of ribbons and medals and awards. But what has Raymond got to call his own?

My brother Raymond, a great runner in the family tradition.

So I stand there with my new plan, laughing out loud by this time as Raymond jumps down from the fence and runs over with his teeth showing and his arms down to the side, which no one before him has quite mastered as a running style. And by the time he comes over, I'm jumping up and down so glad to see him—my brother Raymond, a great runner in the family tradition. But of course everyone thinks I'm jumping up and down because the men on the loudspeaker have finally gotten themselves together and compared notes and are announcing, "In first place–Miss Hazel Elizabeth Deborah Parker." (Dig that.) "In second place–Miss Gretchen P. Lewis." And I look over at Gretchen, wondering what the P. stands for. And I smile. 'Cause she's good, no doubt about it. Maybe she'd like to help me coach Raymond; she obviously is serious about running, as any fool can see. And she nods to congratulate me, and then she smiles. And I smile. We stand there with this big smile of respect between us. It's about as real a smile as girls can do for each other, considering we don't practice real smiling every day you know, 'cause maybe we too busy being flowers or fairies or strawberries instead of something honest and worthy of respect . . . you know . . . like being people. ❧

INSIGHT

For Poets
AL YOUNG

Stay beautiful
but dont stay down underground too long
Dont turn into a mole
or a worm
or a root
or a stone

Come on out into the sunlight
Breathe in trees
Knock out mountains
Commune with snakes
& be the very hero of birds

Dont forget to poke your head up
& blink
Think
Walk all around

Swim upstream
Dont forget to fly

E X P L A I N

Responding to Reading

First Impressions

1. What were your strongest impressions of Squeaky as you read? Briefly note your thoughts in your journal or on a sheet of paper.

Second Thoughts

2. In what ways does Squeaky change by the end of the story?

Think about
- how she sees her rival
- how she feels about Raymond
- how she defines herself

3. What are your feelings about Squeaky's relationship with Raymond?

4. Imagine that Squeaky did not have a brother like Raymond. Would she be a different person? Explain your answer.

Broader Connections

5. What attitudes toward the disabled are revealed in this story? Are these attitudes typical of the way people respond to those with disabilities? Use examples from your own experience and from your reading to support your answer.

Literary Concept: External Conflict

Perhaps you recall that **conflict** is the struggle between two opposing forces in a story. An **external conflict** takes place between a character and some outside person or force. Explain the external conflict in "Raymond's Run." Do you think that Squeaky also has an **internal conflict?** Explain.

Writing Options

1. Think about two siblings who get along well. You might be one of the two. Write a **feature article** about the relationship of the siblings. Focus your article around a particular event or incident.

2. Reread Squeaky's description of her race, and picture the race in your mind. Then write a **play-by-play commentary** of the race.

Options for Learning

1 • Winners All Research the Special Olympics and report your findings to the class. Incorporate answers to questions such as Where are they held? Who competes? What events are included?

2 • A Whole New Career With a partner, design a newspaper ad for a new business—Squeaky and Gretchen's coaching service. Decide on a catchy name for the business. Think about the people you want to attract and the statements and pictures that will persuade them to try the service.

3 • Sprint Technique Research the topic of sprinting. How do the top sprinters train for their events? What must they keep in mind during a race's three phases—the start, the middle, and the finish? Prepare an oral report for your class.

4 • Raymond's Rap Tell the story of "Raymond's Run" in a rap song. If you like, perform the composition for your class.

FACT FINDER MATH

Today many running events are measured in meters, not yards. How much longer is fifty meters than the fifty yards of Squeaky's race?

Toni Cade Bambara
1939-

Toni Cade Bambara was born and educated in New York City, where "Raymond's Run" takes place. She also studied in Italy at the University of Florence's Commedia dell' Arte and in Paris, France, at a mime school.

In addition to her writing career, Bambara has worked as a welfare investigator, a project director for social programs, a college instructor, and a lecturer. Bambara writes novels, screenplays, and short stories. Three of her short stories have been adapted for film. She won an American Book Award for her novel *The Salt Eaters*.

Bambara credits her mother as a major influence on her work, recalling, "She gave me permission to wonder, to dawdle, to daydream," Barbara recalls. "My most indelible memory of 1948 is my mother coming upon me in the middle of the kitchen floor with my head in the clouds and my pencil on the paper and her mopping around me. . . . She thought it was wonderful that I could write things that almost made some kind of sense."

WRITER'S WORKSHOP

DESCRIPTIVE WRITING

What makes a person special? Think about Connie and Poppa in "Dancing for Poppa"—or perhaps Squeaky and Raymond in "Raymond's Run." What did they do or say that revealed their personalities? As you got to know these characters, a picture emerged about the qualities that made them unique. In this workshop you will get a chance to write a character sketch about a special person in your life. A **character sketch** is a type of descriptive writing that focuses on a person's personality traits and behavior patterns.

USE DESCRIPTIVE WRITING IN

essays
reports
letters
editorials
scripts
advertisements
stories
character sketches

GUIDED ASSIGNMENT: CHARACTER SKETCH

Write a character sketch about an unforgettable person. Describe the qualities that make her or him special.

Here is one writer's PASSkey to this assignment.

P URPOSE: To describe the qualities of a special person

A UDIENCE: Classmates, friends, family

S UBJECT: An unforgettable character

S TRUCTURE: A character sketch

STUDENT MODEL
Before you write, read how one student responded to the assignment.

Elena! What a Girl!

by Yoshiko Sagami

"We are here today to say goodbye to Elena Rodriguez, who will soon be going home to her native land, Argentina. We've all grown to know and respect Elena. She's a true friend AND a fantastic soccer player. As a special honor the soccer team has voted to make Elena honorary team captain. We feel she deserves this honor because of her great contribution to the team. Elena, come up and say a few words."

I sat in the crowded auditorium and cheered along with the other kids as an amazed--and a little embarrassed--Elena walked quietly to

As you read, notice how the writer described her subject through the use of **flashback,** a technique in which a writer tells about something that happened earlier.

the podium. I couldn't help but think of the day last September when we first met Elena. She certainly has changed!

On the first day of school, Ms. Oliver, our homeroom teacher, introduced us to a plain-looking girl dressed in a very drab outfit made up of a white shirt and pleated gray skirt. "I'd like you all to meet Elena Rodriguez. She's an exchange student from Argentina and will be with us this year."

We tried to be cordial, but she just stared at us. She sat down and carefully unpacked her school bag. She lined up her pens like a row of soldiers and stacked her notebooks neatly on her desk. This went on day after day just like clockwork. Once we arranged the equipment on our desks just like she did. We thought maybe we'd get her to laugh. Instead, she just stared at us. We really wondered if we could ever be friends with her. To us, she was just this superneat, superpolite "nobody."

Vivid and precise word choice brings the subject to life.

Things began to change, however, when soccer season started. We soon learned that beneath Elena's polite--and seemingly cold--exterior was an absolutely incredible soccer player. She taught us a great soccer move called "give and go," which works like this: Elena would kick the ball to me and then bolt down the field to meet the ball flying back from me. You've never seen anyone move so fast! She was a four-foot-two-inch whirlwind.

Our poor coach had been struggling to pound this soccer skill into our heads, but we just couldn't master it. Elena made it click. We began nailing goals and winning games.

We discovered that Elena wasn't unfriendly, just shy. Soccer seemed to be just the thing to make the real Elena come alive. She turned out to be an interesting person--and fun to be with. She not only taught us soccer but also some wild Argentine music and the fancy footwork to go with it.

> Elena and I soon became close friends. We listened to music together, we shopped, we did our homework together. If I needed to borrow something, she would gladly lend it to me. Elena's going to leave soon. I'm not sad, though, because with a little luck, I'LL be going to ARGENTINA as an exchange student next year. Getting to know Elena has been quite an experience. She's a terrific girl and a good friend.

◀ The writer builds an overall picture of Elena as admirable and likable.

Now begin your own character sketch.

Prewrite and Explore

1 **Recall unforgettable moments**   If you need some writing ideas, think about memorable people from your life. Try remembering special events at school or in your family. Were you affected by anyone in particular? Did you identify with someone's experience? Choose a person you know well, or would like to know well. Your enthusiasm will liven up your writing.

◀ WRITER'S CHOICE
Try looking through letters and postcards you've received. Perhaps one is from that "special" person.

GATHERING INFORMATION

   Begin by observing and recording details about your subject. If you're writing about a person from your past, you can "observe" through your memories, photos, and the recollections of others who knew your subject. Next, use a **category chart** such as the one that follows to organize details. As you write, think about what it is that makes your subject special. Look at the chart that Yoshiko used.

```
        Subject Observed--Elena Rodriguez

Unforgettable Traits    Background
taught us "give and go"  exchange student
incredible soccer player    from Argentina
arranges desk same
  way each day
ignores jokes
generous
Interests                Appearance
Argentine music and dance 4 ft. 2 in. tall
soccer                   wears plain clothes
```

◀ STUDENT MODEL

◀ NEED HELP?
Will your subject be interesting to readers? Ask a peer reader to look at your notes and highlight areas where you need more detail.

Draft and Discover

WRITER'S CHOICE

If you can't find a method of organization that will work, try beginning with a brief physical description of your subject. Then discuss the character traits that make this person special.

▶ **1** **Begin drafting**   As you write, think about the order in which you will present information. Character sketches often begin by identifying the trait that is most significant to the writer. Then, the picture is expanded with other traits and supporting details such as anecdotes that illustrate the qualities of the subject.

2 **Use flashback to set the scene**   You might also consider using **flashback** to set the scene for your character sketch. Flashback is a technique in which a writer begins a story at one point in time and then "flashes back" to something that happened earlier in the sequence of events. With flashback, you can tell readers about your subject's history. Think about the opening scene in the story "Dancing For Poppa." Connie stands near Poppa's graveside and starts thinking back to the time that he brought her a ballet outfit. What did this flashback scene tell you about the role ballet played in Connie's life?

LITERARY MODEL

Revise Your Writing

ASK FOR HELP

Does it sound right? Read your description aloud to a classmate. See if the way your words sound supports the overall picture you want to create. You may also be able to identify awkward phrases or sentences when you hear them spoken.

▶ **1** **Clarify your language**   As you review your draft, consider the language you've chosen to describe your subject. Now that your basic ideas are on paper, you may want to fine-tune the descriptive details to sharpen the image you want to present. Study some of the ways Yoshiko revised her description of Elena.

First Draft	She's a friend and a good soccer player, too.
Revised Draft	She's a true friend AND a fantastic soccer player.
First Draft	a plain-looking girl who wears dull clothes
Revised Draft	a plain-looking girl dressed in a very drab outfit made up of a white shirt and pleated gray skirt
First Draft	To us, she was dull and boring.
Revised Draft	To us, she was just this superneat, superpolite "nobody."
First Draft	a very good soccer player
Revised Draft	an absolutely incredible soccer player

2 **Evaluate your draft**   Ask a friend to respond to your draft. The questions on the next page will help you.

Revision Questions

For You	For a Peer Reader
1. Is my language vivid and specific?	1. How do you think you would respond to my subject?
2. Should I order the details differently?	2. What descriptive language created vivid images? Was any language vague?
3. Does my description create an overall impression of why my subject is special?	3. Why do you think I found my subject unforgettable?

Proofread

As you proofread your draft, look for errors in grammar and punctuation. Working with a classmate, review your choice of verbs to be sure you've chosen those that accurately convey your meaning.

COMPUTER TIP

Try using the "spell checking" feature of your software to spotlight any mistakes. Remember, if you spell a word correctly but use it incorrectly, spell checkers will not notice.

NEED MORE HELP?

See the Language Workshop that follows (pages 120-122).

THE EDITOR'S EYE: CONFUSING VERBS

Avoid misusing verbs with related meanings.

Many verbs with related meanings are commonly confused.

Problem She *learned* us a great move called "give and go."

Correct She *taught* us a great move called "give and go."

Publish and Present

Here is a suggestion for sharing your work with others.

A Yearbook As a class, review all the sketches. Assign yearbook-style titles such as "Most Likely to Succeed" and "Hardest Worker" to the various subjects. Add photographs or drawings and collect the material in a yearbook-style notebook.

Reflect on Your Writing

Briefly answer the following questions. Put your answers with your paper and add both to your portfolio.

FOR YOUR PORTFOLIO

1. Which elements of descriptive writing did you find the easiest?
2. Do you think you captured the unforgettable personality traits of your subject? Explain.

LANGUAGE
WORKSHOP

COMMONLY CONFUSED VERBS

Many verbs with similar spellings or related meanings are commonly confused with each other. Use verbs that convey your intended meaning.

Verbs with Related Meanings

The chart that follows shows the verb forms for three pairs of commonly confused verbs with related meanings.

	Present	Past	Past Participle
Learn/Teach	learn	learned	(have) learned
	teach	taught	(have) taught
Borrow/Lend	borrow	borrowed	(have) borrowed
	lend	lent	(have) lent
Let/Leave	let	let	(have) let
	leave	left	(have) left

learn and *teach*

Learn and *teach* both involve an exchange of knowledge. *Learn* means "to gain knowledge or skill." *Teach* means "to show how or explain" or "to help someone learn."

> Yoshiko wanted to *learn* the "give and go" soccer move.
> Elena wanted to *teach* her the soccer move.

borrow and *lend*

Borrow means "to receive something from." *Lend* means "to give out to."

> Yoshiko wanted to *borrow* a pen from Elena.
> Elena was happy to *lend* her new friend a pen.

let and *leave*

Let means "to allow or to permit." *Leave* means "to go away from."

> After the funeral, Connie's parents *let* her stay home alone.
> Connie did not have to *leave* home after the funeral.

Exercise 1   Concept Check   Write the correct verb from the
two given in parentheses.

1. Von and his father wanted to (let, leave) Vietnam.
2. The Vietnamese government (let, left) Von and his father go.
3. Von wanted to (learn, teach) about life in the United States.
4. Von's sponsor (learned, taught) Von about American food.
5. Von tried to (learn, teach) his American friends about Vietnam.
6. Did the lady at the airport (borrow, lend) money to Von?
7. What vocabulary did Von (learn, teach) at the school?
8. The rabbi (borrowed, lent) several things to Von's father.
9. Von's father did not want to (borrow, lend) money from the rabbi.
10. Did the Vietnamese government (let, leave) the rest of Von's family
    go to the United States?

Verbs with Similar Spellings and Related Meanings

The following chart shows the verb forms for three pairs of commonly
confused verbs with similar spellings and related meanings.

	Present	**Past**	**Past Participle**
Sit/Set	sit	sat	(have) sat
	set	set	(have) set
Rise/Raise	rise	rose	(have) risen
	raise	raised	(have) raised
Lie/Lay	lie	lay	(have) lain
	lay	laid	(have) laid

◀ NOTE . . . .
In the present form,
the verbs *sit, rise,* and
lie do not take a direct
object. *Set, raise,* and
lay always have a
direct object. *Set* the
spoon on the table.
Raise the cup. *Lay* the
hot cup on the saucer.

sit and set

Sit and *set* both involve movement toward places. *Sit* means "to rest
in a seated position." *Set* means "to put or place."

> Did Raymond *sit* on the fire hydrant?
> Squeaky *set* her first-place medal on her dresser.

rise and raise

Rise and *raise* both involve upward movement. *Rise* means "to move
upward by itself." *Raise* means "to move or lift something upward."

> Squeaky began to *rise* from the ground like a missile.
> She was able to *raise* her hands in victory at the end of the race.

TIP

To distinguish between *lie* and *lay,* remember that chickens *lay* eggs. People *lie* down.

lie and *lay*

Lie means "to rest in a flat position." *Lay* means "to place."

> After each race, she would *lie* down and rest.
> She would *lay* her head on the soft grass.

Exercise 2   Concept Check   Write the correct verb.

1. Flowers were (lain, laid) on the tombs near Poppa's grave.
2. Connie thought about the time when Poppa (sat, set) a gift-wrapped box in front of her.
3. Connie's excitement (rose, raised) when she saw the gift—pink tights, a black leotard, and pink ballet slippers.
4. Orphelia Bell's School of Dance (sat, set) in a quaint shopping area.
5. Connie tried to (rise, raise) her leg over the wooden rail.
6. When Connie had finished performing, Poppa (rose, raised) out of his seat and applauded.
7. After Poppa's funeral, Connie wanted to (sit, set) by herself.
8. Later, Connie went to her room to (lie, lay) down.
9. While listening to music she (rose, raised) and danced.
10. The dancing made her so tired that she (lay, laid) on her bed and dreamed of ballet—and of Poppa.

Exercise 3   Proofreading Skill   Rewrite the following paragraph, paying special attention to the use of correct verb forms. Correct any errors in verb usage that you find.

> Paul Revere told a friend to sat one or two lanterns in the belfry of the North Church tower as signal lights. The friend was to let people know whether the British were coming by land or by sea. When Revere learned that they were coming by sea, he bravely set out on a midnight ride to warn the colonists. As he galloped through the countryside, his shouted message rose the alarm for battle. The colonists lay waiting for the British, ready to learn them a lesson they would not soon forget.

Exercise 4   Revising Your Writing

1. Proofread the character sketch you wrote for the Writer's Workshop on pages 115–119. Lightly underline any verbs you used and correct any errors you find.
2. Pay special attention to the commonly confused verbs you have learned in this workshop.
3. Remember to check for correct verb use each time you proofread.

LANGUAGE HANDBOOK

For review and practice: Section 5, Using Verbs, pages 786–788.

READER'S WORKSHOP

AUTHOR BIAS

Authors have opinions that influence how they present their subject matter. Sometimes an author slants facts toward her or his own personal beliefs. Subsequently, the written material reflects the biases of that author. A **bias** is a prejudice, a mental leaning, or an inclination. As a reader, it is useful to recognize the ways in which an author uses bias to slant a piece of writing. Very often an author uses **loaded words**—words that trigger strong emotions—to slant the presentation a certain way. Study the example below to see how this can work.

> Von is a remarkable young man. He valiantly battled the Vietnamese government to get to the United States. Later, this courageous young man overcame tremendous odds to become a U.S. citizen.

Was the writer of the passage impressed by Von? The writer showed a very favorable bias toward Von by using words such as *remarkable, valiantly,* and *courageous* when talking about him. Suppose the writer had described Von as a "nice young man" rather than a "remarkable young man"? Or that Von faced "high odds" instead of "tremendous odds"? Do you think the impact would have been the same?

When reading a selection, try to figure out the author's biases. Don't always accept her or his views and beliefs, but keep an open mind and decide afterward. Bias is not necessarily wrong, but readers need to be alerted to the possibility of a slanted presentation.

Exercise   Read the following passages, which describe the same incident. Explain the biases toward the characters expressed by the writer of each passage. Then identify any words that reflect those biases.

> Sheila was always poking her nose into other people's lives. Finally, she paid the price for her nosiness. Tom told her he preferred to keep his problems private. He politely asked her to respect his wishes by never approaching him again.

> Sheila gave generously of her time and her energy. Unfortunately, people were not always grateful for her hard work. Tom, for example, told her to get lost and rudely slammed the door in her face.

TIP
As you review your own writing in this and future workshops, pay careful attention to words and expressions that may reflect your own biases.

Reading on Your Own

Suggested Novels for Unit One

The novels introduced on these pages allow you to explore the unit theme, "Personal Codes," in more depth and in different ways.

JOHNNY TREMAIN
ESTHER FORBES ©1943

What would you do if you knew that your community was in danger of being attacked by a foreign power? This is the situation a young man faces in the historical novel *Johnny Tremain*. Set in Boston in the 1770s, the novel brings to life one of the most memorable periods in the history of the United States. Along with historical characters such as Paul Revere and Samuel Adams, Johnny Tremain, a silversmith's apprentice, plays an important role in the American Revolution. Find out how Tremain faces his own moment of truth and defines himself through his actions. As you read, put yourself in his place by thinking about the following questions:

• What role might you play in the defense of your community?

• How would you help your land win its freedom?

• How would you feel if your own freedom were threatened?

A DELL YEARLING BOOK
Winner of the Newbery Medal
44250-8•U.S. $3.99 CAN. $4.99

Johnny Tremain
Esther Forbes

THE TRUE CONFESSIONS OF CHARLOTTE DOYLE

AVI ©1990

How would you feel if you were accused of murder and put on trial? How would you feel if you were found guilty? This is the situation a girl your age faces in *The True Confessions of Charlotte Doyle*. Set in England in 1832, the novel relates the story of Charlotte Doyle, who is to sail to the United States to be reunited with her parents. During the voyage, she unwillingly gets involved in a plot to overthrow the ship's captain. Through her struggles, Charlotte learns a great deal about herself. Read to find out...

• why she is accused of murder

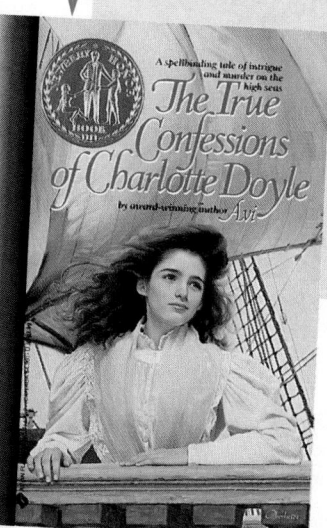

• why she is unable to prove her innocence

• whether she is ever reunited with her parents

THE HONORABLE PRISON

LYLL BECERRA DE JENKINS ©1988

Have you ever thought about the privileges and freedoms that we have in the United States? How would your life be different if you lived in a country in which your personal beliefs were against the law? This is the situation faced by the young heroine in *The Honorable Prison*. Partially based on the author's own experiences in Colombia, this novel describes a fictitious South American country where *freedom* is not a common word. Read to discover . . .

• what personal beliefs are held by the heroine

• whether her beliefs give her enough strength to resist the threats she faces

• what steps she takes to survive the tyranny of the government

Other Recommended Books

The Bumblebee Flies Anyway by Robert Cormier (©1983). Barney, a sixteen-year-old patient in a terminal care facility, faces an important moment in his life when he realizes his treatment is only experimental and he is actually dying.

I, Juan de Pareja by Elizabeth Borton de Treviño (©1965). This classic tale depicts the life of the famous seventeenth-century Spanish artist Diego Velázquez and his devoted slave Juan de Pareja.

We the People: The Story of the United States Constitution Since 1787 by Doris and Harold Faber (©1987). In this nonfictional book, the authors discuss the changes in the U.S. Constitution since its signing in 1787.

The American Revolutionaries: A History in Their Own Words by Milton Meltzer (©1987). This nonfictional text includes letters, diaries, journals, speeches, and other writings by people whose personal codes shaped the formation of the United States.

ALL OR
NOTHING

*L*ife is either a

daring adventure

or nothing.

Helen Keller

DOWNHILL SKIER
1991 Todd Doney
The Image Bank.

127

OBSESSIONS

A once-popular song begins with "All or nothing at all . . ." The sentiment expressed in the line suggests an impulsive and passionate approach to life. The title of Unit Two, "All or Nothing," refers to situations involving all-or-nothing approaches to life.

A person with such an approach to life is said to have an obsession. By definition, an obsession is a strong feeling that "takes over" a person's thoughts, words, and actions. She or he feels compelled to do a particular thing. An obsession may be healthy or unhealthy. For example, practicing day and night to become a great gymnast might be considered to be a healthy obsession. On the other hand, buying expensive new clothes every month might be considered to be an unhealthy obsession.

In the following selections you will read about people with obsessions. Some of these obsessions are healthy; others are not.

Fiction

The Tell-Tale Heart

EDGAR ALLAN POE

Examine What You Know

You thought you were home alone, but now you're starting to wonder. An old door creaks, a windowpane rattles, and when you pick up the ringing phone, no one answers. Now the sound you hear is the rapid beat of your heart, because clutched in your cold hands is . . . a horror story! In small groups discuss what makes a good horror story. Then, in a word web like the one below, jot down words and phrases related to these stories.

Types of Characters		Settings		Plots

HORROR STORIES

Emotions Produced		Titles		Authors

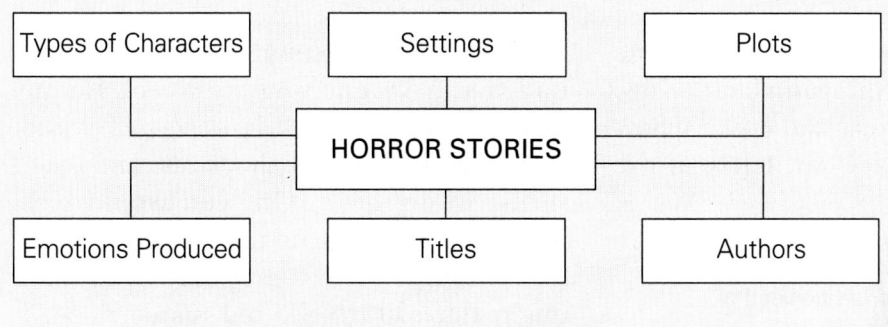

Expand Your Knowledge

The best horror story writers are masters at scaring the wits out of us. The father of the horror tale, Edgar Allan Poe, understood how chilling a story could be if told by a killer. Today's master of horror, Stephen King, understands the frightening power of the unknown and the supernatural. Why are horror stories so popular? As one critic put it, "There is no delight the equal of dread."

Enrich Your Reading

Challenging Vocabulary One reason Poe's horror stories are effective is his very rich choice of words. Don't, however, let yourself get stuck on an unfamilar word. You can enjoy the story even if you don't know what every word means. Read the entire story, then reread parts with interesting or unfamiliar words. Use context clues, definitions, and word parts to figure out the meanings.

■ *Author biography on Extend page*

The Tell-Tale Heart

EDGAR ALLAN POE

True!—nervous—very, very dreadfully nervous I had been and am; but why *will* you say that I am mad? The disease had sharpened my senses—not destroyed—not dulled them. Above all was the sense of hearing acute. I heard all things in the heaven and in the earth. I heard many things in hell. How, then, am I mad? Hearken! and observe how healthily—how calmly I can tell you the whole story.

question | What is your first impression of the narrator?

It is impossible to say how first the idea entered my brain; but once conceived, it haunted me day and night. Object there was none. Passion there was none. I loved the old man. He had never wronged me. He had never given me insult. For his gold I had no desire. I think it was his eye! Yes, it was this! He had the eye of a vulture—a pale blue eye, with a film over it. Whenever it fell upon me, my blood ran cold; and so by degrees—very gradually—I made up my mind to take the life of the old man, and thus rid myself of the eye forever.

Now this is the point. You fancy me mad. Madmen know nothing. But you should have seen *me*. You should have seen how wisely I proceeded—with what caution—with what foresight—with what dissimulation[1] I went to work! I was never kinder to the old man than during the whole week before I killed him. And every night, about midnight, I turned the latch of his door and opened it—oh, so gently! And then, when I had made an opening sufficient for my head, I put in a dark lantern, all closed, closed, so that no light shone out, and then I thrust in my head. Oh, you would have laughed to see how cunningly I thrust it in! I moved it slowly—very, very slowly, so that I might not disturb the old man's sleep. It took me an hour to place my whole head within the opening so far that I could see him as he lay upon his bed. Ha!—would a madman have been so wise as this? And then, when my head was well in the room, I undid the lantern cautiously—oh, so cautiously—cautiously (for the hinges creaked)—I undid it just so much that a single, thin ray fell upon the vulture eye. And this I did for seven long nights—every night just at midnight—but I found the eye always closed; and so it was impossible to do the work; for it was not the old man who vexed[2] me, but

---

1. **dissimulation:** a hiding of one's true feelings.
2. **vexed:** disturbed; annoyed.

Words to Know and Use | **acute** (ə kyo͞ot′) *adj.* sharp; keen
conceived (kən sēvd′) *adj.* thought of **conceive** *v.*
cunningly (kun′ iŋ lē) *adv.* cleverly and slyly

his Evil Eye. And every morning, when the day broke, I went boldly into the chamber, and spoke courageously to him, calling him by name in a hearty tone, and inquiring how he had passed the night. So you see he would have been a very profound old man, indeed, to suspect that every night, just at twelve, I looked in upon him while he slept.

Upon the eighth night I was more than usually cautious in opening the door. A watch's minute hand moves more quickly than did mine. Never before that night, had I *felt* the extent of my own powers—of my sagacity.[3] I could scarcely contain my feelings of triumph. To think that there I was, opening the door, little by little, and he not even to dream of my secret deeds or thoughts. I fairly chuckled at the idea; and perhaps he heard me; for he moved on the bed suddenly, as if startled. Now you may think that I drew back—but no. His room was as black as pitch with the thick darkness (for the shutters were close fastened, through fear of robbers), and so I knew that he could not see the opening of the door, and I kept pushing it on steadily, steadily.

I had my head in, and was about to open the lantern, when my thumb slipped upon the tin fastening, and the old man sprang up in bed, crying out—"Who's there?"

review   Does the old man suspect anything?

I kept quite still and said nothing. For a whole hour I did not move a muscle, and in the meantime I did not hear him lie down. He was still sitting up in the bed listening; just as I have done, night after night, hearkening to the deathwatches[4] in the wall.

Presently I heard a slight groan, and I knew it was the groan of mortal terror. It was not a groan of pain or grief—oh, no!—it was the low, stifled sound that arises from the bottom of the soul when overcharged with awe. I knew the sound well. Many a night, just at midnight, when all the world slept, it has welled up from my own bosom, deepening, with its dreadful echo, the terrors that distracted me. I say I knew it well. I knew what the old man felt, and pitied him, although I chuckled at heart. I knew that he had been lying awake ever since the first slight noise, when he had turned in the bed. His fears had been ever since growing upon him. He had been trying to fancy them causeless, but could not. He had been saying to himself—"It is nothing but the wind in the chimney—it is only a mouse crossing the floor," or "it is merely a cricket which has made a single chirp." Yes, he had been trying to comfort himself with these suppositions: but he had found all in vain. *All in vain;* because Death, in approaching him, had stalked with his black shadow before him, and enveloped the victim. And it was the mournful influence of the unperceived shadow that caused him to feel—although he neither saw nor heard—to *feel* the presence of my head within the room.

When I had waited a long time, very patiently, without hearing him lie down, I resolved to open a little, a very, very little

---

3. **sagacity:** sound judgment; intelligence.
4. **deathwatches:** wood-burrowing beetles that make a tapping sound with their heads.

Words to Know and Use | **stifled** (stī′ fəld) *adj.* held back **stifle** *v.*
stalk (stôk) *v.* to pursue or follow in a grim way
resolve (ri zälv′) *v.* to make up one's mind

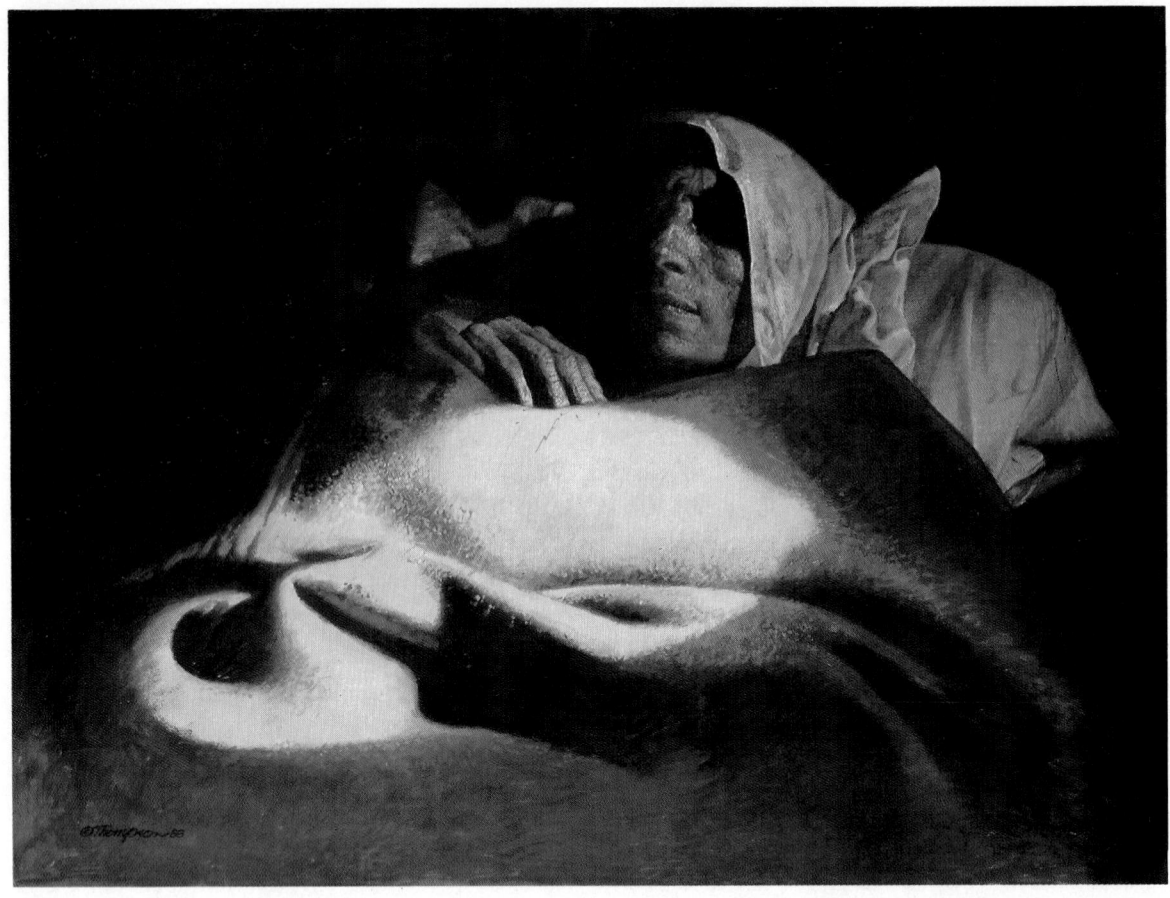

Illustration by John Thompson.

crevice in the lantern. So I opened it—you cannot imagine how stealthily, stealthily—until at length a single dim ray, like the thread of the spider, shot from out the crevice and fell full upon the vulture eye.

It was open—wide, wide open—and I grew furious as I gazed upon it. I saw it with perfect distinctness—all a dull blue, with a hideous veil over it that chilled the very marrow in my bones; but I could see nothing else of the old man's face or person; for I had directed the ray, as if by instinct, precisely upon the damned spot.

And have I not told you that what you mistake for madness is but overacuteness of the senses?—now, I say, there came to my ears a low, dull, quick sound, such as a watch makes when enveloped in cotton. I knew *that* sound well, too. It was the beating of the old man's heart. It increased my fury, as the beating of a drum stimulates the soldier into courage.

But even yet I refrained and kept still. I scarcely breathed. I held the lantern motionless. I tried how steadily I could maintain the ray upon the eye. Meantime the hellish

Words
to Know
and Use

132

crevice (krev′ is) *n.* a crack
hideous (hid′ ē əs) *adj.* ugly and horrifying
refrain (ri frān′) *v.* to hold oneself back

tattoo[5] of the heart increased. It grew quicker and quicker, and louder and louder every instant. The old man's terror *must* have been extreme! It grew louder, I say, louder every moment!–do you mark me well? I have told you that I am nervous; so I am. And now at the dead hour of the night, amid the dreadful silence of that old house, so strange a noise as this excited me to uncontrollable terror. Yet, for some minutes longer I refrained and stood still. But the beating grew louder, louder! I thought the heart must burst. And now a new anxiety seized me—the sound would be heard by a neighbor! The old man's hour had come! With a loud yell, I threw open the lantern and leaped into the room. He shrieked once—once only. In an instant I dragged him to the floor, and pulled the heavy bed over him. I then smiled gaily, to find the deed so far done. But, for many minutes, the heart beat on with a muffled sound. This, however, did not vex me; it would not be heard through the wall. At length it ceased. The old man was dead. I removed the bed and examined the corpse. Yes, he was stone, stone dead. I placed my hand upon the heart and held it there many minutes. There was no pulsation. He was stone dead. His eye would trouble me no more.

predict — What's going to happen now?

If still you think me mad, you will think so no longer when I describe the wise precautions I took for the concealment of the body. The night waned,[6] and I worked hastily, but in silence. First of all I dismembered the corpse. I cut off the head and the arms and the legs.

I then took up three planks from the flooring of the chamber, and deposited all between the scantlings.[7] I then replaced the boards so cleverly, so cunningly, that no human eye—not even *his*—could have detected anything wrong. There was nothing to wash out—no stain of any kind—no blood spot whatever. I had been too wary for that. A tub had caught all—ha! ha!

The beating grew louder, louder!

When I had made an end of these labors, it was four o'clock—still dark as midnight. As the bell sounded the hour, there came a knocking at the street door. I went down to open it with a light heart,—for what had I *now* to fear? There entered three men, who introduced themselves, with perfect suavity, as officers of the police. A shriek had been heard by a neighbor during the night; suspicion of foul play had been aroused; information had been lodged at the police office, and they (the officers) had been deputed to search the premises.

I smiled,—for *what* had I to fear? I bade the gentlemen welcome. The shriek, I said,

---

5. **hellish tattoo:** awful sound like a drum beating.
6. **waned:** approached its end.
7. **scantlings:** small wooden beams supporting the floor.

Words to Know and Use | **anxiety** (aŋ zī´ ə tē) *n.* a feeling of worry, nervousness, and fear

was my own in a dream. The old man, I mentioned, was absent in the country. I took my visitors all over the house. I bade them search—search *well*. I led them, at length, to *his* chamber. I showed them his treasures, secure, undisturbed. In the enthusiasm of my confidence, I brought chairs into the room, and desired them *here* to rest from their fatigues, while I myself, in the wild audacity of my perfect triumph, placed my own seat upon the very spot beneath which reposed[8] the corpse of my victim.

I foamed—I raved—I swore!

The officers were satisfied. My *manner* had convinced them. I was singularly at ease. They sat, and while I answered cheerily, they chatted of familiar things. But, ere long, I felt myself getting pale and wished them gone. My head ached, and I fancied a ringing in my ears: but still they sat and still chatted. The ringing became more distinct;—it continued and became more distinct; I talked more freely to get rid of the feeling; but it continued and gained definiteness—until, at length, I found that the noise was *not* within my ears.

No doubt I now grew *very* pale;—but I talked more fluently, and with a heightened voice. Yet the sound increased—and what could I do? It was *a low, dull, quick sound—much such a sound as a watch makes when enveloped in cotton.* I gasped for breath—and yet the officers heard it not. I talked more

quickly—more vehemently; but the noise steadily increased. I arose and argued about trifles, in a high key and with violent gesticulations;[9] but the noise steadily increased. Why *would* they not be gone? I paced the floor to and fro with heavy strides, as if excited to fury by the observations of the men—but the noise steadily increased. Oh God; what *could* I do? I foamed—I raved—I swore! I swung the chair upon which I had been sitting, and grated it upon the boards, but the noise arose over all and continually increased. It grew louder—louder—*louder!* And still the men chatted pleasantly, and smiled. Was it possible they heard not? Almighty God!—no, no! They heard!—they suspected!—they *knew!*—they were making a mockery of my horror!—this I thought, and this I think. But anything was better than this agony! Anything was more tolerable than this derision! I could bear those hypocritical smiles no longer! I felt that I must scream or die! and now—again!—hark! louder! louder! louder! *louder!*

"Villains!" I shrieked. "Dissemble[10] no more! I admit the deed!—tear up the planks! here, here!—it is the beating of his hideous heart!" ❧

It was almost a perfect crime. Why didn't the murderer keep quiet?

---

8. **reposed:** rested.
9. **gesticulations:** energetic gestures of the hands or arms.
10. **dissemble:** to pretend.

Responding to Reading

First Impressions

1. In your journal describe the part of this story that is most memorable.

Second Thoughts

2. What are your impressions of the narrator?

> **Think about**
> * his insistence that he is sane
> * his claim that he loves the old man
> * his obsession with the old man's Evil Eye
> * his care in planning the murder
> * the way he deals with the police

3. Why do you think the narrator puts his chair directly over the dead body?

4. What do you think might have happened to the narrator if the police had not come on the night of the murder?

5. Consider your discussion of horror stories in Examine What You Know. How does "The Tell-Tale Heart" measure up to other horror stories?

Broader Connections

6. Under most systems of criminal law, an insane person cannot be found guilty of a crime. Defendants declared not guilty by reason of insanity are usually hospitalized until they are no longer considered mentally ill and dangerous. Do you think murderers like the narrator of "The Tell-Tale Heart" should be able to use an insanity defense to avoid prison or the death penalty? Explain your opinion.

Literary Concepts: Mood and Irony

The **mood** of a literary work is the feeling or atmosphere that the writer creates for the reader. A story's events and setting and the way these are described all contribute to the mood of the story. One element of "The Tell-Tale Heart" that creates a mood of horror is the description of sounds, such as the victim's groan and the heartbeat. What other details in the story help produce its mood of horror?

Irony is a contrast between what is expected and what actually happens. For example, one wouldn't expect a murderer to invite the police to stay longer in the murder room; it is ironic when the narrator does just that. Find another example of irony in this story.

Writing Options

1. Imagine that, like the narrator of "The Tell-Tale Heart," you found one of your senses greatly intensified. What would it be like? Write a **description** of one hour in your day.

2. Consider how two different newspapers might report the murder in "The Tell-Tale Heart." One is a city's reputable daily newspaper. Its articles are factual, telling *who, what, when, where,* and *why.* The second newspaper is a tabloid known for outrageous stories, full of sensational details. Write the **lead paragraph** of the murder story for each of the two newspapers.

3. Imagine you are one of the police officers assigned to the tell-tale-heart case. Write your **police report,** detailing the investigation and the arrest of the murderer.

4. Write the **dialogue** that the narrator of Poe's story might have had with the three police officers in the room where the murder took place. Visualize your speakers and think of how to make them sound "in character."

Vocabulary Practice

Exercise   On your paper write the letter of the word that differs in meaning from the other words in the set.

1. (a) sharp   (b) acute   (c) dull   (d) keen
2. (a) calm   (b) fear   (c) worry   (d) anxiety
3. (a) boldness   (b) audacity   (c) caution   (d) nerve
4. (a) destroyed   (b) wrecked   (c) ruined   (d) conceived
5. (a) ray   (b) crack   (c) crevice   (d) cranny
6. (a) stupidly   (b) cleverly   (c) shrewdly   (d) cunningly
7. (a) clear   (b) blurred   (c) sharp   (d) distinct
8. (a) fluently   (b) smoothly   (c) roughly   (d) eloquently
9. (a) elevated   (b) lifted   (c) heightened   (d) lowered
10. (a) beautiful   (b) hideous   (c) gorgeous   (d) lovely
11. (a) insincere   (b) truthful   (c) hypocritical   (d) phony
12. (a) start   (b) refrain   (c) stop   (d) halt
13. (a) determine   (b) ignore   (c) decide   (d) resolve
14. (a) pace   (b) stalk   (c) stride   (d) climb
15. (a) stifled   (b) muffled   (c) heightened   (d) smothered

Words to Know and Use

acute
anxiety
audacity
conceived
crevice
cunningly
distinct
fluently
heightened
hideous
hypocritical
refrain
resolve
stalk
stifled

Options for Learning

1 • **The Beat Goes On** An insistent beat is at the heart of Edgar Allan Poe's horror story. Capture this throbbing sound in a rap song about the tell-tale heart.

2 • **Murder Trial** With a group of your classmates, stage the trial of the old man's murderer. What arguments would the defense attorney and the prosecuting attorney use? Determine whether the narrator will use the insanity defense. What people would be called to testify? The classmates who observe can be the jury.

3 • **A Thrill a Minute** Draw the plans for an amusement-park house of horrors called House of the Tell-Tale Heart. Describe the setting, scares, thrills, and shocks the visitors would experience as they made their way through the house.

4 • **With Your Good Eye** Imagine that you have been commissioned by a publisher to illustrate "The Tell-Tale Heart." Choose any memorable scene or image from the story (except the one already illustrated in this book), and interpret it in a painting or drawing.

 FACT FINDER SCIENCE

How many times per minute does a healthy, resting person's heart beat?

Edgar Allan Poe
1809–1849

Edgar Allan Poe is one of America's greatest poets, short story writers, and literary critics. He is widely considered to be the father of the modern detective story as well as of the horror story.

Poe's writings about the dark side of existence reflect the loss, bitterness, and depression of his own life. His father deserted the family and his mother died before the boy's third birthday. Never adopted by his foster family, Poe later broke all ties with his foster father, who resented his appeals for money. Poe was determined to be a writer.

The young writer's poetry, stories, and criticism brought him increasing recognition, but never enough money to live comfortably. Although he was a brilliant magazine editor, he was prone to quarrels and to excessive drinking. Poe's happy marriage to his thirteen-year-old cousin ended tragically when she died of tuberculosis.

Poe's life ended in a mystery that recalls his own stories. The writer had planned to remarry, but disappeared before his wedding. He was later found sick and disoriented in a Baltimore tavern. Poe died four days later.

Fiction

Petty Larceny

JESSICA SAIKI

(jes' i kə sä ē' kē)

Examine What You Know

If you could wake up tomorrow as anyone else in the world, whose face would greet you from your mirror? Would it be a performer's? an athlete's? a politician's? an astronaut's? Think about the person you would like to be—or be like. What makes that person so attractive to you? In small groups compare your choices and your reasons for making them.

Expand Your Knowledge

During the 1930s every little girl, including author Jessica Saiki, dreamed of being just like Shirley Temple. From her dimples and blonde curls to her adorable dresses, Temple was admired by fans throughout the world. Born in 1928 in Santa Monica, California, Temple made her movie debut at the age of three. At six, she sang her signature song, "On the Good Ship Lollipop." At twenty-one, Temple retired from films, and later pursued a career in politics.

Enrich Your Reading

Comparison and Contrast When you **compare and contrast** two things or people, you determine how they are similar and how they are different. In this story the narrator, Tamako, who idolizes Shirley Temple, contrasts herself with Sheila, a classmate who also idolizes Temple. When you finish reading, use a chart like the one below to compare and contrast Tamako and Sheila. Consider how the attitude, appearance, and upbringing of each girl affects the way she views herself and others.

	Appearance	Upbringing	Attitude toward others
Tamako			
Sheila			

■ *Author biography in Reader's Handbook*

Petty Larceny

JESSICA SAIKI

With a Shirley Temple dress I could do anything. In it I would be this shoe-button cute, dimpled darling with golden sausage curls and a voice with a built-in grip. I would live in a shamefully huge house, where my parents would throw parties one after another. At my own Saturday afternoon shindigs, everyone in my class would be invited. Words like charming, adorable, and marvelous would spill from my parents' mouths as they stood in their store-bought finery greeting everybody with toothpaste ad smiles.

I believed that. Back when I was a child, Shirley Temple, the Good Ship Lollipop Kid, was a mania.[1] All girls tried to look like her. The blondes begged for twisted curls held in place by satin bows. Tap-dancing lessons were a must. Songs were sung with a choked-up cuteness, usually ending with "boop boop de-boop." All of this was in faraway Hawaii; even in Lunalilo, Shirley Temple was a disease infecting all of us.

Sheila, a fair-haired girl in my class, had hair so fine that when her mother took her to a beauty parlor for a Shirley Temple perm, frizz instead of curls resulted. Daughter to one of the wealthiest merchants in town, her family owned the largest dry goods department store on Main Street, and it was Sheila who brought the brand-new Miss T. dress to school one day.

The moment the rest of us set eyes on it, we gasped in wonderment, envy, and longing. To Sheila, it was just another pretty dress, as she had two closetsful at home, she promptly informed us. But to me, an eight-year-old at the time, the dress meant much, much more.

To this day I remember everything about the garment. Under a certain angle of light, its sherbet orange glistened with a soft sheen. Party dresses in those days were made of organdy, which wilted into a limp mass when laundered in water. All the tiers of flounces and ruffles that made a Miss T. dress impossible to sit down in were flattened. Diligent mothers revived these ruffles with thick starch and tedious ironing. With it came a matching panty which would be well exposed beneath the triple-tiered skirt flared out like a fat umbrella. Sheila had brought the dress to school for our May Day program calling for a dance of pastel-colored flowers, blossoms unfolding in a

---

1. **mania:** a craze; fad.

139

Illustration by Phil Huling.

spring garden. To me, it stood for something as wondrous as Cinderella's ball gown. The more I saw it, the more magical appeared its possibilities, like a genie opening doors to treasure-laden rooms. Although the hand-me-downs I usually wore to school were OK, still, faint telltale creases ringed their hemlines, and they were certainly not the kind of clothes you could wear to a fancy party.

After school, Sheila and the other rich kids whose parents could afford to send them home on private jitney buses[2] made ceremonial exits from the school yard while the remainder of us "walkers" stood around saying goodbye before straggling home on foot. My after-school route took me past bungalow homes, their trim walkways gardenia lined, their landscaped properties crowded with unpicked fruit trees. I also passed the town's mausoleum-gray stone library, my favorite haunt.

---

2. jitney buses: small local buses.

Next to the library was Donald's house. Four-eyed and studious, he was a kid who had just moved into town from Connecticut. The sad thing about him was that Prince, his pet dog, had been run over by a milkman's truck shortly after they moved here. Prince was buried in their front yard. I knew this because I watched Donald's dad dig the grave. It was an especially deep hole, I remember. For a long time after, you could still see a fresh dirt mound in their yard where the grass hadn't grown back in yet. You could tell something lay beneath by the way it bulged upward like an ant hill.

Past Donald's house, across the river was where I lived. Home for me was a shabby, paint-peeled house in the rental section of town. With kids who walked the route with me, I exchanged good-byes at the foot of the hill. That way they couldn't see which house was ours. I was afraid they might puncture me with embarrassing questions like "Do you have your own bedroom?" or "Your folks own a radio?" Stuff like that I didn't want to answer.

Most days I hurriedly dropped off my school books at home, where my mom would be either pedaling her Singer sewing machine[3] in our kitchen or else sweeping off the front sidewalk like someone in a cleanup crew. Small and neat in plain cotton dresses, her hair pulled back tightly into a round, gray bun, she held her broom in her hand like a weapon. She swept outside the house almost as much as she swept inside, attacking both as the dreaded enemy. Cigarette butts, gum wrappers, or just plain dirt horrified her; she just couldn't stand them.

"We need kerosene, Tamako." My mother's small voice coming from the kitchen would shatter the afternoon quiet. She had a midget-type voice. No matter how long she lived in Hawaii, she still acted like a timid stranger trespassing in a foreign land. "Quarter's on the table. Make sure Ah Ping fills it up to the top this time," she said.

"OK," I answered in a deadpan voice, disguising any feeling I had about carrying out the order.

"And don't spill any on your dress, you hear? You need to wear it again tomorrow."

"OK." My answer was muffled as if filtered through cotton wadding.

I lifted the oily glass container by its thin metal handle and carried its fuel smell with me across the kitchen and out the house through the back screen door. Up the street I sped the two blocks to Ah Ping's Grocery. After that obligatory errand, I rushed to Philamina's house, which was only three houses in back of ours. Best friend Philamina was most likely to be home, listening to the Orphan Annie program on their new radio. Ear to the domed brown box,[4] she wore her usual faded coveralls, its frayed bib top barely hanging onto a button about to fall off. Her clothes, unfancy like mine, her house, pretty much a duplicate of ours, offering only bone essentials of living,

---

3. **Singer sewing machine:** a brand of sewing machine, named for its inventor, Isaac Merritt Singer (1811–1875).

4. **domed brown box:** the wooden radio cabinet.

made it comfortable to be with Philamina. We didn't have to cover up about anything, telling stories. We could talk about things we wished we had or things we didn't have. We both considered Orphan Annie an intimate friend. That particular day's episode had her running away from a cruel superintendent in the orphanage. It was winter, I could tell by the bitter wind moaning loudly like for real. Annie, wearing only rags, of course, was shivering in the cold. Her poverty was something we understood, and we could hardly wait to hear about her next bit of hard luck.

After weeks of rehearsals and preparation, the long-awaited May Day arrived. The entire school met at assembly for the Special Program, in which each class would participate. Lilting spring songs we in the chorus had assiduously[5] put to memory were sung. Donald read aloud a poem he had written:

On this May Day we welcome spring.
It makes us glad, it makes us sing,
For winter now has gone away,
Hawaiians say it with a lei.[6]

It had won first prize in a contest. The sixth graders, who had studied Hawaiian history all year, presented a play about Maui[7] and the sun. Their program came before our third-grade Flower Dance, which our teacher, Miss Bowerbox, said went off perfectly. Everyone commented on how pretty the flower girls looked in their matching pastel dresses. Mrs. Walker, whom we called "Witch Walker" because of her pointed nose, played the piano. Altogether it was a swell celebration, but my favorite by far was our own Flower Dance. For a long time afterward, I kept on hearing Mrs. Walker's

tinkly piano music. Clear as anything, I could see the dancers, their skirts twirling in time to the music, how they spun like tops, like Japanese paper flowers exploding when wet into rainbow blooms.

After school on that particular day, Miss Bowerbox had asked me to erase all blackboards in our classroom. No one else was around. I couldn't even hear Mr. Gonzalez, the janitor who I knew would be cleaning up as he usually did after school. Atop one of the tables, I saw several paper bags. Names of students were penciled on them in large letters. Then I noticed Sheila's name on one of them. Orange ruffles bulged out.

At first I thought to myself, There's that Shirley Temple dress, all right. Sheila, in her rush to the jitney, probably forgot all about it. I know she was excited. It was an exciting day for everybody!

As instructed, I erased all the day's assignments, then clapped out chalk powder from the erasers into a metal wastebasket. All the while, emptying clouds of white dust, I thought about my discovery. I grabbed the bag containing my dream dress, clutched it tightly in a sweaty palm, then walked out of the classroom on rubberized legs.

It was all too simple. No one witnessed my crime. Was this what was meant by Getting Away with Murder? Only after walking outside in bright daylight, where the sun's glare felt like spotlights centered on me, did I begin to think clearly about what I had done . . . *What could I do with the dress now?*

---

5. **assiduously:** diligently; carefully.

6. **lei** (lā): in Hawaii, a wreath of flowers worn around the neck.

7. **Maui** (mou′ ē): a god for whom one of the Hawaiian Islands is named.

Retracing a familiar path home, one along which I knew every loose pebble, odd plant, friendly or hostile dog, cracked fence, state of a fruiting tree, or crack in the sidewalk, I trudged gingerly.[8] With each step I felt a cloud of Sunday-school guilt like a hot water bag on my hand. It burned. What I had done was sin, all right.

The neat bungalow houses I passed every day like old friends now threatened me with eyes peeping behind every curtained window. A lady collecting mail from her mailbox turned to stare at me. Besides Superman, were there others who had X-ray vision? She acted like she did. She acted like she knew by the way she squinted at me.

Even the people I saw streaming out of the old library with books under their arms were suspicious of the brown bag I carried. They probably knew too.

Beyond the river, past Donald's house, my walk quickened. What if someone I knew saw me now? "Whatcha got there?" would be the first thing they would ask . . . In panic I found myself running the rest of the way home. Avoiding the front part of the house where I knew my mother would surely see me, I sneaked through a tangle of guava bushes, banana, and avocado trees. Under the lapped cover of their deep green leaves, there was a darkness like being under a bridge. Suddenly I felt shivery even though it had been a warm day. Overhead the wind shook leaves like tissue paper kites into a scary rattle. In the stillness, a mosquito buzzed with a high pitch, sirenlike. I

Illustration by Barbara Maslen.

became aware of my own excitement beating inside my chest where a health teacher had just told us our heart is located. What to do? The fear, the awful fear now churning inside, made pin pricks shoot up from my feet to my head as I crouched there trying to decide what to do next.

Among limp remains of old taro roots and ginger stalks, I found a rusty shovel in one corner of the yard, where I began digging. ❧

---

8. gingerly: carefully and cautiously.

Responding to Reading

First Impressions

1. What are your reactions to what Tamako does? Jot them down in your journal or on a sheet of paper.

Second Thoughts

2. What could Tamako do with the stolen dress besides bury it?

3. Why do you think Tamako is obsessed with the orange dress?

4. Compare Tamako's thoughts on her walk home with the thoughts of the narrator of "The Tell-Tale Heart" during his visit from the police.

5. What kind of person do you think Tamako is?

   Think about
   - how she feels about herself
   - how she contrasts herself with Sheila
   - her dreams of being like Shirley Temple

Broader Connections

6. Some people use experiences such as Tamako's to argue that schools should have dress codes or require uniforms. These people claim that such regulations would help students stop comparing themselves with others who have more or less than they do. Explain why you think your school should or should not have a dress code or require uniforms.

Literary Concept: Allusion

An **allusion** is a reference to a famous person, place, event, or literary work that the author assumes will be familiar to most readers. For example, at the beginning of this story, the narrator makes an extended allusion to Shirley Temple, who was a popular phenomenon in the 1930s and 1940s. To what other literary or movie characters does the author allude in this story?

Writing Options

1. Rewrite a **scene** from Tamako's story, using the style of the narrator of "The Tell-Tale Heart." You may want to begin with the words "It was all too simple. . . ."

2. Do you think Tamako actually buries the orange dress? Does she ever confess her petty larceny? If you were Tamako, what might you do? Think about a possible solution or ending to Tamako's story. Then write a **sequel** that tells what you think might happen next.

3. Is there something you want as much as Tamako wants Sheila's orange dress? What is it? Why do you want it? How would having the item make things better or different for you? Write a vivid **description** of the object you would love to have.

4. A petty larceny is a theft of personal property that is of value to the person from whom it was stolen but not of considerable monetary value. What instances of petty larceny have you heard or read about? Write an **account** of the details of the crime.

Vocabulary Practice

Exercise   Decide whether or not the boldfaced word in each sentence is used correctly. On a sheet of paper, write *Correct* or *Incorrect*.

1. The May Day Special Program promised to be a **tedious** and festive occasion.

2. Our class was **diligent,** carefully rehearsing our songs for weeks before the assembly.

3. As we waited eagerly to perform, our **deadpan** expressions reflected our excitement.

4. We performed so well that the dazzled crowd listened in **wonderment.**

5. When we finished singing, they jumped to their feet in **obligatory** applause.

Words to Know and Use

deadpan
diligent
obligatory
tedious
wonderment

Fiction

The Banana Tree

JAMES BERRY

Examine What You Know

Each year powerful, destructive storms called hurricanes threaten many parts of the world. What do you know about hurricanes? Have you ever been in one yourself? In small groups organize your knowledge about hurricanes into a web such as the one below.

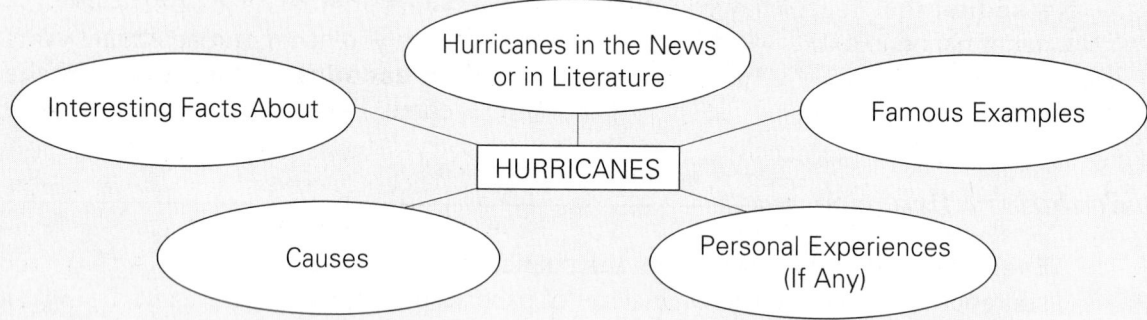

- Interesting Facts About
- Hurricanes in the News or in Literature
- Famous Examples
- HURRICANES
- Causes
- Personal Experiences (If Any)

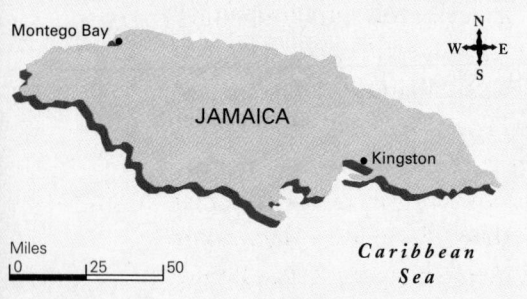

Montego Bay

JAMAICA

Kingston

Miles
0   25   50

Caribbean Sea

Expand Your Knowledge

If you lived in Jamaica, where "The Banana Tree" takes place, you would probably know a lot about hurricanes. These storms frequently bring death and destruction to the Caribbean Sea. Hurricanes develop from regions of low pressure in the atmosphere. In a hurricane, torrents of rain fall and the winds swirl at least seventy-five miles per hour around a calm spot in the center, called the eye.

Enrich Your Reading

Dialect   In describing the hurricane, Mr. Bass says, "The storm's bad, chil'run. Really bad. But it'll blow off. It'll spen' itself out. . . ." Like most Jamaicans, Mr. Bass speaks in a **dialect** in which English words are mixed with African words, pronunciations, and expressions. In many cases the last letter of a word is missing—as in *han'* for *hand*—or a vowel sound is changed in a word, such as *mek* for *make*. Reading the dialogue aloud may help you figure out unfamiliar words.

■ *Author biography in Reader's Handbook*

The *Banana Tree*

JAMES BERRY

In the hours the hurricane stayed, its presence made everybody older. It made Mr. Bass see that not only people and animals and certain valuables were of most importance to be saved.

From its very buildup the hurricane meant to show it was merciless, unstoppable, and, with its might, changed landscapes.

All day the Jamaican sun didn't come out. Then, ten minutes before, there was a swift shower of rain that raced by and was gone like some urgent messenger-rush of wind. And again everything went back to that quiet, that unnatural quiet. It was as if trees crouched quietly in fear. As if, too, birds knew they should shut up. A thick and low black cloud had covered the sky and shadowed everywhere, and made it seem like night was coming on. And the cloud deepened. Its deepening spread more and more over the full stretch of the sea.

The doom-laden afternoon had the atmosphere of Judgment Day[1] for everybody in all the districts about. Everybody knew the hour of disaster was near. Warnings printed in bold lettering had been put up at post offices, police stations, and school-yard entrances and in clear view on shop walls in village squares.

Carrying children and belongings, people hurried in files and in scattered groups, headed for the big, strong, and safe community buildings. In Canerise Village, we headed for the schoolroom. Loaded with bags and cases, with bundles and lidded baskets, individuals carrying or leading an animal, parents shrieking for children to stay at their heels, we arrived there. And looking around, anyone would think the whole of Canerise was here in this vast superbarn of a noisy chattering schoolroom.

With violent gusts and squalls the storm broke. Great rushes, huge bulky rushes, of wind struck the building in heavy, repeated thuds, shaking it over and over and carrying on.

Families were huddled together on the floor. People sang, sitting on benches, desks, anywhere there was room. Some people knelt in loud prayer. Among the refugees' noises a goat bleated,[2] a hen fluttered or cackled, a dog whined.

Mr. Jetro Bass was sitting on a soap box. His broad back leaned on the blackboard against the wall. Mrs. Imogene Bass, largely pregnant, looked a midget beside him. Their children were sitting on the floor. The eldest boy, Gustus, sat farthest from his father. Altogether, the children's heads made seven different levels of height around the parents.

---

1. Judgment Day: a religious term for the end of the world.
2. bleated: made a crying sound.

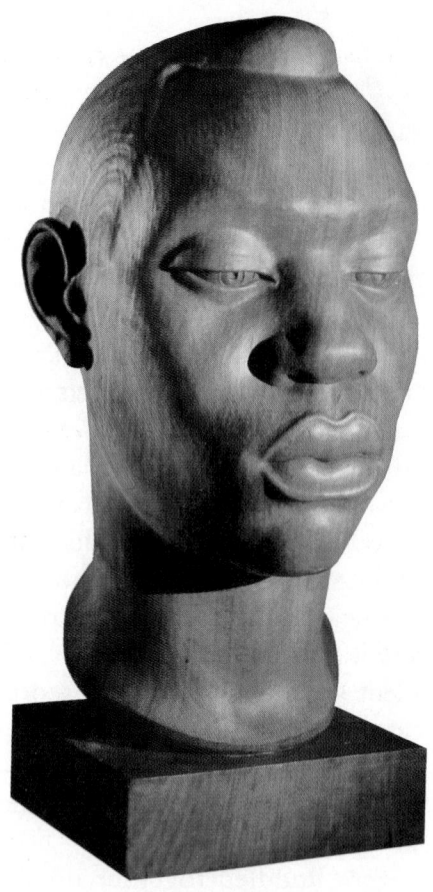

BOYSIE   1962   Alvin Marriott   Private collection.

Mr. Bass forced a reassuring smile. His toothbrush mustache[3] moved about a little as he said, "The storm's bad, chil'run. Really bad. But it'll blow off. It'll spen' itself out. It'll kill itself."

Except for Gustus's, all the faces of the children turned up with subdued fear and looked at their father as he spoke.

"Das true wha' Pappy say," Mrs. Bass said. "The good Lord won' gi' we more than we can bear."

Mr. Bass looked at Gustus. He stretched fully through the sitting children and put a lumpy, blistery hand—though a huge hand—on the boy's head, almost covering it. The boy's clear brown eyes looked straight and unblinkingly into his father's face. "Wha's the matter, bwoy?" his dad asked.

He shook his head. "Nothin', Pappy."

"Wha' mek you say nothin'? I sure somet'ing bodder you, Gustus. You not a bwoy who frighten easy. Is not the hurricane wha' bodder you? Tell Pappy."

"Is nothin'."

"You're a big bwoy now. Gustus—you nearly thirteen. You strong. You very useful fo' you age. You good as mi right han'. I depen' on you. But this afternoon—earlier—in the rush, when we so well push to move befo' storm broke, you couldn' rememba a t'ing! Not one t'ing! Why so? Wha' on you mind? You harborin' t'ings from me, Gustus?"

Gustus opened his mouth to speak but closed it again. He knew his father was proud of how well he had grown. To strengthen him, he had always given him "last milk"[4] straight from the cow in the mornings. He was thankful. But to him his strength was only proven in the number of innings he could pitch for his cricket[5] team. The boy's lips trembled. What's the good of tellin' when Pappy don' like cricket. He only get vex[6] an' say it's an evil game for idle hands! He twisted his head and looked away. "I'm harborin' nothin', Pappy."

"Gustus . . ."

At that moment a man called, "Mr. Bass!" He came up quickly. "Got a hymnbook, Mr. Bass? We want you to lead us singing."

---

3. **toothbrush mustache:** a small, rectangular mustache.
4. **last milk:** the last milk taken from milking a cow.
5. **cricket:** an English game related to baseball.
6. **vex:** dialect for *vexed,* "annoyed."

The people were sitting with bowed heads, humming a song. As the repressed[7] singing grew louder and louder, it sounded mournful in the room. Mr. Bass shuffled, looking around as if he wished to back out of the suggestion. But his rich voice and singing leadership were too famous. Mrs. Bass already had the hymnbook in her hand, and she pushed it at her husband. He took it and began turning the leaves as he moved toward the center of the room.

Immediately Mr. Bass was surrounded. He started with a resounding chant over the heads of everybody. "Abide wid me; fast fall the eventide. . . ." He joined the singing but broke off to recite the next line. "The darkness deepen; Lord, wid me, abide. . . ." Again, before the last long-drawn note faded from the deeply stirred voices, Mr. Bass intoned musically, "When odder helpers fail, and comfo'ts flee . . ."

In this manner he fired inspiration into the singing of hymn after hymn. The congregation swelled their throats, and their mixed voices filled the room, pleading to heaven from the depths of their hearts. But the wind outside mocked viciously. It screamed. It whistled. It smashed everywhere up.

Mrs. Bass had tightly closed her eyes, singing and swaying in the center of the children who nestled around her. But Gustus was by himself. He had his elbows on his knees and his hands blocking his ears. He had his own worries.

What's the good of Pappy asking all those questions when he treat him so bad? He's the only one in the family without a pair of shoes! Because he's a big boy, he don't need anyt'ing an' must do all the work. He can't stay at school in the evenings an' play cricket because there's work to do at home. He can't have no outings with the other children because he has no shoes. An' now when he was to sell his bunch of bananas an' buy shoes so he can go out with his cricket team, the hurricane is going to blow it down.

It was true: the root of the banana was his "navel string."[8] After his birth the umbilical cord[9] was dressed with castor oil and sprinkled with nutmeg and buried, with the banana tree planted over it for him. When he was nine days old, the nana midwife[10] had taken him out into the open for the first time. She had held the infant proudly and walked the twenty-five yards that separated the house from the kitchen, and at the back showed him his tree. "'Memba when you grow up," her toothless mouth had said, "it's you nable strings feedin' you tree, the same way it feed you from you mudder."

Refuse from the kitchen made the plant flourish out of all proportion. But the rich soil around it was loose. Each time the tree gave a shoot, the bunch would be too heavy for the soil to support; so it crashed to the ground, crushing the tender fruit. This time, determined that his banana must reach the market, Gustus had supported his tree with eight props. And as he watched it night and morning, it had become very close to him. Often he had seriously thought of moving his bed to its root.

---

7. **repressed:** low and soft.
8. **navel string:** a term for the umbilical cord.
9. **umbilical cord** (um bil' i kəl kôrd): the cord through which a fetus receives nourishment; a person's navel marks the place where it was attached.
10. **nana midwife:** a woman who helps other women give birth and care for newborn children.

Muffled cries, and the sound of blowing noses, now mixed with the singing. Delayed impact of the disaster was happening. Sobbing was everywhere. Quickly the atmosphere became sodden[11] with the wave of weeping outbursts. Mrs. Bass's pregnant belly heaved. Her younger children were upset and cried, "Mammy, Mammy, Mammy. . . ."

Realizing that his family, too, was overwhelmed by the surrounding calamity, Mr. Bass bustled over to them. Because their respect for him bordered on fear, his presence quietened all immediately. He looked around. "Where's Gustus! Imogene . . . where's Gustus!"

His shirt was fluttering from his back like a boat sail.

"He was 'ere, Pappy," she replied, drying her eyes. "I dohn know when he get up."

Briskly Mr. Bass began combing the schoolroom to find his boy. He asked; no one had seen Gustus. He called. There was no answer. He tottered, lifting his heavy boots over heads, fighting his way to the jalousie.[12] He opened it, and his eyes gleamed up and down the road but saw nothing of the boy. In despair Mr. Bass gave one last thunderous shout: "Gustus!" Only the wind sneered.

By this time Gustus was halfway on the mile journey to their house. The lone figure in the raging wind and shin-deep road flood was tugging, snapping, and pitching branches out of his path. His shirt was fluttering from his back like a boat sail. And a leaf was fastened to his cheek. But the belligerent wind was merciless. It bellowed into his ears and drummed a deafening commotion. As he grimaced and covered his ears, he was forcefully slapped against a coconut tree trunk that lay across the road.

When his eyes opened, his round face was turned up to a festered[13] sky. Above the tormented trees a zinc sheet writhed, twisted, and somersaulted in the tempestuous flurry. Leaves of all shapes and sizes were whirling and diving like attackers around the zinc sheet. As Gustus turned to get up, a bullet drop of rain struck his temple. He shook his head, held grimly to the tree trunk, and struggled to his feet.

Where the road was clear, he edged along the bank. Once, when the wind staggered him, he recovered with his legs wide apart. Angrily he stretched out his hands with clenched fists and shouted, "I almos' hol' you that time. . . . Come solid like that again, an' we fight like man an' man!"

When Gustus approached the river he had to cross, it was flooded and blocked beyond recognition. Pressing his chest against the gritty road bank, the boy closed his weary eyes on the brink of the spating river. The wrecked footbridge had become the harboring fort for all the debris, branches, and monstrous tree trunks which the river swept along its course. The river was still swelling. More accumulation arrived each moment, ramming and pressing the bridge. Under pressure it was cracking and shifting minutely toward a turbulent forty-foot fall.

---

11. **sodden:** soaked.
12. **jalousie** (jal′ ə sē′): a window covering made of thin slats.
13. **festered:** diseased.

Gustus had seen it! A feeling of dismay paralyzed him, reminding him of his foolish venture. He scraped his cheek on the bank looking back. But how can he go back? He has no strength to go back. His house is nearer than the school. An' Pappy will only strap him for nothin' . . . for nothin' . . . no shoes, nothin', when the hurricane is gone.

With trembling fingers he tied up the remnants of his shirt. He made a bold step, and the wind half lifted him, ducking him in the muddy flood. He sank to his neck. Floating leaves, sticks, coconut husks, dead ratbats, and all manner of feathered creatures and refuse surrounded him. Forest vines under the water entangled him. But he struggled desperately until he clung to the laden bridge and climbed up among leafless branches.

His legs were bruised and bore deep scratches, but steadily he moved up on the slimy pile. He felt like a man at sea, in the heart of a storm, going up the mast of a ship. He rested his feet on a smooth log that stuck to the water-splashed heap like a black torso. As he strained up for another grip, the torso came to life and leaped from under his feet. Swiftly sliding down, he grimly clutched some brambles.

The urgency of getting across became more frightening, and he gritted his teeth and dug his toes into the debris, climbing with maddened determination. But a hard gust of wind slammed the wreck, pinning him like a motionless lizard. For a minute the boy was stuck there, panting, swelling his naked ribs.

He stirred again and reached the top. He was sliding over a breadfruit limb when a flutter startled him. As he looked and saw the clean-head crow and glassy-eyed owl close together, there was a powerful jolt. Gustus flung himself into the air and fell in the expanding water on the other side. When he surfaced, the river had dumped the entire wreckage into the gurgling gully. For once the wind helped. It blew him to land.

Gustus was in a daze when he reached his house. Mud and rotten leaves covered his head and face, and blood caked around a gash on his chin. He bent down, shielding himself behind a tree stump whose white heart was a needly splinter, murdered by the wind.

He could hardly recognize his yard. The terrorized trees that stood were writhing in turmoil. Their thatched house had collapsed like an open umbrella that was given a heavy blow. He looked the other way and whispered, "Is still there! That's a miracle. . . .That's a miracle."

A feeling of dismay paralyzed him.

Dodging the wind, he staggered from tree to tree until he got to his own tormented banana tree. Gustus hugged the tree. "My nable string!" he cried. "My nable string! I know you would stan' up to it, I know you would."

The bones of the tree's stalky leaves were broken, and the wind lifted them and harassed them. And over Gustus's head the heavy fruit swayed and swayed. The props held the tree, but they were squeaking and slipping. And around the plant the roots

SPIRITUALISM   1979   Everald Brown
Wadsworth Atheneum, Hartford, Connecticut, Ella Gallup Sumner and Mary Caitlin Sumner Collection.

stretched and trembled, gradually surfacing under loose earth.

With the rags of his wet shirt flying off his back, Gustus was down busily on his knees, bracing, pushing, tightening the props. One by one he was adjusting them until a heavy rush of wind knocked him to the ground. A prop fell on him, but he scrambled to his feet and looked up at the thirteen-hand bunch of bananas. "My good tree," he bawled, "hol' you fruit. . . . Keep it to you heart like a mudder savin' her baby! Don't let the wicked wind t'row you to the groun' . . . even if it t'row me to the groun'. I will not leave you."

But several attempts to replace the prop were futile. The force of the wind against his weight was too much for him. He thought of a rope to lash the tree to anything, but it was difficult to make his way into the kitchen, which, separate from the house, was still standing. The invisible hand of the wind tugged, pushed, and forcefully restrained him. He got down and crawled on his belly into the earth-floor kitchen. As he showed himself with the rope, the wind tossed him, like washing on the line, against his tree.

The boy was hurt! He looked crucified against the tree. The spike of the wind was slightly withdrawn. He fell, folded on the ground. He lay there unconscious. And the wind had no mercy for him. It shoved him, poked him, and molested his clothes like muddy newspaper against the tree.

As darkness began to move in rapidly, the wind grew more vicious and surged a mighty gust that struck the resisting kitchen. It was heaved to the ground in a rubbled pile. The brave wooden hut had been shielding the banana tree but in its death fall missed it by inches. The wind charged again, and the soft tree gurgled—the fruit was torn from it and plunged to the ground.

The wind was less fierce when Mr. Bass and a searching party arrived with lanterns. Because the bridge was washed away, the hazardous roundabout journey had badly impeded them.

Talks about safety were mockery to the anxious father. Relentlessly he searched. In the darkness his great voice echoed everywhere, calling for his boy. He was wrenching and ripping through the house wreckage when suddenly he vaguely remembered how the boy had been fussing with the banana tree. Desperate, the man struggled from the ruins, flagging the lantern he carried.

The flickering light above his head showed Mr. Bass the forlorn and pitiful banana tree. There it stood, shivering and twitching like a propped-up man with lacerated throat and dismembered head. Half of the damaged fruit rested on Gustus. The father hesitated. But when he saw a feeble wink of the boy's eyelids, he flung himself to the ground. His bristly chin rubbed the child's face while his unsteady hand ran all over his body. "Mi bwoy!" he murmured. "Mi hurricane bwoy! The Good Lord save

you. . . . Why you do this? Why you do this?"

"I did want buy mi shoes, Pappy. I . . . I can't go anywhere 'cause I have no shoes. . . . I didn' go to school outing at the factory. I didn' go to Government House. I didn' go to Ol' Fort in town."

Mr. Bass sank into the dirt and stripped himself of his heavy boots. He was about to lace them to the boy's feet when the onlooking men prevented him. He tied the boots together and threw them over his shoulder.

Gustus's broken arm was strapped to his side as they carried him away. Mr. Bass stroked his head and asked how he felt. Only then grief swelled inside him and he wept. ❧

The Hurricane
PALES MATOS

When the hurricane unfolds
Its fierce accordion of winds,
On the tip of its toes,
Agile dancer, it sweeps whirling
Over the carpeted surface of the sea
With the scattered branches of the palm.

Responding to Reading

First Impressions

1. Jot down your reactions to Gustus's trip to the banana tree.

Second Thoughts

2. Do you think Gustus is courageous or foolish in trying to protect the tree?

   Think about
   - what the tree means to him
   - his reasons for trying to save the tree
   - the dangers he faces

3. How would you describe the relationship between Gustus and his father?

4. Reread the last two paragraphs of the story. Why do you think Gustus's father ties his boots together and throws them over his shoulder?

5. Do you think anything positive comes out of Gustus's trip to the banana tree? Why or why not?

Literary Concept: Setting

Setting is the time and place in which a story's events occur. Although setting is not very important in some stories, it is crucial in others. Think about the setting of "The Banana Tree." How important is the setting in this story? Explain.

Concept Review: Conflict   Most stories contain **conflicts,** or struggles between opposing forces. A conflict may be **internal**—within the mind of a single character—or **external**—between different characters, between a character and society, or between a character and nature. In "The Banana Tree" a major external conflict occurs between Gustus and nature. Who or what do you think triumphs?

Writing Options

1. Have you ever been in a hurricane or another bad storm? Write a **description** of it, using as many details as possible. You may want to use some of the information you included in your web for Examine What You Know.

2. Write a **dialogue** that might take place between Gustus and his father after Gustus's broken arm is treated.

Nonfiction   ## Tracee

ROBERT LIPSYTE

Examine What You Know

Think about the highest, most challenging goal you can see yourself working to achieve. What steps would you have to take to achieve your goal? What sacrifices would you make? If you achieved your goal, what rewards might you expect? Answer these questions and describe your goal in your journal or on a sheet of paper.

Expand Your Knowledge

Olga Korbut, Nadia Comaneci, Mary Lou Retton, Shannon Miller—every four years the women's Olympic gymnastics competition produces a new star who leaps and somersaults straight into the hearts of a worldwide audience. Tracee Talavera, the subject of this selection, dreamed of being an Olympic star—a goal shared by many but achieved by only a very few. The flips and twists that appear so effortless require years of training. The physical and emotional toll of this training can be severe.

In women's gymnastics there are four events: vault, uneven parallel bars, balance beam, and floor exercise. A gymnast's performance is judged on difficulty, originality, composition, execution, amplitude, and general impression. A perfect score is ten points.

Enrich Your Reading

Connecting   When you are reminded of things you have seen or read about as you read a selection, you are developing an important reading strategy. Reading is more fun and interesting when you can connect what is described in a selection to the people, places, and things you know. For example, you may have little knowledge of gymnastics; but the training may remind you of working toward a goal in another area, or Tracee may remind you of someone you know. By making such connections, you get more out of your reading.

■ *Author biography on Extend page*

Tracee

ROBERT LIPSYTE

Dawn breaks chilly and damp, and Tracee Talavera feels crummy. Her muscles ache, her throat is sore, she has a slight headache. She would like to stay burrowed in this warm bed in this cozy room crowded with five other girls and dozens of cuddly stuffed animals. From the muffled groans around her, she can tell that the others feel the same way.

She sits up. There are no days off on the road to the Olympics. Besides, she thinks, a crummy day may be just what she needs. She's been feeling too good lately. Maybe she needs the experience of working out while she feels bad.

That way, if she goes to a championship meet with a sore throat and a headache, she'll be prepared. The difference between winning and losing in gymnastics is sometimes just a sneeze, a twitch, a frown. Maybe this lousy day will pay off.

The difference between Tracee Talavera and the millions of other teenage girls who do gymnastics is more than muscle strength and balance and coordination. It is the willingness to get up at 4:45 A.M. no matter how she feels and, perhaps even more important, the <u>motivation</u> to find a golden glimmer in a gray funk.

By 6 A.M. Tracee and the other young Elite (top competitive level) gymnasts who live together are limbering up for their daily workout in a chilly, chalk-dusty gym in Eugene, Oregon. If Tracee is still feeling crummy, she isn't showing it. Once warmed up, she races across the gym, somersaults over a leather vaulting horse,[1] and plunges into a pond of foam rubber.

She bounds to her feet and glances at coach Dick Mulvihill for approval. He turns away from Tracee to watch another girl.

Tracee's expression hardens, her eyes narrow. She jogs back to her starting position, waits until Mulvihill is looking at her, then starts again, charging down the narrow runway, leaping into the air, flipping over the horse. This time, as she rises from the foam, Mulvihill is nodding at her. Tracee smiles. She hurries away to try it again.

"She's hungry," says Mulvihill a few minutes later. We are standing together in the gym as the camera crew shoots Tracee making an entry in the precise workout journal that every serious gymnast keeps. "She's the first one on the apparatus and just about the

---

1. **vaulting horse:** a padded block on legs, over which gymnasts perform acrobatic leaps.

Words to Know and Use | **motivation** (mōt′ ə vä′ shən) *n.* a driving force; incentive

last to leave. She sets the pace for all the kids, and she hustles all the time."

"Hunger, is that what you look for in a beginning gymnast?" I ask Mulvihill.

"I like to look at their eyes," he says. "If they're looking around and they sort of have a hungry, steely, squinty look, like they're sizing up the other girls."

"You sound like a prizefight manager," I say.

"I used to box myself," he says.

Six hundred miles away, Tracee's parents, Nancy and Rip Talavera, are just getting up. They think about Tracee every day, and their thoughts are mixed with pride and sorrow.

"Tracee went up to Eugene when she was eleven," says Nancy. "She's now sixteen. We've lost five years of her youth that we can never regain. It's a situation where you've given your child to someone else to raise, and it's a loss."

Tracee calls home once a week from Eugene and chitchats with her mother about grandma, the pets, neighbors. Nancy always felt it was important to keep Tracee up to date on family trivia so she wouldn't feel like a stranger when she came home. But Rip rarely talks to Tracee when she calls. He says it's too painful, he misses her so much. And Rip seems to be protecting himself from further hurt when he says, "In fact, when she does come back, it really is disappointing, because she's not the kid who left here." When I ask him about the eleven-year-old Tracee who left, his voice cracks. "That's like a dream."

Allowing Tracee to leave home was an emotionally painful decision, and an expensive one. It cost almost ten thousand

Tracee on balance beam. © 1992 Dave Black.

dollars a year in tuition and living expenses for Tracee to attend Mulvihill's National Academy of Artistic Gymnastics. And the decision was a gamble—balanced against the hope that Tracee would become a champion was the fear that she could be physically hurt or become psychologically stunted, a gym rat instead of a well-rounded person.

But the Talaveras had been heading toward that decision ever since Tracee was an infant, a nonstop crib bouncer, a living-room rug flipper, a trampoline tumbler. She was pure energy looking for an outlet.

She found that outlet when she was five. Like millions of others around the world, she was captivated by Olga Korbut, the tiny gymnast from the Soviet Union who won a gold medal in the 1972 Olympics. Watching the games on television, Tracee and her sister, Coral, who was eight, determined to become gymnasts, too.

This wasn't as easy in 1972 as it would become a few years later, when children's gymnastics classes sprang up like fast-food franchises. The Talaveras found no lessons available in San Francisco. They enrolled their daughters in acrobatics classes (after a year, the girls complained that the classes weren't "hard enough"), ballet ("too slow"), and trampoline before they eventually found a gymnastics club south of the city.

In the next few years, gymnastics came to dominate the Talaveras' family life. The girls moved up the levels of competition, and their parents became their cheerleaders, chauffeurs, trainers. They searched for better coaching. They found a good coach in Walnut Creek, a suburb within driving distance of their San Francisco home. After a while, they moved to Walnut Creek.

During summer vacations they traveled to Eugene so the girls could work out with Mulvihill and his wife, Linda Metheny, a gymnast in three Olympics.

Both sisters were strong and light for their body size, graceful, energetic, and talented. But Tracee had the kid sister advantage of growing up with an older, more advanced gymnast; whatever Coral learned, Tracee

learned too. She also had what one Japanese coach called "konjo," an inner drive, a fighter's fire to keep going, to never quit.

In 1976, Nadia Comaneci of Romania replaced Olga Korbut as the Olympic gymnastic darling, and all over the world strong little girls fantasized about replacing Nadia. Tracee's potential was recognized. She was a California champion at nine; she was on track to the Olympic trials. Excitement grew in the Talavera household. If Tracee continued to develop, she might be the darling of the 1980 Olympics in Moscow. When the girls' Walnut Creek coach left California for a better job, Tracee and Coral went to live at the Academy in Eugene, to train full time with Mulvihill.

"She was the imp," remembers Mulvihill. "The vivacious little teenybopper that darted around and really didn't know what was going on but was having a good time."

Coral was injured and became discouraged. She left after a year. The Talaveras thought that Tracee would come home, too, but she stayed. She began winning local, state, and regional titles. She won two United States championships and a bronze medal at the World Games in Moscow. She won a place on the 1980 Olympic team.

She also seemed to flourish in the cloistered[2] life at the academy, a carefully regulated existence that allows no dating and hardly any activities beyond gymnastics and regular public school. Even school was bent around gymnastics. Tracee attended only

---

2. **cloistered** (klȯisʹ tərd): isolated from the outside world.

Words to Know and Use	**captivate** (kapʹ tə vāt) *v.* to fascinate or charm **dominate** (dämʹ ə nāt′) *v.* to rule or control **vivacious** (vī vāʹ shəs) *adj.* lively **flourish** (flʉrʹ ish) *v.* to thrive; be successful

three or four classes a day, mostly math, English, and foreign languages. She got credit for gym, music, art, and social studies because of gymnastics and the international travel—she got to China, Japan, and Europe even if she never got to the school cafeteria.

"Sometimes you wish you could go to dances and football games and people's parties and stuff," says Tracee, "but then you sort of think, well, I'm getting more out of life right now than they are, and I can always go to parties later. So it's sort of . . . it's worth it, I think."

She got to China, Japan, and Europe.

The girls of the academy work out six days a week, three on the compulsory exercises[3] that every gymnast must perform in competition, three days for the optional exercises that each performs to show off her own particular strength. Six hours a day of the vaulting horse and the tumbling mat and the uneven parallel bars and the balance beams, the endless floor routines practiced until each muscle has a memory of its own, pushing through pain and boredom and the low days when the coach scowls or, worse, ignores her, coming back after sprained ankles and pulled muscles and torn tendons and broken toes, ignoring the clouds of chalk dust and the chilly dawns and the constant "rips," the little skin tears in the palm that plague most gymnasts.

Many girls drop out of high-level competi-

tive gymnastics, particularly those who have been pushed by their parents after their own interest waned. Some of those girls, afraid to confront their parents, will "eat their way out" of competition, or purposely get hurt.

Tracee's conflict was different. Her passion for gymnastics was growing, even as her parents began to doubt that her life was taking the right course.

In the summer of 1980, Tracee's world came apart. First, President Carter canceled United States participation in the Olympics; there would be no trip to Moscow, no chance to become the first American female gymnast to ever win an Olympic medal, no shot at becoming the imp of the world.

Then, her father demanded that she leave the academy and come home to stay.

"She was hooked on gymnastics; she wanted to do gymnastics at all costs," explains Rip now. He wanted her to concentrate on her studies so she could attend a good college. "Tracee has to be prepared for life, and gymnastics isn't going to prepare her for life. It's a good experience in life, but it's not what's essential. Nobody is going to ask her how her double back was when she's looking for a job."

Tracee came home to Walnut Creek in the fall of 1980. She was fourteen. She never stopped nagging her mother and father to send her back to Eugene.

"She made it sufficiently tough," says Nancy, "that my husband and I let her go back. We wanted it to work so bad, but she

---

3. **compulsory exercises:** gymnastic routines made up of a set of required skills.

Words to Know and Use

scowl (skoul) *v.* to frown
confront (kən frunt') *v.* to face up to; oppose boldly

didn't want it to work. She'd go to a local gym and she'd complain about everything."

Nancy's eyes fill with tears when she remembers the four months that Tracee was home. "She made us feel guilty that she wasn't doing her gymnastics in what she felt was the best place. Anytime there was a little problem, she'd say, "Well, in Eugene we did it like this.""

Nancy and Rip wanted Tracee to lead a "normal" life. But Walnut Creek wasn't "normal" for Tracee anymore.

"My gymnastics wasn't going anywhere," remembers Tracee. "I wanted to come back the whole time."

"She made it real impossible," says Rip. The final incident was a meet in Oakland, California. Coach Mulvihill was there, and Rip couldn't help noticing their easy rapport, how Tracee brightened up. After four months, Rip gave up and let Tracee return to Eugene.

"My dad just got sick of my nagging," says Tracee.

When she said that, she gave a little laugh. It sounded cold. I wondered how much guilt might be behind that little laugh. Tracee wanted to become the best that she could be; she obviously burned to be great. Her parents were ambitious for her, too. And yet, the pride they all felt was mixed with so much pain. They had all made sacrifices so Tracee could go for the gold.

When I interviewed Rip in the fall of 1982, he said that he no longer pays any money to the academy. Coach Mulvihill would not discuss his financial arrange-ments. But there was no doubt that Tracee was a prime attraction at the academy. Her picture was on the cover of academy publications; her poster was on sale in the office. The academy has a local booster club of people who donate money.

I wondered how many Eugene girls attended classes at the academy because Tracee was there. How many girls from other cities came to live at the academy because they dreamed of becoming Olympians, too.

But staying there may be harder than getting there.

"It's not for everyone," says Tracee. We're sitting in the upstairs living room of the Mulvihill house rather than the downstairs lounge area of the dormitory, because one of the girls is sick and we don't want to disturb her. The interview, one of an increasing number that Tracee undergoes, is just an interruption in this day that broke chill and damp and crummy. After her workout, she lifted weights, jogged, and went to school.

Meanwhile, six hundred miles to the south, Rip and Nancy are thinking about her, wishing they were there to monitor her studies, wondering if the Mulvihills care as much about her life outside gymnastics as they do.

Rip thinks about the addiction to glory, and what will happen to her psyche[4] and her body as she pounds away toward the next Olympics. Nancy thinks about what will happen to her when her gymnastics career is over.

"I've seen a lot of kids who haven't had the same success they had as a gymnast feel

---

4. **psyche** (sī′ kē): mind or soul.

Words to Know and Use | **rapport** (ra pôr′) *n.* a relationship of understanding and agreement

Tracee completing routine on
uneven parallel bars.
© 1992 Dave Black.

they're a failure," she says. "A couple of kids have gone anorexic[5] because they're still striving to be that cute little gymnast that they were at eleven and twelve and thirteen and now they're seventeen and they're not getting that attention."

The family is still deeply involved in gymnastics. Coral coaches at her college, Nancy judges meets, and Rip teaches at a small local club. He says he is more relaxed with other people's daughters than he ever was with his own.

"So I lose Tracee," he says, glancing around the gym, "but I got about thirty other kids here that I work with. So these are like my, you know, almost like my family."

Nancy nods when I ask her if she ever thinks about that decision they made years ago to let their daughters become gymnasts, and the decisions that followed to let Tracee devote her life to it. "She had a talent, and we were lucky enough to be able to let her pursue it. I don't think what we've done would be much different than what most parents would do. Most parents want to do what's best for their kids. And I feel that's what we've done."

---

5. **anorexic:** having a mental disorder that involves an obsession with weight loss.

Back in Eugene, Tracee does her homework, has supper with the other girls, then watches some television–"General Hospital" or another soap taped earlier in the day. She will go to sleep early. She has to get up tomorrow morning at 4:45.

"Some girls just can't take it," said Tracee when I saw her. "First of all, they're used to their own rooms. They're used to, like, having the whole room, everything of theirs, and they get this little space."

She talked about the trouble she has readjusting to her parents' house when she returns a few times a year on brief vacations.

"It's really weird going back home," she says. "You know, here, all fourteen of us go here, then all fourteen go there. It's done in such large groups, and, like, at home I'm sort of by myself a lot. And you know, there's only four people in my family, so it's just like, gosh, it's so empty you know, there's no one there."

But in June of 1983, Tracee responded to her parents' wishes and came home again. Her grandmother was dying, and her father, Rip, was more upset than ever by Tracee's absence.

Tracee settled into the life of the family. She spent the summer working out in the gym where Rip volunteered. She still planned to try out for the Olympic team.

Was Tracee going to stay home this time? The last time I called, her mother's voice sounded uncertain as she said, "I'm keeping my fingers crossed." ❧

INSIGHT

Watching Gymnasts

ROBERT FRANCIS

Competing not so much with one another
As with perfection
    They follow follow as voices in a fugue[1]
    A severe music.

Something difficult they are making clear
Like the crack teacher
    Demonstrating their paradigms[2] until
    The dumb see.

How flower-light they toss themselves,
    how light
They toss and fall
    And flower-light, precise, and arabesque[3]
    Let their praise be.

---

1. fugue (fyo͞og): a musical composition in which a phrase started by one voice or instrument is imitated and developed by others.
2. paradigms (par′ ə dīmz′): example words used to show the grammatical forms of verbs and nouns.
3. arabesque (ar′ ə besk′): like a complex design of intertwined lines.

E X P L A I N

Responding to Reading

First Impressions

1. What feelings do you have about Tracee after reading the selection? Jot down your thoughts in your journal or on a sheet of paper.

Second Thoughts

2. Do you think Tracee's Olympic goal was worth all the problems she faced in trying to achieve it?

> **Think about**
> • Tracee's personal sacrifices
> • the sacrifices of the Talavera family
> • her father's remark: "gymnastics isn't going to prepare her for life"

3. Tracee's parents felt that what they did wasn't much different from what most parents would do for their children. Do you agree with them? Explain.

4. What are your impressions of Dick Mulvihill and his actions as Tracee's coach?

5. Would you describe Tracee's pursuit of her athletic goal as a healthy obsession? When does someone cross the line from dedication to obsession?

Broader Connections

6. The dream of many young athletes is to someday compete in the Olympic Games. At times, however, countries boycott the Olympics for political reasons. For example, the United States decided not to send its team to the 1980 Moscow Olympics to protest the Soviet invasion of Afghanistan. This boycott prevented Tracee Talavera and many other athletes from competing in the Olympics. Do you think countries should use the Olympics to express their political views?

Literary Concept: Feature Profile

A magazine or newspaper article about a noteworthy person is often called a **feature profile**. This type of article usually includes biographical information about the person, quotes and anecdotes, and an "angle," or slant, conveying a particular attitude about the person by focusing on one aspect of his or her life. How would you describe Robert Lipsyte's angle in his profile of Tracee?

Writing Options

1. Imagine that Tracee Talavera has been invited to your eighth-grade graduation ceremony. She has been asked to talk about her life in sports and her pursuit of excellence. What do you think she would say? Write her **speech.**

2. Organizers of the Olympic Games usually prepare a press guide, a booklet of information about all the sports and all the participants in the games. Write an **informative paragraph** about Tracee Talavera that could have appeared in the Olympic press guide for the 1984 Summer Games in Los Angeles.

3. If Tracee started her own gymnastics academy, what do you think it would be like? How do you think she would advertise her academy? Create an **advertising brochure** that will interest young gymnasts and their parents in Tracee's gymnastics school.

4. In 1983, Tracee had to make a decision about whether to stay home, as her parents wanted, or to return to Eugene, Oregon, to train with Coach Mulvihill. Imagine Tracee's conversation with her parents about her decision. Write this **dialogue** between Tracee and her parents.

Vocabulary Practice

Exercise   On a sheet of paper, write the word from the list that best completes each sentence.

1. The gymnast's goal was to win all major championships and to _?_ in her favorite event—the vault.

2. The athlete decided to _?_ her father and talk to him about returning to the academy.

3. The gymnast's parents worried that their daughter's diet would cause her growth to be _?_.

4. Do you think you would _?_ in the strict atmosphere of a gymnastics academy?

5. The young athlete had an excellent _?_ with her coach; they could talk easily.

6. At times when she did poorly in practice, the coach would look at her and _?_.

7. To get up at 4:45 every morning to train, she must have strong _?_ and a great desire to win.

8. The determined gymnast had a _?_ look in her eyes.

9. The gymnast had grace and a perfect routine, but it was her wonderful smile that would _?_ the audience.

10. Her _?_ personality made the Olympic audiences cheer.

> *Words
> to Know
> and Use*
> ___
> **captivate
> confront
> dominate
> flourish
> motivation
> rapport
> scowl
> steely
> stunted
> vivacious**

*O*ptions for Learning

1 • **Look It Up** Choose a sports-related topic to research, such as a particular sport, event, athlete, or coach. Prepare a report on your topic. You will probably want to begin by making a list of information to include. For example, if you choose a sport, you might want to give a brief history of it, as well as information about its current rules.

2 • **Olympic Pursuits** Design a board game about winning the gold medal in an Olympic sport. Study popular board games to get ideas. Be sure to include various lucky breaks, such as living near a famous sports academy, as well as setbacks, such as injuries.

 FACT FINDER SPORTS

How many gold medals were won by American women gymnasts in the 1984 Olympics? Name the winner(s).

*R*obert Lipsyte 1938–

After Robert Lipsyte graduated from college, he worked as a copy aide and later a reporter at the *New York Times*. His first major writing assignment came in 1962, when he covered the New York Mets.

Lipsyte has won the Dutton Best Sports Stories Award for his feature articles. He has also written several novels for young adults, including *The Contender, The Brave,* and *One Fat Summer.* In addition he has worked as a radio commentator and a television talk-show host, a job for which he won an Emmy.

By writing truthfully about sports, Lipsyte hopes to "encourage kids to relax and have fun . . . to challenge themselves for the pleasure of it, without self-doubt and without fear."

*T*racee Talavera 1966–

Tracee missed her chance to compete at the 1980 Olympics, but she did compete at the 1984 Olympics in Los Angeles on a strong U.S. team that won a silver medal. The same year, she placed fourth in the world in the vault and sixteenth in the overall competition. Reflecting on her career, she has no regrets: "You have to put your social life on hold for a while, but you can catch up quick." Her advice to young gymnasts: "Enjoy whatever it is you're doing. It should be something you really like, not something someone else wants you to do."

NARRATIVE WRITING

USE NARRATIVE WRITING FOR

feature profiles
biographies
movie scripts
poems
personal anecdotes
short stories

What kind of story do you like best? For some people, nothing matches the excitement of a horror story. Some love a good mystery. Others prefer science fiction or romance or sports stories. In this workshop you will have a chance to write the kind of story you like best. In your story you will include the basic ingredients of a good **narrative: characters** that have personality, a **setting** that fits the story, a **plot** that has suspense, and a problem or **conflict** with which the characters struggle. The short stories you have read in this book provide examples of each of these elements.

Here is one writer's PASSkey to this assignment.

GUIDED ASSIGNMENT: GROUP SHORT STORY

With two or more of your classmates, write a short story. Your story should have characters, a setting, a plot, and a conflict.

PURPOSE: To write a group story
AUDIENCE: Students, teachers, parents
SUBJECT: Horror
STRUCTURE: A short story

STUDENT MODEL

Before you write, read how one group of students responded to the assignment. This is the first part of their story.

Mike is characterized through his actions and the narrator's direct comments.

> Was It a Cat?
> by Yolanda Jackson, Fred Giroux, and Sue Hall
>
> Band practice had ended late. Outside, the rain poured down. My twin brother, Mike, and I stood in front of the school, waiting for the rain to let up so that we could ride our bikes home. Mike paced impatiently. He doesn't like to wait for anything. Mike's a good guy most of the time, but he was in a bad mood that day. He was winging some rocks at the bike rack when he saw the cat.
>
> A mangy orange tomcat was slinking near the wall of the school building, trying to stay out of the rain. The weird thing about this

cat was its eyes. One eye was normal, but the other was totally white. Mike scowled at the cat and picked up a rock.

"No, Mike!" I yelled at him, but it was too late. He threw the rock at the cat. The rock grazed the cat's body, and the cat ran away. However, before the cat ran out of sight, it stopped, turned around to face us, and let out a terrible hiss.

Mike felt bad about hitting the cat, but we didn't think too much more about it until later. The rain started to let up, so we got our bikes and took off.

We were putting our bikes in the garage when Mike shouted, "Matt, did you see that?"

"See what?" I asked.

"That orange cat. I think I saw him run into the garage." Mike looked at me nervously.

"You're weird, Mike," I said. I pointed out that we live over a mile from the school.

Later that night Mike and I were doing our homework. "Did you hear that screeching sound?" Mike asked. "I think it's that cat!"

I knew it was just a car, but Mike wanted to check anyway. I followed him to the garage. We looked under the car and searched in the corners. There was no sign of a cat. I felt like an idiot. "Are you satisfied?" I asked, shoving him into the kitchen.

Mike stopped dead in his tracks. "Where's Moby?" Mike was staring at our goldfish bowl on the kitchen counter. Our goldfish was gone. Mike and I stared at each other. Maybe he was right. Maybe there was something strange going on here.

Note the use of action verbs, such as *yelled, threw, grazed,* and *ran.*

Notice that the events in this story are in chronological order.

Dialogue is used to advance the plot and spice up the characterization.

The problem in this story has been made clear by the end of the first part. Suspense is starting to build.

Now it's time to create your own group short story.

Prewrite and Explore

1 **Go to your sources** How do you find an idea for your story? Each group member should first consider his or her own experiences. Even the most ordinary experience can be turned into an interesting story. You might also consider books and newspaper articles. Another writer's plot may trigger ideas.

2 **Brainstorm your ideas** As a group, make decisions about the major elements of your story. What problem or conflict will your main character face? Who are the characters you want in your story. What are their names? What can the characters do or say that will make them unique? Also choose an effective setting.

FOR EXAMPLE

Yolanda, Fred, and Sue really liked Poe's story "The Tell-Tale Heart." What influences of Poe did you see in their story?

COLLABORATION TIP

As you discuss, at first be open to any and all ideas, even far-fetched ones. Then weigh the ideas and come to an agreement on the best ones, using these criteria:
Will this story line make sense?
Will it create interest and suspense?

STUDENT MODEL

Note the chain of strange events building to a climax.

GATHERING INFORMATION

The writers of "Was It a Cat?" decided to organize their work by dividing the story into three parts. First, the group discussed some general goals for each part of their story. Then they decided on the specific events that would take place during each part.

Beginning: Introduce the main characters / a strange
    occurrence scares them / describe a setting
Middle: The main characters encounter additional
    strange happenings
End: The final, scariest event takes place / resolve
    the main characters' fears

Beginning
    Rainy evening / twin brothers wait at school /
    Mike hits strange cat with rock / cat turns,
    hisses / at home Mike thinks he sees cat in garage
    / later Mike hears screech / goldfish missing
Middle
    Both boys have nightmare about killer cat / they
    find two dead mice by their bikes / they hear cat
    sounds at band practice
End
    After practice, dark and stormy / boys hear crash
    in band room / lights go off / Mike is scratched /
    Matt hits at something / lights go on / Is scratch
    from music stand? / they hear cat one last time

Draft and Discover

1 Stick to your goal   One way to simplify the task of drafting is to have each member of your group write one part. As you write, focus on what you want to achieve in your part. For example, if it's the beginning, your goal might be to have something happen that makes the main character's problem clear.

2 Select the point of view   Do you want a character in your story to narrate the events? In this type of narration, called the first-person point of view, the pronouns *I* and *we* are used; it brings your reader close and makes the tone personal. Or do you want the story told by someone outside it? In this type of narration, called the third-person point of view, the pronouns *he, she,* and *they* are used; it enables you to describe everything, including characters' thoughts. Which type of narration did Yolanda, Fred, and Sue choose?

Revise Your Writing

1 Fix the inconsistencies   When you put your three parts together, you may see some mismatches. For example, is a cat described as orange in one part and black in another? In dialogue, does your main character sound different from one part to the next? Does one part fail to lead logically to the next? Iron out these problems.

2 Exchange stories   Ask another group of writers to respond to your story. Consider the following questions.

Revision Questions

For Your Group	For a Peer Reader
1. Do we clearly show conflict?	1. Is the story interesting? Does the plot create suspense?
2. Have we *told* something about a character instead of *showing* it through action?	2. Does the dialogue help you see and hear the characters? Does it sound natural?
3. Have we included any unnecessary details?	3. Are there any inconsistencies between the parts?
4. Do we bring the conflict to a believable resolution?	4. Could we change the ending?

Proofread

When you are satisfied with your revised draft, take turns proofreading for errors in grammar, spelling, and punctuation. Pay special attention to the punctuation of dialogue.

NEED MORE HELP?
For rules about punctuating dialogue, see the Language Workshop that follows (pages 171–173) and pages 817–818 of the Language Handbook.

THE EDITOR'S EYE: USING COMMAS

Use commas to set off direct quotations. Do not use commas to set off indirect quotations.

A direct quotation gives the exact words spoken; an indirect quotation does not. Study the following examples.

Direct Quotation

. . . Mike shouted, "Matt, did you see that?"

Indirect Quotation

I pointed out that we live over a mile from the school.

Publish and Present

Here is a suggestion for sharing your work with others.

New Book for Your Library   Gather the group stories from your class and put them together in a short story collection. Make the collection available for everyone to read by donating it to your school library. Design a poster that advertises the library's new acquisition.

Reflect on Your Writing

FOR YOUR PORTFOLIO ▶

Write brief answers to the following questions. Then add your answers and a copy of your group's story to your portfolio.

1. Which parts of your story are the strongest? What did you do in your writing to make those parts strong?
2. Did you like the fact that this was a group project? Explain. What did you learn about creative writing from the process your group used?

LANGUAGE
WORKSHOP

USING COMMAS CORRECTLY

You might not consider commas very important, but imagine trying to read a story without them. Commas are a little like traffic signals telling the reader to slow down temporarily. They help clarify thoughts.

Commas in Dialogue

> Use commas to set off direct quotations. Do not use commas to set off indirect quotations.

A **direct quotation** gives the speaker's exact words; quotation marks set off these words. Explanatory words such as *he said* or *she asked* are not part of a quotation. They must be set off with commas.

> "She was hooked on gymnastics; she wanted to do gymnastics at all costs," explains Rip now.
> "She made it sufficiently tough," says Nancy, "that my husband and I let her go back."

An **indirect quotation** tells what a speaker said without giving the speaker's exact words. No commas or quotation marks are necessary.

> When I interviewed Rip in the fall of 1982, he said that he no longer pays any money to the academy.

◀ LITERARY MODELS
from "Tracee" by
Robert Lipsyte

Commas with Introductory Words and Direct Address

> Use commas to separate an introductory word or a noun of direct address from the rest of a sentence.

Use a comma after **introductory words** such as *oh, yes, no, well, therefore, however, next, finally, first,* and so on.

> "Yes, I'm competing in all four gymnastic events."
> "However, I don't think these judges will award any perfect 10s."

The name of a person who is spoken to directly is called a **noun of direct address.** Always use a comma to set off a noun of direct address from the rest of your sentence. If the name comes in the middle of the sentence, place commas before and after it.

Amy, your score for the vault was 9.5.
If you receive a perfect 10 from these judges, Elissa, you're a real star.

Exercise 1   Concept Check   Rewrite the following sentences, adding commas where necessary. If a sentence requires no added punctuation, write *Correct.*

1. "José were you in the hurricane?" asked Ms. Page. "Tell us about it."
2. José explained that Hurricane Andrew had trapped him and his family in South Florida for a week.
3. "We were visiting relatives" began José "and we got a warning to evacuate the area."
4. Next, José told us that he and his family had driven an hour north and stayed in a high school for two days.
5. "Were you scared?" asked Sarah.
6. "Yeah everyone was" José admitted. "Ms. Page I've never seen winds so strong—over a hundred miles an hour!"
7. Ms. Page pointed out that a storm is called a hurricane when its winds blow at seventy-five miles an hour or faster.
8. "The rain was unbelievable" said José "and it seemed to go on forever."
9. "José tell us what happened to the town" said Ms. Page.
10. "My uncle's house was not too badly damaged" explained the boy "but some houses in town were completely blown away."

Commas in a Series

Use a comma after every item in a series except the last one.

A series includes three or more items of the same kind. These items may be words, phrases, or clauses.

EXCEPTION
You do not need commas when all the items in a series are joined by *and, or,* or *nor.*
Her dress was orange and white and ruffled.

Words	At the crime scene were a <u>gun</u>, a <u>rope</u>, and a <u>dagger</u>.
Phrases	The detective dusted for fingerprints <u>on the doorknob</u>, <u>around the table</u>, and <u>inside the desk drawer.</u>
Clauses	The criminal <u>left the scene</u>, <u>hid the gun</u>, and <u>returned to work</u>.

> Use commas between adjectives of equal rank.

The gunshot produced a hot, smoky cloud.

To determine whether the adjectives are of equal rank, place the word *and* between them. Does *and* sound natural there? Can you reverse the order of the adjectives without changing the meaning? If the answer to these questions is yes, the adjectives are of equal rank.

> The detective always wore a dark brown overcoat.
> (An *and* between *dark* and *brown* sounds awkward, and the adjectives cannot be reversed. No comma is necessary.)

Exercise 2   Concept Check   Rewrite the following sentences, adding commas where necessary. If a sentence requires no added punctuation, write *Correct*.

1. In "The Murders in the Rue Morgue," Edgar Allan Poe introduces a brilliant eccentric detective named C. Auguste Dupin.
2. Dupin's talents are his imagination his keen eye and his thoroughness.
3. In Poe's story a double murder has taken place.
4. Dupin studies the newspaper report of the murders visits the crime scene and examines the evidence.
5. Dupin's solution proves to be bizarre shocking and accurate.

Exercise 3   Proofreading Skill   Rewrite the following passage. Correct any errors in comma use that you find.

> "Mr. Young were there always big movie stars?" Amanda asked.
> "No in the early days movie acting was not considered respectable" replied Mr. Young. "However moviegoers soon had favorite actors. The star system began about 1910."
> Mr. Young noted that Shirley Temple was the most popular child movie star of the 1930s. "Temple became a star when she was only six years old" explained Mr. Young. "Her talents included acting singing and dancing. She appeared in many films.

Exercise 4   Revising Your Writing   Reread the short story you and your classmates wrote for the Writer's Workshop on pages 166–170. Correct any errors in comma use that you find.

LANGUAGE HANDBOOK
. . . .
For review and practice: Section 9, Punctuation, pages 815–819.

VOCABULARY
WORKSHOP

ANALOGIES

An analogy helps you understand a word's meaning by requiring you to think about the word's relationship to other words. In this way an analogy helps to improve your vocabulary. A typical analogy problem looks like this:

> Choose the lettered word pair that expresses a relationship similar to that of the original word pair.
> HEART : BODY :: (a) jellyfish : porpoise   (b) branch : tree
> (c) truck : car   (d) magazine : newsstand

Another way to express the problem is to say; "A <u>heart</u> is to a <u>body</u> as a ___?___ is to a ___?___."

To solve the analogy, first figure out the relationship between the words in the original pair. Create a sentence that expresses the relationship: "A <u>heart</u> is part of a <u>body</u>." Then try each of the other pairs of words in this sentence. See which pair makes sense. For example, "A <u>truck</u> is part of a <u>car</u>" doesn't make sense. Using this method, you can see that answer *b* is correct: "A <u>branch</u> is part of a <u>tree</u>."

Exercise   Write the letter of the word pair that expresses a relationship similar to that expressed by the capitalized pair.

1. CREVICE : CRACK :: (a) mug : cup   (b) actor : movie   (c) dress : party : (d) radio : television
2. VEX : COMFORT :: (a) study : observe   (b) cut : dismember   (c) refrain : continue   (d) mask : hide
3. BALANCE BEAM : GYMNASTICS :: (a) vault : uneven bars   (b) long jump : track and field   (c) baseball : football   (d) practice : competition
4. JAMAICA : ISLAND :: (a) mountain : valley   (b) New York : California   (c) land : ocean   (d) Mississippi : river
5. HURRICANE : WIND :: (a) leaf : tree   (b) flood : water   (c) snow : blizzard   (d) shoe : foot

DREAMS AND SCHEMES

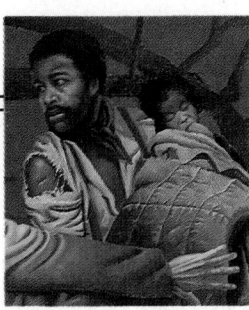

What dreams keep you awake at night or make you stare off into space in the middle of the day? Perhaps you dream of building skyscrapers, of becoming an astronaut, of writing a song that sells a million copies, or of being the swiftest runner in the world. Do you long to make the world a better place? Perhaps you dream of discovering a cure for a fatal disease, combating pollution, or even being president.

Whatever dreams inspire you, you will have to match your dreams with a plan of action in order to make them come true. Schemes, or plans, can help turn your dreams into realities. Of course, some schemes are more realistic and workable than others.

In the following selections you will see how the "dreams and schemes" of the characters unfold.

Nonfiction

from Harriet Tubman:

Conductor on the Underground Railroad

ANN PETRY

*E*xamine What You Know

Four million slaves toiled on the plantations of the southern United States in the years before the Civil War. Each year several thousand of these slaves would attempt to escape north, and many succeeded.

What do you know about these desperate escape attempts? Write the words and phrases that come to mind when you think about what slaves went through as they tried to escape.

*E*xpand Your Knowledge

With no tracks and no trains, the Underground Railroad transported thousands of slaves to freedom. The term *Underground Railroad* became popular after a slave named Tice Davids escaped from his Kentucky master in 1831. Davids's bewildered master said that his slave must have "gone off on an underground railroad."

The Underground Railroad had "stations" where fleeing slaves could get food and drink. "Timetables" told when the fugitives might arrive at particular stations. The "commuter's ticket" was the password: "A friend with friends." Most important, the railroad had "conductors," like Harriet Tubman, who helped escort the slaves to freedom. Conducting slaves to freedom became even more risky after the Fugitive Slave Law of 1850 pronounced it a federal crime to assist a runaway slave.

*E*nrich Your Reading

■ *Author biography on Extend page*

Cause and Effect   Certain events are connected to each other as **cause and effect**—that is, one event causes the other to happen. Touching a flame (cause) will result in a burn (effect). The events in a narrative often reflect this relationship. In this selection, for example, an escape attempt results in a chase. As you read, note various other instances of cause and effect.

from *Harriet Tubman:*

Conductor on the Underground Railroad

ANN PETRY

GENERAL MOSES 1965 Charles White Collection, Golden
State Mutual Company, Courtesy, Heritage Gallery, Los Angeles.

The Railroad Runs to Canada

Along the eastern shore of Maryland, in
Dorchester County, in Caroline County, the
masters kept hearing whispers about the
man named Moses, who was running off
slaves. At first they did not believe in his
existence. The stories about him were fantastic, unbelievable. Yet they watched for
him. They offered rewards for his capture.

They never saw him. Now and then they
heard whispered rumors to the effect that he
was in the neighborhood. The woods were
searched. The roads were watched. There
was never anything to indicate his whereabouts. But a few days afterward, a goodly
number of slaves would be gone from the
plantation. Neither the master nor the overseer had heard or seen anything unusual in
the quarter.[1] Sometimes one or the other
would vaguely remember having heard a
whippoorwill call somewhere in the woods,
close by, late at night. Though it was the
wrong season for whippoorwills.

Sometimes the masters thought they had
heard the cry of a hoot owl repeated and
would remember having thought that the
intervals between the low, moaning cry were

---

1. **quarter:** district or neighborhood.

wrong, that it had been repeated four times in succession instead of three. There was never anything more than that to suggest that all was not well in the quarter. Yet when morning came, they invariably discovered that a group of the finest slaves had taken to their heels.

question Who is helping the slaves escape?

Unfortunately, the discovery was almost always made on a Sunday. Thus a whole day was lost before the machinery of pursuit could be set in motion. The posters offering rewards for the fugitives could not be printed until Monday. The men who made a living hunting for runaway slaves were out of reach, off in the woods with their dogs and their guns, in pursuit of four-footed game, or they were in camp meetings saying their prayers with their wives and families beside them.

Harriet Tubman could have told them that there was far more involved in this matter of running off slaves than signaling the would-be runaways by imitating the call of a whippoorwill or a hoot owl, far more involved than a matter of waiting for a clear night when the North Star was visible.

In December 1851, when she started out with the band of fugitives that she planned to take to Canada, she had been in the vicinity of the plantation for days, planning the trip, carefully selecting the slaves that she would take with her.

She had announced her arrival in the quarter by singing the forbidden spiritual– "Go down, Moses, 'way down to Egypt Land"[2]–singing it softly outside the door of a slave cabin late at night. The husky voice was beautiful even when it was barely more than a murmur <u>borne</u> on the wind.

Once she had made her presence known, word of her coming spread from cabin to cabin. The slaves whispered to each other, ear to mouth, mouth to ear, "Moses is here." "Moses has come." "Get ready. Moses is back again."

What kind of person is Harriet Tubman? *evaluate*

The ones who had agreed to go north with her put ashcake and salt herring in an old bandanna, hastily tied it into a bundle, and then waited patiently for the signal that meant it was time to start.

There were eleven in this party, including one of her brothers and his wife. It was the largest group that she had ever conducted, but she was determined that more and more slaves should know what freedom was like.

She had to take them all the way to Canada. The Fugitive Slave Law[3] was no longer a great many <u>incomprehensible</u> words written down on the country's law books. The new law had become a reality. It

---

2. **"Go down, Moses, 'way down to Egypt Land":** part of a well-known African-American folk song about Moses leading the enslaved Israelites out of Egypt.

3. **Fugitive Slave Law:** a law passed in 1850, allowing slave owners to recover escaped slaves even if the slaves had reached free states.

Words to Know and Use | **borne** (bôrn) *adj.* carried **bear** *v.*
incomprehensible (in′ kăm′ prē hen′ sə bəl) *adj.* not capable of being understood

was Thomas Sims, a boy, picked up on the streets of Boston at night and shipped back to Georgia. It was Jerry and Shadrach, arrested and jailed with no warning.

She had never been in Canada. The route beyond Philadelphia was strange to her. But she could not let the runaways who accompanied her know this. As they walked along she told them stories of her own first flight; she kept painting vivid word pictures of what it would be like to be free.

But there were so many of them this time. She knew moments of doubt when she was half-afraid and kept looking back over her shoulder, imagining that she heard the sound of pursuit. They would certainly be pursued. Eleven of them. Eleven thousand dollars' worth of flesh and bone and muscle that belonged to Maryland planters. If they were caught, the eleven runaways would be whipped and sold south, but she—she would probably be hanged.

They tried to sleep during the day, but they never could wholly relax into sleep. She could tell by the positions they assumed, by their restless movements. And they walked at night. Their progress was slow. It took them three nights of walking to reach the first stop. She had told them about the place where they would stay, promising warmth and good food, holding these things out to them as an <u>incentive</u> to keep going.

When she knocked on the door of a farmhouse, a place where she and her parties of runaways had always been welcome, always been given shelter and plenty to eat, there was no answer. She knocked again, softly. A voice from within said, "Who is it?" There was fear in the voice.

She knew instantly from the sound of the voice that there was something wrong. She said, "A friend with friends," the password on the Underground Railroad.[4]

The door opened slowly. The man who stood in the doorway looked at her coldly, looked with unconcealed astonishment and fear at the eleven <u>disheveled</u> runaways who were standing near her. Then he shouted, "Too many, too many. It's not safe. My place was searched last week. It's not safe!" and slammed the door in her face.

She turned away from the house, frowning. She had promised her passengers food and rest and warmth, and instead of that there would be hunger and cold and more walking over the frozen ground. Somehow she would have to <u>instill</u> courage into these eleven people, most of them strangers; would have to feed them on hope and bright dreams of freedom instead of the fried pork and corn bread and milk she had promised them.

They stumbled along behind her, half-dead for sleep, and she urged them on, though she was as tired and as discouraged as they were. She had never been in Canada, but she kept painting wondrous word pictures of what it would be like. She managed to <u>dispel</u> their fear of pursuit so that they would not become hysterical,

---

4. **Underground Railroad:** a secret system used before the Civil War to help slaves escape from the South to free states in the North or to Canada.

Words to Know and Use | **incentive** (in sent′ iv) *n.* encouragement to make an effort
disheveled (di shev′ əld) *adj.* messy; untidy
instill (in stil′) *v.* to supply gradually
dispel (di spel′) *v.* to drive away

179

panic-stricken. Then she had to bring some of the fear back so that they would stay awake and keep walking though they drooped with sleep.

Yet during the day, when they lay down deep in a thicket, they never really slept, because if a twig snapped or the wind sighed in the branches of a pine tree, they jumped to their feet, afraid of their own shadows, shivering and shaking. It was very cold, but they dared not make fires, because someone would see the smoke and wonder about it.

She kept thinking, eleven of them. Eleven thousand dollars' worth of slaves. And she had to take them all the way to Canada. Sometimes she told them about Thomas Garrett, in Wilmington. She said he was their friend even though he did not know them. He was the friend of all fugitives. He called them God's poor. He was a Quaker[5] and his speech was a little different from that of other people. His clothing was different, too. He wore the wide-brimmed hat that the Quakers wear.

She said that he had thick white hair, soft, almost like a baby's, and the kindest eyes she had ever seen. He was a big man and strong, but he had never used his strength to harm anyone, always to help people. He would give all of them a new pair of shoes. Everybody. He always did. Once they reached his house in Wilmington, they would be safe. He would see to it that they were.

She described the house where he lived, told them about the store where he sold shoes. She said he kept a pail of milk and a loaf of bread in the drawer of his desk so that he would have food ready at hand for any of God's poor who should suddenly appear before him fainting with hunger. There was a hidden room in the store. A whole wall swung open, and behind it was a room where he could hide fugitives. On the wall there were shelves filled with small boxes—boxes of shoes—so that you would never guess that the wall actually opened.

While she talked, she kept watching them. They did not believe her. She could tell by their expressions. They were thinking, New shoes, Thomas Garrett, Quaker, Wilmington—what foolishness was this? Who knew if she told the truth? Where was she taking them, anyway?

That night they reached the next stop—a farm that belonged to a German. She made the runaways take shelter behind trees at the edge of the fields before she knocked at the door. She hesitated before she approached the door, thinking, Suppose that he, too, should refuse shelter, suppose—Then she thought, Lord, I'm going to hold steady on to You, and You've got to see me through—and knocked softly.

She heard the familiar guttural voice say, "Who's there?"

She answered quickly, "A friend with friends."

He opened the door and greeted her warmly. "How many this time?" he asked.

"Eleven," she said and waited, doubting, wondering.

He said, "Good. Bring them in."

He and his wife fed them in the lamplit

---

5. **Quaker:** a member of a religious group known as the Society of Friends.

THE UNDERGROUND RAILROAD 1981 Paul Collins Courtesy of the artist.

kitchen, their faces glowing as they offered food and more food, urging them to eat, saying there was plenty for everybody, have more milk, have more bread, have more meat.

They spent the night in the warm kitchen. They really slept, all that night and until dusk the next day. When they left, it was with reluctance. They had all been warm and safe and well fed. It was hard to exchange the security offered by that clean, warm kitchen for the darkness and the cold of a December night.

"Go on or Die"

Harriet had found it hard to leave the warmth and friendliness, too. But she urged them on. For a while, as they walked, they seemed to carry in them a measure of contentment; some of the serenity and the cleanliness of that big, warm kitchen lingered on inside them. But as they walked farther and farther away from the warmth and the light, the cold and the darkness entered into them. They fell silent, sullen, suspicious. She waited for the moment when some one of them would turn mutinous. It did not happen that night.

Two nights later she was aware that the feet behind her were moving slower and slower. She heard the irritability in their voices, knew that soon someone would refuse to go on.

She started talking about William Still and the Philadelphia Vigilance Committee.[6] No one commented. No one asked any questions. She told them the story of William and Ellen Craft and how they escaped from Georgia. Ellen was so fair that she looked as though she were white, and so she dressed up in a man's clothing, and she looked like a wealthy young planter. Her husband, William, who was dark, played the role of her slave. Thus they traveled from Macon, Georgia, to Philadelphia, riding on the trains, staying at the finest hotels. Ellen pretended to be very ill—her right arm was in a sling, and her right hand was bandaged because she was supposed to have rheumatism. Thus she avoided having to sign the register at the hotels, for she could not read or write. They finally arrived safely in Philadelphia and then went on to Boston.

It is better to be a slave than to suffer like this.

No one said anything. Not one of them seemed to have heard her.

She told them about Frederick Douglass,[7] the most famous of the escaped slaves, of his eloquence, of his magnificent appearance.

Then she told them of her own first, vain effort at running away, evoking the memory of that miserable life she had led as a child, reliving it for a moment in the telling.

But they had been tired too long, hungry too long, afraid too long, footsore too long. One of them suddenly cried out in despair, "Let me go back. It is better to be a slave than to suffer like this in order to be free."

Why did Harriet Tubman and the slaves risk so much? *question*

She carried a gun with her on these trips. She had never used it—except as a threat. Now as she aimed it, she experienced a feeling of guilt, remembering that time, years ago, when she had prayed for the death of Edward Brodas, the Master, and then not too long afterward had heard that great, wailing cry that came from the throats of the field hands, and knew from the sound that the Master was dead.

One of the runaways said again, "Let me go back. Let me go back," and stood still, and then turned around and said over his shoulder, "I am going back."

She lifted the gun, aimed it at the despairing slave. She said, "Go on with us or die." The husky, low-pitched voice was grim.

He hesitated for a moment, and then he joined the others. They started walking

---

6. **Philadelphia Vigilance Committee:** a fund-raising organization set up before the Civil War to help slaves escaping from the South.

7. **Frederick Douglass:** a black leader of the 1800s who worked for the end of slavery in the United States.

Words to Know and Use | **irritability** (ir′ i tə bil′ ə tē) *n.* state of being easily annoyed
eloquence (el′ ə kwəns) *n.* ability to speak forcefully and persuasively
vain (vān) *adj.* useless; worthless

again. She tried to explain to them why none of them could go back to the plantation. If a runaway returned, he would turn traitor; the master and the overseer would force him to turn traitor. The returned slave would <u>disclose</u> the stopping places, the hiding places, the corn stacks they had used with the full knowledge of the owner of the farm, the name of the German farmer who had fed them and sheltered them. These people who had risked their own security to help runaways would be ruined, fined, imprisoned.

She said, "We got to go free or die. And freedom's not bought with dust."

This time she told them about the long agony of the Middle Passage[8] on the old slave ships, about the black horror of the holds, about the chains and the whips. They too knew these stories. But she wanted to remind them of the long, hard way they had come, about the long, hard way they had yet to go. She told them about Thomas Sims, the boy picked up on the streets of Boston and sent back to Georgia. She said when they got him back to Savannah, got him in prison there, they whipped him until a doctor who was standing by watching said, "You will kill him if you strike him again!" His master said, "Let him die!"

Thus she forced them to go on. Sometimes she thought she had become nothing but a voice speaking in the darkness, cajoling,[9] urging, threatening. Sometimes she told them things to make them laugh; sometimes she sang to them and heard the eleven voices behind her blending softly with hers, and then she knew that for the moment all was well with them.

She gave the impression of being a short, muscular, indomitable[10] woman who could never be defeated. Yet at any moment she was liable to be seized by one of those curious fits of sleep,[11] which might last for a few minutes or for hours.

Freedom's not bought with dust.

Even on this trip she suddenly fell asleep in the woods. The runaways, ragged, dirty, hungry, cold, did not steal the gun, as they might have, and set off by themselves, or turn back. They sat on the ground near her and waited patiently until she awakened. They had come to trust her implicitly, totally. They too had come to believe her repeated statement, "We got to go free or die." She was leading them into freedom, and so they waited until she was ready to go on.

Finally, they reached Thomas Garrett's house in Wilmington, Delaware. Just as Harriet had promised, Garrett gave them all new shoes, and provided carriages to take them on to the next stop.

---

8. Middle Passage: the route traders used to transport African slaves across the Atlantic to the Americas.
9. cajoling (kə jōl′ iŋ): coaxing; persuading with promises.
10. indomitable (in däm′ i tə bəl): not able to be discouraged or conquered.
11. curious fits of sleep: refers to mysterious spells of dizziness experienced by Harriet Tubman.

Words to Know and Use | **disclose** (dis klōz′) *v.* to reveal

183

By slow stages they reached Philadelphia, where William Still hastily recorded their names and the plantations whence they had come and something of the life they had led in slavery. Then he carefully hid what he had written, for fear it might be discovered. In 1872 he published this record in book form and called it *The Underground Railroad*. In the foreword to his book, he said: "While I knew the danger of keeping strict records, and while I did not then dream that in my day slavery would be blotted out or that the time would come when I could publish these records, it used to afford me great satisfaction to take them down, fresh from the lips of fugitives on the way to freedom, and to preserve them as they had given them."

William Still, who was familiar with all the station stops on the Underground Railroad, supplied Harriet with money and sent her and her eleven fugitives on to Burlington, New Jersey.

Harriet felt safer now, though there were danger spots ahead. But the biggest part of her job was over. As they went farther and farther north, it grew colder; she was aware of the wind on the Jersey ferry and aware of the cold damp in New York. From New York they went on to Syracuse, where the temperature was even lower.

In Syracuse she met the Reverend J. W. Loguen, known as "Jarm" Loguen. This was the beginning of a lifelong friendship. Both Harriet and Jarm Loguen were to become friends and supporters of Old John Brown.[12]

From Syracuse they went north again, into a colder, snowier city–Rochester. Here they almost certainly stayed with Frederick Douglass, for he wrote in his autobiography:

"On one occasion I had eleven fugitives at the same time under my roof, and it was necessary for them to remain with me until I could collect sufficient money to get them to Canada. It was the largest number I ever had at any one time, and I had some difficulty in providing so many with food and shelter, but, as may well be imagined, they were not very fastidious in either direction, and were well content with very plain food, and a strip of carpet on the floor for a bed, or a place on the straw in the barnloft."

Late in December 1851, Harriet arrived in St. Catharines, Canada West (now Ontario), with the eleven fugitives. It had taken almost a month to complete this journey; most of the time had been spent getting out of Maryland.

That first winter in St. Catharines was a terrible one. Canada was a strange, frozen land, snow everywhere, ice everywhere, and a bone-biting cold the like of which none of them had ever experienced before. Harriet rented a small frame house in the town and set to work to make a home. The fugitives boarded with her. They worked in the forests felling trees, and so did she. Sometimes she took other jobs, cooking or cleaning house for people in the town. She cheered on these newly arrived fugitives, working herself, finding work for them, finding food for them, praying for them, sometimes begging for them.

Often she found herself thinking of the beauty of Maryland, the mellowness of the soil, the richness of the plant life there. The climate itself made for an ease of living that

---

12. **Old John Brown:** an antislavery leader executed for leading a raid on the federal arsenal at Harpers Ferry, Virginia, in 1859.

could never be duplicated in this bleak, barren countryside.

In spite of the severe cold, the hard work, she came to love St. Catharines and the other towns and cities in Canada where black men lived. She discovered that freedom meant more than the right to change jobs at will, more than the right to keep the money that one earned. It was the right to vote and to sit on juries. It was the right to be elected to office. In Canada there were black men who were county officials and members of school boards. St. Catharines had a large colony of ex-slaves, and they owned their own homes, kept them neat and clean and in good repair. They lived in whatever part of town they chose and sent their children to the schools.

When spring came she decided that she would make this small Canadian city her home—as much as any place could be said to be home to a woman who traveled from Canada to the Eastern Shore of Maryland as often as she did.

In the spring of 1852, she went back to Cape May, New Jersey. She spent the summer there, cooking in a hotel. That fall she returned as usual to Dorchester County, and brought out nine more slaves, conducting them all the way to St. Catharines, in Canada West, to the bone-biting cold, the snow-covered forests—and freedom.

She continued to live in this fashion, spending the winter in Canada and the spring and summer working in Cape May, New Jersey, or in Philadelphia. She made two trips a year into slave territory, one in the fall and another in the spring. She now had a definite, crystalized purpose, and in carrying it out her life fell into a pattern which remained unchanged for the next six years. ❧

*R*esponding to Reading

First Impressions

1. What impressed you most about Harriet Tubman? Write your impressions in your journal or on a sheet of paper.

Second Thoughts

2. Why do you think Harriet Tubman repeatedly risked her life to help people realize their dream of freedom?

3. Look back at the words you wrote for Examine What You Know. Now that you have read about Harriet Tubman, what new information about slave escapes could you add?

4. Do you think that if you had been a slave, you would have followed Harriet Tubman to the North? Explain.

   Think about
   - the extreme hardships the "passengers" faced
   - the risk of getting caught and punished
   - Harriet's threat, "Go on with us or die"

Broader Connections

5. The people who opened their homes to the runaways were breaking the Fugitive Slave Law. If caught, they would have faced the possibility of a prison sentence, plus large fines. Would you have broken the law and opened your home to the slaves? Why or why not?

*L*iterary Concept: *Biography*

This selection is an excerpt from a **biography** of Harriet Tubman. A biography is a type of nonfiction in which a writer gives a factual account of someone else's life. Some biographies, while sticking to historical facts, also contain elements of fiction to enliven the subject. *Harriet Tubman: Conductor on the Underground Railroad* contains dialogue as well as some of Tubman's thoughts. The author, Ann Petry, couldn't have known what was actually said and thought, but she made an educated guess. In so doing, she made her biography come alive for the reader.

*W*riting Options

1. Harriet Tubman helped many people escape from slavery. Think about a person who has helped you through a very difficult situation. Write a **description** of this person.

2. Imagine that your town has decided to erect a statue honoring Harriet Tubman. Write the **dedication speech** you will give at the ceremony of unveiling the statue.

3. Imagine that you are one of the slaves who Tubman led safely to Canada. Write a **letter** to your former master in Maryland, telling him your thoughts now that you are free.

4. This selection is in a subunit with the theme "Dreams and Schemes" and a unit with the theme "All or Nothing." In an **essay** explain how this biography of Harriet Tubman reflects those two themes.

*V*ocabulary Practice

Exercise A   Write the letter of the word that differs in meaning from the other words in the set.

1. (a) carried   (b) dropped   (c) borne   (d) supported

2. (a) drive away   (b) eliminate   (c) dispel   (d) increase

3. (a) warning   (b) motivation   (c) encouragement
   (d) incentive

4. (a) supply   (b) provide   (c) ignore   (d) instill

5. (a) profitable   (b) vain   (c) successful   (d) advantageous

> *Words to Know and Use*
>
> **borne
> disclose
> disheveled
> dispel
> eloquence
> incentive
> incomprehensible
> instill
> irritability
> vain**

Exercise B   Some words seem to fit certain subjects or situations. For instance, *pollution* is a word you expect to find in a book on ecology. Read the book titles below. Match each title with a word from the list that you would expect to find in the book. On a sheet of paper, write the matching word next to the title.

1. *Quarks and the Physics of the Atom*

2. *The Latest Fashion Look: Worn and Wrinkled*

3. *A Spy Tells His Story*

4. *The Life of Oscar the Grouch*

5. *How to Be a Great Public Speaker*

Options for Learning

1 • **"Go On with Us or Die"** This selection contains a dramatic scene in which one fugitive wants to turn back. With several classmates, take the roles of the fearful slave, the narrator, and Harriet Tubman. Give a readers' theater presentation of this scene.

2 • **Alias Moses** Create a wanted poster that advertises a reward for the capture and return of Harriet Tubman. To get ideas, look at the wanted posters in your local post office and research other books about Harriet Tubman. Be sure to include a good sketch and a detailed description of "Moses."

3 • **All Aboard** Pick one aspect of the Underground Railroad that interests you, such as the routes, the conductors, or the stations. Research the topic and prepare an oral report for your class.

4 • **Follow the North Star** Plan a walking trip from Dorchester County, Maryland, to St. Catharines, Ontario, in Canada. Research temperatures and elevations to determine the best time of year to travel. Find information about the most suitable trails and roads. Study maps. Figure out how many miles a day you could cover, where you might stay, and how much your trip might cost.

 FACT FINDER HISTORY

Approximately how many slaves did Harriet Tubman help to escape?

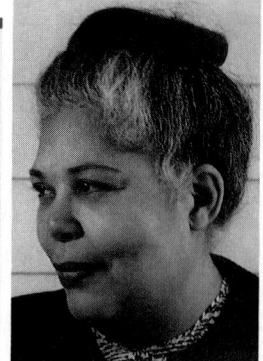

*A***nn Petry**
1912–

Ann Petry grew up in Old Saybrook, Connecticut, where her family owned a drugstore. She trained as a pharmacist, graduating from the College of Pharmacy at the University of Connecticut. This background later inspired Petry to write a children's book called *The Drugstore Cat.*

Petry also worked as an ad saleswoman and a newspaper reporter and editor before she embarked on a successful career of writing novels and short stories. Her first book was *The Street,* a novel about life in a Harlem ghetto. She wrote several novels for young people, including *Tituba of Salem Village* and *Legends of the Saints.* Petry wrote *Harriet Tubman: Conductor on the Underground Railroad* because of her belief that "the majority of textbooks used in high schools do not give an adequate or accurate picture of the history of slavery in the United States."

Fiction

A Cap for Steve

MORLEY CALLAGHAN

Examine What You Know

You recognized your favorite star at the airport, and you asked for an autograph. The star smiled and gave you the autograph, writing it on the back of your T-shirt. Now you are in seventh heaven, and you never want to take off your shirt. Your parents think you are crazy.

Imagine that you have a prized memento of a celebrity. In your journal or on a sheet of paper, write answers to the following questions:

- What did you have to go through to get this memento?

- Do others feel it's as valuable as you think it is? Explain.

- Under what circumstances and for what price would you sell it?

Expand Your Knowledge

Fans, such as the young boy in this story, have always sought souvenirs of their favorite celebrities. In recent times certain celebrity mementos have become valuable collector's items. Can you believe that one rare old baseball card sold for almost half a million dollars? Traditionally, most stars have been glad to oblige their fans with an autograph. Today, however, an eager fan might have to pay for a hero's autograph. In 1992, an all-star outfielder signed a thousand autographs at a baseball-card show in Morristown, New Jersey. Fans who had already paid $4 for admission to the show spent an extra $25 to get the slugger's signature.

Write Before You Read

Use your answers to the questions in Examine What You Know as a starting point for writing about a prized possession. Think about these questions: Why does this object mean so much to you? What is its actual worth? What is its emotional significance? Write in your journal or on a sheet of paper.

■ *Author biography in Reader's Handbook*

A Cap for Steve

MORLEY CALLAGHAN

Dave Diamond, a poor man, a carpenter's assistant, was a small, wiry, quick-tempered individual who had learned how to make every dollar count in his home. His wife, Anna, had been sick a lot, and his twelve-year-old son, Steve, had to be kept in school. Steve, a big-eyed, shy kid, ought to have known the value of money as well as Dave did. It had been ground into him.

But the boy was crazy about baseball, and after school, when he could have been working as a delivery boy or selling papers, he played ball with the kids. His failure to appreciate that the family needed a few extra dollars disgusted Dave. Around the house he wouldn't let Steve talk about baseball, and he scowled when he saw him hurrying off with his glove after dinner.

Steve . . . ought to have known the value of money.

When the Phillies[1] came to town to play an exhibition game with the home team and Steve pleaded to be taken to the ball park,

Dave, of course, was outraged. Steve knew they couldn't afford it. But he had got his mother on his side. Finally Dave made a bargain with them. He said that if Steve came home after school and worked hard helping to make some kitchen shelves, he would take him that night to the ball park.

Steve worked hard, but Dave was still resentful. They had to coax him to put on his good suit. When they started out Steve held <u>aloof</u>, feeling guilty, and they walked down the street like strangers; then Dave glanced at Steve's face and, half-ashamed, took his arm more cheerfully.

As the game went on, Dave had to listen to Steve's recitation of the batting average of every Philly that stepped up to the plate; the time the boy must have wasted learning these averages began to appall him. He showed it so plainly that Steve felt guilty again and was silent.

After the game Dave let Steve drag him onto the field to keep him company while he tried to get some autographs from the Philly players, who were being hemmed in by

---

1. **Phillies:** the major-league baseball team located in Philadelphia, Pennsylvania.

Words to Know and Use

aloof (ə lo͞of') *adj.* distant and uninvolved

BIRDIE TEBBETTS PUTS THE TAG ON BILL BAKER   1978   Lance Richbourg   Courtesy of the artist.

gangs of kids blocking the way to the club-house. But Steve, who was shy, let the other kids block him off from the players. Steve would push his way in, get blocked out, and come back to stand mournfully beside Dave. And Dave grew impatient. He was wasting valuable time. He wanted to get home; Steve knew it and was worried.

Then the big, blond Philly outfielder, Eddie Condon, who had been held up by a gang of kids tugging at his arm and thrust-ing their score cards at him, broke loose and

made a run for the clubhouse. He was jos-tled, and his blue cap with the red peak, tilted far back on his head, fell off. It fell at Steve's feet, and Steve stooped quickly and grabbed it. "OK, son," the outfielder called, turning back. But Steve, holding the hat in both hands, only stared at him.

"Give him his cap, Steve," Dave said, smiling apologetically at the big outfielder, who towered over them. But Steve drew the hat closer to his chest. In an awed trance he looked up at big Eddie Condon. It was an embarrassing moment. All the other kids were watching. Some shouted. "Give him his cap."

"My cap, son," Eddie Condon said, his hand out.

"Hey, Steve," Dave said, and he gave him a shake. But he had to jerk the cap out of Steve's hands.

"Here you are," he said.

The outfielder, noticing Steve's white, worshiping face and pleading eyes, grinned and then shrugged. "Aw, let him keep it," he said.

"No, Mister Condon, you don't need to do that," Steve protested.

"It's happened before. Forget it," Eddie Condon said, and he trotted away to the clubhouse.

Dave handed the cap to Steve; envious kids circled around them, and Steve said, "He said I could keep it, Dad. You heard him, didn't you?"

"Yeah, I heard him," Dave admitted. The wonder in Steve's face made him smile. He took the boy by the arm, and they hurried off the field.

On the way home Dave couldn't get him to talk about the game; he couldn't get him to take his eyes off the cap. Steve could hardly believe in his own happiness. "See," he said suddenly, and he showed Dave that Eddie Condon's name was printed on the sweatband. Then he went on dreaming. Finally he put the cap on his head and turned to Dave with a slow, proud smile. The cap was way too big for him; it fell down over his ears. "Never mind," Dave said. "You can get your mother to take a tuck in the back."

When they got home Dave was tired, and his wife didn't understand the cap's impor-

tance, and they couldn't get Steve to go to bed. He swaggered around wearing the cap and looking in the mirror every ten minutes. He took the cap to bed with him.

Dave and his wife had a cup of coffee in the kitchen, and Dave told her again how they had got the cap. They agreed that their boy must have an attractive quality that showed in his face, and that Eddie Condon must have been drawn to him—why else would he have singled Steve out from all the kids?

But Dave got tired of the fuss Steve made over that cap and of the way he wore it from the time he got up in the morning until the time he went to bed. Some kid was always coming in, wanting to try on the cap. It was childish, Dave said, for Steve to go around assuming that the cap made him important in the neighborhood and to keep telling them how he had become a leader in the park a few blocks away where he played ball in the evenings. And Dave wouldn't stand for Steve's keeping the cap on while he was eating. He was always scolding his wife for accepting Steve's explanation that he'd forgotten he had it on. Just the same, it was remarkable what a little thing like a ball cap could do for a kid, Dave admitted to his wife as he smiled to himself.

One night Steve was late coming home from the park. Dave didn't realize how late it was until he put down his newspaper and watched his wife at the window. Her restlessness got on his nerves. "See what comes from encouraging the boy to hang around with those park loafers," he said. "I don't encourage him," she protested. "You do," he insisted irritably, for he was really worried now. A gang hung around the park until midnight. It was a bad park. It was true that on one side there was a good district with fine, expensive apartment houses, but the kids from that neighborhood left the park to the kids from the poorer homes. When his wife went out and walked down to the corner, it was his turn to wait and worry and watch at the open window. Each waiting moment tortured him. At last he heard his wife's voice and Steve's voice, and he relaxed and sighed; then he remembered his duty and rushed angrily to meet them.

*H*e alone recognized the cap's value.

"I'll fix you, Steve, once and for all," he said. "I'll show you you can't start coming into the house at midnight."

"Hold your horses, Dave," his wife said. "Can't you see the state he's in?" Steve looked utterly exhausted and beaten.

"What's the matter?" Dave asked quickly.

"I lost my cap," Steve whispered; he walked past his father and threw himself on the couch in the livingroom and lay with his face hidden.

"Now, don't scold him, Dave," his wife said.

"Scold him. Who's scolding him?" Dave asked indignantly. "It's his cap, not mine. If it's not worth his while to hang on to it, why should I scold him?" But he was implying resentfully that he alone recognized the cap's value.

"So you are scolding him," his wife said. "It's his cap. Not yours. What happened, Steve?"

Steve told them he had been playing ball, and he found that when he ran the bases, the cap fell off; it was still too big despite the tuck his mother had taken in the band. So the next time he came to bat, he tucked the cap in his hip pocket. Someone had lifted it, he was sure.

"And he didn't even know whether it was still in his pocket," Dave said sarcastically.

"I wasn't careless, Dad," Steve said. For the last three hours he had been wandering around to the homes of the kids who had been in the park at the time; he wanted to go on, but he was too tired. Dave knew the boy was apologizing to him, but he didn't know why it made him angry.

"If he didn't hang on to it, it's not worth worrying about now," he said, and he sounded offended.

An official Phillies cap used between 1947 and 1949.

193

After that night they knew that Steve didn't go to the park to play ball; he went to look for the cap. It irritated Dave to see him sit around listlessly or walk in circles, trying to force his memory to find a particular incident which would suddenly recall to him the moment when the cap had been taken. It was no attitude for a growing, healthy boy to take, Dave complained. He told Steve firmly once and for all that he didn't want to hear any more about the cap.

One night two weeks later, Dave was walking home with Steve from the shoemaker's. It was a hot night. When they passed an ice cream parlor, Steve slowed down. "I guess I couldn't have a soda, could I?" Steve said. "Nothing doing," Dave said firmly. "Come on now," he added as Steve hung back, looking in the window.

"Dad, look!" Steve cried suddenly, pointing at the window. "My cap! There's my cap! He's coming out!"

A well-dressed boy was leaving the ice cream parlor; he had on a blue ball cap with a red peak, just like Steve's cap. "Hey, you!" Steve cried, and he rushed at the boy, his small face fierce and his eyes wild. Before the boy could back away, Steve had snatched the cap from his head. "That's my cap!" he shouted.

"What's this?" the bigger boy said. "Hey, give me my cap, or I'll give you a poke on the nose."

Dave was surprised that his own shy boy did not back away. He watched him clutch the cap in his left hand, half crying with

excitement as he put his head down and drew back his right fist: he was willing to fight. And Dave was proud of him.

"Wait, now," Dave said. "Take it easy, son," he said to the other boy, who refused to back away.

"My boy says it's his cap," Dave said.

"Well, he's crazy. It's my cap."

"I was with him when he got this cap. When the Phillies played here. It's a Philly cap."

"Eddie Condon gave it to me," Steve said. "And you stole it from me, you jerk."

"Don't call me a jerk, you little squirt. I never saw you before in my life."

"Look," Steve said, pointing to the printing on the cap's sweatband. "It's Eddie Condon's cap. See? See, Dad?"

"Yeah. You're right, son. Ever see this boy before, Steve?"

"No," Steve said reluctantly.

The other boy realized he might lose the cap. "I bought it from a guy," he said. "I paid him. My father knows I paid him." He said he got the cap at the ball park. He groped for some magically impressive words and suddenly found them. "You'll have to speak to my father," he said.

"Sure, I'll speak to your father," Dave said. "What's your name? Where do you live?"

"My name's Hudson. I live about ten minutes away on the other side of the park." The boy appraised Dave, who wasn't any bigger than he was and who wore a faded blue windbreaker and no tie. "My father is a lawyer," he said boldly. "He wouldn't let me keep the cap if he didn't think I should."

Words to Know and Use | **reluctantly** (ri luk′ tənt lē) *adv.* unwillingly
appraise (ə prāz′) *v.* to judge the worth or significance of

"Is that a fact?" Dave asked belligerently. "Well, we'll see. Come on. Let's go." And he got between the two boys, and they walked along the street. They didn't talk to each other. Dave knew the Hudson boy was waiting to get to the protection of his home, and Steve knew it, too, and he looked up apprehensively at Dave. And Dave, reaching for his hand, squeezed it encouragingly and strode along, cocky and belligerent, knowing that Steve relied on him.

No one's putting anything over on us.

The Hudson boy lived in that row of fine apartment houses on the other side of the park. At the entrance to one of these houses, Dave tried not to hang back and show he was impressed, because he could feel Steve hanging back. When they got into the small elevator, Dave didn't know why he took off his hat. In the carpeted hall on the fourth floor, the Hudson boy said, "Just a minute," and entered his own apartment. Dave and Steve were left alone in the corridor, knowing that the other boy was preparing his father for the encounter. Steve looked anxiously at his father, and Dave said, "Don't worry, son," and he added resolutely, "No one's putting anything over on us."

A tall, balding man in a brown velvet smoking jacket suddenly opened the door. Dave had never seen a man wearing one of those jackets, although he had seen them in department store windows. "Good evening," he said, making a deprecatory[2] gesture at the cap Steve still clutched tightly in his left hand. "My boy didn't get your name. My name is Hudson."

"Mine's Diamond."

"Come on in," Mr. Hudson said, putting out his hand and laughing good-naturedly. He led Dave and Steve into his livingroom. "What's this about that cap?" he asked. "The way kids can get excited about a cap. Well, it's understandable, isn't it?"

"So it is," Dave said, moving closer to Steve, who was awed by the broadloom rug[3] and the fine furniture. He wanted to show Steve he was at ease himself, and he wished Mr. Hudson wouldn't be so polite. That meant Dave had to be polite and affable, too, and it was hard to manage when he was standing in the middle of the floor in his old windbreaker.

"Sit down, Mr. Diamond," Mr. Hudson said. Dave took Steve's arm and sat him down beside him on the chesterfield.[4] The Hudson boy watched his father. And Dave looked at Steve and saw that he wouldn't face Mr. Hudson or the other boy; he kept looking up at Dave, putting all his faith in him.

"Well, Mr. Diamond, from what I gathered from my boy, you're able to prove this cap belonged to your boy."

"That's a fact," Dave said.

---

2. **deprecatory** (dep′ rə kə tôr′ ē): belittling.
3. **broadloom rug:** a woven woolen carpet.
4. **chesterfield:** a heavily stuffed sofa with upright armrests.

Words to Know and Use | **belligerently** (bə lij′ ər ənt lē) *adv.* in a combative way

"Mr. Diamond, you'll have to believe my boy bought that cap from some kid in good faith."

"I don't doubt it," Dave said. "But no kid can sell something that doesn't belong to him. You know that's a fact, Mr. Hudson."

"Yes, that's a fact," Mr. Hudson agreed. "But that cap means a lot to my boy, Mr. Diamond."

"It means a lot to my boy, too, Mr. Hudson."

Sure it does. But supposing we called in a policeman. You know what he'd say? He'd ask you if you were willing to pay my boy what he paid for the cap. That's usually the way it works out," Mr. Hudson said, friendly and smiling, as he eyed Dave shrewdly.

"But that's not right. It's not justice," Dave protested. "Not when it's my boy's cap."

"I know it isn't right. But that's what they do."

"All right. What did you say your boy paid for the cap?" Dave said reluctantly.

"Two dollars."

"Two dollars!" Dave repeated. Mr. Hudson's smile was still kindly, but his eyes were shrewd, and Dave knew the lawyer was counting on his not having the two dollars; Mr. Hudson thought he had Dave sized up; he had looked at him and decided he was broke. Dave's pride was hurt, and he turned to Steve. What he saw in Steve's face was more powerful than the hurt to his pride: it was the memory of how difficult it had been to get an extra nickel, the talk he heard about the cost of food, the worry in his mother's face as she tried to make ends meet, and the bewildered embarrassment that he was here in a rich man's home,

forcing his father to confess that he couldn't afford to spend two dollars. Then Dave grew angry and reckless. "I'll give you the two dollars," he said.

Steve looked at the Hudson boy and grinned brightly. The Hudson boy watched his father.

"I suppose that's fair enough," Mr. Hudson said. "A cap like this can be worth a lot to a kid. You know how it is. Your boy might want to sell—I mean be satisfied. Would he take five dollars for it?"

"Five dollars?" Dave repeated. "Is it worth five dollars, Steve?" he asked uncertainly.

Steve shook his head and looked frightened.

"No, thanks, Mr. Hudson," Dave said firmly.

"I'll tell you what I'll do," Mr. Hudson said. "I'll give you ten dollars. The cap has a sentimental value for my boy, a Philly cap, a big-leaguer's cap. It's only worth about a buck and a half, really," he added. But Dave shook his head again. Mr. Hudson frowned. He looked at his own boy with indulgent concern, but now he was embarrassed. "I'll tell you what I'll do," he said. "This cap—well, it's worth as much as a day at the circus to my boy. Your boy should be recompensed.[5] I want to be fair. Here's twenty dollars," and he held out two ten-dollar bills to Dave.

That much money for a cap, Dave thought, and his eyes brightened. But he knew what the cap had meant to Steve; to deprive him of it now that it was within his reach would be unbearable. All the things

---

5. **recompensed** (rek′ əm penst′): paid to make up for a loss.

he needed in his life gathered around him; his wife was there, saying he couldn't afford to reject the offer, he had no right to do it; and he turned to Steve to see if Steve thought it wonderful that the cap could bring them twenty dollars.

"What do you say, Steve?" he asked uneasily.

"I don't know," Steve said. He was in a trance. When Dave smiled, Steve smiled too, and Dave believed that Steve was as impressed as he was, only more bewildered, and maybe even more aware that they could not possibly turn away that much money for a ball cap.

"Well, here you are," Mr. Hudson said, and he put the two bills in Steve's hand. "It's a lot of money. But I guess you had a right to expect as much."

With a dazed, fixed smile Steve handed the money slowly to his father, and his face was white.

Laughing jovially, Mr. Hudson led them to the door. His own boy followed a few paces behind.

I n the elevator Dave took the bills out of his pocket. "See, Stevie," he whispered eagerly. "That windbreaker you wanted! And ten dollars for your bank! Won't Mother be surprised?"

"Yeah," Steve whispered, the little smile still on his face. But Dave had to turn away quickly so their eyes wouldn't meet, for he saw that it was a scared smile.

Outside, Dave said, "Here, you carry the money home, Steve. You show it to your mother."

"No, you keep it," Steve said, and then there was nothing to say. They walked in silence.

"It's a lot of money," Dave said finally. When Steve didn't answer him, he added angrily, "I turned to you, Steve. I asked you, didn't I?"

"That man knew how much his boy wanted that cap," Steve said.

"Sure. But he recognized how much it was worth to us."

"No, you let him take it away from us," Steve blurted.

"That's unfair," Dave said. "Don't dare say that to me."

"I don't want to be like you," Steve muttered, and he darted across the road and walked along on the other side of the street.

"It's unfair," Dave said angrily, only now he didn't mean that Steve was unfair, he meant that what had happened in the prosperous Hudson home was unfair, and he didn't know quite why. He had been trapped, not just by Mr. Hudson, but by his own life. Across the road Steve was hurrying along with his head down, wanting to be alone. They walked most of the way home on opposite sides of the street, until Dave could stand it no longer. "Steve," he called, crossing the street. "It was very unfair. I mean, for you to say . . ." but Steve started to run. Dave walked as fast as he could, and Steve was getting beyond him, and he felt enraged, and suddenly he yelled, "Steve!" and he started to chase his son. He wanted to get hold of Steve and pound him, and he didn't know why. He gained on him, he gasped for breath, and he almost got him by the shoulder. Turning, Steve saw his father's face in the street light and was terrified; he circled away, got to the house, and rushed in, yelling, "Mother!"

"Son, son!" she cried, rushing from the kitchen. As soon as she threw her arms

Illustration © 1991 Greg
Spalenka/The Image Bank.

around Steve, shielding him, Dave's anger left him and he felt stupid. He walked past them into the kitchen.

"What happened?" she asked anxiously. "Have you both gone crazy? What did you do, Steve?"

"Nothing," he said sullenly.

"What did your father do?"

"We found the boy with my ball cap, and he let the boy's father take it from us."

"No, no," Dave protested. "Nobody pushed us around. The man didn't put anything over us." He felt tired, and his face was burning. He told what had happened;

*Words
to Know
and Use*

sullenly (sul′ ən lē) *adv.* in a sulky, resentful way

then he slowly took the two ten-dollar bills out of his wallet and tossed them on the table and looked up guiltily at his wife.

It hurt him that she didn't pick up the money and that she didn't rebuke him. "It is a lot of money, son," she said slowly. "Your father was only trying to do what he knew was right, and it'll work out, and you'll understand." She was soothing Steve, but Dave knew she felt that she needed to be gentle with him, too, and he was ashamed.

When she went with Steve to his bedroom, Dave sat by himself. His son had contempt for him, he thought. His son, for the first time, had seen how easy it was for another man to handle him, and he had judged him and had wanted to walk alone on the other side of the street. He looked at the money, and he hated the sight of it.

His wife returned to the kitchen, made a cup of tea, talked soothingly, and said it was incredible that he had forced the Hudson man to pay him twenty dollars for the cap, but all Dave could think of was, Steve was scared of me.

Finally, he got up and went into Steve's room. The room was in darkness, but he could see the outline of Steve's body on the bed, and he sat down beside him and whispered, "Look, son, it was a mistake. I know why. People like us—in circumstances where money can scare us. No, no," he said, feeling ashamed and shaking his head apologetically; he was taking the wrong way of showing the boy they were together; he was covering up his own failure. For the failure had been his, and it had come out of being so separated from his son that he had been blind to what was beyond the price in a boy's life. He longed now to show Steve he could be with him from day to day. His hand went out hesitantly to Steve's shoulder. "Steve, look," he said eagerly. "The trouble was I didn't realize how much I enjoyed it that night at the ball park. If I had watched you playing for your own team—the kids around here say you could be a great pitcher. We could take that money and buy a new pitcher's glove for you, and a catcher's mitt. Steve, Steve, are you listening? I could catch you, work with you in the lane. Maybe I could be your coach . . . watch you become a great pitcher." In the half-darkness he could see the boy's pale face turn to him.

Steve, who had never heard his father talk like this, was shy and wondering. All he knew was that his father, for the first time, wanted to be with him in his hopes and adventures. He said, "I guess you do know how important that cap was." His hand went out to his father's arm. "With that man the cap was—well, it was just something he could buy, eh, Dad?" Dave gripped his son's hand hard. The wonderful generosity of childhood—the price a boy was willing to pay to be able to count on his father's admiration and approval—made him feel humble, then strangely exalted. ❧

Words to Know and Use

contempt (kən tempt') *n.* a feeling of scorn and disgust
humble (hum' bəl) *adj.* not proud; modest
exalted (eg zôlt' id) *adj.* uplifted; elated **exalt** *v.*

*R*esponding to Reading

First Impressions

1. How do you feel about the deal Steve's father made with Mr. Hudson?

Second Thoughts

2. If you were Steve and your father asked you whether to accept the money for the cap, what would you say?

3. Why do you think Mr. Diamond often seems so angry about Steve's obsession with baseball and the cap?

4. Compare and contrast the two fathers, Mr. Hudson and Mr. Diamond.

   Think about
   • their feelings toward their sons
   • the examples they set for their sons
   • their social and economic status

5. Why do you think Dave Diamond hates the sight of the twenty dollars after he and Steve come home from the Hudsons'?

6. How do you think the relationship between Steve and Dave changes during the story? How do you think they will get along in the future?

Broader Connections

7. According to property law, a stolen item that is sold still belongs to its original owner. However, in disputes like the one in the story, the police are seldom brought into the situation; people handle such disputes among themselves. What would you do if you found that you had bought something that actually belonged to someone else?

*L*iterary Concepts: Elements of a Short Story

Many short stories share certain **elements. Characters** participate in a story's action. That action occurs in a particular time and place, called the **setting.** The story's characters face one or more **conflicts** in a series of events that make up the **plot.** The story's plot reaches a peak, or **climax,** in which a crucial event occurs. At the end of the story, there may be a **resolution,** a scene that resolves remaining questions. Identify each of these elements in "A Cap for Steve."

Writing Options

1. Imagine that when Steve Diamond is thirty years old, he is a top professional baseball player. Write an **informative paragraph** for the back of his baseball card. Include his biographical information.

2. Think about a time when your parent or guardian stood up for you—or a time when he or she failed to come through for you. Write a **personal narrative** that tells about this experience.

3. Imagine that years later Steve Diamond and Mr. Hudson's son go off to college. Each father writes his son a letter, giving advice and words of wisdom. Write the **letters** these two fathers would send.

4. Write an **essay,** comparing Steve and his father with the father and son in "The Banana Tree." Explain how the father and son in each story become closer.

Vocabulary Practice

Exercise A   Write the letter of the word that is most nearly *opposite* in meaning to the capitalized word.

1. INDIGNANTLY: (a) angrily   (b) slowly   (c) badly   (d) happily

2. ALOOF: (a) friendly   (b) wounded   (c) standoffish   (d) alarmed

3. EXALTED: (a) excellent   (b) fast   (c) sad   (d) excited

4. BELLIGERENTLY: (a) badly   (b) peacefully   (c) comically   (d) combatively

5. SULLENLY: (a) sneakily   (b) resentfully   (c) cheerfully   (d) suddenly

> *Words to Know and Use*
>
> **aloof**
> **appraise**
> **belligerently**
> **contempt**
> **exalted**
> **humble**
> **imply**
> **indignantly**
> **reluctantly**
> **sullenly**

Exercise B   Write the word from the list that is most clearly related to the situation described.

1. The young boy looked fearfully at the strong-armed pitcher. The boy got a bat and moved slowly, haltingly toward the plate.

2. Though Bart had been the top home-run hitter for three years, he never let his success go to his head. He remained modest.

3. The collector looked at both sides of the baseball card to determine its worth.

4. The owner never actually said that she would fire the team's manager, but her comments suggested that the manager had to go.

5. Many of the fans hated the owner for trading the team's best player. At the games they treated the owner with scorn.

Poetry

Pole Vault
SHIRO MURANO

400-Meter Freestyle
MAXINE W. KUMIN

Examine What You Know

Though pole-vaulting and swimming are both competitive sports, each one requires a different kind of training and set of skills. What do you know about each sport? Make a Venn diagram like the one below. In the left oval write several words or phrases that describe pole-vaulting; in the right oval write several words or phrases that describe swimming. In the overlapping area of the two ovals, write some words or phrases that apply to both sports.

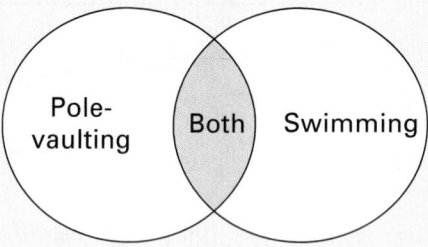

Expand Your Knowledge

A pole-vaulter sprints at full speed toward the crossbar, plants a twelve-foot to sixteen-foot flexible fiberglass pole in the takeoff box, rises into a handstand as the pole straightens, and then swings his or her body up and over the crossbar. After clearing the bar, a vaulter releases the pole and falls as much as twenty feet back to the ground.

Competitive swimmers must swim at maximum speed up and down the length of a pool. In a 400-meter freestyle, competitors swim the length of a 25-meter pool sixteen times, somersaulting quickly to turn at the end of each length.

Enrich Your Reading

Concrete Poetry In **concrete poetry,** typography—the arrangement of words on a page—is used to make the poem look like or suggest a particular subject. As you read the concrete poem "400-Meter Freestyle," think about why the poet chose to write it in its particular design.

■ *Author biography in Reader's Handbook*

Pole Vault

SHIRO MURANO

He is running like a wasp,
Hanging on a long pole.
As a matter of course he floats in the sky,
Chasing the ascending horizon.
5 Now he has crossed the limit,
And pushed away his support.
For him there is nothing but a descent.
Oh, he falls helplessly.
Now on that runner, awkwardly fallen on the ground,
10 Once more
The horizon comes down,
Beating hard on his shoulders.

Responding to Reading

First Impressions of "Pole Vault"

1. What images, or pictures, in the poem stand out in your mind?
Describe or sketch your favorite image in your journal or on paper.

Second Thoughts on "Pole Vault"

2. Why do you think the speaker compares the pole vaulter to a wasp?

3. What other words or images could you use to describe a pole vault?

4. What do you think the horizon represents for the vaulter in this poem?

Think about
- the meanings of the terms *ascending horizon, limit,* and
  support
- what "The horizon comes down" means
- dictionary definitions of *horizon* as "the apparent junction of
  earth and sky" or "something that might be attained"

400-Meter Freestyle

MAXINE W. KUMIN

THE GUN full swing the swimmer catapults[1] and cracks

        s
        i
        x

5   feet away onto that perfect glass he catches at

a
n
d

throws behind him scoop after scoop cunningly moving

10   t
               h
               e

water back to move him forward. Thrift is his wonderful

s

15   e

c

ret; he has schooled out all extravagance. No muscle

               r
               i

20   p

ples without compensation wrist cock to heel snap[2] to

h
i
s

25   mobile mouth that siphons in the air that nurtures

               h
               i
               m

at half an inch above sea level so to speak.

---

1. catapults (kat′ ə pults′): leaps outward.

2. wrist cock to heel snap: the tilting of the wrist to the
abrupt upward movement of the heel.

30   T

      h

      e

astonishing whites of the soles of his feet rise

                                                     a

35   n

                                                   d

salute us on the turns. He flips, converts, and is gone

    a

    l

40   l

in one. We watch him for signs. His arms are steady at

                                                    t

                                                 h

                                                 e

45 catch, his cadent[3] feet tick in the stretch, they know

    t

  h

    e

lesson well. Lungs know, too; he does not list[4] for

50   a

                                                 i

                                               r

he drives along on little sips carefully expended

    b

55 u

    t

that plum red heart pumps hard cries hurt how soon

                                                   i

                                                 t

60   s

near one more and makes its final surge TIME: 4:25:9

---

3. **cadent** (kād′ ′nt): having a regular, rhythmic movement.
4. **list:** lean to the side.

E X P L A I N

*R*esponding *to Reading*

First Impressions of "400-Meter Freestyle"

1. What words or phrases in this poem stick with you the most?

Second Thoughts on "400-Meter Freestyle"

2. Would you enjoy this poem more or less if it were written in traditional stanzas? Why?

Comparing the Poems

3. Look back at the Venn diagram you constructed for Examine What You Know. In what ways is each poem like the sport it describes?

4. Which poem do you like better? Why?

*L*iterary *Concept: Imagery*

Imagery consists of words and phrases that appeal to the reader's senses. Most imagery appeals to the sense of sight, but imagery can appeal to other senses as well. Careful word choice enables a poet to create fresh and striking images, such as Kumin's "plum red heart" and Murano's "running like a wasp." Note at least one other example of imagery in each poem.

Concept Review: Simile   Have you ever said, "My hair feels like straw" or "He's as big as a house"? Each of those expressions is a **simile**—a comparison of unlike things by means of words such as *like, as, than,* or *resembles.* As you know, poets frequently use similes to convey things more vividly. Find the simile in "Pole Vault."

*W*riting *Options*

1. Take another look to see how "400-Meter Freestyle" represents a swimming race. Now rewrite "Pole Vault" as a **concrete poem.**

2. Choose a sport that you enjoy watching or playing, and write your own **poem** about it. If you like, you can use your poem to explain how the game is played or how a particular move in it should be executed.

Elements of
Elements of
DRAMA

Have you watched any good movies lately? If you have, you are already familiar with drama. A **drama,** or **play,** is a form of literature that is performed for an audience, either on stage or before a camera. We can see drama on television, in movies, in videos, and on stage. Occasionally we listen to drama in the form of radio plays, which were a very popular form of entertainment before the coming of television.

The elements of drama are similar to the elements of fiction. Like fiction, drama usually tells a story with characters, plot, and setting. Unlike fiction, drama is written to be performed for an audience. For this reason, drama is written in a special form called a **script,** in which lines are written out for the characters to speak. The script has various parts, which are described below.

Understanding Drama

Cast of Characters   A script usually begins with a list of the characters in the play presented in the order of their appearance. Often a short description appears next to a character's name.

Dialogue   A play consists almost entirely of dialogue—conversation between the characters. Both the plot of the play and the characters' personalities are revealed through dialogue. The dialogue appears in lines next to the characters' names, as in this example from *The Million-Pound Bank Note,* page 212:

Henry. I'd like to discuss the matter.

Gordon. There is nothing to discuss at the moment.

Henry. Is this a joke?

Abel. Not at all. And now good day.

Gordon. And good luck.

Stage Directions   In addition to dialogue, a play includes instructions for the director, the performers, and the stage crew. These are called stage directions and are printed in italics in this book; often they are also enclosed in parentheses. Most stage directions tell actors how to speak or move. Many stage directions describe **sound effects.** These directions are especially important in radio plays, in which the success of the play depends entirely on dialogue and sound.

Stage directions also describe the **scenery**—all the decorations on stage that help create the setting. Some stage directions describe **props**—the objects that actors need during the play. Notice how these stage directions from *Rip Van Winkle,* page 344, tell the actor what to do and what props to use.

Rip *(hesitating).* I don't know. Dame Van Winkle sent me for a bucket of water, but—maybe *one* game. *(He sets down the bucket and draws a stool up to the table as* Vanderdonk *rises.)*

Acts and Scenes The action of a play is sometimes divided into scenes. A scene changes whenever the setting—time, place, or both time and place—changes. Sometimes scenes are grouped into acts. In *The Diary of Anne Frank*, pages 493–571, ten scenes are grouped into two acts.

Strategies for Reading Drama

1. **Read the play silently.** Before you try to read the play aloud, read it to yourself. You need to know the entire plot and understand the characters before you can perform the play.

2. **Figure out what is happening.** When you watch a movie, it usually takes you a while to understand exactly what the movie is about. The same is true when you read a play. Since the plot and the characters are revealed through dialogue, you will need to read several pages to understand what is happening.

3. **Read the stage directions carefully.** If you were watching a drama on stage or on television, you would see the action and the scenery. When you read a drama, you have to imagine both. The stage directions tell exactly where and when each scene is happening and help you visualize the action. If you skip over the stage directions, you will miss important information.

4. **Get to know the characters.** Drama does not contain descriptions of characters and their personalities. You get to know the characters through dialogue—through the characters' own words and actions and through what others say to and about them. Analyze the characters' words carefully and try to discover the feelings behind them, just as if you were reading fiction.

5. **Keep track of the plot.** As in fiction, the plot in drama centers around a main conflict. Look for the conflict and let yourself become involved in the story. Watch for the action to build to a climax, and evaluate how the conflict is resolved.

6. **Read the play aloud with others.** When drama is performed, it takes on a whole new aspect; it becomes almost like real life. When you read the part of a character, you become an actor. You will play the part differently than anyone else because you bring your own interpretation to the role. Let yourself "get into" the part and become that character for a while. React to what other characters say and do. Be ready with your character's lines and read only the words your character says. Do not read the stage directions aloud. You may find that you really enjoy playing the part of someone different from yourself.

Drama

The *Million-Pound Bank Note*

MARK TWAIN
Dramatized by WALTER A. HACKETT

Examine What You Know

Unsure of who your visitor may be, you slowly open your front door. The unfamiliar face that greets you belongs to a messenger for an express mail service. The slim envelope she hands you contains a money order with your name on it. The number on the money order is a one followed by six zeros. Congratulations—you have just won a million dollars! What will you do with all that money? How much will you spend, and how much will you save? How do you think your life will change? Discuss your answers with your classmates.

Expand Your Knowledge

The million-pound bank note referred to in this play was worth 5 million dollars when Mark Twain first published his short story in 1893. Today, however, a British pound is worth less than two dollars in U.S. currency.

Another denomination mentioned in the play is a shilling. A shilling used to be worth one twentieth of a pound, so two shillings would have equaled a tenth of a pound, or fifty cents, in 1893.

Enrich Your Reading

Predicting Predicting what will happen next as you read helps keep your interest high. Sometimes your predictions will be confirmed, but at other times you will enjoy the pleasure of surprise. Read the title *The Million-Pound Bank Note* and the first section of the play, up to Hastings's line "Very well, but I know you're making a mistake, Henry" on page 211. What do you think might happen next? Jot your ideas in your journal or on a sheet of paper.

■ *Author biography on Extend page*

The Million-Pound Bank Note

MARK TWAIN
Dramatized by WALTER A. HACKETT

Henry. When I was twenty-seven years old, I was a mining broker's[1] clerk in San Francisco. I was alone in the world and had nothing to depend upon but my wits and a clean reputation. These were setting my feet in the road to eventual fortune, and I was content with the prospect. During my spare time, I did outside work. One of my part-time employers was Lloyd Hastings, a mining broker. During this period, I was helping Hastings to verify the Gould and Curry Extension papers, covering what seemed to be a highly valuable gold mine. One morning at two, after six hard hours of work on these papers, Lloyd Hastings and I went to the What Cheer restaurant in Frisco.[2] As we lingered over our coffee, he offered me a proposition.

Hastings. Henry, how would you like to go to London?

Henry. Thank you, no.

Hastings. Listen to me. I'm thinking of taking a month's option on the Gould and Curry Extension for the locators.

Henry. And—?

Hastings. They want one million dollars for it.

Henry. Not too much—if the claim works out the way it appears it may.

Hastings. I'm going to try to sell it to London interests, which means a trip there, and I want you to go with me because you know more about these papers than I.

Henry. No, thanks.

Hastings. I'll make it well worth your while. I'll pay all your expenses and give you something over if I make the sale.

Henry. I have a job.

Hastings. I'll arrange for you to get a leave of absence. What do you say?

Henry. No.

Hastings. Why?

Henry. If I go to London, I'll get out of touch with my work and with mining conditions here, and that means months getting the hang of things again.

---

1. **mining broker:** a person who acts as an agent in the buying and selling of mineral rights.
2. **Frisco:** short for "San Francisco."

Hastings. That's a pretty slim excuse, Henry.

Henry. More important, perhaps, I think you're doomed to failure.

Hastings. But you just said the claim is valuable.

Henry. It may well turn out that way, but right now its real value can't be proved. And even so, a month's option may leave you too little time to sell it; unless you sell it within the option time, you'll go stone broke.

Hastings. I'm willing to gamble.

Henry. Well, I'm not.

Hastings. Think—a free trip to London.

Henry. I've no desire to go to London. I'll remain right here in Frisco.

Hastings *(fading)*. Very well, but I know you're making a mistake, Henry.

Henry. One of my few diversions was sailing in the bay. One day I ventured too far and was carried out to sea. Late that night, I was picked up by a freighter which was bound for London. It was a long voyage, and the captain made me work my passage without pay, as a common sailor. When I stepped ashore at London, my clothes were ragged and shabby, and I had only a dollar in my pocket. This money fed and sheltered me for twenty-four hours. During the next twenty-four, I went without food and shelter. I tried to get a job, doing manual labor. But the reply was always the same.

First Cockney. I'm not sure you'd do. You ain't the sort. *(suspiciously)* Look, 'ere, you're a Yank, ain't you?

Henry. The next morning, seedy and hungry, I was dragging myself along Portland Place when my desiring eye fell on a tempting treasure lying in the gutter. It was a luscious big pear—minus one bite. My mouth watered for it. But every time I made a move to get it, some passing eye detected my purpose. I was just getting desperate enough to brave all the shame when a window behind me was raised.

Gordon *(away)*. I say, you there, will you step in here, please?

Henry. It was a very sumptuous house and an equally sumptuous room into which I was ushered by a servant. A couple of elderly gentlemen were sitting by the window. At that moment, if I had known what they had in mind, undoubtedly I would have bolted for the door. They looked me over very thoroughly.

Gordon. He looks poor enough, don't you think, Brother?

Abel. Very. Er, young man, you are poor?

Henry. Extremely!

Abel. Good! And honest, too?

Henry. Honesty is about all I have left; that, and character.

Abel. Splendid!

Gordon. If my brother and I are judges of people, we'd say you are just the man for whom we have been searching. By the way, you are also intelligent, I would say.

Henry. Yes, sir, I am. But what do you mean by saying that I appear to be just the man for whom you have been searching?

Gordon. And we don't know you. You're a perfect stranger. And better still, an American.

Henry. It's very kind of you gentlemen to call me into your home, but I'm a bit puzzled. Could you tell me what you have in mind?

Abel. Might we inquire into your background?

Henry. Pretty soon they had my full story. Their questions were complete and searching, and I gave them straightforward answers. Finally one said:

Gordon. Oh, yes, we're certain you will do, eh, Brother?

Abel. Definitely! He is elected.

Henry. To what am I elected, please?

Gordon. This envelope will explain everything. Here, take it. *(hastily)* No, don't open it now. Take it to your lodgings and look it over carefully.

Abel. Being sure not to be rash or hasty.

Henry. I'd like to discuss the matter.

Gordon. There is nothing to discuss at the moment.

Henry. Is this a joke?

Abel. Not at all. And now good day.

Gordon. And good luck.

Abel. Cheerio!

Henry. As soon as I was out of sight of the house, I opened my envelope and saw it contained money. I lost not a moment but shoved note and money into my pocket and broke for the nearest cheap eating-house. How I did eat! Finished, I took out my money and unfolded it. I took one glimpse and nearly fainted. It was a single million-pound bank note. Five millions of dollars! It made my head swim. The next thing I noticed was the owner of the eating house. His eyes were on the note, and he was petrified. He couldn't stir hand or foot. I tossed the note toward him in careless fashion.

Hawkins. I—is it real, sir? A million-pound note?

Henry *(casually)*. Certainly. Let me have my change, please.

Hawkins. Oh, I'm very sorry, sir, but I can't break the bill.

Henry. Look here—

Hawkins. Hawkins is the name, Albert Hawkins, proprietor. It's only a matter of two shillings[3] you owe, a trifling sum. Please owe it to me.

Henry. I may not be in this neighborhood again for a good time.

Hawkins. It's of no consequence, sir. And you can have anything you want, any time you choose, and let the account run as long as you please. I'm not afraid to trust as rich a gentleman as you just because you choose to play larks[4] by dressing as a tramp.

Henry. Well, thank you. I shall take advantage of your kindness.

Hawkins. Not at all, sir, *(fading)* and please, sir, enter my humble restaurant place any time you wish. I shall be honored to receive you.

---

3. **two shillings:** two former British coins, with a total value of one-tenth of a pound.

4. **play larks:** play pranks; joke around.

Words to Know and Use | **consequence** (kän′ si kwens′) *n.* importance

Henry. I was frightened, afraid that the police might pick me up. I was afraid of the two brothers' reaction when they discovered they had given me a million-pound note instead of what they must have intended giving—a one-pound note. I hurried to their house and rang the bell. The same servant appeared. I asked for the brothers.

Servant. They are gone.

Henry. Gone! Where?

Servant. On a journey.

Henry. But whereabouts?

Servant. To the Continent,[5] I think.

Henry. The Continent?

Servant. Yes, sir.

Henry. Which way—by what route?

Servant. I can't say, sir.

Henry. When will they be back?

Servant. In a month, they said.

Henry. A month! This is awful! Tell me how to get word to them. It's of great importance.

Servant. I can't, indeed. I've no idea where they've gone, sir.

Henry. Then I must see some member of the family.

Servant. Family's been away too; been abroad months—in Egypt and India, I think.

Henry. There's been an immense mistake made. They'll be back before night. Tell them I've been here, and that I'll keep coming till it's all made right, and they needn't worry.

Servant. I'll tell them, if they come back, but I'm not expecting them. They said you'd be here in an hour to make inquiries, but I must tell you it's all right, they'll be here on time to meet you. *(fading)* And that's all they said.

Henry *(slowly)*. I had to give it up and go away. What a riddle it all was! They would be here "on time." What could that mean? Then I thought of the letter. I got it out and read it. It said: "You are an intelligent and honest man, as one can see by your face. We conceive you to be poor and a stranger. Enclosed you will find a sum of money. It is lent to you for thirty days, without interest. Report to this house at the end of that time. I have a bet on you. If I win it, you shall have any situation that is in my gift, any, that is, that you shall be able to prove yourself familiar with and competent to fill." That was all. No signature, no address, no date. I hadn't the least idea what the game was, nor whether harm was meant me or kindness. The letter said there was a bet on me. What kind of a bet? Was the bet that I would abscond with the million-pound bank note? Which brother was betting on my honesty? I reasoned this way: if I ask the Bank of England to deposit it to the credit of the man it belongs to, they'll ask me how I came by it, and if I tell the truth, they'll put me in the asylum; on the other hand, if I lie, they'll put me in jail. The same result would follow if I try to bank it anywhere or borrow money on it.

---

5. **the Continent:** mainland Europe.

Therefore, I have to carry this burden around until those men come back. A month's suffering without wages or profit—unless I help win that bet, whatever it may be. If I do, I will get the situation I am promised. My hopes began to rise high. Then I looked at my rags. Could I afford a new suit? No, for I had nothing in the world but a million pounds. Finally I gave in and entered a fashionable tailor shop. The clerk looked at me very arrogantly.

Tod *(icily)*. No chores to be done here. Get out!

Henry. Perhaps you have a misfit suit.

Tod: We don't give away suits, even misfits.

Henry. I can pay for it.

Tod. Follow me.

Henry. He took me into a back room and overhauled a pile of rejected suits. He tossed the rattiest-looking one at me. I put it on. It didn't fit. It wasn't in any way attractive.

Tod. You may have that for four pounds, cash.

Henry. It would be an <u>accommodation</u> to me if you could wait some days for the money. I haven't any small change about me.

Tod *(sarcastically)*. Oh, you haven't? Well, of course, I didn't expect it. I'd only expect gentlemen like you to carry large change.

Henry *(<u>nettled</u>)*. My friend, you shouldn't judge a stranger always by the clothes he wears. I am quite able to pay for this suit.

Tod. Hah!

Henry. I simply don't wish to put you to the trouble of changing a large note.

Tod. As long as <u>rebukes</u> are going around, I might say that it wasn't quite your affair to infer that we couldn't change any note that you might happen to be carrying around. On the contrary, we *can*.

Henry. Oh, very well. I apologize. Here you are.

Tod. Thank you. *(A complete change. He stutters and fumbles.)* Ah—it's—ah—that is—we—ah—you see— It's— *(quickly)* Take it back, please. *(raising voice)* Mr. Smedley! Mr. Smedley! Help! Oh, Mr. Smedley.

Smedley *(Coming in. A fussy man.)*. What is it, Tod, what is it? Stop shouting!

Tod. Oh, but Mr. Smedley, I can't control myself.

Smedley. What's up? What's the trouble? What's wanting? Who's this?

Henry. I am a customer, and I am waiting for my change.

Smedley. Change, change! Tod, give him his change. Get it for him.

Tod. Get him his change! It's easy for you to say that, Mr. Smedley, but look at the bill yourself.

Smedley. Bill, bill! Let me see it! *(pause)* Tod, you fool, selling an eccentric millionaire such an unspeakable suit as that. Tod, you're a fool—a born fool! Drives every millionaire away from this place because he can't tell a millionaire from a tramp. Here, sir, are some suits more in keeping with your position.

---

*Words
to Know
and Use* | **accommodation** (ə käm′ ə dā′ shən) *n.* a favor or convenience
nettled (net′ ′ld) *adj.* irritated **nettle** *v.*
rebuke (ri byook′) *n.* a sharp criticism

Henry. Thank you, but this one will do.

Smedley. Of course it won't do! I shall burn it. Tod, burn this suit at once.

Tod. Yes, Mr. Smedley.

Smedley. We shall be honored to outfit you completely, sir . . . morning clothes, evening dress, sack suits, tweeds, shetlands—[6] everything you need. Come, Tod, book and pen. Now—length of leg, thirty-two inches; sleeve—

Henry. But look here, I can't give you an order for suits unless you can wait indefinitely or change this bill.

Smedley. *Indefinitely,* sir. It's a weak word, a weak word. *Eternally, that's* the word, sir. Tod, rush these things through. Let the minor customers wait. Set down the gentleman's address and—

Henry. I'm changing my quarters. I'll drop in and leave the new address.

Smedley. Quite right, sir, quite right. One moment—allow me to show you out, sir. And don't worry about paying us. *(fading)* Your credit is the highest. Good day, sir, good day. You honor us greatly, sir.

Henry *(as though sighing).* Well, don't you see what was bound to happen? I drifted naturally into whatever I wanted. Take my hotel, for example. I merely showed the resident manager my million-pound note, and he said:

Manager. We are honored to have you as a guest, sir. Now, I have just the suite for you. It consists of a bedroom, a sitting room, a dressing room, a dining room, two baths and—

Henry. I'll pay you a month in advance with this.

Manager *(laughing).* You honor our simple hotel, sir. Pray, don't worry about the bill.

Henry. But it may be several months before I can pay you.

Manager. We're not worried, Mr.—er—

Henry. Henry Adams.

Manager. Mr. Adams, you are a most distinguished guest. *(fading)* Anything you desire, please name it, and we shall procure it for you immediately. Thank you, sir.

Henry. And there I was, sumptuously housed in an expensive hotel in Hanover Square. I took my dinners there, but for breakfast I stuck by Hawkins's humble feeding-house, where I had got my first meal on my million-pound bank note. I was the making of Hawkins.

Sound. *Rattle of dishes and silver, customers' voices ad-libbing in background.*

Hawkins. Business is brisk, sir, very brisk, indeed, and has been ever since you and your million-pound bank note became patrons of my humble establishment. I've had to hire extra help, put in additional tables. Look for yourself, sir. There's a long queue[7] waiting to get in. Why, I'm famous and fair on my way to becoming wealthy.

Second Cockney. Pardon me, Guv'ner, but aren't you the gentleman what owns the million-pound bank note?

---

6. **morning clothes . . . sack suits . . . shetlands:** men's garments—formal daytime dress, business suits with loose-fitting jackets, and suits made of wool from the Shetland Islands.

7. **queue** (kyo͞o): a line of people.

Hawkins. Look here, you, go away and stop bothering Mr.—Mr.—

Henry. Adams.

Hawkins. Mr. Adams.

Second Cockney. I was just anxious to get a look at him.

Hawkins. Who? Mr. Adams?

Second Cockney. No. The bank note.

Henry. Glad to oblige. There you are.

Second Cockney. By George, it *is* real. *(fading)* Now I can go home and tell me old lady I've seen it with me own eyes. I hopes she believes me, but she won't.

Hawkins. Mr. Adams, I wonder if I couldn't force upon you a small loan—even a large one.

Henry. Oh, no.

Hawkins. Please allow me, sir.

Henry *(relenting)*. Well, as a matter of fact, I haven't gotten around to changing this note.

Hawkins. Fifty pounds might help tide you over. You know, a little spending money?

Henry. It would help a bit.

Hawkins. I consider it a great honor. *(fading)* Indeed, a very great honor. Here you are, Mr. Adams, fifty pounds it is. *(fading)* And don't worry about repaying me.

Henry. I was in, now, and must sink or swim. I walked on air. And it was natural, for I had become one of the notorieties[8] of London. It turned my head, not just a little, but a great deal. The newspapers referred to me as "the Vest-Pocket Millionaire." Then came the climaxing

stroke: *Punch*[9] caricatured me! Wherever I went, people cried:

First Man. There he goes!

Second Man. That's him!

First Woman. Morning, Guv'ner.

Third Man. He's a bit of all right, he is.

Henry. Why, I just swam in glory all day long. About the tenth day of my fame, I fulfilled my duty to my country by calling upon the American ambassador. He received me with enthusiasm and insisted that I attend a dinner party he was giving the following night. Two important things happened at that dinner. I met two people who were to play important roles in the little drama I was living. Among the guests was a lovely English girl named Portia Langham, whom I fell in love with in two minutes, and she with me; I could see it without glasses. And just before dinner, the butler announced:

(Guests ad-libbing in background, very politely.)

Butler *(calling out)*. Mr. Lloyd Hastings.

Henry. I stared at Hastings and he at me, his mouth open in surprise.

Hastings. I, er—pardon me, but are you? No, of course you can't be.

Henry *(chuckling)*. But I am, Lloyd.

Hastings. Henry, I'm speechless. *(suddenly)* Don't tell me that you're also the Vest-Pocket Millionaire?

Henry. Correct!

---

8. **notorieties:** famous people; celebrities.
9. ***Punch:*** an English humor magazine famous for its cartoons poking fun at noted people.

Words to Know and Use | **caricature** (kar′ i kə chər) *v.* to depict features or mannerisms in an exaggerated way.

Hastings. I've seen your own name coupled with the nickname, but it never occurred to me you were *the* Henry Adams. Why, it isn't six months since you were clerking in Frisco and sitting up nights helping me verify the Gould and Curry Extension papers. The idea of your being in London, and a vast millionaire, and a colossal celebrity! It's out of The Arabian Nights!

Henry. I can't realize it myself.

Hastings. It was just three months ago that we were eating together and I tried to persuade you to come to London with me. You turned me down, and now here you are. How did you happen to come, and what gave you this incredible start?

Henry. I'll tell you all about it, but not now.

Hastings. When?

Henry. The end of this month.

Hastings. Make it a week.

Henry. I can't. How's your business venture coming along?

Hastings *(sighing).* You were a true prophet, Henry. I wish I hadn't come.

Henry. Stop with me when we leave here, and tell me all about it. I want to hear the whole story.

Hastings. You'll hear it, every last, dismal word. *(fading a bit)* I'm so grateful to find a willing and sympathetic ear.

Background ad-libbing out.
A pause, then:

Piano. *Playing semiclassical tune in background.*

Henry. After dinner there was coffee and an informal piano recital and dear Miss Langham—lovely Portia Langham, the English girl. I eased her away from the

QUERELLE D'AMOUREUX (Quarreling)   1876
Jacques-Joseph Tissot   Location unknown.

music and the guests to the library, where we talked.

Piano. *Out.*

Portia. I'm really quite excited, Mr. Adams, meeting you like this. A millionaire!

Henry. But I'm not one.

Portia. B-but of course you are.

Henry. You're wrong.

Portia. I don't understand.

Henry. You will! You will, that is, if you allow me to see you tomorrow.

Portia *(as though smiling).* Well, Mr. Adams—

Henry. Henry.

Portia. Henry, then. I will give the invitation serious thought.

Henry. Tomorrow is going to be a sunny day, just right for a picnic in the country. Yes?

Portia. Yes.

Henry. I'll tell you the whole story then.

Portia. Do you think you should?

Henry. Certainly! After all, we're going to be married.

Portia (amazed). We—we're—going to—marry!

Henry. Absolutely! I'll call for you at noon. Where?

Portia. Meet me here.

Henry. You're a guest here?

Portia. N—no, but it will be more convenient.

Henry. Do you like me?

Portia. Yes, Henry. (fading) You're a very unusual young man, even if you are a millionaire and even if you claim you aren't.

Henry. All the way home I was in the clouds, Hastings talking and I not hearing a word. When we reached my suite, he said to me:

Hastings. This luxury makes me realize how poor, how defeated I am. Even the drippings of your daily income would seem like a tremendous fortune to me.

Henry. Unreel your story, Lloyd.

Hastings. I told you the whole story on the way over here.

Henry. You did?

Hastings. Yes.

Henry. I'll be hanged if I heard a word of it.

Hastings. Are you well?

Henry. Yes. I'm in love.

Hastings. That English girl you were speaking to?

Henry. Yes. I'm going to marry her.

Hastings. Small wonder you didn't hear a word I said.

Henry. Now I'm all attention.

Hastings. I came here with what I thought was a grand opportunity. I have an option to sell the Gould and Curry Mine and keep all I can get over a million dollars.

Henry. Sounds like a good proposition.

Hastings. Yes, it's a fine claim.

Henry. Well?

Hastings. The parties here whom I tried to interest have backed down. And so here I am trying to peddle a gold mine but with nary a[10] buyer in sight. In addition, I am almost penniless.

Henry. Surely you'll find a buyer.

Hastings. My option on the mine expires in a matter of days; in fact, at the end of this month.

Henry. You *are* in a fix.

Hastings. Henry, you can save me. Will you do it?

Henry. I? How?

Hastings. Give me a million dollars and my passage home for my option.

Henry. I can't.

---

10. **nary a:** not one.

Hastings. But you're wealthy.

Henry. I—I—not really.

Hastings. You have a million pounds— five millions of dollars. Buy the mine and you'll double, maybe triple, your investment.

Henry. I'd like to help, but I can't.

Hastings. You know the value of this mine as well as I do.

Henry *(tired)*. Oh, Lloyd, I wish I could explain, but I can't. What you ask is impossible.

Hastings. That's quite all right. I'm sorry to have bothered you, Henry. *(fading)* You must have a good reason in turning me down, I'm sure.

Henry. It hurt me to have to refuse Lloyd, but it made me comprehend my delicate and precarious position. Here I was, deep in debt, not a cent in the world, in love with a lovely girl, and nothing in front of me but a promise of a position, if, *if* I won the bet for the nameless brother. Nothing could save me. The next day, Portia and I went on our picnic in the country. I told her the whole story, down to the last detail. Her reaction wasn't exactly what I thought it would be.

Sound. *Bird singing in background. Weave in and out of this scene.*

Portia *(laughs)*. Oh, Henry, that's priceless.

Henry *(a bit stiffly)*. I fail to see the humor.

Portia. But I do, more than you can imagine.

Henry. Here I am mixed up in a bet between two eccentric old men, and for all they care I might well be in jail.

Portia *(still laughing)*. Wonderful, the funniest thing I've ever heard.

Henry. Pardon me if I don't laugh.

Portia *(stops laughing)*. Sorry, but it is both funny and pathetic. But you say that one of the men is going to offer you a position?

Henry. If I win the bet.

Portia. Which one is he?

Henry. I don't know. But I have one solution. If I win, I get the position. Now, I've kept very careful track of every cent I either owe or have borrowed, and I'm going to pay it back from my salary. If the position pays me six hundred pounds a year, I'll—I'll—

Portia. You'll what?

Henry. I'll—*(He whistles.)* To date I owe exactly six hundred pounds, my whole year's salary.

Portia. And the month isn't ended.

Henry. If I'm careful, my second year's salary may carry me through. Oh, dear, that *is* going to make it difficult for us to get married immediately, isn't it?

Portia *(dreamily)*. Yes, it is. *(suddenly)* Henry, what are you talking about? Marriage! You don't know me.

Henry. I know your name, your nationality, your age, and, most important, I know that I love you. I also know that you love me.

Portia. Please be sensible.

Henry. I can't. I'm in love.

Portia. All this sounds like a play.

Henry. It is—a wonderful one. I'll admit my owing my first two years' pay is going to pose a problem insofar as our getting married is concerned. *(suddenly)* I have it! The day I confront those two old gentlemen, I'll take you with me.

Portia. Oh, no. It wouldn't be proper.

Henry. But so much depends upon that meeting. With you there, I can get the old boys to raise my salary—say, to a thousand pounds a year. Perhaps fifteen hundred. Say you'll go with me.

Portia. I'll go.

Henry. In that case, I'll demand two thousand a year, so we can get married immediately.

Portia. Henry.

Henry. Yes?

Portia. Keep your expenses down for the balance of the month. Don't dip into your third year's salary.

Henry. And that is how matters stood at that point. Thoughts raced through my mind. What if I lost the bet for my nameless <u>benefactor</u>? What if he failed to give me a position? Then the answer came to me like a flash of lightning. I roused Lloyd Hastings from bed. He was a bit bewildered.

Hastings. I don't understand you. What are you getting at?

Henry. Lloyd, I'm going to save you. Save you—understand!

Hastings. No.

Henry. I'll save you, but not in the way you ask, for that wouldn't be fair after your hard work and the risks you've run. Now, I don't need to buy a mine. I can keep my capital moving without that; it's what I'm doing all the time. I know all about your mine; I know its immense value and can swear to it if anybody wishes it. You shall sell it inside of the fortnight[11] for three million cash.

Hastings. Three million!

Henry. Right!

Hastings. But how?

Henry. By using my name freely—and right now my name is on the tip of everybody's tongue. We'll divide the profits, share and share alike.

Hastings *(overjoyed)*. I may use your name! Your name—think of it! Man, they'll flock in <u>droves</u>, these rich English. They'll fight for that stock. I'm a made man, a made man forever. *(fading)* I'll never forget you as long as I live . . . never, never . . .

Henry. In less than twenty-four hours, London was abuzz! I hadn't anything to do, day after day, but sit home and wait for calls.

Sir Alfred. Then I may assume, Mr. Adams, that you consider this mining property a sound investment?

Henry. A very sound investment, Sir Alfred.

Sir Alfred. And what of this American chap, Hastings?

Henry. I know him very well, and he is as sound as the mine.

---

11. **fortnight:** two weeks.

Words to Know and Use | **benefactor** (ben' ə fak' tər) *n.* a person who provides money or help
drove (drōv) *n.* a mob or crowd

Sir Alfred. Then I think I shall invest in this property. Your recommendation does it.

Sound. *Telephone bell.*

Henry. Excuse me, Sir Alfred.

Sound. *Receiver lifted from hook.*

Henry *(into phone).* Yes, this is Henry Adams. Who? Sir John Hardcastle. Yes, Sir John. The Gould and Curry Extension? Yes, I know a great deal about it. I certainly would recommend it as a shrewd investment. The mine is worth far more than the asking price. Yes, Mr. Hastings is very well-known in the States. Honest as the day is long, as they say. Yes, I suggest you contact Mr. Hastings. Thank you. Not at all. Good day, Sir John.

Sound. *Receiver replaced onto hook.*

Sir Alfred. That clinches it. If Sir John is in, so am I. Do you suppose that your Mr. Hastings would mind if I brought in a few discreet friends on this venture?

Henry. Er, no, in fact I'm sure he wouldn't. Mr. Hastings is a very democratic chap.

Sir Alfred. Directly I shall go and call upon Mr. Hastings. By the way, exactly where is this mine?

Henry. California.

Sir Alfred. Is that near Washington, D.C.?

Henry. Not exactly.

Sir Alfred. A pity, for I had thought of asking the British ambassador to look at it. *(fading)* Well, I'm off. Thank you for your advice. Good day, Mr. Adams.

Henry. And that's the way it went—a steady stream of wealthy Londoners asking my advice, which, of course, I gave freely. Meanwhile, I said not a word to Portia about the possible sale of the mine. I wanted to save it as a surprise, and then there always was the possibility the sale might fall through. The day the month was up, she and I, dressed in our best, went to the house on Portland Place. As we waited for the two old gentlemen to enter, we talked excitedly.

Portia. You're certain you have the bank note with you?

Henry. Right here. Portia, dearest, the way you look it's a crime to ask for a salary a single penny under three thousand a year.

Portia. You'll ruin us.

Henry. Just trust in me. It'll come out all right.

Portia *(worried).* Please remember, if we ask for too much, we may get no salary at all; and then what will become of us with no way in the world to earn our living? *(fading)* Please handle this delicately, Henry.

Henry. When the two old gentlemen entered, of course they were surprised to see Portia with me. I asked them to introduce themselves, which they did.

Gordon. I am Gordon Featherstone.

Abel. And I am Abel Featherstone.

Henry. Gentlemen, I am ready to report, but first may I ask which of you bet on me?

Gordon. It was I. Have you the million-pound note?

Henry. Here it is, sir.

Gordon. Ah! I've won. *Now* what do you say, Abel?

ASHER WERTHEIMER 1898 John Singer Sargent
The Tate Gallery, London / Art Resource, New York.

Abel. I say he did survive, and I've lost twenty thousand pounds. I never would have believed it.

Henry. Perhaps you might enlighten me as to the terms of the bet.

Gordon. Gladly! The Bank of England once issued two notes of a million pounds each. Only one of these had been used and canceled; the other lay in the vaults. Well, Abel and I got to wondering what would happen to a perfectly honest and intelligent stranger turned adrift in London without a friend and with no money in the world but the million-pound bank note. Abel said he would starve to death, and I claimed he wouldn't. My brother said he would be arrested if he offered the note at a bank. Well, we went on arguing until I bet him twenty thousand pounds that the man would live thirty days, *anyway,* on that million, and keep out of jail, too.

Abel. And I took him up.

Henry. How did you know I was the right choice?

Abel. After talking with you, we decided you had all the qualifications.

Gordon. And that pear incident—if you had picked it up very boldly, it would have proved to us you were nothing but a tramp.

Henry. You don't know how tempted I was to do just that.

Gordon. And so you shall receive your reward—a choice of any position you can fill.

Henry. First I ask that you look at this scrap of paper, all of you. You, too, Portia.

Gordon. A certificate of deposit in the London and County Bank—

Abel. In the sum of—

Gordon. Two hundred thousand pounds.

Portia. Henry, is it yours?

Henry. It is. It represents my share of the sale of a mining property in California, sold by my friend Lloyd Hastings; a sort of commission, as it were. It all came about by thirty days' judicious use of that little loan you gentlemen let me have.

And the only use I made of it was to buy trifles and offer the bill in change.

Abel. Come, this is astonishing.

Gordon. It's incredible.

Henry *(laughing)*. I can prove it.

Portia. Henry, is that really your money? Have you been fibbing to me?

Henry. I have, indeed. But you'll forgive me, I know.

Portia *(half smiling)*. Don't you be so sure.

Henry. Oh, you'll get over it. Come, let's be going.

Gordon. Wait! I promised to give you a situation, you know.

Henry. Thank you, but I really don't want one.

Portia. Henry, I'm ashamed of you. You don't even thank the good gentleman. May I do it for you?

Henry. If you can improve upon it.

Portia. I shall. Uncle Abel, first, thank you for making this possible. And, dear Father—

Henry. Hold on. You're her uncle?

Abel. I am.

Henry. And you—

Gordon. Yes, I'm her stepfather.

Portia. And the dearest one that ever was. You understand now, don't you, Henry, why I was able to laugh when you told me the story of the bet with the two nameless gentlemen. Of course I couldn't miss knowing that it was this house and that the two men were Father and Uncle Abel.

Henry. Sir, you *have* got a situation open that I want.

Gordon. Name it.

Henry. Son-in-law.

Gordon. Well, well, well! But if you haven't ever served in that capacity, you of course can't furnish satisfactory recommendations to satisfy the conditions of the contract.

Henry. Only just try me for thirty or forty years.

Gordon. What do you think, Abel?

Abel. Well, he does look to be a satisfactory sort.

Gordon. And you, Portia?

Portia. I agree—heartily.

Gordon. Very well. Take her along. If you hurry, you can reach the license bureau before it closes. *(fading)* Hop to it now.

Henry. Happy, we two? Indeed, yes! And when London got the whole history of my adventure for a month, how it did talk. My Portia's father took the million-pound bank note to the Bank of England, cashed it, had it canceled, and gave it to us at our wedding. Framed, it now hangs in our home. It gave me my Portia; but for it I could not have remained in London, would not have appeared at the American ambassador's, never should have met her. And so I always say: Yes, it's a million-pounder; but it made but one purchase in its life and then got the article for only about a tenth part of its value.

The End ❧

*R*esponding to Reading

First Impressions

1. Which part of the play did you enjoy most? Write down your thoughts in your journal or on a sheet of paper.

Second Thoughts

2. What is your opinion of the scheme that the two brothers devise?

3. How does having the million-pound note affect Henry?

   Think about
   - his initial response to getting the money
   - his clever use of other people's reactions to his money
   - his reaction to Lloyd's scheme

4. Why do you think people's attitudes toward Henry change when they think he is rich?

5. Henry and Portia keep important information from each other. Do you agree with their decisions to keep secrets? Why or why not?

Broader Connections

6. Think about the ideas you discussed for Examine What You Know. As this play shows, people with a lot of money are often treated with a great deal of respect and attention. On the negative side, however, they may lose their privacy, as Henry does after he is featured in *Punch.* Do you think wealthy or famous people owe the public a certain amount of information about their lives? Why or why not?

*L*iterary Concept: Resolution

After the climax or turning point of a story, the **resolution** tells how the conflict or conflicts are resolved and how the story ends. The climax of *The Million-Pound Bank Note* comes when Henry reveals his own fortune of 200,000 pounds (1,000,000 dollars). What do you think is the resolution of this play?

*W*riting Options

1. The Vest-Pocket Millionaire is the biggest piece of news to hit London this season. Write a **newspaper article** featuring the lucky young man who became the Vest-Pocket Millionaire.

2. Wedding bells are ringing for the Vest-Pocket Millionaire and his English bride. Write about Henry and Portia's wedding plans in a **society column** for your local newspaper.

3. Imagine you are one of the characters in the play and you have been reading about and observing the Vest-Pocket Millionaire. Compose a **character sketch** of Henry from your character's point of view.

4. Write Henry's **last will and testament.** Be sure to include how he spent or invested his money and how his assets and possessions should be distributed to family, friends, and charities.

*V*ocabulary Practice

Exercise Decide if the following pairs of words are synonyms or antonyms. On a sheet of paper, write *S* for synonyms and *A* for antonyms.

1. accommodation—favor
2. benefactor—enemy
3. caricature—exaggerate
4. competent—unfit
5. consequence—importance
6. drove—crowd
7. judicious—foolish
8. nettled—irritated
9. precarious—secure
10. rebuke—compliment

Words to Know and Use

accommodation
benefactor
caricature
competent
consequence
drove
judicious
nettled
precarious
rebuke

Options for Learning

1 • Lights! Camera! Action! *The Million-Pound Bank Note* was adapted as a radio play, which explains why it contains no instructions on how the characters or settings should look. Research some ideas for costumes and settings, and turn this radio play into a full-scale dramatization. You may enjoy videotaping your efforts.

2 • This Is Your Life! Henry made an extraordinary splash when he arrived on the London scene. Suddenly people wanted to know everything about him, including what he was like when he was young. Stage a television show about Henry. Have the host interview people from Henry's life, both before and after he became the Vest-Pocket Millionaire.

3 • Just Ask Henry Suppose Henry regularly donates a portion of his earnings to special causes or to individuals in need. Write a letter to Henry, telling him why your cause or need deserves his help. Have the class read their letters aloud and vote to select the three causes or needs to which Henry should donate money.

4 • Easy Money You talked with your classmates about what you would do with a million dollars. Now take a survey or poll to find out what other people would do with that much money. Share the responses in a chart or a graph.

 FACT FINDER Economics

What is the largest bill in circulation in the United States today?

Samuel Clemens (Mark Twain)
1835–1910

Samuel Clemens took his pen name, Mark Twain, from a cry used by boatmen on the Mississippi River. "Mark twain" refers to water that is two fathoms deep, or deep enough for safe travel. The Mississippi also provided inspiration for some of Twain's masterpieces—*The Adventures of Huckleberry Finn, The Adventures of Tom Sawyer,* and *Life on the Mississippi.* Twain published these works between 1876 and 1884.

Twain's courtship was almost as romantic as Henry and Portia's in *The Million-Pound Bank Note.* In 1867, Twain fell in love with the picture of a beautiful woman, Olivia Langdon. When Twain met Livy in person, he determined to win her hand in marriage, but his busy lecture schedule kept him traveling. In one year Twain wrote Livy well over one hundred love letters. She finally consented to become Mrs. Samuel Clemens in 1870.

WRITER'S WORKSHOP

INFORMATIVE WRITING

To carry out a scheme successfully, you need an effective process. If you have ever tried to make a cake or program a VCR, you understand the importance of carefully following the steps of a process. Think about the athlete in the poem "Pole Vault." To clear the bar at higher and higher heights, the pole vaulter needs to gain mastery of each step of a process that includes sprinting, planting the pole, rocking back on the pole, turning, and clearing the bar. In this workshop you will write a **process report,** a type of informative writing that explains how to do something. In your process report you may teach a personal skill, such as making a great spaghetti sauce, or you may explain a process that intrigues you, such as the making of animated films.

USE INFORMATIVE
WRITING FOR

research papers
science lab reports
comparison papers
newspaper articles
biographies
process reports
demonstration
speeches

GUIDED ASSIGNMENT:
EXPLAINING A PROCESS

Write a report that explains a particular process. Describe each of the steps of this process clearly and thoroughly.

Here is one writer's PASSkey to this assignment.

P URPOSE: To explain a process

A UDIENCE: Classmates, teacher

S UBJECT: How to sprint

S TRUCTURE: A process report

How to Sprint
by Lisa Washington

You probably think that running a sprint is just a matter of pointing yourself in the right direction and then running as fast as you can. Actually, there is a certain way to do each part of a sprint. You can improve your performance if you try the following process.

Sprints are races of 400 meters or less. Because a sprint is short, the start is important. A sprinter uses two metal <u>starting blocks</u> that are attached to a rail set into

STUDENT MODEL

Before you begin, read how one student responded to the assignment.

The topic of this process report is clearly stated in the opening paragraph.

The term *starting blocks* is explained because it may be unfamiliar to readers.

The writer uses precise language to describe exactly how the sprinter should move.

"On your marks" position

Note the use of the transition word *when*. It helps to indicate the sequence of events.

Note that each paragraph groups the steps that go together. This paragraph describes the end of the race.

the track. The blocks give the feet a firm base to push against at the start. The first thing you do at the starting line is adjust the blocks. The front block should be about two foot-lengths from the starting line, and the back block should be about one foot-length behind the front block. Which foot should you have in front? That's up to you. Experiment until you feel comfortable.

When the starting official says, "On your marks," get down on all fours in front of your blocks. Place each foot securely against a block. Your hands should be shoulder-width apart. Your thumbs should make a bridge with your other fingers behind the starting line. When the starter says, "Set," raise your hips, and move your shoulders over your hands. Raise your back knee off the ground, and partially straighten your back leg. Fix your gaze a little in front of the starting line.

When the gun goes off, you should explode out of the blocks. The winner in a sprint is the runner who gets to top speed fastest and holds it longest. Drive with your arms, and don't stand up too fast. During the race make sure you stay relaxed. Don't grit your teeth or clench your fists. Relaxed muscles work faster than tense ones. Remember that all your motion should be straight ahead. Arms that fly around or a head that wags is not getting you where you want to go.

Always, always, sprint through the finish line. Don't slow up at the end. Just before the line, lean forward. The officials judge a race by when a runner's chest crosses the line.

If you follow these steps, you will improve your race. You may not win an Olympic gold medal, but then again, who knows?

Now it's time to begin your own process report.

Prewrite and Explore

1 **Consider the possibilities**   What activities do you do well? Think about hobbies, chores, and sports. What processes do you go through that might be interesting to readers? Broaden your search. Walk through your neighborhood, and consider the processes that occur around you. Have you ever wondered about the steps involved in delivering the mail or supplying electricity? Make a list of ideas.

2 **Select a topic**   Here are some questions to ask yourself when you are choosing a process to explain: Will the information be useful and interesting to my audience? Can I clearly explain the process? Can the process be broken down into clear and logical steps? Do I have enough knowledge of the subject or can I find out enough from library books or other sources, to be able to explain it?

TIP . . . .

Think about the kind of *how* and *why* questions a younger sibling or friend might ask. ("How does hail form?") Such questions may trigger topic ideas.

GATHERING INFORMATION

If you can, go through the process yourself. Take notes about each step as you go. Perhaps you can watch an expert perform the steps of the process. Consult a video library—there may be an instructional videotape on your subject. Read about the process as well, and add to your notes. Here are the notes that Lisa wrote as she gathered information about how to run a sprint.

Before Race	1.	Adjust blocks.
	2.	Find a comfortable position.
"On Your Marks"	3.	Place feet securely.
	4.	Hands are shoulder-width apart.
	5.	Position of hands
"Set"	6.	Raise hips; move shoulders over hands.
	7.	Raise back knee, front thigh perpendicular to track.
	8.	Where to look
Start of Race	9.	Drive with arms.
	10.	Come up gradually.
Middle of Race	11.	Stay relaxed.
	12.	Ignore other runners.
	13.	All parts of body move straight ahead.
End of Race	14.	Run through the finish line.
	15.	Lean at the finish line.

◀ **STUDENT MODEL** . . . .

Note how Lisa divided her material into six groups of steps according to the various stages of a sprint. Also notice that she did not use all of her notes in her report.

Draft and Discover

1 **Begin drafting**   Write a short introductory paragraph that identifies the process and suggests why the reader might be interested in it. Then, using your notes, flesh out each of the steps with clear explanation. Group the steps that go together into paragraphs. For each step ask yourself, How much do my readers need to know? In the conclusion suggest how the information may help the reader.

2 **Use transitions**   To clarify when each step occurs, use transition words such as *before, first, then, when, after, next, while, finally,* and *last.* Notice how transitions are used in the following example:

3 **Consider using a graphic**   A picture is "worth a thousand words." If you describe a complicated step, think about including an illustration, a diagram, or a flowchart. Lisa decided to show a picture of a sprinter in the "on your marks" position.

Revise Your Writing

1 **Clarify your descriptions**   You have the basic process on paper now, but how clear is your explanation? Can the wording be simplified or made more accurate? Be sure to clarify any unfamiliar terms, as Lisa did with *sprint* and *starting blocks.*

► **2** **Enlist a peer reader**   Ask a classmate to read your draft. The following questions can help.

LITERARY MODEL
from "A Cap for Steve" by Morley Callaghan

COMPUTER TIP
If you have software that can be used to create graphics, experiment with diagrams or flowcharts that illustrate your process.

ASK FOR HELP
Not sure if your explanation is clear? Read it to a friend. Then see if he or she can explain the process to you. You may notice that parts of your report are unclear.

Revision Questions

For You	For a Peer Reader
1. Did I explain the process in a clear and thorough way?	1. Could you complete the process that I explained?
2. Did I include all the steps in the correct order?	2. Were any parts of my explanation unclear?
3. Did I use transition words effectively?	3. Are there any unfamiliar terms?

Proofread

Check your draft for spelling, grammar, and punctuation errors. As a double-check, ask a friend to proofread your draft. In this assignment, look carefully at your sentence structure.

THE EDITOR'S EYE: AVOIDING RUN-ONS

Avoid run-on sentences by using punctuation correctly.

In explaining a series of steps, a writer may mistakenly run thoughts together in one sentence, rather than using two or more sentences. Here are two common ways of correcting a run-on sentence:

1. Find the end of the first thought, add a period, and start a new sentence.

2. Join the two sentences with a comma and a conjunction.

Run-on	Drive with your arms don't stand up too fast.
Correct	Drive with your arms. Don't stand up too fast.
Also Correct	Drive with your arms, and don't stand up too fast.

NEED MORE HELP?

See the Language Workshop that follows (pages 232–234) and pages 766–768 of the Language Handbook.

Publish and Present

Here is an idea for sharing your work with others.

Demonstration Speech Using your written report, present a demonstration of your process. Summarize the main points on note cards, and refer to these notes in your speech. If possible, enlarge your graphics to poster size and be prepared to physically demonstrate the process. Present your demonstration to a group of classmates.

Reflect on Your Writing

Write answers to the following questions. Then place them in your portfolio with your process report.

◀ FOR YOUR PORTFOLIO

1. Which parts of your process do you think you explained most effectively?

2. What thoughts and feelings do you have about the idea of teaching a subject?

LANGUAGE
WORKSHOP

AVOIDING FRAGMENTS AND RUN-ONS

Expressing complete thoughts and moving clearly from thought to thought are two of the basics of good writing. When a writer forgets these basics, the result is often a sentence fragment or a run-on sentence.

Sentence Fragments

> A **sentence fragment** is a group of words that does not express a complete thought. It lacks a subject, a predicate, or both.

WHERE'S THE SUBJECT?

In a sentence that is a request or command, the subject is not stated. For example, in the sentence "Now revise the draft" the subject *you* is not stated. It is said to be understood.

Complete sentences have a **subject** (the *who* or *what* in the sentence) and a **predicate** (what the subject *does*). If a group of words is missing either of these two parts, it is a fragment.

Fragment   Had intelligence and luck. (*Who* had intelligence and luck? Here the subject is missing.)

Sentence   The millionaire in Twain's story had intelligence and luck.

Fragment   John D. Rockefeller and Andrew Carnegie. (Rockefeller and Carnegie *did what?* Here the predicate is missing.)

Sentence   John D. Rockefeller and Andrew Carnegie made their huge fortunes in oil and steel.

Fragments Caused by Incomplete Thoughts

BREAKING THE RULES

Fragments are acceptable in some types of writing. Short story writers often use fragments to make dialogue sound more realistic. If you purposely use a fragment in your writing, check carefully to see that the meaning is clear.

When you write quickly, you may not complete your thoughts, and fragments can result. Check each "sentence" with these two questions: Who or what did something? What happened? If it doesn't answer both these questions, it is a fragment, not a sentence.

Fragments   In his later years Mark Twain's money problems. Lost almost $200,000. Investing in a typesetting machine. In 1895, unable to pay his debts.

Sentences   In his later years Mark Twain had money problems. He lost almost $200,000 investing in a typesetting machine. In 1895, Twain was unable to pay his debts.

Fragments Caused by Incorrect Punctuation

When you use an end mark before your thought is complete, a fragment is the result. You can correct fragments of this type by revising the punctuation and capitalization.

◀ **REMINDER**
An end mark can be a period, a question mark, or an exclamation point.

Fragment	According to *Forbes* magazine. There are 101 billionaires in the United States.
Sentence	According to *Forbes* magazine, there are 101 billionaires in the United States.

Exercise 1   Concept Check   Write *S* for each word group that is a sentence. Write *F* for each word group that is a fragment. Then make each fragment a complete sentence by adding words.

1. Money is anything people accept for the things they sell.
2. Historically, many different types of payment.
3. At one time, grain, furs, salt, and even nails.
4. Trade a hundred pounds of tobacco for medical treatment.
5. By 1800, people in the United States used coins for money.
6. Later, in the 1860s, paper money.
7. Nowadays, most coins mixtures of metals.
8. Many people today personal checks.
9. Another common form of payment is the credit card.
10. Several different credit cards.

Run-on Sentences

A **run-on sentence** is two sentences written as though they were one.

A run-on sentence, as its name suggests, keeps going when it should stop. Run-ons make it difficult to tell where one idea ends and another begins. One type of run-on occurs when the punctuation marking the end of the first thought is missing. Another type is the **comma splice,** in which a comma is used instead of a period. There are several ways to correct run-on sentences.

SAY IT ALOUD
Not sure it's a run-on? Try reading the group of words aloud. Often you will naturally pause at the end of a complete thought. Add the correct punctuation at that point.

Run-on	One of Lincoln's goals in the Civil War was to keep the country unified another was to end slavery.
Correct	One of Lincoln's goals in the Civil War was to keep the country unified. **A**nother was to end slavery.

There are three main
ways to correct a run-
on:
1. Insert an end mark,
and begin a new
sentence.
2. Insert a comma and
a conjunction.
3. Insert a semicolon.

Run-on	The Civil War lasted four years, it was the bloodiest war in United States history.
Correct	The Civil War lasted four years**, and** it was the bloodiest war in United States history.
Correct	The Civil War lasted four years**;** it was the bloodiest war in United States history.

Exercise 2   Concept Check   Correct the following run-on sentences.

1. Frederick Douglass was the leading voice for American blacks in the 1800s, he was one of the great speakers and reformers of his era.
2. Douglass was born into slavery he learned to read and write while he was a house servant.
3. He made one unsuccessful attempt to escape, on his second try he escaped to the North disguised as a sailor.
4. He worked at several unskilled jobs eventually he gained fame as a speaker for black rights.
5. Douglass spoke out against unfair hiring practices, he also protested against various forms of segregation.
6. He founded an antislavery newspaper called the *North Star* he also published his autobiography, *Narrative of the Life of Frederick Douglass.*
7. His home was a station for runaway slaves on the Underground Railroad this is where he met Harriet Tubman.
8. During the Civil War, Douglass met with President Abraham Lincoln they discussed the problems of slavery.
9. Douglass helped recruit Union soldiers, the 54th and 55th Massachusetts Negro regiments fought with distinction.
10. In later life Douglass held several political posts his highest post was U.S. consul general in Haiti.

Exercise 3   Proofreading Skill   Rewrite the following paragraph. Correct any sentence fragments or run-on sentences.

I remember the first time my mom and dad took me to a baseball game. Our seats in the bleachers what a view. I watched the outfielders run for a high fly ball, it floated almost like a balloon. Our team won. 3 to 2. After the game we went down near the dugout, I got a baseball signed by my favorite player. I couldn't believe it an autograph from the best hitter in baseball. Still have that baseball.

LANGUAGE HANDBOOK
For review and
practice: Section 2,
Writing Complete
Sentences.

Exercise 4   Revising Your Writing   Reread the process report you wrote for the Writer's Workshop on pages 227–231. Correct any sentence fragments and run-on sentences that you find.

SPEAKING AND LISTENING
WORKSHOP

ORAL PRESENTATION SKILLS

When the time comes to present a speech to your class, will you be up all night worrying? Through careful preparation you can spare yourself this worry. Study the suggestions below.

Prepare

Review your information. Reread your written report plus any other information you have about your subject. You'll feel more comfortable knowing you have more than enough material to present.

Organize your speaking notes. Outline the main points of your speech on numbered index cards. Keep the points short and simple. Refer to them if and when you need to during your speech.

Rehearse

Practice, practice, practice. Rehearse your speech several times—in front of the mirror, in the shower, as you walk to school. If you are using visual aids, practice handling them. Speak at a comfortable pitch. Place extra stress on important words. Let your enthusiasm show.

Test your speech on a real audience. Ask your friends or family members to listen to your speech and offer their suggestions.

Present

It's show time! Take a deep breath and begin. Start with an interesting question or statement to hook your audience. Remember to smile.

Make eye contact. Look people in the eye as if you were having a one-on-one conversation. Stand up straight and avoid nervous movements. Watch the audience's response. If people seem distracted, you may want to jump to a visual aid.

Finish strong. Restate your main ideas, adding a powerful anecdote or example to reinforce your point.

Exercise Prepare, rehearse, and deliver a speech on your process report on a topic of your choice.

TIP
Use charts, slides, or props to illustrate your points. As you refer to them, the visual aids will vary the rhythm of your presentation.

HINT
Try tape-recording your speech. Listening to yourself speak will help you spot any *um*'s and *ah*'s. Your tape will also tell you if certain parts of your speech are too long or complicated.

Reading on Your Own

Suggested Novels for Unit Two

The novels introduced on these pages reflect the theme of Unit Two, "All or Nothing." The main characters in all these novels devise schemes to achieve their greatest dreams.

THE REMARKABLE JOURNEY OF PRINCE JEN

LLOYD ALEXANDER ©1991

Everyone has dreams; everyone makes choices. The consequences of these choices may have a great impact. In *The Remarkable Journey of Prince Jen*, Prince Jen goes in search of the legendary court of T'ien-Kuo. Along the way he encounters a mysterious man who tells him to bring six very special gifts to the court—a saddle, a sword, a paint box, a bowl, a kite, and a flute. Despite being puzzled by this unusual request, Prince Jen continues on his journey. While trying to learn more about the gifts, Jen is surprised to learn of his true destiny. Read to find out . . .

- what is special about the court of T'ien-Kuo

- why Prince Jen is asked to carry the six unusual gifts

- what Prince Jen's destiny is

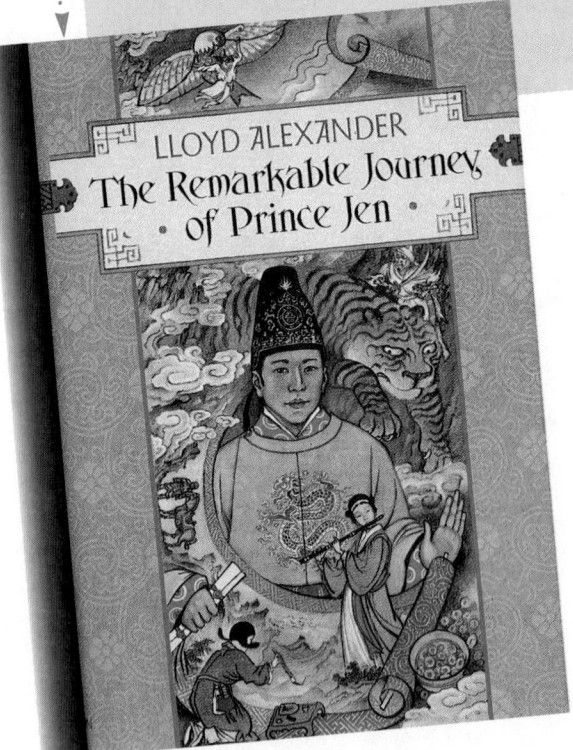

CARRY ON, MR. BOWDITCH
JEAN LEE LATHAM ©1955

Have you ever dreamed of accomplishing something wonderful? What if you were unable to receive the education that would allow your dream to come true? In *Carry On, Mr. Bowditch*, Nathaniel Bowditch, born in Salem, Massachusetts, in 1773, wants to learn about astronomy and navigation. Bowditch not only makes his dream come true but also researches navigation principles and writes a book that changes the history of navigation. As you read this historical novel, look for answers to the following questions:

• What must Bowditch do in order to achieve his dream?

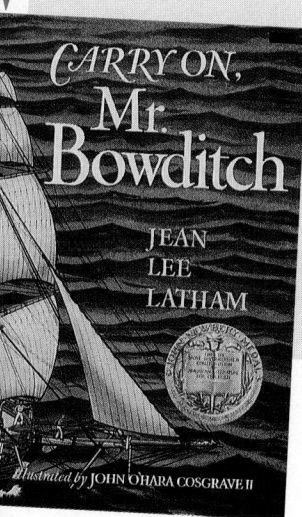

• Would you be willing to make the kinds of sacrifices Bowditch makes?

• Are Bowditch's achievements worth the effort he makes?

LEGEND DAYS
JAMAKE HIGHWATER ©1984

When a smallpox epidemic destroys her tribe, eleven-year-old Amana is abandoned in the wilderness and left to die. She is taken in by Grandfather Fox, who gives her a sacred gift—the courage to become a warrior. Amana, however, must keep the gift a secret. The years pass, but Amana does not forget the secret gift and eventually decides to use it. Like most Native Americans, however, Amana has been taught to value ancient traditions and beliefs—traditions and beliefs that do not allow for female warriors. Read to discover . . .

• why Amana decides to become a warrior

• what struggles she endures to achieve her goal

• how she faces the prejudices of her people

Other Recommended Books

Columbus and the World Around Him by Milton Meltzer (©1990). This fascinating biography relates the story of Christopher Columbus, obsessed with the idea of finding a new route to the Orient. The author presents both the positive and the negative side of Columbus's character and actions.

Rebels of the Heavenly Kingdom by Katherine Paterson (©1983). In this novel, set in China during the 1850s, a group of Chinese citizens struggle to achieve their greatest dream—the overthrow of the Manchu government.

A Nation Torn: The Story of How the Civil War Began by Delia Ray (©1990). This book relates the history of the Civil War. The book, which focuses on the years 1860 and 1861, includes newspaper articles, speeches, diaries, letters, and photographs.

Speeding Bullet by Neal Shusterman (©1992). In this contemporary novel a boy is obsessed with the idea that he can rescue people who are in great peril.

NOTHING STAYS THE SAME

Observe always

that everything is

the result of change.

Marcus Aurelius

COTOPAXI
1863   Frederick Church
The Detroit Institute of the Arts.

$\mathcal{M}$ETAMORPHOSES

Look at yourself in a mirror. You may look the same as you did yesterday, but you're actually changing all the time. Everything in the universe is in a state of constant change. Think, for example, of the caterpillar that emerges from its cocoon as an iridescent butterfly. The buds on an apple tree change first into flowers and then into fruits.

These transformations, or changes in form, can be described by the word *metamorphoses*. This word comes from the Greek language—the prefix *meta-*, meaning "from one to another," and the word *morphē*, meaning "form."

When you read the selections that make up this subunit, you will encounter some amazing metamorphoses.

Fiction

The Enchanted Raisin

JACQUELINE BALCELLS

Examine What You Know

Superman, Charlotte's Web, Mary Poppins—what do these three stories have in common? One of the things they share is a mixture of fantasy and reality. Think about the realism and fantasy in these stories and in others that you have read, heard, or seen. Then fill in a chart like the one below.

Story	Elements of Realism	Elements of Fantasy
Superman		
Charlotte's Web		
Mary Poppins		

Expand Your Knowledge

What makes stories like the ones listed above so popular? Perhaps one of the reasons is that people can easily relate to realistic fiction. Its plots imitate real life, and its characters are ordinary people with ordinary problems. Yet when a writer mixes realism with a little fantasy, the solutions to those ordinary problems can be exciting and even outrageous! How many of us have wished that we could see through walls, fight off evil with superhuman powers, or fly?

Write Before You Read

The following words refer to events in "The Enchanted Raisin." Do any of them suggest an element of fantasy? Use the words to predict the plot of the story. Then read the story to see how your predictions match the writer's ideas.

disobedient children ➤ shrinking mother ➤ raisin
matchbox ➤ cruel stepmother ➤ raisin cake ➤ attic ➤ hunger
tears ➤ laughter ➤ family reunion ➤ fruitcake

■ *Author biography in Reader's Handbook*

The Enchanted Raisin

JACQUELINE BALCELLS

Once upon a time, there was a mom who had three absolutely unbearable children. They did every bad and stupid thing imaginable, as well as the unimaginable ones. Several times they almost burned down the house, and they flooded it a hundred times. They broke the furniture, smashed the plates, fought and screamed like crazy people, spilled ink on the white sheets, and swung from the curtains as if they were monkeys in the jungle. And why bother saying what happened when they were sent outside: they spread panic throughout the neighborhood.

Their dad was almost never home, and their poor mother couldn't manage these three little devils. She was completely exhausted at the end of the day from chasing after them.

> *The poor woman continued to wrinkle and shrink at an incredible rate.*

"My children," she said to them, "please stop your foolishness, if only this once. Look at me: each one of your pranks and screams is a wrinkle on my face. I am becoming an old lady."

And it was true. This woman, who had been tall and beautiful, was wrinkling and shrinking from one day to the next.

Her children didn't notice anything. But one day, when she went to meet them after school, their friends asked with astonishment, "Why does your grandmother come to get you now?"

The children felt bad for a moment; they were upset that their mother was mistaken for their grandmother. But they didn't think about it for long—they had so much to do!

The poor woman continued to wrinkle and shrink at an incredible rate. The moment arrived when she could no longer walk: her legs had become two little sticks that were so skinny they were like cherry stems, and her back was so curved she could barely see in front of her. Nevertheless, her three children did not stop inventing more and more horrible pranks:

"Let's take the feathers out of the pillows!"

"Let's pull out the dog's fur!"

"Let's cut off the cat's ears!"

"Let's dig a hole in the field for the gardener to fall into!"

By now, their mother was so small that, standing, she did not reach her youngest child's knees. She sighed, "Children, enough! Look at my size, my wrinkles. If this continues, I will shrink so much that you won't even be able to see me." But she never thought this would happen.

One night after supper, she dragged herself to her room, exhausted. She put on her nightgown, which was now one hundred times too big. She climbed on her bed, rolled herself into a ball, and fell deeply asleep.

The next morning when they woke up, the children did what they always did. They jumped on their beds like devils and began to yell, "Moooooommm, bring us our breakfast!"

There was no response. They yelled louder, with no success. They began to howl, once, twice, ten times, thirty times. After the fifty-first shout, with their throats sore, they decided to go to their mother's room.

Her bed was unmade, but she was nowhere to be found. The children realized that something strange was happening. Suddenly, the youngest child bent over the pillow and screamed.

"What's the matter?" his brother asked.

"Look, look there!" he shouted.

Between the folds of their mother's nightgown was a small, dark ball. It was a raisin.

The children were frightened. They called louder and louder, "Moooooommy, Mooooommy, . . .!"

Like the other times, there was no answer, but the oldest child realized that with each shout, the raisin on the pillow moved slightly. They were quiet and watched it: the raisin didn't move. They shouted "Mom!" and the raisin shook a little.

Then they remembered their mother's words: "If this continues, I will shrink so much that you won't be able to see me." And horrified, they realized that this raisin that moved when they yelled "Mom" was all that remained of their mother, who in that way tried to make them recognize her. How they cried and wailed!

"Poor us! What are we going to do now that Mom is a raisin? What is Dad going to say when he gets home and sees her?"

Their father had been on a business trip for several weeks but was due to return home that very night. The children, frightened and not knowing what to do, waited for him in their room all day long. Once in a while, to reassure themselves, they approached the raisin and called "Mom!" The raisin invariably moved.

That evening, their father arrived home. He opened the door, dropped his briefcase, took off his hat and coat, and called his wife from the hall: "Hello, are you there? Aren't you going to welcome me home? Aren't you going to give me a hug and bring me a glass of wine?"

Instead of his wife, his children appeared walking one behind the other with their heads bowed. The oldest held a matchbox in his hands.

"What's going on? Why aren't you in bed? And where's your mother?"

"She's in this box," the oldest answered in a mournful tone. "She turned into a raisin."

His father became angry. "You know that I hate jokes! Go to bed immediately!"

He searched the house for his wife. It was useless to tell him he would not find her. He then said, "She must have gone out for a walk!" But an hour later, as she had not appeared, he began to worry.

and drowned! And the worst thing is, I will never know the truth!" he <u>lamented</u> in anguish.[1]

The months passed with no news. Feeling very lonely, the man finally decided to remarry.

"A new wife would help me take care of these wild animals. . . ."

So he chose a wife who was not as pretty as the first one—not to say frightful—but she seemed sweet and self-sacrificing. In reality, her face was as ugly as her heart was hard: she led him to believe that she adored the children, but the truth is that she <u>detested</u> them.

The father didn't realize anything. But the three children immediately understood that their stepmother was evil, and they did not trust her. Also, they knew that their real mother was still alive in the matchbox that they guarded so carefully. They were certain she would stop being a raisin and return to her former self.

From time to time at night, the children circled the box, removed the cover, and called softly, "Mom, Mom."

And each time, the raisin responded by rocking gently.

One day when their father was in a good mood, they again asked him to go to their room to see what happened with the raisin. Perhaps he would understand! But their father didn't want to know anything; on the contrary, he became furious: "How long is this stupid joke going to continue? Little

WALKING WOMAN 1956 © George Spaventa
Collection, Linda and Robert Schimer.

He put on his hat and left. He walked around the neighborhood, went to the houses of his neighbors, relatives, and friends. He asked everyone, "Have you seen my wife?" Then he went to the police station. But they couldn't tell him anything either.

One night passed, a day and another night. And while the time passed and his wife continued to be missing, the father began to ask himself with great pain if his wife had died.

"She must have taken a walk by the lake

---

1. **anguish** (aŋ′ gwish): pain.

Words to Know and Use

lament (lə ment′) *v.* to express grief
detest (dē test′) *v.* to hate
contrary (kän′ trer′ ē) *n.* the opposite point of view

devils . . . if you keep up these stories, you are going to get it. I don't want to hear you mention that raisin again!"

Frightened, the children watched over the box.

But, horrors, the stepmother overheard the conversation from behind the door, and she believed them! For a while, she had had her suspicions about the matchbox that the children watched over with such anxiety.

At the beginning, she didn't say anything. But a few days later, one afternoon when the father wasn't home, she called the children and said to them: "Children, I am going to make a raisin cake and I am short one raisin. I believe you have one. Go get it right now!" The stepmother had an evil expression on her face. The children didn't dare protest. They went to their room and asked each other, "What should we do? We can't give her our mother so she can throw her in the oven!" The oldest decided, "Let's go up to the attic. We will hide the box and tell our stepmother that we lost it."

Unfortunately, the evil woman had followed them and once again listened to their conversation from behind the door. She entered the room like a whirlwind and yelled, "Don't you dare trick me! Give me the raisin now; I already have the oven hot!"

The oldest child had just enough time to grab the box. He yelled for his brothers to follow him, and ran upstairs as fast as he could. On his way out, he pushed the stepmother, who fell to the floor with a loud rattling of her bones because she was very thin.

The children ran up to the attic, closed the door, and blocked the entrance with a large bureau. Meanwhile, the stepmother got up painfully, brushed herself off, and quickly headed toward the attic. "Open the door, brats! Open it up, little monsters! You'll see what will happen when your father gets home!" But the children, mute with fear, didn't budge.

Then, a cold, wicked, and terrible fury invaded her.

I am short one raisin. I believe you have one.

"You don't want to open the door? Very well, you will stay locked there as long as it takes. And when you are dying from hunger . . . you will eat the raisin!" She took a key from her pocket and turned it in the lock. Then she laughed three times, "Ha, ha, ha," with a sharp and evil crackle that was unlike the musical laughs she let her husband hear.

At nightfall, her husband came home and asked, "Where are the children?"

She answered, feigning[2] surprise, "Don't you remember? They left to visit their grandmother in the country for a few days." She lied so convincingly that he said, distracted, "That's true, I had forgotten."

Meanwhile, above in the attic, the three children celebrated the victory of having escaped from the cruel woman. But as the hours passed and they became tired of being prisoners, they began to think about how they would escape. The only opening besides the sealed door was a small skylight that was difficult to reach since it was high above the floor in the rafters. And it was at least ten meters above the ground, over the garden.

---

2. **feigning** (fān′ iŋ): pretending.

"We could never jump," they said. "We would need a parachute or a rope."

But in the attic, they couldn't find anything. Suddenly, in the middle of their reflections, the three children realized with surprise that they hadn't fought, whined, or played pranks for a long time. It was possible for them to behave! They were so happy with this discovery that they hugged each other and promised to continue their good behavior as long as they could.

But now it was vital that they find a way to escape. Night was falling, and with it they felt the first signs of cold and hunger. The oldest sighed, "If only I had my bed and a good blanket." "And a large glass of warm milk," added the second. "And our beautiful mother," murmured the youngest. Not knowing what else to do, the children curled up on the floor in a corner, cuddling each other, with the matchbox in the middle. They stayed like that until they fell asleep.

In the morning, the growling of their stomachs woke them. They had never been so hungry before. "We must eat something!" they said. Then they looked at the matchbox. "Oh no," said the oldest, "We are not going to eat the raisin, never!" After thinking for a moment, he continued in a serious tone, "Brothers, remember the stories of lost explorers or shipwrecked people who are left without food? They end up eating anything or anyone. . . . This must not happen to us!"

The youngest then said, "Let's separate ourselves from our mother so we can be sure we will not eat her."

"Yes," said the middle child. "If we throw her from the skylight, she will land on the grass in the garden, and since it is soft, she won't get hurt."

The children looked at the small raisin for the last time. Their eyes filled with tears. It was hard for them to separate from their mother!

But how could they reach the skylight to throw her into the garden? They could drag over the bureau that was against the door and climb on top of it, but they ran the risk that the evil stepmother would choose that moment to search for them. No! The best thing was to try to climb on top of each other to reach the skylight. The oldest would stand on a chair; the middle child would balance on the very top and open the skylight.

And that is what they did. Or it is what they almost did, because the chair was broken, which did not help the operation.

"Can you reach it? Can you touch the skylight?" the older children asked the youngest, who was balancing on top of them.

"Yes . . . , I found it . . . pass me the box!"

"What? Don't you have it?"

"No! I left it on the floor . . ."

They had to start over!

There was a small argument: each accused the other of having forgotten the box. But they soon made up.

"We'll just begin again," said the oldest child.

And they climbed on top of each other again: the oldest on the chair, the middle child on top of the oldest, and the youngest on top of the middle child, like acrobats. The youngest child reached the window and was about to open it when suddenly, crack, the chair broke in two and the children fell to the floor with a great crash.

ALBORADO DE FIESTA
(The Dawning of a Party)
Arturo Estrada
Courtesy of the artist.

At that very moment their father was entering the house. He heard the noise and said to his wife, "Go see what is happening!"

She disappeared for a moment and returned saying, "It isn't anything, just some mice running through the attic."

Meanwhile, in the attic, the three children were crying. Large tears of pain ran down their cheeks: tears of pain, because they had hurt themselves in the fall, and of frustration, because how were they going to reach the skylight now that the chair was broken? To <u>console</u> themselves, they opened the matchbox and looked at the raisin. But just seeing the raisin made them even sadder, and they started to cry over it as hard as they could.

The children's tears fell in torrents on the matchbox, so that it flooded, and the raisin was left floating in a small, warm puddle.

Suddenly, the oldest child shouted, "Look! It's growing!"

Words to Know and Use | **console** (kən sōl´) *v.* to comfort

247

It was true. The raisin, swollen from the children's tears, had begun to grow. The more they cried, the more the raisin grew. And seeing it grow, the children cried more, but now from happiness.

The raisin continued inflating, stretching, enlarging, growing more and more. Until . . . before the children's disbelieving eyes, it changed form and . . .

"Mommmmmmm!" they yelled.

It was their mother, as tall and as beautiful as before she had shriveled up. The mother took her children in her arms and, laughing and crying, hugged them against her for a long time.

Meanwhile, on the first floor, the father was wondering about the strange noises that were coming from the attic. Finally, he could stand it no longer, and he said to his wife, "Those mice in the attic have a strange way of squeaking. It is as if they were crying. Give me the keys. . . . I am going to see what is happening."

His wife tried every way to stop him, but her efforts were in vain. He went upstairs, tried to open the door with the key, and, when it wouldn't open, pushed it with all his might. Imagine his surprise to find his three children in the arms of his first, beautiful wife! The four, hugging tightly, looked at him without saying anything.

Then this man, who wasn't as bad as he seemed, felt as if he would die from remorse and joy. He covered his children with kisses, and then, kneeling at his wife's feet, he begged forgiveness for having doubted her.

He was immediately forgiven, and father, mother, and children walked downstairs hand in hand to have dinner, with their hearts full of happiness.

The stepmother hadn't waited for them. Guessing what had happened, she had run off at full speed with her bags.

The raisin cake in the oven was completely burnt.

The mother threw it in the trash and quickly made another, delicious cake full of candied fruit.

The whole family happily and hungrily ate this new cake that didn't contain a single raisin. ❧

INSIGHT

The World Is Not a Pleasant Place to Be
NIKKI GIOVANNI

the world is not a pleasant place
to be without
someone to hold and be held by

a river would stop
its flow if only
a stream were there
to receive it

an ocean would never laugh
if clouds weren't there
to kiss her tears

the world is not
a pleasant place to be without
someone

Words to Know and Use | **remorse** (ri môrs') *n.* deep regret for past wrongdoing

Responding to Reading

First Impressions

1. What were you thinking about when you finished this story? Jot down your thoughts in your journal or on a sheet of paper.

Second Thoughts

2. What is a possible message, or moral, of this story?

3. Consider the subunit title, "Metamorphoses." What metamorphoses, or changes, take place in this story?

4. Why do you suppose it takes the children's tears to bring their mother back to her former self?

5. Look back at the ideas you developed in Examine What You Know. What elements of realism and fantasy does this story contain?

Broader Connections

6. Many traditional stories portray stepparents—especially stepmothers—as evil characters. Why do you think stepmothers are typically cast in the role of villain in these stories? Do you think modern stories should portray stepparents as villains? Why or why not?

Literary Concept: Protagonist and Antagonist

The **protagonist** of a story is the main character. Most of the important action in the story centers on that character. Often, the protagonist changes in some way after the climax of the story.

An **antagonist** is a character who opposes or competes with the protagonist. Who do you think are the protagonist and the antagonist in "The Enchanted Raisin"? Why?

Writing Options

1. Imagine that the husband in this story wants to file a police report on his missing wife. What should it say? Assume the husband's role and write a **missing-person report.** Be sure to include details about your wife's height, weight, appearance, and clothing, as well as where she was last seen and by whom.

2. At the end of "The Enchanted Raisin," the family is given a chance for an improved life. Write a **sequel** that describes a day in the life of the "new" family.

3. Tabloid newspapers are often filled with sensational reports that are as fantastic as "The Enchanted Raisin." In the style of a tabloid, write a **newspaper article** that tells the story of the woman who turned into a raisin.

4. Imagine that a person really could change into a raisin and back. Write a "scientific" explanation of this remarkable metamorphosis in the style of an imaginary **medical report.**

Vocabulary Practice

Exercise   On a sheet of paper, write the letter of the word or phrase that best completes each sentence.

1. When the father began to **lament** his lost wife, he probably needed   (a) a newspaper   (b) a clock   (c) a handkerchief.

2. When he said, "On the **contrary,**" the children could tell that   (a) he agreed with them   (b) he did not understand what they were talking about   (c) he disagreed with them.

3. The children knew that their stepmother must **detest** them when she wanted   (a) to greet them with hugs and kisses   (b) to take them to the park   (c) to take their mother away from them.

4. The children showed their **remorse** by   (a) crying bitterly   (b) going to the playground   (c) buying a bag of candy.

5. In an attempt to **console** themselves, the children (a) swung from the curtains like monkeys   (b) smashed plates on the floor   (c) opened the matchbox and looked inside.

Words to Know and Use

---

console
contrary
detest
lament
remorse

Poetry

The *Creation*

JAMES WELDON JOHNSON

A *Loaf of Poetry*

NAOSHI KORIYAMA

Examine What You Know

How do you get from the spark of a great idea to the satisfaction of a finished product such as a poem or a short story? What steps do you take, and in what order? On a staircase like the one below, write the steps of the process you follow when you create something.

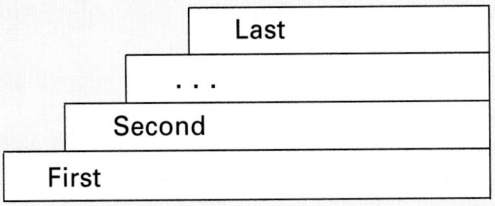

```
                    Last
                ...
            Second
        First
```

Expand Your Knowledge

The authors of the poems you are about to read follow their own creative steps when they write. James Weldon Johnson says that his creative process usually involves writing and rewriting his poems many times. The only exception to this occurred when he had what he calls his "poetic inspiration." That time, he got out of bed, wrote a sonnet, and sent it out in the morning to be published.

When you read "A Loaf of Poetry," see if you can determine the creative process Naoshi Koriyama (nä ō' shē kō rē yä' mä) follows. Do you think it is similar to or different from Johnson's process?

Enrich Your Reading

Poetic Form   During the process of creating a poem, a poet may make several choices about the poem's form. The **form** of a poem is the way it looks—the arrangement of its parts on a page. You have probably noticed that poetry is written in **lines,** which may or may not be sentences. These lines are sometimes separated into groups called **stanzas.** Sometimes all the stanzas of a poem have the same number of lines; at other times, the number of lines varies. After reading "The Creation" and "A Loaf of Poetry," compare the forms of the two poems to see how they are alike and how they are different. Why do you think the poets might have chosen these forms?

■ *Author biographies in Reader's Handbook*

The *Creation*

JAMES WELDON JOHNSON

And God stepped out on space,
And He looked around and said:
I'm lonely—
I'll make me a world.

5 And far as the eye of God could see
Darkness covered everything,
Blacker than a hundred midnights
Down in cypress swamp.

Then God smiled,
10 And the light broke,
And the darkness rolled up on one side,
And the light stood shining on the other,
And God said: That's good!

Then God reached out and took the light in His hands,
15 And God rolled the light around in His hands
Until He made the sun;
And He set that sun a-blazing in the heavens.
And the light that was left from making the sun
God gathered it up in a shining ball
20 And flung it against the darkness,
Spangling the night with the moon and stars.
Then down between
The darkness and the light
He hurled the world;
25 And God said: That's good!

Then God himself stepped down—
And the sun was on His right hand,
And the moon was on His left;
The stars were clustered about His head,
30 And the earth was under His feet.
And God walked, and where He trod
His footsteps hollowed the valleys out
And bulged the mountains up.

Then He stopped and looked and saw
35 That the earth was hot and barren.
So God stepped over to the edge of the world
And He spat out the seven seas—
He batted His eyes, and the lightnings flashed—
He clapped His hands, and the thunders rolled—
40 And the waters above the earth came down,
The cooling waters came down.

Then the green grass sprouted,
And the little red flowers blossomed,
The pine tree pointed his finger to the sky,
45 And the oak spread out his arms,
The lakes cuddled down in the hollows of the ground,
The rivers ran down to the sea;
And God smiled again,
And the rainbow appeared,
50 And curled itself around His shoulder.

Then God raised His arm and He waved His hand
Over the sea and over the land,
And He said: Bring forth! Bring forth!
And quicker than God could drop His hand,
55 Fishes and fowls
And beasts and birds
Swam the rivers and the seas,
Roamed the forests and the woods,
And split the air with their wings.
60 And God said: That's good!

Then God walked around,
And God looked around
On all that He had made.
He looked at His sun,
65 And He looked at His moon,
And He looked at His little stars;
He looked on His world
With all its living things,
And God said: I'm lonely still.
70 Then God sat down
On the side of a hill where He could think;
By a deep wide river He sat down;
With His head in His hands,
God thought and thought,
75 Till He thought: I'll make me a man!

THE CREATION   1935   Aaron Douglas
Howard University Gallery of Art,
Washington, D.C.

Up from the bed of the river
God scooped the clay;
And by the bank of the river
He kneeled Him down;
80 And there the great God Almighty
Who lit the sun and fixed it in the sky,
Who flung the stars to the most far corner of the night,
Who rounded the earth in the middle of His hand;
The Great God,
85 Like a mammy bending over her baby,
Kneeled down in the dust
Toiling over a lump of clay
Till He shaped it in His own image;

Then into it He blew the breath of life,
90 And man became a living soul.
Amen. Amen.

*R*esponding to Reading

First Impressions of "The Creation"

1. What details of this poem stand out most in your mind? Jot them down or sketch them in your journal or on a sheet of paper.

Second Thoughts on "The Creation"

2. Do you think the speaker actually believes that the world was created in the way he describes it? Why or why not?

3. The speaker says that God shaped man "into His own image." What details does the poet include that show how people and God are alike?

4. Why do you think the stanzas of this poem are of different lengths?

A Loaf of Poetry

NAOSHI KORIYAMA

SUNRISE   1924   Arthur Dove
Milwaukee Art Museum, Gift of Mrs. Edward L. Wehr.

you mix
the dough
of experience
with
5 the yeast
of inspiration
and knead it well
with love
and pound it
10 with all your might
and then
leave it
until
it puffs out big
15 with its own inner force
and then
knead it again
and
shape it
20 into a round form
and bake it
in the oven
of your heart

Responding to Reading

First Impressions of "A Loaf of Poetry"

1. What thoughts or feelings are you left with after reading this poem? Jot them down in your journal or on a sheet of paper.

Second Thoughts on "A Loaf of Poetry"

2. How do you think creating a poem is like baking a loaf of bread?

3. How does the "recipe" in this poem match the creative process you described in Examine What You Know?

4. For what else could this poem be a "recipe"?

Literary Concept: Figurative Language

Poets use **figurative language** when they choose words and phrases that help the reader picture familiar things in fresh ways. These words and phrases are called figures of speech. Three common figures of speech are similes, metaphors, and personification.

As you know, a **simile** is a comparison that contains a word such as *like, as, than,* or *resembles.* **Metaphors** are also comparisons but they do not contain words such as *like, as, than,* or *resembles.* In **personification** an animal or an object is described as if it were human or had human qualities. Look through "The Creation" and "A Loaf of Poetry" and find examples of similes, metaphors, and personification.

Writing Options

1. Imagine that the mother in "The Enchanted Raisin" wants to make a new cake for her family, from a recipe like the one in "A Loaf of Poetry." What real or fantasy "ingredients" do you think she might use? Write the **recipe** that she might follow, explaining why she would include each ingredient.

2. Imagine you are a talk-show host interviewing the man God created in "The Creation." Write a **transcript** of the interview, including your questions and his answers.

Nonfiction

The *Home Front: 1941–1945*

HAZEL SHELTON ABERNETHY

Examine What You Know

"I'll never forget where I was when . . ." Do these words remind you of a momentous event in your life? Can you picture the event? Where were you when the event took place? What were you doing? Did you personally experience the event, or was it something you heard about on the evening news? Take a moment or two to collect your thoughts about this event in a chart like the one below.

- Date of the event:
- Where I was and what I was doing at the time:
- What happened:
- Why this event was important:
- How my life changed as a result:

Expand Your Knowledge

Like many others of her generation, Hazel Shelton Abernethy will always remember exactly where she was and what she was doing on December 7, 1941—the day Pearl Harbor was bombed by the Japanese. This momentous event, which forced the United States to enter World War II, affected not only the U.S. military forces but also civilians living on the home front. Every part of civilian life was changed. Factories across the country began producing goods for the war in record amounts. Products important to the war effort—such as gasoline, tires, and almost anything made from metal—were rationed.

Write Before You Read

■ *Author biography in Reader's Handbook*

Use the chart you developed in Examine What You Know as a starting point for describing a momentous event in your life. Write in your journal or on a sheet of paper.

The Home Front: 1941–1945

HAZEL SHELTON ABERNETHY

I was fourteen years old and a sophomore at Nacogdoches High School on Sunday, December 7, 1941. Like all people old enough to have any memory of that day, I can tell you exactly where I was and what I was doing when I heard the news about Pearl Harbor.[1] A group of friends and I had gone to the double-feature movie at the Stone Fort Theatre on the west side of the square. The movies were *Till We Meet Again* with George Brent and Merle Oberon and one of the "Maisie" movies with Ann Southern and Robert Sterling. When we came out of the theater, about four thirty, they were selling "extra" editions of the *Sentinel* that announced the Japanese attack. Most people were not completely sure at that time just where Pearl Harbor was, but our geographical knowledge widened significantly over the next few months.

On Monday, December 8, we gathered in the high school auditorium, the present-day middle school, and heard President Roosevelt ask for a declaration of war against Japan. When "The Star-Spangled Banner" was played, there were few dry eyes.

Almost immediately our lives began to change in response to the national war effort.

At school we had war-bond drives and scrap drives.[2] Tuesday was Stamp Day, and students saved their pennies to buy savings stamps.[3] The stamp books came in denominations of ten and twenty-five cents. When a student had bought $18.75 worth of stamps, he could purchase a savings bond that would mature in ten years at $25.00. There was competition between home rooms, and the room that sold the most stamps each week would receive some special recognition.

We had a scrap-metal drive that could have competed with any school in the country. The entire Mound Street campus was covered with metal scrap. High school students responded enthusiastically with discarded pots and pans, junked jalopies, an entire old bus "carcass," and parts of a locomotive. The drive lasted for six weeks and dominated our activities. This, too, was conducted as a home-room competition. We were in Miss Dora Grant's home room, and we won the prize—an entire page in the school annual.

---

1. **Pearl Harbor:** the site of a U.S. naval base in Hawaii, attacked by Japan on December 7, 1941.

2. **war-bond drives and scrap drives:** nationwide campaigns during World War II encouraging people in the United States to buy government bonds and save recyclable materials to aid the war effort.

3. **savings stamps:** inexpensive stamps sold during World War II to raise money for military expenses.

At the government's request we began to save everything. Paper, tin cans, and bacon grease headed the list of vital "recyclables." We also learned to "make it do, wear it out, and do without." When clothing wore out completely, we saved everything salvageable. Buttons, snaps, and hooks and eyes were hoarded away. Silk stockings were a thing of the past, and nylons were a treasure rarely to be found, so we painted our legs with pancake makeup and drew a seam up the back with eyebrow pencil and prayed we wouldn't get caught out in the rain.

Gold stars represented the boys who would not come home again.

With the exception of shoes, clothing was never rationed, but there were shortages, especially of quality clothes. As wartime weddings increased, mothers of brides searched frantically for white satin or tulle.[4] My mother bought three pre-war evening dresses at the Episcopal Church rummage sale and constructed two seminew formals for my freshman year in college. Shoe rationing allowed each person one pair of shoes for each season. This was particularly hard on families with young children whose growth was not seasonal, so there was pooling of shoe stamps among people according to need. Many a grandparent contributed his shoe stamp to a grandchild.

We worked for the Red Cross and rolled bandages and knitted socks and mufflers, and even Nacogdoches, with a population under ten thousand, had a USO.[5] The high school and college girls acted as hostesses and gave dances there. It alternated as a youth center. The social clubs at the college went to Harmon Military Hospital in Longview and gave programs to entertain the recovering wounded. If they survived that entertainment, they were considered fit for active duty. We wrote letters, baked cookies to send to the boys in service, took strangers in uniform home for dinner, and never passed up a serviceman thumbing a ride on the highway. We followed the war news in the newspapers, radio, and newsreels with anxious hearts. Sometimes we would catch a glimpse of a loved one in a newsreel. Once we saw my cousin's face on the screen, and we came to the theater everytime the newsreel appeared. Who knew when or if we would see him again?

The real cost of the war was being brought sharply home by blue star banners, which were hung in the windows of businesses, schools, and homes. Each of these stars represented a hometown boy who was serving in the military. More and more gold stars began to appear on these banners. Gold stars represented the boys who would not come home again.

Our lives revolved around the comings and goings of our friends in the service. As my own group of friends began to leave in 1944, we developed almost a ritual of their leaving. We would give an all-day picnic for them at Fern Lake, and the night before they left we would have a family party for them. Our parents, brothers and sisters, and friends would all go with them to the station

---

4. **tulle** (tool): a fine, stiff netting used for veils and gowns.

5. **USO**: the United Service Organization, a volunteer-staffed group offering recreational services to U.S. military personnel.

Collage showing typical "home-front" scenes during World War II.

HOW TO USE YOUR GASOLINE RATION BOOK

This book has six pages of eight coupons each. Each coupon is numbered and is good only as follows: Coupons numbered 1, during first and second months. Coupons numbered 2, during third and fourth months. Coupons numbered 3, during fifth and sixth months. Coupons numbered 4, during seventh and eighth months. Coupons numbered 5, during ninth and tenth months. Coupons numbered 6, during eleventh and twelfth months.

Each coupon is good for *ONE UNIT* of gasoline. The number of gallons which each coupon gives you the right to buy will depend upon the available supply of gasoline; therefore, the value of the unit may be changed. Any change in value will be publicly announced by the Office of Price Administration.

Do not loosen or tear coupons from the book. Detached coupons will not be honored. When buying gasoline, hand the book to the service station attendant. Only he is allowed to remove coupons. He must remove enough coupons to cover the number of gallons of gasoline purchased. If your purchase is less than one unit, the attendant must nevertheless remove an entire coupon.

The station attendant is permitted to deliver gasoline only into the tank of a vehicle for which you are entitled to use this book. Do not ask him to violate the law.

A PERMITS DELIVERY OF ONE UNIT OFFICE OF PRICE ADM. - FUEL RATIONING BRANCH 1 THIS COUPON DETACHED AT TIME OF SALE

To conserve fuel during World War II, drivers were required to use gasoline ration books.

to see them off. The train to Houston left at two o'clock in the morning, and there were some emotional send-offs down at that old depot. We were lucky; all of those boys did come home.

The restrictions on transportation probably had the most immediate effect on the conduct of our daily lives. On January 1, 1942, an order was issued banning the production of civilian cars. The last civilian car rolled off the assembly line on February 10, 1942. A limit of five tires for each automobile was strictly enforced; garages and basements were checked for hoarding. Only retread tires could be purchased, and dire need had to be proved through many miles of red tape.

Gasoline rationing began on December 1, 1942, and the national speed limit was set at thirty-five miles an hour to conserve fuel.

Stickers were placed on cars to show how much gas we were allowed to buy, and we were issued books of ration stamps to obtain our quota. Everyone with a car qualified for an A sticker, which allowed us to buy four gallons of gas a week, which was enough to drive about sixty miles a week. B and C stamps allowed more gas for salesmen, delivery men, essential war workers, and for carpools. About one-half the drivers in the country qualified for these stamps. E stamps were for doctors, emergency vehicles, ambulances, and Home Guard vehicles, and a T sticker for trucks approved unlimited gasoline mileage.

In 1943 all pleasure driving was banned—"Is this trip really necessary?"—and the use of public transportation greatly increased. A bus or train trip was never certain. Trains, especially, frequently were sidetracked for more essential uses. All public transportation was cramped and crowded.

In 1943, with SFA's[6] enrollment dipping dangerously low, the Board of Regents obtained a contract to establish the first WAAC school in the nation on our local campus. The Women's Army Auxiliary Corps was on the SFA campus for about twelve months, and two thousand WACs were graduated there. My father, who was the basketball coach at SFA, was not happy. He said we were the only school in the Lone Star Conference who did not get some sort of military unit with men who could play basketball. The high school girls and college girls were not very happy either.

There were several prisoner-of-war camps in the area.

The last thing this community needed was more females injected into the population. When the high school class of 1944 entered SFA in the fall, there were about 25 or 30 men on campus out of a school population of around 300-350. It was bleak.

Food rationing came in gradually. There were periodical sugar and coffee shortages, and sugar was rationed in April of 1942. Food ration books were issued in May of 1942, one to each family member. Prices were frozen on 60 percent of all food items that same spring. As time went on, almost every item that we ate, wore, used, or lived in was subject to rationing or price controls.

Victory gardens[7] grew on almost every vacant lot. One of the best ones was on the corner of King and Raguet where the Raguet Apartments are now. Every family in the neighborhood took its turn tending to this garden. The Demonstration School children dug up the backyard of SFA President Dr. Birdwell's on the SFA Campus and had a flourishing garden. One summer a group of ladies in Central Heights canned vegetables for a nickel a can and no ration stamps if the customer furnished the vegetables. My mother and I used precious gasoline scouring the county for vegetables. They made a delicious soup mix at those kitchens, and my father said we still had some of those canned vegetables in our attic in the late 1950s.

There were several prisoner-of-war camps in the area. Prisoners worked primarily in the forest areas harvesting wood for the lumber companies. There were always rumors of escaped POWs at large but most of these internees did not want to escape. At the camp in Chireno one evening, two prisoners were missing, but when the truck went back to the work area, there they were.

They had been left behind, and they were waiting for the truck to return and take them to supper. Several years after the war some of these men returned to visit; they had very warm memories of their treatment here.

For three and a half years our lives revolved around the comings and goings of our servicemen. After D-Day[8] and the rapid advance of the Allies toward Germany, we were sure the boys would be home to stay, maybe even by Christmas, but the German

---

6. **SFA:** Stephen F. Austin State University in Nacogdoches, Texas.
7. **Victory gardens:** vegetable gardens cultivated during World War II to help relieve food shortages.
8. **D-Day:** June 6, 1944, the day Allied forces landed in Western France.

breakthrough that developed into the Battle of the Bulge[9] ended that hope. The American forces suffered seventy-seven thousand casualties, and that was the grimmest Christmas of the war. As the spring of 1945 arrived, our hopes for victory increased, and even the blow of President Roosevelt's death could not completely dim our optimism. When VE Day[10] came we rejoiced, but the total victory was a few months away.

In the early morning of August 14, 1945, we heard the civil defense siren sound, along with the fire trucks and all five of the mill whistles going full blast. People dressed and went down to the Square and just hugged each other. Just as on the day that began the war, there were extra editions of the *Sentinel* being distributed that said the war was over.

Since the military point system provided for a gradual demobilization,[11] the real impact of the returning veterans was not felt until 1946. On the campus of SFA, the change was dramatic. The enrollment jumped to one thousand that fall, and the ratio of men to women was over three to one. For those girls who had attended school while it was almost an all-girl campus, this was nothing short of miraculous. College life was what it was meant to be. Dances with MEN, and stag lines, football games and MEN, normal college life and MEN. Life was wonderful!

---

9. **Battle of the Bulge:** a World War II battle that began in December 1944; the German army advanced into Belgium, temporarily causing a bulge in the line of Allied military forces.

10. **VE Day:** Short for Victory in Europe Day; May 8, 1945, when Germany officially surrendered and the European phase of World War II ended.

11. **point system . . . demobilization:** refers to a system used to release U.S. military personnel from active duty after World War II, based on a person's accumulation of points awarded for various achievements.

from Wear It Proudly

WILLIAM TSUCHIDA

William Shinji Tsuchida was a medic during the invasion of Germany. His parents, born in Japan, were interned by the United States during the war. Tsuchida wrote often to his brother and sister in the internment camp.[1]

France, 23 Oct. 1944
Dear H and E,

Hello again while I have a chance to write. The other day we were supposed to have our first rest period, but we were called back. From that you can surmise to what degree we are having casualties, since I can't tell you that directly. Anyway we got as far as the showers, and I had my first shower in about two months. You should see us now. We are caked with mud from head to toe, and my clothes are ready to be peeled off me. My underclothes are oily black, and I sure would like to change. The shower point is about twenty minutes away. No ducking, no shrapnel.[2] I guess that was about the most enjoyable five minutes in my life.

What a mess the whole business is. My mind is one confused conglomeration[3] of incidents, the basic fears of night, and the waiting for daylight. I hope everybody with the soft war jobs realizes the horrible days and nights the line company men have to spend out here.

Got your letters regularly, with the pictures. Thanks, and keep it up. Please send me jars of jellies, preserves. Our diet lacks vegetables, so send small cans of tomato juice, soups, fruit, and be sure to make the packages in a variety, not just one item in one box. So long for now,

Shinji

---

1. internment camp: a prisonlike facility set up in the western United States to confine Japanese Americans during World War II.
2. shrapnel (shrap′ nəl): the metal balls and fragments that shoot out from an exploding artillery shell.
3. conglomeration (kən gläm′ ər ā′ shən): a mixture of different things.

Responding to Reading

First Impressions

1. What change in the lives of civilians surprised you the most?

Second Thoughts

2. If you had been living during World War II, what part of rationing would have seemed the worst to you?

3. Reread William Tsuchida's letter to his family on page 265. Compare and contrast his war experience with Abernethy's.

Broader Connections

4. "Make it do, wear it out, and do without." This World War II slogan could have been written yesterday by people concerned about the environment. Recycling, similar in some ways to that during World War II, has become a national movement. Would you favor a national law requiring recycling?

Literary Concept: Memoir

A **memoir** is a first-person recollection of an experience. It relates the details of an event that the writer participated in or witnessed. The writer must convey why the event was personally important and what impact it had on his or her life. Do you think Abernethy succeeds in conveying why her experience was so meaningful? Explain.

Writing Options

1. Imagine that it is 1942 and your school is having a scrap-metal drive to help the war effort. Write a **publicity notice** for your school newspaper. Explain the rules of the scrap-metal contest and motivate students to participate.

2. Think about the momentous event you described in the Write Before You Read activity. How does that event compare with Abernethy's experience? In a **comparison essay** discuss the similarities and differences.

Fiction

*F*lowers for *A*lgernon

DANIEL KEYES

*E*xamine What You Know

What if you woke up tomorrow and realized you had become a genius overnight? In your journal or on a sheet of paper, answer the following questions:

- What personal goals could you achieve if you were a genius?

- What drawbacks, if any, might there be to becoming a genius?

- How might your friends and family react to your intelligence?

*E*xpand Your Knowledge

What if we could increase our intelligence? Researchers are currently exploring drugs that might help us do just that. These drugs—"smart drugs" or "brain drugs"—are combinations of vitamins, nutrients, amino acids, and prescription drugs. Some people say that smart drugs improve people's memory as well as boost their intelligence. Smart drugs, however, have not yet been thoroughly tested by the Food and Drug Administration for safety and effectiveness.

*E*nrich Your Reading

Character Change   In this story Charlie Gordon goes through some dramatic changes. His personality and intelligence change—as does the way others treat him. To better understand and keep track of what happens to Charlie, fill in a chart like the one below as you read.

	March 5–March 10	March 15–June 4	June 5–July 28
What is Charlie's personality like?			
What is his intelligence like?			
How do others see and treat him?			
What does he think about other people?			

■ *Author biography on Extend page*

Flowers for Algernon

DANIEL KEYES

Part 1

progris riport 1—martch 5 1965

Dr. Strauss says I shud rite down what I think and evrey thing that happins to me from now on. I dont know why but he says its importint so they will see if they will use me. I hope they use me. Miss Kinnian says maybe they can make me smart. I want to be smart. My name is Charlie Gordon. I am 37 years old and 2 weeks ago was my birthday. I have nuthing more to rite now so I will close for today.

progris riport 2—martch 6

I had a test today. I think I failed it. and I think that maybe now they wont use me. What happind is a nice young man was in the room and he had some white cards with ink spilled all over them. He sed Charlie what do you see on this card. I was very skared even tho I had my rabits foot in my pockit because when I was a kid I always faled tests in school and I spillled ink to.

predict   What are they using him for?

I told him I saw a inkblot. He said yes and it made me feel good. I thot that was all but when I got up to go he stopped me. He said now sit down Charlie we are not thru yet. Then I dont remember so good but he wantid me to say what was in the ink. I dint see nuthing in the ink but he said there was picturs there other pepul saw some picturs. I coudnt see any picturs. I reely tryed to see. I held the card close up and then far away. Then I said if I had my glases I coud see better I usally only ware my glases in the movies or TV but I said they are in the closit in the hall. I got them. Then I said let me see that card agen I bet Ill find it now.

I tryed hard but I still coudnt find the picturs I only saw the ink. I told him maybe I need new glases. He rote something down on a paper and I got skared of faling the test. I told him it was a very nice inkblot with littel points all around the eges. He looked very sad so that wasnt it. I said please let me try agen. Ill get it in a few minits becaus Im not so fast somtimes. Im a slow reeder too in Miss Kinnians class for slow adults but Im trying very hard.

He gave me a chance with another card that had 2 kinds of ink spillled on it red and blue.

He was very nice and talked slow like Miss Kinnian does and he explained it to me that it was a *raw shok*.[1] He said pepul see

---

1. **raw shok:** Charlie's way of writing *Rorschach*, the name of a test by which people's personalities are judged based on what the people see in various inkblot designs.

things in the ink. I said show me where. He said think. I told him I think a inkblot but that wasnt rite eather. He said what does it remind you—pretend something. I closd my eyes for a long time to pretend. I told him I pretend a fowntan pen with ink leeking all over a table cloth. Then he got up and went out.

I dont think I passd the *raw shok* test.

progris riport 3—martch 7

Dr Strauss and Dr Nemur say it dont matter about the inkblots. I told them I dint spill the ink on the cards and I coudnt see anything in the ink. They said that maybe they will still use me. I said Miss Kinnian never gave me tests like that one only spelling and reading. They said Miss Kinnian told that I was her bestist pupil in the adult nite scool becaus I tryed the hardist and I reely wantid to lern. They said how come you went to the adult nite scool all by yourself Charlie. How did you find it. I said I askd pepul and sumbody told me where I shud go to lern to read and spell good. They said why did you want to. I told them becaus all my life I wantid to be smart and not dumb. But its very hard to be smart. They said you know it will probly be tempirery. I said yes. Miss Kinnian told me. I dont care if it herts.

Later I had more crazy tests today. The nice lady who gave it me told me the name and I asked her how do you spellit so I can rite it in my progris riport. THEMATIC APPERCEPTION TEST.[2] I dont know the frist 2 words but I know what *test* means. You got to pass it or you get bad marks. This test lookd easy becaus I coud see the picturs. Only this time she dint want me to tell her the picturs. That mixd me up. I said the

man yesterday said I shoud tell him what I saw in the ink she said that dont make no difrence. She said make up storys about the pepul in the picturs.

I told her how can you tell storys about pepul you never met. I said why shud I make up lies. I never tell lies any more becaus I always get caut.

She told me this test and the other one the raw shok was for getting personalty. I laffed so hard. I said how can you get that thing from inkblots and fotos. She got sore and put her picturs away. I dont care. It was sily. I gess I faled that test too.

Later some men in white coats took me to a difernt part of the hospitil and gave me a game to play. It was like a race with a white mouse. They called the mouse Algernon. Algernon was in a box with a lot of twists and turns like all kinds of walls and they gave me a pencil and a paper with lines and lots of boxes. On one side it said START and on the other end it said FINISH. They said it was *amazed*[3] and that Algernon and me had the same *amazed* to do. I dint see how we could have the same *amazed* if Algernon had a box and I had a paper but I dint say nothing. Anyway there wasnt time because the race started.

One of the men had a watch he was trying to hide so I woudnt see it so I tryed not to look and that made me nervus.

Anyway that test made me feel worser than all the others because they did it over 10 times with diferent *amazeds* and Algernon won every time. I dint know that mice were

---

2. **Thematic Apperception Test** (thē mat′ ik ap′ ər sep′ shən): a test by which personality is analyzed based on the stories people make up about a series of pictures.
3. **amazed:** Charlie's way of writing *a maze.*

so smart. Maybe thats because Algernon is a white mouse. Maybe white mice are smarter than other mice.

progris riport 4—Mar 8

Their going to use me! Im so exited I can hardly write. Dr Nemur and Dr Strauss had a argament about it first. Dr Nemur was in the office when Dr Strauss brot me in. Dr Nemur was worryed about using me but Dr Strauss told him Miss Kinnian rekemmended me the best from all the pepul who she was teaching. I like Miss Kinnian becaus shes a very smart teacher. And she said Charlie your going to have a second chance. If you volenteer for this experament you mite get smart. They dont know if it will be perminint but theirs a chance. Thats why I said ok even when I was scared because she said it was an operashun. She said dont be scared Charlie you done so much with so little I think you deserv it most of all.

review   Why does he feel so excited?

So I got scaird when Dr Nemur and Dr Strauss argud about it. Dr Strauss said I had something that was very good. He said I had a good *motor-vation*.[4] I never even knew I had that. I felt proud when he said that not every body with an eye-q[5] of 68 had that thing. I dont know what it is or where I got it but he said Algernon had it too. Algernons *motor-vation* is the cheese they put in his box. But it cant be that because I didnt eat any cheese this week.

Then he told Dr Nemur something I dint understand so while they were talking I wrote down some of the words.

He said Dr Nemur I know Charlie is not what you had in mind as the first of your new brede of intelek** (coudnt get the word) superman. But most pepul of his low ment** are host** and uncoop** and they are usualy dull apath** and hard to reach. He has a good natcher hes intristed and eager to please.

Dr Nemur said remember he will be the first human beeng ever to have his intelijence trippled by surgicle meens.

Dr Strauss said exakly. Look at how well hes lerned to read and write for his low mentel age its as grate an acheve** as you and I lerning einstines therey of **vity[6] without help. That shows the intenss motorvation. Its comparat** a tremen** achev** I say we use Charlie.

I dint get all the words and they were talking to fast but it sounded like Dr Strauss was on my side and like the other one wasnt.

Then Dr Nemur nodded he said all right maybe your right. We will use Charlie. When he said that I got so exited I jumped up and shook his hand for being so good to me. I told him thank you doc you wont be sorry for giving me a second chance. And I mean it like I told him. After the operashun Im gonna try to be smart. Im gonna try awful hard.

---

4. **motor-vation:** Charlie's way of writing *motivation*, the inner drive causing someone to take a certain action.

5. **eye-q:** Charlie's way of writing I.Q., short for intelligence quotient, the number used to indicate one's mental ability relative to a normal level.

6. **einstines therey of **vity:** Charlie's way of writing *Einstein's theory of relativity*, a scientific theory of space and time developed by Albert Einstein.

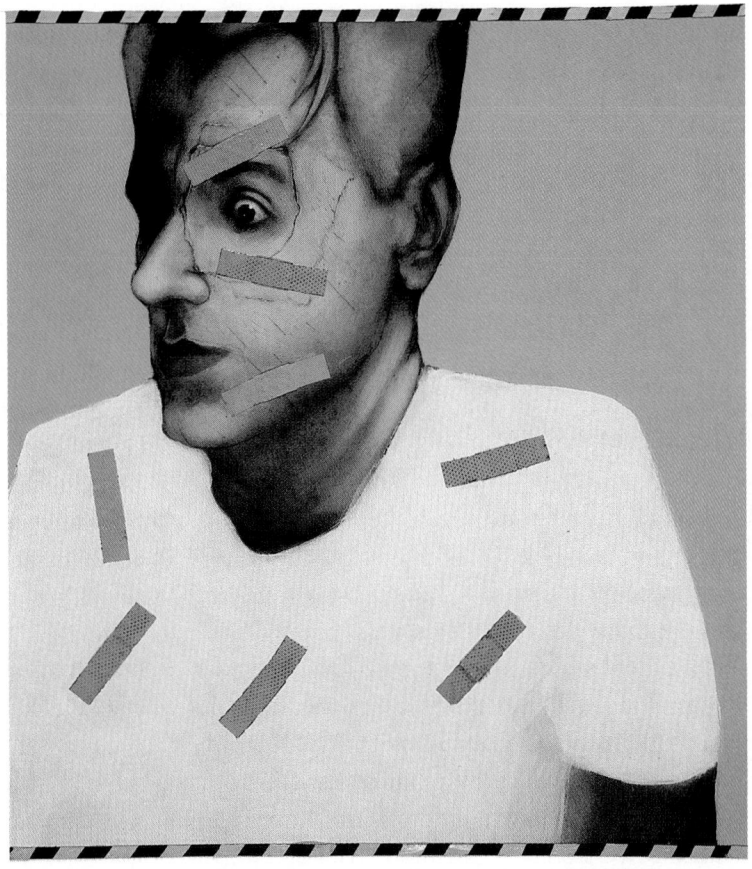

Illustration by Joel Peter Johnson.

progris riport 5—Mar 10

Im skared. Lots of people who work here and the nurses and the people who gave me the tests came to bring me candy and wish me luck. I hope I have luck. I got my rabits foot and my lucky penny and my horse shoe. Only a black cat crossed me when I was comming to the hospitil. Dr Strauss says dont be supersitis Charlie this is sience. Anyway Im keeping my rabits foot with me.

I asked Dr Strauss if Ill beat Algernon in the race after the operashun and he said maybe. If the operashun works Ill show that mouse I can be as smart as he is. Maybe smarter. Then Ill be abel to read better and spell the words good and know lots of things and be like other people. I want to be smart like other people. If it works perminint they will make everybody smart all over the wurld.

They dint give me anything to eat this morning. I dont know what that eating has to do with getting smart. Im very hungry and Dr Nemur took away my box of candy. That Dr Nemur is a grouch. Dr Strauss says I can have it back after the operashun. You cant eat befor a operashun. . . .

What's going to happen to him now?

Progress Report 6—Mar 15

The operashun dint hurt. He did it while I was sleeping. They took off the bandijis from my eyes and my head today so I can make a PROGRESS REPORT. Dr Nemur who looked at some of my other ones says I spell PROGRESS wrong and he told me how to spell it and REPORT too. I got to try and remember that.

A lgernon beats me all the time because he had that operashun too.

I have a very bad memary for spelling. Dr Strauss says its ok to tell about all the things that happin to me but he says I shoud tell more about what I feel and what I think. When I told him I dont know how to think he said try. All the time when the bandijis were on my eyes I tryed to think. Nothing happened. I dont know what to think about. Maybe if I ask him he will tell me how I can think now that Im suppose to get smart. What do smart people think about. Fancy things I suppose. I wish I knew some fancy things already.

Progress Report 7—Mar 19

Nothing is happining. I had lots of tests and different kinds of races with Algernon. I hate that mouse. He always beats me. Dr Strauss said I got to play those games. And he said some time I got to take those tests over again. Those inkblots are stupid. And those pictures are stupid too. I like to draw a picture of a man and a woman but I wont make up lies about people.

I got a headache from trying to think so much. I thot Dr Strauss was my frend but he dont help me. He dont tell me what to think or when Ill get smart. Miss Kinnian dint come to see me. I think writing these progress reports are stupid too.

Progress Report 8—Mar 23

Im going back to work at the factery. They said it was better I shud go back to work but I cant tell anyone what the operashun was for and I have to come to the hospitil for an hour evry night after work. They are gonna pay me mony every month for lerning to be smart.

Im glad Im going back to work because I miss my job and all my frends and all the fun we have there.

Dr Strauss says I shud keep writing things down but I dont have to do it every day just when I think of something or something speshul happins. He says dont get discoridged because it takes time and it happins slow. He says it took a long time with Algernon before he got 3 times smarter than he was before. Thats why Algernon beats me all the time because he had that opera-shun too. That makes me feel better. I could probly do that *amazed* faster than a reglar mouse. Maybe some day Ill beat Algernon. Boy that would be something. So far Alger-non looks like he mite be smart perminent.

Mar 25

(I dont have to write PROGRESS REPORT on top any more just when I hand it in once a week for Dr Nemur to read. I just have to put the date on. That saves time)

We had a lot of fun at the factery today. Joe Carp said hey look where Charlie had his operashun what did they do Charlie put some brains in. I was going to tell him but I remembered Dr Strauss said no. Then Frank Reilly said what did you do Charlie forget your key and open your door the hard way. That made me laff. Their really my friends and they like me.

Sometimes somebody will say hey look at Joe or Frank or George he really pulled a Charlie Gordon. I dont know why they say that but they always laff. This morning Amos Borg who is the 4 man at Donnegans used my name when he shouted at Ernie the office boy. Ernie lost a packige. He said Ernie for godsake what are you trying to be a Charlie Gordon. I dont understand why he said that. I never lost any packiges.

Mar 28

Dr Strauss came to my room tonight to see why I dint come in like I was suppose to. I told him I dont like to race with Algernon any more. He said I dont have to for a while but I shud come in. He had a present for me only it wasnt a present but just for lend. I thot it was a little television but it wasnt. He said I got to turn it on when I got to sleep. I said your kidding why shud I turn it on when Im going to sleep. Who ever herd of a thing like that. But he said if I want to get smart I got to do what he says. I told him I dint think I was going to get smart and he put his hand on my sholder and said Charlie you dont know it yet but your getting smarter all the time. You wont notice for a while. I think he was just being nice to make me feel good because I dont look any smarter.

Oh yes I almost forgot. I asked him when I can go back to the class at Miss Kinnians school. He said I wont go their. He said that soon Miss Kinnian will come to the hospitil to start and teach me speshul. I was mad at her for not comming to see me when I got the operashun but I like her so maybe we will be frends again.

Mar 29

That crazy TV kept me up all night. How can I sleep with something yelling crazy things all night in my ears. And the nutty pictures. Wow. I dont know what it says when Im up so how am I going to know when Im sleeping.

Dr Strauss says its ok. He says my brains are lerning when I sleep and that will help me when Miss Kinnian starts my lessons in the hospitl (only I found out it isnt a hospitil its a labatory). I think its all crazy. If you can get smart when your sleeping why do people go to school. That thing I dont think will work. I use to watch the late show and the late late show on TV all the time and it never made me smart. Maybe you have to sleep while you watch it.

Progress Report 9—April 3

Dr Strauss showed me how to keep the TV turned low so now I can sleep. I don't hear a thing. And I still dont understand what it says. A few times I play it over in the morning to find out what I lerned when I was sleeping and I don't think so. Miss Kinnian says Maybe its another langwidge or something. But most times it sounds american. It talks so fast faster then even Miss Gold who was my teacher in 6 grade and I remember she talked so fast I coudnt understand her.

I told Dr Strauss what good is it to get smart in my sleep. I want to be smart when Im awake. He says its the same thing and I have two minds. Theres the *subsconscious* and the *conscious*[7] (thats how you spell it). And

---

7. **subsconscious and the conscious** (kän′ shəs): psychological terms used for two kinds of mental activity. The *subconscious* (which Charlie misspelled) is mental activity that the person is not aware of. The *conscious* is mental activity that the person is aware of.

© Garry Gay/The Image Bank.

one dont tell the other one what its doing. They dont even talk to each other. Thats why I dream. And boy have I been having crazy dreams. Wow. Ever since that night TV. The late late late late late show.

I forgot to ask him if it was only me or if everybody had those two minds.

(I just looked up the word in the dictionary Dr Strauss gave me. The word is *subconscious. adj. Of the nature of mental operations yet not present in consciousness; as, subconscious conflict of desires.*) There's more but I still dont know what it means. This isnt a very good dictionary for dumb people like me.

Anyway the headache is from the party. My frends from the factery Joe Carp and Frank Reilly invited me to go with them to Muggsys Saloon for some drinks. I dont like to drink but they said we will have lots of fun. I had a good time.

Joe Carp said I should show the girls how I mop out the toilet in the factory and he got me a mop. I showed them and everyone laffed when I told that Mr Donnegan said I was the best janiter he ever had because I like my job and do it good and never come late or miss a day except for my operashun.

I said Miss Kinnian always said Charlie be proud of your job because you do it good.

Everybody laffed and we had a good time and they gave me lots of drinks and Joe said Charlie is a card when hes potted. I dont know what that means but everybody likes me and we have fun. I cant wait to be smart like my best frends Joe Carp and Frank Reilly.

I dont remember how the party was over but I think I went out to buy a newspaper and coffe for Joe and Frank and when I came back there was no one their. I looked for them all over till late. Then I dont remember so good but I think I got sleepy or sick. A nice cop brot me back home. Thats what my landlady Mrs Flynn says.

But I got a headache and big lump on my head and black and blue all over. I think maybe I fell but Joe Carp says it was the cop they beat up drunks some times. I dont think so. Miss Kinnian says cops are to help people. Anyway I got a bad headache and Im sick and hurt all over. I dont think Ill drink anymore.

April 6

I beat Algernon! I dint even know I beat him until Burt the tester told me. Then the second time I lost because I got so exited I fell off the chair before I finished. But after that I beat him 8 more times. I must be getting smart to beat a smart mouse like Algernon. But I dont *feel* smarter.

I wanted to race Algernon some more but Burt said thats enough for one day. They let me hold him for a minit. Hes not so bad. Hes soft like a ball of cotton. He blinks and when he opens his eyes their black and pink on the eges.

I said can I feed him because I felt bad to beat him and I wanted to be nice and make frends. Burt said no Algernon is a very specshul mouse with an operashun like mine, and he was the first of all the animals to stay smart so long. He told me Algernon is so smart that every day he has to solve a test to get his food. Its a thing like a lock on a door that changes every time Algernon goes in to eat so he has to lern something new to get his food. That made me sad because if he coudnt lern he would be hungry.

I dont think its right to make you pass a test to eat. How would Dr Nemur like it to have to pass a test every time he wants to eat. I think Ill be frends with Algernon.

April 9

Tonight after work Miss Kinnian was at the laboratory. She looked like she was glad to see me but scared. I told her dont worry Miss Kinnian Im not smart yet and she laffed. She said I have confidence in you Charlie the way you struggled so hard to read and right better than all the others. At werst you will have it for a littel wile and your doing somthing for sience.

We are reading a very hard book. I never read such a hard book before. Its called *Robinson Crusoe* about a man who gets merooned on a dessert Iland. Hes smart and figers out all kinds of things so he can have a house and food and hes a good swimmer. Only I feel sorry because hes all alone and has no frends. But I think their must be somebody else on the iland because theres a picture with his funny umbrella looking at footprints. I hope he gets a frend and not be lonly.

April 10

Miss Kinnian teaches me to spell better. She says look at a word and close your eyes and say it over and over until you remember. I have lots of truble with *through* that you say *threw* and *enough* and *tough* that you dont say *enew* and *tew*. You got to say *enuff* and *tuff*. Thats how I use to write it before I started to get smart. Im confused but Miss Kinnian says theres no reason in spelling.

Apr 14

Finished *Robinson Crusoe*. I want to find out more about what happens to him but Miss Kinnian says thats all there is. *Why*

Apr 15

Miss Kinnian says Im lerning fast. She read some of the Progress Reports and she looked at me kind of funny. She says Im a fine person and Ill show them all. I asked her why. She said never mind but I shoudnt feel bad if I find out that everybody isnt nice like I think. She said for a person who god gave so little to you done more then a lot of people with brains they never even used. I said all my frends are smart people but there good. They like me and they never did anything that wasnt nice. Then she got something in her eye and she had to run out to the ladys room.

There, are lots! of rules? to lern;

Apr 16

Today, I lerned the comma, this is a *comma* (,) a period, with a tail, Miss Kinnian, says its importent, because, it makes writing, better, she said, somebody, coud lose, a lot of money, if a comma, isnt, in the, right place, I dont have, any money, and I dont see, how a comma, keeps you, from losing it,

But she says, everybody, uses commas, so Ill use, them too,

Apr 17

I used the comma wrong. Its punctuation. Miss Kinnian told me to look up long words in the dictionary to lern to spell them. I said whats the difference if you can read it anyway. She said its part of your education so now on Ill look up all the words Im not sure how to spell. It takes a long time to write

that way but I think Im remembering. I only have to look up once and after that I get it right. Anyway thats how come I got the word *punctuation* right. (Its that way in the dictionary.) Miss Kinnian says a period is punctuation too, and there are lots of other marks to lern. I told her I thot all the periods had to have tails but she said no.

You got to mix them up. she showed? me" how. to mix! them(up,. and now; I can! mix up all kinds" of punctuation, in! my writing? There, are lots! of rules? to lern; but Im gettin'g them in my head.

One thing I? like about, Dear Miss Kinnian: (thats the way it goes in a business letter if I ever go into business) is she, always gives me' a reason" when—I ask. She's a gen'ius! I wish! I cou'd be smart" like, her;

(Punctuation, is; fun!)

Apr 18

What a dope I am! I didn't even understand what she was talking about. I read the grammar book last night and it explanes the whole thing. Then I saw it was the same way as Miss Kinnian was trying to tell me, but I didn't get it, I got up in the middle of the night, and the whole thing straightened out in my mind.

Miss Kinnian said that the TV working in my sleep helped out. She said I reached a plateau. Thats like the flat top of a hill.

After I figgered out how punctuation worked, I read over all my old Progress Reports from the beginning. Boy, did I have crazy spelling and punctuation! I told Miss Kinnian I ought to go over the pages and fix all the mistakes but she said, "No, Charlie, Dr. Nemur wants them just as they are. That's why he let you keep them after they were photostated, to see your own progress. You're coming along fast, Charlie."

That made me feel good. After the lesson I went down and played with Algernon. We don't race any more.

April 20

I feel sick inside. Not sick like for a doctor, but inside my chest it feels empty like getting punched and a heartburn at the same time.

I wasn't going to write about it, but I guess I got to, because its important. Today was the first time I ever stayed home from work.

Last night Joe Carp and Frank Reilly invited me to a party. There were lots of girls and some men from the factory. I remembered how sick I got last time I drank too much, so I told Joe I didn't want anything to drink. He gave me a plain coke instead. It tasted funny, but I thought it was just a bad taste in my mouth.

We had a lot of fun for a while. Joe said I should dance with Ellen and she would teach me the steps. I fell a few times and I couldn't understand why because no one else was dancing besides Ellen and me. And all the time I was tripping because somebody's foot was always sticking out.

Then when I got up I saw the look on Joe's face and it gave me a funny feeling in my stomack. "He's a scream," one of the girls said. Everybody was laughing.

Frank said, "I ain't laughed so much since we sent him off for the newspaper that night at Muggsy's and ditched him."

"Look at him. His face is red."

"He's blushing. Charlie is blushing."

"Hey, Ellen, what'd you do to Charlie? I never saw him act like that before."

I didn't know what to do or where to turn. Everyone was looking at me and laughing and I felt naked. I wanted to hide myself. I ran out into the street and threw up. Then I walked home. It's a funny thing I never knew that Joe and Frank and the others liked to have me around all the time to make fun of me. Now I know what it means when they say "to pull a Charlie Gordon."

I'm ashamed.

Progress Report 10
April 21

Still didn't go into the factory. I told Mrs. Flynn my landlady to call and tell Mr. Donnegan I was sick. Mrs. Flynn looks at me very funny lately like she's scared of me.

I think it's a good thing about finding out how everybody laughs at me. I thought about it a lot. It's because I'm so dumb and I don't even know when I'm doing something dumb. People think it's funny when a dumb person can't do things the same way they can.

Anyway, now I know I'm getting smarter every day. I know punctuation and I can spell good. I like to look up all the hard words in the dictionary and I remember them. I'm reading a lot now, and Miss Kinnian says I read very fast. Sometimes I even understand what I'm reading about, and it stays in my mind. There are times when I can close my eyes and think of a page and it all comes back like a picture.

Besides history, geography, and arithmetic, Miss Kinnian said I should start to learn a few foreign languages. Dr. Strauss gave me some more tapes to play while I sleep. I still don't understand how that conscious and unconscious mind works, but Dr.

Strauss say not to worry yet. He asked me to promise that when I start learning college subjects next week I wouldn't read any books on psychology[8]—that is, until he gives me permission.

I feel a lot better today, but I guess I'm still a little angry that all the time people were laughing and making fun of me because I wasn't so smart. When I become intelligent like Dr. Strauss says, with three times my I.Q. of 68, then maybe I'll be like everyone else and people will like me and be friendly.

I'm not sure what an *I.Q.* is. Dr. Nemur said it was something that measured how intelligent you were—like a scale in the drugstore weighs pounds. But Dr. Strauss had a big argument with him and said an I.Q. didn't weigh intelligence at all. He said an I.Q. showed how much intelligence you could get, like the numbers on the outside of a measuring cup. You still had to fill the cup up with stuff.

Then when I asked Burt, who gives me my intelligence tests and works with Algernon, he said that both of them were wrong (only I had to promise not to tell them he said so). Burt says that the I.Q. measures a lot of different things including some of the things you learned already, and it really isn't any good at all.

So I still don't know what I.Q. is except that mine is going to be over 200 soon. I didn't want to say anything, but I don't see how if they don't know *what* it is, or *where* it is—I don't see how they know *how much* of it you've got.

Dr. Nemur says I have to take a *Rorshach Test* tomorrow. I wonder what *that* is.

April 22

I found out what a *Rorshach* is. It's the test I took before the operation—the one with the inkblots on the pieces of cardboard. The man who gave me the test was the same one.

I was scared to death of those inkblots. I knew he was going to ask me to find the pictures and I knew I wouldn't be able to. I was thinking to myself, if only there was some way of knowing what kind of pictures were hidden there. Maybe there weren't any pictures at all. Maybe it was just a trick to see if I was dumb enough to look for something that wasn't there. Just thinking about that made me sore at him.

"All right, Charlie," he said, "you've seen these cards before, remember?"

"Of course I remember."

The way I said it, he knew I was angry, and he looked surprised. "Yes, of course. Now I want you to look at this one. What might this be? What do you see on this card? People see all sorts of things in these inkblots. Tell me what it might be for you— what it makes you think of."

I was shocked. That wasn't what I had expected him to say at all. "You mean there are no pictures hidden in those inkblots?"

He frowned and took off his glasses. "What?"

"Pictures. Hidden in the inkblots. Last time you told me that everyone could see them and you wanted me to find them too."

He explained to me that the last time he had used almost the exact same words he was using now. I didn't believe it, and I still have the suspicion that he misled me at the

---

8. **psychology** (sī käl′ ə jē): the study of mental processes and behavior.

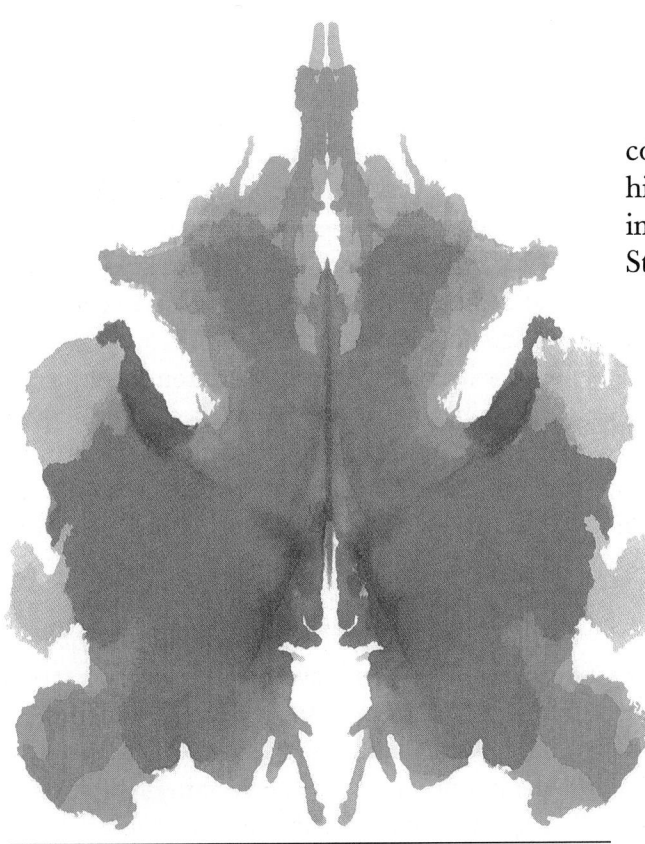

Inkblot similar to those used in Rorschach test.

could he know I wasn't making a fool of him by mentioning things that I didn't really imagine? Maybe I'll understand it when Dr. Strauss lets me read up on psychology.

April 25

I figured out a new way to line up the machines in the factory, and Mr. Donnegan says it will save him ten thousand dollars a year in labor and increased production. He gave me a $25 bonus.

I wanted to take Joe Carp and Frank Reilly out to lunch to celebrate, but Joe said he had to buy some things for his wife, and Frank said he was meeting his cousin for lunch. I guess it'll take a little time for them to get used to the changes in me. Everybody seems to be frightened of me. When I went over to Amos Borg and tapped him on the shoulder, he jumped up in the air.

People don't talk to me much any more or kid around the way they used to. It makes the job kind of lonely.

April 27

I got up the nerve today to ask Miss Kinnian to have dinner with me tomorrow night to celebrate my bonus.

At first she wasn't sure it was right, but I asked Dr. Strauss and he said it was okay. Dr. Strauss and Dr. Nemur don't seem to be getting along so well. They're arguing all the time. This evening when I came in to ask Dr. Strauss about having dinner with Miss Kinnian, I heard them shouting. Dr. Nemur was saying that it was *his* experiment and *his* research, and Dr. Strauss was shouting back that he contributed just as much, because he found me through Miss Kinnian and he performed the operation. Dr. Strauss said that

time just for the fun of it. Unless—I don't know any more—could I have been *that* feeble-minded?

We went through the cards slowly. One of them looked like a pair of bats tugging at something. Another one looked like two men fencing with swords. I imagined all sorts of things. I guess I got carried away. But I didn't trust him any more, and I kept turning them around and even looking on the back to see if there was anything there I was supposed to catch. While he was making his notes, I peeked out of the corner of my eye to read it. But it was all in code that looked like this:

WF + A DdF-Ad orig. WF-A SF + obj

The test still doesn't make sense to me. It seems to me that anyone could make up lies about things that they didn't really see. How

someday thousands of neurosurgeons[9] might be using his technique all over the world.

Dr. Nemur wanted to publish the results of the experiment at the end of this month. Dr. Strauss wanted to wait a while longer to be sure. Dr. Strauss said that Dr. Nemur was more interested in the Chair of Psychology at Princeton[10] than he was in the experiment. Dr. Nemur said that Dr. Strauss was nothing but an opportunist who was trying to ride to glory on *his* coattails.

When I left afterward, I found myself trembling. I don't know why for sure, but it was as if I'd seen both clearly for the first time. I remember hearing Burt say that Dr. Nemur had a shrew of a wife, who was pushing him all the time to get things published so that he could become famous. Burt said that the dream of her life was to have a big shot husband.

Was Dr. Strauss really trying to ride on his coattails?

question | What does he mean by this?

April 28

I don't understand why I never noticed how beautiful Miss Kinnian really is. She has brown eyes and feathery brown hair that comes to the top of her neck. She's only thirty-four! I think from the beginning I had the feeling that she was an unreachable genius—and very, very old. Now, every time I see her she grows younger and more lovely.

We had dinner and a long talk. When she said that I was coming along so fast that soon I'd be leaving her behind, I laughed.

"It's true, Charlie. You're already a better reader than I am. You can read a whole page at a glance, while I can take in only a few lines at a time. And you remember every single thing you read. I'm lucky if I can recall the main thoughts and the general meaning."

"I don't feel intelligent. There are so many things I don't understand."

She took out a cigarette, and I lit it for her. "You've got to be a *little* patient. You're accomplishing in days and weeks what it takes normal people to do in half a lifetime. That's what makes it so amazing. You're like a giant sponge now, soaking things in. Facts, figures, general knowledge. And soon you'll begin to connect them, too. You'll see how the different branches of learning are related. There are many levels, Charlie, like steps on a giant ladder that take you up higher and higher to see more and more of the world around you.

"I can see only a little bit of that, Charlie, and I won't go much higher than I am now, but you'll keep climbing up and up, and see more and more, and each step will open new worlds that you never even knew existed." She frowned. "I hope . . . I just hope to God—"

---

9. neurosurgeons (nōō′ rō sʉr′ jənz): doctors who perform operations on the brain and other parts of the nervous system.

10. Chair of Psychology at Princeton: the position of head of the Psychology Department at Princeton University.

Words to Know and Use	**opportunist** (äp′ ər tōōn′ ist) *n.* a person who takes advantage of any opportunity for self-advancement, even if it means ignoring moral principles **shrew** (shrōō) *n.* a mean, nagging woman

"What?"

"Never mind, Charles. I just hope I wasn't wrong to advise you to go into this in the first place."

I laughed. "How could that be? It worked, didn't it? Even Algernon is still smart."

We sat there silently for a while, and I knew what she was thinking about as she watched me toying with the chain of my rabbit's foot and my keys. I didn't want to think of that possibility any more than elderly people want to think of death. I *knew* that this was only the beginning. I knew what she meant about levels, because I'd seen some of them already. The thought of leaving her behind made me sad.

I'm in love with Miss Kinnian.

Part 2

Progress Report 11
April 30

I've quit my job with Donnegan's Plastic Box Company. Mr. Donnegan insisted that it would be better for all concerned if I left. What did I do to make them hate me so?

The first I knew of it was when Mr. Donnegan showed me the petition. Eight hundred and forty names, everyone connected with the factory, except Fanny Girden. Scanning the list quickly, I saw at once that hers was the only missing name. All the rest demanded that I be fired.

Joe Carp and Frank Reilly wouldn't talk to me about it. No one else would either, except Fanny. She was one of the few people I'd known who set her mind to something and believed it no matter what the rest of the world proved, said, or did—and Fanny did not believe that I should have been fired. She had been against the petition on principle and despite the pressure and threats she'd held out.

"Which don't mean to say," she remarked, "that I don't think there's something mighty strange about you, Charlie. Them changes. I don't know. You used to be a good, dependable, ordinary man—not too bright maybe, but honest. Who knows what you done to yourself to get so smart all of a sudden. Like everybody around here's been saying, Charlie, it's not right."

"But how can you say that, Fanny? What's wrong with a man becoming intelligent and wanting to acquire knowledge and understanding of the world around him?"

She stared down at her work, and I turned to leave. Without looking at me, she said: "It was evil when Eve listened to the snake and ate from the tree of knowledge. It was evil when she saw that she was naked. If not for that none of us would ever have to grow old and sick, and die."[11]

Once again now I have the feeling of shame burning inside me. This intelligence has driven a wedge between me and all the people I once knew and loved. Before, they laughed at me and despised me for my ignorance and dullness; now, they hate me for my knowledge and understanding. What in God's name do they want of me?

They've driven me out of the factory. Now I'm more alone than ever before. . . .

_____

11. **It was evil . . . die:** refers to the Biblical story of Eve who, along with Adam, was banished from the Garden of Eden. They became mortal, subject to illness and death, and passed on the same fate to all their descendants.

May 15

Dr. Strauss is very angry at me for not having written any progress reports in two weeks. He's justified because the lab is now paying me a regular salary. I told him I was too busy thinking and reading. When I pointed out that writing was such a slow process that it made me impatient with my poor handwriting, he suggested that I learn to type. It's much easier to write now because I can type nearly seventy-five words a minute. Dr. Strauss continually reminds me of the need to speak and write simply so that people will be able to understand me.

I'll try to review all the things that happened to me during the last two weeks. Algernon and I were presented to the American Psychological Association sitting in convention with the World Psychological Association last Tuesday. We created quite a sensation. Dr. Nemur and Dr. Strauss were proud of us.

I suspect that Dr. Nemur, who is sixty-ten years older than Dr. Strauss—finds it necessary to see tangible results of his work. Undoubtedly, the result of pressure by Mrs. Nemur.

Contrary to my earlier impressions of him, I realize that Dr. Nemur is not at all a genius. He has a very good mind, but it struggles under the specter of self-doubt. He wants people to take him for a genius. Therefore, it is important for him to feel that his work is accepted by the world. I believe that Dr. Nemur was afraid of further delay because he worried that someone else might make a discovery along these lines and take the credit from him.

Dr. Strauss, on the other hand, might be called a genius, although I feel that his areas of knowledge are too limited. He was educated in the tradition of narrow specialization; the broader aspects of background were neglected far more than necessary—even for a neurosurgeon.

I was shocked to learn that the only ancient languages he could read were Latin, Greek, and Hebrew and that he knows almost nothing of mathematics beyond the elementary levels of the calculus of variations.[12] When he admitted this to me, I found myself almost annoyed. It was as if he'd hidden this part of himself in order to deceive me, pretending—as do many people I've discovered—to be what he is not. No one I've ever known is what he appears to be on the surface.

Dr. Nemur appears to be uncomfortable around me. Sometimes when I try to talk to him, he just looks at me strangely and turns away. I was angry at first when Dr. Strauss told me I was giving Dr. Nemur an inferiority complex. I thought he was mocking me, and I'm oversensitive at being made fun of.

How was I to know that a highly respected psychoexperimentalist like Nemur was unacquainted with Hindustani and Chinese? It's absurd when you consider the work that is being done in India and China today in the very field of his study.

---

12. **calculus of variations** (kal′ kyōō ləs): a branch of higher mathematics that deals with the problem of finding a value representing the highest or lowest limit for a given expression.

Words to Know and Use

sensation (sen sā′ shən) n. something that causes people to become very interested and enthusiastic
undoubtedly (un dout′ id lē) adv. definitely
specialization (spesh′ əl ə zā′ shən) n. focusing on a particular study or activity
absurd (ab surd′) adj. ridiculously false

I asked Dr. Strauss how Nemur could refute Rehajamati's attack on his method and results if Nemur couldn't even read them in the first place. That strange look on Dr. Strauss's face can mean only one of two things. Either he doesn't want to tell Nemur what they're saying in India, or else—and this worries me—Dr. Strauss doesn't know either. I must be careful to speak and write clearly and simply so that people won't laugh.

Thank God for books and music and things I can think about.

May 18

I am very disturbed. I saw Miss Kinnian last night for the first time in over a week. I tried to avoid all discussions of intellectual concepts and to keep the conversation on a simple, everyday level, but she just stared at me blankly and asked me what I meant about the mathematical variance equivalent in Dorbermann's *Fifth Concerto*.

When I tried to explain she stopped me and laughed. I guess I got angry, but I suspect I'm approaching her on the wrong level. No matter what I try to discuss with her, I am unable to communicate. I must review Vrostadt's equations on *Levels of Semantic Progression*. I find that I don't communicate with people much any more. Thank God for books and music and things I can think about. I am alone in my apartment at Mrs. Flynn's boarding house most of the time and seldom speak to anyone.

May 20

I would not have noticed the new dishwasher, a boy of about sixteen, at the corner diner where I take my evening meals if not for the incident of the broken dishes.

They crashed to the floor, shattering and sending bits of white china under the tables. The boy stood there, dazed and frightened, holding the empty tray in his hand. The whistles and catcalls from the customers (the cries of "Hey, there go the profits!" . . . *"Mazeltov!"* . . . and "Well, *he* didn't work here very long . . ." which invariably seem to follow the breaking of glass or dishware in a public restaurant) all seemed to confuse him.

When the owner came to see what the excitement was about, the boy cowered as if he expected to be struck and threw up his arms as if to ward off the blow.

"All right! All right, you dope," shouted the owner, "don't just stand there! Get the broom and sweep that mess up. A broom . . . a broom, you idiot! It's in the kitchen. Sweep up all the pieces."

The boy saw that he was not going to be punished. His frightened expression disappeared, and he smiled and hummed as he came back with the broom to sweep the floor. A few of the rowdier customers kept up the remarks, amusing themselves at his expense.

"Here, sonny, over here there's a nice piece behind you. . . ."

"C'mon, do it again. . . ."

Words to Know and Use | **catcall** (kat′ kôl′) *n.* a harsh cry or whistle intended as an insult
cower (kou′ ər) *v.* to cringe in fear

"He's not so dumb. It's easier to break 'em than to wash 'em. . . ."

As his vacant eyes moved across the crowd of amused onlookers, he slowly mirrored their smiles and finally broke into an uncertain grin at the joke which he obviously did not understand.

I felt sick inside as I looked at his dull, vacuous smile, the wide, bright eyes of a child, uncertain but eager to please. They were laughing at him because he was mentally retarded.

And I had been laughing at him too.

Suddenly, I was furious at myself and all those who were smirking at him. I jumped up and shouted, "Shut up! Leave him alone! It's not his fault he can't understand! He can't help what he is! But for God's sake . . . he's still a human being!"

The room grew silent; I cursed myself for losing control and creating a scene. I tried not to look at the boy as I paid my check and walked out without touching my food. I felt ashamed for both of us.

How strange it is that people of honest feelings and sensibility, who would not take advantage of a man born without arms or legs or eyes—how such people think nothing of abusing a man born with low intelligence. It infuriated me to think that not too long ago, I, like this boy, had foolishly played the clown. And I had almost forgotten.

I'd hidden the picture of the old Charlie Gordon from myself because now that I was intelligent, it was something that had to be pushed out of my mind. But today in looking at that boy, for the first time I saw what I had been. *I was just like him!*

Only a short time ago, I learned that people laughed at me. Now I can see that unknowlingly I joined with them in laughing at myself. That hurts most of all.

I have often reread my progress reports and seen the illiteracy, the childish naïveté— the mind of low intelligence peering from a dark room, through the keyhole, at the dazzling light outside. I see that even in my dullness I knew that I was inferior, and that other people had something I lacked—something denied me. In my mental blindness, I thought that it was somehow connected with the ability to read and write, and I was sure that if I could get those skills I would automatically have intelligence too.

Who else has lived in both worlds?

Even a feeble-minded man wants to be like other men.

A child may not know how to feed itself or what to eat, yet it knows of hunger.

This, then, is what I was like. I never knew. Even with my gift of intellectual awareness, I never really knew.

This day was good for me. Seeing the past more clearly, I have decided to use my knowledge and skills to work in the field of increasing human intelligence levels. Who is better equipped for this work? Who else has lived in both worlds? These are my people. Let me use my gift to do something for them.

Words to Know and Use | **naïveté** (nä ēv tā′) *n.* natural simplemindedness

Tomorrow, I will discuss with Dr. Strauss the manner in which I can work in this area. I may be able to help him work out the problems of widespread use of the technique which was used on me. I have several good ideas of my own.

There is so much that might be done with this technique. If I could be made into a genius, what about thousands of others like myself? What fantastic levels might be achieved by using this technique on normal people? on *geniuses*?

There are so many doors to open. I am impatient to begin.

Progress Report 12
May 23

It happened today. Algernon bit me. I visited the lab to see him, as I do occasionally, and when I took him out of his cage, he snapped at my hand. I put him back and watched him for a while. He was unusually disturbed and vicious.

May 24

Burt, who is in charge of the experimental animals, tells me that Algernon is changing. He is less cooperative; he refuses to run the maze anymore; general motivation has decreased. And he hasn't been eating. Everyone is upset about what this may mean.

May 25

They've been feeding Algernon, who now refuses to work the shifting-lock problem. Everyone identifies me with Algernon. In a way we're both the first of our kind. They're all pretending that Algernon's behavior is not necessarily significant for me. But it's hard to hide the fact that some of the other animals who were used in this experiment are showing strange behavior.

Everyone identifies me with Algernon. In a way we're both the first of our kind.

Dr. Strauss and Dr. Nemur have asked me not to come to the lab any more. I know what they're thinking, but I can't accept it. I am going ahead with my plans to carry their research forward. With all due respect to both of these fine scientists, I am well aware of their limitations. If there is an answer, I'll have to find it out for myself. Suddenly, time has become very important to me.

May 29

I have been given a lab of my own and permission to go ahead with the research. I'm onto something. Working day and night. I've had a cot moved into the lab. Most of my writing time is spent on the notes which I keep in a separate folder, but from time to time I feel it necessary to put down my moods and my thoughts out of sheer habit.

I find the *calculus of intelligence* to be a fascinating study. Here is the place for the application of all the knowledge I have acquired. In a sense it's the problem I've been concerned with all my life.

May 31

Dr. Strauss thinks I'm working too hard. Dr. Nemur says I'm trying to cram a lifetime of research and thought into a few weeks. I know I should rest, but I'm driven on by something inside that won't let me stop. I've got to find the reason for the sharp regression in Algernon. I've got to know *if* and *when* it will happen to me.

June 4
Letter to Dr. Strauss (copy)

Dear Dr. Strauss:

Under separate cover I am sending you a copy of my report entitled "The Algernon-Gordon Effect: A Study of Structure and Function of Increased Intelligence," which I would like to have you read and have published.

As you see, my experiments are completed. I have included in my report all of my formulae, as well as mathematical analyses in the appendix. Of course, these should be verified.

Because of its importance to both you and Dr. Nemur (and need I say to myself, too?) I have checked and rechecked my results a dozen times in the hope of finding an error. I am sorry to say the results must stand. Yet for the sake of science, I am grateful for the little bit that I here add to the knowledge of the human mind and the laws governing the artificial increase of human intelligence.

I recall your once saying to me that an experimental *failure* or the *disproving* of a theory was as important to the advancement of learning as a success would be. I know now that this is true. I am sorry, however, that my own contribution to the field must rest upon the ashes of the work of two men I regard so highly.

Yours truly,
Charles Gordon

encl.: rept.

June 5

I must not become emotional. The facts and the results of my experiments are clear, and the more sensational aspects of my own rapid climb cannot obscure the fact that the tripling of intelligence by the surgical technique developed by Drs. Strauss and Nemur must be viewed as having little or no practical applicability (at the present time) to the increase of human intelligence.

As I review the records and data on Algernon, I see that although he is still in his physical infancy, he has regressed mentally. Motor activity[13] is impaired; there is a general reduction of glandular activity; there is an accelerated loss of coordination.

There are also strong indications of progressive amnesia.[14]

As will be seen by my report, these and other physical and mental deterioration syndromes can be predicted with statistically significant results by the application of my formula.

The surgical stimulus to which we were both subjected has resulted in an intensification and acceleration of all mental processes. The unforeseen development, which I have taken the liberty of calling the Algernon-Gordon Effect, is the logical extension of the

---

13. motor activity: movement caused by nerves carrying impulses from the central nervous system to the muscles.

14. progressive amnesia (am nē′ zhə): a steadily worsening loss of memory.

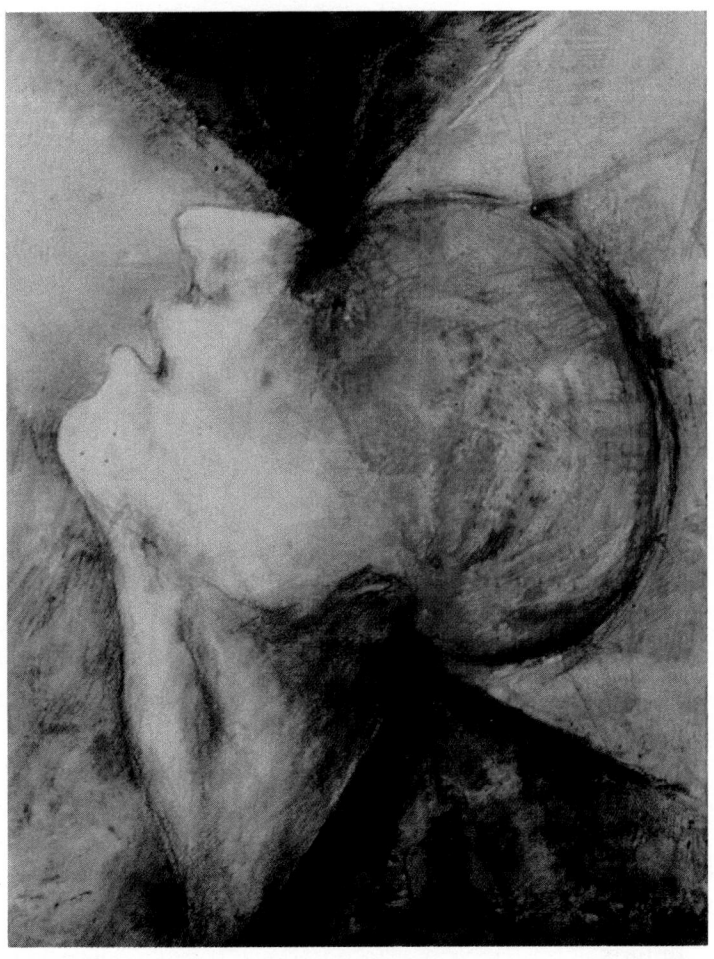

Illustration by Rebekah Raye.
Courtesy Sandoz Pharmaceuticals Corporation.

entire intelligence speedup. The hypothesis here proven may be described simply in the following terms: Artificially increased intelligence deteriorates at a rate of time directly proportional to the quantity of the increase.

I feel that this, in itself, is an important discovery.

As long as I am able to write, I will continue to record my thoughts in these progress reports. It is one of my few pleasures.

However, by all indications, my own mental deterioration will be very rapid.

I have already begun to notice signs of emotional instability and forgetfulness, the first symptoms of the burn-out.

June 10

Deterioration progressing. I have become absentminded. Algernon died two days ago. Dissection shows my predictions were right.

His brain had decreased in weight, and there was a general smoothing out of cerebral convolutions as well as a deepening and broadening of brain fissures.[15]

I've got to try to hold on to some of it. Some of the things I've learned.

I guess the same thing is or will soon be happening to me. Now that it's definite, I don't want it to happen.

I put Algernon's body in a cheese box and buried him in the backyard. I cried.

June 15

Dr. Strauss came to see me again. I wouldn't open the door, and I told him to go away. I want to be left to myself. I have become touchy and irritable. I feel the darkness closing in. It's hard to throw off thoughts of suicide. I keep telling myself how important this introspective journal will be.

It's a strange sensation to pick up a book that you've read and enjoyed just a few months ago and discover that you don't remember it. I remembered how great I thought John Milton was, but when I picked up *Paradise Lost* I couldn't understand it at all. I got so angry I threw the book across the room.

I've got to try to hold on to some of it. Some of the things I've learned. Oh, God, please don't take it all away.

June 19

Sometimes, at night, I go out for a walk. Last night I couldn't remember where I lived. A policeman took me home. I have the strange feeling that this has all happened to me before—a long time ago. I keep telling myself I'm the only person in the world who can describe what's happening to me.

June 21

Why can't I remember? I've got to fight. I lie in bed for days, and I don't know who or where I am. Then it all comes back to me in a flash. Fugues[16] of amnesia. Symptoms of senility—second childhood. I can watch them coming on. It's so cruelly logical. I learned so much and so fast. Now my mind is deteriorating rapidly. I won't let it happen. I'll fight it. I can't help thinking of the boy in the restaurant, the blank expression, the silly smile, the people laughing at him. No—please—not that again. . . .

June 22

I'm forgetting things that I learned recently. It seems to be following the classic pattern—the last things learned are the first things forgotten. Or is that the pattern? I'd better look it up again. . . .

I reread my paper on the Algernon-Gordon Effect, and I get the strange feeling that it was written by someone else. There are parts I don't even understand.

Motor activity impaired. I keep tripping over things, and it becomes increasingly difficult to type.

---

15. cerebral (ser´ ə brəl) **convolutions, brain fissures** (fish´ ərz): parts of the brain. Cerebral convolutions are the parts of the brain that bulge outward. Brain fissures are the grooves that divide the brain into lobes, or sections.

16. fugues (fyo͞ogz): psychological states in which people seem to be acting consciously, although later they have no memory of the activity.

June 23

I've given up using the typewriter completely. My coordination is bad. I feel that I'm moving slower and slower. Had a terrible shock today. I picked up a copy of an article I used in my research, Krueger's "Uber psychische Ganzheit," to see if it would help me understand what I had done. First I thought there was something wrong with my eyes. Then I realized I could no longer read German. I tested myself in other languages. All gone.

June 30

A week since I dared to write again. It's slipping away like sand through my fingers. Most of the books I have are too hard for me now. I get angry with them because I know that I read and understood them just a few weeks ago.

I keep telling myself I must keep writing these reports so that somebody will know what is happening to me. But it gets harder to form the words and remember spellings. I have to look up even simple words in the dictionary now, and it makes me impatient with myself.

Dr. Strauss comes around almost every day, but I told him I wouldn't see or speak to anybody. He feels guilty. They all do. But I don't blame anyone. I knew what might happen. But how it hurts.

July 7

I don't know where the week went. Todays Sunday I know because I can see through my window people going to church. I think I stayed in bed all week but I remember Mrs. Flynn bringing food to me a few times. I keep saying over and over Ive got to do something but then I forget and maybe its just easier not to do what I say Im going to do.

I think of my mother and father a lot these days. I found a picture of them with me taken at a beach. My father has a big ball under his arm and my mother is holding me by the hand. I dont remember them the way they are in the picture. All I remember is my father drunk most of the time and arguing with mom about money.

I keep saying over and over I've got to do something but then I forget.

He never shaved much and he used to scratch my face when he hugged me. My mother said he died but Cousin Miltie said he heard his mom and dad say that my father ran away with another woman. When I asked my mother she slapped my face and said my father was dead. I dont think I ever found out which was true but I dont care much. (He said he was going to take me to see cows on a farm once but he never did. He never kept his promises. . . .)

July 10

My landlady Mrs Flynn is very worried about me. She says the way I lay around all day and dont do anything I remind her of her son before she threw him out of the house. She said she doesnt like loafers. If Im sick its one thing, but if Im a loafer thats another thing and she wont have it. I told her I think Im sick.

HAND WITH FLOWERS
about 1957 Andy Warhol
Courtesy, Andy Warhol
Studio.

I try to read a little bit every day, mostly stories, but sometimes I have to read the same thing over and over again because I dont know what it means. And its hard to write. I know I should look up all the words in the dictionary but its so hard and Im so tired all the time.

Then I got the idea that I would only use the easy words instead of the long hard ones. That saves time. I put flowers on Algernons grave about once a week. Mrs Flynn thinks Im crazy to put flowers on a mouses grave but I told her that Algernon was special.

July 14

Its Sunday again. I dont have anything to do to keep me busy now because my television set is broke and I dont have any money to get it fixed. (I think I lost this months check from the lab. I dont remember)

I get awful headaches and asperin doesnt help me much. Mrs Flynn knows Im really sick and she feels very sorry for me. Shes a wonderful woman whenever someone is sick.

July 22

Mrs Flynn called a strange doctor to see me. She was afraid I was going to die. I told the doctor I wasnt too sick and that I only forget sometimes. He asked me did I have any friends or relatives and I said no I dont have any. I told him I had a friend called Algernon once but he was a mouse and we used to run races together. He looked at me kind of funny like he thought I was crazy.

He smiled when I told him I used to be a genius. He talked to me like I was a baby and he winked at Mrs Flynn. I got mad and chased him out because he was making fun of me the way they all used to.

July 24

I have no more money and Mrs Flynn says I got to go to work somewhere and pay the rent because I havent paid for over two months. I dont know any work but the job I used to have at Donnegans Plastic Box Company. I dont want to go back there because they all knew me when I was smart and maybe they'll laugh at me. But I dont know what else to do to get money.

July 25

I was looking at some of my old progress reports and its very funny but I cant read what I wrote. I can make out some of the words but they dont make sense.

Miss Kinnian came to the door but I said go away I dont want to see you. She cried and I cried too but I wouldnt let her in because I didnt want her to laugh at me. I told her I didn't like her any more. I told her I didnt want to be smart any more. Thats not true. I still love her and I still want to be smart but I had to say that so shed go away. She gave Mrs. Flynn money to pay the rent. I dont want that. I got to get a job.

Please . . . please let me not forget how to read and write. . . .

July 27

Mr. Donnegan was very nice when I came back and asked him for my old job of janitor. First he was very suspicious but I told him what happened to me then he looked very sad and put his hand on my shoulder and said Charlie Gordon you got guts.

Everybody looked at me when I came downstairs and started working in the toilet sweeping it out like I used to. I told myself Charlie if they make fun of you dont get sore because you remember their not so smart as you once thot they were. And besides they were once your friends and if they laughed at you that doesnt mean anything because they liked you too.

One of the new men who came to work there after I went away made a nasty crack he said hey Charlie I hear your a very smart fella a real quiz kid. Say something intelligent. I felt bad but Joe Carp came over and grabbed him by the shirt and said leave him alone you lousy cracker or Ill break your neck. I didnt expect Joe to take my part so I guess hes really my friend.

Later Frank Reilly came over and said Charlie if anybody bothers you or trys to take advantage you call me or Joe and we will set em straight. I said thanks Frank and I got choked up so I had to turn around and go into the supply room so he wouldnt see me cry. Its good to have friends.

July 28

I did a dumb thing today I forgot I wasnt in Miss Kinnians class at the adult center any more like I use to be. I went in and sat down in my old seat in the back of the room and she looked at me funny and she said Charles. I dint remember she ever called me that before only Charlie so I said hello Miss Kinnian Im redy for my lesin today only I lost my reader that we was using. She startid to cry and run out of the room and everybody looked at me and I saw they wasnt the same pepul who use to be in my class.

Then all of a suddin I remembered some things about the operashun and me getting smart and I said holy smoke I reely pulled a Charlie Gordon that time. I went away before she come back to the room.

Thats why Im going away from New York for good. I dont want to do nothing like that agen. I dont want Miss Kinnian to feel sorry for me. Evry body feels sorry at the factery and I dont want that eather so Im going someplace where nobody knows that Charlie Gordon was once a genius and now he cant even reed a book or rite good.

Im taking a cuple of books along and even if I cant reed them Ill practise hard and maybe I wont forget every thing I lerned. If I try reel hard maybe Ill be a littel bit smarter then I was before the operashun. I got my rabits foot and my luky penny and maybe they will help me.

If you ever reed this Miss Kinnian dont be sorry for me Im glad I got a second chanse to be smart becaus I lerned a lot of things I never even new were in this world and Im grateful that I saw it all for a littel bit. I dont know why Im dumb agen or what I did wrong maybe its becaus I dint try hard enuff. But if I try and practis very hard maybe Ill get a littl smarter and know what all the words are. I remember a little bit how nice I had a feeling with the blue book that has the torn cover when I red it. Thats why Im gonna keep trying to get smart so I can have that feeling agen. Its a good feeling to know things and be smart. I wish I had it rite now if I did I woud sit down and reed all the time. Anyway I bet Im the first dumb person in the world who ever found out somthing importent for sience. I remember I did something but I dont remember what. So I gess its like I did it for all the dumb pepul like me.

Goodby Miss Kinnian and Dr. Strauss and evreybody. And P.S. please tell Dr Nemur not to be such a grouch when pepul laff at him and he woud have more frends. Its easy to make frends if you let pepul laff at you. Im going to have lots of frends where I go.

P.P.S. Please if you get a chanse put some flowers on Algernons grave in the bak yard. . . . ❧

*R*esponding to Reading

First Impressions

1. What events in this story affected you the most? Write about them in your journal or on a sheet of paper.

Second Thoughts

2. Look back at the chart you made for Enrich Your Reading. Which of the changes that Charlie goes through do you think are most difficult for him? Why?

3. Why do you think Charlie's co-workers and acquaintances treat him the way they do before and after his operation?

4. If Charlie were asked to participate in another experiment to increase his intelligence, do you think he would accept? Why or why not?

   Think about
   - whether Charlie is happier before or after becoming a genius
   - Charlie's reaction to Fanny Girden's reference to the tree of knowledge
   - the relationship, if any, between intelligence and happiness

5. Have your ideas about being a genius changed after reading this story? Why or why not?

Broader Connections

6. Giving "informed consent" means agreeing to undergo a medical procedure only when one thoroughly understands the possible risks and benefits of the procedure. Do you think Charlie was capable of giving informed consent to his surgery? Do you feel that it was right for the doctors to have operated on him? Why or why not?

*L*iterary Concept: Foreshadowing

Giving hints to suggest events that will happen later in a story is called **foreshadowing**. In "Flowers for Algernon," for example, since Algernon is operated on before Charlie, what happens afterward to Algernon foreshadows what will happen to Charlie. Find and explain one other example of foreshadowing in this story.

Writing Options

1. In his progress report for April 28, Charlie writes that he is in love with Miss Kinnian. If Miss Kinnian were also writing progress reports, what might she write about Charlie? Write her **entry** for that day.

2. What do you think will happen when Charlie leaves New York? Will he find another job and make new friends? Imagine it is one year later. Write a **description** of a typical day in Charlie Gordon's new life.

3. At the end of the story, Charlie says he is going away from New York to a place where people don't feel sorry for him. Imagine that Charlie asks Mr. Donnegan to write him a letter that he can use to help him get another job. Assume the identity of Mr. Donnegan and write a **letter of recommendation** for Charlie.

4. Charlie goes through many changes in the weeks after his operation. Write an "official" **medical report** that explains the changes in Charlie and the effects of those changes.

Vocabulary Practice

Exercise On a sheet of paper, write the letter of the word that differs most in meaning from the other words in the set.

1. (a) crazy   (b) foolish   (c) sensible   (d) absurd
2. (a) boo   (b) cheer   (c) catcall   (d) hiss
3. (a) embrace   (b) crouch   (c) cringe   (d) cower
4. (a) dissection   (b) analysis   (c) inspection   (d) invention
5. (a) fact   (b) actuality   (c) truth   (d) hypothesis
6. (a) impair   (b) damage   (c) improve   (d) hurt
7. (a) naïveté   (b) sophistication   (c) poise   (d) refinement
8. (a) lady   (b) nag   (c) shrew   (d) witch
9. (a) balanced   (b) proportional   (c) equal   (d) uneven
10. (a) certainly   (b) possibly   (c) undoubtedly   (d) surely
11. (a) commotion   (b) boredom   (c) sensation (d) excitement
12. (a) opportunist   (b) humanitarian   (c) scoundrel (d) double-dealer
13. (a) concentration   (b) specialization   (c) expertise   (d) generality
14. (a) statistically   (b) factually   (c) objectively   (d) emotionally
15. (a) relapse   (b) regression   (c) improvement   (d) deterioration

Words to Know and Use

absurd
catcall
cower
dissection
hypothesis
impair
naïveté
opportunist
proportional
regression
sensation
shrew
specialization
statistically
undoubtedly

Options for Learning

1 • Dare to Compare With your classmates, watch the film version of "Flowers for Algernon," called *Charly*. Then get together in small groups and write a comparison of the film and the short story. When you have finished, share your group's comparison with the other groups.

2 • Look into It Choose a topic related to this story and research and write about it. You may want to study some aspect of psychological testing, such as *Rorschach* or IQ tests, or you may prefer to find out more about "smart drugs." To share your report, put it in a large binder with the reports of other classmates who chose this activity.

3 • Clean Up His Act Rewrite Charlie's progress report for "Martch 6," using correct spelling, punctuation, and grammar. When you have finished, compare your entry with the entries of others who chose this activity.

4 • To Be or Not to Be Hold a debate about whether or not the operation should have been performed on Charlie. To begin preparing for the debate, you may want to think back to what you and your classmates said in response to the Broader Connections question on page 293.

 FACT FINDER SCIENCE
What part of the brain is responsible for intelligence?

Daniel Keyes
1927–

Daniel Keyes grew up in Brooklyn, New York. Keyes has taught high school in New York and is presently the director of the creative writing center at Ohio University.

Keyes is interested in abnormal psychology. Since he is, as he says, "fascinated by the complexities of the human mind," Keyes has written several books on psychological themes, such as multiple personalities. One of his books on this subject, *The Minds of Billy Milligan,* came about in a unique way. Billy Milligan, who had twenty-four personalities, chose Keyes to write the book because several of his "selves" had read "Flowers for Algernon" and agreed that Keyes was the perfect author to tell their story.

The short story "Flowers for Algernon" won Keyes a Hugo Award at the World Science Fiction Convention in 1959. Later, when he developed the story into a novel, the Science Fiction Writers of America awarded the new, longer version the coveted Nebula Award. Even the feature film based on "Flowers for Algernon," called *Charly,* was an award winner. Cliff Robertson, the star of the film, won an Academy Award in 1968 for his portrayal of Charlie.

WRITER'S WORKSHOP

INFORMATIVE WRITING

LITERARY MODEL

▶ The characters in this subunit experience all kinds of metamorphoses, or changes. In "The Home Front: 1941-1945," Hazel Shelton Abernethy describes how World War II brought about some major changes in her life, including the development of new products. Even today, products are constantly being created to meet the needs and desires of consumers. One way to educate the public about these products is with consumer reports. A **consumer report** is a brief report that informs consumers about a type of product.

Here is one writer's PASSkey to this assignment.

GUIDED ASSIGNMENT: CONSUMER REPORT

Write a consumer report that describes and evaluates a new product of interest to people your age.

PURPOSE: To describe and evaluate

AUDIENCE: Young consumers

SUBJECT: A new product

STRUCTURE: An informative report

STUDENT MODEL

Gloria chose to write about a video camera because she thought consumers her age would be interested in this product.

▶

Bargain or Bust? The Fisher-Price PXL2000
by Gloria Castro

Have you ever wanted to make a music video, or tape a basketball game? Well, maybe the PXL2000 Camcorder is just the thing for you. Discover what I learned about this surprising new video camera made by Fisher-Price.

THE GOOD POINTS
  The PXL2000 is affordable. Most video cameras cost between $600 and $1000; the PXL2000 costs about $150. For this price, you get a video camera with a built-in sound recorder and a separate $4^1/_2$-inch TV monitor.
  The operating expenses are low. Surprisingly, the PXL2000 records on audiotapes that are made

for tape decks. These tapes are cheaper than the videotapes used with other video cameras. In addition, the PXL2000 runs on six low-priced AA batteries instead of more expensive batteries.

The PXL2000 is easy to operate. Just aim the camera at a subject and shoot. You don't even have to focus! As you shoot, a built-in microphone records sounds automatically.

The PXL2000 is sturdy. Even though the camera was purposely dropped ten times, it didn't break, and it kept on working. Furthermore, weighing under two pounds, the PXL2000 can be carried anywhere.

The PXL2000 is fun to use. The tapes can be played back on the little TV. You can see the images and hear the sounds as soon as they're recorded! With an inexpensive attachment you can play the tape on a regular TV.

THE BAD POINTS

The PXL2000 produces poor images. The images, which are in black-and-white only, are tiny and blurry. In addition, many images on my test tape had white streaks across the middle.

The PXL2000 wastes tape. The PXL2000 records ten minutes of video on a tape designed for ninety minutes of sound recording.

MY RECOMMENDATION

Consumers, think twice before buying the PXL2000. In some ways, the PXL2000 is more like a toy than a useful video camera. While $150 is not expensive for a camcorder, it is a lot to pay for a toy. The PXL2000 is great if you are only interested in learning how to use a video camera, but if you want high quality videotapes worth saving, try waiting until you can afford to buy a better camera. In the meantime, you might consider renting a camcorder for special events or projects.

◀ Notice how Gloria tried to be objective in this part of her report, describing both the good points and the bad points of the PXL2000.

◀ In the final paragraph, the writer is subjective, giving her opinion about the value of the product to consumers.

Now begin your own report.

Prewrite and Explore

WRITER'S CHOICE

Still need an idea? Form a small group with classmates or friends and brainstorm a list of products. You might also consider "inventing" a product that is not actually on the market.

1 **Survey the marketplace**   If you need some writing ideas, think about inventions that have changed people's lives in recent years. You might also find ideas by skimming through newspapers, science magazines, or consumer magazines. Make notes on any products that interest you.

2 **Consider your audience**   As you review your ideas, think about your readers. Choose a product you and others your age will find interesting. After you've chosen a topic, start gathering details that will help you write.

RESEARCH TIP

Keep in mind that new developments in technology occur very rapidly. A good source of information is the *Readers' Guide to Periodical Literature* because it lists recent titles.

STUDENT MODEL

GATHERING INFORMATION

Begin by researching your product thoroughly. Look through books, magazines, and newspapers to find information that describes your product or similar products. If at all possible, visit a store that actually sells your product. Quiz the salesperson and study any advertising material that is available. Jot down notes about the product's main features as well as details such as cost, weight, and so on. Look at the notes Gloria made about the PXL2000.

```
           THE GOOD POINTS
• affordable (costs $150, comes with tiny TV)
• low expenses (low-cost tapes/AA batteries)
• easy to operate (built-in microphone, focus)
• sturdy (won't break, still works after dropping)
• fun to use (immediately see images, hear sounds)

            THE BAD POINTS
• poor images (tiny, black-and-white, streaks)
• wastes tape (records for 10 min. on a 90-min. tape)
```

WRITER'S CHOICE

There are many ways to organize information in a consumer report. You might consider doing a comparison of two similar products in your report.

Draft and Discover

1 **Organize your report**   Think about the best way to organize your report. Gloria organized her information by first introducing the PXL2000, then listing its good points and its bad points, and then making a final recommendation. Note also that she used subheads to organize her information.

2 **Identify the need**   Think about the reasons people your age might be interested in your product. Choose the most important reasons and state them briefly in the opening paragraph.

3 **State the facts**   Present the most helpful details to your audience. Which details are most important? Which ones will most clearly explain what the product does? What are the product's good points and bad points?

4 **Sum up with your opinion**   Feel free to give your honest opinion about the value of the product to consumers. Try contrasting successful aspects with any that are not.

Revise Your Writing

1 **Tighten your language**   Now that you have the facts and reasons down on paper, you can focus on using clear, concise language. Work at using words that give readers specific information about the product. Try for a businesslike, informative tone, and weed out slang or other informal language. You might model your style after some of the sources you used.

2 **Check with a peer reader**   Try exchanging papers with a classmate. The following questions can help each of you respond to the report that you have written.

GRAPHIC AIDS

Try organizing and emphasizing the details by using graphic features, such as capitalized subheads, underlining, charts, and illustrations. If you use a computer, try using "style" functions (boldface, italic, etc).

COMPUTER TIP

Use the "copy" function in your software to make a second copy of your draft. You can then experiment with word choice and sentence structure while still preserving your original version.

Revision Questions

For You

1. Did I use clear, concise language and a businesslike tone to describe my product?
2. Did my supporting facts focus on what readers want to know about this product?
3. Is my evaluation logical and based on the facts I gathered?

For a Peer Reader

1. Did I include enough details about the product's features? If not, what would you like to know more about?
2. Were the details organized clearly and concisely? Did you find the report easy to follow?
3. Would consumers have enough information to make a wise decision?

Proofread

After reviewing your peer reader's comments, proofread your paper for errors in grammar, spelling, capitalization, and punctuation. If possible, ask another friend to review your work. For this assignment, focus on the length and flow of your sentences.

NEED MORE HELP?

See the Language Workshop that follows (pages 301–303).

THE EDITOR'S EYE: SENTENCE COMBINING

Make your writing concise and businesslike by combining sentences.

When two sentences are related, move important information from the second sentence to the first.

Separate   For this price, you get a video camera with a built-in sound recorder. You also get a separate 4½-inch TV monitor.

Combined   For this price, you get a video camera with a built-in sound recorder and a separate 4½-inch TV monitor.

Publish and Present

Here is a suggestion for sharing your work with others.

Consumer Magazine   Along with your classmates, use your reports to create a "consumer magazine." Divide the magazine into sections that reflect different interests, such as transportation, sports, photography, and so on. If you like, illustrate the reports with photographs, drawings, and other graphic aids such as charts and diagrams.

Reflect on Your Writing

Briefly answer the following questions. Place your answers and your paper in your portfolio.

FOR YOUR PORTFOLIO ▶

1. What part of writing a consumer report did you find the easiest? the most difficult?
2. Do you think you did a good job evaluating your product? Explain.

LANGUAGE
WORKSHOP

SENTENCE COMBINING

The more you write, the more comfortable you will feel varying the length and complexity of your sentences. You can vary your sentence rhythms and avoid having too many short, choppy sentences by using the techniques described below.

Combining Sentences

You can combine two sentences when the thoughts in both are related. For example, since the thoughts in these two sentences are related, the sentences can be combined:

> When VE Day came we rejoiced. The total victory was a few months away.
> When VE Day came we rejoiced, **but** the total victory was a few months away.

The thoughts in the following two sentences are not closely related, so they should not be combined:

> We had a scrap-metal drive at school. Scrap-metal drives were held throughout the country.

When two related sentences contain equally important ideas, you can join the sentences by using a comma and a conjunction (*and, but,* or *or*).

> Silk stockings were a thing of the past. Nylons were a treasure to be found.
> Silk stockings were a thing of the past, **and** nylons were a treasure to be found.

> Most people were not sure where Pearl Harbor was. Our geographical knowledge widened over the next few months.
> Most people were not sure where Pearl Harbor was, **but** our geographical knowledge widened over the next few months.

> We could write letters. We could bake cookies.
> We could write letters, **or** we could bake cookies.

REMEMBER

If ideas are similar, use a comma and the word *and*. If ideas contrast, use a comma and the word *but*. If ideas show choice, use a comma and the word *or*.

Combining Sentence Parts

NOTE

Also try using these coordinating conjunctions to join sentence parts: *yet, however, with, while,* or *although.*

PUNCTUATION NOTE

When only sentence parts are joined, no comma is used with the conjunction.

Sometimes, instead of joining two entire sentences, you can combine only their subjects, verbs, or objects. In this case, use conjunctions and leave out words or ideas that are repeated. Note that a comma is not used before the conjunction.

> At school we had war-bond drives. We also had scrap drives.
> At school we had war-bond **and** scrap drives.

> Mothers of brides searched for white satin. Some searched for tulle.
> Mothers of brides searched for white satin **or** tulle.

Exercise 1 Concept Check Combine each pair of sentences, using the conjunctions shown in parentheses. Eliminate italicized words.

1. Harry Truman became Vice-President in 1945. He became President after Franklin Roosevelt's death. (**, and**)
2. Truman faced a difficult choice. He finally decided to use the atomic bomb against Japan. (**, but**)
3. Many people died. Many more might have died in a land war. (**, but**)
4. He could have tried a land invasion. He might have used conventional bombs. (**, or**)
5. Was Truman's choice the right one? *Was it* the wrong one? (**or**)
6. After the war, Truman fought with Congress. He didn't accomplish much at home. (**, and**)
7. In 1948, Truman faced Thomas Dewey in the presidential election. Although he was behind in the polls, he won. (**, and**)
8. Did people lie in the polls? Did they change their minds at the last minute? (**, or**)
9. Truman spoke plainly. He made tough choices. (**and**)
10. People have questioned Truman's use of the atomic bomb. Today he is admired by many U.S. citizens. (**, but**)

Adding Words to Sentences

Sometimes the ideas in two sentences are not equally important. If you want to combine the sentences, you may see that only one word (or word group) in the second sentence adds new meaning. Add that part to the first sentence.

> The oldest held a matchbox. He held it in his hands.
> The oldest held a matchbox **in his hands.**

When you move words from one sentence to another, you may need to change some words slightly. You might add *-ly, -ing, -ed,* or other new endings.

> The raisin grew at a fast rate. The rate was surprising.
> The raisin grew at a **surprisingly** fast rate.

Exercise 2   Concept Check   To the first sentence of each pair below, add the italicized words from the second sentence. Decide where they fit best, make needed changes, and write new sentences.

1. The story of the comic-book hero Superman contains elements of realism. It also contains elements of *fantasy.*
2. Superman made his first appearance in 1938. He *was created by Jerry Siegel and Joe Shuster.*
3. Kal-el, as he was first called, lived on a faraway planet. The planet was *called Krypton.*
4. Kal-el was sent to Earth and raised in Smallville. It was *a small Midwestern town.*
5. Jonathan and Martha Kent raised him. They were *his foster parents.*
6. As an adult, "Clark Kent" moved to a large city. Clark moved to *Metropolis.*
7. He worked as a newspaper reporter. He worked *with Perry White, Jimmy Olsen, and Lois Lane.*
8. As Superman, he worked as a crime fighter. This work was a *secret* to the people of Metropolis.
9. Superman's appearance at crime scenes shocked many criminals. His appearance was usually a *surprise.*
10. Superman could fly. He could also *see through many objects.*

Exercise 3   Revision Skill   Revise each set of sentences below, using techniques from this workshop. Then share your work with classmates.

> (The Rorschach test is a special test. It was developed by a German psychologist, Hermann Rorschach.) (The test is made up of a series of inkblot shapes. There are ten shapes.) (Patients describe what they think the inkblot shapes look like. A trained examiner interprets the descriptions.) (The Rorschach test helps doctors. They learn what is going on in the minds of their patients.)

Exercise 4   Revising Your Writing   Reread the consumer report you wrote for the Writer's Workshop on pages 296–300. Use techniques from this workshop to vary the rhythms of your sentences and remove repetition.

READER'S WORKSHOP

SUMMARIZING

When you do research on a topic, you often need to draw information from many sources and summarize it. A **summary** is a short retelling of written or spoken material. Summarizing can help you understand and remember what you have learned.

When you summarize, restate in your own words the main points and significant details of what you have read. Study the following guidelines for writing a useful summary.

1. Read the material quickly. Get a sense of its overall meaning.
2. Study the material in detail. Note or underline key words.
3. Try to locate the main ideas. Jot these down along with important supporting details.
4. Check your summary with the following questions.
   a. Is it in your own words? Have you made sure not to copy the exact words of the original material?
   b. Have you stated the main idea of the original material in the first sentence?
   c. Have you included only significant details?
   d. Is the information presented in the same order of importance in which it appears in the original material?

Exercise   Summarize the following paragraphs.

ASK FOR HELP
Not sure if you can spot the main idea? Try telling a friend about what you read. You will naturally identify the main points. Ask your friend to make notes as you talk.

Millions of women in the United States and Canada joined the labor force during World War II, after men left for combat. Women worked in shipyards and aircraft factories and filled many jobs previously held only by men. The number of working women in the United States climbed from about 15 million in 1941 to about 19 million in 1945. Canadian women replaced men on farms as well as in factories. They helped raise the crops that fed Allied troops.

New opportunities opened up for American blacks during World War II. In 1941, [President] Roosevelt created the Fair Employment Practices Committee to prevent job discrimination in U.S. defense industries. Large numbers of Southern blacks moved to the North to work in war plants.

Excerpted from *The World Book Encyclopedia.*
© 1992 World Book, Inc. By permission of the publisher.

ACROSS TIME AND PLACE

If you could choose to be alive at any time in any place in the world, what time and place would you choose? What do you think your new life would be like? What would be the same? What would be different? In this subunit, you'll get a chance to travel "across time and place," transporting yourself to lands both near and far. You'll travel to ancient Italy and sixteenth-century Japan. You'll see life in the United States during the late 1700s and the middle 1800s.

You may think people in the past and in other places felt or acted differently from the way you do. They certainly dressed differently and their speech was different too. Still, as you read, you may be surprised to see how similar these people's reactions and feelings are to what yours would be in similar situations. Pleasant journeys!

Nonfiction

Pompeii

ROBERT SILVERBERG

Examine What You Know

How much do you know about volcanoes? In a small-group discussion, use a chart like the one below to consider what you already know about volcanoes, what you want to know, and then what you learned from reading the following article.

What We Know	What We Want to Learn	What We Learned
volcanoes are mountains that erupt		

Expand Your Knowledge

When Mount Vesuvius exploded nearly two thousand years ago, it buried not only Pompeii but also two smaller cities nearby. Even though Vesuvius has erupted on numerous occasions since, many people still choose to live near the mountain.

Enrich Your Reading

SQ3R   You can better understand and remember a nonfiction selection if you use a technique known as **SQ3R**. It has five steps.

- **Survey**   Look over "Pompeii" to get an idea of what it is about. Read all the subheadings and study the pictures.

- **Question**   Jot down questions that you want answered.

- **Read**   Now read "Pompeii," looking for answers to your questions. Note the main ideas.

- **Recite**   After you read, recite the answers to your questions. Then write your answers in the form of notes.

- **Review**   Try to answer your original questions without using your notes. This review will help you retain the information.

■ *Author biography on Extend page*

Pompeii

ROBERT SILVERBERG

Not very far from Naples a strange city sleeps under the hot Italian sun. It is the city of Pompeii, and there is no other city quite like it in all the world. No one lives in Pompeii but crickets and beetles and lizards, yet every year thousands of people travel from distant countries to visit it.

Pompeii is a dead city. No one has lived there for nearly two thousand years—not since the summer of the year A.D. 79, to be exact.

Until that year Pompeii was a prosperous city of twenty-five thousand people. Nearby was the Bay of Naples, an arm of the blue Mediterranean. Rich men came down from wealthy Rome, 125 miles to the north, to build luxurious seaside villas.[1] Fertile farmlands occupied the fields surrounding Pompeii. Rising sharply behind the city was the four-thousand-foot bulk of Mount Vesuvius, a grass-covered slope where the shepherds of Pompeii took their goats to graze. Pompeii was a busy city and a happy one.

It died suddenly, in a terrible rain of fire and ashes.

The tragedy struck on the twenty-fourth of August, A.D. 79. Mount Vesuvius, which had slumbered quietly for centuries, exploded with savage violence. Death struck on a hot summer afternoon. Tons of hot ashes fell on Pompeii, smothering it, hiding it from sight. For three days the sun did not break through the cloud of volcanic ash that filled the sky. And when the eruption ended, Pompeii was buried deep. A thriving city had perished in a single day.

It died suddenly, in a terrible rain of fire and ashes.

Centuries passed. Pompeii was forgotten. Then, fifteen hundred years later, it was discovered again. Beneath the protecting shroud of ashes, the city lay intact. Everything was as it had been the day Vesuvius erupted. There were still loaves of bread in the ovens of the bakeries. In the wine shops, the wine jars were in place, and on one counter could be seen a stain where a customer had thrown down his glass and fled.

---

1. **villas:** large, luxurious country houses.

307

Pompeii today. © Peter Menzel/Stock Boston.

Modern archaeology[2] began with the discovery of buried Pompeii. Before then, the digging of treasures from the ground had been a haphazard and unscholarly affair. But the excavation of Pompeii was done in a systematic, scientific manner, and so the science of serious archaeology can be said to have begun there. Since the year 1748, generations of skilled Italian workmen have been carefully removing the ashes that buried Pompeii, until today almost four-fifths of the city has been uncovered.

Other Roman cities died more slowly. Wind and rain and fire wore them away. Later peoples tore down the ancient monuments, using the stone to build houses and churches. Over the centuries, the cities of the Caesars[3] vanished, and all that is left of them today are scattered fragments.

Not so with Pompeii. It was engulfed in an instant, and its people's tragedy was our great gain. The buildings of Pompeii still stand as they stood two thousand years ago, and within the houses we can still see the pots and pans, the household tools, the hammers and nails. On the walls of the

---

2. **archaeology** (är′ kē äl′ ə jē): the study of ancient cultures by examining buried objects.
3. **Caesars** (sē′ zərz): emperors of ancient Rome.

Words to Know and Use | **haphazard** (hap′ haz′ ərd) *adj.* without planning; random
excavation (eks′ kə vā′ shən) *n.* something unearthed by digging

buildings are election slogans and the scrawlings of unruly boys. Pompeii is like a photograph in three dimensions. It shows us exactly what a city of the Roman Empire was like, down to the smallest detail of everyday life.

To go to Pompeii today is to take a trip backward in a time machine.[4] The old city comes to vivid life all around you. You can almost hear the clatter of horses' hoofs on the narrow streets, the cries of children, the loud, hearty laughter of the shopkeepers. You can almost smell meat sizzling over a charcoal fire. The sky is cloudlessly blue, with the summer sun almost directly overhead. The grassy slopes of great Vesuvius pierce the heavens behind the city, and sunlight shimmers on the water of the bay a thousand yards from the city walls. Ships from every nation are in port, and the babble of strange languages can be heard in the streets.

*T*o go to Pompeii today is to take a trip backward in a time machine.

Such was Pompeii on its last day. And so it is today, now that the volcanic ash has been cleared away. A good imagination is all you need to restore it to bustling vitality. . . .

At dawn on the twenty-fourth of August in the year 79, Pompeii's twenty-five thousand people awakened to another hot day in that hot summer. There was going to be a performance in the arena that night, and the whole town was looking forward to the bloody contests of the gladiators. The rumble of heavy wooden wheels was heard as carts loaded with grain entered the city from the farms outside the walls. Over the centuries the steady stream of carts had worn ruts deep into the pavement of Pompeii's narrow streets.

Wooden shutters were drawn back noisily. The grocers and sellers of fruit opened their shops, displaying their wares on trays set out on the sidewalk. In the wine shops, the girls who sold wine to the thirsty sailors got ready for another busy day. . . .

Outside, children headed toward school, carrying slates and followed by their dogs. Nearly everyone in Pompeii had a dog, and barking could be heard everywhere as the Pompeiian pets greeted one another. A small boy who had just learned the Greek alphabet stopped in front of a blank wall and took a piece of charcoal from his tunic. Hastily he scribbled the Greek letters: *alpha, beta, gamma.*

In the Forum, the town's important men had gathered after breakfast to read the political signs that were posted during the night. Elsewhere in the Forum, the wool merchants talked business, and the men who owned the vineyards were smiling to each other about the high quality of this year's wine, which would fetch a good price in other countries. . . .

---

4. **time machine:** an imaginary machine for traveling backward and forward in time.

Words to Know and Use | **unruly** (un rool' ē) *adj.* hard to control; disobedient
vivid (viv' id) *adj.* producing clear mental images
restore (ri stôr') *v.* to bring back to a former condition

309

The quiet morning moved slowly along. There was nothing very unusual about Pompeii. . . .

But tragedy was on its way. Beneath Vesuvius' vine-covered slopes, a mighty force was about to break loose.

No one in Pompeii knew the dangerous power imprisoned in Vesuvius. For fifteen hundred years the mountain had slept quietly, but far beneath the crest a boiling fury of molten lava had gradually been gathering strength. The solid rock of Vesuvius held the hidden forces in check. An earthquake sixteen years before had been the first sign that the trapped fury beneath the mountain was struggling to break free. Pressure was building up. In the city at the base of the mountain, life went on in complete ignorance of the looming catastrophe.

Portrait of Paquio Proculo with his wife.
Naples National Museum / Art Resource, New York.

Vesuvius Explodes

At one o'clock in the afternoon on the twenty-fourth of August, A.D. 79, the critical point was reached. The walls of rock could hold no longer.

The mountain exploded, raining death on thousands.

Like many tragedies, this one was misunderstood at first. Down in Pompeii, four miles from Vesuvius, a tremendous explosion was heard, echoing ringingly off the mountains on the far side of the city.

"What was that?" people cried from one end of town to another. They stared at each other, puzzled, troubled. Were the gods fighting in heaven? Is that what the loud explosion was?

"Look!" somebody shouted. "Look at Vesuvius!"

Thousands of eyes swiveled upward. Thousands of arms pointed. A black cloud was rising from the shattered crest of the mountain. Higher and higher it rose. An eyewitness, the Roman philosopher Pliny, described the cloud as he saw it from Misenum, twenty-two miles from Pompeii on the opposite side of the bay.

"Better than any other tree, the pine can give an idea of the shape and appearance of this cloud," Pliny wrote in his notebook later that day. "In fact it was projected into the air like an enormous trunk and then spread into many branches, now white, now black, now spotted, according to whether earth or ashes were thrown up."

Words to Know and Use | **catastrophe** (kə tas′ trə fē) *n.* a sudden disaster or calamity

Minutes passed. The sound of the great explosion died away, but it still tingled in everyone's ears. The cloud over Vesuvius still rose, black as night, higher and higher.

"The cloud is blotting out the sun!" someone cried in terror.

Still no one in Pompeii had perished. The fragments of rock thrown up when the mountain exploded all fell back on the volcano's slopes. Within the crater, sizzling masses of molten rock were rushing upward, and upwelling gas drove small blobs of liquefied stone thousands of feet into the air. They cooled high above the gaping mouth of the volcano and plummeted[5] earthward.

A strange rain began to fall on Pompeii—a rain of stone.

The stones were light. They were pumice[6] stones, consisting mostly of air bubbles. They poured down as though there had been a sudden cloudburst. The pumice stones, or lapilli, did little damage. They clattered against the wooden roofs of the Pompeiian houses. They fell by the hundreds in the streets. The people who had rushed out of houses and shops and thermopolia[7] to see what had caused the explosion now scrambled to take cover as the weird rain of lapilli continued.

"What is happening?" Pompeiians asked one another. They rushed to the temples—the Temple of Jupiter, the Temple of Apollo, the Temple of Isis. Bewildered priests tried to calm bewildered citizens. Darkness had come at midday, and a rain of small stones fell from the sky, and who could explain it?

Some did not wait for explanation. In a tavern near the edge of the city, half a dozen gladiators who were scheduled to compete in that night's games decided to flee quickly. They had trumpets with them that were used to sound a fanfare at the amphitheater.[8] But they tossed the trumpets aside, leaving them to be found centuries later. Covering their heads with tiles and pieces of wood, the gladiators rushed out into the hail of lapilli and sprinted toward the open country beyond the walls, where they hoped they would be safe.

Vesuvius was rumbling ominously now. The sky was dark. Lapilli continued to pour down, until the streets began to clog with them.

"The eruption will be over soon!" a hopeful voice exclaimed.

But it did not end. An hour went by, and darkness still shrouded everything; and still the lapilli fell. All was confusion now. Children struggled home from school, panicky in the midday darkness.

The people of Pompeii knew that doom was at hand now. Their fears were doubled when an enormous rain of hot ashes began to fall on them, along with more lapilli. Pelted with stones, half smothered by the ashes, the Pompeiians cried out to the gods for mercy. The wooden roofs of some of the houses began to catch fire as the heat of the

---

5. **plummet:** to fall quickly.
6. **pumice:** a spongy, light rock ejected by volcanoes.
7. **thermopolia** (ther´ mō pō´ lē ä): shops selling wine.
8. **amphitheater:** a stadium where gladiators fought.

Words to Know and Use | **ominously** (äm´ ə nəs lē) *adv.* in a threatening way

311

ashes reached them. Other buildings were collapsing under the weight of the pumice stones that had fallen on them.

In those first few hours, only the quick-witted managed to escape. Vesonius Primus, a wealthy wool merchant, called his family together and piled jewelry and money into a sack. Lighting a torch, Vesonius led his little band out into the nightmare of the streets. Overlooked in the confusion was Vesonius' black watchdog, chained in the courtyard. The terrified dog barked wildly as lapilli struck and drifting white ash settled around him. The animal struggled with his chain, battling fiercely to get free; but the chain held, and no one heard the dog's cries. The humans were too busy saving themselves.

The entire city seemed to shake in the grip of a giant fist.

Many hundreds of Pompeiians fled in those first few dark hours. Stumbling in the darkness, they made their way to the city gates, then out, down to the harbor. They boarded boats and got away, living to tell the tale of their city's destruction. Others preferred to remain within the city, huddling inside the temples or in the public baths[9] or in the cellars of their homes. They still hoped that the nightmare would end—that the tranquillity of a few hours ago would return. . . .

It was evening now, and new woe was in store for Pompeii. The earth trembled and quaked! Roofs that had somehow withstood the rain of lapilli went crashing in ruin, burying hundreds who had hoped to survive the eruption. In the Forum, tall columns toppled as they had in A.D. 63. Those who remembered that great earthquake screamed in new terror as the entire city seemed to shake in the grip of a giant fist.

Three feet of lapilli now covered the ground. Ash floated in the air. Gusts of poisonous gas came drifting from the belching crater, though people could still breathe. Roofs were collapsing everywhere. The cries of the dead and dying filled the air. Rushing throngs,[10] blinded by the darkness and the smoke, hurtled madly up one street and down the next, trampling the fallen in a crazy, fruitless dash toward safety. Dozens of people plunged into dead-end streets and found themselves trapped by crashing buildings. They waited there, too frightened to run farther, expecting the end.

The rich man Diomedes was another of those who decided not to flee at the first sign of alarm. Rather than risk being crushed by the screaming mobs, Diomedes calmly led the members of his household into the solidly built basement of his villa. Sixteen people altogether, as well as his daughter's dog and her beloved little goat. They took enough food and water to last for several days.

But for all his shrewdness and foresight, Diomedes was undone anyway. Poison gas

---

9. **public baths:** large, elaborate buildings containing pools for bathing, favorite places for socializing in the Roman Empire.

10. **throngs:** large crowds.

Words to Know and Use

tranquillity (tran kwil′ ə tē) *n.* calmness
hurtle (hʉrt′ ′l) *v.* to dash recklessly
fruitless (frōōt′ lis) *adj.* unsuccessful
shrewdness (shrōōd′ nis) *n.* cleverness

was creeping slowly into the underground shelter! He watched his daughter begin to cough and struggle for breath. Vesuvius was giving off vast quantities of deadly carbon monoxide that was now settling like a blanket over the dying city. . . .

The poison gas thickened as the terrible night continued. It was possible to hide from the lapilli but not from the gas, and Pompeiians died by the hundreds. Carbon monoxide gas keeps the body from absorbing oxygen. Victims of carbon monoxide poisoning get sleepier and sleepier until they lose consciousness, never to regain it. All over Pompeii, people lay down in the beds of lapilli, overwhelmed by the gas, and death came quietly to them. . . .

Two prisoners, left behind in the jail when their keepers fled, pounded on the sturdy wooden doors. "Let us out!" they called. But no one heard, and the gas entered. They died, not knowing that the jailers outside were dying as well.

In a lane near the Forum, a hundred people were trapped by a blind-alley wall. Others hid in the stoutly built public bathhouses, protected against collapsing roofs but not against the deadly gas. Near the house of Diomedes, a beggar and his little goat sought shelter. The man fell dead a few feet from Diomedes' door; the faithful goat remained by his side, its silver bell tinkling, until its turn came.

All through the endless night, Pompeiians wandered about the streets or crouched in their ruined homes or clustered in the

Pompeiians caught by the lava flow.
©Krafft/Explorer/Photo Researchers

temples to pray. By morning, few remained alive. Not once had Vesuvius stopped hurling lapilli and ash into the air, and the streets of Pompeii were filling quickly. At midday on August 25, exactly twenty-four hours after the beginning of the holocaust,[11] a second eruption racked the volcano. A second cloud of ashes rose above Vesuvius' summit. The wind blew ash as far as Rome and Egypt. But most of the new ashes descended on Pompeii.

---

11. **holocaust:** great or total destruction of life, especially by fire.

The deadly shower of stone and ashes went unslackening into its second day. But it no longer mattered to Pompeii whether the eruption continued another day or another year. For by midday on August 25, Pompeii was a city of the dead. . . .

Pompeii Today

Arriving at Pompeii today, you leave your car outside and enter through an age-old gate. Just within the entrance is a museum that has been built in recent years to house many of the smaller antiquities[12] found in the ruins. Here are statuettes and toys, saucepans and loaves of bread. The account books of the banker Caecilius Jucundus are there, noting all the money he had lent at steep interest rates. Glass cups, coins, charred beans and peas and turnips, baskets of grapes and plums and figs, a box of chestnuts—the little things of Pompeii have all been miraculously preserved for your startled eyes.

Then you enter the city proper. The streets are narrow and deeply rutted with the tracks of chariot wheels. Only special narrow Pompeiian chariots could travel inside the town. Travelers from outside were obliged to change vehicles when they reached the walls of the city. This provided a profitable monopoly for the Pompeiian equivalent of cab drivers twenty centuries ago!

At each intersection, blocks of stone several feet high are mounted in the roadway, so designed that chariot wheels could pass on either side of them.

"Those are steppingstones for the people of Pompeii," your guide tells you. "Pompeii had no sewers, and during heavy rainfalls the streets were flooded with many inches of water. The Pompeiians could keep their feet dry by walking on those stones." . . .

The houses and shops are of stone. The upper stories, which were wooden, were burned away in the holocaust or simply crumbled with the centuries. The biggest of the shops are along the Street of Abundance, which must have been the Fifth Avenue[13] of its day. Silversmiths, shoemakers, manufacturers of cloth—all had their shops here. And every few doors, there is another thermopolium, or wine shop. In many of these, the big jars of wine are still intact, standing in holes in marble counters just the way bins of ice cream are stored in a soda fountain today. . . .

The center of the city's life was the Forum, a large square which you enter not far from the main gate of the city. Before the earthquake of A.D. 63, Pompeii's Forum must have been a truly imposing place, enclosed on three sides by a series of porticoes supported by huge columns. At the north end, on the fourth side, stood the temple of Jupiter, Juno, and Minerva, raised on a podium ten feet high. But the earthquake toppled the temple and most of the columns, and not much rebuilding had been done at the time of the eruption. Pompeii's slowness to rebuild was our eternal loss, for little remains of the Forum except the stumps of massive columns. . . .

Many public buildings were on the main square: the headquarters of the wool industry and several other temples, including one dedicated to Vespasian (father of Titus), a

---

12. **antiquities:** ancient objects.
13. **Fifth Avenue:** a street in New York City, famous for its fine shops.

Interior of room
showing wine jars.
© Marcel Eskenazy
Photography/Photo Edit.

Roman emperor who was worshiped as a deity.[14] Near the Forum was a macellum, or market, where foodstuffs were sold and where beggars wandered.

Pompeii had many beggars. One of them was found in April 1957 at the gate of the road leading to the town of Nocera. A cast taken of him shows him to have been less than five feet tall and deformed by the bone disease known as rickets. On the last day of Pompeii's life, this beggar had gone about asking for alms, and some generous citizen had given him a bone with a piece of meat still adhering to it. When the eruption came, the beggar tried to flee, jealously guarding his precious sack containing the cutlet—and he was found with it two thousand years later.

Pompeii was a city of many fine temples,

both around the Forum and in the outlying streets. One of the most interesting is one dating from the sixth century B.C., the oldest building in the city. Only the foundation and a few fragmented columns remain, but this temple was evidently regarded with great <u>reverence</u>, since it was located in the center of a fairly large triangular space adjoining the main theater. Nearby is the Temple of Isis, which was rebuilt after the earthquake and so is in fairly good preservation. Isis, an Egyptian goddess, was one of the many foreign gods and goddesses who had come to be worshiped in the Roman Empire by the time of the destruction of Pompeii. Her gaudily decorated temple at Pompeii is the only European temple of

14. **deity:** a god or goddess.

Isis that has come down to us from the ancient world.

But many temples, bathhouses, amphitheaters, and government buildings have survived in other places. What makes Pompeii uniquely significant is the wealth of knowledge it gives us about the *private* lives of its people. Nowhere else do we have such complete information about the homes of the ancients, about their customs and living habits, about their humble pots and pans.

The houses in Pompeii show the evolution of styles over a period of several centuries. Many of the houses are built to the same simple plan: a central court, known as the atrium, around which a living room, bedrooms, and a garden are arrayed. This was the classic Roman style of home. Some of the later and more impressive houses show the influence of Greek styles, with paintings and mosaic[15] decorations as well as baths, reception rooms, huge gardens, and sometimes a second atrium.

The houses of Pompeii are known by name, and a good deal is known of their occupants. One of the most famous is the House of the Vetti Brothers, which is lavishly decorated with paintings, mosaics, and sculptures. The inscriptions on these houses are often amusing today. One businessman had written on the walls of his villa WELCOME PROFITS! Another greeted his visitors with the inscribed words PROFITS MEAN JOY!

At the so-called House of the Tragic Poet, a mosaic shows a barking dog, with the inscription *cave canem*—"Beware of the dog." On the building known as the House of the Lovers, which received its name because the newly married Claudius Elogus lived there, someone had written a line of verse, dedicated to the newlyweds, on the porch: *Amantes,* *ut apes, vitam mellitem exigunt.* ("Lovers, like bees, desire a life full of honey.") . . .

One interesting house uncovered since World War II is the Villa of Giulia Felix ("Happy Julia"), which was of exceptional size. Apparently Giulia found the expense of this elegant house too much for her budget because she had opened her baths to the public and advertised the fact with a sign on the gate. For a fee, Pompeiians who scorned the crowds at the public baths could bathe at Giulia's in privacy and comfort. Even this income does not seem to have been enough, for another sign uncovered in 1953 announced that the magnificent villa was for rent. . . .

One of the truly fascinating aspects of Pompeii is the multitude of scribbled street signs. Notices were painted directly on the stone and have come down to us. At the big amphitheater, an inscription tells us, "The troupe of gladiators owned by Suettius Centus will give a performance at Pompeii on May 31st. There will be an animal show. The awnings will be used." And at the theater where plays were given, a message to a popular actor reads, "Actius, beloved of the people, come back soon; fare thee well!"

There are inscriptions at the taverns, too. "Romula loves Staphyclus" is on one wall. Elsewhere there is a poem that sounds like one of today's hit tunes: "Anyone could as well stop the winds blowing, / And the waters from flowing, / As stop lovers from loving." . . .

---

15. **mosaic:** a design made by cementing small bits of stone or glass to a surface.

Wherever you turn in Pompeii, echoes of the dead city strike you. In one rich house, a breakfast-set in silver, complete with two egg cups, was found. Shopping lists were discovered. Wall paintings show religious ceremonies, games, and everyday amusements. The vats used for bleaching cloth for togas still remain. In some of the twenty bakeries, newly baked loaves stand on the counters.

To enter Pompeii is to step into the Rome of the Caesars. An entire city, forever frozen in the last moment of its life by a terrible cataclysm,[16] awaits the visitor. Thanks to the painstaking[17] work of generations of devoted Italian archaeologists, we can experience today the most minute details of life twenty centuries ago in a Roman city. So much do we know of the people of Pompeii that they take on vivid life for us—the banker Jucundus, the wool merchant Vesonius, the newlywed Claudius Elogus, the nobleman Diomedes. The dreadful eruption that snatched the life of these people and this city in a single day also gave it a kind of immortality. Pompeii and its people live on today in timeless permanence, their city transformed by Vesuvius' fury into a miraculous survivor of the ancient world. ❧

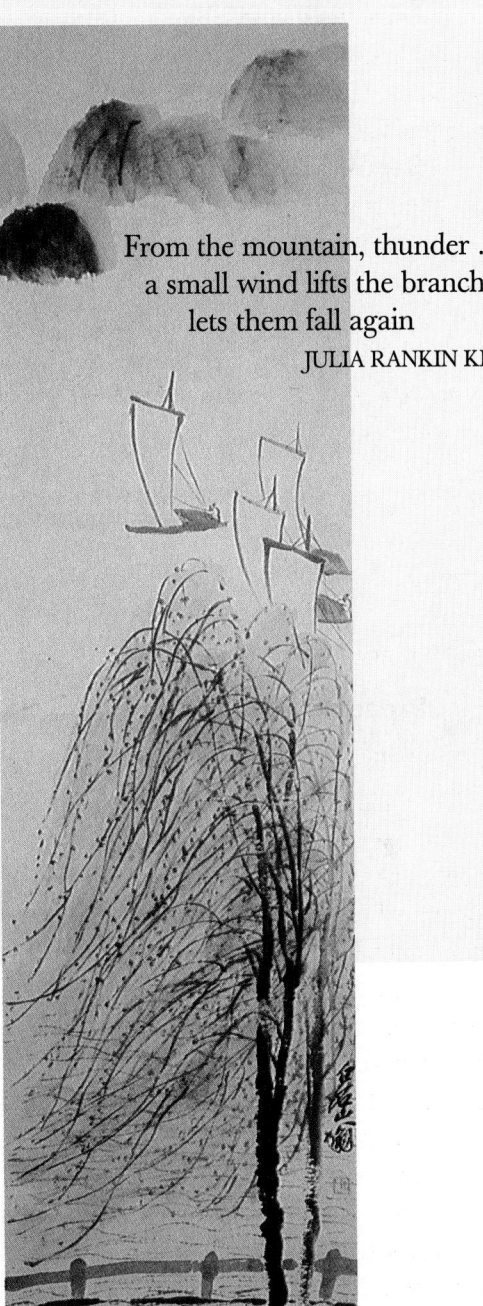

I N S I G H T

From the mountain, thunder . . .
a small wind lifts the branches
lets them fall again
JULIA RANKIN KING

SAILING BOATS IN THE WIND
Ch'i Pai-shih
National Gallery, Prague,
Czechoslovakia.

*R*esponding to Reading

First Impressions

1. What did you find most interesting about Pompeii? Write your impressions in your journal or on a sheet of paper.

Second Thoughts

2. Compare the residents of Pompeii with the people of your town. What similarities and differences do you see?

   Think about
   - the lifestyles of the Pompeiians and the people of your town
   - how Pompeiians reacted to crisis and how your neighbors might react

3. Imagine traveling across time and place to Pompeii and arriving there on August 24, A.D. 79. What do you think you would have done to save yourself and others from the volcanic eruption?

4. Think about a recent natural disaster, such as a hurricane or an earthquake. What advances in technology and government services help people today in such crises?

Broader Connections

5. Why do you suppose thousands of people visit Pompeii every year? Would you want to visit Pompeii? Why or why not?

*L*iterary Concept: Historical Narrative

A **historical narrative** tells a story about something that really happened. This type of writing contains fictional elements, such as dialogue. For example, a Pompeiian in the story shouts "The eruption will be over soon!" Of course, the author doesn't know what anyone in Pompeii actually said. However, he can certainly imagine what the Pompeiians were saying and feeling as the disaster unfolded. Find another example of a fictional element in this nonfiction article.

*W*riting Options

1. Imagine that you are a reporter in Pompeii during the eruption of Vesuvius. You manage to escape on the last boat to leave the harbor. Write an **eyewitness account** describing the disaster.

2. Write a **short story** about traveling to Pompeii to save your ancestors from the Vesuvius catastrophe.

3. Write an **essay test** that covers the material in Silverberg's article. For ideas, use the "What We Learned" information from the Explore page.

4. Imagine that you are a citizen of Pompeii. You have stayed in the city during the eruption, and now you realize you may not survive. Write your thoughts in a **diary entry.**

*V*ocabulary Practice

Exercise A   Match each word on the right with the book in which you would expect to find that word.

1.	*The Mysterious Burial Cloth*	**a.** excavation
2.	*Famous Archaeological Digs*	**b.** fruitless
3.	*When Children Misbehave*	**c.** ominously
4.	*Making Old Furniture New Again*	**d.** restore
5.	*Remember Details Clearly*	**e.** reverence
6.	*My Failed Attempts in Gardening*	**f.** shrewdness
7.	*The Coming Economic Storm*	**g.** shroud
8.	*How to Pray*	**h.** stoutly
9.	*Buildings that Withstand Quakes*	**i.** unruly
10.	*Outsmart Your Competition*	**j.** vivid

> *Words to Know and Use*
>
> catastrophe
> excavation
> fruitless
> haphazard
> hurtle
> ominously
> permanence
> restore
> reverence
> shrewdness
> shroud
> stoutly
> tranquillity
> unruly
> vivid

Exercise B   Write the letter of the word pair that best expresses a relationship similar to that expressed in the original pair.

1. EARTHQUAKE : CATASTROPHE :: (a) bee : garden (b) infection : illness   (c) sunshine : storm   (d) leg : table

2. HAPHAZARD : CAREFUL :: (a) complicated : simple   (b) joyous : happy   (c) excessive : expensive   (d) hazardous : dangerous

3. JOG : HURTLE :: (a) listen : speak   (b) read : write   (c) sing : dance (d) talk : shout

4. TRANQUILLITY : PEACE :: (a) scowl : smile   (b) fear : hope (c) coward : hero   (d) joy : delight

5. EARTH : PERMANENCE :: (a) moon : sky   (b) color : red (c) sun : brightness   (d) clock : time

Options for Learning

1 • Mountains of Fire Research one aspect of volcanoes and prepare a report for your class. For example, you may study different kinds of volcanoes or create a chart displaying active volcanoes around the world.

2 • Time Traveler Imagine that you built a time machine that could take you to any place or time you wanted. Draw a picture of your time machine. In a written or an oral presentation, describe a place and time you would like to visit. Explain why you would want to go there.

3 • See For Yourself Plan an imaginary, one-week class trip to Pompeii. You might want to start by getting some brochures from a local travel agency. Figure out the fares and the schedules. Arrange a complete itinerary for your trip.

4 • Blow Your Top Construct a model volcano. Check a reference book for directions on how to make a safe, working model. You may enjoy videotaping the eruption of your volcano.

 FACT FINDER VOCABULARY

What is the origin of the word volcano?

Robert Silverberg
1935–

This popular author began his writing career while still a student at Columbia University in the 1950s. Silverberg has written a wide variety of nonfiction books, such as *Wonders of Ancient Chinese Science, Ghost Towns of the American West,* and *Lost Cities and Vanished Civilizations,* from which "Pompeii" is taken.

Silverberg described one of his writing goals with the following words, which could easily serve as an introduction to "Pompeii": "To show the reader something he has never been able to see with his own eyes, some-thing strange and unique, beautiful and troubling, which draws him for a moment out of himself, [and] places him in contact with the vastness of the universe. . . ."

Silverberg is also a well-known science fiction writer who won the World Science Fiction "Hugo" award in 1956. He explains that science fiction "opened the universe to me. I feel a sense of obligation to science fiction to replace what I had taken from it, to add to the shelf, to put something else there for someone else that would do for them what other writers had done for me."

Fiction

The Inn of Lost Time

LENSEY NAMIOKA
(nä mē ō' kä)

Examine What You Know

The saying "Things aren't always what they appear to be" can apply to many people, objects, and situations. For example, have you ever formed a first impression of someone, only to change it after you got to know the person better? With your classmates, discuss situations that you know of or have experienced in which things weren't what they had appeared to be.

Expand Your Knowledge

The time is the late 1500s; the place is Japan. Hungry samurai (sam' ə rī), or army officers, roam the war-torn countryside, unable to find work as soldiers for competing warlords. Some find jobs as body-guards for rich merchants. Others, who are more desperate, prey on defenseless farmers.

Troubled times such as these helped bring about a new form of literature that allowed people to turn away from the harshness of the real world and seek the comfort of make-believe and illusion. These popular Japanese tales celebrate a world in which things were not always what they appeared to be.

Write Before You Read

Think about the ideas you developed in Examine What You Know. In your journal or on a sheet of paper, write about a time when a person, an object, or a situation wasn't what it appeared to be.

■ *Author biography in Reader's Handbook*

The Inn of Lost Time

LENSEY NAMIOKA

"Will you promise to sleep if I tell you a story?" said the father. He pretended to put on a stern expression.

"Yes! Yes!" the three little boys chanted in unison. It sounded like a nightly routine.

The two guests smiled as they listened to the exchange. They were wandering ronin, or unemployed samurai,[1] and they enjoyed watching this cozy family scene.

The father gave the guests a helpless look. "What can I do? I have to tell them a story, or these little rascals will give us no peace." Clearing his throat, he turned to the boys. "All right. The story tonight is about Urashima Taro."

Instantly the three boys became still. Sitting with their legs tucked under them, the three little boys, aged five, four, and three, looked like a descending row of stone statuettes. Matsuzo, the younger of the two ronin, was reminded of the wayside half-body statues of Jizo, the God of Travelers and Protector of Children.

Behind the boys the farmer's wife took up a pair of iron chopsticks and stirred the ashes of the fire in the charcoal brazier.[2] A momentary glow brightened the room. The lean faces of the two ronin, lit by the fire, suddenly looked fierce and hungry.

The farmer knew that the two ronin were supposed to use their arms in defense of the weak. But in these troubled times, with the country torn apart by civil wars, the samurai didn't always live up to their honorable code.

Then the fire died down again, and the subdued red light softened the features of the two ronin. The farmer relaxed and began his story.

The tale of Urashima Taro is familiar to every Japanese. No doubt the three little boys had heard their father tell it before—and more than once. But they listened with rapt attention.

Urashima Taro, a fisherman, rescued a turtle from some boys who were battering it with stones. The grateful turtle rewarded Taro by carrying him on his back to the bottom of the sea, where he lived happily with the Princess of the Undersea. But Taro soon became homesick for his native village and asked to go back on land. The princess gave him a box to take with him but warned him not to peek inside.

When Taro went back to his village, he found the place quite changed. In his home

---

1. **samurai** (sam′ ə rī′): warrior knights of feudal Japan.
2. **brazier** (brā′ zhər): a metal pan to hold burning coals for heating or cooking.

he found his parents gone, and living there was another old couple. He was stunned to learn that the aged husband was his own son, whom he had last seen as a baby! Taro thought he had spent only a pleasant week or two undersea with the princess. On land, seventy-two years had passed! His parents and most of his old friends had long since died.

Desolate, Taro decided to open the box given him by the princess. As soon as he looked inside, he changed in an instant from a young man to a decrepit old man of more than ninety.

He had lost the most precious thing of all: time.

At the end of the story, the boys were close to tears. Even Matsuzo found himself deeply touched. He wondered why the farmer had told his sons such a poignant bedtime story. Wouldn't they worry all evening instead of going to sleep?

But the boys recovered quickly. They were soon laughing and jostling each other, and they made no objections when their mother shooed them toward bed. Standing in order of age, they bowed politely to the guests and then lay down on the mattresses spread out for them on the floor. Within minutes the sound of their regular breathing told the guests that they were asleep.

Zenta, the older of the two ronin, sighed as he glanced at the peaceful young faces. "I wish I could fall asleep so quickly. The story of Urashima Taro is one of the saddest that I know among our folk tales."

The farmer looked proudly at his sleeping sons. "They're stout lads. Nothing bothers them much."

The farmer's wife poured tea for the guests and apologized. "I'm sorry this is only poor tea made from coarse leaves."

Zenta hastened to reassure her. "It's warm and heartening on a chilly autumn evening."

"You know what I think is the saddest part of the Urashima Taro story?" said Matsuzo, picking up his cup and sipping the tea. "It's that Taro lost not only his family and friends but a big piece of his life as well. He had lost the most precious thing of all: time."

The farmer nodded agreement. "I wouldn't sell even one year of my life for money. As for losing seventy-two years, no amount of gold will make up for that!"

Why do they think time is so valuable?   *review*

Zenta put his cup down on the floor and looked curiously at the farmer. "It's interesting that you should say that. I had an opportunity once to observe exactly how much gold a person was willing to pay for some lost years of his life." He smiled grimly. "In this case the man went as far as one gold piece for each year he lost."

"That's bizarre!" said Matsuzo. "You never told me about it."

"It happened long before I met you," said Zenta. He drank some tea and smiled ruefully. "Besides, I'm not particularly

---

Words to Know and Use | **decrepit** (dē krep' it) *adj.* broken down; worn out
jostle (jäs' əl) *v.* to bump against or push
heartening (härt' 'n iŋ) *adj.* cheering **hearten** *v.*

323

THE IVY LANE   Fukae Roshu   (1699-1757)   The Cleveland Museum of Art, John L. Severance Fund 54.127.

proud of the part I played in that strange affair."

"Let's hear the story!" urged Matsuzo. "You've made us all curious."

The farmer waited expectantly. His wife sat down quietly behind her husband and folded her hands. Her eyes looked intently at Zenta.

"Very well, then," said Zenta. "Actually, my story bears some resemblance to that of Urashima Taro. . . ."

It happened about seven years ago, when I was a green, inexperienced youngster not quite eighteen years old. But I had had a good training in arms, and I was able to get a job as a bodyguard for a wealthy mer-

chant from Sakai.

As you know, wealthy merchants are relatively new in our country. Traditionally the rich have been noblemen, landowners, and warlords with thousands of followers. Merchants, considered as parasites in our society, are a despised class. But our civil wars have made people unusually mobile and stimulated trade between various parts of the country. The merchants have taken advantage of this to conduct businesses on a scale our fathers could not imagine. Some of them have become more wealthy than a warlord with thousands of samurai under his command.

The man I was escorting, Tokubei, was one of this new breed of wealthy merchants.

He was trading not only with outlying provinces but even with the Portuguese[3] from across the sea. On this particular journey he was not carrying much gold with him. If he had, I'm sure he would have hired an older and more experienced bodyguard. But if the need should arise, he could always write a message to his clerks at home and have money forwarded to him. It's important to remember this.

The second day of our journey was a particularly grueling one, with several steep hills to climb. As the day was drawing to its close, we began to consider where we should spend the night. I knew that within an hour's walking was a hot-spring resort known to have several attractive inns.

But Tokubei, my employer, said he was already very tired and wanted to stop. He had heard of the resort and knew the inns there were expensive. Wealthy as he was, he did not want to spend more money than he had to.

While we stood talking, a smell reached our noses, a wonderful smell of freshly cooked rice. Suddenly I felt <u>ravenous</u>. From the way Tokubei swallowed, I knew he was feeling just as hungry.

We looked around eagerly, but the area was forested and we could not see very far in any direction. The tantalizing smell seemed to grow, and I could feel the saliva filling my mouth.

"There's an inn around here somewhere," muttered Tokubei. "I'm sure of it."

We followed our noses. We had to leave the well-traveled highway and take a narrow, winding footpath. But the mouth-watering smell of the rice and the vision of fluffy, freshly aired cotton quilts drew us on.

The sun was just beginning to set. We passed a bamboo grove,[4] and in the low evening light the thin leaves turned into little golden knives. I saw a gilded clump of bamboo shoots. The sight made me think of the delicious dish they would make when boiled in soy sauce.

We hurried forward. To our delight we soon came to a clearing with a thatched house standing in the middle. The fragrant smell of rice was now so strong that we were certain a meal was being prepared inside.

Standing in front of the house was a pretty girl beaming at us with a welcoming smile. "Please honor us with your presence," she said, beckoning.

There was something a little unusual about one of her hands, but being hungry and eager to enter the house, I did not stop to observe closely.

You will say, of course, that it was my duty as a bodyguard to be suspicious and to look out for danger. Youth and inexperience should not have prevented me from wondering why an inn should be found hidden away from the highway. As it was, my stomach growled, and I didn't even hesitate but followed Tokubei to the house.

What's going to happen next?  *predict*

---

3. **Portuguese:** here, merchants from Portugal, a European country that formerly colonized and traded in Asia, Africa, and America.
4. **bamboo grove:** a group of treelike tropical grasses.

Words to Know and Use | **ravenous** (rav′ ə nəs) *adj.* very hungry

Before stepping up to enter, we were given basins of water to wash our feet. As the girl handed us towels for drying, I saw what was unusual about her left hand: she had six fingers.

question   How did she get six fingers?

Tokubei had noticed it as well. When the girl turned away to empty the basins, he nudged me. "Did you see her left hand? She had——" He broke off in confusion as the girl turned around, but she didn't seem to have heard.

The inn was peaceful and quiet, and we soon discovered the reason why. We were the only guests. Again, I should have been suspicious. I told you that I'm not proud of the part I played.

Tokubei turned to me and grinned. "It seems that there are no other guests. We should be able to get extra service for the same amount of money."

The girl led us to a spacious room which was like the principal chamber of a private residence. Cushions were set out for us on the floor, and we began to shed our traveling gear to make ourselves comfortable.

The door opened and a grizzled-haired man entered. Despite his vigorous-looking face, his back was a little bent, and I guessed his age to be about fifty. After bowing and greeting us, he apologized in advance for the service. "We have not always been innkeepers here," he said, "and you may find the accommodations lacking. Our good intentions must make up for our inexperience.

However, to compensate for our inadequacies, we will charge a lower fee than that of an inn with an established reputation."

Tokubei nodded graciously, highly pleased by the words of our host, and the evening began well. It continued well when the girl came back with some flasks of wine, cups, and dishes of salty snacks.

While the girl served the wine, the host looked with interest at my swords. From the few remarks he made, I gathered that he was a former samurai, forced by circumstances to turn his house into an inn.

Having become a bodyguard to a tight-fisted merchant, I was in no position to feel superior to a ronin-turned-innkeeper. Socially, therefore, we were more or less equal.

We exchanged polite remarks with our host while we drank and tasted the salty snacks. I looked around at the pleasant room. It showed excellent taste, and I especially admired a vase standing in the alcove.

My host caught my eyes on it. "We still have a few good things that we didn't have to sell," he said. His voice held a trace of bitterness. "Please look at the panels of these doors. They were painted by a fine artist."

Tokubei and I looked at the pair of sliding doors. Each panel contained a landscape painting, the right panel depicting a winter scene, and the left one the same scene in late summer. Our host's words were no idle boast. The pictures were indeed beautiful.

Tokubei rose and approached the screens for a closer look. When he sat down again, his eyes were calculating. No doubt he was trying to estimate what price the paintings would fetch.

Words to Know and Use | **compensate** (käm′ pən sāt′) *v.* to make up for

After my third drink, I began to feel very tired. Perhaps it was the result of drinking on an empty stomach. I was glad when the girl brought in two dinner trays and a lacquered container of rice. Uncovering the rice container, she began filling our bowls.

Again I noticed her strange left hand with its six fingers. Any other girl would have tried to keep that hand hidden, but this girl made no effort to do so. If anything, she seemed to use that hand more than her other one when she served us. The extra little finger always stuck out from the hand, as if inviting comment.

The hand fascinated me so much that I kept my eyes on it and soon forgot to eat. After a while the hand looked blurry. And then everything else began to look blurry. The last thing I remembered was the sight of Tokubei shaking his head, as if trying to clear it.

When I opened my eyes again, I knew that time had passed but not how much time. My next thought was that it was cold. It was not only extremely cold but damp.

I rolled over and sat up. I reached immediately for my swords and found them safe on the ground beside me. *On the ground?* What was I doing on the ground? My last memory was of staying at an inn with a merchant called Tokubei.

 What happened to them?

The thought of Tokubei put me into a panic. I was his bodyguard, and instead of watching over him, I had fallen asleep and had awakened in a strange place.

I looked around frantically and saw that he was lying on the ground not far from where I was. Had he been killed?

SUDDEN SHOWER   1917   Ito Shinsui
Courtesy, The Trustees of the British Museum, London.

I got up shakily, and when I stood up, my head was swimming. But my sense of urgency gave some strength to my legs. I stumbled over to my employer and to my great relief found him breathing—breathing heavily, in fact.

When I shook his shoulder, he grunted and finally opened his eyes. "Where am I?" he asked thickly.

It was a reasonable question. I looked around and saw that we had been lying in a bamboo grove. By the light I guessed that it was early morning, and the reason I felt cold and damp was because my clothes were wet with dew.

"It's cold!" said Tokubei, shivering and climbing unsteadily to his feet. He looked around slowly, and his eyes became wide with disbelief. "What happened? I thought we were staying at an inn!"

His words came as a relief. One of the possibilities I had considered was that I had gone mad and that the whole episode with the inn was something I had imagined. Now I knew that Tokubei had the same memory of the inn. I had not imagined it.

But why were we out here on the cold ground instead of on comfortable mattresses in the inn?

"They must have drugged us and robbed us," said Tokubei. He turned and looked at me furiously. "A fine bodyguard you are!"

There was nothing I could say to that. But at least we were both alive and unharmed. "Did they take all your money?" I asked.

Tokubei had already taken his wallet out of his sash and was peering inside. "That's funny! My money is still here!"

This was certainly unexpected. What did the innkeeper and his strange daughter intend to do by drugging us and moving us outside?

At least things were not as bad as we had feared. We had not lost anything except a comfortable night's sleep, although from the heaviness in my head I had certainly slept deeply enough—and long enough too. Exactly how much time had elapsed since we drank wine with our host?

All we had to do now was find the highway again and continue our journey. Tokubei suddenly chuckled. "I didn't even have to pay for our night's lodging!"

As we walked from the bamboo grove, I saw the familiar clump of bamboo shoots, and we found ourselves standing in the same clearing again. Before our eyes was the thatched house. Only it was somehow different. Perhaps things looked different in the daylight than at dusk.

But the difference was more than a change of light. As we approached the house slowly, like sleepwalkers, we saw that the thatching was much darker. On the previous evening the thatching had looked fresh and new. Now it was dark with age. Daylight should make things appear brighter, not darker. The plastering of the walls also looked more dingy.

Tokubei and I stopped to look at each other before we went closer. He was pale, and I knew that I looked no less frightened. Something was terribly wrong. I loosened my sword in its scabbard.[5]

We finally gathered the courage to go up to the house. Since Tokubei seemed unable to find his voice, I spoke out. "Is anyone there?"

After a moment we heard shuffling footsteps, and the front door slid open. The face of an old woman appeared. "Yes?" she inquired. Her voice was creaky with age.

What set my heart pounding with panic, however, was not her voice. It was the sight of her left hand holding on to the frame of the door. The hand was wrinkled and crooked with the arthritis[6] of old age—and it had six fingers.

I heard a gasp beside me and knew that Tokubei had noticed the hand as well.

---

5. **scabbard** (skab′ ərd): a sheath or case for the blade of a sword.
6. **arthritis** (är *thrīt′* is): an inflammation of the joints, causing pain and swelling.

The door opened wider, and a man appeared beside the old woman. At first I thought it was our host of the previous night. But this man was much younger, although the resemblance was strong. He carried himself straighter, and his hair was black, while the innkeeper had been grizzled and slightly bent with age.

"Please excuse my mother," said the man. "Her hearing is not good. Can we help you in some way?"

Tokubei finally found his voice. "Isn't this the inn where we stayed last night?"

The man stared. "Inn? We are not innkeepers here!"

"Yes, you are!" insisted Tokubei. "Your daughter invited us in and served us with wine. You must have put something in the wine!"

The man frowned. "You are serious? Are you sure you didn't drink too much at your inn and wander off?"

"No, I didn't drink too much!" said Tokubei, almost shouting. "I hardly drank at all! Your daughter, the one with six fingers on her hand, started to pour me a second cup of wine . . ." His voice trailed off, and he stared again at the left hand of the old woman.

"I don't have a daughter," said the man slowly. "My mother here is the one who has six fingers on her left hand, although I hardly think it polite of you to mention it."

"I'm getting dizzy," muttered Tokubei, and he began to totter.

"I think you'd better come in and rest a bit," the man said to him gruffly. He glanced at me. "Perhaps you wish to join your friend. You don't share his delusion about the inn, I hope?"

"I wouldn't presume to contradict my elders," I said carefully. Since both Tokubei and the owner of the house were my elders, I wasn't committing myself. In truth I didn't know what to believe, but I did want a look at the inside of the house.

The inside was almost the same as it was before, but the differences were there when I looked closely. We entered the same room with the alcove and the pair of painted doors. The vase I had admired was no longer there, but the doors showed the same landscapes painted by a master. I peered closely at the pictures and saw that the colors looked faded. What was more, the left panel, the one depicting a winter scene, had a long tear in one corner. It had been painstakingly mended, but the damage was impossible to hide completely.

Tokubei saw what I was staring at, and he became even paler. At this stage we had both considered the possibility that a hoax of some sort had been played on us. The torn screen convinced Tokubei that our host had not played a joke: the owner of a valuable painting would never vandalize it for a trivial reason.

As for me, I was far more disturbed by the sight of the sixth finger on the old woman's hand. Could the young girl have disguised herself as an old crone?[7] She could put rice powder in her hair to whiten it, but she could not transform her pretty straight fingers into old fingers twisted with arthritis. The woman here with us now was genuinely old, at least fifty years older than the girl.

It was this same old woman who finally gave us our greatest shock. "It's interesting

---

7. **crone:** an ugly, withered old woman.

that you should mention an inn, gentlemen," she croaked. "My father used to operate an inn. After he died, my husband and I turned this back into a private residence. We didn't need the income, you see."

Some of our guests disappeared, you see.

"Your . . . your . . . f-father?" stammered Tokubei.

"Yes," replied the old woman. "He was a ronin, forced to go into innkeeping when he lost his position. But he never liked the work. Besides, our inn had begun to acquire an unfortunate reputation. Some of our guests disappeared, you see."

Even before she finished speaking, a horrible suspicion had begun to dawn on me. Her *father* had been an innkeeper, she said, her father who used to be a ronin. The man who had been our host was a ronin-turned-innkeeper. Could this mean that this old woman was actually the same person as the young girl we had seen?

I sat stunned while I tried to absorb the implications. What had happened to us? Was it possible that Tokubei and I had slept while this young girl grew into a mature woman, got married, and bore a son, a son who was now an adult? If that was the case, then we had slept for fifty years!

The old woman's next words confirmed my fears. "I recognize you now! You are two of the lost guests from our inn! The other lost ones I don't remember so well, but I remember *you* because your disappearance made me so sad. Such a handsome youth, I thought; what a pity that he should have gone the way of the others!"

A high wail came from Tokubei, who began to keen and rock himself back and forth. "I've lost fifty years! Fifty years of my life went by while I slept at this accursed inn!"

How could they have slept for fifty years?

review

The inn was indeed accursed. Was the fate of the other guests similar to ours? "Did anyone else return as we did, fifty years later?" I asked.

The old woman looked uncertain and turned to her son. He frowned thoughtfully. "From time to time wild-looking people have come to us with stories similar to yours. Some of them went mad with the shock."

Tokubei wailed again. "I've lost my business! I've lost my wife, my young and beautiful wife! We had been married only a couple of months!"

A gruesome chuckle came from the old woman. "You may not have lost your wife. It's just that she's become an old hag like me!"

That did not console Tokubei, whose keening became louder. Although my relationship with my employer had not been characterized by much respect on either side, I did begin to feel very sorry for him. He was right: he had lost his world.

As for me, the loss was less traumatic. I had left home under extremely painful

Words to Know and Use | **implication** (im′ pli kā′ shən) *n.* a possible meaning or significance
accursed (ə kur′ sid) *adj.* under a curse; enchanted

circumstances and had spent the next three years wandering. I had no friends and no one I could call a relation. The only thing I had was my duty to my employer. Somehow, someway, I had to help him.

"Did no one find an explanation for these disappearances?" I asked. "Perhaps if we knew the reason why, we might find some way to reverse the process."

The old woman began to nod eagerly. "The priestess! Tell them about the shrine priestess!"

"Well," said the man, "I'm not sure if it would work in your case. . . ."

"What? What would work?" demanded Tokubei. His eyes were feverish.

"There was a case of one returning guest who consulted the priestess at our local shrine," said the man. "She went into a trance and revealed that there was an evil spirit dwelling in the bamboo grove here. This spirit would put <u>unwary</u> travelers into a long, unnatural sleep. They would wake up twenty, thirty, or even fifty years later."

"Yes, but you said something worked in his case," said Tokubei.

The man seemed <u>reluctant</u> to go on. "I don't like to see you cheated, so I'm not sure I should be telling you this."

"Tell me! Tell me!" demanded Tokubei. The host's reluctance only made him more impatient.

"The priestess promised to make a spell that would undo the work of the evil spirit," said the man. "But she demanded a large sum of money, for she said that she had to burn some very rare and costly incense before she could begin the spell."

At the mention of money, Tokubei sat back. The hectic flush died down on his face, and his eyes narrowed. "How much money?" he asked.

The host shook his head. "In my opinion the priestess is a fraud and makes outrageous claims about her powers. We try to have as little to do with her as possible."

"Yes, but did her spell work?" asked Tokubei. "If it worked, she's no fraud!"

"At least the stranger disappeared again," cackled the old woman. "Maybe he went back to his own time. Maybe he walked into a river."

Tokubei's eyes narrowed further. "How much money did the priestess demand?" he asked again.

"I think it was one gold piece for every year lost," said the host. He hurriedly added, "Mind you, I still wouldn't trust the priestess."

"Then it would cost me fifty gold pieces to get back to my own time," muttered Tokubei. He looked up. "I don't carry that much money with me."

"No, you don't," agreed the host.

Something alerted me about the way he said that. It was as if the host knew already that Tokubei did not carry much money on him.

Meanwhile, Tokubei sighed. He had come to a decision. "I do have the means to obtain more money, however. I can send a message to my chief clerk, and he will <u>remit</u> the money when he sees my seal."

"Your chief clerk may be dead by now," I reminded him.

SAMURAI 16th c.
Courtesy, The Agency for Cultural Affairs, Tokyo

"You're right!" moaned Tokubei. "My business will be under a new management, and nobody will even remember my name!"

"And your wife will have remarried," said the old woman, with one of her chuckles. I found it hard to believe that the gentle young girl who had served us wine could turn into this dreadful harridan.[8]

"Sending the message may be a waste of time," agreed the host.

"What waste of time!" cried Tokubei. "Why shouldn't I waste time? I've wasted fifty years already! Anyway, I've made up my mind. I'm sending that message."

"I still think you shouldn't trust the priestess," said the host.

That only made Tokubei all the more determined to send for the money. However, he was not quite resigned to the amount. "Fifty gold pieces is a large sum. Surely the priestess can buy incense for less than that amount?"

"Why don't you try giving her thirty gold pieces?" cackled the old woman. "Then the priestess will send you back thirty years, and your wife will only be middle-aged."

While Tokubei was still arguing with himself about the exact sum to send for, I decided to have a look at the bamboo grove. "I'm going for a walk," I announced, rising and picking up my sword from the floor beside me.

The host turned sharply to look at me. For an instant a faint, rueful smile appeared on his lips. Then he looked away.

Outside, I went straight to the clump of shoots in the bamboo grove. On the previous night—or what I perceived as the previous

8. **harridan** (har′ i dən): a bad-tempered old woman.

night—I had noticed that clump of bamboo shoots particularly, because I had been so hungry that I pictured them being cut up and boiled.

The clump of bamboo shoots was still in the same place. That in itself proved nothing, since bamboo could spring up anywhere, including the place where a clump had existed fifty years earlier. But what settled the matter in my mind was that the clump looked almost exactly the way it did when I had seen it before, except that every shoot was about an inch taller. That was a reasonable amount for bamboo shoots to grow overnight.

Overnight. Tokubei and I had slept on the ground here overnight. We had not slept here for a period of fifty years.

Once I knew that, I was able to see another inconsistency: the door panels with the painted landscapes. The painting with the winter scene had been on the *right* last night, and it was on the *left* this morning. It wasn't simply a case of the panels changing places because the depressions in the panel for the handholds had been reversed. In other words, what I saw just now was not a pair of paintings faded and torn by age. They were an entirely different pair of paintings.

But how did the pretty young girl change into an old woman? The answer was that if the screens could be different ones, so could the women. I had seen one woman, a young girl, last night. This morning I saw a different woman, an old hag.

The darkening of the thatched roof? Simply blow ashes over the roof. The grizzled-haired host of last night could be the same man who claimed to be his grandson today. It would be a simple matter for a young man to put gray in his hair and assume a stoop.

And the purpose of the hoax? To make Tokubei send for fifty pieces of gold, of course. It was clever of the man to accuse the shrine priestess of fraud and pretend reluctance to let Tokubei send his message.

I couldn't even feel angry toward the man and his daughter—or mother, sister, wife, whatever. He could have killed me and taken my swords, which he clearly admired. Perhaps he was really a ronin and felt sympathetic toward another one.

When I returned to the house, Tokubei was looking resigned. "I've decided to send for the whole fifty gold pieces." He sighed.

"Don't bother," I said. "In fact, we should be leaving as soon as possible. We shouldn't even stop here for a drink, especially not of wine."

Tokubei stared. "What do you mean? If I go back home, I'll find everything changed!"

"Nothing will be changed," I told him. "Your wife will be as young and beautiful as ever."

"I don't understand," he said. "Fifty years . . ."

"It's a joke," I said. "The people here have a peculiar sense of humor, and they've played a joke on us."

The people here have a peculiar sense of humor.

Tokubei's mouth hung open. Finally he closed it with a snap. He stared at the host, and his face became first red and then purple. "You—you were trying to swindle me!"

He turned furiously to me. "And you let them do this!"

"I'm not letting them," I pointed out. "That's why we're leaving right now."

"Are you going to let them get away with this?" demanded Tokubei. "They might try to swindle someone else!"

"They only went to this much trouble when they heard of the arrival of a fine fat fish like you," I said. I looked deliberately at the host. "I'm sure they won't be tempted to try the same trick again."

"And that's the end of your story?" asked Matsuzo. "You and Tokubei just went away? How did you know the so-called innkeeper wouldn't try the trick on some other luckless traveler?"

Zenta shook his head. "I didn't know. I merely guessed that once the trick was exposed, they wouldn't take the chance of trying it again. Of course, I thought about revisiting the place to check if the people there were leading an honest life."

"Why didn't you?" asked Matsuzo. "Maybe we could go together. You've made me curious about that family now."

"Then you can satisfy your curiosity," said Zenta, smiling. He held his cup out for more tea, and the farmer's wife came forward to pour.

Only now she used both hands to hold the pot, and for the first time Matsuzo saw her left hand. He gasped. The hand had six fingers.

"Who was the old woman?" Zenta asked the farmer's wife.

"She was my grandmother," she replied. "Having six fingers is something that runs in my family."

At last Matsuzo found his voice. "You mean this is the very house you visited? This is the inn where time was lost?"

"Where we *thought* we lost fifty years," said Zenta. "Perhaps I should have warned you first. But I was almost certain that we'd be safe this time. And I see that I was right."

He turned to the woman again. "You and your husband are farmers now, aren't you? What happened to the man who was the host?"

"He's dead," she said quietly. "He was my brother, and he was telling you the truth when he said that he was a ronin. Two years ago he found work with another warlord, but he was killed in battle only a month later."

Matsuzo was peering at the pair of sliding doors, which he hadn't noticed before. "I see that you've put up the faded set of paintings. The winter scene is on the left side."

The woman nodded. "We sold the newer pair of doors. My husband said that we're farmers now and that people in our position don't need valuable paintings. We used the money to buy some new farm implements."

She took up the teapot again. "Would you like another cup of tea?" she asked Matsuzo.

Staring at her left hand, Matsuzo had a sudden qualm. "I—I don't think I want any more."

Everybody laughed. 🍂

Responding to Reading

First Impressions

1. What are your reactions to Zenta's story about the hoax?

Second Thoughts

2. Why do you think the hoax worked on other people but not on Zenta?

Think about
- the cleverness of the trick
- people's gullibility
- Zenta's personality

3. Neither Zenta nor Tokubei confronted the innkeepers. If you had been Zenta or Tokubei, would you have punished the innkeepers for their trick? Why or why not?

4. If you had been Zenta, would you have returned to the inn after the hoax? Why or why not?

5. Why might it be sad or frightening to lose years of your life, as Urashima Taro did?

Broader Connections

6. A hoax is defined as "a trick or fraud, especially one meant as a practical joke." Throughout history, hoaxes have been played on individuals as well as on groups of people. What are some hoaxes that you have read about or know about from your own experiences?

Literary Concept: Frame Story

A **frame story** is a story that takes place inside another story. "The Inn of Lost Time" actually contains two frame stories. First the story of Urashima Taro introduces the idea of lost time. What is the second frame story within "The Inn of Lost Time"?

Concept Review: Foreshadowing As you know, using hints or clues to suggest what will happen later in a story is called **foreshadowing.** Foreshadowing can create suspense or set up an expectation that, when met, satisfies the reader. When you finish "The Inn of Lost Time," note examples that you think foreshadowed certain important events in the story.

Writing Options

1. Outwardly, the farmer's wife appeared calm as she sat, hands folded, listening to Zenta. Do you think she really was calm? Write an **interior monologue** that describes what she might have been thinking and feeling.

2. The Urashima Taro story could be adapted to any time and any location. Write a contemporary or futuristic version of this **tale,** placing it in the setting of your choice.

3. Imagine that Zenta and Tokubei really did age fifty years during their night in the bamboo grove. How might their story be different? Rewrite the **story ending** as if the men actually had grown older.

4. Consider other tricks or hoaxes you have read or heard about—or in which you have participated. Choose one and write a detailed **description** of how it worked.

Vocabulary Practice

Exercise   On a sheet of paper, write the word from the list that best completes the sentence.

1. The smell of food from a nearby inn made the two travelers _?_ .

2. When they got to the inn, they were greeted by a girl with a warm and _?_ smile.

3. The hosts were new at innkeeping, so they offered a lower price to _?_ for their inexperience.

4. When one of the men noticed that the girl had six fingers on one hand, he began to nudge and _?_ his companion.

5. Although the men kept staring at the girl's hand, they were _?_ to ask her about it.

6. The innkeepers were so pleasant that the _?_ travelers had no suspicions.

7. The men did not realize what an _?_ hoax the innkeepers had set into motion.

8. How could a beautiful young woman change overnight into a _?_ old hag?

9. The host's _?_ was clear: if the travelers paid the money, they could have their lost years back.

10. If the men did not have the money, they could _?_ it after they returned home.

> *Words to Know and Use*
> ─────────
> **accursed**
> **compensate**
> **decrepit**
> **heartening**
> **implication**
> **jostle**
> **ravenous**
> **reluctant**
> **remit**
> **unwary**

Poetry

Nothing Gold Can Stay

ROBERT FROST

O Captain! My Captain

WALT WHITMAN

Examine What You Know

Think of the last day of summer before school begins again. How do you feel? A little sad that all those golden lazy days are coming to an end? A feeling of loss? The sadness that comes when we lose something or someone wonderful is one of the most common human emotions. What other experiences in life may cause a feeling of loss? In a word web, jot down examples of such events.

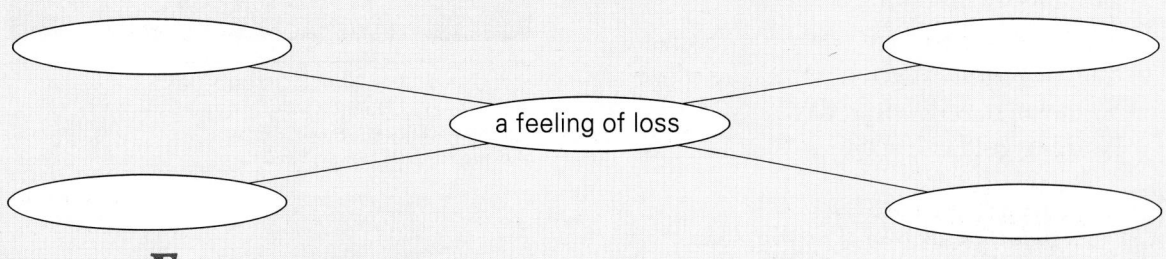

a feeling of loss

Expand Your Knowledge

Sometimes an entire nation experiences a moment of loss. Such was the case in April 1865. The Civil War had just ended, and Americans were enjoying the first week of peacetime in four years. On April 14, President Abraham Lincoln and Mrs. Lincoln went to Ford's Theatre in Washington, D.C., to see *Our American Cousin,* a popular play of the time. Shortly after 10 P.M., a shot rang out. John Wilkes Booth, a famous actor and Confederate sympathizer, had shot Lincoln in the head. The President was carried, unconscious, to a nearby boardinghouse, where he died the next morning. People across the nation grieved the loss of "Father Abraham."

Write Before You Read

■ *Author biographies on Extend page*

Think about the examples of loss that you listed in Examine What You Know. In your journal or on a sheet of paper, write a poem that describes a time when you or someone you know experienced a loss.

Nothing Gold Can Stay

ROBERT FROST

AUTUMN LEAVES, LAKE GEORGE, N.Y.
1924   Georgia O'Keeffe
Columbus (Ohio) Museum of Art:
Museum Purchase Howald Fund II.

Nature's first green[1] is gold,
Her hardest hue[2] to hold.
Her early leaf's a flower;
But only so an hour.
5 Then leaf subsides[3] to leaf.
So Eden[4] sank to grief,
So dawn goes down to day.
Nothing gold can stay.

---

1. **green:** here, the color of growing plants.
2. **hue:** a particular shade of a color.
3. **subside:** to sink down; die down.
4. **Eden:** in the Bible, the garden in which the first
human beings were created and from which they were
expelled for their disobedience to God.

*R*esponding to Reading

First Impressions of "Nothing Gold Can Stay"

1. What does this poem mean to you? Write your impressions in your
journal or on a sheet of paper.

Second Thoughts on "Nothing Gold Can Stay"

2. Look over your writing for the Explore page activities. What
connections can you see between your thoughts and the ideas in this
poem?

3. Do you agree with Robert Frost that "nothing gold can stay" in life?
Why or why not?

O Captain! My Captain!

WALT WHITMAN

O Captain! my Captain! our fearful trip is done,
The ship has weather'd every rack,[1] the prize we sought is won,
The port is near, the bells I hear, the people all exulting,[2]
While follow eyes the steady keel, the vessel grim and daring;
5   But O heart! heart! heart!
            O the bleeding drops of red,
                Where on the deck my Captain lies,
                    Fallen cold and dead.

Captain! my Captain! rise up and hear the bells;
10 Rise up—for you the flag is flung—for you the bugle trills,
For you bouquets and ribbon'd wreaths—for you the shores a-crowding,
For you they call, the swaying mass, their eager faces turning;
            Here Captain! dear father!
                This arm beneath your head!
15   It is some dream that on the deck,
                    You've fallen cold and dead.

My Captain does not answer, his lips are pale and still,
My father does not feel my arm, he has no pulse nor will,
The ship is anchor'd safe and sound, its voyage closed and done,
20 From fearful trip the victor ship comes in with object won:
            Exult O shores, and ring O bells!
                But I with mournful tread,
                    Walk the deck my Captain lies,
                        Fallen cold and dead.

---

1. **rack:** a buffeting, as by a storm.
2. **exulting:** rejoicing.

Responding to Reading

First Impressions of "O Captain! My Captain!"

1. What feelings do you have after reading this poem?

Second Thoughts on "O Captain! My Captain!"

2. In what ways is the captain in this poem like Abraham Lincoln?

3. What do you think makes the captain's death particularly tragic and ironic?

4. For over a hundred years students in the United States have studied and memorized this poem. Why do you think this is the case?

Comparing the Poems

5. How do the two poems compare in terms of rhyme and rhythm?

6. Which poem do you like better? Explain.

Literary Concept: Rhythm

In poetry, the pattern of stressed and unstressed syllables is called **rhythm.** Rhythm makes language sound musical. It can also emphasize ideas or create a particular mood. Notice the rhythm in the following lines from "O Captain! My Captain!" The stressed syllables are marked with a /.

My father does not feel my arm, he has no pulse nor will,

The ship is anchor'd safe and sound, its voyage closed and done,

Write the second line of the first stanza of the poem and mark the stressed and unstressed syllables.

Writing Options

1. Write a **eulogy,** a speech of praise for someone who has died. Think about the qualities of this person, and the main impression you would like to leave.

2. Write a **message** to President Abraham Lincoln, persuading him not to go to Ford's Theatre on the evening of April 14, 1865.

Options for Learning

1 • **Honest Abe** Research one topic related to Abraham Lincoln's life. Prepare a report to present to your class. Try to include visual or audio aids in your presentation.

2 • **Act It Out** Prepare a dramatic reading of Walt Whitman's poem. Tape record your reading and play it for your class. You may choose to add appropriate sound effects or music.

Robert Frost 1874–1963

Robert Frost, the most popular American poet of his time, nearly missed his calling. Long before he achieved success as a poet, he worked as a farmer, an editor, and a teacher. He published his first book of poems, *A Boy's Will,* in England when he was 39 years old.

Frost's poetry is known for its plain language. He believed that a poem "begins in delight and ends in wisdom." Frost won the Pulitzer Prize for poetry in 1924, 1931, 1937, and 1943, the only poet to win this award four times. In 1960, Congress voted him a medal "in recognition of his poetry, which . . . enriched the culture of the United States and the philosophy of the world."

Walt Whitman 1819–1892

Walt Whitman worked as a printer, a teacher, an editor, a housing contractor, a nurse, a government clerk, and a lecturer. He is best known, however, as a poet.

Whitman's first poetry collection, *Leaves of Grass,* contained only twelve poems. During the rest of his life, Whitman revised and expanded this book until the final edition contained more than four hundred poems.

Many of Whitman's poems sing the praises of American life and democracy. In his preface to *Leaves of Grass,* Whitman wrote, "The United States themselves are essentially the greatest poem." Abraham Lincoln reportedly had a copy of Whitman's book in his law office and liked to read aloud from it.

Whitman's new style of poetry was at first criticized as "barbaric," but today critics regard *Leaves of Grass* as one of the great works in American literature.

Drama

Rip Van Winkle

WASHINGTON IRVING
Dramatized by ADELE THANE

*E*xamine *What You Know*

Imagine waking up one morning and finding out that twenty years have passed since you fell asleep. What would you see when you looked in the mirror? Who would greet you when you went to get breakfast? In your journal or on a sheet of paper, list some of the changes that you would expect to have taken place in your appearance, in your family, in your neighborhood, and in your country after your twenty-year nap.

*E*xpand *Your Knowledge*

In the play you are about to read, Rip Van Winkle falls asleep in 1770 and awakens in 1790. During the twenty years that Rip was asleep, many changes took place. Perhaps the biggest change is the one that occurred in America. As a result of the American Revolutionary War (1775–1783), Rip's home changed from a colony ruled by England's King George III to New York, one of the United States of America headed by President George Washington.

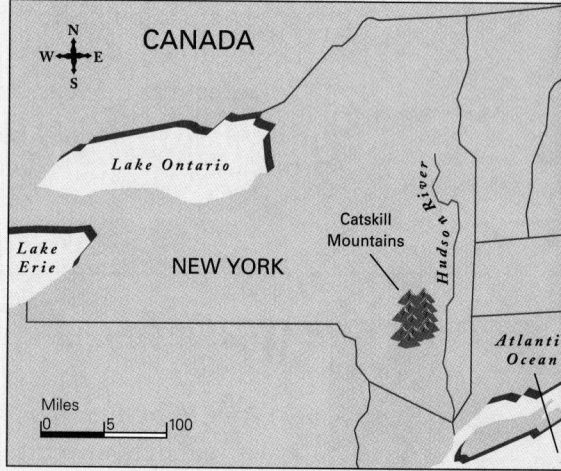

*E*nrich *Your Reading*

Theatrical Conventions   When writing a play, an author must sometimes include certain **theatrical conventions**—such as lighting, makeup, or costume changes—that will let the audience know that time has passed. In *Rip Van Winkle* this is especially true, since twenty years pass while Rip sleeps. As you read, notice the variety of theatrical conventions that Adele Thane uses to suggest the passage of time.

■ *Author biography on Extend page*

Rip Van Winkle

WASHINGTON IRVING
Dramatized by ADELE THANE

Courtesy, Historic Hudson Valley,
Tarrytown, New York.

CHARACTERS

Rip Van Winkle

Dame Van Winkle, his wife

Judy, his daughter

Luke Gardenier

Katchen — Judy's playmates

Meenie, a girl

Jacob

Nicholas Vedder, landlord of the King George Tavern

Derrick Van Bummel, the schoolmaster

Peter Vanderdonk — men of the village

Brom Dutcher

Offstage Voice

Hendrik Hudson

Sailors, Hudson's crew

Orator

Jonathan Doolittle, proprietor of the Union Hotel

Judith Gardenier, Judy grown up

Little Rip, her son

Townspeople

Children

Scene 1

Time: Early autumn, a few years before the Revolutionary War.

Setting: A village in the Catskill Mountains.[1] At left, there is an inn with a sign, KING GEORGE TAVERN, and a picture of King George III.[2] A British Union Jack[3] hangs on the flagpole.

At Rise: Nicholas Vedder, Derrick Van Bummel, Brom Dutcher, and Peter Vanderdonk are seated outside the tavern. Vedder is sprawled back in his chair. Dutcher and Vanderdonk are at the table, playing a game of checkers. Van Bummel is reading aloud from a newspaper. From time to time, a rumble of thunder can be heard in the distance.

Van Bummel *(reading)*. ". . . and it has been learned that Massachusetts favors a Stamp Act Congress to be held in New York to protest English taxation in the colonies."

Dutcher *(looking up from his game)*. Good! It's high time we did something about this English taxation.

Vanderdonk. Taxes and more taxes! The English are a pack of rascals with their hands in our pockets.

Van Bummel. There's even a revenue stamp on our newspapers. One of these days the people here in the American colonies will revolt, you mark my words.

Vedder *(pointing off right as a merry whistle is heard)*. Well, here comes one man who is not troubled by these problems—Rip Van Winkle. *(Rip Van Winkle enters, a wooden bucket in one hand, his gun in the other. He props his gun against the tree trunk, then crosses to the group of men.)*

Rip. Good afternoon, Nick Vedder—Brom—Peter. *(to Van Bummel)* Good afternoon, Mr. Schoolmaster. *(They return his greeting. There is a loud rumble of thunder, and Rip cocks his head.)* Just listen to that, will you!

Dutcher. We're probably in for a storm after this heat all day.

Vedder. Sit down, Rip. Derrick is reading us the news.

Vanderdonk. How about a game of checkers, Rip?

Rip *(hesitating)*. I don't know. Dame Van Winkle sent me for a bucket of water, but—maybe *one* game. *(He sets down the bucket and draws a stool up to the table as Vanderdonk rises.)*

Dutcher. Your move, Rip. *(Suddenly Dame Van Winkle's voice is heard from off right.)*

Dame Van Winkle *(calling from off right)*. Rip! R-i-p! Rip Van Winkle!

Rip. Oh, my galligaskins![4] It's my wife! *(Before he can get to his feet, Dame Van Winkle enters with a broom. She looks at men, then crosses directly to Rip.)*

Dame Van Winkle. So this is how you draw water from the well! Sitting around with a lot of lazy good-for-nothing loafers. *(She tries to hit Rip with the broom.)* Pick

---

1. **Catskill Mountains:** a forested mountain range in southeastern New York.
2. **King George III:** the king of England from 1760 to 1820, during whose rule the American Revolution took place.
3. **Union Jack:** a name for the British flag.
4. **galligaskins:** loose trousers; here the word is used as a mild exclamation.

up that bucket, you dawdling Dutchman, and fill it with water!

Rip (*snatching up the bucket and dodging out of the way*). Hey there, Dame, I'm not an old rug to be beaten with a broomstick.

Dame Van Winkle. Well, you might better be. An old rug is more use than you. At least it would keep our feet warm in winter, which is more than you can do. Little you care that your family is starving and the cow is gone.

Rip. The cow is gone?

Dame Van Winkle. Aye, the cow is gone, and the cabbage trampled down. When are you going to mend the fence?

Rip. It rained yesterday—

Dame Van Winkle. If excuses were shillings,[5] we'd be rich!

Rip. I'll mend the fence—tomorrow.

Dame Van Winkle. Tomorrow, tomorrow! All your work is going to be done tomorrow! (Rip *goes to the well as she starts off right, still talking.*) You show enough energy when there's a husking bee[6] or an errand to run for the neighbors, but here at home. . . . (*She exits.* Rip *lowers his bucket into the well. The other men rise to go into the tavern.*)

---

5. **shillings:** coins of England and colonial America.
6. **husking bee:** a festive gathering of neighbors to remove the leaflike coverings from harvested ears of corn.

Courtesy, Historic Hudson Valley, Tarrytown, New York.

Vedder. Poor Rip! His wife has the scoldingest tongue in the Hudson Valley.

Van Bummel. A sharp tongue is the only tool that grows keener with use.

Dutcher. What would you do, Derrick, if you had a wife like Van Winkle's?

Van Bummel. War could be no worse. I would enlist. *(They all laugh and exit through the door of the tavern. Rip turns to leave, then stops and smiles, as children's voices are heard off left.* Judy, Luke, Katchen, Meenie, *holding a kite, and* Jacob, *carrying a bow, run in, left, and shout with delight when they see* Rip.*)*

Children *(ad lib)*. There he is! There's Rip Van Winkle! *(They surround him, chattering excitedly.)*

Judy. Hello, Father, I've brought some of my friends.

Rip. Glad to see you, children.

> *Words to Know and Use*
>
> **ad lib** (ad′ lib′) *adv.* by improvising; speaking in one's own words

Jacob (*holding out bow*). Oh, Rip, there's something wrong with my bow. Every time I go to shoot, the cord slips. (*Rip takes the bow, draws his knife from his pocket, and cuts the notch deeper for the cord.*)

Rip. There, Jacob, try that, and see if it doesn't work.

Jacob (*pretending to shoot*). Yes, it's all right now.

Meenie (*holding out kite*). My kite won't stay up, Rip.

Rip (*taking off part of the tail*). Now it will, Meenie—and this breeze is just right for it. (*He hands kite to* Meenie.)

Katchen. My mother wants you to plug up her rain barrel so she'll be able to wash next week.

Rip. Tell her I'll fix it tonight, Katchen.

Luke. Rip, will you see what's the matter with my whistle? I made it just the way you showed me, but it isn't any good. (*He hands* Rip *a whistle.*)

Rip (*examining it*). You haven't whittled it right there, Luke. Here, I'll fix it for you. (*He sits on the bench under the tree and begins to whittle.*)

Judy. Tell us a story, Father!

Luke. Yes, you tell better stories than anybody in the Catskills. (*The children all gather around* Rip, *sitting on the ground.*)

Rip. What shall it be about?

Jacob. Indians!

Katchen. I like witches and goblins best. (*A long roll of thunder is heard.*)

Judy. Oh, Father, hear that! Hear the thunder!

Rip. Why, don't you know what that is, Judy? That's Hendrik Hudson and his famous crew playing ninepins[7] up in the mountains. (*More thunder is heard.*)

Meenie. Oh, what a noise they make!

Rip. Yes, they are jolly fellows. They sail the wide sea over in their ship, the Half-Moon, then every twenty years they come back to the Catskills.

Jacob. What do they do that for?

Rip. Oh, old Hendrik Hudson likes to revisit the country he discovered and keep a watchful eye over his river, the Hudson.

Jacob. I wish I could see Hendrik Hudson and his crew.

Rip. Peter Vanderdonk says his father saw them once in their funny breeches playing at ninepins up in the hills. (*A loud peal of thunder is heard.*) Listen to their balls rolling! That must be Hendrik Hudson himself, the Flying Dutchman! (*Dame Van Winkle enters with broom as* Rip *is speaking.*)

Dame Van Winkle. So! Here you are, telling stories without a word of truth in 'em! Oh, *I* could tell a story or two myself—about a <u>shiftless</u> husband who does nothing but whittle and whistle.

---

7. **ninepins:** a bowling game in which nine pins are used.

Whittle and whistle! What a job for a grown man! *(She snatches the whistle from* Rip.*)*

Luke *(pleadingly)*. It's my whistle! Please don't break it, Dame Van Winkle.

Dame Van Winkle. Take it and begone! *(She gives* Luke *the whistle, and he runs off.)* Judy, you go and ask Dame Vedder for an armful of wood. Your father is too busy spinning yarns to split wood for *our* fire. *(Judy goes off behind the tavern.)* As for the rest of you, go home if you have any homes, and don't keep hanging around here like stray dogs looking for bones. *(She sweeps the children off the stage with her broom.)* Get along! Begone, all of you! Go home now! *(With arms akimbo,*[8] *she faces* Rip.*)* Well, what do you have to say for yourself? *(Rip shrugs, shakes his head and says nothing.)* Nothing as usual. *(Rip goes to the tree for his gun.)* What are you getting your gun for? Going off to the mountains, no doubt. Anything to keep you out of the house.

Rip *(Good-naturedly)*. Well, wife, you have often told me—*my* side of the house is the *out*side. Where's my dog? Where's Wolf?

Dame Van Winkle. Wolf is tied up in the cellar.

Rip. You didn't tie up Wolf?

Dame Van Winkle. I certainly did. That dog tracked up my kitchen floor right after I'd finished scrubbing it. Well, if you're going hunting, go, and don't come back until you bring us something for supper. And if you can't bring any supper, don't bring yourself.

Judy *(reentering from up left, her arms full of logs)*. But, Mother, it's going to rain.

Dame Van Winkle *(taking the wood)*. Pooh! Your father won't get as wet as we will in the house, with the roof leaking and the windows broken. You hurry home now. And bring that bucket of water your father managed to get this far. *(Dame Van Winkle starts right, but* Judy *stays behind with* Rip.*)*

Rip *(calling after his wife)*. Wife, turn Wolf loose when you get home. *(Dame Van Winkle looks back at him angrily, tosses her head, and exits right.)*

Judy *(starting to cry as she puts her hand in* Rip's*)*. Father, where will you go if it rains?

Rip. I'll find a place. Don't cry, Judy. Remember your little song? Come, we'll sing it together. *(They sing an appropriate folk song, such as "Rosa, Will We Go Dancing?")*

Judy *(hugging* Rip*)*. Oh, Father, I hope you have wonderful luck. Then Mother won't be so cross.

Rip. I don't blame her for being cross with me sometimes. I guess I don't do much work around here. But I'm going to do better, Judy. I'm going to do all the jobs your mother has been after me about.

Dame Van Winkle *(calling from off)*. Ju-dee! Ju-dee!

Rip. There's your mother. I'd better be off. Goodbye, Judy dear. *(He walks left,*

---

8. **with arms akimbo:** with hands on hips and elbows bent outward.

whistling for his dog.) Come, Wolf! Come, boy! *(A dog's bark is heard off left as* Rip *turns, waves to* Judy, *and exits.)*

Judy *(waving)*. Goodbye, Father. *(Luke enters from right and joins* Judy *as loud crash of thunder is heard. Startled,* Judy *clings to* Luke.) Oh, Luke, listen to that thunder!

Luke. It's only Hendrik Hudson's men playing ninepins. Don't be scared, Judy.

Judy. I'm not—that is, not very.

Dame Van Winkle *(calling from off)*. Judy! Ju-dee!

Luke. You'd better go in or you'll catch it. Your mother is getting awfully free with her broomstick lately. Here, I'll carry your bucket for you. *(He exits right with the bucket of water.* Judy *lingers behind to look off in direction her father has taken as the thunder gets louder. Then humming softly to herself, she exits right.)*

Curtain

Scene 2

Time: *Later the same afternoon.*

Setting: *A forest <u>glade</u>, high in the Catskill Mountains. There is a tree stump at right center and a large bush at far left. This scene may be played before the curtain.*

At Rise: Rip, *carrying his gun, enters left, dragging his feet wearily. He sinks down on the stump.*

Rip. Whew! That was a climb! All the way up the mountain. How peaceful it is up here. No one to scold me, no one to wave a broomstick. Ah, me! *(He gives a big sigh of contentment.)* I wonder where Wolf is. Wolf! Here, boy! *(He whistles, and a dog barks off left.)* That's it, Wolf, sic 'em! I hope we get something this time. We can't go home until we do. *(A loud crash of thunder is heard.)* That thunder sounds much louder up here in the mountains than down in the valley. Maybe it's going to rain after all.

Voice *(calling from off, high-pitched, like a birdcall)*. Rip Van Winkle! *(Rip looks around wonderingly.)* Rip Van Winkle!

Rip *(rising)*. That's my name. Somebody is calling me.

Voice *(off)*. Rip Van Winkle!

Rip. Is it Dame Van Winkle? No—she would never follow me up here. *(Sound of a ship's bell is heard from off right.)* What was that? *(Bell rings again.)* A ship's bell! But how can that be? A ship? Up here in the mountains? *(He gazes off right, in astonishment.)* It is a ship! Look at it! Sails all set—a Dutch flag at the masthead. *(Ship's bell is heard again, fainter.)* There, it's gone. I must have imagined it. *(First Sailor, with a keg on his back, enters from right and goes to center as* Rip *watches him in amazement.)* By my galligaskins, what a funny little man! And how strangely he's dressed. Such old-fashioned clothes! *(First Sailor stops at center.* Rip *goes to meet him.)* Hello, old Dutchman. That

Words to Know and Use | **glade** (glād) *n.* an open space in a forest

keg looks heavy. Let me carry it for you. *(He relieves* First Sailor *of the keg.)* By golly, it is heavy! Why did you bring this keg all the way up here to the top of the mountain? And who are you, anyhow?

First Sailor *(gruffly)*. Don't ask questions. Set it down over there. *(He points left to a spot beside the bush.)*

Rip *(obeying cheerfully)*. Anything to oblige. *(There is a commotion off right, and* Hendrik Hudson *and his crew enter, capering and shouting. They carry bowling balls and ninepins and a drum.* Second Sailor *has a burlap bag containing drinking mugs thrown over his shoulder.* Rip *turns to* First Sailor.*)* Why, bless my soul! Here are a lot of little fellows just like yourself. *(to* Sailors *as they gather at center)* Who are you?

Sailors *(shouting)*. Hendrik Hudson and his merry crew!

Hudson *(stepping forward)*. Set up the ninepins, men, and we'll have a game. *(Two or three* Sailors *set up the ninepins at extreme right.* Hudson *speaks to the* First Sailor.*)* You there, fill up the flagons![9]

---

9. **flagon:** a container for liquids.

Courtesy, Historic Hudson Valley, Tarrytown, New York

(Second Sailor *opens sack and passes out the mugs.* Hudson *turns to* Rip.) Now then, Rip Van Winkle, will you drink with us?

Rip. Why, yes, thank you, Captain Hudson. I'm quite thirsty after my long climb up the mountain. *(The mugs are filled from keg.)*

Second Sailor *(raising his mug in toast)*. To Hendrik Hudson, the Half-Moon, and its merry crew!

All *(as they raise their mugs)*. To Hendrik Hudson, the Half-Moon, and its merry crew!

Rip *(lifting his mug)*. Well, gentlemen, here's to your good health. May you live long and prosper. *(Rip drinks and smacks his lips.)* Ah! This is the best drink I ever tasted, but it makes me feel very sleepy. *(Hudson and his men begin to bowl. As they roll the balls, the thunder increases.* Rip *yawns.)* Ho, hum! I can't keep my eyes open. I guess I'll lie down—*(Carrying his gun, he goes behind bush at left and lies down out of sight. Note: Unseen by audience,* Rip *may go offstage for necessary costume changes and return in time for his awakening.)*

Hudson *(to* Sailors*)*. Now, men, let's stop our game of ninepins and have a merry dance. Then we'll be off, to return again in twenty years. *(One of the men beats the drum, and* Sailors *dance. At the end of the dance,* First Sailor *points to bush where* Rip *is sleeping.)*

First Sailor. Look! Rip Van Winkle is asleep.

Hudson. Peace be with the poor fellow. He needs to take a good long rest from his nagging wife. Sh-h-h-h! *(He places his finger to his lips, and they all go about quietly gathering up the ninepins, balls, mugs, keg, etc.; then they tiptoe off the stage, their voices dying away to a whisper. The lights may dim briefly to indicate the passage of twenty years, and recorded music may be played. When the lights come up,* Rip *is heard yawning behind the bush, then he stands up with great difficulty. He limps to center, carrying a rusty gun. His clothes are shabby, and he has a long white beard.)*

Rip *(groaning)*. Ouch, my back! It's so stiff. And my legs—just like pokers. My, my, but I'm shaky! I feel as if I'd grown to be an old man overnight. It must be rheumatism coming on. Oh, won't I have a blessed time with Dame Van Winkle if I'm laid up with rheumatism. Well, I'd better get along home to Dame Van Winkle. *(He looks at the gun he is carrying.)* Why, this rusty old thing is not my gun! Somebody has played a trick on me. *(suddenly recollecting)* It's that Hendrik Hudson and his men! They've stolen my gun and left this rusty one for me! *(He puts his hand to his head.)* Another scolding in store from the Dame. *(He whistles.)* Wolf! Here, Wolf! Have those scamps stolen my dog, too? He'd never leave me. *(He whistles again.)* Come on, old boy! Maybe he found it too cold and went home to be warmed by his mistress's broomstick. Well, I will follow after and get my hot welcome, too. *(He shoulders the rusty gun and totters off.)*

Curtain

Scene 3

Time: *Twenty years after Scene 1.*

Setting: *Same as Scene 1, except that the sign above the tavern door reads* UNION HOTEL—PROPRIETOR, JONATHAN DOOLITTLE. *A picture of George Washington has replaced that of King George III. Washington's name is printed below the picture, and an American flag flutters on a pole above it.*

At Rise: *An* Orator *is standing on a bench, haranguing a crowd of* Townspeople.

Orator. Remember the Boston Tea Party! Remember Bunker Hill! Who saved this country? Who is the father of this country?

Townspeople. George Washington! Washington for President! *(They sing "Yankee Doodle.")*
Father and I went down to camp
    Along with Captain Good'in,
There we saw the men and boys
    As thick as hasty puddin'.

Yankee Doodle keep it up,
    Yankee Doodle Dandy,
Mind the music and the step
    And with the girls be handy.

(Rip enters with a troop of children, who laugh and jeer at him.)

Children *(ad lib).* Look at him! He looks like a scarecrow! Where did you come from, Daddy Longlegs? Where did you

get that gun? *(Rip and Children go to center. First Child stands in front of Rip and crouches down, pulling on an imaginary beard.)*

First Child. Billy goat, billy goat! *(Children begin stroking imaginary beards until Rip does the same. He is amazed to find he has a beard.)*

Rip. By my galligaskins, what's this?

Second Child. It's a beard, old Father Time. Didn't you know you had a beard?

Rip. But I didn't have one last night. *(Children laugh and mock him.)*

Orator *(to Rip).* What do you mean by coming here at election time with a gun on your shoulder and a mob at your heels? Do you want to cause a riot?

Rip. Oh, no, sir! I am a quiet man and a loyal subject of King George!

Children and Townspeople *(shouting, ad lib).* A spy! Away with him! Lock him up.

Jonathan Doolittle *(stepping forward from crowd).* Hold on a minute! We must get to the bottom of this. *(to Rip)* Aren't you a supporter of Washington for President?

Rip *(puzzled).* Eh? Supporter of Washington? *(shaking his head, wholly bewildered)* I don't understand. I mean no harm. I only want to find my friends. They were here at the tavern yesterday.

Doolittle. Who are these friends of yours? Name them.

Rip *(hesitantly).* Well, one is the landlord—

Words to Know and Use   **jeer** (jir) *v.* to make fun of; mock

Courtesy, Historic Hudson Valley, Tarrytown, New York.

Doolittle. I am the landlord of this hotel—Jonathan Doolittle.

Rip. Why, what happened to Nicholas Vedder?

First Woman *(pushing her way out of the crowd).* Nicholas Vedder? Why, he's dead and gone these eighteen years.

Rip. No, no, that's impossible! Where's Brom Dutcher? And the schoolmaster, Van Bummel—?

First Man. Brom Dutcher was killed in the war at Stony Point.

Second Man. And Van Bummel went off to the war, too. He became a great general, and now he's in Congress.

Rip. War? What war?

Second Man. Why, the war we fought against England, and won, of course.

Rip. I don't understand. Am I dreaming? Congress? Generals? What's happened to me?

Doolittle *(impatiently).* Now, we've had enough of this nonsense. Who are you, anyway? What is your name?

Rip (_utterly_ confused). I don't know. I mean, I was Rip Van Winkle yesterday, but today—

Doolittle. Don't try to make sport of us, my man!

Rip. Oh, indeed, I'm not, sir. I was myself last night, but I fell asleep on the mountain, and Hendrik Hudson and his crew changed my gun, and everything's changed, and I'm changed, and I can't tell what my name is or who I am! _(Townspeople exchange significant glances, nod knowingly, and tap their foreheads.)_

Second Man (_shaking his head_). Hendrik Hudson, he says! Poor chap. He's mad. Let's leave him alone.

Rip (_in great distress_). Isn't there anybody here who knows who I am?

Second Woman (_soothingly_). Why, you're just yourself, old man. Who else do you think you could be? _(Judith Gardenier enters from left, leading_ Little Rip _by the hand. He hangs back, whimpering.)_

Judith. Hush, Rip! The old man won't hurt you.

Rip (_turning in surprise_). Rip? Who said Rip?

Judith. Why, I did. I was just telling my little boy not to be frightened.

Rip (_scanning her face_). And what is your name, my good woman?

Judith. My name is Judith, sir.

Rip. Judith? Did you say Judith? _(in great excitement)_ And your father—what was his name?

Judith. Ah, poor man, his name was Rip Van Winkle. It's twenty years since he went away from home. We never heard of him again.

Rip (_staggered_). Twenty years!

Judith. Yes, it must be all of that. His dog came back without him. I was a little girl then.

Rip. And your mother—where is she?

Judith. My mother is dead, sir.

Rip (_sighing_). Ah, but that woman had a tongue! Well, peace be with her soul. Did you love your father, Judith?

Judith. With all my heart. All the children in the village loved him, too.

Rip. Then look at me. Look closely, my dear Judy. I am your father.

Judith (_incredulously_). You? My father?

Rip. We used to sing a little song together, remember? _(He sings a few lines from the folk song sung in Scene 1.)_

Judith (_slowly_). Yes, my father used to sing that song with me, but many people know it.

Rip. Do you remember, Judy, that I told you the story of how Hendrik Hudson and his crew played ninepins in the mountains just before I went off hunting with Wolf?

Judith (_excitedly_). Yes! And Wolf _was_ our dog's name! Oh, Father, it's really _you_!

Rip (_taking her in his arms_). Yes, my little Judy—young Rip Van Winkle once, old Rip Van Winkle now. _(Townspeople talk_

Words to Know and Use | **utterly** (ut′ ər lē) _adv._ completely

excitedly among themselves as they watch Rip *and* Judith.*)*

Judith. Dearest Father, come home with me. Luke and I will take good care of you.

Rip. Luke?

Judith. Luke Gardenier, my old playmate. You used to make whistles for him and take him fishing. We were married when he came back from the war.

Rip. Ah, the war. There is so much I have to catch up with.

Judith. You will have plenty of time to do that—and you must tell us what happened to you.

Rip. Maybe you won't believe what happened to me, Judy—it was all so strange. *(*Rip *reaches out a hand to* Little Rip, *who shyly takes it, and they start off left,* Judith *following. A loud clap of thunder stops them.* Rip *turns front and shakes his fist toward the mountains.)* Oh, no you don't, Hendrik Hudson! You don't get me back up there again. *(There is an answering roll of thunder that sounds like a deep rumble of laughter as the curtain falls.)*

The End 🐿

*R*esponding to Reading

First Impressions

1. What are your reactions to what happened to Rip Van Winkle? Write them in your journal or on a sheet of paper.

Second Thoughts

2. How would you describe Rip Van Winkle's personality?

3. What do you suppose Dame Van Winkle thought had happened to Rip when he failed to return home?

4. Why do you think Rip did not seem to mind that he had lost twenty years of his life?

   Think about
   - his relationship with his wife
   - his relationships with his children
   - his personality
   - what was happening in the country when he awoke

Broader Connections

5. Both *Rip Van Winkle* and "The Inn of Lost Time" deal with the loss of time. Compare Rip Van Winkle's attitude about losing time to Zenta's attitude in "The Inn of Lost Time." What is the same? What is different? How valuable is time?

*L*iterary Concept: Legend

A **legend** is a story that has been passed down from generation to generation and that is believed to have a historical basis. Frequently, legends are based on real characters and situations, though the happenings in the legends are fictional. Washington Irving created the legend of Rip Van Winkle out of parts of several different stories: American tales, an old Scottish story, and a German narrative. Although legends are not usually true stories, legends live on because they tell some basic truth about human nature. What truth do you think the legend of Rip Van Winkle tells?

Writing Options

1. With its sensational story of a man who slept for twenty years, the legend of Rip Van Winkle seems like something right out of a tabloid newspaper. Write your own **tabloid article** that details Rip's ordeal.

2. If Rip Van Winkle had slept for 220 years instead of 20, he just might be yawning and stretching right about now. Imagine that Rip awoke today in your town. Write a **narrative** that describes his reactions to the things he would see and hear.

3. What do you think Rip was thinking and feeling on the day he awoke? What might some of his discoveries and conversations have been like? Write Rip's **journal entry** for the day of his awakening.

4. All the time that Rip was asleep, his family and friends didn't know what had happened to him. Now that he is awake again, he certainly has a lot of explaining to do! In Rip's words, write a **speech** that he can give to the townspeople to explain what happened to him.

Vocabulary Practice

Exercise   On your paper, write the word from the list that is most clearly related to the situation described in the sentence. Then rewrite the sentences using the related word.

1. A man was hiking in the woods when he decided to take a rest. The clearing ahead seemed like a perfect spot.

2. Since he had been hiking all morning, the man was completely exhausted.

3. Many people thought that the man was lazy and lacked ambition.

4. They often made fun of him and criticized the way he lived his life.

5. Often the man could readily defend himself against their attacks, but there were some times when he had to respond unprepared.

> *Words to Know and Use*
>
> **ad lib**
> **glade**
> **jeer**
> **shiftless**
> **utterly**

Options for Learning

1 • Up Close and Personal Rip Van Winkle is doing the talk-show circuit! With a partner, act out the interview that Rip would give on your favorite TV talk show. You may prefer to write a brief outline of the interview before you perform it for your classmates. Consider asking Rip about his plans for the future.

2 • Check Him Out Who was Hendrik Hudson—also known as Henry Hudson—and what were some of his important accomplishments? Research answers to these and other questions you may have about Hudson, and prepare a report to share with your classmates. You may choose to do your report orally or in writing.

3 • Play It Again, Rip Choose your favorite part or scene from the play to dramatize. Include costumes, props, and sound effects or music. Or, if you prefer, read your version as a radio play. You also may enjoy recording your scene on videotape or audiotape.

4 • You Want a Revolution? Research some of the songs that were popular during the American Revolutionary War and tape them to share with your classmates. Among the songs that you tape, be sure to include the ones mentioned in the play.

 FACT FINDER SPORTS

When and why did the Dutch game of ninepins become the game of bowling with ten pins?

Washington Irving
1783–1859

Washington Irving was born in New York City and was named after George Washington by Irving's stern Scottish father. Though Irving entered a law office and later joined his older brothers in a hardware business, he much preferred to ramble around Sleepy Hollow, an area north of New York City, or sail up the Hudson and Mohawk Rivers and chat with Dutch farmers.

On a trip to England, Irving met the British writer Sir Walter Scott, whose love of folklore sparked Irving's own interest in American folklore—particularly Dutch-American folktales. Irving first published "Rip Van Winkle" in *The Sketch Book* in 1819. A review in the *New York Evening Post* called the story a "master-piece. For that comic spirit which is without any infusion of gall, which delights in what is ludicrous rather than what is ridiculous . . . the story of Rip Van Winkle has few competitors."

INFORMATIVE/PERSUASIVE WRITING

Think about the places and times you read about in this subunit. If you could travel back in time to one of those places, which one would you choose? Now imagine that you could take along a product that could improve the lives of the people of that time. What product would you take? How could you convince the people of the product's value? One way to "sell" a product is through an **infomercial.** An infomercial is an extended television commercial that gives information and "testimonials" about a product's usefulness and effectiveness in order to persuade people to buy it. In this workshop, you will write a script for your own infomercial.

USE INFORMATIVE/
PERSUASIVE
WRITING FOR

editorials
debates
letters to the editor
book reviews
job-application essays
speeches
legal arguments
infomercials

GUIDED ASSIGNMENT: INFOMERCIAL

Write a five-minute script for an infomercial, selling a modern product to people from another time and place.

Here is one writer's PASSkey to this assignment.

PURPOSE: To sell a product

AUDIENCE: People from another time and place

SUBJECT: A new and useful product

STRUCTURE: A five-minute infomercial script

> Personal Tea Bags
> by Ian Roberts
>
> ANNOUNCER: Hey, Road Warriors, when <u>you're</u> on the road, do you ever worry about the quality and purity of the tea you drink? . . . Hello, I'm Ian Roberts, and I'm here with some friends to tell you about an amazing new discovery in travel convenience and safety--Personal Tea Bags.
>
> (<u>Hold product up for close-up camera shot.</u>)
>
> Before we tell you all about how Personal Tea Bags work, let me introduce you to one of our many satisfied customers.

◀ STUDENT MODEL

Before you write, read how one student responded to the assignment. Notice that the model includes only parts of his entire infomercial.

▶

ZENTA: Hi, I'm Zenta. As a samurai warrior, I'm on the road a lot. Sometimes the inns I visit aren't the best--especially the one where some tricky innkeepers put drugs in my tea! I thought I'd have to stop drinking tea altogether, until I found Personal Tea Bags. Now I carry them with me wherever I go. All of the bags have my favorite blend in them, too. All I need to do to brew myself a delicious--and safe--pot of tea is to add boiling water! Personal Tea Bags have made my life safe and pleasant again.

(Introduce and cut to Thomas Sullivan.)

▶

THOMAS SULLIVAN: Thanks, Zenta. My Personal Tea Bags are incredibly simple to use. Each of the bags holds in it the right amount of tea. All you have to do is place the bag into your favorite teapot and pour in boiling water. That's all there is to it! No fuss, no mess--and no worrying about unsafe tea! . . . Now back to you, Ian.

(Cut back to Ian, who introduces other customers. At conclusion of infomercial:)

▶

ANNOUNCER: Because we're so sure that you'll love these new Personal Tea Bags, we're going to make you a special offer: If you order your bags within the next thirty minutes, we'll include a personalized teapot absolutely free. Also, especially for you Road Warriors, we'll throw in a travel-sized, airtight container that you can take with you. So, what are you waiting for? ACT NOW! Take advantage of this incredible offer. Join Zenta and hundreds of others who are already enjoying the convenience and safety of Personal Tea Bags. Remember this offer is limited. ACT NOW!

Now it's time to write your own infomercial.

Prewrite and Explore

1 **Explore another time** With a group of classmates, discuss the times and places described in this subunit: Japan in the 1580s, Pompeii in A.D. 79, and the United States in the 1750s. Try putting yourselves into each selection, and then talk about the problems different characters faced. What kinds of modern products or conveniences might have made their lives easier? Take notes on ideas that interest you.

WRITER'S CHOICE

Still need an idea? Try skimming through books on inventions and machines or through other selections in this book. You may find a product that sparks your imagination.

GATHERING INFORMATION

Once you've decided on a product to "sell," begin collecting factual information about it. If possible, observe the product being used. Otherwise, learn about it through books and magazines. How does the product work? What special features does it have?

Next consider the persuasive techniques that will help sell your product most effectively. List reasons why people would want to buy the product. As you review your notes, consider the facts and reasons that will be most persuasive. Look at Ian's notes. He organized his facts around the selling points they supported best.

<u>Safe from tampering</u>
- individually packaged
- completely sealed
- only you handle the bag

<u>Convenient for travel</u>
- packaged in small, single-serving bags
- can make good, safe tea wherever you go
- only need hot water

<u>Easy to prepare tea</u>
- place in pot; cover with boiling water
- let stand awhile
- remove bag

<u>Special offer</u>
- free personalized teapot
- free airtight container

<u>General Facts</u>
- T. Sullivan "accidentally" invented in 1904
- single serving of tea in sealed gauze bag

◀ **STUDENT MODEL**

Compare Ian's lists of details with what he actually included in his infomercial. Which ones are most effective?

TIP

As you gather facts and list selling points, think about how a visual format can help you explain and sell your product.

Draft and Discover

1 **Focus on the audience** How can you best persuade your audience to buy your product? Some advertising techniques you could try are **testimonials** and **loaded language.** Testimonials are statements by famous people or satisfied customers about a product's effectiveness. Loaded language tries to sell a product by appealing to people's emotions. Ian used both techniques.

WRITER'S CHOICE

Try using storyboards to experiment with the format and sequence of your infomercial script. (Storyboards are boards containing sketches or scenes arranged in sequence and are used for outlining the action.) You may want to create a separate board for each scene. This will allow you to move the scenes around and try different arrangements.

2 **Decide on a format** Often during an infomercial, a "reporter" or spokesperson weaves together factual information, selling points, and testimonials in a kind of news format. You might choose this format, or you might try structuring your script around a dramatic re-enactment of a real-life situation.

Revise Your Writing

1 **Check your message** As you fine-tune your draft, review the information you've presented about your product. Make sure it is accurate and complete. You may want to verify your facts in a secondary source such as an encyclopedia. Ian referred to books about inventions and about tea drinking to fill in factual details.

2 **Use a visual medium** Can your audience *see* themselves using your product? Consider different ways to present information visually. You might insert a step-by-step demonstration.

3 **Role-play your draft** Ask a friend to read your script aloud. As he or she reads, listen to make sure that the tone of the script is natural and conversational. The following questions may help.

Revision Questions

For You	For a Peer Reader
1. Did I present the necessary facts and information?	1. Did I clearly explain how my product works?
2. Did I use advertising techniques effectively?	2. What parts of my infomercial did you find most persuasive?
3. Did I use a visual medium?	3. Would you buy my product?

Proofread

After revising your paper for content, review it for errors in capitalization, punctuation, grammar, and spelling. See if a friend will proofread it for you. For this assignment, pay special attention to how you use pronouns and their antecedents.

COMPUTER TIP

Try using the "grammar checker" on your software program to find errors, including those involving pronoun use. Grammar checkers won't catch every error, however, so be sure you also thoroughly proofread your paper.

THE EDITOR'S EYE: PRONOUN ANTECEDENTS

Use pronouns correctly when referring to indefinite pronoun antecedents.

When you use a pronoun to refer to an indefinite pronoun such as *each, all,* or *anybody,* be sure the pronoun and its antecedent agree in number. Decide if the indefinite pronoun is singular or plural. Choose a singular pronoun to refer to a singular indefinite pronoun antecedent or a plural pronoun to refer to a plural indefinite pronoun antecedent.

Problem   *Each* of the bags holds in *them* the right amount of tea.

Correct   *Each* of the bags holds in *it* the right amount of tea.

Problem   *All* of the bags have my favorite blend in *it,* too.

Correct   *All* of the bags have my favorite blend in *them,* too.

NEED MORE HELP?

See the Language Workshop that follows (pages 364–366) and pages 779–781 of the Language Handbook.

Publish and Present

Here is a suggestion for sharing your work with others.

On the Air   With your classmates, choose the most convincing scripts and perform them with settings, costumes, and props. If possible, use a video camera to tape each infomercial.

Reflect on Your Writing

Consider the following questions. Then write your answers, attach them to your paper, and place them in your portfolio.

FOR YOUR PORTFOLIO

1. Which parts of your infomercial are the most persuasive?
2. Did you enjoy writing an infomercial? Was the persuasive or the informative element easier? Explain.

LANGUAGE
WORKSHOP

PRONOUN-ANTECEDENT AGREEMENT

> A **pronoun** must agree with its **antecedent** in number and gender.

The **antecedent** of a pronoun is the noun or other pronoun for which the pronoun stands. The pronoun must agree with, or correctly refer to, its antecedent. There are two types of pronoun-antecedent agreement that can cause problems.

Noun Antecedents

Pronouns and their antecedents must agree in number and in gender. When your antecedent is a noun, it is relatively simple to check this agreement. First, ask yourself whether the noun antecedent is singular or plural. Choose a singular pronoun to refer to a singular noun antecedent. If the antecedent is plural, choose a plural pronoun.

> Tons of ashes fell on Pompeii, smothering *it,* hiding *it* from sight. (The singular pronoun *it* is used because the noun antecedent, *Pompeii,* is singular.)
>
> Outside, children headed toward school, carrying slates and followed by *their* dogs. (The plural pronoun *their* is used because the noun antecedent, *children,* is plural.)

Next, ask yourself whether the noun is masculine or feminine. Use a masculine pronoun to agree with a masculine noun and a feminine pronoun to agree with a feminine noun.

> There were sixteen people altogether, as well as *his* daughter's dog and *her* beloved little goat. (*Her* refers to the feminine antecedent *his daughter's. His* refers to the masculine antecedent *Diomedes,* which appears in an earlier sentence.)

Exercise 1 Concept Check   Write the correct pronoun or pronouns.

1. Dutch settlers played a special bowling game. (It, They) was called *Dutch pins.*

2. Bowlers arranged nine tall, slender pins in a diamond. (It, They) also spaced the pins far apart.

3. The first bowler to knock down 31 pins won the game; (he or she, they) could also win by knocking over the middle pin.

4. Bowling was very popular until the early 1800s. In 1841, however, the Connecticut legislature passed a special law; (it, they) outlawed "bowling of nine pins."

5. Bowlers had the last word! (It, They) bypassed the law by adding a tenth pin—and thus began the ten-pin bowling game we know today.

◀ HE OR SHE?
. . . .
Notice that *he or she* is sometimes used when the person referred to could be either male or female.

Indefinite Pronoun Antecedents

Most pronoun agreement problems occur when indefinite pronouns are used. **Indefinite pronouns** do not refer to a particular person or thing. Some are singular, some are plural, and some can be either.

You cannot always "hear" whether you are using an indefinite pronoun correctly. The only way to know for sure is to learn which indefinite pronouns are singular, which are plural, and which are singular or plural, depending on the circumstances.

Indefinite Pronouns	
Singular	another anybody anyone anything each either everybody everyone everything neither nobody no one one somebody someone something
Plural	both few many several
Singular or Plural	all any most none some

Pronouns and their antecedents must agree in number. So how can you tell whether an indefinite pronoun is singular or plural? Begin by studying the examples that follow.

Use a singular pronoun if the indefinite pronoun is singular.

Problem   Nobody drank *their* wine after seeing Rip Van Winkle.
Correct   Nobody drank *his or her* wine after seeing Rip Van Winkle.

Use a plural pronoun if the indefinite pronoun is plural.

Problem	Few were willing to take *his* sheep onto the Mountain.
Correct	Few were willing to take *their* sheep onto the Mountain.

Notice that *all, any, most, none,* and *some* may be either singular or plural, depending on their meaning in the sentence. They are singular when they refer to one thing and plural when they refer to several things.

▶
Singular	All of Rip's family welcomed him back to *it.*
Plural	All of the villagers had hats on *their* heads.

Exercise 2   Concept Check   Write the correct pronoun or pronouns.

1. Both thought (their, her) brother would not return.
2. Nobody ever seemed to survive (his or her, their) travels.
3. Each of the mothers worried about (her, their) own children.
4. Many thought that ghosts were stealing (their, its) children.
5. Several remembered the story of (their, his or her) childhood.
6. No one could explain (his or her, their) belief in the legend.
7. One of the villagers returned to tell (his or her, their) story.
8. It seems that most of the missing had slept (their, his or her) lives away without knowing it.
9. Few knew the magic words that kept (their, his or her) memories alive.
10. Still, neither of the boys was pleased when (his, their) mother asked him about the story.

Exercise 3   Proofreading Skill   Rewrite the following paragraph. Correct any errors in pronoun-antecedent agreement that you find.

Japan's music is as ancient as their literature. Other cultures have left its mark on Japanese music. For example, some dates back to the fifth century, when they was borrowed from Chinese traditions. One type includes mouth organ, flute, and oboe in them. Buddhist songs made its appearance in the sixth century. A ceremonial dancer used music from India in his or her work. Few of Japan's musicians may realize that even instruments such as the *koto* have contributed to his or her musical legacy.

Exercise 4   Revising Your Writing   Reread the infomercial you wrote for the Writer's Workshop on pages 359–363. Identify and correct any errors you find in pronoun-antecedent agreement.

NOTE

Don't be confused by a prepositional phrase that appears between an indefinite pronoun and a possessive pronoun.
Problem: Each of the townspeople had their own opinion of Rip. (The possessive pronoun should agree with *each,* not with *townspeople.*)
Correct: Each of the townspeople had *his or her* opinion of Rip.

LANGUAGE HANDBOOK

For review and practice: Section 4, Using Pronouns, pages 779–781.

R EADER'S
WORKSHOP

THE LANGUAGE OF ADVERTISING

Advertising is all around you. Study the ads you hear or read carefully and critically. Watch out for some of the techniques listed below.

Loaded Language   By appealing to your emotions instead of your logic, advertisers hope to sway your thinking before you examine the facts too carefully. To do this, writers use words that strike either a positive or a negative emotional chord.

Testimonials   In testimonials, well-known people or satisfied customers stand behind, or endorse, products. Advertisers hope that because you admire and respect the celebrities or because you can identify with a person who is much like yourself, you will share their opinions of the products. Most celebrities and customers who give testimonials are paid generously for their endorsements. Be sure to evaluate whether or not a celebrity really is an "expert" on a product.

Bandwagon   The bandwagon approach appeals to your desire to fit in with your peers. It suggests that everyone else is using a product, and you'll be left out if you don't join the crowd. This can be done with statements such as "Everybody's using Sparkle Shampoo" or by showing a crowd of people with shining hair. All of the people are popular and attractive, and they are having a great time.

Plain Folks   Often used by politicians, this method associates the speaker with everyday people. It tells the audience that the speaker is "one of them." A campaign commercial or ad, for example, might have a candidate in a hard hat chatting with construction workers to show that he or she understands the workers and their needs.

Exercise   On a sheet of paper, list the persuasive techniques you find in the ad below.

> All the kids at Fenton High agree: The Find-It-Fast notebook makes studying easier and faster. Class valedictorian Sharon Chobaz says: "Find-It-Fast helped me get where I am today!" Whether you rush eagerly to chemistry class, excel in woodworking, or write for the school newspaper, the Find-It-Fast notebook will work for *you!* This durable, stylish binder delivers excellent value. Don't wait another day to join your friends who are already using the Find-It-Fast notebook.

FOR REVIEW
To understand loaded language from the author's viewpoint, look back at "Author Bias," the Reader's Workshop on page 123.

NOTE
One kind of bandwagon technique is **snob appeal.** Here, advertisers tap into your desire to be special, using statements such as "Only those who truly know quality will recognize the richness of Sparkle Shampoo."

WRITER'S CHOICE
To help you further understand the language of advertising, you may want to bring in magazine or newspaper ads that contain examples of the persuasive techniques described in this lesson.

Reading on Your Own

Suggested Novels for Unit Three

The novels introduced on these pages will allow you to explore the unit theme, "Nothing Stays the Same."

DICEY'S SONG

CYNTHIA VOIGT ©1982

Strong characterizations in fine literature show us that nothing stays the same. Characters change and grow as they face great obstacles. One who does so is Dicey, a disabled girl with a flair for music. Besides Dicey, you will meet other very strong characters in Dicey's Song, such as a grandmother whom the townspeople consider eccentric, a young boy who strikes out in anger at those he loves, and a gifted boy who tries to hide his gift. As you read the novel, think about . . .

- what role music plays in the story

- how music reveals important information about the characters

- how Dicey achieves her goals

NOTHING BUT THE TRUTH: A DOCUMENTARY NOVEL

AVI ©1991

Fourteen-year-old Philip Malloy hums along when "The Star-Spangled Banner" is played during homeroom. His teacher, Margaret Narwin, accuses him of being disrespectful. Philip stands firm in his conviction that he has done nothing wrong. Because of this incident, Philip is suspended from school. Sides are drawn as charges and countercharges are leveled at Philip and his teacher. *Nothing But the Truth: A Documentary Novel* takes a hard look at the issues of respect, freedom, and patriotism. Read to find out . . .

• whose version is correct—Philip's or his teacher's

• what motives draw others into the conflict between Philip and his teacher

• how interpretations of an incident can vary so much

SHABANU: DAUGHTER OF THE WIND

SUZANNE FISHER STAPLES ©1989

In *Shabanu, Daughter of the Wind*, you will meet Shabanu and her sister Phulan, daughters of nomads living in the Cholistan Desert of Pakistan. Shabanu, twelve, is to be wed in a year or so. Shabanu's father has arranged this marriage. Shabanu's willingness to obey him is tested when she learns she has been pledged to the brother of a hated landowner. Should she accept her father's decision and live a life of misery, or should she go against his wishes and bring shame on her family? As you read, think about these questions:

• How does someone go about making such an important decision?

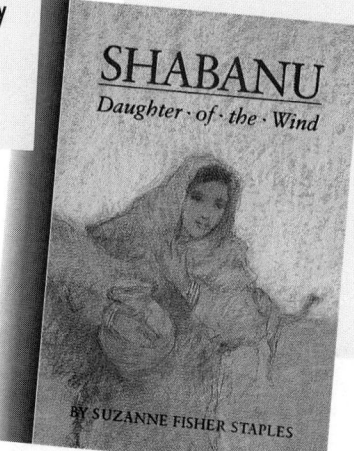

• Which is more important—individual happiness or family obligation?

• What would you do if you were in Shabanu's position?

Other Recommended Books

Eva by Peter Dickinson (©1989). After an automobile accident, thirteen-year-old Eva is left in a coma. Advanced scientific technology enables her to recover.

Pompeii: Exploring a Roman Ghost Town by Ron and Nancy Goor (©1986). This excellent nonfictional book explores ancient Pompeii and the treasures archaeologists have discovered there. Numerous photographs enhance the appeal of the city that launched modern archaeology.

Castle in the Air by Diana Wynne Jones (©1991). In this fantasy novel, Abdullah, a carpet dealer, discovers that his life changes a great deal when he becomes the owner of a magic carpet.

Talking to the Sun edited by Kenneth Koch and Kate Farrell (©1985). This collection of poetry is illustrated with paintings and sculpture from New York City's Metropolitan Museum of Art.

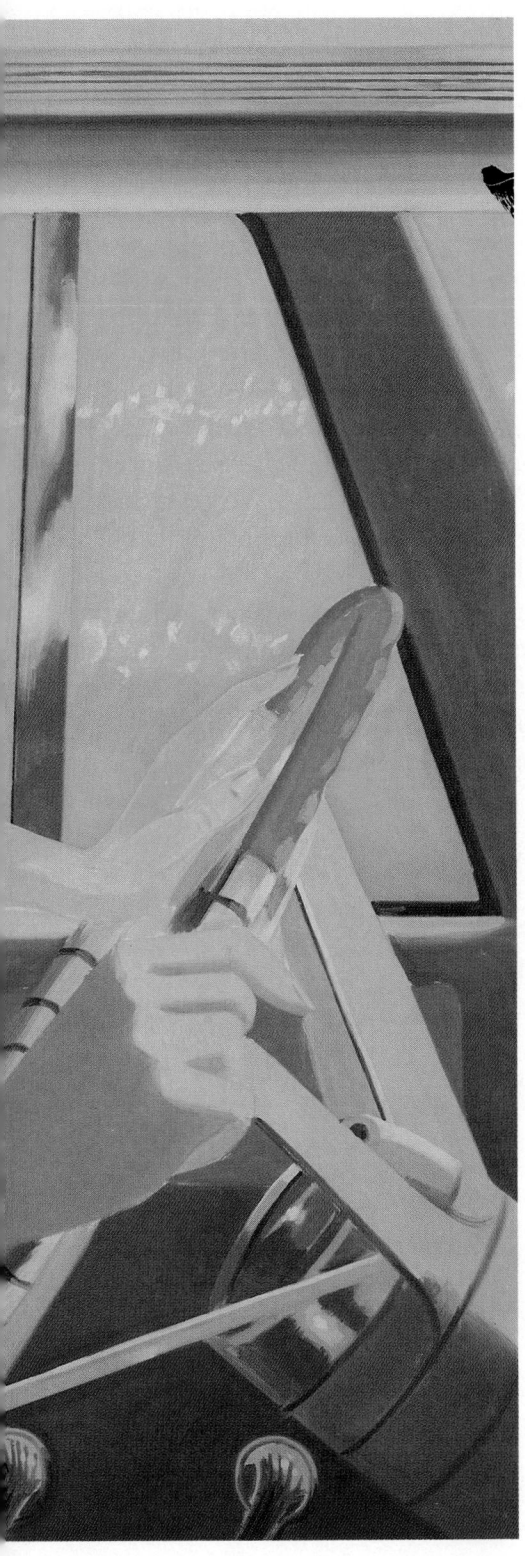

MATTERS OF THE HEART

*L*ove is a battle,

love is a war;

love is a growing up.

James Baldwin

ADA AND VINCENT IN THE CAR
1972   Alex Katz
Collection, the Hirshhorn Museum and Sculpture
Garden, Smithsonian Institution, Washington, D.C.
Courtesy Marlborough Gallery, New York.
© Alex Katz/VAGA, New York 1992.

371

THE STRUGGLE TO CONNECT

For thousands of years people have believed in the special importance of the heart. The ancient Egyptians thought that the heart held the key to both intelligence and emotion. The Chinese maintained that the heart was the dwelling place of happiness. The title of Unit Four, "Matters of the Heart," then, refers to situations that call forth strong feelings.

One of the strongest emotions is "the struggle to connect"—the desire to reach out to someone for emotional fulfillment and affection or the need to connect with someone. For most people this struggle is very challenging. Why is it sometimes hard to talk to a parent or to make a new friend?

In the following selections you will read about people trying, and sometimes failing, to connect with one another. At times the struggles will make you laugh, but at other times you may feel like crying.

Nonfiction

Foul Shots

ROGELIO R. GOMEZ
(rô hā' lyô gô' māz)

Examine What You Know

Think about the term *self-esteem*. What does this term bring to mind? Use a diagram like the one below to organize your ideas.

SELF-ESTEEM

Dictionary Definition

Synonyms

Feelings or Examples That the Word Brings to Mind

In small groups compare your ideas with those of your classmates. Continue your discussion, using the following questions as a guide: (1) How does someone build self-esteem? (2) How might the words *superiority* and *inferiority* relate to self-esteem? (3) How can self-esteem be damaged? (4) Do you think you have strong self-esteem?

Expand Your Knowledge

Many people lack self-esteem because of the ways they have been treated. The writer of this selection felt inferior because his Hispanic language and culture were viewed negatively by many of his teachers and classmates. To make matters worse, he was told that he had a learning disability, a condition that he mistakenly equated with low intelligence.

Enrich Your Reading

Comparison and Contrast **Comparing** two things is showing the similarities between them; **contrasting** two things is pointing out their differences. In "Foul Shots" two teams compete in a sporting event. Self-esteem—how the teammates feel about themselves— plays an important part in the way the two teams interact. As you read, look for ways in which self-esteem creates similarities and differences between the teams.

■ *Author biography in Reader's Handbook*

Foul Shots

ROGELIO R. GOMEZ

Now and then I can still see their faces, snickering and laughing, their eyes mocking me. And it bothers me that I should remember. Time and maturity should have diminished the pain, because the incident happened more than twenty years ago. Occasionally, however, a smug smile triggers the memory, and I think, "I should have done something." Some act of defiance could have killed and buried the memory of the incident. Now it's too late.

review How does the narrator feel about the incident?

In 1969, I was a senior on the Luther Burbank High School basketball team. The school is on the south side of San Antonio, in one of the city's many barrios.[1] After practice one day, our coach announced that we were going to spend the following Saturday scrimmaging with the ball club from Winston Churchill High, located in the city's rich, white north side. After the basketball game, we were to select someone from the opposing team and "buddy up"— talk with him, have lunch with him and generally spend the day attempting friendship. By telling us that this experience would do both teams some good, I suspect our well-intentioned coach was thinking about the possible benefits of integration and of learning to appreciate the differences of other people. By integrating us with this more prosperous group, I think he was also trying to inspire us.

But my teammates and I smiled sardonically at one another, and our sneakers squeaked as we nervously rubbed them against the waxed hardwood floor of our gym. The prospect of a full day of unfavorable comparisons drew from us a collective groan. As "barrio boys," we were already acutely aware of the differences between us and them. Churchill meant "white" to us: It meant shiny new cars, two-story homes with fireplaces, pedigreed dogs and manicured hedges. In other words, everything that we did not have. Worse, traveling north meant putting up a front,[2] to ourselves as well as to the Churchill team. We felt we had to pretend that we were cavalier about it all, tough guys who didn't care about "nothin.'"

It's clear now that we entered the contest with negative images of ourselves. From

---

1. **barrios** (bär′ ē ōz): Hispanic sections of U.S. cities.
2. **putting up a front:** creating a false impression.

374

DOUBLE DRIBBLE © 1988 Brad Holland.

childhood, we must have suspected some-thing was <u>inherently</u> wrong with us. The evidence wrapped itself around our collec-tive psyche[3] like a noose. In elementary school, we were not allowed to speak Spanish. The bladed edge of a wooden ruler once came crashing down on my knuckles for violating this dictum. By high school, however, policies had changed, and we could speak Spanish without fear of physical <u>reprisal</u>. Still, speaking our language before whites brought on spasms of shame—for the supposed inferiority of our language and culture—and guilt at feeling shame. That mixture of emotions fueled our burning sense of inferiority.

After all, our mothers in no way resem-bled the glamorized models of American

---

3. **collective psyche** (sī′ kē): soul or spirit of a group of people.

Words to Know and Use

inherently (in hir′ ənt lē) *adv.* basically; essentially
reprisal (ri prī′ zəl) *n.* an act of revenge

TV mothers—Donna Reed[4] baking cookies in high heels. My mother's hands were rough and chafed; her wardrobe was drab and worn. And my father was preoccupied with making ends meet. His silence starkly contrasted with the glib counsel Jim Anderson[5] offered in *Father Knows Best*. And where the Beaver worried about trying to understand some difficult homework assignment, for me it was an altogether different horror, when I was told by my elementary school principal that I did not have the ability to learn.

After I failed to pass the first grade, my report card read that I had a "learning disability." What shame and disillusion it brought my parents! To have carried their dream of a better life from Mexico to America only to have their hopes quashed by having their only son branded inadequate. And so somewhere during my schooling, I assumed that saying I had a "learning disability" was just another way of saying that I was "retarded." School administrators didn't care that I could not speak English.

As teenagers, of course, my Mexican-American friends and I did not consciously understand why we felt inferior. But we might have understood if we had fathomed our desperate need to trounce Churchill. We viewed the prospect of beating a white north-side squad as a particularly fine coup. The match was clearly racial, our need to succeed born of a defiance against prejudice. I see now that we used the basketball court to prove our "blood." And who better to confirm us if not those whom we considered better? In retrospect, I realize the only thing confirmed that day was that we saw ourselves as negatively as they did.

What does he mean by "prove our 'blood'"?

question

After we won the morning scrimmage, both teams were led from the gym into an empty room where everyone sat on a shiny linoleum floor. We were supposed to mingle—rub the colors together. But the teams sat separately, our backs against concrete walls. We faced one another like enemies, the empty floor between us a no man's land. As the coaches walked away, one reminded us to share lunch. God! The mere thought of offering them a taco from our brown bags when they had refrigerated deli lunches horrified us.

Then one of their players tossed a bag of Fritos at us. It slid across the slippery floor and stopped in the center of the room. With hearts beating anxiously, we Chicanos stared at the bag as the boy said with a sneer, "Y'all probably like 'em"—the "Frito Bandito" commercial[6] being popular then. And we could see them, smiling at each other, giggling, jabbing their elbows into one another's ribs at the joke. The bag seemed to grow before our eyes like a monstrous symbol of inferiority.

---

4. **Donna Reed:** actress who played Donna Stone, a typical TV mother of the 1950s and 1960s.

5. **Jim Anderson:** a typical TV father of the 1950s and 1960s.

6. **"Frito Bandito" commercial:** a television ad featuring an animated Hispanic bandit. Such ads were considered ethnically offensive by many Hispanic Americans.

---

*Words
to Know
and Use*

glib (glib) *adj.* smooth and fluent
quashed (kwäsht) *adj.* ended suddenly   **quash** *v.*
fathom (fath′ əm) *v.* to understand thoroughly

376

We won the afternoon basketball game as well. But winning had accomplished nothing. Though we had wanted to, we couldn't change their perception of us. It seems, in fact, that defeating them made them meaner. Looking back, I feel these young men needed to put us "in our place," to reaffirm the power they felt we had threatened. I think, moreover, that they felt justified, not only because of their inherent sense of superiority but because our failure to respond to their insult underscored our worthlessness in their eyes.

Two decades later, the memory of their gloating lives on in me. When a white person is discourteous, I find myself wondering what I should do and, afterward, if I've done the right thing. Sometimes I argue when a deft comment would suffice. Then I reprimand myself, for I am no longer a boy. But my impulse to argue bears witness to my ghosts. For, invariably, whenever I feel insulted, I'm reminded of that day at Churchill High. And whenever the past encroaches upon the present, I see myself rising boldly, stepping proudly across the years and crushing, underfoot, a silly bag of Fritos. ❧

I N S I G H T

Where the Rainbow Ends

RICHARD RIVE

Where the rainbow ends
There's going to be a place, brother,
Where the world can sing all sorts of songs,
And we're going to sing together, brother,
You and I, though you're white and I'm not.
It's going to be a sad song, brother,
Because we don't know the tune,
And it's a difficult tune to learn.
But we can learn, brother, you and I.
There's no such tune as a black tune.
There's no such tune as a white tune.
There's only music, brother,
And it's music we're going to sing
Where the rainbow ends.

SKY STUDY WITH RAINBOW   1827   John Constable
Yale Center for British Art, Paul Mellon Collection.

Words to Know and Use	**perception** (pər sep′ shən) *n.* impression; understanding **encroach** (en krōch′) *v.* to intrude in a slow, sneaky way

377

Responding to Reading

First Impressions

1. What feelings did you experience as you read this selection? Record them in your journal or on a sheet of paper.

Second Thoughts

2. How do you think the players' self-esteem affected their actions?

3. Assume the role of a player on one of the teams. Would you have done anything differently? Explain.

4. Since foul shots are not mentioned in this selection, why do you think the author chose "Foul Shots" as a title? Explain.

5. Imagine that twenty years later Gomez runs into the player who tossed the Fritos. What do you think Gomez might say or do?

   Think about
   - Gomez's background and the sting of the incident when it happened
   - the lingering anger Gomez still feels
   - Gomez's current success

6. If you haven't already done so, read "Where the Rainbow Ends" on page 377. Compare Gomez's attitude in this selection with the attitude of the speaker in the poem.

Broader Connections

7. Sporting events—such as the basketball games in "Foul Shots"—are often used to help break down barriers between groups. What could the coaches have done to help the teams connect? Consider problems you think the coaches could have avoided, as well as your own experiences.

Literary Concept: Personal Essay

A work of nonfiction that expresses an opinion on a subject is called an essay. A **formal essay** is highly organized and examines a topic in a thorough manner and a serious tone. "Foul Shots" is considered a **personal essay** because it reflects the writer's feelings and personality and has a more casual tone. What elements in "Foul Shots" let you know that the selection is a personal essay?

Writing Options

1. Imagine that you are one of the two basketball coaches from "Foul Shot." Write a **personal essay** telling what you hoped to accomplish by arranging the game.

2. Stereotypes often shape people's behavior. Think about other examples of stereotypes you have encountered in your reading or in your life. Write a **report** that describes one instance in which stereotypes made it difficult for people to understand each other.

3. Imagine that the two teams meet again twenty years later for a rematch. Write a **sequel** to this selection.

4. Consider whether you believe activities designed to bring people from different backgrounds together—such as basketball games—help or hinder people's struggle to connect. Write a **letter** to your school principal, persuading her or him to either stop or continue having such events.

Vocabulary Practice

Exercise Decide if the following pairs of words are synonyms or antonyms. On a sheet of paper, write *S* for synonyms or *A* for antonyms.

1. cavalier—indifferent
2. encroach—intrude
3. fathom—understand
4. glib—stumbling
5. inherently—basically
6. pedigreed—purebred
7. perception—understanding
8. quashed—mended
9. reprisal—forgiveness
10. sardonically—respectfully

Words to Know and Use

cavalier
encroach
fathom
glib
inherently
pedigreed
perception
quashed
reprisal
sardonically

Nonfiction

Conversational Ballgames

NANCY MASTERSON SAKAMOTO

*E*xamine What You Know

Take a few moments to think about these situations:

- You travel to Italy and find all the shops closed at midday.
- You go to a restaurant in Ethiopia only to find that there is no silverware.
- You look for a restroom in a foreign country and realize you don't know the words for "men" and "women."

Some of the strongest memories people have of foreign travel are of the surprises and difficulties they have encountered because of cultural differences. In small groups discuss countries you have read about or traveled to. List any cultural differences or customs that might create confusion or difficulty for a tourist.

*E*xpand Your Knowledge

Different cultures have different "rules" about such things as dress, table manners, and conversation. In Saudi Arabia, for example, most women cover their faces with veils when they go outside the home. In Korea belching is the proper way to compliment a host's fine cooking. The unspoken rules each culture has about conversation can be especially difficult for a foreigner to understand, as the author of this selection learns.

*E*nrich Your Reading

Extended Metaphor   As you may recall, an **extended metaphor** is a series of comparisons between two things that have several elements in common. In "Conversational Ballgames" Nancy Masterson Sakamoto uses an extended metaphor to explain a cultural difference between Americans and Japanese. As you read the selection, think about whether the metaphor is used effectively.

■ *Author biography in Reader's Handbook*

Conversational Ballgames

NANCY MASTERSON SAKAMOTO

After I was married and had lived in Japan for a while, my Japanese gradually improved to the point where I could take part in simple conversations with my husband and his friends and family. And I began to notice that often, when I joined in, the others would look startled, and the conversational topic would come to a halt. After this happened several times, it became clear to me that I was doing something wrong. But for a long time, I didn't know what it was.

Finally, after listening carefully to many Japanese conversations, I discovered what my problem was. Even though I was speaking Japanese, I was handling the conversation in a Western way.[1]

Japanese-style conversations develop quite differently from Western-style conversations. And the difference isn't only in the languages. I realized that just as I kept trying to hold Western-style conversations even when I was speaking Japanese, so my English students kept trying to hold Japanese-style conversations even when they were speaking English. We were unconsciously playing entirely different conversational ballgames.

A Western-style conversation between two people is like a game of tennis. If I introduce a topic, a conversational ball, I expect you to hit it back. If you agree with me, I don't expect you simply to agree and do nothing more. I expect you to add something—a reason for agreeing, another example, or an elaboration to carry the idea further. But I don't expect you always to agree. I am just as happy if you question me, or challenge me, or completely disagree with me. Whether you agree or disagree, your response will return the ball to me.

Western-style conversation is like a game of tennis.

And then it is my turn again. I don't serve a new ball from my original starting line. I hit your ball back again from where it has bounced. I carry your idea further, or answer your questions or objections, or challenge or question you. And so the ball goes back and forth, with each of us doing

---

1. **Western way:** the manner common in Europe and the Americas.

ABSTRACT CONSTRUCTS   Masako Honjo   Courtesy of the artist.

our best to give it a new twist, an original spin, or a powerful smash.

And the more vigorous the action, the more interesting and exciting the game. Of course, if one of us gets angry, it spoils the conversation, just as it spoils a tennis game. But getting excited is not at all the same as getting angry. After all, we are not trying to hit each other. We are trying to hit the ball. So long as we attack only each other's opinions, and do not attack each other personally, we don't expect anyone to get hurt. A good conversation is supposed to be interesting and exciting.

If there are more than two people in the conversation, then it is like doubles in tennis, or like volleyball. There's no waiting in line. Whoever is nearest and quickest hits the ball, and if you step back, someone else will hit it. No one stops the game to give you a turn. You're responsible for taking your own turn.

But whether it's two players or a group, everyone does his best to keep the ball going, and no one person has the ball for very long.

A Japanese-style conversation, however, is not at all like tennis or volleyball. It's like bowling. You wait for your turn. And you always know your place in line. It depends on such things as whether you are older or younger, a close friend or a relative stranger to the previous speaker, in a senior or junior position, and so on.

When your turn comes, you step up to the starting line with your bowling ball and carefully bowl it. Everyone else stands back and watches politely, murmuring encouragement. Everyone waits until the ball has reached the end of the alley and watches to see if it knocks down all the pins, or only some of them, or none of them. There is a pause, while everyone registers your score.

*K*nowing the rules is
not at all the same thing
as playing the game.

Then, after everyone is sure that you have completely finished your turn, the next person in line steps up to the same starting line, with a different ball. He doesn't return your ball, and he does not begin from where your ball stopped. There is no back and forth at all. All the balls run parallel. And there is always a suitable pause between turns. There is no rush, no excitement, no scramble for the ball.

No wonder everyone looked startled when I took part in Japanese conversations. I paid no attention to whose turn it was and kept snatching the ball halfway down the alley and throwing it back at the bowler. Of course the conversation died. I was playing the wrong game.

This explains why it is almost impossible to get a Western-style conversation or discussion going with English students in Japan. I used to think that the problem was

their lack of English language ability. But I finally came to realize that the biggest problem is that they, too, are playing the wrong game.

Whenever I serve a volleyball, everyone just stands back and watches it fall, with occasional murmurs of encouragement. No one hits it back. Everyone waits until I call on someone to take a turn. And when that person speaks, he doesn't hit my ball back. He serves a new ball. Again, everyone just watches it fall.

So I call on someone else. This person does not refer to what the previous speaker has said. He also serves a new ball. Nobody seems to have paid any attention to what anyone else has said. Everyone begins again from the same starting line, and all the balls run parallel. There is never any back and forth. Everyone is trying to bowl with a volleyball.

And if I try a simpler conversation, with only two of us, then the other person tries to bowl with my tennis ball. No wonder foreign English teachers in Japan get discouraged.

Now that you know about the difference in the conversational ballgames, you may think that all your troubles are over. But if you have been trained all your life to play one game, it is no simple matter to switch to another, even if you know the rules. Knowing the rules is not at all the same thing as playing the game.

Even now, during a conversation in Japanese, I will notice a startled reaction and belatedly realize that once again I have rudely interrupted by instinctively trying to hit back the other person's bowling ball. It is no easier for me to "just listen" during a conversation than it is for my Japanese students to "just relax" when speaking with foreigners. Now I can truly sympathize with how hard they must find it to try to carry on a Western-style conversation.

If I have not yet learned to do conversational bowling in Japanese, at least I have figured out one thing that puzzled me for a long time. After his first trip to America, my husband complained that Americans asked him so many questions and made him talk so much at the dinner table that he never had a chance to eat. When I asked him why he couldn't talk and eat at the same time, he said that Japanese do not customarily think that dinner, especially on fairly formal occasions, is a suitable time for extended conversation.

Since Westerners think that conversation is an indispensable part of dining, and indeed would consider it impolite not to converse with one's dinner partner, I found this Japanese custom rather strange. Still, I could accept it as a cultural difference even though I didn't really understand it. But when my husband added, in explanation, that Japanese consider it extremely rude to talk with one's mouth full, I got confused. Talking with one's mouth full is certainly not an American custom. We think it very rude, too. Yet we still manage to talk a lot and eat at the same time. How do we do it?

For a long time, I couldn't explain it, and it bothered me. But after I discovered the conversational ballgames, I finally found the answer. Of course! In a Western-style conversation, you hit the ball, and while someone else is hitting it back, you take a bite, chew, and swallow. Then you hit the ball again and then eat some more. The more people there are in the conversation, the more chances you have to eat. But even with only two of you talking, you still have plenty of chances to eat.

Maybe that's why polite conversation at the dinner table has never been a traditional part of Japanese etiquette. Your turn to talk would last so long without interruption that you'd never get a chance to eat. 🍃

Responding to Reading

First Impressions

1. What are you left thinking about at the end of this selection? Write your thoughts in your journal or on a sheet of paper.

Second Thoughts

2. If you were to visit Japan, how might your behavior be influenced by what you learned from this selection? Explain.

3. What do you think the author means when she says, "Knowing the rules is not at all the same thing as playing the game"?

4. "Conversational Ballgames" shows one person's attempt to understand the customs of another culture. How does Sakamoto's struggle to connect contrast with the struggle depicted in "Foul Shots"?

5. What is your opinion of the way the ballgame metaphor is used?

> **Think about**
> * whether or not the metaphor is effective
> * how the selection would be different without the metaphor

Broader Connections

6. On the basis of what you have learned, who besides tourists would benefit from a better understanding of cultural differences and customs?

Writing Options

1. Observe a family or some other group, and note how they talk to one another. What game is their conversation most like? Write an **extended metaphor** in which you compare the group's way of talking with this game.

2. Recall a time when you discovered a cultural difference between your way of doing something and another person's. Write a **personal narrative** in which you tell about this discovery.

3. Imagine that you are a foreign tourist visiting the United States for the first time. Write a **letter** to a friend back home. Include in your letter a description of Americans and of one of their customs that confuses you.

4. Imagine that you are the head of your school's student-exchange program. Your group is planning a trip to Japan. Write a **speech,** persuading your group to read "Conversational Ballgames" and other articles about Japan, in order to become aware of Japanese customs.

Fiction

White Mice

RUBEN SALAZ–MARQUEZ
(rü bān' sä' läz mär' kāz)

Examine What You Know

No matter how long your ancestors have lived in this country or where they originally came from, your family probably maintains some customs that reflect your cultural and ethnic heritage. If you were to choose just one thing— an object, an article of clothing, a song, a food— to represent your cultural and ethnic heritage, what would it be? Describe your choice in your journal and tell how it represents your heritage.

Expand Your Knowledge

Promoting students' pride in their native languages and cultural heritages is one of the goals of the bilingual education program. This program, which was mandated by the U.S. Supreme Court in 1974, was established to help students who speak little or no English. In this story a group of fourth graders participating in a bilingual education program holds a cultural day to celebrate ethnic heritage. As part of this celebration, the students bring foods representative of their backgrounds.

Enrich Your Reading

Prediction   Mrs. Teubbes, a teacher in this story, is monolingual; she knows only one language—English. She also has a big appetite and is looking forward to the delicious ethnic foods her students are planning to supply for the cultural day. Given these facts, predict what might happen in this story. As you read, see if your predictions change.

■ *Author biography on Extend page*

White Mice

RUBEN SALAZ-MARQUEZ

Mrs. Teubbes thrust her key into the knob, unlocked the door, and swung it open. Her great bulk reacted against bending over to engage the stopper, but the motion was completed without undue strain for a woman her size. The classroom was pleasantly quiet as she walked to her desk and set down the papers she had graded last night. She pulled out another key, the smaller one for her desk drawer, unlocked it and deposited her purse within, shoved it shut and locked it once more. She glanced at the clock. Kids would start coming in after a spell. She sat at her desk and relaxed, as everything was ready for the coming day. *Two more days before Christmas vacation,* she thought. She would weather the storm of student anticipation. She was confident, and all she needed now was the students. Tomorrow she would meet some of the parents for the cultural day her aide, Mrs. Archunde, had set up. Now there was a gem. If Archunde had a college education, she would be a top teacher . . . *too,* she added quietly in her mind. These Hispanics, or Latins or Chicanos or whatever they were going by these days, had as much talent as anybody; they just didn't, well, apply themselves at the proper time or in gainful ways. There were exceptions, of course, nothing being one hundred percent, but Mrs. Archunde could be excellently qualified with a degree. Teubbes wondered why she didn't go to college now, for it was never too late. It wasn't that she couldn't speak English. She knew both languages and used them well. At least Teubbes thought Archunde used Spanish well because she taught the Spanish component for all fourth graders in the school.

Thus far Mrs. Teubbes was enjoying the bilingual component, something new for her classroom, and she was picking up the language right along with the kids. Of course, the students already had a background in it, but the teachers could learn too. If the component would help the kids learn English better, then Teubbes was in favor of it. She had even attended the entire bilingual conference last month in an effort to learn first-hand how to combat code switching[1] and maybe even cultural switching,[2] both of which her students were prone to. Her ardor cooled somewhat when she saw the conference was just a lark for a number of the participants. Some of them must have spent all their time at the lounge, for they

---

1. **code switching:** changing back and forth between two languages as one speaks.
2. **cultural switching:** changing back and forth between two sets of cultural beliefs as one thinks and acts.

Words to Know and Use

prone (prōn) *adj.* having a tendency; inclined
lark (lärk) *n.* a merry adventure

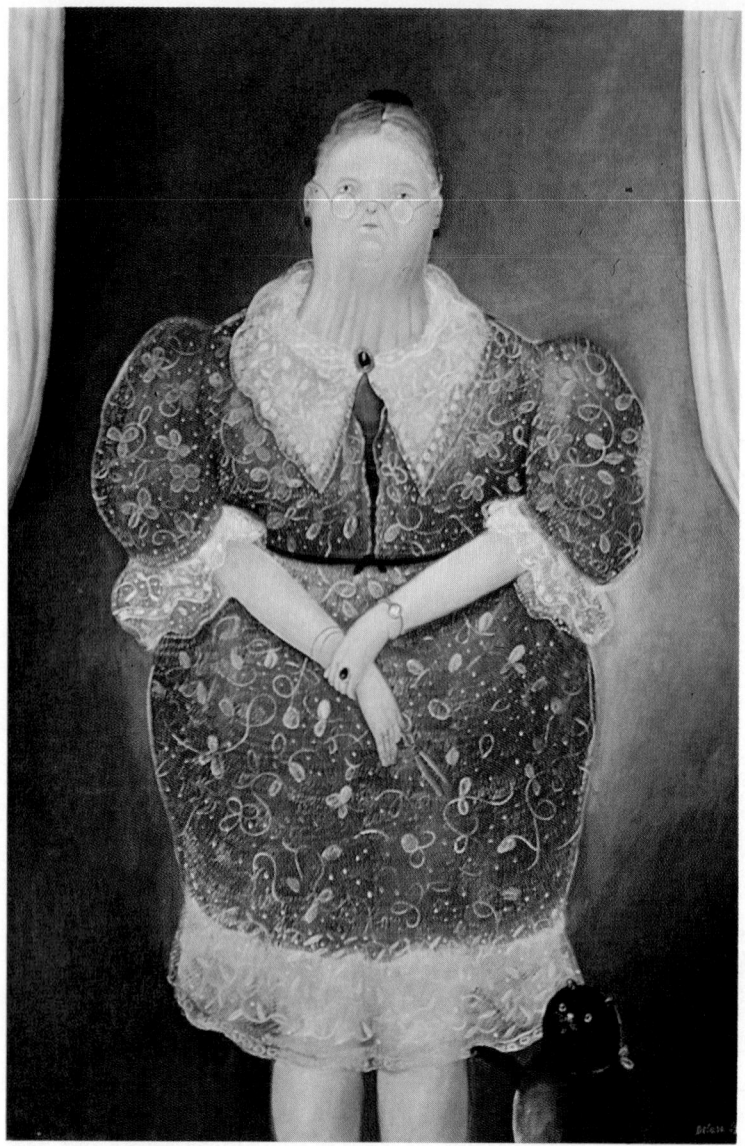

GRANDMOTHER 1969
Fernando Botero Private Collection.

weren't seen at any of the presentations. And she had seen some of them getting rather chummy. Well, no matter. You get out what you put in. But the real tragedy was that the *bilingual* conference had been conducted totally in English. Yes, after a few *Buenos días*'s and such, not a word was spoken in Spanish. Kathy Teubbes had gone prepared to make a herculean[3] effort to catch what would be said, but precious little turned up in Spanish. She still hadn't decided if she was relieved or disappointed, for it was her nature to take up new challenges,

whether she conquered all of them or not. *After all, nobody's perfect.* But now she was quite certain the bilingual program was soft government money[4] being put to use until it ran out. If the language wasn't going to be used all through life, including bilingual conferences, it was just as well to teach the children English and forget about Spanish in school except as a transitional tool. If these

---

3. herculean (hər kyōō′ lē ən): requiring exceptional strength.
4. soft government money: government funds that are not budgeted for a specific purpose.

were the facts of life, and the English bilingual conference proved they were, she didn't feel bad that she had never picked up much Spanish over the years. If Hispanic adults and intellectual leaders didn't use the language in conferences and whatever, they themselves were admitting Spanish isn't necessary in the good old U.S.A. *Why waste taxpayers' money?* Besides, mixing the two languages often trapped students in hilariously embarrassing code and cultural switching.

The thought of "hamburger mice" almost turned her stomach.

"Good morning, Mrs. Teubbes," said Ricardo as he bounced into the room.

"Good morning, Richard," replied the teacher as she came out of her reverie. Oh, that little imp had more energy than anyone, but the only thing he could do right was say good morning when he charged in ahead of everyone else. "Are you ready for another day of learning?"

Ricardo didn't answer. Instead he sat at his desk and looked intently at his teacher.

"Well?" she said.

"Two more days of school," he said, "and tomorrow is our cultural day, huh?"

"Yes, and I'm looking forward to it. We've never done that in this room."

"You like to eat, huh?" observed Ricardo as other students began to fill the room. That impish look was in his eyes, as usual. "I'll bring something good!"

"You like Mexican food?" asked Becky.

"Of course," said Mrs. Teubbes. "Now why don't you review your vocabulary words?" What children! Ah well, at least Richard wasn't vicious. *Of course, none of the children are,* she thought as they trooped into the room. She felt most of them had very good manners, actually, and were quite nice. They were followers more than leaders, but then followers were important too. She wished very sincerely these students were more interested in schoolwork, for the sake of their future.

"Good morning Mrs. Teubbes!" rang out a happy, feminine voice.

"Well, good morning, America!" returned the teacher. Now there was a jewel if there ever was one. That Martinez girl was in a class by herself as far as Kathy Teubbes was concerned. Indeed, it could almost be said the teacher was in awe of America Martinez. She scrutinized the girl as she went over to the cages of gerbils and white mice even before putting down her books. How she loved those little animals! And when there were some to give away, America was sure to take them. The teacher often wondered what she did with them. They couldn't be made into hamburger. Teubbes had worked with such critters for several years, but down deep she had a revulsion for rodents as a species, and even the thought of "hamburger mice" almost turned her stomach. She wondered how the Martinez family could put up with them at home.

"Everybody made it through the night," said America as she went to her desk.

Mrs. Teubbes smiled at the girl. If the teacher were ever to adopt one of her students,

Words to Know and Use | **reverie** (rev′ ər ē) *n.* a daydream
scrutinize (skro͞ot′ 'n īz′) *v.* to observe carefully

389

it would be America Martinez. Not that she was underprivileged or anything like that, of course. She was always clean, well dressed, polite. Her skin was a bit on the olive side, but her jet black hair and pearly teeth went well with her complexion. But what impressed Teubbes the most was America's determined spirit. When she didn't understand something, she'd march right up to the teacher's desk and get help. And if she didn't get it right the next time, she'd come right back with another thoughtful question. She was good at language and had to work harder on her math, but she was usually equal to the task. Teubbes remembered once when she had been outside on recess duty, a couple of little nasties thought they were going to intimidate America. The two had each grabbed an arm, but America broke loose, made a fist and whacked each one on the nose, causing them to bleed profusely. Later in the principal's office America was a picture of confidence and contentment. Lord! Most fourth graders would have been quaking in their little shoes.

Nothing seemed to bother America.

"What would you do in my place?" the principal had asked.

"I'd send you back to class," America had replied matter-of-factly.

"What if those girls jump you again?"

"I'll bloody their noses again."

Heavens! Mrs. Teubbes now began to consider something she had been unable to define before. Something, perhaps bordering on the ineffable, *bothered* her about America. Was it the child's name? How could any parents name their daughter *America?* That was rather sacrilegeous, wasn't it? She had heard children teasing "Miss America!" and "God Bless America!" on the playground. It never seemed to bother the little girl. Or maybe that's what disturbed Mrs. Teubbes: *nothing* seemed to bother America, such was her confidence and aplomb. Why, she could put many an eighteen-year-old to the blush. Somehow it just wasn't fair that a mere child, of a minority at that—

"*Buenos días, Senora Teubbes,*" repeated Mrs. Archunde.

"Oh, yes, *buenos días,* Magdalena. How are you today?"

"Fine, thank you. You seem to have been lost in thought."

"Not lost, just thinking. I'm looking forward to the cultural day tomorrow." Teubbes looked up at the wall clock just as the bell rang for classes to begin.

"You'll enjoy it," assured Archunde, "and unless I miss my guess, a number of parents will be here."

"Will America's be here, do you know?"

"We can ask her."

"Yes, of course," said Teubbes. "All right children, let's take out your mathematics workbooks." There was an audible groan from the class. "Come on; borrowing is not hard, and you have to learn it. How many of you worked on it at home and had your parents help you?" A couple of hands went up, including America's. "And what did your parents have to say about borrowing, America?"

"My Dad said it was what you did after you found a cosigner," replied the girl. Mrs. Archunde chuckled.

"Oh, I see," continued Mrs. Teubbes, "but that's not the kind of borrowing we mean, of course. Well, let's get busy. Richard, stay in your seat. Mrs. Archunde and I will walk around, then you come to the desk when you need help."

The students fell to working quickly, for Mrs. Teubbes believed in discipline and no one was allowed to clown it up. After a vigilant walk around the room, the teacher and her aide sat at their respective desks and tutored one-on-one. Mrs. Teubbes saw America look up with confusion wrinkled into her pretty face. "Come on up if you need help." The girl did. "Yes, dear?"

"Mrs. Teubbes, can you borrow from the dollar sign?"

Now it was the teacher who broke out laughing, everyone stopping what he or she had been doing and staring. "No, dear," said a chuckling Mrs. Teubbes. "The dollar sign just informs us we are dealing with dollars and cents. You can't borrow from it. Now let's take a look at your paper . . ." The problem was discovered and explained away.

After mathematics Mrs. Archunde drilled the class on vocabulary in both English and Spanish. She reviewed the old words and carefully introduced the new. ". . . and what do you buy when you go to the movies?"

"POPCORN!"

"And how do you say that in Spanish?"

"*Maíz*,"[5] said Caroline.

"Yes," encouraged Archunde, "that's part of it. Anybody know the rest?" No one did, so she told them: "*Palomitas de maíz.*"[6]

"Pigeon corn?" asked Martin.

"Yes," encouraged Archunde further, "and can anybody tell me why they call it that in Mexico?" She could tell the kids were trying hard to figure out the riddle, but no hands were up. "Now let's imagine as we think . . . the corn pops up and flies into the air, almost like little . . . white . . . pigeons."

*I*sn't it beautiful to be able to use two languages?

"Ooooh!" chorused the class, impressed with the imagery.

"Yes, now let's review our vegetables quickly," said Archunde as she pointed to a chart on the wall. "Besides *maíz,* what do we have?"

"Cowcumbers!" said Martin.

Mrs. Teubbes almost interrupted to correct the code switching mistake which so many students were prone to make.

"Cucumbers," said Mrs. Archunde.

"My grandfather's are big!" explained Martin. Then to Mrs. Teubbes: "Remember those he sent you?"

"Yes, Martin." His grandfather, Mr. De La O, had sent her some very large cucumbers in September.

"He's coming tomorrow."

"Fine," said Archunde. "Now let's get back to work." When all the vegetables were mentioned in English, they were reviewed in Spanish with equal gusto. "Isn't it beautiful, children, to be able to use two languages?

---

5. *maíz* (mä ēs′) *Spanish.*
6. *palomitas de maíz* (pä lô mē′ täs dä mä ēs′) *Spanish.*

Words to Know and Use	**vigilant** (vij′ ə lənt) *adj.* watchful **gusto** (gus′ tō) *n.* enthusiasm; zest

Each one of you is worth two people if you learn both languages. Your lives will be that much richer. Now I want to teach you three new words. Maybe some of you know them; we'll see. What do you call a person who knows three languages?"

The children concentrated but couldn't come up with an answer.

"Trilingual," said Archunde, then she had everyone repeat it several times. She wrote it on the board and underlined the prefix. "Remember, *tri-* means 'three,' 'three.'" Most of the students wrote it down.

"Now who can tell me the word for a person who speaks *two* languages? You should know that one, children." But no one came up with it. "Bilingual!" said Archunde, then she repeated the procedure as before. "And don't forget: *bi-* means 'two.' Yes, I don't have to tell you to put it in your notebooks. Don't forget it over the Christmas vacation." Mrs. Teubbes walked up and down the rows verifying the notebook work.

"Now," said Archunde, "what is the word for a person who speaks just one language?" One hand instantly went up in the air. "America?"

"Gringo!" said the girl.

Archunde burst out laughing, but she controlled it quickly. "No, not quite," said the aide, who trembled mirthfully as she used to do as a young girl when she got the giggles in church. "The word I was looking for is *monolingual. Mono-* means 'one,' 'one,'" she said as she wrote it on the board.

Ricardo's hand went up. "Mrs. Archunde, what's gringo?" he asked mischievously.

Archunde felt like hitting him with a "cowcumber." She was momentarily at a loss for words.

"*Gringo,*" said Mrs. Teubbes, "is a word used to describe someone who is of American-English descent. It is not the nicest word to use."

"My grandmother uses it all the time and she's nice," said Ricardo.

"It depends on how you use it, how you say it," volunteered Archunde. "Technically it comes from the Spanish word *griego,*[7] which means 'Greek.' *Gringo* just means 'foreigner.' Now let's get back to our lesson so we can finish the details for the cultural day."

Other vocabulary words were introduced, written down, and drilled. When that was done, the aide reinforced the cultural unit from three days before. "All right, now let's see who can lead the class in a little Christmas carol. Who wants to do it?"

"In English or Spanish?" asked a student.

"Well, let me see, how should I do it?"

"I know," said Martin, "eenie, meenie, minie, moe."

"I like the way you taught it to us in Spanish," said America.

"All right, go ahead," encouraged the aide.

America got up from her desk and turned to face the class. She pointed to a different student with each syllable she uttered: *"Tela mela, teplatí, como sal que es para ti!*[8] Becky is it!" She sat down again.

---

7. *griego* (grye′ gô) *Spanish.*
8. *Tela mela, teplatí, como sal que es para ti!* (te′ lä me′ lä te plä tē′ cô′ mô säl kä es pä′ rä tē): a Spanish counting-out rhyme.

Becky put on a persevering face, shrugged her shoulders a bit, and went up in front of the class. "But which one shall we sing?" she asked in mild protestation. Other students called out a number of carols.

"You pick it, dear," said Mrs. Archunde.

"Well, let's do 'Alarrú,' but you all have to sing!"

The class was enthusiastic as Archunde picked up her guitar and everyone joined voices with the Christmas lullaby:

> No temas a Herodes
> Que nada te ha de hacer;
> Duérmete, Niño lindo;
> No tienes que temer.
> Alarrú, alamé,
> Alarrú, alamé, mi Señor.[9]

As the class finished the carol, contentment was expressed on the children's faces. They felt good about themselves, a sentiment the two professionals had labored strenuously to achieve.

"That was beautiful, children!" said Mrs. Teubbes. "I could listen to you all day. But let's take some time to review who is going to bring what for tomorrow. I am so excited about our cultural day!" Quickly she wrote the students' names on the board, then gave the chalk to Mrs. Archunde to jot down the names of the foods, since she was more familiar with the spelling. When the task was completed, Mrs. Teubbes said, "Children, I'm looking forward to seeing your parents tomorrow, those who can come, and everything sounds so good I'm not even going to eat breakfast at home."

"That's OK; I'll bring you some *atole*,"[10] said Ricardo.

"Wonderful, Richard," Mrs. Teubbes sighed. One never knew what that boy was going to say.

"I'm a wonderful boy," admitted Ricardo as the bell sounded for recess. "I can hardly wait for tomorrow!"

The following day no one realized how memorable the cultural day would be as the students got to class earlier than usual because of the food they brought. By the time the final bell rang to start the day, the food table was covered with all sorts of aromatic steaming crock-pots, ovenware, and gaily painted dishes, which lent even more personality to the foods with which Mrs. Teubbes was becoming acquainted. Indeed, this experience would do a tremendous job of broadening her cultural perspectives as well as her palate.

The children were remarkably well-behaved, especially with so much temptation at hand. Archunde put on a tape of Spanish-language Christmas carols to start the festivities. *A choir of angels couldn't sound more heavenly,* thought Mrs. Teubbes. She was glad she was able to make a contribution, for she had taken the time to go out and purchase the tape by José Feliciano, and afterward she would play it for everyone and maybe even lead them in his "Feliz Navidad!"[11]

---

9. *No temas . . . mi Señor* Spanish: Have no fear of Herod,/Who has nothing to do with you;/Sleep, beautiful boy;/You have nothing to fear./Lullaby, lullay,/Lullaby, lullay, my Lord.

10. *atole* (ä tô′ lä) *Spanish:* a Mexican drink made of corn meal.

11. *"Feliz Navidad!"* (fe lēs′ nä vē däd′): the title of a popular song, from the Spanish for "Merry Christmas."

Words to Know and Use	**persevering** (pʉr′ se vir′ iŋ) *adj.* determined to continue **persevere** *v.* **perspective** (per spek′ tiv) *n.* a point of view **palate** (pal′ ət) *n.* sense of taste

393

Mrs. Teubbes saw Martin's grandfather, Mr. De La O, entering the room. Immediately she went to thank him for his gift from back in September. "I'm so glad you could come, Mr. De La Zero," she blurted as she shook the man's hand. "I wanted to express in person how much my family and I appreciated your thoughtfulness."

"Thank you, *señora,*" said the old gentleman, warmly receptive to the woman's intent. "I'm glad you enjoyed our little gift."

"We have a chair for you right over here," she said as she led him across the room.

Mrs. Archunde was mixing with everyone, but she went to America and her father when they walked into the room.

"I hope you won't throw us out for being fashionably late," said the man to Mrs. Archunde.

"Of course not," she replied.

"I brought the *pozole,*"[12] chirped America. "We even grew the corn that's in it."

"Oh oh; if it's no good, they'll throw us out for sure," said the father, making Archunde smile. Little wonder America had such a sense of humor. "I'll put it right over here," he said as he placed the large pot on the last remaining space on the table.

"We were saving it for you," said Archunde.

"I guess we're ready to start," said Mrs. Teubbes. "Children, you all make a line on that side of the table with your parents, and Mrs. Archunde and I will serve from this side if you need help." A second invitation was unnecessary, and everyone cooperated in an orderly fashion.

Mrs. Teubbes had not eaten breakfast, usually a very large meal for her, so she was quite hungry to begin with; and as she helped serve the different dishes, her mouth literally watered in expectation. She controlled herself by making pleasant comments on how good everything looked, but she could hardly wait to begin her own meal.

"Is this porridge or cement?" asked Denise as she looked at a white crock-pot full of light blue *atole.*

The people talked, music played, and when everyone had been through the line once, the two teachers finally served themselves. Mrs. Teubbes was not shy about sampling a little of everything, starting with the items familiar to her, devouring them in as dainty a fashion as possible. Then she began with the unfamiliar dishes, and this is where she got herself into a bit of difficulty. A *relleno*[13] had some hot chili in it, and the unsuspecting woman had to make a quick exit to the drinking fountain for some cold water. Undaunted, she returned to the food table and continued her adventures amid the happiness and jovial spirit which everyone shared. The good food, beautiful music, and happy people enriched the holiday season as nothing else could.

"Mrs. Teubbes, have you tasted my *pozole* yet?" asked America of her teacher.

"Your what?"

"This dish over here," said the girl, "the *pozole.*"

"No, dear," admitted Mrs. Teubbes, "but hand me a bowl and it will be next. I've never had such delicious food in my life!"

"Really?" said the smiling girl.

---

12. *pozole* (pô zô′ lā) *Spanish:* a Mexican stew.
13. *relleno* (re ye′ nô) *Spanish:* stuffing.

Words to Know and Use | **jovial** (jō′ vē əl) *adj.* jolly and sociable

TAMALADA
© 1987
Carmen Lomas Garza
Courtesy of the artist.
Photo by Wolfgang Dietz.

"Can you imagine that?" continued Mrs. Teubbes. "Of course, I grew up in a different part of the country. But they couldn't drag me away now." She took the bowl America handed to her and filled it generously. "Hmm, smells delicious." She was ever so slightly wary because of the chili relleno, but the woman was unable to discover anything potentially <u>deleterious</u> to her palate as she tasted a little. "Hmm, it's good." She looked at America, put a hand on her shoulder momentarily, and said, "You know, my dear, I've been wondering something for a long time . . . I mean, I have a question for you." She continued to eat the tasty *pozole*.

"I have always wondered, what do you do with all those little rodents you take home?"

"We put them to good use; we don't waste anything," replied America as she smiled.

"Heavens, this has such flavor!" said Mrs. Teubbes as she ate the *pozole*. "Quite unlike anything I've ever eaten. What do you call it again?"

After America told her, Mrs. Teubbes <u>waxed</u> rather poetic and said happily, "One thing is certain: this taste is not a waste! What is this that gives it such flavor?"

America couldn't see the bits of white pork meat the teacher was moving about with her spoon, so she assumed Mrs. Teubbes was referring to the white corn, for to her that was the best part of the *pozole*.

"Oh, *that's* the white *maíz!*" replied America.

Mrs. Teubbes's eyes opened wide as saucers, and an expression of terror swept into her face as she blurted: "WHITE MICE?!" She dropped the <u>leprous</u> bowl of *pozole*, clamped a hand over her mouth, and raced out of the room. ❧

*R*esponding to Reading

First Impressions

1. What was your reaction to what happened at the end of the story?

Second Thoughts

2. What do you think causes the incident at the end of the story?

    Think about
    • Mrs. Teubbes's attitude toward her students and others
    • her appetite
    • her lack of knowledge of Spanish

3. Would you want to have Mrs. Teubbes for a teacher? Why or why not?

4. How do you think Mrs. Archunde and the students feel about Mrs. Teubbes? Use evidence from the story to support your answer.

5. Why do you think Mrs. Archunde laughs when America answers "Gringo" to her question "What is the word for a person who speaks just one language?"

Broader Connections

6. From its beginning people have had mixed feelings about bilingual education. Many people feel that students should learn English before taking a particular course of study, and others think that students learn English and other school subjects better if they become more proficient in their first language. What might be some of the benefits and the drawbacks of bilingual education?

*L*iterary Concept: Surprise Ending

An unexpected twist in the plot at a story's conclusion can provide a **surprise ending** like the one in "White Mice." For a surprise ending to be most effective, it must be based on facts and clues given earlier in the story. Find at least two clues in "White Mice" that lead up to its surprise ending.

Concept Review: Stereotype As you know, an oversimplified mental picture of a person, a group, or an institution is called a **stereotype.** Mrs. Teubbes stereotypes Hispanics, for example, by thinking that they "had as much talent as anybody; they just didn't, well, apply themselves at the proper time or in gainful ways." Can you find some other examples of stereotyping in this story?

Writing Options

1. Imagine that you are a visitor to a foreign land. You have just been handed a bowl of steaming hot and fragrant food. You have no idea what the ingredients are. Write a **narrative,** telling what you will do next.

2. Imagine that Mrs. Teubbes has just met the author of "Conversational Ballgames." Write a **dialogue** that the two women might have.

3. Imagine that you are a faculty evaluator for the school in "White Mice." Write **performance reviews** for Mrs. Teubbes and Mrs. Archunde.

4. Like the school in "White Mice," your school probably has many students from different cultural backgrounds. Write a **letter** to persuade your principal to hold a Cultural Awareness Day.

Vocabulary Practice

Exercise   On a sheet of paper, write the word from the list that best completes each sentence.

1. Mrs. Teubbes fell into a dreamy _?_ as she waited for her students to arrive in the classroom.

2. Her appetite began to _?_ as she thought of the foods she would be tasting during the cultural day.

3. She knew that the foods would be pleasing to her _?_ .

4. As she thought, Mrs. Teubbes told herself that she needed to look at her students from a new _?_ .

5. She must not _?_ them in a judgmental way.

6. Instead, she must keep a _?_ watch for the positive things they said and did.

7. Otherwise, she would be _?_ to look at her students' weaknesses instead of their strengths.

8. Yes, she would continue in her _?_ attempts to change her attitude.

9. After all, her students were not dirty, _?_ individuals.

10. Mrs. Teubbes also would try to maintain a _?_ attitude.

11. Just then, the children began entering the room, singing their favorite song with _?_ .

12. On a _?_ one of the students asked Mrs. Teubbes to dance.

13. Suddenly Mrs. Teubbes was filled with an _?_ feeling that overwhelmed her.

14. She had such a nice group of students; how could she let them _?_ her?

15. Certainly they would never do anything remotely _?_ to her!

> ### Words to Know and Use
>
> **deleterious**
> **gusto**
> **ineffable**
> **intimidate**
> **jovial**
> **lark**
> **leprous**
> **palate**
> **persevering**
> **perspective**
> **prone**
> **reverie**
> **scrutinize**
> **vigilant**
> **wax**

*O*ptions for Learning

1 • Bilingual Education Is there a bilingual education program in your school? What do you know about it? Write a list of questions that you would like to ask about bilingual education. Then interview your principal or a teacher in your school's bilingual program, and share your findings with the rest of the class.

2 • One, Two, Three, Go! For each of the prefixes *mono-*, *bi-*, and *tri-*, find five examples of words containing the prefix. With your classmates compile a list of words that include these prefixes, and put them on a poster or a large sheet of paper. If you wish, add illustrations for some of the words or use them in sentences.

3 • Fiesta! With your classmates plan a cultural day similar to the one in "White Mice." Think back to the item you chose to represent yourself and your heritage in Examine What You Know. Bring it in to share during the celebration.

4 • White Mice II What do you think will happen when Mrs. Teubbes returns to the classroom? What might she say and do? What might Mrs. Archunde and the children say and do? Dramatize the scene (or a few alternative scenes) that might take place.

 FACT FINDER SOCIAL STUDIES

Where was corn first grown, and what are at least three uses for this versatile vegetable?

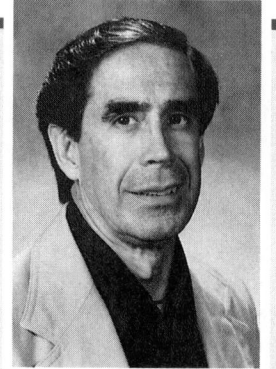

*R*ubén Sálaz-Márquez
1935-

Rubén Sálaz-Márquez claims that his inspiration for "White Mice" stemmed from an anecdote he once heard: "A woman told me that her daughter had been asked to name her favorite food and the little girl answered, 'At my house, we like white *maíz* best of all.' The surprised questioner wanted to know how they cooked the mice—and whether they ate gray mice too!"

In addition to teaching for over twenty years, Sálaz-Márquez has written several books, including *Cosmic: The La Raza Sketchbook* and *Heartland: Stories of the Southwest*. He is currently working on a trilogy about the Native American leader Tecumseh.

A lifelong native of New Mexico, Sálaz-Márquez enjoys his home state's unique blend of Native American, Hispanic, and European-American cultures. "Living in New Mexico is a tremendous experience," he says, "because we have a long history of getting along without racial hatred."

Fiction

Checkouts

CYNTHIA RYLANT

Examine What You Know

Have you ever moved to a new home? If so, you probably had strong feelings about the move. On the one hand, you might have felt sad about leaving close friends and familiar places. On the other hand, you might have been excited about living in a new place and making new friends. Even if you've never moved, you have no doubt had new students enter your classroom from other schools. In small groups consider the advantages and the disadvantages of moving. After discussing in groups, meet as a class to complete a chart like this:

MOVING	
Advantages	Disadvantages
making new friends	missing old friends

Expand Your Knowledge

Millions of Americans move each year. Most migration in the United States during the past decade has been from the East and the North to the South, the Midwest, and the West. Years ago, moving far away often meant leaving family and friends behind for good. Fortunately, today's conveniences, such as fax machines, modems, telephones, and ever-improving modes of transportation have allowed people to move farther away while still remaining in close contact.

Write Before You Read

Choose one of the following topics and write about it in your journal or on a sheet of paper:

- Have you ever moved? If so, how did you feel?
- How would you feel if you found out that you had to move?
- What was it like when a new student entered your classroom?

■ *Author biography in Reader's Handbook*

Checkouts

CYNTHIA RYLANT

Her parents had moved her to Cincinnati, to a large house with beveled glass windows and several porches and the *history* her mother liked to emphasize. You'll love the house, they said. You'll be lonely at first, they admitted, but you're so nice you'll make friends fast. And as an impulse tore at her to lie on the floor, to hold to their ankles and tell them she felt she was dying, to offer anything, anything at all, so they might allow her to finish growing up in the town of her childhood, they firmed their mouths and spoke from their chests, and they said, It's decided.

They moved her to Cincinnati, where for a month she spent the greater part of every day in a room full of beveled glass windows, sifting through photographs of the life she'd lived and left behind. But it is difficult work, suffering, and in its own way a kind of art, and finally she didn't have the energy for it anymore, so she emerged from the beautiful house and fell in love with a bag boy at the supermarket. Of course, this didn't happen all at once, just like that, but in the sequence of things that's exactly the way it happened.

She liked to grocery shop. She loved it in the way some people love to drive long country roads, because doing it she could think and relax and wander. Her parents wrote up the list and handed it to her, and off she went without complaint to perform what they regarded as a great sacrifice of her time and a sign that she was indeed a very nice girl. She had never told them how much she loved grocery shopping, only that she was "willing" to do it. She had an intuition which told her that her parents were not safe for sharing such strong, important facts about herself. Let them think they knew her.

Once inside the supermarket, her hands firmly around the handle of the cart, she would lapse into a kind of reverie and wheel toward the produce. Like a Tibetan monk in solitary meditation, she calmed to a point of deep, deep happiness; this feeling came to her, reliably, if strangely, only in the supermarket.

Then one day the bag boy dropped her jar of mayonnaise, and that is how she fell in love.

He was nervous—first day on the job—and along had come this fascinating girl, standing in the checkout line with the unfocused stare one often sees in young children, her face turned enough away that he might take several full looks at her as he packed sturdy bags full of food and the goods of modern life. She interested him because her hair was red and thick, and in it she had placed a huge orange bow, nearly the size of a small hat. That was enough to distract him, and when finally it was her groceries he was packing, she looked at him and smiled, and he could respond only by busting her jar of mayonnaise on the floor, shards of glass and oozing cream decorating the area around his feet.

She loved him at exactly that moment, and if he'd known this, perhaps he wouldn't have fallen into the brown depression he fell into, which lasted the rest of his shift. He believed he must have looked a fool in her eyes, and he envied the sureness of everyone around him: the cocky cashier at the register, the grim and harried[1] store manager, the bland butcher, and the brazen bag boys who smoked in the warehouse on their breaks. He wanted a second chance. Another chance to be confident and say witty things to her as he threw tin cans into her bags, persuading her to allow him to help her to her car so he might learn just a little about her, check out the floor of the car for signs of hobbies or fetishes[2] and the bumpers for clues as to beliefs and loyalties.

But he busted her jar of mayonnaise, and nothing else worked out for the rest of the day.

Strange, how attractive clumsiness can be. She left the supermarket with stars in her eyes, for she had loved the way his long, nervous fingers moved from the conveyor belt to the bags, how deftly (until the mayonnaise) they had picked up her items and placed them into her bags. She had loved the way the hair kept falling into his eyes as he leaned over to grab a box or a tin. And the tattered brown shoes he wore with no socks. And the left side of his collar turned in rather than out.

The bag boy seemed a wonderful contrast to the perfectly beautiful house she had

PEACHES, TOMATOES AND WATERMELONS 1973
Don Eddy Museum of Art, Rhode Island School of Design,
The Albert Pilavin Collection of Twentieth Century Art
Photo by Cathy Carver.

been forced to accept as her home, to the *history* she hated, to the loneliness she had become used to, and she couldn't wait to come back for more of his awkwardness and dishevelment.

Incredibly, it was another four weeks before they saw each other again. As fate would have it, her visits to the supermarket never coincided with his schedule to bag. Each time she went to the store, her eyes scanned the checkouts at once, her heart in her mouth. And each hour he worked, the bag boy kept one eye on the door, watching for the red-haired girl with the big orange bow.

---

1. harried: constantly bothered or pestered by others.
2. fetishes: things to which a person is irrationally attached.

Yet in their disappointment these weeks, there was a kind of ecstasy. It is reason enough to be alive, the hope you may see again some face which has meant something to you. The anticipation of meeting the bag boy eased the girl's painful transition into her new and jarring life in Cincinnati. It provided for her an anchor amid all that was impersonal and unfamiliar, and she spent less time on thoughts of what she had left behind as she concentrated on what might lie ahead. And for the boy, the long and often tedious hours at the supermarket, which provided no challenge other than that of showing up the following workday . . . these hours became possibilities of mystery and romance for him as he watched the electric doors for the girl in the orange bow.

And when finally they did meet up again, neither offered a clue to the other that he, or she, had been the object of obsessive thought for weeks. She spotted him as soon as she came into the store, but she kept her eyes strictly in front of her as she pulled out a cart and wheeled it toward the produce. And he, too, knew the instant she came through the door—though the orange bow was gone, replaced by a small but bright yellow flower instead—and he never once turned his head in her direction but watched her from the corner of his vision as he tried to swallow back the fear in his throat.

It is odd how we sometimes deny ourselves the very pleasure we have longed for and which is finally within our reach. For some perverse reason she would not have been able to articulate, the girl did not bring her cart up to the bag boy's checkout when her shopping was done. And the bag boy let her leave the store, pretending no notice of her.

This is often the way of children, when they truly want a thing, to pretend that they don't. And then they grow angry when no one tries harder to give them this thing they so casually rejected, and they soon find themselves in a rage simply because they cannot say yes when they mean yes. Humans are very complicated. (And perhaps cats, who have been known to react in the same way, though the resulting rage can only be guessed at.)

The girl hated herself for not checking out at the boy's line, and the boy hated himself for not catching her eye and saying hello, and they most sincerely hated each other without having ever exchanged even two minutes of conversation.

Eventually—in fact, within the week—a kind and intelligent boy who lived very near her beautiful house asked the girl to a movie, and she gave up her fancy for the bag boy at the supermarket. And the bag boy himself grew so bored with his job that he made a desperate search for something better and ended up in a bookstore where scores of fascinating girls lingered like honeybees about a hive. Some months later the bag boy and the girl with the orange bow again crossed paths, standing in line with their dates at a movie theater, and, glancing toward the other, each smiled slightly, then looked away, as strangers on public buses often do when one is moving off the bus and the other is moving on. ❧

Responding to Reading

First Impressions

1. What memories or feelings does this story trigger in you?

Second Thoughts

2. Why do you think the girl and the boy are attracted to each other?

3. Why do you think the girl and the boy ignore each other the second time they meet at the store?

4. What do you think the girl would have thought of the boy if she had met him while she still lived in "the town of her childhood"?

   Think about
   - the effect that the family's move has on the girl
   - her feeling that he provides a contrast to her new home
   - her struggle to connect in a new town

5. Recall the selection "Memories of Dating" on page 42. What advice might Dave Barry give the girl and the boy?

Literary Concept: Third-Person Omniscient Point of View

Point of view is the perspective from which a story is told. "Checkouts" is told from a **third-person omniscient point of view**— that is, the narrator is someone outside the action rather than a character within the story. It is an omniscient, or all-knowing, viewpoint because the narrator knows everything about the characters. Give one example of a detail the narrator could not have known if the story had been told in the first-person voice of the girl.

Writing Options

1. Recall the thoughts about moving that you listed before reading the story. Then write a **letter** that the girl might write to a friend back home, describing the advantages and the disadvantages of her move.

2. Imagine you will be moving soon. Write an **annotated list** of the mementos and pictures that you want to put in a scrapbook to help you remember your old home. In each annotation include a detailed description of the item and your reasons for including it.

Drama

The Kid Nobody Could Handle

KURT VONNEGUT, JR.
Dramatized by CHRISTOPHER SERGEL

Examine What You Know

Imagine that a student has vandalized one of the classrooms at your school. What reasons do you think a student might have for such vandalism? With three of your classmates, role-play a meeting of the student, the student's parent or guardian, the teacher whose classroom was damaged, and the principal. Discuss what happened and why. Also discuss the student's punishment and how to correct his or her behavior. Try to agree on a suitable course of action.

Expand Your Knowledge

Vandalism is often associated with juvenile delinquency. The legal category of juvenile delinquency was established so that lawbreakers under a certain age—eighteen in most states—could get help rather than punishment and not be classified as criminals. Juvenile delinquency accounts for an increasing share of crime in the United States. Each year, about 4 percent of children between the ages of ten and eighteen appear in juvenile court at least once.

Enrich Your Reading

Stage Directions   In this play the action takes place in two areas of the stage. One area represents a restaurant; the other represents a high school where a serious act of vandalism takes place. As you read, use the drawing below to help you imagine where the characters are in each scene.

■ *Author biography on Extend page*

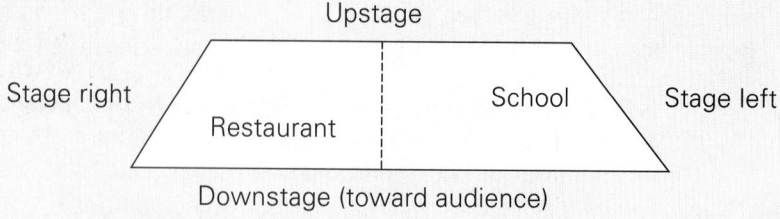

The Kid Nobody Could Handle

KURT VONNEGUT, JR.
Dramatized by CHRISTOPHER SERGEL

CHARACTERS

Newt, *observer*

Margie, *waitress*

George Helmholtz, *high school music teacher*

Grace Helmholtz, *his wife*

Bert Quinn, *restaurant owner*

Jim Donnini, *a problem young man*

Mrs. Crane, *English teacher*

The curtain is rising to reveal a stage with several playing areas.

At right, there's a suggestion of a portion of a quite ordinary small restaurant. All that's required is a small table with a checked cloth and two chairs. If desired, however, this can be <u>elaborated</u> with another table or so and perhaps a section of counter. There should be a parking meter standing in front and to the side of the restaurant area.

At upstage center and to stage left, there are several chairs arranged as classroom seats, teacher's desk, and a locker. A small podium at left, facing front, and any other available props that would suggest a high school music room. A few instrument cases placed beside the locker would be helpful.

A small, humorless man, Bert Quinn, is revealed sitting at the restaurant table toying sourly with some food on the plate before him. If desired, a few extras may be seen crossing downstage, either to right or left, apparently on the sidewalk.

| *Words to Know and Use* | **elaborate** (ē lab′ ə rāt′) *v.* to add details to |

405

Newt *(as curtain is rising)*. It's early morning—some people going to work, some to school. *(indicates right)* That's Bert Quinn's restaurant. Bert eats his own food—not because he likes it, but because he saves money that way.

(Margie is entering right with a Silex full of coffee.)

Bert *(calling right without looking up)*. Margie——

Margie *(as she's pouring more coffee into his cup)*. Yes, Mr. Quinn?

Bert. I'd like more— *(realizing)* Thank you. Did the Kid finish mopping?

Margie. No, sir.

Bert *(irritated)*. Tell him—hurry, and then get to school.

Margie *(as she's going; casually)*. I tell him every morning.

Newt. Bert isn't really a well man. He can't sleep, can't digest his food, and can't stop working. He has only two moods: one suspicious, the other arrogant. The first applies when he's losing money, the second when he's making it.

(Newt steps upstage a few steps and nods left.)

Newt. Over here is Lincoln High School—that large classroom is for the band—run by George Helmholtz—whose head is always filled with band music.

(George Helmholtz, holding a car steering wheel as though driving, comes shuffling on left. His wife, Grace, as though in the seat beside him, shuffles with him.)

Newt. George is driving his wife to the bus before school this morning because she's going to spend a few days with relatives. *(George apparently turns the car toward the audience and then apparently stops.)*

George *(to his wife)*. Before you go, I'd like a kiss.

Grace *(looking about, embarrassed)*. I kissed you before we left the house.

George. I'd like another.

(With a sigh, she gives him a brief kiss.)

Newt *(summing up)*. Very affectionate fellow.

Grace. Try to collect from the school for the money you paid to get the music copied.

George. The minute I get there.

Grace *(concerned)*. I could've fixed breakfast for you.

George. I'll stop at Bert's restaurant.

Grace. After he took such advantage of you on that land deal?

George. What's the difference? *(affectionately)* How about another—

Grace *(amused, apparently hopping out of car, carrying overnight bag)*. Back in a few days.

George *(calling after her)*. Phone me tonight.

(Grace goes off left while George apparently continues slowly right in car.)

Words to Know and Use | **casually** (kazh′ o͞o əl ē) *adv.* in an informal or relaxed way
arrogant (ar′ ə gənt) *adj.* proud and scornful

Newt *(meanwhile)*. Each year George dreams the same big dream. He dreams of leading as fine a band as there is on the face of the earth. And, in a sense, each year his dream comes true. It comes true because George is sure that a man couldn't have a better dream. Faced by his <u>unnerving</u> sureness, Kiwanians, Rotarians, and Lions pay for band uniforms that cost twice as much as their best suits, school administrators let George raid the budget, and youngsters play their hearts out for him.

(During this, George *has apparently parked the car near the restaurant—don't let the actor be elaborate—by propping the wheel against a standing parking meter.)*

Newt. And when the youngsters don't have any talent, George gets them to play on guts alone.

(Before going into restaurant, George *glances about, sees he's alone, takes a step forward, and then raises his arms as though to lead a band.)*

George. A-one, a-two, a-three—*(He brings arms down, and there's a burst of beautiful band music that he apparently leads for several seconds. He gestures for the end, the sound cuts out—and humming the continuation of whatever music was played, he walks into restaurant.)*

(Note: A rousing Sousa[1] march would be a good choice, and the sound cues should be carefully rehearsed.)

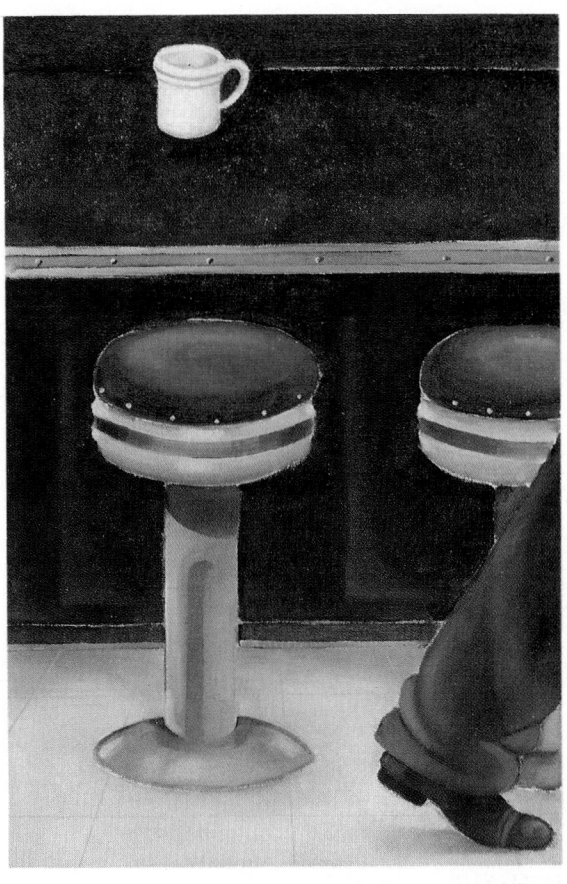

Illustration by Terry Widener.

Newt *(smiling)*. That music was all in George's head. But he cares so much he makes everyone hear it.

(George is seating himself at the table with Bert, *and the sounds of heavy construction work may begin here, though kept as background.)*

---

1. **Sousa** (soo′ zə): John Philip Sousa, U.S. band conductor famous for the marches he composed in the late 1800s and early 1900s.

407

Bert *(calling right).* Fried eggs, coffee, and toast for Mr. Helmholtz.

Newt *(wryly, toward sounds).* The noise of real life. Waddling, clanking, muddy machines tearing the hill behind the restaurant to pieces, with trucks hauling the pieces away. Those sounds put Bert in his arrogant and boastful mood.

Bert. How many eyes saw that hill back there before I did? Thousands, I'll bet. And not one saw what I saw. *(in wonder, chewing on toothpick)* How many eyes?

George. Mine, at least.

Bert *(amused).* Yours.

(Margie, the waitress, is bringing tray to George.)

George *(pleasantly).* All the hill meant to me was a hard climb, some free blackberries, taxes, and a place for band picnics. *(to Margie)* Thank you. *(She exits.)*

Bert. You inherit the hill, and it's nothing but a pain in the neck. So you figure you'll stick me with it.

George. The price was more than fair.

Bert *(gleefully).* You say that now—now you see the shopping district's got to grow. Now you see what I saw.

(A wiry young man, sullen, withdrawn, wearing jeans and gaudy shiny black boots with a jingling chain on them, is coming on, mopping mechanically.)

George *(as he's eating; not really interested).* Yes, but too late. Too late.

Bert. What do I do when I get your hill? *(gestures toward sound)* I'm tearing down your hill. And now everybody wants to build a store where the hill was.

George. Um. *(nodding to boy)* Hello. *(Without response, the boy keeps mopping.)*

Bert. We all got something. You got music, I got vision.

Newt *(smiling).* And it's perfectly clear to Bert which one has the money.

Bert. Think big. That's what vision is. Keep your eyes wider than anybody else's.

George *(still regarding the mopper).* That boy. I've seen him around school, but I never knew his name.

Bert *(smiling cheerfully).* Billy the Kid. The storm trooper.[2] Flash Gordon. *(calling)* Hey, Jim! Come here a minute.

Newt *(as the sullen boy is approaching them, the mop dragging after).* George is pretty sensitive. What appalled him was to see that the boy's eyes were as expressionless as oysters.

Bert. This is my brother-in-law's kid by another marriage—before he married my sister. His name's Jim Donnini, and he's from the south side of Chicago, and he's very tough.

George. How do you do?

Jim. *(looking past him; emptily).* Hi.

---

2. **storm trooper:** a member of the brutal militia of Nazi Germany.

Words to Know and Use	**wryly** (rī′ lē) *adv.* in an ironic way; using dry humor **wiry** (wīr′ ē) *adj.* thin but strong **gaudy** (gôd′ ē) *adj.* showy and tasteless

Bert. He's living with me now. He's my baby now.

George. You want a lift to school, Jim?

Bert *(as Jim doesn't reply)*. He won't talk to me, either. But, yeah, he wants a lift to school. *(To Jim. Shortly.)* Go on, kid, wash up and shave. *(Robotlike, Jim goes off right, trailing the mop.)*

George *(concerned)*. Where are his parents?

Bert. His mother's dead. His old man married my sister, walked out on her, and stuck her with him. Then the court didn't like the way she was raising him and put him in foster homes for a while. Then they decided to get him clear of Chicago, so they stuck me with him. (shaking his head) Life's a funny thing, Helmholtz.

George *(pushing his eggs away)*. Not very funny, sometimes.

Bert *(chewing toothpick)*. Like some whole new race of people coming up. He's nothing like the decent kids we got around here. Did you notice those boots he wears? And he won't talk, won't run around with other kids, won't study. I don't think he can even read or write very good.

George. Does he like music at all? Or drawing? Does he collect anything?

Bert. You know what he likes—he likes to polish those boots. The only enjoyment he gets is when he's alone, comic books spread around, and polishing those boots. *(remembering)* Oh, he had a collection, too. I took it away from him and threw it in the river.

George. Threw it in the river?

Bert. Yeah. Eight knives—some with blades as long as your hand.

George. Oh. *(concerned)* This is a new problem at some schools, I guess. *(wanting to sort it out)* It's kind of a sickness, isn't it? That's the way to look at it, wouldn't you say?

Bert. Yes, sick. *(tapping his chest)* And Doctor Bert is just the man to give him what's good for his ailment.

George. What's that?

Bert *(hard)*. For a start—no more talk about poor little sick boy. That's all he's heard from social workers and the juvenile court.

(Jim, still expressionless, is reentering right, now wearing a leather jacket.)

George. But actually—

Bert. Actually he's a bum. Well, I'm going to ride his tail until he straightens up and flies right or winds up in the can[3] for life.

George *(nodding toward Jim; warning)*. Bert—

Bert *(going right on)*. One way or the other. *(directly to Jim)* Believe it, boy!

George. I see. *(to Jim)* I'm parked in front. *(Without a response, Jim goes out to stand by the parking meter. George gets up, putting some money on the table.)* That right? *(Bert nods, and George puts a separate coin by coffee cup. He's depressed.)* If I knew anything to say to that boy.

Bert *(picking up money)*. What's to say? Listen to those bulldozers—really tearing into it.

---

3. **can:** a slang term for jail.

George (*preoccupied*). They are—they really are.

(*As he's going to join* Jim, Bert *reaches across, picks up the other coin, considers an instant, then goes out right.*)

Bert (*holding coin for her*). Margie—

(*Without talk,* George *takes up wheel, and he and* Jim *are apparently driving left. The construction sounds, if used, fade.*)

Newt. George tried baseball, football, anything to get a conversation going, but nothing happened. And, of course, he couldn't help trying the most important subject in the world to him.

George (*glancing at* Jim *and clearing his throat*). Do you—do you like listening to music? (Jim *sighs heavily with boredom.*) (George *tries again.*) Ever drum with your fingers or keep time with your feet? (Jim *leans his head back, closing his eyes, waiting for* George *to give up.*) (George *tries another approach.*) Those boots—what's the function of the chains? Are they to jingle? (Jim *looks away, but* George *presses on.*) At least you whistle. Even whistling—it can be like picking up the keys to a whole new world.

Jim (*contemptuously*). A new world—

George (*eagerly*). A world as beautiful as any world can be. (Jim *makes a soft Bronx cheer,[4] but* George *continues* <u>undaunted</u>.) There! You've illustrated the basic principle of the family of brass wind instruments. The glorious voice of every one of them starts with a buzz on the lips.

(*Apparently they've reached a parking place at left, and they're both facing forward.*)

Jim (*fishing out a cigarette from inside of his leather jacket*). Any time.

George (*noticing as* Jim *lights cigarette, keeping casual*). That—that won't do your lungs much good. (Jim's *reply is to expel some smoke.* George *speaks carefully.*) Sometimes I get disgusted, too, and I don't see how I can stand it. I feel like doing all kinds of crazy things—things that might even be bad for me. (Jim *expels more smoke.*) And then—(*snaps fingers of left hand and grabs wheel again enthusiastically*) And then, Jim, I remember I've got at least one tiny corner of the universe I can make just the way I want it. I can go to it and enjoy it till I'm brand-new and happy again.

Jim. Aren't you the lucky one?

George. I am, for a fact. My corner of the universe happens to be the air around my head. I can fill it with music. (Jim *is yawning, apparently getting out of the car.* George *continues eagerly.*) Mr. Beeler, in zoology, has his butterflies. Mr. Trottman, in physics, has his pendulum. Mrs. Crane, in English, her books—

Jim (*contemptuously*). Mrs. Crane—

George. Making sure everybody has a corner like that is about the biggest job we teachers have. I—(*But he's stopped as* Jim *drops cigarette and walks out left.*) Jim—

---

4. Bronx cheer: a ridiculing sound, made by placing the tongue between the lips and blowing out air.

(But the boy is gone. Unhappily, George places wheel by post or sets it off left, then steps on the remainder of Jim's cigarette, scoops it into his hand, and takes it with him into his classroom, where he puts it in a wastebasket.)

Newt *(meanwhile)*. George Helmholtz's first class of the morning was C Band. C Band is where beginners thumped and wheezed and tooted as best they could, and looked down the long, long road through B Band to A Band, the Lincoln High School Ten Square Band, the finest school band in the world.

(George is coming up onto the podium left, holding a baton.)

George *(speaking front, addressing imaginary class)*. Good morning, C Band. I know it's early—none of us warmed up yet. *(raising his baton)* But remember this— *(believing it)* You're better than you think you are! A-one, a-two, a-three . . . *(Down comes the baton, and with it there's the sound of magnificent band music.)*

Newt *(as George continues to lead)*. Sounds great for C Band, doesn't it? *(shaking his head)* That music you're hearing isn't C Band. What that is—it's what George was hearing—in his head—the music as it was going to be—some day! Actually C Band set out in its quest for beauty—set out like a rusty switch engine, with valves stuck, pipes clogged, unions leaking, bearings dry—

(George is singing yump-yumps along with band as he brings this passage to a close.)

JERRY ON A STOOL 1957 Fairfield Porter
Collection of Arthur M. Bullowa.

Newt. And George was still smiling at the end of that class hour.

George *(front)*. Thanks. Thank you very much. See you tomorrow.

Words to Know and Use | **quest** (kwest) *n.* a search

411

(With this, he's getting off the podium and coming forward into what is the beginning of some student traffic—extras—crossing downstage to left or to right, talking excitedly to each other as they cross.)

(Note: Margie *and* Grace, *with minor costume changes to look like students, may do this.)*

Students *(generally).* No, it's true! . . . How do you know? . . . Mr. Beeler was telling Mr. Trottman . . . I heard Mrs. Crane was crying . . . You're outa your mind . . . Can't be true . . . So how come her classes are canceled? Tomorrow, too.

Newt *(during above).* George had gone into the hall for a drink of water, but he couldn't figure out what the students were talking about.

(The students are going off, leaving a confused George *behind. As he looks left,* Jim *walks in, pausing to polish his boots on his pants leg.)*

George. Hello, Jim. What's going on? *(Jim shrugs.)* I have to get back for rehearsal with B Band—but I was thinking about you. The school has a lot of clubs and teams that meet after classes. It's a good way to get to know a lot of the other students.

Jim *(coldly).* Maybe I don't want to know a lot of the other students. *(walking past* George; *heading right.)* Ever think of that? *(As he's going off right,* Jim *walks hard to make the boot chains jingle.)*

(Mrs. Crane, a worried English teacher, is coming on left.)

Mrs. Crane *(keeping herself calm with an effort).* George—

George. Mrs. Crane—I just heard your name—some of the students—

Mrs. Crane *(unhappily).* Can't hush it up. I suppose it's all over the school. Will you be at the faculty meeting?

George. Meeting?

Mrs. Crane. A special meeting this afternoon—on vandalism.

George *(with casual concern).* I hear that some schools—

Mrs. Crane *(cutting in).* My office was wrecked last night.

George *(stunned).* Your office? Here?

Mrs. Crane *(swallowing with difficulty).* I keep searching my mind—whom I might've offended—where I might've done less than I should for some student.

George *(incredulous).* You said—wrecked?

Mrs. Crane. Books, diplomas, records, even the snapshots of my trip to England—ripped, crumpled, trampled, drenched with ink!

George *(aghast).* No—

Mrs. Crane *(with an unhappy laugh).* Also the beginnings of eleven novels. I don't suppose they were very good, but I'd rather destroy them myself.

George *(can hardly talk).* I can't believe it!

Mrs. Crane. The meeting—for whatever it's worth—is at four. *(Starting right. Speaking mainly to herself.)* Is it my fault? Is it their fault? What's happening?

(As she is going off right, and as the shocked George is going off left, the lights are dimming except for a spot on Newt at downstage right.)

Newt *(during this).* George was sickened. He couldn't believe it. And with his wife away, he had no one to discuss it with. It didn't become real to George until late that night, in a dream. In the dream, George saw a boy with barracuda teeth, with claws like baling hooks.[5] The monster climbed into the band rehearsal-room and started clawing to tatters the heads of the biggest and best drums in the state. George woke up terrified. There was nothing to do but to dress and go to school.

(The stage is still dark, but George has come into the classroom area at left with a lighted flashlight.)

Newt. George let himself in with his key and used a flashlight, as he didn't want to attract attention. *(The flashlight is exploring the band instrument-cases.)* His treasures were safe. And with the contentment of a miser counting his money, George looked over the instruments one by one. Even now—even under these circumstances, he could hear the great horns roaring, could see them flashing in the

sunlight, with the Stars and Stripes and the banner of Lincoln High going before!

George *(happy with relief).* Thank Heaven!

Newt. Then George heard a noise in the chemistry lab next door. *(The flashlight snaps out.)* George went out into the hall, then jerked open the lab door.

(The flashlight comes on again, revealing Jim holding a bottle that he has tilted over to pour.)

George. You! You!

Newt. Jim Donnini was splashing acid over the periodic table of the elements, over the books, over the bust of Lavoisier.[6] It was the most repulsive thing George had ever seen.

George *(horrified).* Put that down and get out of there!

Jim. What're you gonna do?

George *(in shock).* I don't know. Clean up. Save what I can. But come out of there—come to my classroom.

(They're moving left.)

Jim. You gonna call the fuzz?

George *(bewildered).* Call the fuzz?

Jim *(George is so stupid).* The cops!

---

5. **baling hooks:** large hooks attached to handles, used for moving crates and bundles.

6. **Lavoisier** (lȧ vwȧ zyā′): Antoine Laurent Lavoisier, an eighteenth-century French scientist known as the founder of modern chemistry.

© Tom Voss / Stockworks.

George. Is it? *(struggling with concern)* That must be so, if one of our students wants to murder it.

Jim. What good is it?

George. Not much, I guess. *(unhappily)* But it's the best thing human beings have managed to do yet.

Jim *(with contempt)*. The best thing—

George *(swallowing)*. Jim, if you smashed up all the schools, we wouldn't have any hope.

Jim. What hope?

(George considers a moment.)

George. The hope that someday everybody will be glad they're alive. *(takes a breath)* Even you.

Jim. That's a laugh. All I ever got out of this garbage pile was a hard time. *(calculating)* So what're you gonna do?

George *(realizing)*. I have to do something, don't I?

Jim *(contemptuously polishing a boot on his pants leg)*. I don't care what you do!

George. Isn't there anything you care about? Anything, but those boots?

Jim *(challenging)*. Go on. Call up whoever you're gonna call—Go ahead!

George *(an agony of indecision; speaking mainly to himself)*. I don't want to turn you in! I want to find some way to reach—*(Breaks off as he's struck by new thought. Rushing to get something from his locker nearby. As he takes something from locker)* I'll show you—you'll see—maybe this will convince—*(He brings velvet-cov-*

(George apparently turns on the lights in his classroom area.)

George. I—I don't know. Put down the bottle of acid. *(Jim does. George is confused and miserable. No thoughts come.)* If I'd caught you hurting the band instruments, probably I'd have hit you. *(bothered by himself)* But I wouldn't have had any intelligent thoughts about what you were—what you thought you were doing.

Jim *(bravado)*. It's about time this place got set on its ear.

ered object toward Jim*)* There! *(He takes velvet away, revealing a brightly polished trumpet.)* There's my treasure! It's the dearest thing I own. *(He thrusts it into* Jim's *hands.)* I give it to you. Do what you please with it. If you want, you can smash it—and I won't move a muscle to stop you. It's yours! *(*Jim *is holding the trumpet uncertainly.)* Go on! If the world has treated you so badly, it deserves to have that trumpet smashed.

Jim *(tossing trumpet on desk; polishing boot again)*. I—I don't want it.

George. Jim—*(exploding)* Those—boots! *(*George *grabs* Jim's *belt, puts a foot behind him, and dumps him onto the floor.)*

Jim. Hey! What are you—

*(*George *is jerking* Jim's *gaudy boots off—they should fit loosely to come off easily—and throwing them in corner.)*

George *(as he's doing it; savagely)*. I'll show you! There! *(He pulls* Jim *to his feet again.)* All right—I've taken them!

*(*Jim *has apparently lost his socks with the boots. He stands looking down at his bare feet, shivering as though intensely cold.* George *shoves the trumpet back into* Jim's *hands.)*

George. Listen to me. You have to know what you have in your hand. That trumpet? *(*Jim *just stands, holding it.)* The special thing about it—it belonged to John Philip Sousa! And I'm trading it to you—

for your boots. It's yours, Jim. John Philip Sousa's trumpet! It's worth hundreds of dollars, maybe thousands—

Jim *(in a tight voice)*. I don't want—

George. It's better than boots. You can learn to play it. You're somebody, Jim. You're the boy with John Philip Sousa's trumpet.

(They stand facing each other for a moment. The energy goes out of George. *He expels a breath.)*

George *(subdued)*. I'll drive you home. I won't say a word about tonight. *(crossing to apparent light switch)* I better turn these lights out.

Jim. Can I have my boots?

George. No. I don't think they're good for you.

(Apparently he turns off the lights, and for a moment the stage is dark. Then the industrial sound of bulldozers, if used, comes on again and so do the stage lights, generally revealing George *and* Bert *eating breakfast again, and* Newt *standing at downstage right.)*

Newt. The next morning the waddling, clanking muddy machines were making the vision of Bert Quinn true. They were smoothing off the place where the hill had been behind the restaurant.

Bert. Eating out two mornings in a row? Something wrong at home?

George. My wife's still visiting relatives.

Bert *(winking)*. While the cat's away—

Words to Know and Use | **subdued** (səb dōōd´) *adj.* calmed down **subdue** *v.*

415

George. When the cat's away, this mouse gets hungry.

(Jim *is coming on mopping as before, except now he wears some old gym shoes. The industrial noise, once registered, fades.*)

Bert (*leaning forward*). Is that what got you out of bed in the middle of the night? (*jerks head toward* Jim.) Kid! Go get Mr. Helmholtz his horn.

(Jim *raises his head and looks directly at* George *for an instant, then goes off right again, trailing the mop after him.*)

Newt (*during this*). What upset George—the boy's eyes were again as expressionless as oysters.

Bert (*irritated*). You take away his boots and give him a horn, and I'm not supposed to get curious? I'm not supposed to start asking questions?

George. I was going to—

Bert (*going right on; his voice rising*). I'm not supposed to find out you caught him taking the school apart? And it wasn't the first time.

George. I know, but—

Bert (*interrupting again*). You'd make a lousy crook. You'd leave your baton, sheet music, and your driver's license at the scene of the crime.

George. I don't think about hiding clues.

Bert (*derisively*). You don't think about anything.

George. I just do what I do. The reason I came for breakfast, I wanted to discuss with you about—

Bert (*sharply*). Nothing to discuss.

George (*uneasily*). What do you mean?

Bert. All over with Jim and me. Last night was the payoff.

George. What will you do?

Bert. I'm sending him back where he came from.

George. To another string of foster homes?

Bert. Whatever the experts figure out to do with such a kid.

(*He sits back, relieved that he's said it.* George *takes this in, and he's very concerned.*)

George (*a decision*). You can't.

Bert (*almost laughter*). I can.

George. But that will be the end of him.

Bert. Why?

George (*strong*). Because he can't stand to be thrown away like that one more time.

Bert (*getting up angrily*). Him? He can't feel anything. I can't help him—I can't hurt him.

(Jim *is coming on right, impassively holding the trumpet.*)

Bert. There isn't a nerve or feeling in him.

George. A bundle of scar tissue.

Bert (*aware of him*). Kid—give back the horn.

(Jim *puts the trumpet on the table.*)

George. No, Jim. (*forcing a smile*) It's yours.

Bert. He doesn't want it. Take it while you got the chance.

George (*continuing, to* Jim). I gave it to you.

Bert. All he'll do is swap it for a knife or a pack of cigarettes.

George (*without turning to* Bert). He doesn't know what it is yet. It takes awhile to find out.

Bert. Is it any good?

George. Any good? (*incredulous*) It belonged to John Philip Sousa.

Bert. Who?

George (*getting up uncertainly, his voice hushed with emotion*). Who was John Philip Sousa? (George *picks up the trumpet, utterly inarticulate.*)

Newt. The subject was too big, and George was too exhausted to cover it.

(*As* Bert *and* Jim *watch, each in his way bewildered,* George *kisses the cold mouthpiece and fingers the valves professionally.*)

Newt (*during this*). There was nothing George could say or show them. They were deaf to him, and blind. And all George could see was the futility of men and their treasures. He'd thought this greatest treasure he owned could buy a soul for a troubled boy. But his trumpet was worthless.

(*With a cry,* George *suddenly bangs the trumpet on the edge of the table, then again.*)

(*Note: This can be done with a substitute piece of metal so it can't be seen by audience.*)

Bert. Hey! What are ya—(George *is banging trumpet on floor behind table and then apparently stamps on it.*)

Bert. You crazy? Nuts! (George, *totally exhausted, tosses trumpet back onto table.*)

Bert. Ya busted it! Why'dya do that? (George *is shaking his head.*) What's that prove?

George. I—I don't know. I—excuse me—I want to go.

Bert. You're leaving the busted—

George (*sharply*). Yes!

Bert. Why?

George (*welling out of him*). Because life's no good. (George, *utterly miserable, is going off left uncertainly as the others watch.*)

Newt (*quietly*). There was one thing George didn't notice. He didn't notice the eyes of Jim Donnini. Suddenly those eyes filled with pity and with alarm. They became human. They came alive.

(Jim *picks up the trumpet and goes out right.* Bert *looks after him thoughtfully and then follows him off.*)

Newt (*as this happens*). The surprising thing—somehow Bert Quinn caught the change—and something like hope flickered for the first time in Bert's bitterly lonely face. (Newt *is alone now on the stage.*) There were some unanswered questions when the new semester began two weeks later at Lincoln High. (*smiles as he goes off right*) But life was about to deal with them.

(*With his exit, students are crossing downstage to right and left, moving energetically and talking to each other as they go. This can*

Words to Know and Use | **futility** (fy$\overline{oo}$ til′ ə tē) *n.* uselessness

417

REHEARSAL 1949–1950 David Park The Oakland Museum
Gift of the Anonymous Donor program of the American Federation of Arts. Photo by M. Lee Fatherree.

include Grace, Margie, *and* Mrs. Crane, *all dressed as students.)*

Students *(generally).* Is there practice for C Band or not? . . . How do I know? . . .

There was supposed to be an announcement if it was canceled . . . Well, check the bulletin board . . . How can I check when C Band is the first practice? . . .

What's wrong with Mr. Helmholtz? . . . Beats me. You'd think he had a death in his family!

(During this last exchange, George is coming on left, holding his baton. The students, afraid he's overheard—which he has—hurry on off left. George turns to face the podium, his back to the audience, considering what to do.)

(Jim, holding the apparently repaired trumpet, enters right, crossing unseen toward George.)

Jim *(speaking quietly)*. Mr. Helmholtz—Mr. Helmholtz—(George *turns slowly to see him.)* Is this where I come for C Band practice?

George. Yes. Yes, this is the place.

Jim *(indicating horn)*. It was just bent a little. No trouble getting it fixed.

(Happiness is coming back into George, but he speaks carefully.)

George. I see.

Jim *(looking off left front)*. Where should I sit?

George *(beginning to smile)*. For a start—the last seat of the worst trumpet section of the worst band in school.

Jim *(agreeably)*. Right—

George *(cheerfully)*. But with that trumpet—

(Suddenly filling with his old enthusiasm, he hurries up onto the podium.)

George. Let's get started, C Band. What are we waiting for? Maybe you're C Band now, but—

(In a moment, he's stopped by his own happiness and enthusiasm flooding back. Jim *still stands left, watching.)*

George *(speaking front; starting over)*. Think of it this way. Our aim is to make the world sound more beautiful than it did when we came into it. *(with* conviction*)* It can be done. You can do it.

Jim *(bursting out of him)*. How?

George *(pointing off left front)*. You should be sitting in the trumpet section.

Jim *(backing off; as he goes)*. But how?

(Jim has gone off left, now apparently a part of C Band.)

George *(after him)*. Just—love yourself—and make your instrument sing about it. *(He raises his baton.)* A-one, a-two, a-three—

(Down comes the baton, and with this, rousing and triumphant band music—the magnificent band music George hears in his head—fills the theater.)

(The curtain falls.) ❧

Responding to Reading

First Impressions

1. What were your impressions of George Helmholtz?

Second Thoughts

2. Why do you think George is able to help "the kid nobody could handle" when everyone else has failed?

3. Contrast the characters of George Helmholtz and Bert Quinn. Use examples from the play to support your opinions.

    Think about
    - their dreams of success
    - their feelings about Jim

4. Why do you think Jim decides to join the band?

    Think about
    - the effect of George's not reporting Jim for vandalism
    - the effect of George's trading Jim the trumpet for the boots
    - the effect of George's breaking the trumpet

5. Consider the ideas about suitable punishments for vandalism you discussed in Examine What You Know. How effective do you think your course of action would have been for Jim? Explain.

6. What similarities do you see between the characters in this drama and those in the story "Dancer" on pages 32–39?

Broader Connections

7. Activities such as band, art, and sports are usually the first to be eliminated when school budgets are cut. Do you think eliminating these activities is the best or most logical solution to budget problems? Think about the play as well as your own experiences.

Literary Concept: Motivation

The reasons a character acts a certain way are referred to as the **motivation.** To understand a character's behavior, you must think about his or her psychological and cultural background, as well as the circumstances he or she faces. What do you think motivates Jim Donnini to act the way he does? What motivates George Helmholtz?

Writing Options

1. Most schools keep a file on each student—information about the student's grades, test scores, and behavior. As Jim's counselor, write a **summary** of Jim's background and behavior for his school file.

2. Choose one of the following statements. Write an **essay** explaining what the statement means and to what extent you agree or disagree with it.

   • If you smashed up all the schools, we wouldn't have any hope.

   • Think big. That's what vision is.

3. George Helmholtz likes to fill his "corner of the universe"—a place to go and to enjoy until he feels brand-new and happy—with music. In a **personal narrative** describe your own special "corner of the universe."

4. Imagine that the superintendent of your school district has proposed eliminating the school band in order to cut the budget. Write a **letter to the editor,** either defending or rejecting this idea.

Vocabulary Practice

Exercise   Write the letter of the word that is most different in meaning from the other words in the set.

1. (a) improve   (b) supplement   (c) elect   (d) elaborate
2. (a) informally   (b) carefully   (c) casually   (d) simply
3. (a) arrogant   (b) respectful   (c) humble   (d) modest
4. (a) frightening   (b) upsetting   (c) unnerving   (d) calming
5. (a) amusingly   (b) wryly   (c) ironically   (d) quickly
6. (a) wiry   (b) stocky   (c) fat   (d) chubby
7. (a) gaudy   (b) simple   (c) flashy   (d) showy
8. (a) undaunted   (b) confident   (c) fearful   (d) encouraged
9. (a) pursuit   (b) search   (c) vacation   (d) quest
10. (a) disbelieving   (b) doubtful   (c) incredulous   (d) trusting
11. (a) surprised   (b) serious   (c) shocked   (d) aghast
12. (a) repulsive   (b) odd   (c) disgusting   (d) calm
13. (a) excited   (b) subdued   (c) quiet   (d) calm
14. (a) uselessness   (b) hopelessness   (c) concern   (d) futility
15. (a) certainty   (b) intensity   (c) conviction   (d) doubt

> *Words to Know and Use*
>
> aghast
> arrogant
> casually
> conviction
> elaborate
> futility
> gaudy
> incredulous
> quest
> repulsive
> subdued
> undaunted
> unnerving
> wiry
> wryly

Options for Learning

1 • The Kid: 1990s Update With a partner choose one scene of this play. Rewrite the scene, updating the language and situation to make the story seem typical of the 1990s. Then do a dramatic reading of the scene for your class.

2 • Cutouts Find pictures that illustrate the theme of this subunit— "The Struggle to Connect." Your pictures may show struggles between social or ethnic groups, between young and old, between male and female, or between authority and anti-authority. Find at least one picture to represent each selection in this subunit. You might also like to cut out words or phrases related to the subunit theme. Put the pictures and words together as a collage.

3 • Story vs. Play Read the Kurt Vonnegut short story on which this play is based. Create a chart showing the differences between the story and the play. At the bottom of the chart, explain which one you prefer and why.

4 • Name That Tune George Helmholtz hears great music in his head, music that he dreams his band can play. Imagine that you are the director of this drama. Choose the music that George hears. Play a recording of it for your class. Be prepared to lead a discussion of why this music is so good.

 FACT FINDER MUSIC

Name three marches written by the famous U.S. composer John Philip Sousa.

Kurt Vonnegut, Jr.
1922–

In his Indiana high school, Kurt Vonnegut edited the school newspaper, and he enjoyed writing about real events and people. After attending Cornell University and the Carnegie Institute of Technology, Vonnegut served in the U.S. infantry during World War II.

As a prisoner of war in World War II, Vonnegut witnessed the firebombing of Dresden, Germany. His experiences left him with a hatred of war that strongly influenced his writing. Much of his work deals with the large questions of war, peace, and human kindness. Vonnegut often uses humor, poking fun at people, their foibles, and their institutions.

Vonnegut's writing ranges from novels and short stories to screenplays and essays. Much of his early writing was science fiction. His novels, including *Player Piano, Cat's Cradle,* and *Slaughterhouse Five,* have sold millions of copies and have been translated into numerous foreign languages.

WRITER'S WORKSHOP

PERSUASIVE WRITING

Many people find it difficult to connect with others. Why? No two people are alike. We all have different experiences, and more important, we all have different opinions. **Persuasive writing,** which attempts to convince people to follow a particular idea, goal, or course of action, has long been a way to confront our differences of opinion. The **editorial,** a statement of opinion in a newspaper or other medium, is one important form of persuasive writing. In this workshop you will write an editorial that could be published in a school newspaper. You will use facts, quotes, and examples to persuade readers to see an issue your way.

USE PERSUASIVE
WRITING IN
speeches
advertisements
book reviews
debates
letters to the editor
editorials

Here is one writer's PASSkey
to this assignment.

GUIDED ASSIGNMENT:
EDITORIAL

Write an editorial in which you take a stand on an important issue in your school or community. Support your argument with persuasive reasons.

P URPOSE: To persuade
A UDIENCE: The school community
S UBJECT: A significant issue
S TRUCTURE: An editorial

Save Our Sports and Clubs
by Diana Gaudiani

You may be holding the final edition of our school newspaper. Last week the School Board discussed cutting all extracurricular activities. Board President Hines said there is not enough money for all the programs we have and something has to give. If the School Board decides to go ahead with the cuts, you can say goodbye to all sports and clubs at our school. We can't let this happen. Here are the reasons why.

First, the after-school sports and clubs here at Franklin Junior High are very popular. According to our principal,

STUDENT MODEL
The writer uses a dramatic opening sentence.

The writer clearly defines the issue and states her position.

The first of three reasons is explained.

A statistic and a quote are given to support the writer's point.

78 percent of our students participate in these programs. Eighth-grade basketball player Jerry Viti says, "I really look forward to practice at the end of the day. I can't imagine our school without sports teams."

A second reason is given and then supported with a personal anecdote.

Many people think that the extracurricular programs are not as important as regular school subjects. I disagree. The values that sports and clubs teach are tremendously important. Discipline and pride are just two of these values. On the newspaper staff we often work very long hours. We push each other, we rely on each other, and we get a lot of satisfaction from the final product. Everything I've learned about teamwork, I've learned from working on the school paper.

The writer uses a quote from the opposition to lead into the third reason.

Board member Mark Turner said that "there isn't enough money to support these clubs." The money CAN be found. I'm no expert, but if we pool our ideas and efforts, we can find ways to get the money. Cut expenses in school maintenance. How? Ask each student to work one afternoon a month cleaning classrooms and hallways. When asked about such a proposal,

The writer offers solutions to the opposition's major argument (no money).

seventh grader Becky Romano said, "I would gladly help around the school if it would save our clubs. I'm great with a paintbrush." The School Board claims we need $50,000 to keep our after-school programs going. Why not get everyone involved in a giant fund-raiser?

In her conclusion, the writer restates her position and calls for specific action.

School Board members, don't take our sports and clubs away. There have to be other ways to solve our money problem. Students, the next School Board meeting is Thursday at 7 P.M. in the school cafeteria. Go to it. Encourage your parents to go. Voice your opinions. Let the board know we want to--we HAVE to--save our sports and clubs.

Now it's time to begin your own editorial.

Prewrite and Explore

1 **Listen for people disagreeing**   Try going to places in your school where students gather and talk. What issues do students complain or argue about? If this search doesn't yield much, visit gathering places in your town, keeping your eyes and ears open. Bring a notebook or tape recorder. Bring a classmate along. Each of you may see possibilities the other missed.

2 **Select and define an issue**   If you can answer *yes* to the following three questions, then you have a topic and you are ready to gather the material that will support your view:

Can you clearly express your position?
Can you list three strong reasons to support your opinion?
Do you feel strongly about your position?

◀ WRITER'S CHOICE ....
Think about the selections in this unit. One might give you an idea for an editorial. The editorial pages of your local newspaper may also give you ideas.

◀ TIP ....
Use the following statement to help: "On the issue of _____ , I believe _____."

◀ ASK FOR HELP ....
Find a classmate who has an opposing opinion on your issue. Have this person help you develop the *Con* side of your notes.

◀ STUDENT MODEL ....

GATHERING INFORMATION

Gather information that will support at least three reasons. Explanation, quotes, statistics, examples, and anecdotes are the ingredients that support reasons. Consider the other side of the argument. What can you say to counter the points the other side would raise? A chart can help you organize your information.

Position: <u>The extracurricular programs should be saved. They are an essential part of our school.</u>

Pro	Con
1.78% participate. Use Jerry's quote.	1.Sports and clubs--not as important as regular school subjects.
2.Sports, clubs teach discipline, hard work. My newspaper experience.	
3.Counterargument: Find other ways to cut expenses. Help with maintenance. Use Becky's quote. Have big fundraiser.	2.$50,000 must be cut from budget. No more places to cut, except extracurricular programs.
4.Call to action: Come to Board Meeting.	

◀ Notice Diana's counterargument.

Draft and Discover

1 **Consider the shape**   Look over your material and think about how you will organize it. Most editorials have three parts: a beginning, which clearly states the issue and the writer's stand; a middle, which thoroughly explains reasons for the position; and a conclusion, which restates the opinion and may call for a specific action.

2 **Begin your draft**   Working from your notes, get down your ideas steadily, without worrying about perfection. Remind yourself, this is only a Draft, not your Final Product. State your case simply, clearly, and forcefully.

3 **Make decisions**   As you write and think about what to say next, you will make many decisions. For instance, how many of your notes will you use? The rule here is—Keep the strong material and forget the weak.

COMPUTER TIP

If your computer has a split-screen function, use this function to incorporate your prewriting notes into your draft.

WRITER'S CHOICE

Another decision you make is how to order your arguments. Some writers save their best point for last, while others present their best first.

COMPUTER TIP

Need stronger wording? Try using the thesaurus function in your software to search for more vivid and precise words.

Revise Your Writing

1 **Check your arguments**   As you revise your draft, look carefully at how you explained and supported each of your reasons. Think about your audience. Are your explanations persuasive? Could a statistic add more strength to an argument? Could you insert a quote to make your point livelier and more personal?

Check for faulty reasoning. A common mistake is **circular reasoning,** trying to prove a statement simply by repeating it in different words.

Be precise. The more precise your wording, the more believable your arguments. Sentences with phrases such as *all people* are often inaccurate. The use of limiting words such as *some* or *most* can help you be more accurate.

2 **Throw out deadwood**   Read your draft to see if there are any unnecessary words or phrases that can be cut. Beginning writers of persuasion often pepper their work with *I feel* and *I believe.* These phrases are usually unnecessary. Your readers already know that you are giving your opinions.

3 **Form an editorial board**   Gather a small group of your classmates and review one another's drafts. Consider the revision questions on the next page.

Proofread

Correct errors in grammar. Pay attention to subject-verb agreement.

THE EDITOR'S EYE: SUBJECT-VERB AGREEMENT

Use singular verbs when your subject is singular.
Use plural verbs when your subject is plural.

If you are unsure of whether to use a singular or plural verb, find the subject. Is it singular or plural?

Problem Here <u>is</u> the reasons why.
Revised Here <u>are</u> the reasons why.

<u>Reasons</u> is the subject. It is plural; therefore, use a plural verb.

NEED MORE HELP?

See the Language Workshop that follows (pages 428–430) and pages 798–799 of the Language Handbook.

Publish and Present

Create an Editorial Review   First, organize small groups to evaluate the editorials of their members. Next, decide which editorial from the group should be included in the review. Choose three class members to serve as "managing editors." They will organize the editorials, plan the layout, and assign tasks, such as typing the final copies. Post the review on a school bulletin board.

Reflect on Your Writing

Write brief answers to the questions below.

◀ FOR YOUR PORTFOLIO

1. Did your position change as a result of writing this editorial?
2. Were you comfortable trying to persuade others of your views?

LANGUAGE
WORKSHOP

SUBJECT-VERB AGREEMENT

REMINDER
1. The pronoun *you* can be singular or plural, but it always takes a plural verb.
2. Except in *I am* and *I was,* the pronoun *I* always takes a plural verb.

A verb and its subject must agree in number.

Using a singular verb with a plural subject is like singing off-key. Neither the sentence nor the song will sound right.

A word's **number** simply refers to whether it is singular or plural. A word is **singular** if it refers to one thing and **plural** if it refers to more than one thing. If the subject of a sentence is singular, then its verb must be singular. If the subject is plural, then its verb must be plural.

> The <u>American</u> (singular) <u>learns</u> (singular) about Japanese customs.

> <u>Americans</u> (plural) <u>learn</u> (plural) about Japanese customs.

Usually, your ear will tell you whether the subject and verb in a sentence agree. However, in certain sentences you may be unsure about whether to use a singular or plural verb.

Problems with Phrases

The object of a preposition cannot be the subject of a sentence.

Prepositional phrases that come between the subject and the verb present a common stumbling block to subject-verb agreement. Remember, the subject is never part of such a phrase. To check the subject-verb agreement in this kind of sentence, use the "drop-out" strategy: Drop the phrase out of the sentence, and your ear will usually tell you the correct verb.

TIP
Need help identifying phrases that come between the subject and verb? Look for commas coming before and after a group of words. This punctuation suggests that the words are not part of the subject.

> The <u>proposal</u> from the School Board members <u>makes</u> us angry. (<u>Proposal,</u> not <u>members,</u> is the subject.)

> <u>Sports</u> at Franklin Junior High <u>are</u> very popular. (<u>Sports,</u> not <u>Franklin Junior High,</u> is the subject.)

Phrases that are set off by commas and begin with words such as *with, along with, together with, including, as well as,* or *in addition to* are often not part of the subject.

The School Board <u>president,</u> along with the other Board members, <u>makes</u> the final decision on the budget cuts.

All <u>sports,</u> including basketball, <u>are</u> on the list of cuts.

Exercise 1   Concept Check   On your paper, write the verb that agrees with the subject.

1. Juvenile delinquency (exists, exist) in all countries.
2. Juvenile delinquency (is, are) not a new problem; street gangs existed in the United States in the 1800s.
3. Most states (defines, define) juveniles as people less than eighteen years old.
4. Burglary, as well as arson, (is, are) a common form of delinquency.
5. One out of three thefts (is, are) committed by juveniles.
6. An increasing number of girls (is, are) involved in juvenile delinquency.
7. Some youths (commits, commit) crimes to try to escape poverty or boredom.
8. What (is, are) the solutions to juvenile delinquency?
9. A treatment program, including counseling and work experience, sometimes (helps, help) delinquents stay out of trouble.
10. Recreation centers, as well as clubs, (provides, provide) positive activities for youths.

Verbs with Compound Subjects

A compound subject is two or more subjects used with the same verb.
Compound subjects joined by the word *and* are plural and take a plural verb.

NEED MORE HELP?

For help in understanding compound subjects containing pronouns, see "Using Pronouns Correctly," the Language Workshop on pages 61–63.

<u>Relleno</u> and <u>pozole</u> <u>were</u> the favorite foods on cultural day.

If the compound subject is joined by the conjunction *or* or *nor,* the verb agrees with the subject nearer to the verb.

Neither <u>Mrs. Teubbes</u> nor the other full-time <u>teachers</u> <u>understand</u> Spanish.

Either the <u>students</u> or <u>Mrs. Archunde</u> <u>writes</u> the new Spanish words on the blackboard.

Exercise 2   Concept Check   Some of the following sentences contain errors in subject-verb agreement. On your paper, rewrite those sentences correctly. If a sentence has no error, write *Correct.*

1. Next Thursday and Friday are the days for our Ethnocenter Festival.
2. Liz and Carmen are the organizers of the Festival.
3. Neither Mrs. Robinson nor the other teachers knows what to expect.
4. Can you believe that Ralph and Alex is coming in lederhosen?
5. Wilson and his sister have some incredible ivory figures from Africa.
6. Either Britt or her sisters is making Swedish pancakes.
7. Hector and Sonia is bringing blue *atole* and a piñata.
8. Neither Hector nor his parents likes *atole,* but other people love it.
9. Rich and Sam are bringing in a cricket bat and a giant model of the Big Ben clock tower in London.
10. Either the school newsletter or a special memo is informing the parents of the Ethnocenter Festival.

PROOFREADING TIP

Try listening for errors in subject-verb agreement. Working alone or with a peer, read passages aloud. You may find that you hear errors that you missed when reading silently.

▶ **Exercise 3   Proofreading Skill**   Rewrite the following paragraph, correcting any errors in subject-verb agreement.

My older sister and I are in Japan for the first time. Either my sister or my parents has arranged a visit with relatives. My Uncle Noboru and my Aunt Aki welcomes us politely. Before dinner he gives a speech about how happy he is to see us, but then no one talks. I decide to break the ice. I give my opinion on Japan's high prices. Neither my uncle nor my other relatives says a word. One of the rules of conversation have been broken, but I don't really understand what I did wrong.

Exercise 4   Revising Your Writing

1. Reread the editorial you wrote for the Writer's Workshop on pages 423–427.
2. Look for errors in subject-verb agreement, particularly in sentences containing prepositional phrases or compound subjects.
3. Correct any errors in subject-verb agreement that you find.
4. Remember to check for errors in subject-verb agreement each time you proofread your work.

LANGUAGE HANDBOOK

For review and practice: Section 7, Subject-Verb Agreement, pages 798–801.

READER'S WORKSHOP

FACT AND OPINION

When you write persuasively, you use both fact and opinion. Statements of fact support opinions; statements of opinion introduce facts. To be effective, you must know the difference between them.

A **fact** is a statement that can be proved. An **opinion** cannot be proved.

Fact   On Saturday our basketball team beat Churchill High School. (A local newspaper could give proof of this statement.)

Opinion   Having sports competitions between teams from different areas of the city is the best way to fight juvenile delinquency. (This statement cannot be proved. It can, however, be supported by facts.)

How can you check to see whether a statement is a fact or an opinion? Here are some guidelines for facts:

- Can you and others prove the statement through direct observation?
- Can the statement be verified by reliable reference sources?
- Can the statement be verified by an expert?

If you answer yes to any of these guidelines, your statement is probably a fact; if you answer no to all three guidelines, then it is probably an opinion.

Exercise   Mark those statements which are fact with an *F* and those statements which are opinion with an *O*. If a statement is a fact, tell how you could prove the statement.

1. The best sport at our school is basketball.
2. More spectators come to our basketball games than to any other school sport.
3. Our team has a six-foot-ten-inch center named Abdul.
4. He is awesome.
5. The sportswriters voted Abdul our conference's Most Valuable Player.
6. I have the top free-throw percentage on the team.
7. Last year our team won the City Tournament by a score of 51 to 50.
8. The players on the losing team were awfully poor sports.
9. After the game our fans came running onto the court to celebrate.
10. That was the most wonderful game ever played!

IN OTHER CLASSES

When you write reports in science and social studies, you will give primarily factual information. Use the fact questions to judge the information you give on these kinds of reports.

JUDGMENT WORDS

One way to identify opinions is to look for **judgment words.** These words express personal feelings.

terrible	useful
fantastic	brilliant
ridiculous	inspiring
difficult	friendly
better	important

What judgment words do you see in the exercise?

SECRETS AND SACRIFICES

Listen, do you want to know a secret? Have you ever been tempted to tell someone else a secret? Secrets sometimes arouse powerful emotions. You have probably discovered how difficult it is to keep a secret.

Keeping or telling a secret sometimes involves personal sacrifice. Have you ever sacrificed anything that was important to you?

"Secrets and Sacrifices" refers to personal choices involving matters of the heart. In the following selections you will read about characters who experience the effects of keeping secrets and making sacrifices.

Fiction

The Gift of the Magi

O. HENRY

Examine What You Know

Think about gifts you've given and received. What has made some of them special? Create a chart of the most unforgettable gifts you have given or received. The chart below shows some categories that you may want to include. Compare your gifts with those in this story.

Most Unforgettable Gifts				
Most Meaningful	Most Humorous	Most Expensive	Most Inappropriate	Most Valuable

Expand Your Knowledge

O. Henry refers to the magi in this story. According to Christian tradition, the **magi** were three wise men or kings named Balthasar, Melchior, and Gaspar. They traveled from the East to Bethlehem, guided by a miraculous star, to pay homage to the infant Jesus. The gifts the magi gave to Jesus were gold, frankincense, and myrrh.

Enrich Your Reading

Context Clues This story contains words that you may not recognize immediately. You can find the meanings of some of these words in footnotes. However, you will have to figure out the meanings of others yourself. You can use a dictionary, or you can use **context clues,** hints in the words or sentences surrounding an unknown word. For example, you may not know the meaning of the word *sterling,* but when you read that a character in the story wants to give a gift that is "fine and rare and sterling," you probably can figure out that *sterling* means "of high quality" or "excellent."

■ *Author biography on Extend page*

The Gift of the Magi

O. HENRY

One dollar and eighty-seven cents. That was all. And sixty cents of it was in pennies. Pennies saved one and two at a time by bulldozing the grocer and the vegetable man and the butcher until one's cheeks burned with the silent imputation of parsimony[1] that such close dealing implied. Three times Della counted it. One dollar and eighty-seven cents. And the next day would be Christmas.

There was clearly nothing to do but flop down on the shabby little couch and howl. So Della did it. Which instigates the moral reflection that life is made up of sobs, sniffles, and smiles, with sniffles predominating.

While the mistress of the home is gradually subsiding from the first stage to the second, take a look at the home. A furnished flat at $8 per week. It did not exactly beggar description, but it certainly had that word on the lookout for the mendicancy squad.[2]

In the vestibule below was a letter box into which no letter would go, and an electric button from which no mortal finger could coax a ring. Also appertaining[3] thereunto was a card bearing the name "Mr. James Dillingham Young."

The "Dillingham" had been flung to the breeze during a former period of prosperity when its possessor was being paid $30 per week. Now, when the income was shrunk to $20, the letters of "Dillingham" looked blurred, as though they were thinking seriously of contracting to a modest and unassuming D. But whenever Mr. James Dillingham Young came home and reached his flat above he was called "Jim" and greatly hugged by Mrs. James Dillingham Young, already introduced to you as Della. Which is all very good.

Della finished her cry and attended to her cheeks with the powder rag. She stood by the window and looked out dully at a gray cat walking a gray fence in a gray backyard. Tomorrow would be Christmas Day, and she had only $1.87 with which to buy Jim a present. She had been saving every penny she could for months, with this result. Twenty dollars a week doesn't go far. Expenses had been greater than she had calculated. They always are. Only $1.87 to buy a present for Jim. Her Jim. Many a happy

---

1. imputation of parsimony (im pyōō tā′ shən, pär′ sə mō′ nē): suggestion of being stingy.

2. mendicancy squad (men′ di kən sē): a police unit assigned to arrest beggars. The author here is making a play on the word *beggar,* used earlier to mean "make inadequate."

3. appertaining (ap′ ər tān′ iŋ): connected; attached.

Words to Know and Use

instigate (in′ stə gāt′) *v.* to stir up; provoke
predominating (prē däm′ ə nāt′ iŋ) *adj.* most important or frequent **predominate** *v.*
subside (səb sīd′) *v.* to lessen in activity or intensity

hour she had spent planning for something nice for him. Something fine and rare and sterling–something just a little bit near to being worthy of the honor of being owned by Jim.

There was a pier glass[4] between the windows of the room. Perhaps you have seen a pier glass in an $8 flat. A very thin and very agile person may, by observing his reflection in a rapid sequence of longitudinal strips, obtain a fairly accurate conception of his looks. Della, being slender, had mastered the art.

Suddenly she whirled from the window and stood before the glass. Her eyes were shining brilliantly, but her face had lost its color within twenty seconds. Rapidly she pulled down her hair and let it fall to its full length.

Now, there were two possessions of the James Dillingham Youngs in which they both took a mighty pride. One was Jim's gold watch that had been his father's and his grandfather's. The other was Della's hair. Had the Queen of Sheba[5] lived in the flat across the air shaft, Della would have let her hair hang

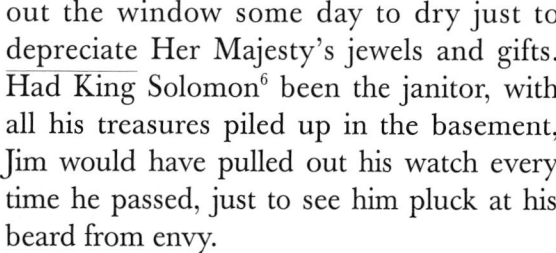

out the window some day to dry just to depreciate Her Majesty's jewels and gifts. Had King Solomon[6] been the janitor, with all his treasures piled up in the basement, Jim would have pulled out his watch every time he passed, just to see him pluck at his beard from envy.

So now Della's beautiful hair fell about her rippling and shining like a cascade of brown waters. It reached below her knee and made itself almost a garment for her. And then she did it up again nervously and quickly. Once she faltered for a minute and stood still while a tear or two splashed on the worn red carpet.

On went her old brown jacket; on went her old brown hat. With a whirl of skirts and with the brilliant sparkle still in her eyes, she fluttered out the door and down the stairs to the street.

Where she stopped the sign read: "Mme. Sofronie. Hair Goods of All Kinds." One flight up Della ran, and collected herself, panting. Madame, large, too white, chilly, hardly looked the "Sofronie."

"Will you buy my hair?" asked Della.

"I buy hair," said Madame. "Take yer hat off and let's have a sight at the looks of it."

Down rippled the brown cascade.

"Twenty dollars," said Madame, lifting the mass with a practiced hand.

---

4. **pier glass:** a narrow mirror set in a wall section between windows.
5. **Queen of Sheba:** in the Bible, a rich Arabian queen.
6. **King Solomon:** a Biblical king of Israel, known for his wisdom and wealth.

GIRL COMBING HER HAIR   1909   William McGregor Paxton   Private Collection   Courtesy, Gallery Vose, Boston.

"Give it to me quick," said Della.

Oh, and the next two hours tripped by on rosy wings. Forget the hashed metaphor. She was ransacking the stores for Jim's present.

She found it at last. It surely had been made for Jim and no one else. There was no other like it in any of the stores, and she had turned all of them inside out. It was a platinum fob chain[7] simple and chaste in design, properly proclaiming its value by substance alone and not by meretricious ornamentation[8]—as all good things should do. It was even worthy of The Watch. As soon as she saw it she knew that it must be Jim's. It was like him. Quietness and value—the description applied to both. Twenty-one dollars they took from her for it, and she hurried home with the eighty-seven cents. With that chain on his watch Jim might be properly anxious about the time in any company. Grand as the watch was, he sometimes looked at it on the sly on account of the old leather strap that he used in place of a chain.

When Della reached home her intoxication gave way a little to prudence and reason. She got out her curling irons and lighted the gas and went to work repairing the ravages made by generosity added to love. Which is always a tremendous task, dear friends—a mammoth task.

Within forty minutes her head was covered with tiny, close-lying curls that made her look wonderfully like a truant schoolboy. She looked at her reflection in the mirror long, carefully, and critically.

"If Jim doesn't kill me," she said to herself, "before he takes a second look at me, he'll say I look like a Coney Island chorus girl. But what could I do—oh! what could I do with a dollar and eighty-seven cents?"

At seven o'clock the coffee was made and the frying pan was on the back of the stove hot and ready to cook the chops.

Jim was never late. Della doubled the fob chain in her hand and sat on the corner of the table near the door that he always entered. Then she heard his step on the stair away down on the first flight, and she turned white for just a moment. She had a habit of saying little silent prayers about the simplest everyday things, and now she whispered: "Please God, make him think I am still pretty."

The door opened and Jim stepped in and closed it. He looked thin and very serious. Poor fellow, he was only twenty-two—and to be burdened with a family! He needed a new overcoat and he was without gloves.

Jim stopped inside the door, as immovable as a setter at the scent of quail. His eyes were fixed upon Della, and there was an expression in them that she could not read, and it terrified her. It was not anger, nor surprise, nor disapproval, nor horror, nor any of the sentiments that she had been prepared for. He simply stared at her fixedly with that peculiar expression on his face.

Della wriggled off the table and went for him.

---

7. **fob chain:** a short chain for a pocket watch.
8. **meretricious ornamentation** (mer′ ə trish′ əs): cheap, gaudy decoration.

"Jim, darling," she cried, "don't look at me that way. I had my hair cut off and sold it because I couldn't have lived through Christmas without giving you a present. It'll grow out again—you won't mind, will you? I just had to do it. My hair grows awfully fast. Say 'Merry Christmas,' Jim, and let's be happy. You don't know what a nice—what a beautiful, nice gift I've got for you."

"You've cut off your hair?" asked Jim, laboriously, as if he had not arrived at that patent fact yet even after the hardest mental labor.

"Cut it off and sold it," said Della. "Don't you like me just as well, anyhow? I'm me without my hair, ain't I?"

Jim looked about the room curiously.

"You say your hair is gone?" he said, with an air almost of idiocy.

"You needn't look for it," said Della. "It's sold, I tell you—sold and gone, too. It's Christmas Eve, boy. Be good to me, for it went for you. Maybe the hairs of my head were numbered," she went on with a sudden serious sweetness, "but nobody could ever count my love for you. Shall I put the chops on, Jim?"

Out of his trance Jim seemed quickly to wake. He enfolded his Della. For ten seconds let us regard with <u>discreet</u> scrutiny[9] some <u>inconsequential</u> object in the other direction. Eight dollars a week or a million a year—what is the difference? A mathematician or a wit would give you the wrong answer. The magi[10] brought valuable gifts, but that was not among them. This dark <u>assertion</u> will be <u>illuminated</u> later on.

Jim drew a package from his overcoat pocket and threw it upon the table.

"Don't make any mistake, Dell," he said, "about me. I don't think there's anything in the way of a haircut or a shave or a shampoo that could make me like my girl any less. But if you'll unwrap that package you may see why you had me going awhile at first."

White fingers and nimble tore at the string and paper. And then an <u>ecstatic</u> scream of joy; and then, alas! a quick feminine change to hysterical tears and wails, necessitating the immediate employment of all the comforting powers of the lord of the flat.

For there lay The Combs—the set of combs, side and back, that Della had worshipped for long in a Broadway window. Beautiful combs, pure tortoise shell, with jeweled rims—just the shade to wear in the beautiful vanished hair. They were expensive combs, she knew, and her heart had simply craved and yearned over them without the least hope of possession. And now, they were hers, but the tresses[11] that should have adorned the coveted adornments[12] were gone.

But she hugged them to her bosom, and at length she was able to look up with dim eyes and a smile and say: "My hair grows so fast, Jim!"

---

9. **scrutiny** (skr o͞ot′ 'n ē): careful observation.

10. **magi** (mā′ jī′): the wise men from the East who brought gifts to the infant Jesus.

11. **tresses**: a woman's long, unbound hair.

12. **adornments**: ornaments of beauty and splendor.

And then Della leaped up like a little singed cat and cried, "Oh, oh!"

Jim had not yet seen his beautiful present. She held it out to him eagerly upon her open palm. The dull precious metal seemed to flash with a reflection of her bright and ardent spirit.

"Isn't it a dandy, Jim? I hunted all over town to find it. You'll have to look at the time a hundred times a day now. Give me your watch. I want to see how it looks on it."

Instead of obeying, Jim tumbled down on the couch and put his hands under the back of his head and smiled.

"Dell," said he, "let's put our Christmas presents away and keep 'em awhile. They're too nice to use just at present. I sold the watch to get the money to buy your combs. And now suppose you put the chops on."

The magi, as you know, were wise men—wonderfully wise men—who brought gifts to the Babe in the manger. They invented the art of giving Christmas presents. Being wise, their gifts were no doubt wise ones, possibly bearing the privilege of exchange in case of duplication. And here I have lamely related to you the uneventful chronicle of two foolish children in a flat who most unwisely sacrificed for each other the greatest treasures of their house. But in a last word to the wise of these days let it be said that of all who give gifts these two were the wisest. Of all who give and receive gifts, such as they are wisest. Everywhere they are wisest. They are the magi. ❧

Responding to Reading

First Impressions

1. What were your thoughts about Della and Jim as you finished reading? Write them down in your journal or on a sheet of paper.

Second Thoughts

2. Reread the last paragraph. Why do you think O. Henry compares Della and Jim to the magi?

3. O. Henry calls Della and Jim both foolish and wise. Do you agree with this description? Why or why not?

4. Describe Della and Jim's relationship.

   Think about
   • the way they greet each other every day
   • the sacrifices each character makes
   • their reactions at the end of the story
   • the relationships of other couples you know or have read about

5. Think about what Della and Jim did for each other. Would you do something similar for a person you loved? Why or why not?

Broader Connections

6. For most people, exchanging gifts is a very different experience from the one that Della and Jim had. In small groups discuss your attitudes toward giving and receiving gifts. Do people expect too much? Do they spend too much? Use your own experiences with gifts, like the ones you listed in Examine What You Know, as examples of the kinds of gifts that matter to you

Literary Concept: Irony

Irony—a contrast between what is thought or said and what actually exists or happens—sometimes involves the upsetting of expectations. A character thinks one thing will happen, but something completely different takes place instead. One of the major ironies of this story is that Della sells her treasured hair to buy Jim's gift, but his gift to her is a set of combs for her hair. What is the other major irony of the story?

Writing Options

1. Review the chart you made about gifts. Then write a **personal essay** about a meaningful gift that you have given or received. Explain why the gift was special.

2. What might Jim have been thinking as he stood staring at Della's haircut? Write an **interior monologue** that expresses his point of view.

3. Write a **magazine article,** describing some gifts that you could buy today for $1.87.

4. If Jim took another cut in salary, he and Della might have to sell the fob chain and the set of combs. Write a **persuasive ad** for Jim and Della to put in a local newspaper telling what is for sale and the ways in which the items are valuable.

Vocabulary Practice

Exercise   On a sheet of paper, write the letter of the word that is most unlike the other words in the set.

1. (a) stop   (b) stir   (c) urge   (d) instigate
2. (a) predominating   (b) dominating   (c) ruling   (d) missing
3. (a) increase   (b) subside   (c) lessen   (d) decline
4. (a) limber   (b) agile   (c) clumsy   (d) flexible
5. (a) decrease   (b) praise   (c) depreciate   (d) lessen
6. (a) substance   (b) gift   (c) essence   (d) material
7. (a) stream   (b) river   (c) brook   (d) cascade
8. (a) spotless   (b) chaste   (c) pure   (d) dirty
9. (a) approvingly   (b) intently   (c) steadily   (d) fixedly
10. (a) discreet   (b) careful   (c) cautious   (d) careless
11. (a) important   (b) vital   (c) inconsequential   (d) significant
12. (a) assertion   (b) declaration   (c) denial   (d) statement
13. (a) darken   (b) illuminate   (c) obscure   (d) dim
14. (a) sad   (b) thrilled   (c) ecstatic   (d) delighted
15. (a) history   (b) poem   (c) chronicle   (d) report

Words to Know and Use

agile
assertion
cascade
chaste
chronicle
depreciate
discreet
ecstatic
fixedly
illuminate
inconsequential
instigate
predominating
subside
substance

Options for Learning

1 • A Gift for You People in different cultures exchange gifts for particular reasons. Research a culture of your choice and tell when and why the people give gifts and what kinds of gifts they give.

2 • Before and After Draw pictures of Della before and after her haircut. Base your pictures on the descriptions O. Henry provides in the story.

3 • A Slice of the Pie If you received an allowance of twenty dollars a week, how would you budget it? How much of it would you spend on clothes, food, entertainment, and gifts? How much would you save? Draw a pie chart that allots a certain amount of money for each purpose.

4 • Tell It Like It Is Make a comic strip that tells the whole story of or illustrates a particular scene from "The Gift of the Magi."

 FACT FINDER CONSUMER EDUCATION

How much does a plain platinum fob chain cost today?

O. Henry
1862–1910

William Sydney Porter wrote nearly three hundred short stories under the pen name O. Henry. Porter lived a life that was an exciting story in itself.

When he was twenty, Porter moved to Texas from Greensboro, North Carolina. In Texas he tried various jobs. At different times, he worked as a ranch hand, a newspaper publisher and columnist, and a bank teller.

While working as a teller, Porter was accused of stealing funds. To avoid trial he fled to Central America. When he sneaked back to Austin, Texas, to visit his dying wife, however, Porter was captured and had to spend three years in jail.

Porter began to write short stories in prison. Like "The Gift of the Magi," many of his stories contain ironic humor and surprise endings. After he was released from prison, Porter moved to New York City, where he worked as a newspaper columnist and fiction writer.

Fiction

*M*other and *D*aughter

GARY SOTO

*E*xamine *What You Know*

How are decisions about spending money made in your family? Consider the following scenario:

> A son or daughter wants something special, such as some nice clothes or a new bike. The son or daughter tries to persuade a parent or guardian to buy the item. "All my friends have this," is one argument. The parent or guardian cannot afford to spend money on this item right now for several reasons and is inclined to say no.

With a partner, role-play this situation. Assume the roles of the son or daughter and the parent or guardian, and discuss the problem until you reach a suitable decision. Be prepared to explain your decision to the class.

*E*xpand *Your Knowledge*

In this story the Moreno family is, in some ways, like some other Mexican-American families you might know. Mrs. Moreno tells stories of her childhood, when she and her parents left Mexico. Now in the United States, she retains some of the old ways, such as speaking her native Spanish language at home and preparing Mexican dishes. Like many immigrants, Mrs. Moreno places a great value on saving money for the future and making sure her child gets a good education. The Morenos do not have much money; as in many families, this lack of money can cause problems.

*E*nrich *Your Reading*

Problem Solving   A story plot is often based on a **conflict,** or problem, that the characters face. By the end of the story, the characters often arrive at some kind of solution to the conflict. As you read "Mother and Daughter," think about the problem that the Morenos encounter, their attempt to resolve it, and their ultimate solution.

■ *Author biography in Reader's Handbook*

Mother and Daughter

GARY SOTO

Yollie's mother, Mrs. Moreno, was a large woman who wore a muumuu[1] and butterfly-shaped glasses. She liked to water her lawn in the evening and wave at low-riders, who would stare at her behind their smoky sunglasses and laugh. Now and then a low-rider from Belmont Avenue would make his car jump and shout "*Mamacita*!" But most of the time they just stared and wondered how she got so large.

Mrs. Moreno had a strange sense of humor. Once, Yollie and her mother were watching a late-night movie called *They Came to Look*. It was about creatures from the underworld who had climbed through molten lava to walk the earth. But Yollie, who had played soccer all day with the kids next door, was too tired to be scared. Her eyes closed but sprang open when her mother screamed, "Look, Yollie! Oh, you missed a scary part. The guy's face was all ugly!"

But Yollie couldn't keep her eyes open. They fell shut again and stayed shut, even when her mother screamed and slammed a heavy palm on the arm of her chair.

"Mom, wake me up when the movie's over so I can go to bed," mumbled Yollie.

"OK, Yollie, I wake you," said her mother through a mouthful of popcorn.

But after the movie ended, instead of waking her daughter, Mrs. Moreno laughed under her breath, turned the TV and lights off, and tiptoed to bed. Yollie woke up in the middle of the night and didn't know where she was. For a moment she thought she was dead. Maybe something from the underworld had lifted her from her house and carried her into the earth's belly. She blinked her sleepy eyes, looked around at the darkness, and called, "Mom? Mom, where are you?" But there was no answer, just the throbbing hum of the refrigerator.

Finally, Yollie's grogginess cleared, and she realized her mother had gone to bed, leaving her on the couch. Another of her little jokes.

But Yollie wasn't laughing. She tiptoed into her mother's bedroom with a glass of water and set it on the night stand next to the alarm clock. The next morning, Yollie woke to screams. When her mother reached to turn off the alarm, she had overturned the glass of water.

Yollie burned her mother's morning toast and gloated. "Ha! Ha! I got you back. Why

---

1. **muumuu** (mōo' mōo'): a long, loose dress, often brightly colored.

> *Words to Know and Use*
>
> **gloat** (glōt) *v.* to show triumph or delight

PORTRAIT OF DORA MAAR
Pablo Picasso
© 1993 ARS, New York / SPADEM, Paris.

did you leave me on the couch when I told you to wake me up?"

Despite their jokes, mother and daughter usually got along. They watched bargain matinees together and played croquet[2] in the summer and checkers in the winter. Mrs. Moreno encouraged Yollie to study hard because she wanted her daughter to be a doctor. She bought Yollie a desk, a typewriter, and a lamp that cut glare so her eyes would not grow tired from hours of studying.

Yollie was slender as a tulip, pretty, and one of the smartest kids at Saint Theresa's. She was captain of crossing guards, an altar girl, and a whiz in the school's monthly spelling bees.

"Tienes que estudiar mucho," Mrs. Moreno said every time she propped her work-weary feet on the hassock. "You have to study a lot, then you can get a good job and take care of me."

"Yes, Mama," Yollie would respond, her face buried in a book. If she gave her mother any sympathy, she would begin her stories

---

2. **croquet** (krō kā'): an outdoor game in which players use mallets to hit wooden balls through a series of wire arches.

about how she had come with her family from Mexico with nothing on her back but a sack with three skirts, all of which were too large by the time she crossed the border because she had lost weight from not having enough to eat.

Everyone thought Yollie's mother was a riot. Even the nuns laughed at her antics. Her brother Raul, a nightclub owner, thought she was funny enough to go into show business.

But there was nothing funny about Yollie needing a new outfit for the eighth-grade fall dance. They couldn't afford one. It was late October, with Christmas around the corner, and their dented Chevy Nova had gobbled up almost one hundred dollars in repairs.

*E*veryone thought Yollie's mother was a riot.

"We don't have the money," said her mother, genuinely sad because they couldn't buy the outfit, even though there was a little money stashed away for college. Mrs. Moreno remembered her teenage years and her hard-working parents, who picked grapes and oranges and chopped beets and cotton for <u>meager</u> pay around Kerman. Those were the days when "new clothes" meant limp and out-of-style dresses from Saint Vincent de Paul.[3]

The best Mrs. Moreno could do was buy Yollie a pair of black shoes with velvet bows and fabric dye to color her white summer dress black.

"We can color your dress so it will look brand-new," her mother said brightly, shaking the bottle of dye as she ran hot water into a plastic dish tub. She poured the black liquid into the tub and stirred it with a pencil. Then, slowly and carefully, she lowered the dress into the tub.

Yollie couldn't stand to watch. She *knew* it wouldn't work. It would be like the time her mother stirred up a batch of molasses for candy apples on Yollie's birthday. She'd dipped the apples into the goo and swirled them and seemed to taunt Yollie by singing *"Las Mañanitas"* to her. When she was through, she set the apples on wax paper. They were hard as rocks and hurt the kids' teeth. Finally they had a contest to see who could break the apples open by throwing them against the side of the house. The apples shattered like grenades, sending the kids scurrying for cover, and in an odd way the birthday party turned out to be a success. At least everyone went home happy.

To Yollie's surprise, the dress came out shiny black. It looked brand-new and sophisticated, like what people in New York wear. She beamed at her mother, who hugged Yollie and said, "See, what did I tell you?"

The dance was important to Yollie because she was in love with Ernie Castillo, the third-best speller in the class. She bathed, dressed, did her hair and nails, and <u>primped</u> until her mother yelled, "All right

---

3. **Saint Vincent de Paul:** a reference to the Society of Saint Vincent de Paul, a Roman Catholic organization that operates stores where donated goods are sold cheaply.

Words to Know and Use	**meager** (mē′ gər) *adj.* small in quantity **sophisticated** (sə fis′ tə kāt′ id) *adj.* mature; stylish **primp** (primp) *v.* to fuss over one's appearance

already." Yollie sprayed her neck and wrists with Mrs. Moreno's Avon perfume and bounced into the car.

Mrs. Moreno let Yollie out in front of the school. She waved and told her to have a good time but behave herself, then roared off, blue smoke trailing from the tailpipe of the old Nova.

Yollie ran into her best friend, Janice. They didn't say it, but each thought the other was the most beautiful girl at the dance; the boys would fall over themselves asking them to dance.

The evening was warm but thick with clouds. Gusts of wind picked up the paper lanterns hanging in the trees and swung them, blurring the night with reds and yellows. The lanterns made the evening seem romantic, like a scene from a movie. Everyone danced, sipped punch, and stood in knots of threes and fours, talking. Sister Kelly got up and jitterbugged[4] with some kid's father. When the record ended, students broke into applause.

Janice had her eye on Frankie Ledesma, and Yollie, who kept smoothing her dress down when the wind picked up, had her eye on Ernie. It turned out that Ernie had his mind on Yollie, too. He ate a handful of cookies nervously, then asked her for a dance.

"Sure," she said, nearly throwing herself into his arms.

They danced two fast ones before they got a slow one. As they circled under the lanterns, rain began falling, lightly at first. Yollie loved the sound of the raindrops ticking against the leaves. She leaned her head on Ernie's shoulder, though his sweater was scratchy. He felt warm and tender. Yollie could tell that he was in love, and with her,

of course. The dance continued successfully, romantically, until it began to pour.

"Everyone, let's go inside—and, boys, carry in the table and the record player," Sister Kelly commanded.

The girls and boys raced into the cafeteria. Inside, the girls, drenched to the bone, hurried to the restrooms to brush their hair and dry themselves. One girl cried because her velvet dress was ruined. Yollie felt sorry for her and helped her dry the dress off with paper towels, but it was no use. The dress was ruined.

Yollie went to a mirror. She looked a little gray now that her mother's makeup had washed away but not as bad as some of the other girls. She combed her damp hair, careful not to pull too hard. She couldn't wait to get back to Ernie.

Yollie bent over to pick up a bobby pin, and shame spread across her face. A black puddle was forming at her feet. Drip, black drip. Drip, black drip. The dye was falling from her dress like black tears. Yollie stood up. Her dress was now the color of ash. She looked around the room. The other girls, unaware of Yollie's problem, were busy grooming themselves. What could she do? Everyone would laugh. They would know she dyed an old dress because she couldn't afford a new one. She hurried from the restroom with her head down, across the cafeteria floor and out the door. She raced through the storm, crying as the rain mixed with her tears and ran into twig-choked gutters.

---

4. **jitterbugged:** danced in a lively, acrobatic style popular in the early 1940s.

STUDIO c. 1928 Bernard von Eichman
Collection of the Oakland Museum
Gift of the artist.
Courtesy, Nancy Boas, author of
The Society of Six: California Colorists,
Chronicle Books, San Francisco, 1988.
Photo by Cecile Keefe.

When she arrived home, her mother was on the couch eating cookies and watching TV.

"How was the dance, *m'ija?*[5] Come watch the show with me. It's really good."

Yollie stomped, head down, to her bedroom. She undressed and threw the dress on the floor.

Her mother came into the room. "What's going on? What's all this racket, baby?"

"The dress. It's cheap! It's no good!" Yollie kicked the dress at her mother and watched it land in her hands. Mrs. Moreno studied it closely but couldn't see what was wrong. "What's the matter? It's just little bit wet."

"The dye came out, that's what."

Mrs. Moreno looked at her hands and saw the grayish dye puddling in the shallow lines of her palms. Poor baby, she thought, her brow darkening as she made a sad face.

---

5. *m'ija* (mē′ hä) *Spanish:* a shortened version of *mi hija,* meaning "my daughter."

She wanted to tell her daughter how sorry she was, but she knew it wouldn't help. She walked back to the living room and cried.

The next morning, mother and daughter stayed away from each other. Yollie sat in her room turning the pages of an old *Seventeen*, while her mother watered her plants with a Pepsi bottle.

"Drink, my children," she said loud enough for Yollie to hear. She let the water slurp into pots of coleus and cacti. "Water is all you need. My daughter needs clothes, but I don't have no money."

Yollie tossed her *Seventeen* on her bed. She was embarrassed at last night's tirade. It wasn't her mother's fault that they were poor.

When they sat down together for lunch, they felt awkward about the night before. But Mrs. Moreno had made a fresh stack of tortillas and cooked up a pan of *chile verde,* and that broke the ice. She licked her thumb and smacked her lips.

"You know, honey, we gotta figure a way to make money," Yollie's mother said. "You and me. We don't have to be poor. Remember the Garcias. They made this stupid little tool that fixes cars. They moved away because they're rich. That's why we don't see them no more."

"What can we make?" asked Yollie. She took another tortilla and tore it in half.

"Maybe a screwdriver that works on both ends? Something like that." The mother looked around the room for ideas, but then shrugged. "Let's forget it. It's better to get an education. If you get a good job and have spare time, then maybe you can invent something." She rolled her tongue over her lips and cleared her throat. "The county fair hires people. We can get a job there. It will be here next week."

Yollie hated the idea. What would Ernie say if he saw her pitching hay at the cows? How could she go to school smelling like an armful of chickens? "No, they wouldn't hire us," she said.

The phone rang. Yollie lurched from her chair to answer it, thinking it would be Janice wanting to know why she had left. But it was Ernie wondering the same thing. When he found out she wasn't mad at him, he asked if she would like to go to a movie.

"I'll ask," Yollie said, smiling. She covered the phone with her hand and counted to ten. She uncovered the receiver and said, "My mom says it's OK. What are we going to see?"

After Yollie hung up, her mother climbed, grunting, onto a chair to reach the top shelf in the hall closet. She wondered why she hadn't done it earlier. She reached behind a stack of towels and pushed her chubby hand into the cigar box where she kept her secret stash of money.

"I've been saving a little every month," said Mrs. Moreno. "For you, *m'ija.*" Her mother held up five twenties, a blossom of green that smelled sweeter than flowers on that Saturday. They drove to Macy's and bought a blouse, shoes, and a skirt that would not bleed in rain or any other kind of weather. ❧

How to Die of Embarrassment

DELIA EPHRON

On a Date

Pick up a piece of pizza and take a bite. Watch the mozzarella cheese stretch. Bite down harder. It is still stretching. Move slice farther away from mouth. The strands are growing thinner and longer. You can see three spaghetti-like strands of mozzarella cheese extending out of your mouth. They are hanging between the slice and your mouth like jump ropes. You do not know what to do. With the hand that is not holding the pizza, grab cheese with fingers, break off, and stuff ends in mouth. Chew, swallow, do not look at date, and begin again.

Between Classes

On the way to your class on the third floor, detour down to the first floor to pass the room where he has his next class. Is he there? He is! Smile and say, "Hi." He says hi back. Ask if he did the English assignment. Ask if he's ready for the test. Say that you'll see him later. Smile and say, "Bye." He is so cute!

Continue down the hall, swinging your hips. Then, as you start up the stairs to the second floor, start running. Just make it to class in time. Flop down in seat, drop books on floor, take mirror out of purse, and look at yourself. There's a piece of apple between your two front teeth.

At Your Boyfriend's House for Dinner

Salad: With fork, pick up a piece of lettuce and look at it. Will it fit in your mouth? Put it back on the plate. Attempt to cut it with fork. Wonder if it's OK to use a knife on salad. Look around the table to see if anyone else is using his knife. No one is. Pick up the lettuce again. Put it down. Pick it up. Put it down. Pick it up, open mouth, close eyes, and cram it in. Open eyes and realize that your boyfriend's mother is looking at you strangely. You are eating her salad.

Roll: Remembering what your mother told you about the correct way to eat rolls, break off a small piece, scattering crumbs on the table. Butter, place in mouth. While chewing, answer a question, spraying a shower of crumbs across the table.

(Alternative: Mistake roll for baked potato—cut slit in top and stuff butter in.)

Responding to Reading

First Impressions

1. What did you think of Mrs. Moreno at the end of the story? Jot down your thoughts about her in your journal or on a sheet of paper.

Second Thoughts

2. Discuss the story from Mrs. Moreno's point of view.

3. In what ways is the relationship of Yollie and her mother like or unlike that of the teens and their parents you know?

4. What do you think of Yollie's desire for nice clothes?

   Think about
   - whether she should have gotten a new dress before the dance
   - whether she should have sacrificed the college money for new clothes

5. What do you think Yollie will tell her friends and Ernie about her disappearance from the dance?

Broader Connections

6. Yollie has a desire for nice clothes despite the fact that her family is poor. How important are clothes to you? Do you have to be well dressed to be popular? How important is it to have the right jacket or the "in" athletic shoes? Think about the role-playing situation that you acted out in Examine What You Know. Then brainstorm some ideas on this issue.

Literary Concept: Resolution

Often the final part of a story's plot is the **resolution.** The resolution explains how the conflict is resolved, or settled. Think about the conflict in "Mother and Daughter." How is this conflict resolved? Do you think this scene is an effective way of resolving the conflict?

Writing Options

1. Imagine that Mrs. Moreno's brother Raul asked her to do a comedy routine at his night club. Write Mrs. Moreno's **comedy monologue.** Have her tell about the night Yollie's dress was ruined.

2. Consider Yollie's embarrassing moment and those described in Delia Ephron's "How to Die of Embarrassment." Write a **personal narrative** about your most embarrassing moment.

3. Write two **diary entries** for Ernie Castillo, one that describes the night of the dance and one that describes the day Yollie agrees to go to the movies with him.

4. Imagine that a local radio station is giving a big cash prize for the funniest mom. Assume the role of Yollie and write an **essay** describing your mother. Through the essay persuade the officials that your mother is indeed a very funny person.

Vocabulary Practice

Exercise On your paper write the letter of the sentence that best demonstrates the meaning of the boldfaced word.

1. **gloat**
   a. A rival bragged about beating you in a race.
   b. A boat glided over the water.
   c. All the farm animals escaped from the barn.

2. **meager**
   a. Thanksgiving dinner was a huge feast.
   b. Her salary barely supported her three children.
   c. The butcher loved his job and was good at it.

3. **sophisticated**
   a. The new dress and hairdo made my sister look like a movie star.
   b. Bill tried very hard to convince us that he was right.
   c. The baby sucked his thumb contentedly.

4. **primp**
   a. She cared nothing for her appearance.
   b. What could that new boy in the second row be thinking?
   c. He spent hours combing his hair to make sure it was just right.

5. **tirade**
   a. She packed the emergency tools in the trunk of the car.
   b. He drank the entire pitcher of fruit punch.
   c. After the defeat the coach yelled at his team for an hour.

Words to Know and Use

gloat
meager
primp
sophisticated
tirade

Poetry

The Burden

FRANCESCA YETUNDE PEREIRA

(frän chäs' kä yā tōōn'də pə rä' ē rə)

The Choice

DOROTHY PARKER

Examine What You Know

Think about a poem that has made an impression on you. What thoughts and emotions did it trigger and why? Now consider the poems you have read that had little effect on you. Why did the poems fail for you? Use a word map like the one below to examine your thoughts about poetry.

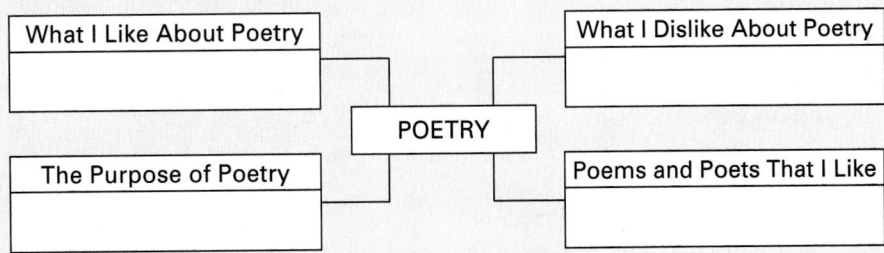

What I Like About Poetry		What I Dislike About Poetry
	POETRY	
The Purpose of Poetry		Poems and Poets That I Like

Expand Your Knowledge

The author of "The Burden," Francesca Pereira, is a contemporary African poet and folk singer. "The Choice" was written by Dorothy Parker, a New Yorker who wrote witty poems for popular magazines in the 1920s and 1930s. "The Burden" and "The Choice" differ in tone and style. Pereira's poem has a serious **tone** and uses no **rhyme,** but Parker's poem is light and rhyming. Both, however, are examples of **lyric poems,** short poems that express the thoughts or feelings of a single **speaker.**

Write Before You Read

The words below relate to the poems "The Burden" and "The Choice." Choose one of the two lists and write a short poem, using each of the words in the list at least once.

- "The Burden"—friend, secret, heart, maze, mute, speech, loyalty
- "The Choice"—two men, a woman, pearls, houses of marble, a song, swift, lace, ribbons, horses, a queen, a whistle, crazy

■ *Author biographies in Reader's Handbook*

The Burden

FRANCESCA YETUNDE PEREIRA

Tell me no secret, friend,
My heart will not sustain
Its load, too heavily
On my mind to weigh

5 Involve me not, friend,
Make not of me a mute.[1]
Like a labyrinth[2]
The road from my heart
Winds round and round,
10 Yet leads to an avenue–
The boulevard of speech.

Tell me no secret, friend,
To you I'll still be true.
For you I'll fight
15 No matter where–
But make not a mute of me.

---

1. **mute** (myo͞ot): one who is unable to speak.
2. **labyrinth** (lab′ ə rinth′): a maze.

Responding to Reading

First Impressions of "The Burden"

1. What were your thoughts as you finished reading this poem? Write your impressions in your journal or on a sheet of paper.

Second Thoughts on "The Burden"

2. What did the poem bring to mind about your own experiences with friends and secrets?

Think about

• how hard it is to keep a secret
• what happens to friendships when secrets are not kept
• what kind of friendship exists when secrets are not shared

3. How do you think the image of a labyrinth relates to keeping or telling a secret?

The Choice

DOROTHY PARKER

He'd have given me rolling lands,
    Houses of marble, and billowing farms,
Pearls, to trickle between my hands,
    Smoldering rubies, to circle my arms.
5 You—you'd only a lilting song,
    Only a melody, happy and high,
You were sudden and swift and strong—
    Never a thought for another had I.

He'd have given me laces rare,
10   Dresses that glimmered with frosty sheen,
Shining ribbons to wrap my hair,
    Horses to draw me, as fine as a queen.
You—you'd only to whistle low,
    Gayly I followed wherever you led.
15 I took you, and I let him go—
    Somebody ought to examine my head!

BIRTHDAY 1914 Marc Chagall
Oil on cardboard, 31¾ x 39¼ inches
Collection, The Museum of Modern Art,
New York, through the Lillie P. Bliss Bequest.
Photograph © 1992 The Museum of
Modern Art, New York.

*R*esponding to Reading

First Impressions of "The Choice"

1. What is your feeling about the speaker of this poem?

Second Thoughts on "The Choice"

2. Do you think the speaker really regrets her choice? Explain.

3. The ending of the poem is a surprise to most readers. How does the poet accomplish this?

Comparing the Poems

4. Consider the thoughts about poetry you developed in Examine What You Know. Which poem do you like better? Why?

5. How do the ideas about friendship and love in these poems compare with your ideas on these subjects?

*L*iterary Concept: Rhyme Scheme

The pattern of rhymes in a poem is called the poem's **rhyme scheme.** In these lines from "Nothing Gold Can Stay," on page 338, notice the rhyming words. Rhyme scheme can be noted by using a different letter for every rhyming sound.

> Nature's first green is *gold,*   *a*
> Her hardest hue to *hold.*   *a*
> Her early leaf's a *flower;*   *b*
> But only so an *hour.*   *b*

On a sheet of paper, write the letters indicating the rhyme scheme of the first stanza of "The Choice."

*W*riting Options

1. Write a **personal narrative** about a time when you revealed a secret. What was the outcome of your revelation? Were you happy or sorry?

2. Imagine that you are the mother or father of the speaker in "The Choice." You are upset with your daughter's choice. Write a **letter** explaining the foolishness of her decision and persuading her to forget the poor man and choose the rich man.

Nonfiction

Battle by the Breadfruit Tree

THEODORE WALDECK

Examine What You Know

Imagine that you and a friend are walking at night. You hear a noise and turn around suddenly to find a menacing creature behind you. What would you be willing to do to protect yourself and your friend from harm? Would you think about your actions first, or would you act solely on instinct? With your classmates discuss instances that you have read about, heard about, or experienced firsthand in which a person or an animal acted out of instinct to protect another person or animal.

Expand Your Knowledge

In the wild some animals live in herds for protection. Baboons, for example, have a system in which dominant males rest or march in the center of the group and watch the others. When the group is threatened, the males leave the center to face the danger. Occasionally, a mother and her infant get separated from the group. Although the average female baboon is less than half the size of a male, she often gets the best of her opponent. Baboon mothers have such fierce protective instincts that they will sacrifice their own lives rather than allow harm to come to their babies.

Enrich Your Reading

Description   In "Battle by the Breadfruit Tree" Theodore Waldeck uses **description** to tell about a battle between a mother baboon and a leopard. Descriptive writing contains words that appeal to the senses, and it often compares one thing to another. Note the details Waldeck uses to describe the battle: "We could tell they were together because they formed a ball of fighting fury, and the sounds of the two animals came out of the pinwheel of murderous action." When you finish reading, look for other examples of descriptive writing and jot them down on a sheet of paper or in your journal.

■ *Author biography in Reader's Handbook*

Battle by the Breadfruit Tree

THEODORE WALDECK

Smith and I were anxious to procure motion pictures of a herd of baboons. We had tried and tried, with no success whatever, though we saw many of these creatures. Our camp was some miles from a little ravine through which a stream ran. Beyond the ravine was a plateau leading back to thick woods. The baboons, scores of them, came out of these woods with their young to play on the plateau, to drink from the stream, and to fight for the favors of the females. Often Smith and I watched them, tried to photograph them, but could never get close enough. The baboons enjoyed what we were doing. They thought it was a game of some sort.

Once we set up the camera at the edge of the plateau in order to take them when they came through the woods at dawn to greet the sun. We didn't even come close, for when the baboons saw us, they charged like a shrieking army of savages. They threw sticks and stones at us, and we fled as though the devil and all his imps were at our heels. A grown bull baboon could have torn either of us to shreds. We didn't even stop to take our camera. We felt sure that our camera would be a wreck when we returned, which could not be until the baboons had retired from the plateau. We went back then, to find it exactly as we had left it. They had not so much as touched it.

"We *must* get those pictures," said Smith, "and I think I know the answer. Those breadfruit trees[1] this side of the ravine. That big one, with the leafy top. . ."

"Yes?"

"We go there now and build a platform, up among the leaves, set up our camera, take blankets, a thermos bottle filled with hot tea, and spend the night. Then, when they come out in the morning, we'll be looking right down on them."

I saw that he was right, and we set about it. The trekkers[2] got boards from the camp and carried them to the tree. Big limbs were cut off and lashed high among the leaves at the top of the breadfruit tree. Then the

---

1. **breadfruit trees:** tropical trees with seedless round fruit.
2. **trekkers:** in South Africa, people who travel on foot or in wagons and carry equipment.

Words to Know and Use | **procure** (prō kyoor') *v.* to get; acquire

458

boards were laid across the limbs, the camera set up. We had supper, took our blankets, and went to the tree to spend an uncomfortable night; but however uncomfortable it might be, it would not matter if we got our pictures.

Night. We sat hunched up with our blankets over us listening to the sounds of the night. Now and again we dozed off. I'd have a cigarette; Smith would smoke a pipe. Then we'd waken. The wind blew steadily toward us from the plateau, which we could see dimly in the moonlight. The hours wore on.

Finally, animals began to greet the growing morning, though it would be some time, if they stuck to schedule, before the baboons appeared. I sat back on my blanket now—it was already warm enough to do without it—and watched the day break. I never tired of doing that. The sun comes up in a different way in Africa. First the leaves would be black. Then a grayish haze would outline their shapes. Then the gray would lighten into the green of the leaves. Then the sun itself would strike through, and morning would be with us, covering that part of Africa with a mixture of colors that ran through all the spectrum. Sunlight played upon colors like a mighty organist upon the keys, and the keys were everything the sunlight touched; when the dawn was come, it was music made visible. Not just the music that men played, but the music of Nature herself, with all the sounds that Nature used. A great sword of crimson was like a bloodcurdling scream you could not hear

because you came before it sounded or after the sound had passed—and the sword struck deeply into the ravine and raised itself to slash across the plateau on which the baboons usually played. The green of the trees was light and like a touch of agony somehow—not the agony of pain, but the agony of an unexplainable kind of ecstasy. Far away and all around were the mounded hills, with the veldt[3] between them, and some of the hills wore caps of crimson or orange or gold, and some were still touched with the mystery of distance or the night that had not yet left them. Whatever color or combination of colors you cared to mention, you could find there. And they came out of the east in a magical rush, like paint of all colors flung across the world by a painter bigger than all the earth itself.

I sighed and drank it in. Smith was looking out through the leaves, watching for the baboons to appear. Then he nudged me, and I made an end, for the moment, of dreaming. I parted the leaves in utter silence, making sure that my lens was uncovered and aimed at the plateau, and looked through. The baboon herd had not come, but a single baboon and her baby. Smith had not actually seen her coming. One moment he had been watching, seeing nothing. Then he had blinked his eyes, and she was there. He signaled me to start the camera. I noted that the wind was toward us. I felt sure that the rest of the baboons would come, following this one. The mother baboon, while her baby played across the

---

3. **veldt** (velt): an open grassland in South Africa.

Mother and baby baboon. © Marvin E. Newman / The Image Bank.

could see her nose wrinkling as she tried to get our scent. But the wind was toward us, and she got nothing. She even looked several times at the breadfruit tree that hid us.

I was about to start grinding again when a terrific squall came from the baby. It caught at my heart, that sound. I know it caught at the heart of Smith, too, for I could see it in his face. The mother baboon whirled around, so fast one could scarcely see the movement. The baby was jumping swiftly to the top of a rock, which was all too low to be of any use to him, as protection against the creature that was close behind him.

That creature was a hunting leopard, and it, like the baboon, had come so softly and silently that we had not seen it. It was simply there, a murderous streak behind the baby baboon. Did the female hesitate for a single moment? Not at all. If the leopard were a streak, so was the mother baboon. She shot toward that leopard and was in the air above him, reaching for his neck, while he was in midleap behind the baby, which now sat upon the rock and uttered <u>doleful</u> screams of terror.

The great cat instantly had his work cut out for him. For the baboon, by gripping his neck from behind, beyond reach of those <u>talons</u>, could break it. And that was what she tried, with hands and feet and killing <u>incisors</u>. But while I knew nothing of this fighting combination, the leopard must have, for he did what any cat would <u>instinctively</u> do in such a case. He spun to his back and reached for the baboon with all four of his brutally armed paws. One stroke across

plateau behind her, came down to its edge to peer into the ravine, perhaps to dash down for a drink. I started the camera. It was almost silent but not quite. And with the first whirring sound, which we ourselves could scarcely hear, though we were right beside it, the mother jumped up and looked around. Her ears had caught the little sound. She looked in all directions, twisting her head swiftly, and even in this her eyes kept darting to her young one. I stilled the whirring. We did not move or make a sound, even a whisper. She was so close we

460

the abdomen of the baboon, and she would be killed outright. But she knew something of leopards.

Smith did not make a sound, nor did I. I don't think we even breathed. The great cat recovered himself as the baboon jumped free of the leopard and ran toward her baby. The leopard charged the baboon. The baboon waited until the last minute, shot into the air, allowed the cat to go under her, turned in the air, and dropped back for the killing hold on the back of the neck again.

They formed a ball of fighting fury.

She got some hair in her mouth, which she spat out disgustedly. The baby kept on squalling. As nearly as I could tell—though I probably would not have heard even the trumpeting of elephants or the roaring of lions—there was no sound other than the screaming of the female baboon, the squalling of her baby, and the spitting and snarling of the leopard.

This time, when the leopard whirled to his back to dislodge the baboon, he managed to sink his claws into the baboon. I saw the blood spurt from the baboon's body, dyeing her fur. I knew that the smell of blood would drive the leopard mad, and it did. He would just as soon eat the meat of a grown baboon if he could not have the baby.

Both stood off for a second, regarding each other, to spit out fur and hair. Then the leopard charged once more. Again the baboon leaped high, started down, reaching for that neck. And this time, when she came down, the leopard had already turned, and

she could not entirely avoid landing among those fearful talons. Even a baboon could not jump from a spot in midair. For a brief moment there was a terrific flurry of infighting, from which came the snarling of the leopard, the screaming of the she-baboon. Now we could see the leopard, now the baboon, the latter trying with all her strength and agility to escape a disemboweling stroke from one of the four feet of the killer. Then both were so mixed up, and fighting so much all over the plateau, that we could not distinguish them. We could tell they were together because they formed a ball of fighting fury, and the sounds of the two animals came out of the pinwheel of murderous action.

How long it lasted I do not know. To the she-baboon and her baby it must have seemed ages. It may have been seconds, even a minute. And then they were standing off, catching their breath, spitting out fur, regarding each other again. Both were tired. To my utter amazement the baboon was holding her own with the leopard. At that moment I would not have known which one had the edge, if either. For both were panting, weary, and stained with blood.

Neither gave ground. By common consent they stood for a few seconds, the baboon on her hind legs, the leopard crouching on all fours. Then the leopard charged. Again the baboon went into the air to let the leopard go under her. She knew better, at this stage of the game, than to run away or jump to either side. The leopard could overtake her if she ran, could turn instantly and follow her if she jumped to either side. So up and over was her only chance. Again she came down. But this time she was expecting the cat to whip upon his back and present his talons, and was ready. She twisted aside a little, and to the front, perhaps with some idea of reaching for the neck from the underside, now uppermost. The forepaws of the leopard lashed at her. The sun gleamed on the exposed talons and showed that they were red with baboon blood. I could see long weals[4] across the abdomen of the baboon. She had <u>evaded</u> those slashes at the last moment, each time. Feeling the talons' touch she had got away, just enough to escape disemboweling, not enough to escape deep, parallel gashes that reached inward for her life.

Her screaming still informed him that she was ready for more.

Now I began to see how the fight was going to go, though neither Smith nor I could have done anything about it because we were spellbound, rooted to our place in the breadfruit tree, watching something that few explorers had ever seen: a battle between a leopard and a baboon! And for the best reason in the world—the baboon to protect her baby.

But now the she-baboon was tiring. It was obvious in all her movements, though I knew and the leopard knew that as long as she stood upright and could see him, she was dynamite—fury incarnate,[5] capable of slaying if she got in the blows she wanted. So far she had not made it.

Now she panted more than the leopard did. She did not entirely evade his rushes, though she jumped over him as before. But she did not go as high or twist as quickly in the air. She couldn't. Her body was beginning to weigh too much for her tiring muscles. She was like an arm-weary prizefighter who has almost fought himself out. But her little eyes still glared defiance, her screaming still informed him that she was ready for more. Now there were other slashes upon her face, her head, her chest, and her abdomen—clear down even to her hands and feet. She was a bloody mess. But she never even thought of quitting. They drew apart once more, spitting fur. They glared at each other. Several times I saw the orange eyes of the leopard, and there was hell in them—the hell of hate and fury and <u>thwarted</u> hunger.

Now he charged before the baboon had rested enough. He was getting stronger, the baboon weaker. His second wind[6] came sooner perhaps, and he sorely needed it. Even yet the baboon could break his neck, given the one chance.

Again the baboon went into the air, came down, and was caught in the midst of those four paws. Again the battle raged, the two animals all mixed up together, all over the plateau. The little one squalled from his boulder, and there was despair in his voice. He cried hopeless encouragement to his mother. She heard, I knew she did, and tried

---

4. weals: ridges on the skin that result from being struck.
5. incarnate: made a reality; in the flesh.
6. second wind: a burst of energy following a period of exhaustion.

Leopard and baboon fighting.　John Dominis, *Life* magazine, © 1967 Time Warner, Inc.

to find some reserve with which to meet the attacks of the killer.

That last piece of infighting lasted almost too long. There was no relief from it, and the nerves of the two men who watched were strained to the breaking point, though neither was aware of it. How long they had held their breath they did not know.

The two beasts broke apart, and I saw instantly that the leopard had at last succeeded, managing the stroke he had been trying for since the battle began. He had raked deeply into the abdomen of the baboon. The result may be well imagined. The baboon drew off slowly and looked down at herself. What she saw told her the truth—that even if the leopard turned and ran away this minute, she was done.

But did she expect mercy? Death did not grant mercy in Africa—certainly not on this particular morning.

The baboon noted the direction of the leopard's glance. The great cat was crouched well back but facing the rock on which the baby squalled. He licked his chops, looked at the dying she-baboon, and growled, and it was as though he said:

"Not much time now. And when you are gone, nothing will keep me from getting him!"

As if the leopard had actually screamed those words, I got the thought which raced through his evil head. And the baboon got it too. For she turned slowly, like a dead thing walking, and moved to turn her back toward the rock, so that now the baby was almost over her head.

Then she looked at the leopard once more and screamed as though she answered: "Perhaps, but over my dead body!"

The leopard charged again, for the last time. It would be easy now. And as the she-baboon set herself against that last charge, the strangest, most nearly human cry I ever heard went keening[7] out across the veldt. It bounced against the breadfruit trees, dipped into the ravine; it went back through the forest whence the other baboons usually came to play and drink. It went out in all directions, that cry, across the plain. It rolled across the mounded hills. It was a cry that could never be forgotten by those that heard it.

And then, in the midst of the cry—like none she had uttered while the fight had been so fierce—the leopard struck her down. She sprawled, beaten to a pulp, at the base of the boulder, while that last cry of hers still moved across the veldt.

And now, sure that the she-baboon was dead, the leopard backed away, crouched, lifted his eyes to the baby on the rock.

I came to life then, realizing for the first time what I was seeing. I couldn't have moved before. But now, somehow, my rifle was in my hands, at my shoulder, and I was getting the leopard in my sights. Why had I not done it before, saved the life of the mother? I'll never know. Certainly, and sincerely, I had not allowed the fight to continue simply in order to see which would win out. I had simply become a statue, possessing only eyes and ears.

I got the leopard in my sights as he crouched to spring. I had his head for a target. I'd get him before he moved, before he sprang. The baby—looking down, sorrow in his cries, with a knowledge of doom too—had nowhere to go. I tightened the trigger. And then . . .

On the instant, the leopard was blotted out, and for several seconds I could not understand what had happened, what the mother's last cry had meant. But now I did. For living baboons, leaping, screaming, had appeared out of nowhere. They came, the whole herd of them, and the leopard was invisible in their midst. I did not even hear the leopard snarl and spit. I heard nothing save the baboons, saw nothing save the big blur of their bodies, over and around the spot where I had last seen the leopard.

How long that lasted I do not know. But when it was over, another she-baboon jumped to the rock, gathered up the baby, and was gone. After her trailed all the other baboons. Smith and I looked at each other, and if my face was as white and shocked as his, it was white and shocked indeed. Without a word, because we both understood, we slipped down from the tree, crossed the ravine, climbed its far side, crossed the plateau, looked down at the dead she-baboon, then looked away again. One mother had fought to the death for the life of her baby and had saved that life. We looked around for the leopard who had slain her. We couldn't find a piece of it as big as an average man's hand! So the baboons had <u>rallied</u> to the dying cry of the mother baboon.

We went slowly back to the tree, got our camera down, returned with it to our camp. Not until we were back did we realize that neither of us, from the beginning of that fight to its <u>grim</u> and savage end, had thought of the camera, much less touched it.

One of the greatest fights any explorer ever saw was unrecorded. 🖎

---

7. **keening:** wailing.

Words to Know and Use | **rally** (ral′ ē) *v.* to come together to provide help
grim (grim) *adj.* fierce; cruel

*R*esponding to Reading

First Impressions

1. How did you feel when the baboon herd appeared at the end of the selection?

Second Thoughts

2. Do you think Waldeck would have been justified in shooting the leopard? Why or why not?

   Think about
   - whether the timing would have made a difference
   - whether people should interfere in natural events
   - whether you would have shot the leopard
   - what Waldeck would have gained and lost by shooting the leopard

3. What effects do you think the men's experience might have had on them?

4. What part of the battle affected you most?

5. How do you think the impact of the battle might have been different if you had seen it rather than read about it?

Broader Connections

6. Do you think "shooting" game should be limited to photographic shooting only? Before you answer, consider ideas from the selection as well as your personal feelings about animals and hunting.

*L*iterary Concept: Eyewitness Reporting

Selections such as "Battle by the Breadfruit Tree" are often written as **eyewitness reports.** In such writing the writer tells what he or she saw, just as a witness does in a trial. In **subjective eyewitness reports** the thoughts and feelings of the writer play an important role in the writing. In **objective eyewitness reports** the writer strives to report what happened without sharing his or her feelings. Give one example of a phrase or sentence in Waldeck's eyewitness report that tells how he felt about the outcome of the battle.

Writing Options

1. Observe an animal or some natural phenomenon such as a thunderstorm. Write an **eyewitness report,** describing exactly what you saw. You may choose to share your feelings as Waldeck did, or you may want to keep your description completely objective.

2. The baboon mother's saving her baby is a good example of instinctive behavior. Write your own **definition** of *instinct* and give several other examples of instinctive behavior.

3. What if the baboon had won the battle? Starting with the paragraph on page 462 that begins "Again the baboon . . .," rewrite the **account** of the ending of the battle.

4. Imagine that the baboon and the leopard could talk. Write the **conversation** that the two animals might have had as they battled by the breadfruit tree.

Vocabulary Practice

Exercise   On a sheet of paper, write the word from the list that best completes each sentence.

1. As the sun was setting on the plateau, the sky shone with every color of the __?__ .

2. A mother baboon heard a strange sound in the distance and __?__ drew her baby nearer.

3. The sound was made by a leopard, coming to __?__ its next meal.

4. Upon seeing the leopard, the frightened baby baboon let out a __?__ wail.

5. The leopard gave the baboons a __?__ look as it moved closer to attack.

6. The sun glistened off its sharp __?__ as it curled its lip and bared its teeth.

7. As the leopard swiped at the baboons, its __?__ came perilously close to the baby's head.

8. At the last second, the baby pulled its head back and was able to __?__ the leopard's crushing blow.

9. The leopard's __?__ attempts at attacking the baboons caused it to grow angrier and angrier.

10. The mother baboon let out a cry, causing the rest of her group to __?__ to her and her baby's aid.

Words to Know and Use

doleful
evade
grim
incisors
instinctively
procure
rally
spectrum
talons
thwarted

Fiction

The Moustache

ROBERT CORMIER

Examine What You Know

What do you know about the elderly? How do you feel about being around older people? What problems do they face? Have you ever visited a nursing home? Do you have any aged relatives? How do they act? How do you feel about growing old? In your journal or on a sheet of paper, jot down some of your images of and thoughts about the elderly and the problems they face.

Expand Your Knowledge

Most elderly people in the United States live on their own or with their families. However, about 5 percent of the nation's elderly reside in nursing homes. An older person may decide to live in such a facility if he or she has health problems requiring constant medical attention. Such care is needed for many conditions that afflict the aged, including arteriosclerosis (är tir′ ē ō′ sklə rō′ sis)—commonly known as hardening of the arteries—a disease that affects one of the characters in this story. Because arteriosclerosis thickens the artery walls and decreases blood flow to vital organs, such as the brain, its effects can range from dizziness and slurred speech to forgetfulness.

Enrich Your Reading

Inference To **infer,** or make **inferences,** is to figure out something from evidence rather than from information told outright. For example, if your best friend suddenly started to ignore you, you might infer that your friend was angry at you. Sometimes an author will not directly describe an event or a character in a story, yet will supply enough evidence for you to make inferences. "The Moustache" concerns a visit to an elderly person in a nursing home. As you read the story, you will discover that some details about the characters and the setting are only hinted at. You will have to "read between the lines" to understand what is happening.

■ *Author biography on Extend page*

The Moustache

ROBERT CORMIER

At the last minute Annie couldn't go. She was invaded by one of those twenty-four-hour flu bugs that sent her to bed with a fever, moaning about the fact that she'd also have to break her date with Handsome Harry Arnold that night. We call him Handsome Harry because he's actually handsome; but he's also a nice guy, cool, and he doesn't treat me like Annie's kid brother, which I am, but like a regular person. Anyway, I had to go to Lawnrest alone that afternoon. But first of all I had to stand inspection. My mother lined me up against the wall. She stood there like a one-man firing squad, which is kind of funny because she's not like a man at all; she's very feminine, and we have this great relationship—I mean, I feel as if she really likes me. I realize that sounds strange, but I know guys whose mothers love them and cook special stuff for them and worry about them and all, but there's something missing in their relationship.

Anyway. She frowned and started the routine.

"That hair," she said. Then admitted: "Well, at least you combed it."

I sighed. I have discovered that it's better to sigh than argue.

"And that moustache." She shook her head. "I still say a seventeen-year-old has no business wearing a moustache."

"It's an experiment," I said. "I just wanted to see if I could grow one." To tell the truth, I had proved my point about being able to grow a decent moustache, but I also had learned to like it.

"It's costing you money, Mike," she said.

"I know, I know."

The money was a reference to the movies. The Downtown Cinema has a special Friday night offer—half-price admission for high school couples seventeen or younger. But the woman in the box office took one look at my moustache and charged me full price. Even when I showed her my driver's license. She charged full admission for Cindy's ticket, too, which left me practically broke and unable to take Cindy out for a hamburger with the crowd afterward. That didn't help matters, because Cindy has been getting impatient recently about things like the fact that I don't own my own car and have to concentrate on my studies if I want to win that college scholarship, for instance. Cindy wasn't exactly crazy about the moustache, either.

Now it was my mother's turn to sigh.

"Look," I said, to cheer her up. "I'm thinking about shaving it off." Even though I wasn't. Another discovery: You can build a way of life on postponement.

"Your grandmother probably won't even recognize you," she said. And I saw the shadow fall across her face.

Let me tell you what the visit to Lawnrest was all about. My grandmother is seventy-three years old. She is a resident—which is supposed to be a better word than *patient*—at the Lawnrest Nursing Home. She used to make the greatest turkey dressing in the world and was a nut about baseball and could even quote batting averages, for crying out loud. She always rooted for the losers. She was in love with the Mets until they started to win. Now she has arteriosclerosis, which the dictionary says is "a chronic disease characterized by abnormal thickening and hardening of the arterial walls." Which really means that she can't live at home anymore or even with us, and her memory has betrayed her as well as her body. She used to wander off and sometimes didn't recognize people. My mother visits her all the time, driving the thirty miles to Lawnrest almost every day. Because Annie was home for a semester break from college, we had decided to make a special Saturday visit. Now Annie was in bed, groaning theatrically—she's a drama major—but I told my mother I'd go, anyway. I hadn't seen my grandmother since she'd been admitted to Lawnrest. Besides, the place is located on the Southwest Turnpike, which meant I could barrel along in my father's new Le Mans. My ambition was to see the speedometer hit seventy-five. Ordinarily, I used the old station wagon, which can barely stagger up to fifty.

Frankly, I wasn't too crazy about visiting a nursing home. They reminded me of hospitals, and hospitals turn me off. I mean, the smell of ether[1] makes me nauseous, and I

EVA'S ALMA MATER © 1988 Deidre Scherer.

feel faint at the sight of blood. And as I approached Lawnrest—which is a terrible cemetery kind of name, to begin with—I was sorry I hadn't avoided the trip. Then I felt guilty about it. I'm loaded with guilt <u>complexes</u>. Like driving like a madman after promising my father to be careful. Like sitting in the parking lot, looking at the nursing home with dread and thinking how I'd rather be with Cindy. Then I thought of all

---

1. **ether** (ē′ thər): a chemical formerly used by surgeons to make patients unconscious.

the Christmas and birthday gifts my grandmother had given me, and I got out of the car, guilty, as usual.

Inside, I was surprised by the lack of hospital smell, although there was another odor or maybe the absence of an odor. The air was antiseptic, sterile. As if there was no atmosphere at all or I'd caught a cold suddenly and couldn't taste or smell.

A nurse at the reception desk gave me directions—my grandmother was in East Three. I made my way down the tiled corridor and was glad to see that the walls were painted with cheerful colors like yellow and pink. A wheelchair suddenly shot around a corner, self-propelled by an old man, white-haired and toothless, who cackled merrily as he barely missed me. I jumped aside—here I was, almost getting wiped out by a two-mile-an-hour wheelchair after doing seventy-five on the pike. As I walked through the corridor seeking East Three, I couldn't help glancing into the rooms, and it was like some kind of wax museum[2]—all these figures in various stances and attitudes, sitting in beds or chairs, standing at windows, as if they were frozen forever in these postures. To tell the truth, I began to hurry because I was getting depressed. Finally, I saw a beautiful girl approaching, dressed in white, a nurse or an attendant; and I was so happy to see someone young, someone walking and acting normally, that I gave her a wide smile and a big hello, and I must have looked like a kind of nut. Anyway, she looked right through me as if I were a window, which is about par for the course whenever I meet beautiful girls.

I finally found the room and saw my grandmother in bed. My grandmother looks like Ethel Barrymore.[3] I never knew who Ethel Barrymore was until I saw a terrific movie, *None But the Lonely Heart,* on TV, starring Ethel Barrymore and Cary Grant.[4] Both my grandmother and Ethel Barrymore have these great craggy faces like the side of a mountain and wonderful voices like syrup being poured. Slowly. She was propped up in bed, pillows puffed behind her. Her hair had been combed out and fell upon her shoulders. For some reason, this flowing hair gave her an almost girlish appearance, despite its whiteness.

She saw me and smiled. Her eyes lit up, and her eyebrows arched, and she reached out her hands to me in greeting. "Mike, Mike," she said. And I breathed a sigh of relief. This was one of her good days. My mother had warned me that she might not know who I was at first.

I took her hands in mine. They were fragile. I could actually feel her bones, and it seemed as if they would break if I pressed too hard. Her skin was smooth, almost slippery, as if the years had worn away all the roughness the way the wind wears away the surfaces of stones.

"Mike, Mike, I didn't think you'd come," she said, so happy, and she was still Ethel Barrymore, that voice like a caress. "I've been waiting all this time." Before I could

---

2. **wax museum:** a museum that displays wax statues of famous people.

3. **Ethel Barrymore:** 1879–1959; U.S. stage and screen actress.

4. **Cary Grant:** 1904–1986; U.S. movie star.

Words to Know and Use | **antiseptic** (an′ tə sep′ tik) *adj.* thoroughly clean

reply, she looked away, out the window. "See the birds? I've been watching them at the feeder. I love to see them come. Even the blue jays. The blue jays are like hawks—they take the food that the small birds should have. But the small birds, the chickadees, watch the blue jays and at least learn where the feeder is."

She lapsed into silence, and I looked out the window. There was no feeder. No birds. There was only the parking lot and the sun glinting on car windshields.

She turned to me again, eyes bright. Radiant, really. Or was it a medicine brightness? "Ah, Mike. You look so grand, so grand. Is that a new coat?"

"Not really," I said. I'd been wearing my Uncle Jerry's old army-fatigue jacket for months, practically living in it, my mother said. But she insisted that I wear my raincoat for the visit. It was about a year old but looked new because I didn't wear it much. Nobody was wearing raincoats lately.

"You always loved clothes, didn't you, Mike?" she said.

I was beginning to feel uneasy because she regarded me with such intensity. Those bright eyes. I wondered—are old people in places like this so lonesome, so abandoned that they go wild when someone visits? Or was she so happy because she was suddenly <u>lucid</u>, and everything was sharp and clear? My mother had described those moments when my grandmother suddenly emerged from the fog that so often obscured her mind. I didn't know the answers, but it felt kind of spooky, getting such an emotional welcome from her.

"I remember the time you bought the new coat—the chesterfield,"[5] she said, looking away again, as if watching the birds that weren't there. "That lovely coat with the velvet collar. Black, it was. Stylish. Remember that, Mike? It was hard times, but you could never resist the glitter."

I was about to protest—I had never heard of a chesterfield, for crying out loud. But I stopped. Be patient with her, my mother had said. Humor her. Be gentle.

We were interrupted by an attendant who pushed a wheeled cart into the room. "Time for juices, dear," the woman said. She was the standard forty- or fifty-year-old woman: glasses, nothing hair, plump cheeks. Her manner was cheerful but a businesslike kind of cheerfulness. I'd hate to be called "dear" by someone getting paid to do it. "Orange or grape or cranberry, dear? Cranberry is good for the bones, you know."

My grandmother ignored the interruption. She didn't even bother to answer, having turned away at the woman's arrival, as if angry about her appearance.

The woman looked at me and winked. A conspiratorial kind of wink. It was kind of horrible. I didn't think people winked like that anymore. In fact, I hadn't seen a wink in years.

"She doesn't care much for juices," the woman said, talking to me as if my grandmother weren't even there. "But she loves

---

5. **chesterfield**: an overcoat with concealed buttons and a velvet collar.

her coffee. With lots of cream and two lumps of sugar. But this is juice time, not coffee time." Addressing my grandmother again, she said, "Orange or grape or cranberry, dear?"

"Tell her I want no juices, Mike," my grandmother commanded regally, her eyes still watching invisible birds.

Ah, Mike, I thought I'd lost you forever.

The woman smiled, patience like a label on her face. "That's all right, dear. I'll just leave some cranberry for you. Drink it at your leisure. It's good for the bones."

She wheeled herself out of the room. My grandmother was still absorbed in the view. Somewhere a toilet flushed. A wheelchair passed the doorway—probably that same old driver fleeing a hit-run accident. A television set exploded with sound somewhere, soap-opera voices filling the air. You can always tell soap-opera voices.

I turned back to find my grandmother staring at me. Her hands cupped her face, her index fingers curled around her cheeks like parenthesis marks.

"But you know, Mike, looking back, I think you were right," she said, continuing our conversation as if there had been no interruption. "You always said, 'It's the things of the spirit that count, Meg.' The spirit! And so you bought the baby-grand piano—a baby grand in the middle of the Depression. A knock came on the door, and it was the deliveryman. It took five of them

to get it into the house." She leaned back, closing her eyes. "How I loved that piano, Mike. I was never that fine a player, but you loved to sit there in the parlor, on Sunday evenings, Ellie on your lap, listening to me play and sing." She hummed a bit, a fragment of melody I didn't recognize. Then she drifted into silence. Maybe she'd fallen asleep. My mother's name is Ellen, but everyone always calls her Ellie. "Take my hand, Mike," my grandmother said suddenly. Then I remembered—my grandfather's name was Michael. I had been named for him.

Who does Mike's grandmother think he is?

review

"Ah, Mike," she said, pressing my hands with all her feeble strength. "I thought I'd lost you forever. And here you are, back with me again. . . ."

Her expression scared me. I don't mean scared as if I were in danger but scared because of what could happen to her when she realized the mistake she had made. My mother always said I favored her side of the family. Thinking back to the pictures in the old family albums, I recalled my grandfather as tall and thin. Like me. But the resemblance ended there. He was thirty-five when he died, almost forty years ago. And he wore a moustache. I brought my hand to my face. I also wore a moustache now, of course.

"I sit here these days, Mike," she said, her voice a lullaby, her hand still holding mine, "and I drift and dream. The days are fuzzy sometimes, merging together. Sometimes it's like I'm not here at all but somewhere else altogether. And I always think of you. Those years we had. Not enough years, Mike, not enough. . . ."

Her voice was so sad, so mournful that I made sounds of sympathy, not words exactly but the kind of soothings that mothers murmur to their children when they awaken from bad dreams.

"And I think of that terrible night, Mike, that terrible night. Have you ever really forgiven me for that night?"

"Listen . . .," I began. I wanted to say: "Nana, this is Mike your grandson, not Mike your husband."

"Sh . . . sh . . .," she whispered, placing a finger as long and cold as a candle against my lips. "Don't say anything. I've waited so long for this moment. To be here. With you. I wondered what I would say if suddenly you walked in that door like other people have done. I've thought and thought about it. And I finally made up my mind—I'd ask you to forgive me. I was too proud to ask before." Her fingers tried to mask her face. "But I'm not proud anymore, Mike." That great voice quivered and then grew strong again. "I hate you to see me this way—you always said I was beautiful. I didn't believe it. The Charity Ball when we led the grand march and you said I was the most beautiful girl there . . ."

"Nana," I said. I couldn't keep up the pretense any longer, adding one more burden to my load of guilt, leading her on this way, playing a pathetic game of make-believe with an old woman clinging to memories.

She didn't seem to hear me.

"But that other night, Mike. The terrible one. The terrible accusations I made. Even Ellie woke up and began to cry. I went to her and rocked her in my arms, and you came into the room and said I was wrong. You were whispering, an awful whisper, not wanting to upset little Ellie but wanting to make me see the truth. And I didn't answer you, Mike. I was too proud. I've even forgotten the name of the girl. I sit here, wondering now—was it Laura or Evelyn? I can't remember. Later, I learned that you were telling the truth all the time, Mike. That I'd been wrong . . ." Her eyes were brighter than ever as she looked at me now, but tear-bright, the tears gathering. "It was never the same after that night, was it, Mike? The glitter was gone. From you. From us. And then the accident . . . and I never had the chance to ask you to forgive me . . ."

My grandmother. My poor, poor grandmother. Old people aren't supposed to have those kinds of memories. You see their pictures in the family albums, and that's what they are: pictures. They're not supposed to come to life. You drive out in your father's Le Mans doing seventy-five on the pike, and all you're doing is visiting an old lady in a nursing home. A duty call. And then you find out that she's a person. She's *somebody*. She's my grandmother, all right, but she's also herself. Like my own mother and father. They exist outside of their relationship to me. I was scared again. I wanted to get out of there.

MOOSE 1956 Alice Neel
Courtesy, Robert Miller Gallery,
New York.

"Mike, Mike," my grandmother said. "Say it, Mike."

I felt as if my cheeks would crack if I uttered a word.

"Say you forgive me, Mike. I've waited all these years …"

I was surprised at how strong her fingers were.

"Say, *'I forgive you, Meg.'*"

I said it. My voice sounded funny, as if I were talking in a huge tunnel. "I forgive you, Meg."

Her eyes studied me. Her hands pressed mine. For the first time in my life, I saw love at work. Not movie love. Not Cindy's sparkling eyes when I tell her that we're going to the beach on a Sunday afternoon. But love like something alive and tender, asking nothing in return. She raised her face, and I knew what she wanted me to do. I bent and brushed my lips against her cheek. Her flesh was like a leaf in autumn, crisp and dry.

She closed her eyes, and I stood up. The

sun wasn't glinting on the cars any longer. Somebody had turned on another television set, and the voices were the show-off voices of the panel shows. At the same time you could still hear the soap-opera dialogue on the other television set.

Finally I left. Just like that. I didn't say goodbye or anything.

I waited awhile. She seemed to be sleeping, her breathing <u>serene</u> and regular. I buttoned my raincoat. Suddenly she opened her eyes again and looked at me. Her eyes were still bright, but they merely stared at me. Without recognition or curiosity. Empty eyes. I smiled at her, but she didn't smile back. She made a kind of moaning sound and turned away on the bed, pulling the blankets around her.

I counted to twenty-five and then to fifty and did it all over again. I cleared my throat and coughed <u>tentatively</u>. She didn't move; she didn't respond. I wanted to say, "Nana, it's me." But I didn't. I thought of saying, "Meg, it's me." But I couldn't.

Finally I left. Just like that. I didn't say goodbye or anything. I stalked through the corridors, looking neither to the right nor the left, not caring whether that wild old man with the wheelchair ran me down or not.

On the Southwest Turnpike I did seventy-five—no, eighty—most of the way. I turned the radio up as loud as it could go. Rock music—anything to fill the air. When I got home, my mother was vacuuming the living-room rug. She shut off the cleaner, and the silence was deafening. "Well, how was your grandmother?" she asked.

I told her she was fine. I told her a lot of things. How great Nana looked and how she seemed happy and had called me Mike. I wanted to ask her—hey, Mom, you and Dad really love each other, don't you? I mean—there's nothing to forgive between you, is there? But I didn't.

Instead I went upstairs and took out the electric razor Annie had given me for Christmas and shaved off my moustache. ❧

INSIGHT

If There Be Sorrow
MARI EVANS

If there be sorrow
let it be
for things undone
undreamed
    unrealized
        unattained
to these add one:
love withheld
    restrained

Words to Know and Use | **serene** (se rēn') *adj.* calm
tentatively (ten' tə tiv lē) *adv.* in an uncertain or hesitant way

475

Responding to Reading

First Impressions

1. What did this story make you think about? Write your response in your journal or on a sheet of paper.

Second Thoughts

2. How do Mike's feelings about his grandmother change during the course of the story?

> **Think about**
> - Mike's guilt as he goes to the nursing home
> - Mike's feelings when Meg thinks he is her husband
> - Mike's thoughts at the end of the story

3. Why do you think Mike shaves off his moustache?

4. If you were Mike, would you go along with your grandmother's fantasy about her husband? Explain.

5. In your opinion what is the **theme** of this story?

> **Think about**
> - the guilt both Mike and his grandmother feel
> - attitudes toward the elderly—both Mike's and your own

Broader Connections

6. When people like Mike's grandmother can no longer take care of themselves, what should they do? Some feel that they should live with their children or grandchildren—that whatever the costs to the family, their rightful place is with family members. Others believe that the elderly receive better care and attention in nursing homes and that the government should pay for nursing-home care for patients who cannot afford it. What is your opinion on this issue?

Literary Concept: Symbolism

Sometimes a writer uses a concrete object—a **symbol**—to stand for an idea. For example, in "The Moustache" the piano **symbolizes** certain things about the grandfather—it seems to represent his generous spirit and his love of life. Similarly, a concrete object associated with Mike is his moustache. What do you think Mike's moustache symbolizes?

Writing Options

1. What do you suppose Mike is thinking about as he leaves the nursing home? Write an **interior monologue** expressing his thoughts. Remember that thoughts often wander and do not always come in complete sentences.

2. Use inference skills to write a **character sketch** of Mike's grandmother before and after her husband died. Be sure to include information about her outlook on life.

3. Reread "If There Be Sorrow," on page 475, or "The Burden," on page 454. Write an **explanation,** telling how you think the speaker of the poem would have reacted if he or she had been in Mike's situation.

4. Write a **letter to the editor** of your school newspaper to persuade readers of the importance of communicating and socializing with the elderly. Urge your fellow students to visit an elderly friend or relative.

Vocabulary Practice

Exercise   On a sheet of paper, write the word from the list that best completes each sentence.

1. With slow and quiet steps, Mike walked _?_ down the hall of the nursing home.

2. Nursing homes made him feel uncomfortable, with their _?_ smells and ailing patients.

3. Mike had thought some patients might be shouting or groaning, but Lawnrest was surprisingly _?_.

4. It had been a long time since Mike last saw his grandmother, and he had a strong guilt _?_.

5. Mike wasn't sure if his grandmother would be _?_ enough to recognize him when she saw him.

6. He wouldn't know what to do if she had a memory _?_ while he was there.

7. As Mike entered his grandmother's room, he was struck by how small and _?_ she was.

8. Mistaking Mike for her husband, she gave him a _?_ wink and asked him for a kiss.

9. Mike felt all kinds of emotions _?_ together at once.

10. He wondered if he should go along with the _?_ or tell his grandmother who he was.

> **Words to Know and Use**
>
> antiseptic
> complex
> conspiratorial
> lapse
> lucid
> merging
> pathetic
> pretense
> serene
> tentatively

Options for Learning

1 • Snapshot of Family History

Interview one of your older relatives. Find a photo showing him or her as a young person. Ask the relative to tell you some memorable family anecdotes from the time when the picture was taken. Later, use your interview notes to write a biographical sketch. Attach the photo to your writing and show the sketch to your family.

2 • Community Elder Care

With a partner look into the kinds of care provided for the elderly in your community. The care may include nursing homes, retirement centers, and day-care centers. If possible, visit these places and study their brochures. Make an evaluation of the quality of the care offered in your community. Present your findings to your class.

3 • Show time

With two partners choose from "The Moustache" a scene that includes dialogue. Decide who will read Mike's lines, his grandmother's lines, and the narrator's lines. Share the scene with your class as a readers' theater presentation.

4 • Student Doctor

Research one medical problem that mainly affects elderly people. For example, you might choose arteriosclerosis or Alzheimer's disease. Study the symptoms, the causes, and the treatments. Prepare an oral report for your class.

 FACT FINDER MATH

If Mike drove home at eighty miles per hour and his home was thirty miles from the nursing home, how many minutes did the drive take?

Robert Cormier
1925-

A former journalist, Robert Cormier has written more than a dozen novels about young adults. Three of his books—*The Chocolate War, I Am the Cheese,* and *After the First Death*—have won Outstanding Book of the Year awards from the New York Times. Cormier's most recent novel, *We All Fall Down,* was published in 1991.

Cormier lives in Leominster, Massachusetts, the town where he was born. There he and his wife have raised four children. The idea for the short story "The Moustache" came from one of Cormier's children, Peter. Cormier explains, "Peter's grandmother was in a nursing home. He had visited her. He was a teenager and had recently grown a moustache. His grandmother had had little recognition of him. He had been shaken by the visit." Drawing on these few realities and the emotion of the situation, Cormier created "The Moustache."

WRITER'S WORKSHOP

WRITING ABOUT LITERATURE

Were you moved by Della and Jim's bittersweet gestures of love? Did you find the ending of "The Moustache" satisfying? What kinds of selections work for you? One way to express your feelings about a selection is through a **critical review.** As a critic you can tell readers why you did or did not like a selection. In this workshop you will write a critical review that analyzes your favorite selection in this book.

Here is one writer's PASSkey to this assignment.

GUIDED ASSIGNMENT: CRITIC'S CORNER REVIEW

Write a critical review of your favorite selection in this book.

PURPOSE: To analyze a literary selection

AUDIENCE: Classmates, teachers

SUBJECT: A favorite selection

STRUCTURE: A critical review

Oh, Mamacita! Not Again!
by Hector Colón

Do you remember a time when your mom or dad embarrassed you? Maybe you got kissed in front of all your friends or were made to wear the ugliest jacket in the world. You probably wanted to shrivel up and die, right? We've all had moments like these, and so does Yollie Moreno, the main character in Gary Soto's "Mother and Daughter." The author makes her seem so real that I felt I knew exactly what was going on in her head. This true-to-life quality is one reason the story is so enjoyable. It is also humorous, and above all, it contains two very likable characters.

◄ **STUDENT MODEL**

Before you write, read how one student responded to the assignment.

◄ The writer states which selection he likes and why he likes it—it's true to life, and it contains humor and likeable characters.

Notice how the writer uses a quotation from the selection to describe a character.

The relationship between Yollie and her mother is very special. First, picture Yollie's mother--"a large woman who wore a muumuu and butterfly-shaped glasses." She enjoys watching scary late-night movies, playing practical jokes on Yollie, and talking to plants. Yollie enjoys watching TV with her mother; when she gets a chance, <u>she</u> plays practical jokes on her mother.

Relevant details strengthen the writer's position.

Yollie doesn't completely understand her mother, but she accepts her crazy ways--even when they lead to disaster. For example, one time Mrs. Moreno made candy apples for Yollie's birthday; the apples were so hard that they "shattered like grenades" when tossed against the side of a building. I felt sorry for Mrs. Moreno, but I couldn't help laughing when I pictured exploding candy apples.

The writer hints at the plot without giving away the final outcome.

Another incident--the main event in the plot--happens because Yollie wants a new dress for a school dance but her mother can't afford to buy her one. Instead, Mrs. Moreno promises to fix an old dress "so it will look brand-new." Yollie shudders with horror at this idea, and who could blame her?

Dance night arrives, and to no one's surprise, Mrs. Moreno's efforts lead to catastrophe. Something very embarrassing happens to Yollie, and she runs home in tears, upset at the way her mother has "helped" her. Yollie's anger eventually dies down. In turn, Mrs. Moreno understands how painful the incident at the dance was for Yollie and does something to make things better.

In the final paragraph the writer sums up his thoughts about the selection.

This relationship between the characters is one of the best things about this story. "Mother and Daughter" is satisfying because it is about people you know, people next door, maybe even people in your house.

Now begin a critical review of your favorite selection.

Prewrite and Explore

1 **Develop your criteria**   How do you go about choosing a selection? How do you know whether it's good or not? To answer these questions, you need to develop some basic criteria for recommending one selection over the others.

For openers, write down the titles of three or four selections you have read and enjoyed. Jot down the first impressions that come to mind about these selections. Think about what qualities make the selections worth reading. List the most important three or four of these qualities as your criteria. These criteria will serve as the basis for your evaluation.

2 **Make a final choice**   Review the selections you have chosen and rate them according to the criteria you have developed. Rate each selection for each criterion. Give a rating of 3 if you think a selection meets the criterion very well. Write 2 if it partially meets the criterion and 1 if it fails to meet the criterion. The selection with the highest total score is probably the one you will want to write about.

◀ LEARNING OPTION

You may wish to study the Reader's Workshop (page 487) before developing your criteria.

◀ WRITER'S CHOICE

You may find that one selection outweighs the merits of a more highly-rated selection. Feel free to disregard your rating chart if you feel strongly about a particular selection.

GATHERING INFORMATION

Once you've made your choice, you can revisit the selection to gather supporting evidence. Make a list of details that support each of your criteria. Look at the list of details that Hector made.

<u>It's true to life.</u>
  Yollie embarrassed by parent
  concern about appearance, what others will think
  Mother and daughter share special moments.

<u>It's humorous.</u>
  funny incidents (exploding candy apples)
  practical jokes

<u>It has likable characters.</u>
  Mrs. Moreno: dresses funny
                has some crazy ways
                plays practical jokes on Yollie
                talks to plants
                tells stories about childhood
  Yollie: is typical teenager
                plays practical jokes on mother
                is in love with Ernie Castillo

◀ STUDENT MODEL

◀ COMPUTER TIP

You can use a windows function to bring up your supporting details when gathering your information.

Draft and Discover

1 Begin drafting Look over the notes you have gathered. Work at developing the main ideas you want to get across to your readers. Focus on finding details and examples in the selection to support the criteria you have established. Try mixing your own interpretations with specific quotations or descriptions from the story.

NEED MORE DETAILS? ▶

Use the "why" test to add more details to your review. State a position, then ask yourself why you feel that way. Find evidence to support your opinion. Continue asking *why* and supporting your answers until you have sufficient details.

2 Check your evidence Be accurate and relevant. Ask yourself if all the details you've gathered are important to the points you're trying to make. Be sure you quote and paraphrase accurately.

3 Consider your organization You may want to begin by listing your criteria and describing how the selection meets each one. Once you have drafted your ideas, add a brief plot summary. Be sure not to give away too much of the plot.

Revise Your Writing

1 Provide a strong introduction Start your critical review with thought-provoking questions or relevant information that will attract the interest of your readers.

TIP ▶

Remember that the title is the first thing your readers will read. Look through your critical review a few times before making a final choice.

2 Go for a strong title After you are satisfied with your draft, work at developing a catchy title. Try a line from the selection itself or one that captures your focus. If you don't like your first ideas, put the draft aside and tackle the title problem again later.

3 Ask a peer to respond With a peer reader discuss areas in which your writing is most and least effective. Consider the following questions.

Revision Questions	
For You	**For a Peer Reader**
1. Are my criteria sound?	**1.** Do you know what my criteria are?
2. Did I show *why* this selection is my favorite?	**2.** Did I include good examples?
3. Did I choose convincing details and reasons?	**3.** What kinds of details should I have added?

Proofread

Check your draft for errors in grammar, spelling, and punctuation. Review your choice of words to be sure you've chosen ones that accurately convey your meaning. If possible, ask a classmate to proofread your work.

HE EDITOR'S EYE: COMMON USAGE ERRORS

Avoid misusing words with similar sounds or spellings.

Many words with similar sounds or spellings are commonly confused.

Problem Yollie . . . *excepts* her crazy ways . . .

Correct Yollie . . . *accepts* her crazy ways . . .

Accept means "to take" or "to agree to." *Except* means "other than" or "if it were not."

NEED MORE HELP?
See the Language Workshop that follows (pages 484–486).

Publish and Present

Here is a suggestion for sharing your work with others.

A Class Anthology Invite a few teachers, classmates, and the school principal to serve on an anthology committee. Have them read all the reviews and decide which selections they feel are recommended most effectively. Compile those selections into an anthology that includes one or two reviews of each selection. If you wish, share the anthology with other classes.

Reflect on Your Writing

Briefly answer the following questions. Include your responses with your review when you add it to your portfolio.

1. What part of writing a critical review did you find the easiest?

2. Do you think you did a good job reviewing your selection? Explain.

◀ FOR YOUR PORTFOLIO

LANGUAGE
WORKSHOP

COMMON USAGE ERRORS

> Words with similar sounds, similar spellings, or related meanings are often confused. Study these words to avoid misusing them.

Words with Similar Sounds or Spellings

accept and except

Accept means "to take" or "to agree to." *Except* means "other than" or "if it were not."

> We watched the baby baboon *accept* some food from its mother.
> *Except* for the mother's sacrifice, the baby baboon would have died.

affect and effect

Affect means "to influence." *Effect* means "the result of an action."

> Smith and I were unable to *affect* the outcome of the fight.
> The baboon's sacrifice had an emotional *effect* on us.

all ready and already

All ready means "completely prepared." *Already* means "by that time."

> The camera and the telescope were *all ready* to be used.
> When the baboons arrived, we were *already* in the breadfruit tree.

desert and dessert

A *desert* (dez' ərt) is a dry, sandy region with little vegetation. *Desert* (di zʉrt') means "to abandon or leave." A *dessert* (di zʉrt') is a sweet food, such as cake or pie, served at the end of a meal.

> Some baboons live near the *desert* regions of Africa.
> Baboons do not *desert* their young.
> Do baboons eat fruit and grass for *dessert?*

farther and further

Farther means "at a greater distance." Further means "more."

> The breadfruit tree was farther up the hill than the baboons.
> The battle we witnessed prompted us to begin further study.

◄ SPELLING TIP ....
Remember, when spelling farther, think about how far you will go.

past and passed

Past means "beyond" or "former." Passed means "moved beyond."

> The leopard had to get past the mother baboon.
> We watched silently as the baboon herd passed by.

stationary and stationery

Stationary means "not moving" or "unchanged." Stationery is the paper and other material used for writing.

> Smith anchored the camera in a stationary position.
> He pulled out his stationery to take notes.

◄ SPELLING TIP ....
Remember, something stationary stays in one place, whereas stationery includes paper.

Words with Related Meanings

amount and number

Amount is used to refer to a quantity of something that doesn't consist of countable parts. Number is used to refer to a quantity of individual items that can be counted.

> I couldn't believe the amount of energy the baboon had.
> The number of people in our research group varied from year to year.

fewer and less

Fewer is used with things that can be counted. Less is used with things that cannot be counted.

> The mother baboon had fewer reasons to live than to die.
> The baboon had less hope of winning the battle.

Exercise 1 Concept Check On your paper write the correct word of the two given in parentheses.

1. Many baboons live near the (desert, dessert) regions of Africa.
2. Others live (farther, further) east on the Arabian Peninsula.
3. The (amount, number) of individuals in baboon groups ranges from thirty to two hundred.
4. A few groups, however, have (fewer, less) than thirty baboons.
5. Most baboons live in groups made up of a number of baboon families—(accept, except) chacma baboons, which live in smaller groups ruled by several large males.
6. Female baboons have a great (affect, effect) on their young.
7. Male baboons are fierce fighters; they never (desert, dessert) the other baboons in the group.
8. When baboons are (all ready, already) to fight, they band together to protect one another.
9. The males often stand in (stationary, stationery) positions to protect the group from enemies.
10. Most enemies find it extremely difficult to get (past, passed) the baboon "guards."

Exercise 2 Proofreading Skill Rewrite the following paragraph. Correct any errors in word usage that you find.

What do you know about the breadfruit? You may all ready know that it is a tropical fruit. Further research would show that breadfruits usually weigh about three pounds and that they grow on huge trees, none of which is fewer than 65 feet tall! Breadfruit would make a great desert accept for one thing—it has a very bland taste. If you can get passed the bland taste, you will be able to except that the breadfruit is an important food. Like potatoes, breadfruits can be baked, boiled, and fried. Even the seeds are edible! All in all, eating breadfruit might have a great affect on you.

Exercise 3 Revising Your Writing Reread the critical review you wrote for the Writer's Workshop on pages 479–483. Lightly underline and correct any errors in word usage that you find.

READER'S WORKSHOP

MAKING JUDGMENTS

In writing your critical review for the Writer's Workshop on pages 479–483, you needed to evaluate a selection and make a judgment about it. When you make a judgment about anything—a story, an idea, a music performance, a political candidate—you are expressing the reasons why you like or dislike it.

There are certain steps you need to follow when making a judgment. First, develop a set of **criteria**—standards for assessing the thing you are evaluating. In evaluating the selection for your critical review, for example, you probably asked yourself questions such as the following: Was the plot interesting? Were the characters realistic? Was the dialogue moving? These were the criteria you used to evaluate your selection. Second, ask yourself if your criteria are both sound and relevant. If your criteria are not sound and relevant, your judgment may not be reasonable. For example, if Hector had chosen "Mother and Daughter" because the author won literary awards for *other* writings, his judgment of *this* selection might have been affected by an irrelevant consideration. Third, once you are satisfied with your criteria, you need to gather data to see whether the evidence meets your standards. Next, organize the evidence you've gathered. Finally, review the data and draw a conclusion about the topic on the basis of your criteria.

Here are examples of conclusions you might reach if you used sound and relevant criteria to judge a sports leader, a school course, and a film.

◀ TIP
Remember, use these four steps when you are called upon to make a judgment about a topic.
1. Develop criteria.
2. Use criteria to evaluate topic.
3. Gather data.
4. Review data.

1. I recommend Elaine for team captain because she is the most experienced player and gets along well with her teammates.
2. I have chosen Spanish as my elective course because Spanish is spoken by more people in my community than any other language.
3. I don't recommend that film because the plot was not believable and the special effects were amateurish.

Exercise   Choose one of the following topics or a topic of your own. Write criteria for evaluating the topic. Then make a judgment about the topic on the basis of your criteria.

- physical safety in your school environment
- the best teacher in your school
- the last movie you watched
- the most interesting trip you've ever taken

Reading on Your Own

Suggested Novels for Unit Four

The novels introduced on these pages reflect the theme of Unit Four, "Matters of the Heart."

THE HERO AND THE CROWN

ROBIN MCKINLEY ©1984

Aerin is the only daughter of King Damar and heir to his throne. Aerin's destiny, however, is much greater than either she or her father's people know—she must battle with Maur, the Black Dragon. Before the battle Aerin ventures into the Damarian Hills, where she meets the wizard Luthe. It is Luthe who reveals to Aerin the secret of the Blue Sword, which she uses in an attempt to reclaim the Hero's Crown, Damar's greatest treasure and the source of his strength. The steps of her quest are increasingly severe tests of fortitude and dedication. As a consequence, Aerin makes a discovery about herself and learns the true role of responsibility and love. Read to find out . . .

- what obstacles Aerin faces in her epic quest

- how she is able to outwit her opponents

- whether she succeeds in her quest

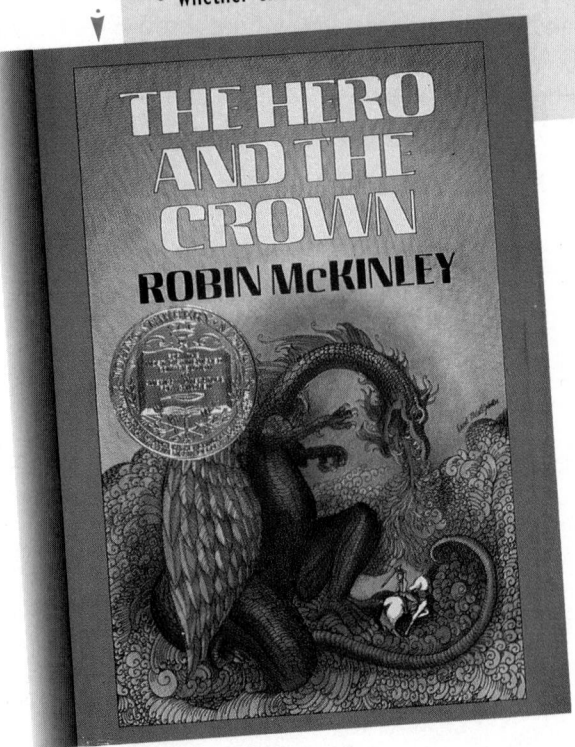

TAKING SIDES
GARY SOTO ©1991

Lincoln Mendoza has just moved to Columbus and attends Columbus Junior High. Lincoln is saddened because he can no longer play on the basketball team at Franklin, his former school, but he manages to retain his friendship with his former teammates. Later, he tries out for basketball at Columbus and is pleased when he makes the team, becoming its only Hispanic player. Things are fine until scheduling pits Columbus against Franklin. Because of the game, Lincoln learns about winning—and about loyalty, change, and friendship. As you read, put yourself in Lincoln's place by thinking about these questions:

* How would you feel about leaving your school and friends?

* What would it be like to play your former teammates in a basketball game?

* How can a person make the adjustments needed to survive in a new school?

LOUISA MAY: THE WORLD AND WORKS OF LOUISA MAY ALCOTT
NORMA JOHNSTON ©1991

The author Louisa May Alcott (1832-1888) wrote many books that became classics. Among her works are *Little Women* and *Little Men*. What inspired this popular author to write? What was life like for an author during the mid-1800s? In *Louisa May: The World and Works of Louisa May Alcott*, you will learn about Louisa May Alcott—her childhood, her inspirations, her hardships, and her triumphs. As you read, think about . . .

* the forces that motivated Louisa May Alcott to write

* how she was able to support her family with her writing

* how different her life was from the life of a female writer today

Other Recommended Books

Ghost Brother by C. S. Adler (©1990). In this story twelve-year-old Wally struggles to live up to the athletic abilities of his older brother, Jon, who was killed in an accident.

Preposterous: Poems of Youth edited by Paul Janeczko (©1991). This collection of poetry contains many poems related to the unit theme, "Matters of the Heart."

The Civil Rights Movement in America from 1865 to the Present by Patricia and Frederick McKissack (©1991). This nonfictional book reveals the struggles and sacrifices of people who became involved in the civil rights movement.

The Day That Elvis Came to Town by Jan Marino (©1991). In this novel set in the South during the early 1960s, a young girl makes a discovery about a famous boarder and faces the truth about her family and herself.

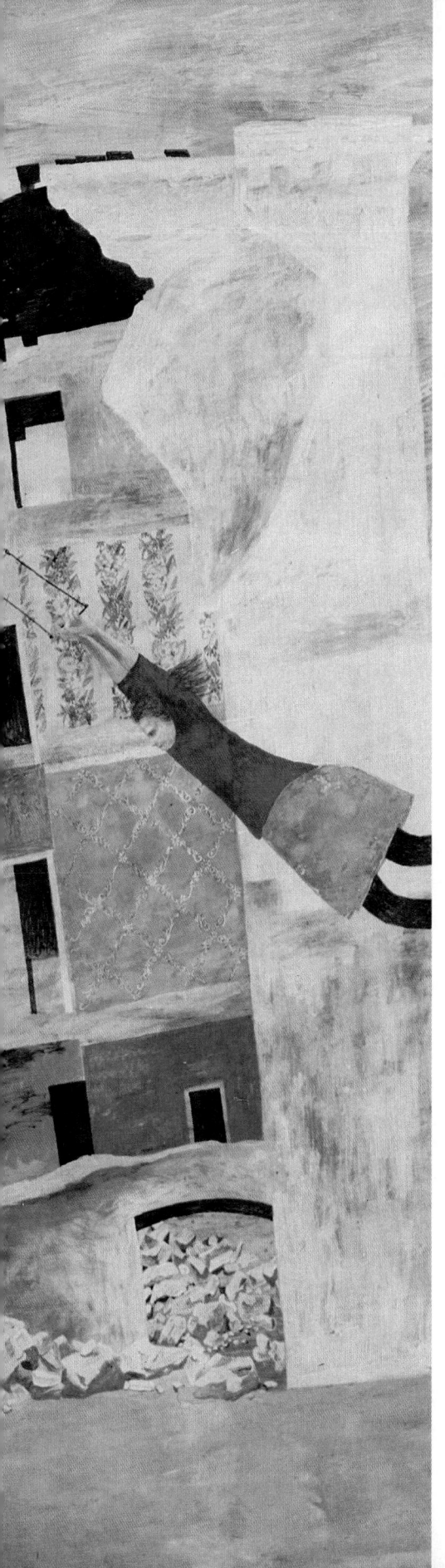

THE WILL TO SURVIVE

There is a place

in you where

nothing is impossible.

Tara Singh

LIBERATION   1945   Ben Shahn
Tempera on cardboard mounted on
composition board, 29¾ in. x 40 in.
Collection, The Museum of Modern Art,
New York, James Thrall Soby Bequest.
Photograph © 1992 The Museum of
Modern Art, New York.

THE INVINCIBLE SPIRIT

You sense danger. Immediately, your heartbeat quickens, your blood pressure rises, your pupils dilate, and blood rushes to your muscles. Because the will to survive is one of the most basic human instincts, your body is perfectly programmed to respond to fight or flee in cases of sudden threat. You can count on it. The title of Unit Five, "The Will to Survive," then, refers to situations that require great mental and physical alertness.

Survival, however, is not always a matter of a single decisive moment. Sometimes people find themselves caught in a situation that demands that they rely more on their spirit than on their instincts. People who live through war, for example, frequently find internal strengths they never knew they possessed.

Can you imagine having to hide out for two years from powerful enemies? Your foes have all the power on their side. All you have to help you survive are your own wits, the support of your family, and the kindness of a few loyal friends. Where do you think you could find the inner strength you would need to survive? If you kept a record of your years in hiding, how might such a record read?

In this subunit, "The Invincible Spirit," you will meet a group who successfully hid for over two years in Nazi-occupied Amsterdam during World War II.

Drama

The Diary of Anne Frank

FRANCES GOODRICH AND ALBERT HACKETT

Examine What You Know

World War II was the most destructive war of all time. In addition to the millions of military deaths, a large-scale, systematic killing of innocent civilians took place. In small groups pool your knowledge about World War II and the tragic fate of the victims, especially the European Jews. For each term in the following list, jot down the words that come to mind when you consider the term's meaning and importance.

Hitler	concentration camps	deportation	Ayran race
Nazi	Normandy—D-day	Holocaust	Auschwitz
Allies	Nuremberg trials	antisemitism	Gestapo

Expand Your Knowledge

Adolf Hitler, the dictator who ruled Germany from 1933 to 1945, dreamed of a world empire led by a "master race." Part of Hitler's plan involved the extermination of all European Jews in what was termed the final solution to the Jewish problem. Despite being defeated by the Allied powers—led by the United States, the United Kingdom, and the Soviet Union—Hitler and his Nazi war machine left behind a terrible legacy. By the time World War II ended in 1945, over 6 million Jews had been murdered, as well as 5 million Gypsies, Slavs, and Poles.

When Hitler's war machine overran the Netherlands in 1940, Jews living there were subjected to increased restrictions.

Soon, Jews were rounded up and shipped to concentration camps, where most of them died of starvation or were killed in gas chambers. Among the Jewish families affected by Hitler's tyranny were the Franks, a German Jewish family that had fled to the Netherlands in 1933. When Margot Frank was called to report "for work in the East," the Franks knew they must go into hiding. This play, based on a diary left by thirteen-year-old Anne Frank, tells of the events that followed.

*E*nrich Your Reading

Stage Set   The cramped rooms in the warehouse where the Franks and their friends hid needed to be represented by a stage set that would suggest the crowding and also allow each room to be plainly visible to the audience. The illustration below shows the stage set.

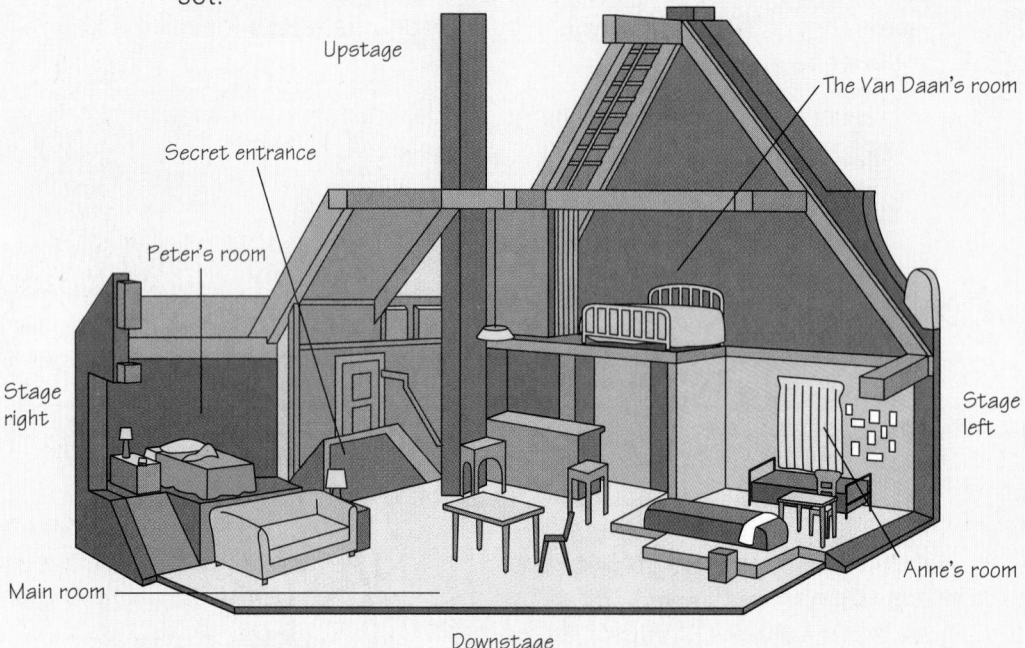

Upstage

The Van Daan's room

Secret entrance

Peter's room

Stage right

Stage left

Main room

Anne's room

Downstage

*W*rite Before You Read

The Franks, the Van Daan family, and Dr. Dussel—eight people in all—spent over two years in hiding. There were only four rooms. Food was scarce, and strict silence had to be maintained during the daytime. If you were in a similar situation and had to spend two years shut up with your family and another family, what problems do you think you would face? Write down your thoughts in your journal or on a sheet of paper.

■ *Author biographies on Extend page*

The Diary of Anne Frank

FRANCES GOODRICH AND ALBERT HACKETT

CHARACTERS

Mr. Frank

Miep

Mrs. Van Daan

Mr. Van Daan

Peter Van Daan

Mrs. Frank

Margot Frank

Anne Frank

Mr. Kraler

Dr. Dussel

ACT ONE

Scene 1

The scene remains the same throughout the play. It is the top floor of a warehouse and office building in Amsterdam, Holland. The sharply peaked roof of the building is outlined against a sea of other rooftops, stretching away into the distance. Nearby is the belfry of a church tower, the Westertoren, whose carillon[1] rings out the hours. Occasionally faint sounds float up from below: the voices of children playing in the street, the tramp of marching feet, a boat whistle from the canal.

The three rooms of the top floor and a small attic space above are exposed to our view. The largest of the rooms is in the center, with two small rooms, slightly raised,

on either side. On the right is a bathroom, out of sight. A narrow, steep flight of stairs at the back leads up to the attic. The rooms are sparsely furnished with a few chairs, cots, a table or two. The windows are painted over or covered with makeshift blackout curtains.[2] In the main room there is a sink, a gas ring for cooking, and a wood-burning stove for warmth.

The room on the left is hardly more than a closet. There is a skylight in the sloping ceiling. Directly under this room is a small,

---

1. carillon: a set of tuned bells.
2. makeshift blackout curtains: improvised curtains for concealing lights from enemy bombers.

steep stairwell, with steps leading down to a door. This is the only entrance from the building below. When the door is opened, we see that it has been concealed on the outer side by a bookcase attached to it.

The curtain rises on an empty stage. It is late afternoon, November 1945.

The rooms are dusty, the curtains in rags. Chairs and tables are overturned.

The door at the foot of the small stairwell swings open. Mr. Frank *comes up the steps into view. He is a gentle, cultured European in his middle years. There is still a trace of a German accent in his speech.*

He stands looking slowly around, making a supreme effort at self-control. He is weak, ill. His clothes are threadbare.

After a second he drops his rucksack[3] on the couch and moves slowly about. He opens the door to one of the smaller rooms and then abruptly closes it again, turning away. He goes to the window at the back, looking off at the Westertoren as its carillon strikes the hour of six; then he moves restlessly on.

From the street below we hear the sound of a barrel organ[4] and children's voices at play. There is a many-colored scarf hanging from a nail. Mr. Frank *takes it, putting it around his neck. As he starts back for his rucksack, his eye is caught by something lying on the floor. It is a woman's white glove. He holds it in his hand and suddenly all of his self-control is gone. He breaks down, crying.*

We hear footsteps on the stairs. Miep Gies *comes up, looking for* Mr. Frank. Miep *is a Dutch girl of about twenty-two. She wears a coat and hat, ready to go home.*

She is pregnant. Her attitude toward Mr. Frank *is protective,* compassionate.

Miep. Are you all right, Mr. Frank?

Mr. Frank *(quickly controlling himself).* Yes, Miep, yes.

Miep. Everyone in the office has gone home . . . It's after six. *(then pleading)* Don't stay up here, Mr. Frank. What's the use of torturing yourself like this?

Mr. Frank. I've come to say goodbye . . . I'm leaving here, Miep.

Miep. What do you mean? Where are you going? Where?

Mr. Frank. I don't know yet. I haven't decided.

Miep. Mr. Frank, you can't leave here! This is your home! Amsterdam is your home. Your business is here, waiting for you . . . You're needed here . . . Now that the war is over, there are things that . . .

Mr. Frank. I can't stay in Amsterdam, Miep. It has too many memories for me. Everywhere there's something . . . the house we lived in . . . the school . . . that street organ playing out there . . . I'm not the person you used to know, Miep. I'm a bitter old man. *(breaking off)* Forgive me. I shouldn't speak to you like this . . . after all that you did for us . . . the suffering . . .

---

3. **rucksack:** a small knapsack.
4. **barrel organ:** a mechanical musical instrument played by turning a crank.

Words to Know and Use | **compassionate** (kəm pash′ ən it) *adj.* sympathizing deeply

Miep. No. No. It wasn't suffering. You can't say we suffered. (*As she speaks, she straightens a chair which is overturned.*)

Mr. Frank. I know what you went through, you and Mr. Kraler. I'll remember it as long as I live. (*He gives one last look around.*) Come, Miep. (*He starts for the steps, then remembers his rucksack, going back to get it.*)

Miep (*hurrying up to a cupboard*). Mr. Frank, did you see? There are some of your papers here. (*She brings a bundle of papers to him.*) We found them in a heap of rubbish on the floor after . . . after you left.

Mr. Frank. Burn them. (*He opens his rucksack to put the glove in it.*)

Miep. But, Mr. Frank, there are letters, notes . . .

Mr. Frank. Burn them. All of them.

Miep. Burn *this*? (*She hands him a paperbound notebook.*)

Mr. Frank (*quietly*). Anne's diary. (*He opens the diary and begins to read.*) "Monday, the sixth of July, nineteen forty-two." (*to* Miep) Nineteen forty-two. Is it possible, Miep? . . . Only three years ago. (*As he continues his reading, he sits down on the couch.*) "Dear Diary, since you and I are going to be great friends, I will start by telling you about myself. My name is Anne Frank. I am thirteen years old. I was born in Germany the twelfth of June, nineteen twenty-nine. As my family is Jewish, we emigrated to Holland when Hitler came to power."

(*As* Mr. Frank *reads on, another voice joins his, as if coming from the air. It is* Anne's *voice.*)

Anne Frank's diary.

Mr. Frank and **Anne.** "My father started a business, importing spice and herbs. Things went well for us until nineteen forty. Then the war came, and the Dutch capitulation,[5] followed by the arrival of the Germans. Then things got very bad for the Jews."

(Mr. Frank's *voice dies out.* Anne's *voice continues alone. The lights dim slowly to darkness. The curtain falls on the scene.*)

Anne's Voice. You could not do this and you could not do that. They forced Father out of his business. We had to wear yellow stars.[6] I had to turn in my bike. I couldn't go to a Dutch school anymore. I couldn't go to the movies, or ride

---

5. **capitulation:** surrender.

6. **yellow stars:** the six-pointed Stars of David that the Nazis ordered all Jews to wear for identification.

Mr. and Mrs. Van Daan
and Mr. Kraler.

in an automobile or even on a streetcar, and a million other things. But somehow we children still managed to have fun. Yesterday Father told me we were going into hiding. Where, he wouldn't say. At five o'clock this morning Mother woke me and told me to hurry and get dressed. I was to put on as many clothes as I could. It would look too suspicious if we walked along carrying suitcases. It wasn't until we were on our way that I learned where we were going. Our hiding place was to be upstairs in the building where Father used to have his business. Three other people were coming in with us . . . the Van Daans and their son, Peter . . . Father knew the Van Daans but we had never met them . . .

(During the last lines, the curtain rises on the scene. The lights dim on. Anne's voice fades out.)

Scene 2

It is early morning, July 1942. The rooms are bare, as before, but they are now clean and orderly.

Mr. Van Daan, *a tall, portly man in his late forties, is in the main room, pacing up and down, nervously smoking a cigarette. His clothes and overcoat are expensive and well cut.*

Mrs. Van Daan *sits on the couch, clutching her possessions, a hatbox, bags, and so forth. She is a pretty woman in her early forties. She wears a fur coat over her other clothes.*

Peter Van Daan *is standing at the window of the room on the right, looking down at the street below. He is a shy, awkward boy of sixteen. He wears a cap, a raincoat, and long Dutch trousers, like "plus fours."[7] At his feet is a black case, a carrier for his cat.*

---

7. plus fours: short, loose trousers gathered at the knees; knickers.

The yellow Star of David is conspicuous on all of their clothes.

Mrs. Van Daan *(rising, nervous, excited).* Something's happened to them! I know it!

Mr. Van Daan. Now, Kerli!

Mrs. Van Daan. Mr. Frank said they'd be here at seven o'clock. He said . . .

Mr. Van Daan. They have two miles to walk. You can't expect . . .

Mrs. Van Daan. They've been picked up. That's what's happened. They've been taken . . .

(Mr. Van Daan indicates that he hears someone coming.)

Mr. Van Daan. You see?

(Peter takes up his carrier and his school bag, and so forth, and goes into the main room as Mr. Frank comes up the stairwell from below. Mr. Frank looks much younger now. His movements are brisk, his manner confident. He wears an overcoat and carries his hat and a small cardboard box. He crosses to the Van Daans, shaking hands with each of them.)

Mr. Frank. Mrs. Van Daan, Mr. Van Daan. Peter. *(then, in explanation of their lateness)* There were too many of the Green Police[8] on the streets . . . we had to take the long way around.

(Up the steps come Margot Frank, Mrs. Frank, Miep (not pregnant now), and Mr. Kraler. All of them carry bags, packages, and so forth. The Star of David is conspicuous on all of the Franks' clothing. Margot is eighteen, beautiful, quiet, shy. Mrs. Frank is a young mother, gently bred, reserved. She, like Mr. Frank, has a slight German accent. Mr. Kraler is a Dutchman, dependable, kindly.

As Mr. Kraler and Miep go upstage to put down their parcels, Mrs. Frank turns back to call Anne.)

Mrs. Frank. Anne?

(Anne comes running up the stairs. She is thirteen, quick in her movements, interested in everything, mercurial[9] in her emotions. She wears a cape and long wool socks and carries a school bag.)

Mr. Frank *(introducing them).* My wife, Edith. Mr. and Mrs. Van Daan . . . their son, Peter . . . my daughters, Margot and Anne.

(Mrs. Frank hurries over, shaking hands with them.)

(Anne gives a polite little curtsy as she shakes Mr. Van Daan's hand. Then she immediately starts off on a tour of investigation of her new home, going upstairs to the attic room.

Miep and Mr. Kraler are putting the various things they have brought on the shelves.)

Mr. Kraler. I'm sorry there is still so much confusion.

Mr. Frank. Please. Don't think of it. After all, we'll have plenty of leisure to arrange everything ourselves.

---

8. **Green Police:** the Nazi police who wore green uniforms.
9. **mercurial:** changing quickly and unpredictably.

The Frank family. Anne (center), Mr. Frank (with hat), Margot (right), and family friends.

Miep *(to* Mrs. Frank*).* We put the stores of food you sent in here. Your drugs are here . . . soap, linen here.

Mrs. Frank. Thank you, Miep.

Miep. I made up the beds . . . the way Mr. Frank and Mr. Kraler said. *(She starts out.)* Forgive me. I have to hurry. I've got to go to the other side of town to get some ration books for you.

Mrs. Van Daan. Ration books? If they see our names on ration books, they'll know we're here.

Mr. Kraler. There isn't anything . . .

Miep. Don't worry. Your names won't be on them. *(as she hurries out)* I'll be up later.

Mr. Frank. Thank you, Miep.

Mrs. Frank *(to* Mr. Kraler*).* It's illegal, then, the ration books? We've never done anything illegal.

Mr. Frank. We won't be living here exactly according to regulations.

(As Mr. Kraler *reassures* Mrs. Frank, *he takes various small things, such as matches, soap, and so forth, from his pockets, handing them to her.)*

Mr. Kraler. This isn't the black market,[10] Mrs. Frank. This is what we call the white market . . . helping all of the hundreds and hundreds who are hiding out in Amsterdam.

---

10. **black market:** a system for selling goods illegally, in violation of rationing or other restrictions.

(The carillon is heard playing the quarter-hour before eight. Mr. Kraler looks at his watch. Anne stops at the window as she comes down the stairs.)

It's the Westertoren!

Mr. Kraler. I must go. I must be out of here and downstairs in the office before the workmen get here. *(He starts for the stairs leading out.)* Miep or I, or both of us, will be up each day to bring you food and news and find out what your needs are. Tomorrow I'll get you a better bolt for the door at the foot of the stairs. It needs a bolt that you can throw yourself and open only at our signal. *(to Mr. Frank)* Oh . . . You'll tell them about the noise?

Mr. Frank. I'll tell them.

Mr. Kraler. Goodbye, then, for the moment. I'll come up again, after the workmen leave.

Mr. Frank. Goodbye, Mr. Kraler.

Mrs. Frank *(shaking his hand)*. How can we thank you?

(The others murmur their goodbyes.)

Mr. Kraler. I never thought I'd live to see the day when a man like Mr. Frank would have to go into hiding. When you think—

(He breaks off, going out. Mr. Frank follows him down the steps, bolting the door after him. In the interval before he returns, Peter goes over to Margot, shaking hands with her. As Mr. Frank comes back up the steps, Mrs. Frank questions him anxiously.)

Mrs. Frank. What did he mean, about the noise?

Mr. Frank. First let us take off some of these clothes.

(They all start to take off garment after garment. On each of their coats, sweaters, blouses, suits, dresses, is another yellow Star of David. Mr. and Mrs. Frank are underdressed quite simply. The others wear several things, sweaters, extra dresses, bathrobes, aprons, nightgowns, and so forth.)

Mr. Van Daan. It's a wonder we weren't arrested, walking along the streets . . . Petronella with a fur coat in July . . . and that cat of Peter's crying all the way.

Anne. A cat?

(Finally, as they have all removed their surplus clothes, they look to Mr. Frank, waiting for him to speak.)

Mr. Frank. Now. About the noise. While the men are in the building below, we must have complete quiet. Every sound can be heard down there, not only in the workrooms, but in the offices too. The men come at about eight-thirty and leave at about five-thirty. So, to be perfectly safe, from eight in the morning until six in the evening we must move only when it is necessary, and then in stockinged feet. We must not speak above a whisper. We must not run any water. We cannot use the sink or even, forgive me, the w.c.[11] The pipes go down through the workrooms. It would be heard. No trash . . .

(Mr. Frank stops abruptly as he hears the sound of marching feet from the street below. Everyone is motionless, paralyzed with fear. Mr. Frank goes quietly into the room on the right to look down out of the window. Anne runs after him, peering out with him. The

---

11. **w.c.:** water closet; toilet.

tramping feet pass without stopping. The tension is relieved. Mr. Frank, followed by Anne, returns to the main room and resumes his instructions to the group.)

. . . No trash must ever be thrown out which might reveal that someone is living up here . . . not even a potato paring. We must burn everything in the stove at night. This is the way we must live until it is over, if we are to survive.

(There is silence for a second.)

Mrs. Frank. Until it is over.

Mr. Frank *(reassuringly)*. After six we can move about . . . we can talk and laugh and have our supper and read and play games . . . just as we would at home. *(He looks at his watch.)* And now I think it would be wise if we all went to our rooms and were settled before eight o'clock. Mrs. Van Daan, you and your husband will be upstairs. I regret that there's no place up there for Peter. But he will be here, near us. This will be our common room, where we'll meet to talk and eat and read, like one family.

Mr. Van Daan. And where do you and Mrs. Frank sleep?

Mr. Frank. This room is also our bedroom.

⌐**Mrs. Van Daan.** That isn't right. We'll sleep here, and you take the room upstairs.

Together

└**Mr. Van Daan.** It's your place.

Mr. Frank. Please. I've thought this out for weeks. It's the best arrangement. The only arrangement.

Mrs. Van Daan *(to* Mr. Frank*)*. Never, never can we thank you. *(then to* Mrs. Frank*)* I don't know what would have happened to us if it hadn't been for Mr. Frank.

Mr. Frank. You don't know how your husband helped me when I came to this country . . . knowing no one . . . not able to speak the language. I can never repay him for that. *(going to* Van Daan*)* May I help you with your things?

Mr. Van Daan. No. No. *(to* Mrs. Van Daan*)* Come along, *liefje.*[12]

Mrs. Van Daan. You'll be all right, Peter? You're not afraid?

Peter *(embarrassed)*. Please, Mother.

(They start up the stairs to the attic room above. Mr. Frank *turns to* Mrs. Frank*.)*

Mr. Frank. You too must have some rest, Edith. You didn't close your eyes last night. Nor you, Margot.

Anne. I slept, Father. Wasn't that funny? I knew it was the last night in my own bed, and yet I slept soundly.

Mr. Frank. I'm glad, Anne. Now you'll be able to help me straighten things in here. *(to* Mrs. Frank *and* Margot*)* Come with me . . . You and Margot rest in this room for the time being.

(He picks up their clothes, starting for the room on the right.)

Mrs. Frank. You're sure . . . ? I could help . . . And Anne hasn't had her milk . . .

---

12. *liefje* (lēf yə) *Dutch:* little darling.

Mr. Frank. I'll give it to her. *(to* Anne *and* Peter*)* Anne, Peter . . . it's best that you take off your shoes now, before you forget.

(He leads the way to the room, followed by Margot.)

Mrs. Frank. You're sure you're not tired, Anne?

Anne. I feel fine. I'm going to help Father.

Mrs. Frank. Peter, I'm glad you are to be with us.

Peter. Yes, Mrs. Frank.

*(*Mrs. Frank *goes to join* Mr. Frank *and* Margot.)*

(During the following scene, Mr. Frank *helps* Margot *and* Mrs. Frank *to hang up their clothes. Then he persuades them both to lie down and rest. The Van Daans, in their room above, settle themselves. In the main room* Anne *and* Peter *remove their shoes.* Peter *takes his cat out of the carrier.)*

Anne. What's your cat's name?

Peter. Mouschi.

Anne. Mouschi! Mouschi! Mouschi! *(She picks up the cat, walking away with it. To* Peter.*)* I love cats. I have one . . . a darling little cat. But they made me leave her behind. I left some food and a note for the neighbors to take care of her . . . I'm going to miss her terribly. What is yours? A him or a her?

Peter. He's a tom. He doesn't like strangers. *(He takes the cat from her, putting it back in its carrier.)*

Badge required to be worn by Dutch Jews.

Anne *(unabashed).*[13] Then I'll have to stop being a stranger, won't I? Where did you go to school?

Peter. Jewish Secondary.

Anne. But that's where Margot and I go! I never saw you around.

Peter. I used to see you . . . sometimes . . .

Anne. You did?

Peter. . . . in the schoolyard. You were always in the middle of a bunch of kids. *(He takes a penknife from his pocket.)*

Anne. Why didn't you ever come over?

Peter. I'm sort of a lone wolf. *(He starts to rip off his Star of David.)*

Anne. What are you doing?

Peter. Taking it off.

Anne. But you can't do that. They'll arrest you if you go out without your star.

---

13. **unabashed:** not embarrassed.

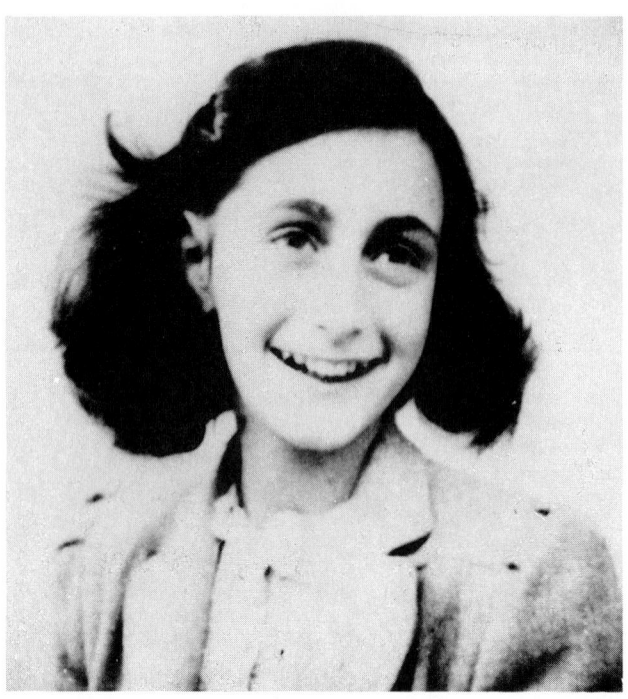

Anne Frank.

we'd suddenly been called away . . . breakfast dishes in the sink . . . beds not made . . . *(As she pulls off her star, the cloth underneath shows clearly the color and form of the star.)* Look! It's still there! *(Peter goes over to the stove with his star.)* What're you going to do with yours?

Peter. Burn it.

Anne *(starts to throw hers in and cannot).* It's funny, I can't throw mine away. I don't know why.

Peter. You can't throw . . . ? Something they branded you with . . . ? That they made you wear so they could spit on you?

Anne. I know. I know. But after all, it *is* the Star of David, isn't it?

(In the bedroom, right, Margot *and* Mrs. Frank *are lying down.* Mr. Frank *starts quietly out.)*

Peter. Maybe it's different for a girl.

(Mr. Frank comes into the main room.)

Mr. Frank. Forgive me, Peter. Now let me see. We must find a bed for your cat. *(He goes to a cupboard.)* I'm glad you brought your cat. Anne was feeling so bad about hers. *(getting a used small washtub)* Here we are. Will it be comfortable in that?

Peter *(gathering up his things).* Thanks.

Mr. Frank *(opening the door of the room on the left).* And here is your room. But I warn you, Peter, you can't grow any more. Not an inch, or you'll have to sleep with your feet out of the skylight. Are you hungry?

Peter. No.

Mr. Frank. We have some bread and butter.

(He tosses his knife on the table.)

Peter. Who's going out?

Anne. Why, of course! You're right! Of course we don't need them any more. *(She picks up his knife and starts to take her star off.)* I wonder what our friends will think when we don't show up today?

Peter. I didn't have any dates with anyone.

Anne. Oh, I did. I had a date with Jopie to go and play Ping-Pong at her house. Do you know Jopie de Waal?

Peter. No.

Anne. Jopie's my best friend. I wonder what she'll think when she telephones and there's no answer? . . . Probably she'll go over to the house . . . I wonder what she'll think . . . we left everything as if

Peter. No, thank you.

Mr. Frank. You can have it for luncheon then. And tonight we will have a real supper . . . our first supper together.

Peter. Thanks. Thanks. *(He goes into his room. During the following scene he arranges his possessions in his new room.)*

Mr. Frank. That's a nice boy, Peter.

Anne. He's awfully shy, isn't he?

Mr. Frank. You'll like him, I know.

Anne. I certainly hope so, since he's the only boy I'm likely to see for months and months.

*(*Mr. Frank *sits down, taking off his shoes.)*

Mr. Frank. Annele,[14] there's a box there. Will you open it?

(He indicates a carton on the couch. Anne brings it to the center table. In the street below there is the sound of children playing.)

Anne *(as she opens the carton).* You know the way I'm going to think of it here? I'm going to think of it as a boarding house. A very peculiar summer boarding house, like the one that we—*(She breaks off as she pulls out some photographs.)* Father! My movie stars! I was wondering where they were! I was looking for them this morning . . . and Queen Wilhelmina![15] How wonderful!

Mr. Frank. There's something more. Go on. Look further. *(He goes over to the sink, pouring a glass of milk from a thermos bottle.)*

Anne *(pulling out a pasteboard-bound book).* A diary! *(She throws her arms around her father.)* I've never had a diary. And I've

always longed for one. *(She looks around the room.)* Pencil, pencil, pencil, pencil. *(She starts down the stairs.)* I'm going down to the office to get a pencil.

Mr. Frank. Anne! No! *(He goes after her, catching her by the arm and pulling her back.)*

Anne *(startled).* But there's no one in the building now.

Mr. Frank. It doesn't matter. I don't want you ever to go beyond that door.

Anne *(sobered).* Never . . . ? Not even at nighttime, when everyone is gone? Or on Sundays? Can't I go down to listen to the radio?

Mr. Frank. Never. I am sorry, Anneke. It isn't safe. No, you must never go beyond that door.

(For the first time Anne *realizes what "going into hiding" means.)*

Anne. I see.

Mr. Frank. It'll be hard, I know. But always remember this, Anneke. There are no walls, there are no bolts, no locks that anyone can put on your mind. Miep will bring us books. We will read history, poetry, mythology. *(He gives her the glass of milk.)* Here's your milk. *(With his arm about her, they go over to the couch, sitting down side by side.)* As a matter of fact, between us, Anne, being here has certain advantages for you. For instance, you remember the battle you had with your mother the other day on the subject of

---

14. **Annele/Anneke:** a nickname for Anne.
15. **Queen Wilhelmina** (wil′ hel mē′ nə): the queen of the Netherlands from 1890 to 1948.

overshoes? You said you'd rather die than wear overshoes? But in the end you had to wear them? Well now, you see, for as long as we are here, you will never have to wear overshoes! Isn't that good? And the coat that you inherited from Margot, you won't have to wear that anymore. And the piano! You won't have to practice on the piano. I tell you, this is going to be a fine life for you!

(Anne's *panic is gone.* Peter *appears in the doorway of his room with a saucer in his hand. He is carrying his cat.*)

Peter. I . . . I . . . I thought I'd better get some water for Mouschi before . . .

Mr. Frank. Of course.

(*As he starts toward the sink, the carillon begins to chime the hour of eight. He tiptoes to the window at the back and looks down at the street below. He turns to* Peter, *indicating in pantomime that it is too late.* Peter *starts back for his room. He steps on a creaking board. The three of them are frozen for a minute in fear. As* Peter *starts away again,* Anne *tiptoes over to him and pours some of the milk from her glass into the saucer for the cat.* Peter *squats on the floor, putting the milk before the cat.* Mr. Frank *gives* Anne *his fountain pen and then goes into the room at the right. For a second* Anne *watches the cat, then she goes over to the center table and opens her diary.*

In the room at the right, Mrs. Frank *has sat up quickly at the sound of the carillon.* Mr. Frank *comes in and sits down beside her on the settee, his arm comfortingly around her.*

Upstairs, in the attic room, Mr. *and* Mrs. Van Daan *have hung their clothes in the closet*

The building where the secret annex was located.

and are now seated on the iron bed. Mrs. Van Daan *leans back exhausted.* Mr. Van Daan *fans her with a newspaper.*

Anne *starts to write in her diary. The lights dim out; the curtain falls.*

In the darkness Anne's *voice comes to us again, faintly at first and then with growing strength.)*

Anne's Voice. I expect I should be describing what it feels like to go into hiding. But I really don't know yet myself. I only know it's funny never to be able to go outdoors . . . never to breathe fresh air . . . never to run and shout and jump. It's the silence in the nights that frightens me most. Every time I hear a creak in the house or a step on the street outside, I'm sure they're coming for us. The days aren't so bad. At least we know that Miep and Mr. Kraler are down there below us in the office. Our protectors, we call them. I asked Father what would happen to them if the Nazis found out they were hiding us. Pim said that they would suffer the same fate that we would . . . Imagine! They know this, and yet when they come up here, they're always cheerful and gay, as if there were nothing in the world to bother them . . . Friday, the twenty-first of August, nineteen forty-two. Today I'm going to tell you our general news. Mother is unbearable. She insists on treating me like a baby, which I loathe. Otherwise things are going better. The weather is . . .

(As Anne's *voice is fading out, the curtain rises on the scene.)*

Responding to Reading

1. You have read Mr. Frank's words both in Scene 1 and in Scene 2. What conclusions can you draw about him?

2. What are your initial impressions of Anne?

3. What special things would you want to take with you if you had to go into hiding?

Scene 3

It is a little after six o'clock in the evening, two months later.

Margot is in the bedroom at the right, studying. Mr. Van Daan is lying down in the attic room above.

The rest of the "family" is in the main room. Anne and Peter sit opposite each other at the center table, where they have been doing their lessons. Mrs. Frank is on the couch. Mrs. Van Daan is seated with her fur coat, on which she has been sewing, in her lap. None of them are wearing their shoes.

Their eyes are on Mr. Frank, waiting for him to give them the signal which will release them from their day-long quiet. Mr. Frank, his shoes in his hand, stands looking down out of the window at the back, watching to be sure that all of the workmen have left the building below.

After a few seconds of motionless silence, Mr. Frank turns from the window.

Mr. Frank *(quietly, to the group)*. It's safe now. The last workman has left.

(There is an immediate stir of relief.)

Anne *(her <u>pent-up</u> energy explodes)*. WHEE!

Mrs. Frank *(startled, amused)*. Anne!

Mrs. Van Daan. I'm first for the w.c.

(She hurries off to the bathroom. Mrs. Frank puts on her shoes and starts up to the sink to prepare supper. Anne sneaks Peter's shoes from under the table and hides them behind her back. Mr. Frank goes into Margot's room.)

Mr. Frank *(to Margot)*. Six o'clock. School's over.

(Margot gets up, stretching. Mr. Frank sits down to put on his shoes. In the main room Peter tries to find his.)

Peter *(to Anne)*. Have you seen my shoes?

Anne *(innocently)*. Your shoes?

Peter. You've taken them, haven't you?

Anne. I don't know what you're talking about.

Peter. You're going to be sorry!

Anne. Am I?

(Peter goes after her. Anne, with his shoes in her hand, runs from him, dodging behind her mother.)

Mrs. Frank *(protesting)*. Anne, dear!

Peter. Wait till I get you!

Anne. I'm waiting! *(Peter makes a lunge for her. They both fall to the floor. Peter pins her down, wrestling with her to get the shoes.)* Don't! Don't! Peter, stop it. Ouch!

Mrs. Frank. Anne! . . . Peter!

(Suddenly Peter becomes self-conscious. He grabs his shoes roughly and starts for his room.)

Anne *(following him)*. Peter, where are you going? Come dance with me.

Peter. I tell you I don't know how.

Anne. I'll teach you.

Words to Know and Use | **pent-up** (pent′ up′) *adj.* held in check; restrained

508

Peter. I'm going to give Mouschi his dinner.

Anne. Can I watch?

Peter. He doesn't like people around while he eats.

Anne. Peter, please.

Peter. No! *(He goes into his room. Anne slams his door after him.)*

Mrs. Frank. Anne, dear, I think you shouldn't play like that with Peter. It's not dignified.

Anne. Who cares if it's dignified? I don't want to be dignified.

(Mr. Frank and Margot come from the room on the right. Margot goes to help her mother.

Mr. Frank *starts for the center table to correct* Margot's *school papers.)*

Mrs. Frank *(to Anne).* You complain that I don't treat you like a grown-up. But when I do, you resent it.

Anne. I only want some fun . . . someone to laugh and clown with . . . After you've sat still all day and hardly moved, you've got to have some fun. I don't know what's the matter with that boy.

Mr. Frank. He isn't used to girls. Give him a little time.

Anne. Time? Isn't two months time? I could cry. *(catching hold of* Margot) Come

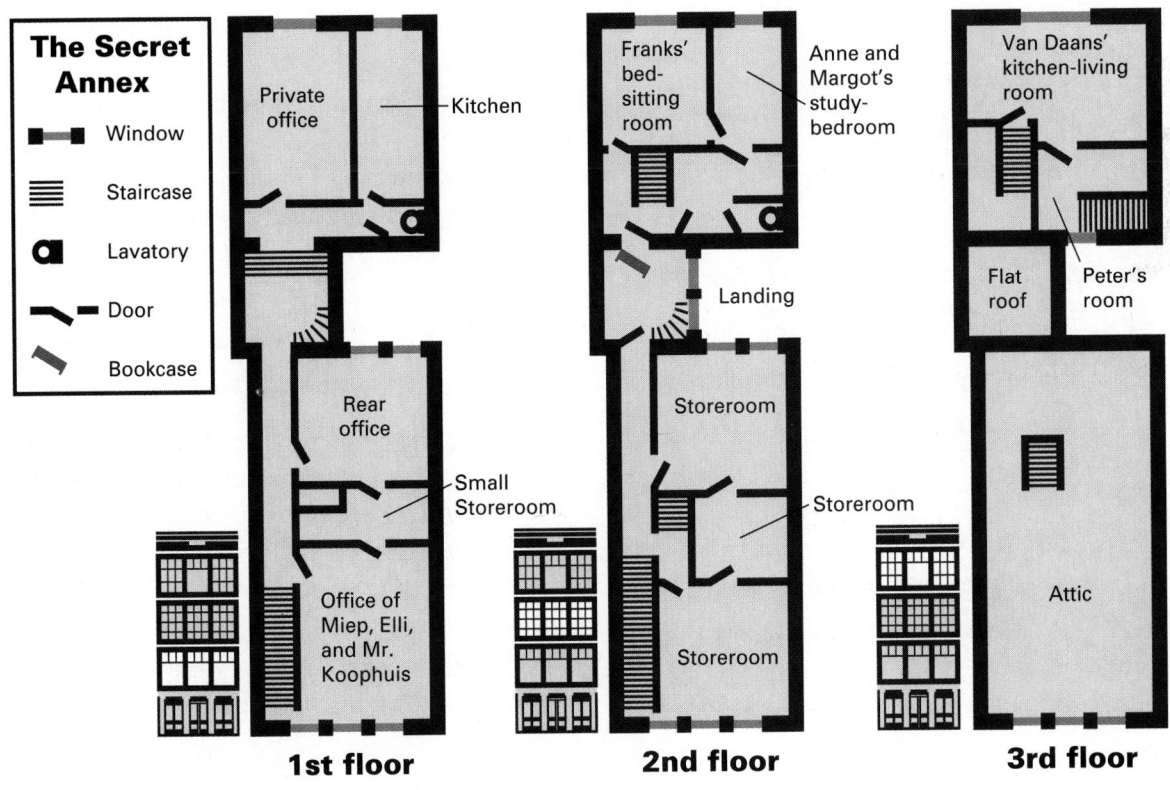

Floor plan of the secret annex.

on, Margot . . . dance with me. Come on, please.

Margot. I have to help with supper.

Anne. You know we're going to forget how to dance . . . When we get out, we won't remember a thing.

(She starts to sing and dance by herself. Mr. Frank takes her in his arms, waltzing with her. Mrs. Van Daan comes in from the bathroom.)

Mrs. Van Daan. Next? *(She looks around as she starts putting on her shoes.)* Where's Peter?

Anne *(as they are dancing)*. Where would he be!

Mrs. Van Daan. He hasn't finished his lessons, has he? His father'll kill him if he catches him in there with that cat and his work not done. *(Mr. Frank and Anne finish their dance. They bow to each other with extravagant formality.)* Anne, get him out of there, will you?

Anne *(at Peter's door)*. Peter? Peter?

Peter *(opening the door a crack)*. What is it?

Anne. Your mother says to come out.

Peter. I'm giving Mouschi his dinner.

Mrs. Van Daan. You know what your father says. *(She sits on the couch, sewing on the lining of her fur coat.)*

Peter. For heaven's sake, I haven't even looked at him since lunch.

Mrs. Van Daan. I'm just telling you, that's all.

Anne. I'll feed him.

Peter. I don't want you in there.

Mrs. Van Daan. Peter!

Peter *(to Anne)*. Then give him his dinner and come right out, you hear?

(He comes back to the table. Anne shuts the door of Peter's room after her and disappears behind the curtain covering his closet.)

Mrs. Van Daan *(to Peter)*. Now is that any way to talk to your little girlfriend?

Peter. Mother . . . for heaven's sake . . . will you please stop saying that?

Mrs. Van Daan. Look at him blush! Look at him!

Peter. Please! I'm not . . . anyway . . . let me alone, will you?

Mrs. Van Daan. He acts like it was something to be ashamed of. It's nothing to be ashamed of, to have a little girlfriend.

Peter. You're crazy. She's only thirteen.

Mrs. Van Daan. So what? And you're sixteen. Just perfect. Your father's ten years older than I am. *(to Mr. Frank)* I warn you, Mr. Frank, if this war lasts much longer, we're going to be related and then . . .

Mr. Frank. *Mazel tov!*[16]

Mrs. Frank *(deliberately changing the conversation)*. I wonder where Miep is. She's usually so prompt.

(Suddenly everything else is forgotten as they hear the sound of an automobile coming to a screeching stop in the street below. They are tense, motionless in their terror. The car starts away. A wave of relief sweeps over them. They pick up their occupations again. Anne flings open the door of Peter's room, making a dra-

---

16. **mazel tov** (mä′ zəl tōv′) *Hebrew:* good luck.

matic entrance. She is dressed in Peter's *clothes.* Peter *looks at her in fury. The others are amused.*)

Anne. Good evening, everyone. Forgive me if I don't stay. *(She jumps up on a chair.)* I have a friend waiting for me in there. My friend Tom. Tom Cat. Some people say that we look alike. But Tom has the most beautiful whiskers, and I have only a little fuzz. I am hoping . . . in time . . .

Peter. All right, Mrs. Quack Quack!

Anne (outraged *jumping down*). Peter!

Peter. I heard about you . . . How you talked so much in class they called you Mrs. Quack Quack. How Mr. Smitter made you write a composition . . . "'Quack, quack,' said Mrs. Quack Quack."

Anne. Well, go on. Tell them the rest. How it was so good he read it out loud to the class and then read it to all his other classes!

Peter. Quack! Quack! Quack . . . Quack . . . Quack . . .

(Anne pulls off the coat and trousers.)

Anne. You are the most intolerable, insufferable boy I've ever met!

(She throws the clothes down the stairwell. Peter goes down after them.)

Peter. Quack, quack, quack!

Mrs. Van Daan *(to* Anne*).* That's right, Anneke! Give it to him!

Anne. With all the boys in the world . . . Why I had to get locked up with one like you! . . .

Peter. Quack, quack, quack, and from now on stay out of my room!

(As Peter *passes her,* Anne *puts out her foot, tripping him. He picks himself up and goes on into his room.)*

Mrs. Frank *(quietly).* Anne, dear . . . your hair. *(She feels* Anne's *forehead.)* You're warm. Are you feeling all right?

Anne. Please, Mother. *(She goes over to the center table, slipping into her shoes.)*

Mrs. Frank *(following her).* You haven't a fever, have you?

Anne *(pulling away).* No. No.

Mrs. Frank. You know we can't call a doctor here, ever. There's only one thing to do . . . watch carefully. Prevent an illness before it comes. Let me see your tongue.

Anne. Mother, this is perfectly absurd.

Mrs. Frank. Anne, dear, don't be such a baby. Let me see your tongue. *(As* Anne *refuses,* Mrs. Frank *appeals to* Mr. Frank.*)* Otto . . . ?

Mr. Frank. You hear your mother, Anne.

(Anne flicks out her tongue for a second, then turns away.)

Mrs. Frank. Come on—open up! *(as* Anne *opens her mouth very wide)* You seem all right . . . but perhaps an aspirin . . .

Mrs. Van Daan. For heaven's sake, don't give that child any pills. I waited for

511

Anne Frank at her desk.

Mr. Van Daan. What's for dinner tonight?

Mrs. Van Daan. Beans.

Mr. Van Daan. Not again!

Mrs. Van Daan. Poor Putti! I know. But what can we do? That's all that Miep brought us.

(Mr. Van Daan *starts to pace, his hands behind his back.* Anne *follows behind him, imitating him.*)

Anne. We are now in what is known as the bean cycle. Beans boiled, beans en casserole, beans with strings, beans without strings . . .

(Peter *has come out of his room. He slides into his place at the table, becoming immediately absorbed in his studies.*)

Mr. Van Daan (to Peter). I saw you . . . in there, playing with your cat.

Mrs. Van Daan. He just went in for a second, putting his coat away. He's been out here all the time, doing his lessons.

Mr. Frank (looking up from the papers). Anne, you got an excellent in your history paper today . . . and very good in Latin.

Anne (sitting beside him). How about algebra?

Mr. Frank. I'll have to make a confession. Up until now I've managed to stay ahead of you in algebra. Today you caught up with me. We'll leave it to Margot to correct.

fifteen minutes this morning for her to come out of the w.c.

Anne. I was washing my hair!

Mr. Frank. I think there's nothing the matter with our Anne that a ride on her bike or a visit with her friend Jopie de Waal wouldn't cure. Isn't that so, Anne?

(Mr. Van Daan *comes down into the room. From outside we hear faint sounds of bombers going over and a burst of ack-ack.[17]*)

Mr. Van Daan. Miep not come yet?

Mrs. Van Daan. The workmen just left a little while ago.

---

17. **ack-ack:** a slang term referring to antiaircraft gunfire.

Anne. Isn't algebra *vile*, Pim!

Mr. Frank. Vile!

Margot *(to* Mr. Frank*).* How did I do?

Anne *(getting up).* Excellent, excellent, excellent, excellent!

Mr. Frank *(to* Margot*).* You should have used the subjunctive[18] here . . .

Margot. Should I? . . . I thought . . . look here . . . I didn't use it here . . .

(The two become absorbed in the papers.)

Anne. Mrs. Van Daan, may I try on your coat?

Mrs. Frank. No, Anne.

Mrs. Van Daan *(giving it to* Anne*).* It's all right . . . but careful with it. *(*Anne *puts it on and struts with it.)* My father gave me that the year before he died. He always bought the best that money could buy.

Anne. Mrs. Van Daan, did you have a lot of boyfriends before you were married?

Mrs. Frank. Anne, that's a personal question. It's not courteous to ask personal questions.

Mrs. Van Daan. Oh, I don't mind. *(to* Anne*)* Our house was always swarming with boys. When I was a girl, we had . . .

Mr. Van Daan. Oh, no. Not again!

Mrs. Van Daan *(good-humoredly).* Shut up! *(Without a pause, to* Anne, Mr. Van Daan *mimics* Mrs. Van Daan, *speaking the first few words in unison with her.)* One summer we had a big house in Hilversum. The boys came buzzing around like bees around a jam pot. And when I was sixteen! . . . We were wearing our skirts very short those days, and I had good-looking legs. *(She pulls up her skirt, going to* Mr. Frank.*)* I still have 'em. I may not be as pretty as I used to be, but I still have my legs. How about it, Mr. Frank?

Mr. Van Daan. All right. All right. We see them.

Mrs. Van Daan. I'm not asking you. I'm asking Mr. Frank.

Peter. Mother, for heaven's sake.

Mrs. Van Daan. Oh, I embarrass you, do I? Well, I just hope the girl you marry has as good. *(then to* Anne*)* My father used to worry about me, with so many boys hanging around. He told me, if any of them gets fresh, you say to him . . . "Remember, Mr. So-and-So, remember I'm a lady."

Anne. "Remember, Mr. So-and-So, remember I'm a lady." *(She gives* Mrs. Van Daan *her coat.)*

Mr. Van Daan. Look at you, talking that way in front of her! Don't you know she puts it all down in that diary?

Mrs. Van Daan. So, if she does? I'm only telling the truth!

(Anne stretches out, putting her ear to the floor, listening to what is going on below. The sound of the bombers fades away.)

---

18. **subjunctive:** a verb form used to express wishes, possibilities, and so forth.

Words to Know and Use | **vile** (vīl) *adj.* disgusting

Mrs. Frank (*setting the table*). Would you mind, Peter, if I moved you over to the couch?

Anne (*listening*). Miep must have the radio on.

(Peter *picks up his papers, going over to the couch beside* Mrs. Van Daan.)

Mr. Van Daan (*accusingly, to* Peter). Haven't you finished yet?

Peter. No.

Mr. Van Daan. You ought to be ashamed of yourself.

Peter. All right. All right. I'm a dunce. I'm a hopeless case. Why do I go on?

Mrs. Van Daan. You're not hopeless. Don't talk that way. It's just that you haven't anyone to help you like the girls have. (*to* Mr. Frank) Maybe you could help him, Mr. Frank?

Mr. Frank. I'm sure that his father . . . ?

Mr. Van Daan. Not me. I can't do anything with him. He won't listen to me. You go ahead . . . if you want.

Mr. Frank (*going to* Peter). What about it, Peter? Shall we make our school coeducational?

Mrs. Van Daan (*kissing* Mr. Frank). You're an angel, Mr. Frank. An angel. I don't know why I didn't meet you before I met that one there. Here, sit down, Mr. Frank . . . (*She forces him down on the couch beside* Peter.) Now, Peter, you listen to Mr. Frank.

Mr. Frank. It might be better for us to go into Peter's room.

(Peter *jumps up eagerly, leading the way.*)

Mrs. Van Daan. That's right. You go in there, Peter. You listen to Mr. Frank. Mr. Frank is a highly educated man.

(As Mr. Frank *is about to follow* Peter *into his room,* Mrs. Frank *stops him and wipes the lipstick from his lips. Then she closes the door after them.*)

Anne (*on the floor, listening*). Shh! I can hear a man's voice talking.

Mr. Van Daan (*to* Anne). Isn't it bad enough here without your sprawling all over the place?

(Anne *sits up.*)

Mrs. Van Daan (*to* Mr. Van Daan). If you didn't smoke so much, you wouldn't be so bad-tempered.

Mr. Van Daan. Am I smoking? Do you see me smoking?

Mrs. Van Daan. Don't tell me you've used up all those cigarettes.

Mr. Van Daan. One package. Miep only brought me one package.

Mrs. Van Daan. It's a filthy habit anyway. It's a good time to break yourself.

Mr. Van Daan. Oh, stop it, please.

Mrs. Van Daan. You're smoking up all our money. You know that, don't you?

Mr. Van Daan. Will you shut up? (*During this,* Mrs. Frank *and* Margot *have studiously kept their eyes down. But* Anne, *seated on the floor, has been following the discussion interestedly.* Mr. Van Daan *turns to see her staring up at him.*) And what are you staring at?

Anne. I never heard grown-ups quarrel before. I thought only children quarreled.

Mr. Van Daan. This isn't a quarrel! It's a discussion. And I never heard children so rude before.

Anne *(rising, indignantly)*. I, rude!

Mr. Van Daan. Yes!

Mrs. Frank *(quickly)*. Anne, will you get me my knitting? *(Anne goes to get it.)* I must remember, when Miep comes, to ask her to bring me some more wool.

Margot *(going to her room)*. I need some hairpins and some soap. I made a list. *(She goes into her bedroom to get the list.)*

Mrs. Frank *(to Anne)*. Have you some library books for Miep when she comes?

Anne. It's a wonder that Miep has a life of her own, the way we make her run errands for us. Please, Miep, get me some starch. Please take my hair out and have it cut. Tell me all the latest news, Miep. *(She goes over, kneeling on the couch beside Mrs. Van Daan.)* Did you know she was engaged? His name is Dirk, and Miep's afraid the Nazis will ship him off to Germany to work in one of their war plants. That's what they're doing with some of the young Dutchmen . . . they pick them up off the streets—

Mr. Van Daan *(interrupting)*. Don't you ever get tired of talking? Suppose you try keeping still for five minutes. Just five minutes.

(He starts to pace again. Again Anne follows him, mimicking him. Mrs. Frank jumps up and takes her by the arm up to the sink and gives her a glass of milk.)

Mrs. Frank. Come here, Anne. It's time for your glass of milk.

Mr. Van Daan. Talk, talk, talk. I never heard such a child. Where is my . . . ? Every evening it's the same talk, talk, talk. *(He looks around.)* Where is my . . .?

Mrs. Van Daan. What're you looking for?

Mr. Van Daan. My pipe. Have you seen my pipe?

Mrs. Van Daan. What good's a pipe? You haven't got any tobacco.

Mr. Van Daan. At least I'll have something to hold in my mouth! *(opening Margot's bedroom door)* Margot, have you seen my pipe?

Margot. It was on the table last night.

(Anne puts her glass of milk on the table and picks up his pipe, hiding it behind her back.)

Mr. Van Daan. I know. I know. Anne, did you see my pipe? . . . Anne!

Mrs. Frank. Anne, Mr. Van Daan is speaking to you.

Anne. Am I allowed to talk now?

Mr. Van Daan. You're the most aggravating . . . The trouble with you is, you've been spoiled. What you need is a good old-fashioned spanking.

Anne *(mimicking Mrs. Van Daan)*. "Remember, Mr. So-and-So, remember I'm a lady." *(She thrusts the pipe into his mouth, then picks up her glass of milk.)*

Mr. Van Daan *(restraining himself with difficulty)*. Why aren't you nice and quiet like your sister Margot? Why do you have to show off all the time? Let me give you a little advice, young lady. Men don't like that kind of thing in a girl. You know that? A man likes a girl who'll listen to him once in a while . . . a domestic girl, who'll keep her house shining for her husband . . . who loves to cook and sew and . . .

Anne. I'd cut my throat first! I'd open my veins! I'm going to be remarkable! I'm going to Paris . . .

Mr. Van Daan (scoffingly). Paris!

Anne. . . . to study music and art.

Mr. Van Daan. Yeah! Yeah!

Anne. I'm going to be a famous dancer or singer . . . or something wonderful.

(She makes a wide gesture, spilling the glass of milk on the fur coat in Mrs. Van Daan's lap. Margot rushes quickly over with a towel. Anne tries to brush the milk off with her skirt.)

Mrs. Van Daan. Now look what you've done . . . you clumsy little fool! My beautiful fur coat my father gave me . . .

Anne. I'm so sorry.

Mrs. Van Daan. What do you care? It isn't yours . . . So go on, ruin it! Do you know what that coat cost? Do you? And now look at it! Look at it!

Anne. I'm very, very sorry.

Mrs. Van Daan. I could kill you for this. I could just kill you!

(Mrs. Van Daan goes up the stairs, clutching the coat. Mr. Van Daan starts after her.)

Mr. Van Daan. Petronella . . . *liefje! Liefje!* . . . Come back . . . the supper . . . come back!

Mrs. Frank. Anne, you must not behave in that way.

Anne. It was an accident. Anyone can have an accident.

Mrs. Frank. I don't mean that. I mean the answering back. You must not answer back. They are our guests. We must always show the greatest courtesy to them. We're all living under terrible tension. (She stops as Margot indicates that Van Daan can hear. When he is gone, she continues.) That's why we must control ourselves . . . You don't hear Margot getting into arguments with them, do you? Watch Margot. She's always courteous with them. Never familiar. She keeps her distance. And they respect her for it. Try to be like Margot.

Anne. And have them walk all over me, the way they do her? No, thanks!

Mrs. Frank. I'm not afraid that anyone is going to walk all over you, Anne. I'm afraid for other people, that you'll walk on them. I don't know what happens to you, Anne. You are wild, self-willed. If I had ever talked to my mother as you talk to me . . .

Anne. Things have changed. People aren't like that anymore. "Yes, Mother." "No, Mother." "Anything you say, Mother." I've got to fight things out for myself! Make something of myself!

Mrs. Frank. It isn't necessary to fight to do it. Margot doesn't fight, and isn't she . . .?

Anne (violently rebellious). Margot! Margot! Margot! That's all I hear from everyone

. . . how wonderful Margot is . . . "Why aren't you like Margot?"

Margot (protesting). Oh, come on, Anne, don't be so . . .

Anne (paying no attention). Everything she does is right, and everything I do is wrong! I'm the goat around here! . . . You're all against me! . . . And you worst of all!

(She rushes off into her room and throws herself down on the settee, stifling her sobs. Mrs. Frank sighs and starts toward the stove.)

Mrs. Frank (to Margot). Let's put the soup on the stove . . . if there's anyone who cares to eat. Margot, will you take the bread out? (Margot gets the bread from the cupboard.) I don't know how we can go on living this way . . . I can't say a word to Anne . . . she flies at me . . .

Margot. You know Anne. In half an hour she'll be out here, laughing and joking.

Mrs. Frank. And . . . (She makes a motion upwards, indicating the Van Daans.) . . . I told your father it wouldn't work . . . but no . . . no . . . he had to ask them, he said . . . he owed it to him, he said. Well, he knows now that I was right! These quarrels! . . . This bickering!

Margot (with a warning look). Shush. Shush.

(The buzzer for the door sounds. Mrs. Frank gasps, startled.)

Mrs. Frank. Every time I hear that sound, my heart stops!

Margot (starting for Peter's door). It's Miep. (She knocks at the door.) Father?

(Mr. Frank comes quickly from Peter's room.)

Mr. Frank. Thank you, Margot. (as he goes down the steps to open the outer door) Has everyone his list?

Margot. I'll get my books. (giving her mother a list) Here's your list. (Margot goes into her and Anne's bedroom on the right. Anne sits up, hiding her tears, as Margot comes in.) Miep's here.

(Margot picks up her books and goes back. Anne hurries over to the mirror, smoothing her hair.)

Mr. Van Daan (coming down the stairs). Is it Miep?

Margot. Yes. Father's gone down to let her in.

Mr. Van Daan. At last I'll have some cigarettes!

Mrs. Frank (to Mr. Van Daan). I can't tell you how unhappy I am about Mrs. Van Daan's coat. Anne should never have touched it.

Mr. Van Daan. She'll be all right.

Mrs. Frank. Is there anything I can do?

Mr. Van Daan. Don't worry.

(He turns to meet Miep. But it is not Miep who comes up the steps. It is Mr. Kraler, followed by Mr. Frank. Their faces are grave. Anne comes from the bedroom. Peter comes from his room.)

Mrs. Frank. Mr. Kraler!

Mr. Van Daan. How are you, Mr. Kraler?

Margot. This is a surprise.

Mrs. Frank. When Mr. Kraler comes, the sun begins to shine.

Mr. Van Daan. Miep is coming?

Mr. Kraler. Not tonight.

(Kraler *goes to* Margot *and* Mrs. Frank *and* Anne, *shaking hands with them.*)

Mrs. Frank. Wouldn't you like a cup of coffee? . . . Or, better still, will you have supper with us?

Mr. Frank. Mr. Kraler has something to talk over with us. Something has happened, he says, which demands an immediate decision.

Mrs. Frank (*fearful*). What is it?

(Mr. Kraler *sits down on the couch. As he talks, he takes bread, cabbages, milk, and so forth, from his briefcase, giving them to* Margot *and* Anne *to put away.*)

Mr. Kraler. Usually, when I come up here, I try to bring you some bit of good news. What's the use of telling you the bad news when there's nothing that you can do about it? But today something has happened . . . Dirk . . . Miep's Dirk, you know, came to me just now. He tells me that he has a Jewish friend living near him. A dentist. He says he's in trouble. He begged me, could I do anything for this man? Could I find him a hiding place? . . . So I've come to you . . . I know it's a terrible thing to ask of you, living as you are, but would you take him in with you?

Mr. Frank. Of course we will.

Mr. Kraler (*rising*). It'll be just for a night or two . . . until I find some other place. This happened so suddenly that I didn't know where to turn.

Mr. Frank. Where is he?

Mr. Kraler. Downstairs in the office.

Mr. Frank. Good. Bring him up.

Mr. Kraler. His name is Dussel . . . Jan Dussel.

Mr. Frank. Dussel . . . I think I know him.

Mr. Kraler. I'll get him.

(He goes quickly down the steps and out. Mr. Frank *suddenly becomes conscious of the others.*)

Mr. Frank. Forgive me. I spoke without consulting you. But I knew you'd feel as I do.

Mr. Van Daan. There's no reason for you to consult anyone. This is your place. You have a right to do exactly as you please. The only thing I feel . . . there's so little food as it is . . . and to take in another person . . .

(Peter *turns away, ashamed of his father.*)

Mr. Frank. We can stretch the food a little. It's only for a few days.

Mr. Van Daan. You want to make a bet?

Mrs. Frank. I think it's fine to have him. But, Otto, where are you going to put him? Where?

Peter. He can have my bed. I can sleep on the floor. I wouldn't mind.

Mr. Frank. That's good of you, Peter. But your room's too small . . . even for *you.*

Anne. I have a much better idea. I'll come in here with you and Mother, and Margot can take Peter's room, and Peter can go in our room with Dr. Dussel.

Margot. That's right. We could do that.

Mr. Frank. No, Margot. You mustn't sleep in that room . . . neither you nor Anne.

Mouschi has caught some rats in there. Peter's brave. He doesn't mind.

Anne. Then how about *this?* I'll come in here with you and Mother, and Dr. Dussel can have my bed.

Mrs. Frank. No. No. *No!* Margot will come in here with us, and he can have her bed. It's the only way. Margot, bring your things in here. Help her, Anne.

(Margot hurries into her room to get her things.)

Anne *(to her mother).* Why Margot? Why can't I come in here?

Mrs. Frank. Because it wouldn't be proper for Margot to sleep with a . . . Please, Anne. Don't argue. Please.

(Anne starts slowly away.)

Mr. Frank *(to* Anne*).* You don't mind sharing your room with Dr. Dussel, do you, Anne?

Anne. No. No, of course not.

Mr. Frank. Good. *(Anne goes off into her bedroom, helping* Margot. Mr. Frank *starts to search in the cupboards.)* Where's the cognac?[19]

Mrs. Frank. It's there. But, Otto, I was saving it in case of illness.

Mr. Frank. I think we couldn't find a better time to use it. Peter, will you get five glasses for me?

(Peter goes for the glasses. Margot *comes out of her bedroom carrying her possessions, which she hangs behind a curtain in the main room.* Mr. Frank *finds the cognac and pours it into the five glasses that* Peter *brings him.* Mr. Van Daan *stands looking on sourly.* Mrs. Van

Daan *comes downstairs and looks around at all the bustle.)*

Mrs. Van Daan. What's happening? What's going on?

Mr. Van Daan. Someone's moving in with us.

Mrs. Van Daan. In here? You're joking.

Margot. It's only for a night or two . . . until Mr. Kraler finds him another place.

Mr. Van Daan. Yeah! Yeah!

(Mr. Frank hurries over as Mr. Kraler *and* Dr. Dussel *come up.* Dr. Dussel *is a man in his late fifties, meticulous, finicky . . . bewildered now. He wears a raincoat. He carries a briefcase, stuffed full, and a small medicine case.)*

Mr. Frank. Come in, Dr. Dussel.

Mr. Kraler. This is Mr. Frank.

Dr. Dussel. Mr. Otto Frank?

Mr. Frank. Yes. Let me take your things. *(He takes the hat and briefcase, but* Dr. Dussel *clings to his medicine case.)* This is my wife, Edith . . . Mr. and Mrs. Van Daan . . . their son, Peter . . . and my daughters, Margot and Anne.

(Dr. Dussel shakes hands with everyone.)

Mr. Kraler. Thank you, Mr. Frank. Thank you all. Dr. Dussel, I leave you in good hands. Oh . . . Dirk's coat.

(Dr. Dussel hurriedly takes off the raincoat, giving it to Mr. Kraler. *Underneath is his white dentist's jacket, with a yellow Star of David on it.)*

----

19. cognac: (kän′ yak′): a brandy.

Dr. Dussel *(to* Mr. Kraler*)*. What can I say to thank you . . . ?

Mrs. Frank *(to* Dr. Dussel*)*. Mr. Kraler and Miep . . . They're our lifeline. Without them we couldn't live.

Mr. Kraler. Please. Please. You make us seem very heroic. It isn't that at all. We simply don't like the Nazis. *(to* Mr. Frank, *who offers him a drink)* No, thanks. *(then going on)* We don't like their methods. We don't like . . .

Mr. Frank *(smiling)*. I know. I know. "No one's going to tell us Dutchmen what to do with our Jews!"

Mr. Kraler *(to* Dr. Dussel*)*. Pay no attention to Mr. Frank. I'll be up tomorrow to see that they're treating you right. *(to* Mr. Frank*)* Don't trouble to come down again. Peter will bolt the door after me, won't you, Peter?

Peter. Yes, sir.

Mr. Frank. Thank you, Peter, I'll do it.

Mr. Kraler. Good night. Good night.

Group. Good night, Mr. Kraler. We'll see you tomorrow.

*(*Mr. Kraler *goes out with* Mr. Frank. Mrs. Frank *gives each one of the grown-ups a glass of cognac.)*

Mrs. Frank. Please, Dr. Dussel, sit down.

*(Dr. Dussel *sinks into a chair.* Mrs. Frank *gives him a glass of cognac.)*

Dr. Dussel. I'm dreaming. I know it. I can't believe my eyes. Mr. Otto Frank here! *(to* Mrs. Frank*)* You're not in Switzerland then? A woman told me . . . She said she'd gone to your house . . . the door was open, everything was in disorder, dishes in the sink. She said she found a piece of paper in the wastebasket with an address scribbled on it . . . an address in Zurich. She said you must have escaped to Zurich.

Anne. Father put that there purposely . . . just so people would think that very thing!

Dr. Dussel. And you've been *here* all the time?

Mrs. Frank. All the time . . . ever since July.

*(Anne *speaks to her father as he comes back.)*

Anne. It worked, Pim . . . the address you left! Dr. Dussel says that people believe we escaped to Switzerland.

Mr. Frank. I'm glad . . . And now let's have a little drink to welcome Dr. Dussel. *(Before they can drink,* Dr. Dussel *bolts his drink.* Mr. Frank *smiles and raises his glass.)* To Dr. Dussel. Welcome. We're very honored to have you with us.

Mrs. Frank. To Dr. Dussel, welcome.

*(The Van Daans *murmur a welcome. The grown-ups drink.)*

Mrs. Van Daan. Um. That was good.

Mr. Van Daan. Did Mr. Kraler warn you that you won't get much to eat here? You can imagine . . . three ration books among the seven of us . . . and now you make eight.

*(Peter *walks away, humiliated. Outside, a street organ is heard dimly.)*

Dr. Dussel *(rising)*. Mr. Van Daan, you don't realize what is happening outside that you should warn me of a thing like

that. You don't realize what's going on
. . . *(As* Mr. Van Daan *starts his characteristic pacing,* Dr. Dussel *turns to speak to
the others.)* Right here in Amsterdam
every day, hundreds of Jews disappear . . .
They surround a block and search house
by house. Children come home from
school to find their parents gone.
Hundreds are being deported . . . people
that you and I know . . . the Hallensteins
. . . the Wessels . . .

Mrs. Frank *(in tears).* Oh, no. No!

Dr. Dussel. They get their call-up notice . . .
come to the Jewish theater on such and
such a day and hour . . . bring only what
you can carry in a rucksack. And if you
refuse the call-up notice, then they come
and drag you from your home and ship
you off to Mauthausen.[20] The death
camp!

Mrs. Frank. We didn't know that things
had gotten so much worse.

Dr. Dussel. Forgive me for speaking so.

Anne *(coming to* Dr. Dussel*).* Do you know
the de Waals? . . . What's become of
them? Their daughter Jopie and I are in
the same class. Jopie's my best friend.

Dr. Dussel. They are gone.

Anne. Gone?

Dr. Dussel. With all the others.

Anne. Oh, no. Not Jopie!

(She turns away, in tears. Mrs. Frank *motions
to* Margot *to comfort her.* Margot *goes to*
Anne, *putting her arms comfortingly around
her.)*

Mrs. Van Daan. There were some people
called Wagner. They lived near us . . . ?

Dr. Dussel.

Mr. Frank *(interrupting, with a glance at*
Anne*).* I think we should put this off until
later. We all have many questions we
want to ask . . . But I'm sure that Dr.
Dussel would like to get settled before
supper.

Dr. Dussel. Thank you. I would. I brought
very little with me.

Mr. Frank *(giving him his hat and
briefcase).* I'm sorry we can't give you a
room alone. But I hope you won't be too
uncomfortable. We've had to make strict

---

20. **Mauthausen** (mout' hou' zən): a Nazi concentration camp in Austria.

rules here . . . a schedule of hours . . . We'll tell you after supper. Anne, would you like to take Dr. Dussel to his room?

Anne *(controlling her tears)*. If you'll come with me, Dr. Dussel? *(She starts for her room.)*

Dr. Dussel *(shaking hands with each in turn)*. Forgive me if I haven't really expressed my gratitude to all of you. This has been such a shock to me. I'd always thought of myself as Dutch. I was born in Holland. My father was born in Holland, and my grandfather. And now . . . after all these years . . . *(He breaks off.)* If you'll excuse me.

(Dr. Dussel gives a little bow and hurries off after Anne. Mr. Frank and the others are subdued.)

Anne *(turning on the light)*. Well, here we are.

(Dr. Dussel looks around the room. In the main room Margot speaks to her mother.)

Margot. The news sounds pretty bad, doesn't it? It's so different from what Mr. Kraler tells us. Mr. Kraler says things are improving.

Mr. Van Daan. I like it better the way Kraler tells it.

(They resume their occupations, quietly. Peter goes off into his room. In Anne's room, Anne turns to Dr. Dussel.)

Anne. You're going to share the room with me.

Dr. Dussel. I'm a man who's always lived alone. I haven't had to adjust myself to others. I hope you'll bear with me until I learn.

Anne. Let me help you. *(She takes his briefcase.)* Do you always live all alone? Have you no family at all?

Dr. Dussel. No one. *(He opens his medicine case and spreads his bottles on the dressing table.)*

Anne. How dreadful. You must be terribly lonely.

Dr. Dussel. I'm used to it.

Anne. I don't think I could ever get used to it. Didn't you even have a pet? A cat or a dog?

Dr. Dussel. I have an allergy for fur-bearing animals. They give me asthma.

Anne. Oh, dear. Peter has a cat.

Dr. Dussel. Here? He has it here?

Anne. Yes. But we hardly ever see it. He keeps it in his room all the time. I'm sure it will be all right.

Dr. Dussel. Let us hope so. *(He takes some pills to fortify himself.)*

Anne. That's Margot's bed, where you're going to sleep. I sleep on the sofa there. *(indicating the clothes hooks on the wall)* We cleared these off for your things. *(She goes over to the window.)* The best part about this room . . . you can look down and see a bit of the street and the canal. There's a houseboat . . . you can see the end of it . . . a bargeman lives there with his family . . . They have a baby, and he's just beginning to walk, and I'm so afraid he's going to fall into the canal some day. I watch him. . . .

Dr. Dussel *(interrupting)*. Your father spoke of a schedule.

Anne *(coming away from the window)*. Oh, yes. It's mostly about the times we have to be quiet. And times for the w.c. You can use it now if you like.

Dr. Dussel *(stiffly)*. No, thank you.

Anne. I suppose you think it's awful, my talking about a thing like that. But you don't know how important it can get to be, especially when you're frightened . . . About this room, the way Margot and I did . . . she had it to herself in the afternoons for studying, reading . . . lessons, you know . . . and I took the mornings. Would that be all right with you?

Dr. Dussel. I'm not at my best in the morning.

Anne. You stay here in the mornings then. I'll take the room in the afternoons.

Dr. Dussel. Tell me, when you're in here, what happens to me? Where am I spending my time? In there, with all the people?

Anne. Yes.

Dr. Dussel. I see. I see.

Anne. We have supper at half past six.

Dr. Dussel *(going over to the sofa)*. Then, if you don't mind . . . I like to lie down quietly for ten minutes before eating. I find it helps the digestion.

Anne. Of course. I hope I'm not going to be too much of a bother to you. I seem to be able to get everyone's back up.

(Dr. Dussel lies down on the sofa, curled up, his back to her.)

Dr. Dussel. I always get along very well with children. My patients all bring their children to me because they know I get on well with them. So don't you worry about that.

(Anne leans over him, taking his hand and shaking it gratefully.)

Anne. Thank you. Thank you, Dr. Dussel.

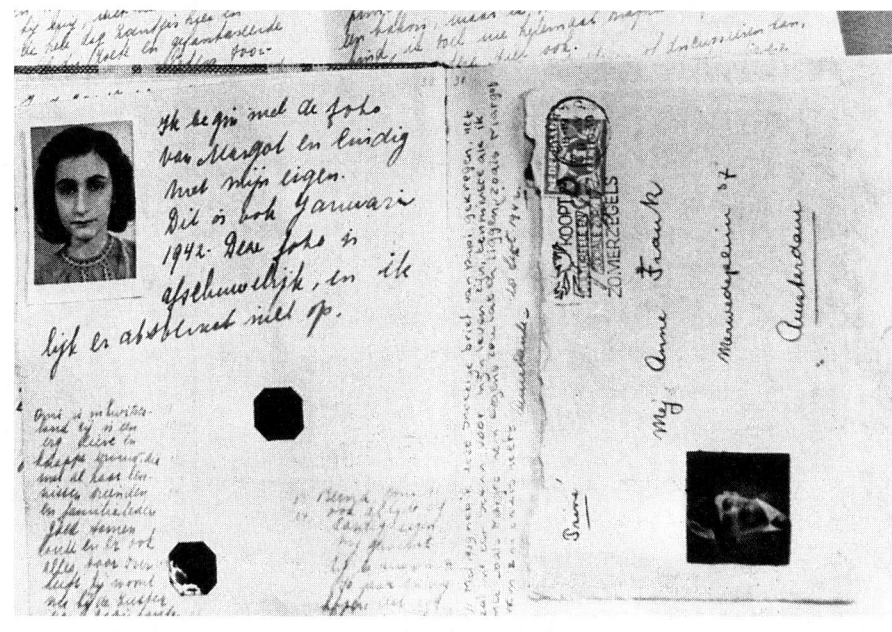

View of diary opened.

(The lights dim to darkness. The curtain falls on the scene. Anne's voice comes to us, faintly at first and then with increasing power.)

Anne's Voice.. . . . And yesterday I finished Cissy Van Marxvelt's latest book. I think she is a first-class writer. I shall definitely let my children read her. Monday the twenty-first of September, nineteen forty-two. Dr. Dussel and I had another battle yesterday. Yes, Dr. Dussel! According to him, nothing, I repeat . . . nothing, is right about me . . . my appearance, my character, my manners. While he was going on at me, I thought . . . sometime I'll give you such a smack that you'll fly right up to the ceiling! Why is it that every grown-up thinks he knows the way to bring up children? Particularly the grown-ups that never had any. I keep wishing that Peter was a girl instead of a boy. Then I would have someone to talk to. Margot's a darling, but she takes everything too seriously. To pause for a moment on the subject of Mrs. Van Daan. I must tell you that her attempts to flirt with Father are getting her nowhere. Pim, thank goodness, won't play.

(As she is saying the last lines, the curtain rises on the darkened scene. Anne's voice fades out.)

Responding to Reading

1. Do you think Mr. Frank is right in letting Dr. Dussel live with the two families? Explain your answer.

2. What was your reaction to the news Dr. Dussel brings from the outside?

3. Compare and contrast the characters of Anne and Peter.

4. The people in hiding are beginning to get on one another's nerves. What advice would you give individual characters to lessen the conflicts that are occurring?

Scene 4

It is the middle of the night, several months later. The stage is dark except for a little light which comes through the skylight in Peter's room.

Everyone is in bed. Mr. and Mrs. Frank lie on the couch in the main room, which has been pulled out to serve as a makeshift double bed.

Margot is sleeping on a mattress on the floor in the main room, behind a curtain stretched across for privacy. The others are all in their accustomed rooms.

From outside we hear two soldiers singing "Lili Marlene." A girl's high giggle is heard. The sound of running feet is heard coming closer and then fading in the distance. Throughout the scene there is the distant sound of airplanes passing overhead.

A match suddenly flares up in the attic. We dimly see Mr. Van Daan. *He is getting his bearings. He comes quickly down the stairs and goes to the cupboard where the food is stored. Again the match flares up and is as quickly blown out. The dim figure is seen to steal back up the stairs.*

There is quiet for a second or two, broken only by the sound of airplanes and running feet on the street below.

Suddenly, out of the silence and the dark, we hear Anne *scream.*

Anne (*screaming*). No! No! Don't . . . don't take me!

(*She moans, tossing and crying in her sleep. The other people wake, terrified.* Dr. Dussel *sits up in bed, furious.*)

Dr. Dussel. Shush! Anne! Anne, for God's sake, shush!

Anne (*still in her nightmare*). Save me! Save me!

(*She screams and screams.* Dr. Dussel *gets out of bed, going over to her, trying to wake her.*)

Dr. Dussel. Quiet! Quiet! You want someone to hear?

(*In the main room* Mrs. Frank *grabs a shawl and pulls it around her. She rushes in to* Anne, *taking her in her arms.* Mr. Frank *hurriedly gets up, putting on his overcoat.* Margot *sits up, terrified.* Peter's *light goes on in his room.*)

Mrs. Frank (*to* Anne, *in her room*). Hush, darling, hush. It's all right. It's all right. (*over her shoulder to* Dr. Dussel) Will you be kind enough to turn on the light, Dr. Dussel? (*back to* Anne) It's nothing, my darling. It was just a dream.

(Dr. Dussel *turns on the light in the bedroom.* Mrs. Frank *holds* Anne *in her arms. Gradually* Anne *comes out of her nightmare, still trembling with horror.* Mr. Frank *comes into the room and goes quickly to the window, looking out to be sure that no one outside has heard* Anne's *screams.* Mrs. Frank *holds* Anne, *talking softly to her. In the main room* Margot *stands on a chair, turning on the center hanging lamp. A light goes on in the* Van Daans' *room overhead.* Peter *puts his robe on, coming out of his room.*)

Dr. Dussel (*to* Mrs. Frank, *blowing his nose*). Something must be done about that child, Mrs. Frank. Yelling like that! Who knows but there's somebody on the streets? She's endangering all our lives.

Mrs. Frank. Anne, darling.

Dr. Dussel. Every night she twists and turns. I don't sleep. I spend half my night shushing her. And now it's nightmares!

(*Margot comes to the door of* Anne's *room, followed by* Peter. *Mr. Frank goes to them, indicating that everything is all right.* Peter *takes* Margot *back.*)

Mrs. Frank (*to* Anne). You're here, safe, you see? Nothing has happened. (*to* Dr. Dussel) Please, Dr. Dussel, go back to bed. She'll be herself in a minute or two. Won't you, Anne?

Dr. Dussel (*picking up a book and a pillow*). Thank you, but I'm going to the w.c. The one place where there's peace!

(*He stalks out.* Mr. Van Daan, *in underwear and trousers, comes down the stairs.*)

Mr. Van Daan (*to* Dr. Dussel). What is it? What happened?

Dr. Dussel. A nightmare. She was having a nightmare!

Mr. Van Daan. I thought someone was murdering her.

Dr. Dussel. Unfortunately, no.

(*He goes into the bathroom.* Mr. Van Daan *goes back up the stairs.* Mr. Frank, *in the main room, sends* Peter *back to his own bedroom.*)

Mr. Frank. Thank you, Peter. Go back to bed.

(*Peter goes back to his room.* Mr. Frank *follows him, turning out the light and looking out the window. Then he goes back to the main room and gets up on a chair, turning out the center hanging lamp.*)

Mrs. Frank (*to* Anne). Would you like some water? (Anne *shakes her head.*) Was it a very bad dream? Perhaps if you told me . . . ?

Anne. I'd rather not talk about it.

Mrs. Frank. Poor darling. Try to sleep then. I'll sit right here beside you until you fall asleep. (*She brings a stool over, sitting there.*)

Anne. You don't have to.

Mrs. Frank. But I'd like to stay with you . . . very much. Really.

Anne. I'd rather you didn't.

Mrs. Frank. Good night, then. (*She leans down to kiss* Anne. Anne *throws her arm up over her face, turning away.* Mrs. Frank, *hiding her hurt, kisses* Anne's *arm.*) You'll be all right? There's nothing that you want?

Anne. Will you please ask Father to come.

Mrs. Frank (*after a second*). Of course, Anne dear. (*She hurries out into the other room.* Mr. Frank *comes to her as she comes in.*) *Sie verlangt nach Dir!*[21]

Mr. Frank (*sensing her hurt*). Edith, *Liebe, schau . . .* [22]

Mrs. Frank. *Es macht nichts! Ich danke dem lieben Herrgott, dass sie sich wenigstens an Dich wendet, wenn sie Trost braucht! Geh hinein, Otto; sie ist ganz hysterisch vor Angst.*[23] (*as* Mr. Frank *hesitates*) *Geh zu*

---

21. *Sie verlangt nach Dir* (zē fer länt′ näkh dir) *German:* She is asking for you.

22. *Liebe, schau* (lē′ bə shou) *German:* Dear, look.

23. *Es macht . . . vor Angst* (es mäkht nikhts ikh dänk′ ə däm lē′ bən her′ gôt′ däs zē zikh vān′ ikh stəns än dikh ven′ dət ven zē trôst broukht gā hin in′ ät tô zē ist gänts hü ster′ ish fôr änst) *German:* It's all right. I thank dear God that at least she turns to you when she needs comfort. Go in, Otto; she is hysterical with fear.

German occupation forces marching through a Dutch city.

ihr.[24] *(He looks at her for a second and then goes to get a cup of water for* Anne. Mrs. Frank *sinks down on the bed, her face in her hands, trying to keep from sobbing aloud.* Margot *comes over to her, putting her arms around her.)* She wants nothing of me. She pulled away when I leaned down to kiss her.

Margot. It's a phase . . . You heard Father . . . Most girls go through it . . . they turn to their fathers at this age . . . they give all their love to their fathers.

Mrs. Frank. You weren't like this. You didn't shut me out.

Margot. She'll get over it . . .

(She smooths the bed for Mrs. Frank *and sits beside her a moment as* Mrs. Frank *lies down. In* Anne's *room* Mr. Frank *comes in, sitting down by* Anne. Anne *flings her arms around him, clinging to him. In the distance we hear the sound of ack-ack.)*

Anne. Oh, Pim. I dreamed that they came to get us! The Green Police! They broke down the door and grabbed me and

---

24. **Geh zu ihr** (gā tsōō ēr) *German:* Go to her.

started to drag me out the way they did Jopie.

Mr. Frank. I want you to take this pill.

Anne. What is it?

Mr. Frank. Something to quiet you.

(She takes it and drinks the water. In the main room Margot turns out the light and goes back to her bed.)

Mr. Frank *(to Anne).* Do you want me to read to you for a while?

Anne. No. Just sit with me for a minute. Was I awful? Did I yell terribly loud? Do you think anyone outside could have heard?

Mr. Frank. No. No. Lie quietly now. Try to sleep.

Anne. I'm a terrible coward. I'm so disappointed in myself. I think I've conquered my fear . . . I think I'm really grown-up . . . and then something happens . . . and I run to you like a baby . . . I love you, Father. I don't love anyone but you.

Mr. Frank *(reproachfully).*[25] Annele!

Anne. It's true. I've been thinking about it for a long time. You're the only one I love.

Mr. Frank. It's fine to hear you tell me that you love me. But I'd be happier if you said you loved your mother as well . . . She needs your help so much . . . your love . . .

Anne. We have nothing in common. She doesn't understand me. Whenever I try to explain my views on life to her, she asks me if I'm constipated.

Mr. Frank. You hurt her very much just now. She's crying. She's in there crying.

Anne. I can't help it. I only told the truth. I didn't want her here . . . *(then, with sudden change)* Oh, Pim, I was horrible, wasn't I? And the worst of it is, I can stand off and look at myself doing it and know it's cruel, and yet I can't stop doing it. What's the matter with me? Tell me. Don't say it's just a phase! Help me.

Mr. Frank. There is so little that we parents can do to help our children. We can only try to set a good example . . . point the way. The rest you must do yourself. You must build your own character.

Anne. I'm trying. Really I am. Every night I think back over all of the things I did that day that were wrong . . . like putting the wet mop in Dr. Dussel's bed . . . and this thing now with Mother. I say to myself, that was wrong. I make up my mind, I'm never going to do that again. Never! Of course I may do something worse . . . but at least I'll never do *that again!* . . . I have a nicer side, Father . . . a sweeter, nicer side. But I'm scared to show it. I'm afraid that people are going to laugh at me if I'm serious. So the mean Anne comes to the outside and the good Anne stays on the inside, and I keep on trying to switch them around and have the good Anne outside and the bad Anne inside and be what I'd like to be . . . and might be . . . if only . . . only . . .

(She is asleep. Mr. Frank watches her for a moment and then turns off the light and starts out. The lights dim out. The curtain falls on the scene. Anne's voice is heard, dimly at first and then with growing strength.)

---

25. reproachfully: in a way intended to make someone feel ashamed.

Anne's Voice. . . . The air raids are getting worse. They come over day and night. The noise is terrifying. Pim says it should be music to our ears. The more planes, the sooner will come the end of the war. Mrs. Van Daan pretends to be a fatalist. What will be, will be. But when the planes come over, who is the most frightened? No one else but Petronella! . . . Monday, the ninth of November, nineteen forty-two. Wonderful news! The Allies have landed in Africa. Pim says that we can look for an early finish to the war. Just for fun he asked each of us what was the first thing we wanted to do when we got out of here. Mrs. Van Daan longs to be home with her own things, her needle-point chairs, the Beckstein piano her father gave her . . . the best that money could buy. Peter would like to go to a movie. Dr. Dussel wants to get back to his dentist's drill. He's afraid he is losing his touch. For myself, there are so many things . . . to ride a bike again . . . to laugh till my belly aches . . . to have new clothes from the skin out . . . to have a hot tub filled to overflowing and <u>wallow</u> in it for hours . . . to be back in school with my friends . . .

(As the last lines are being said, the curtain rises on the scene. The lights dim on as Anne's voice fades away.)

Responding to Reading

1. What are your thoughts about Anne's nightmare and the reactions that other characters have to it?

2. What are your impressions of Anne's mother?

3. In the lines above, Anne describes the first thing each of the people would like to do after getting out of the hidden quarters. If you were free after many months of hiding, what would be the first thing you would like to do?

Words to Know and Use | **wallow** (wäl′ ō) *v.* to lie relaxed in water

529

Scene 5

It is the first night of the Hanukkah[26] celebration. Mr. Frank is standing at the head of the table on which is the menorah.[27] He lights the shamas,[28] or servant candle, and holds it as he says the blessing. Seated listening is all the "family," dressed in their best. The men wear hats; Peter *wears his cap.*

Mr. Frank *(reading from a prayer book).* "Praised be Thou, oh Lord our God, Ruler of the universe, who has sanctified us with Thy commandments and bidden us kindle the Hanukkah lights. Praised be Thou, oh Lord our God, Ruler of the universe, who has wrought wondrous deliverances for our fathers in days of old. Praised be Thou, oh Lord our God, Ruler of the universe, that Thou has given us life and <u>sustenance</u> and brought us to this happy season." *(Mr. Frank lights the one candle of the menorah as he continues.)* "We kindle this Hanukkah light to celebrate the great and wonderful deeds wrought through the zeal with which God filled the hearts of the heroic Maccabees, two thousand years ago. They fought against <u>indifference</u>, against <u>tyranny</u> and <u>oppression</u>, and they restored our Temple to us. May these lights remind us that we should ever look to God, whence cometh our help." Amen.

All. Amen.

(Mr. Frank hands Mrs. Frank *the prayer book.)*

Mrs. Frank *(reading).* "I lift up mine eyes unto the mountains, from whence cometh my help. My help cometh from the Lord who made heaven and earth. He will not suffer thy foot to be moved. He that keepeth thee will not slumber. He that keepeth Israel doth neither slumber nor sleep. The Lord is thy keeper. The Lord is thy shade upon thy right hand. The sun shall not smite thee by day, nor the moon by night. The Lord shall keep thee from all evil. He shall keep thy soul. The Lord shall guard thy going out and thy coming in, from this time forth and forevermore." Amen.

All. Amen.

*(*Mrs. Frank *puts down the prayer book and goes to get the food and wine.* Margot *helps her.* Mr. Frank *takes the men's hats and puts them aside.)*

Dr. Dussel *(rising).* That was very moving.

Anne *(pulling him back).* It isn't over yet!

Mrs. Van Daan. Sit down! Sit down!

Anne. There's a lot more, songs and presents.

Dr. Dussel. Presents?

Mrs. Frank. Not this year, unfortunately.

Mrs. Van Daan. But always on Hanukkah everyone gives presents . . . everyone!

---

26. **Hanukkah** (kä′ noo kä′): a Jewish holiday, celebrated in December and lasting eight days.

27. **menorah** (mə nō′ rə): a candleholder with nine branches. One of the candles is lit on each day of Hanukkah.

28. **shamas** (shä′ məs): the candle used to light the others in a menorah.

Words to Know and Use | **sustenance** (sus′ tə nəns) *n.* comfort; nourishment
indifference (in dif′ ər əns) *n.* a lack of concern or feeling
tyranny (tir′ ə nē) *n.* cruel and unjust government
oppression (ə presh′ ən) *n.* domination by the cruel use of power

Dr. Dussel. Like our St. Nicholas's Day.[29]

(There is a chorus of noes from the group.)

Mrs. Van Daan. No! Not like St. Nicholas! What kind of a Jew are you that you don't know Hanukkah?

Mrs. Frank *(as she brings the food)*. I remember particularly the candles . . . First one, as we have tonight. Then the second night you light two candles, the next night three . . . and so on until you have eight candles burning. When there are eight candles, it is truly beautiful.

Mrs. Van Daan. And the potato pancakes.

Mr. Van Daan. Don't talk about them!

Mrs. Van Daan. I make the best latkes[30] you ever tasted!

Mrs. Frank. Invite us all next year . . . in your own home.

Mr. Frank. God willing!

Mrs. Van Daan. God willing.

Margot. What I remember best is the presents we used to get when we were little . . . eight days of presents . . . and each day they got better and better.

Mrs. Frank *(sitting down)*. We are all here, alive. That is present enough.

Anne. No, it isn't. I've got something . . .

(She rushes into her room, hurriedly puts on a little hat improvised from the lampshade, grabs a satchel bulging with parcels, and comes running back.)

Mrs. Frank. What is it?

Anne. Presents!

Mrs. Van Daan. Presents!

Dr. Dussel. Look!

Menorah.

Mr. Van Daan. What's she got on her head?

Peter. A lampshade!

Anne *(picks out one at random)*. This is for Margot. *(She hands it to* Margot, *pulling her to her feet.)* Read it out loud.

Margot *(reading)*.
"You have never lost your temper.
You never will, I fear.
You are so good.
But if you should,
Put all your cross words here."

29. **St. Nicholas's Day:** December 6, the day Christian children in the Netherlands receive gifts.
30. **latkes** (lät′ kəz): potato pancakes.

Mrs. Edith Frank.

(*She tears open the package.*) A new crossword puzzle book! Where did you get it?

Anne. It isn't new. It's one that you've done. But I rubbed it all out, and if you wait a little and forget, you can do it all over again.

Margot (*sitting*). It's wonderful, Anne. Thank you. You'd never know it wasn't new.

(*From outside we hear the sound of a streetcar passing.*)

Anne (*with another gift*). Mrs. Van Daan.

Mrs. Van Daan (*taking it*). This is awful . . . I haven't anything for anyone . . . I never thought . . .

Mr. Frank. This is all Anne's idea.

Mrs. Van Daan (*holding up a bottle*). What is it?

Anne. It's hair shampoo. I took all the odds and ends of soap and mixed them with the last of my toilet water.

Mrs. Van Daan. Oh, Anneke!

Anne. I wanted to write a poem for all of them, but I didn't have time. (*offering a large box to* Mr. Van Daan) Yours, Mr. Van Daan, is *really* something . . . something you want more than anything. (*as she waits for him to open it*) Look! Cigarettes!

Mr. Van Daan. Cigarettes!

Anne. Two of them! Pim found some old pipe tobacco in the pocket lining of his coat . . . and we made them . . . or rather, Pim did.

Mrs. Van Daan. Let me see . . . Well, look at that! Light it, Putti! Light it.

(Mr. Van Daan *hesitates.*)

Anne. It's tobacco, really it is! There's a little fluff in it, but not much.

(*Everyone watches intently as* Mr. Van Daan *cautiously lights it. The cigarette flares up. Everyone laughs.*)

Peter. It works!

Mrs. Van Daan. Look at him.

Mr. Van Daan (*spluttering*). Thank you, Anne. Thank you.

(Anne *rushes back to her satchel for another present.*)

Anne (*handing her mother a piece of paper*). For Mother, Hanukkah greeting.

(*She pulls her mother to her feet.*)

Mrs. Frank (*reading*).

"Here's an IOU that I promise to pay. Ten hours of doing whatever you say. Signed, Anne Frank." (*Mrs. Frank, touched, takes* Anne *in her arms, holding her close.*)

Dr. Dussel (*to* Anne). Ten hours of doing what you're told? *Anything* you're told?

Anne. That's right.

Dr. Dussel. You wouldn't want to sell that, Mrs. Frank?

Mrs. Frank. Never! This is the most precious gift I've ever had!

(*She sits, showing her present to the others.* Anne *hurries back to the satchel and pulls out a scarf, the scarf that* Mr. Frank *found in the first scene.*)

Anne (*offering it to her father*). For Pim.

Mr. Frank. Anneke . . . I wasn't supposed to have a present! (*He takes it, unfolding it and showing it to the others.*)

Anne. It's a muffler . . . to put round your neck . . . like an ascot, you know. I made it myself out of odds and ends . . . I knitted it in the dark each night, after I'd gone to bed. I'm afraid it looks better in the dark!

Mr. Frank (*putting it on*). It's fine. It fits me perfectly. Thank you, Annele.

(Anne *hands* Peter *a ball of paper with a string attached to it.*)

Anne. That's for Mouschi.

Peter (*rising to bow*). On behalf of Mouschi, I thank you.

Anne. (*hesitant, handing him a gift*). And . . . this is yours . . . from Mrs. Quack

Quack. (*as he holds it gingerly in his hands*) Well . . . open it . . . Aren't you going to open it?

Peter. I'm scared to. I know something's going to jump out and hit me.

Anne. No. It's nothing like that, really.

Mrs. Van Daan (*as he is opening it*). What is it, Peter? Go on. Show it.

Anne (*excitedly*). It's a safety razor!

Dr. Dussel. A what?

Anne. A razor!

Mrs. Van Daan (*looking at it*). You didn't make that out of odds and ends.

Anne (*to* Peter). Miep got it for me. It's not new. It's secondhand. But you really do need a razor now.

Dr. Dussel. For what?

Anne. Look on his upper lip . . . you can see the beginning of a mustache.

Dr. Dussel. He wants to get rid of that? Put a little milk on it and let the cat lick it off.

Peter (*starting for his room*). Think you're funny, don't you.

Dr. Dussel. Look! He can't wait! He's going in to try it!

Peter. I'm going to give Mouschi his present!

(*He goes into his room, slamming the door behind him.*)

Mr. Van Daan (*disgustedly*). Mouschi, Mouschi, Mouschi.

(*In the distance we hear a dog persistently barking.* Anne *brings a gift to* Dr. Dussel.)

Anne. And last but never least, my roommate, Dr. Dussel.

Dr. Dussel. For me? You have something for me?

(He opens the small box she gives him.)

Anne. I made them myself.

Dr. Dussel *(puzzled)*. Capsules! Two capsules!

Anne. They're earplugs!

Dr. Dussel. Earplugs?

Anne. To put in your ears so you won't hear me when I thrash around at night. I saw them advertised in a magazine. They're not real ones . . . I made them out of cotton and candle wax. Try them . . . See if they don't work . . . see if you can hear me talk . . .

Dr. Dussel *(putting them in his ears)*. Wait, now, until I get them in . . . so.

Anne. Are you ready?

Dr. Dussel. Huh?

Anne. Are you ready?

Dr. Dussel. Oh! They've gone inside! I can't get them out! *(They laugh as Dr. Dussel jumps about, trying to shake the plugs out of his ears. Finally he gets them out. Putting them away.)* Thank you, Anne! Thank you!

Mr. Van Daan. A real Hanukkah!

Mrs. Van Daan. Wasn't it cute of her?

Together

Mrs. Frank. I don't know when she did it.

Margot. I love my present.

Anne *(sitting at the table)*. And now let's have the song, Father . . . please . . . *(to Dr. Dussel)* Have you heard the Hanukkah song, Dr. Dussel? The song is the whole thing! *(She sings.)* "Oh, Hanukkah! Oh Hanukkah! The sweet celebration . . . "

Mr. Frank *(quieting her)*. I'm afraid, Anne, we shouldn't sing that song tonight. *(to Dr. Dussel)* It's a song of jubilation, of rejoicing. One is apt to become too enthusiastic.

Anne. Oh, please, please. Let's sing the song. I promise not to shout!

Mr. Frank. Very well. But quietly now . . . I'll keep an eye on you and when . . .

(As Anne starts to sing, she is interrupted by Dr. Dussel, who is snorting and wheezing.)

Dr. Dussel *(pointing to Peter)*. You . . . You! *(Peter is coming from his bedroom, ostentatiously holding a bulge in his coat as if he were holding his cat and dangling Anne's present before it.)* How many times . . . I told you . . . Out! Out!

Mr. Van Daan *(going to Peter)*. What's the matter with you? Haven't you any sense? Get that cat out of here.

Peter *(innocently)*. Cat?

Mr. Van Daan. You heard me. Get it out of here!

Peter. I have no cat. *(Delighted with his joke, he opens his coat and pulls out a bath towel. The group at the table laugh, enjoying the joke.)*

Dr. Dussel *(still wheezing)*. It doesn't need to be the cat . . . his clothes are enough . . . when he comes out of that room . . .

Words to Know and Use

534

jubilation (jōō′ bə lā′ shən) *n.* a happy celebration
ostentatiously (äs′ tən tā′ shəs lē) *adv.* with great show

Mr. Van Daan. Don't worry. You won't be bothered anymore. We're getting rid of it.

Dr. Dussel. At last you listen to me. *(He goes off into his bedroom.)*

Mr. Van Daan *(calling after him)*. I'm not doing it for you. That's all in your mind . . . all of it! *(He starts back to his place at the table.)* I'm doing it because I'm sick of seeing that cat eat all our food.

Peter. That's not true! I only give him bones . . . scraps . . .

Mr. Van Daan. Don't tell me! He gets fatter every day! That cat looks better than any of us. Out he goes tonight!

Peter. No! No!

Anne. Mr. Van Daan, you can't do that! That's Peter's cat. Peter loves that cat.

Mrs. Frank *(quietly)*. Anne.

Peter *(to Mr. Van Daan)*. If he goes, I go.

Mr. Van Daan. Go! Go!

Mrs. Van Daan. You're not going, and the cat's not going! Now please . . . this is Hanukkah . . . Hanukkah . . . this is the time to celebrate . . . What's the matter with all of you? Come on, Anne. Let's have the song.

Anne *(singing)*.
"Oh, Hanukkah! Oh, Hanukkah!
The sweet celebration."

Mr. Frank *(rising)*. I think we should first blow out the candle . . . then we'll have something for tomorrow night.

Margot. But, Father, you're supposed to let it burn itself out.

Mr. Frank. I'm sure that God understands shortages. *(before blowing it out)* "Praised be Thou, oh Lord our God, who has sus-tained us and permitted us to celebrate this joyous festival."

(He is about to blow out the candle when suddenly there is a crash of something falling below. They all freeze in horror, motionless. For a few seconds there is complete silence. Mr. Frank slips off his shoes. The others noiselessly follow his example. Mr. Frank turns out a light near him. He motions to Peter to turn off the center lamp. Peter tries to reach it, realizes he cannot, and gets up on a chair. Just as he is touching the lamp, he loses his balance. The chair goes out from under him. He falls. The iron lampshade crashes to the floor. There is a sound of feet below, running down the stairs.)

Mr. Van Daan *(under his breath)*. Oh. oh! *(The only light left comes from the Hanukkah candle. Dr. Dussel comes from his room. Mr. Frank creeps over to the stairwell and stands listening. The dog is heard barking excitedly.)* Do you hear anything?

Mr. Frank *(in a whisper)*. No. I think they've gone.

Mrs. Van Daan. It's the Green Police. They've found us.

Mr. Frank. If they had, they wouldn't have left. They'd be up here by now.

Mrs. Van Daan. I know it's the Green Police. They've gone to get help. That's all. They'll be back!

Mr. Van Daan. Or it may have been the Gestapo,[31] looking for papers . . .

---

31. **Gestapo** (gə stä′ pō): the Nazi secret police force, known for its terrorism and brutality.

Mr. Frank (*interrupting*). Or a thief, looking for money.

Mrs. Van Daan. We've got to do something . . . Quick! Quick! Before they come back.

Mr. Van Daan. There isn't anything to do. Just wait.

(*Mr. Frank holds up his hand for them to be quiet. He is listening intently. There is complete silence as they all strain to hear any sound from below. Suddenly Anne begins to sway. With a low cry she falls to the floor in a faint. Mrs. Frank goes to her quickly, sitting beside her on the floor and taking her in her arms.*)

Mrs. Frank. Get some water, please! Get some water!

(*Margot starts for the sink.*)

Mr. Van Daan (*grabbing* Margot). No! No! No one's going to run water!

Mr. Frank. If they've found us, they've found us. Get the water. (*Margot starts again for the sink. Mr. Frank, getting a flashlight.*) I'm going down.

(*Margot rushes to him, clinging to him. Anne struggles to consciousness.*)

Margot. No, Father, no! There may be someone there, waiting . . . It may be a trap!

Mr. Frank. This is Saturday. There is no way for us to know what has happened until Miep or Mr. Kraler comes on Monday morning. We cannot live with this uncertainty.

Margot. Don't go, Father!

Mrs. Frank. Hush, darling, hush. (Mr. Frank *slips quietly out, down the steps and out through the door below.*) Margot! Stay close to me. (Margot *goes to her mother.*)

Mr. Van Daan. Shush! Shush!

(*Mrs. Frank whispers to* Margot *to get the water.* Margot *goes for it.*)

Mrs. Van Daan. Putti, where's our money? Get our money. I hear you can buy the Green Police off, so much a head. Go upstairs quick! Get the money!

Mr. Van Daan. Keep still!

Mrs. Van Daan (*kneeling before him, pleading*). Do you want to be dragged off to a concentration camp? Are you going to stand there and wait for them to come up and get you? Do something, I tell you!

Mr. Van Daan (*pushing her aside*). Will you keep still!

(*He goes over to the stairwell to listen.* Peter *goes to his mother, helping her up onto the sofa. There is a second of silence, then* Anne *can stand it no longer.*)

Anne. Someone go after Father! Make Father come back!

Peter (*starting for the door*). I'll go.

Mr. Van Daan. Haven't you done enough?

(*He pushes* Peter *roughly away. In his anger against his father,* Peter *grabs a chair as if to hit him with it, then puts it down, burying his face in his hands.* Mrs. Frank *begins to pray softly.*)

Anne. Please, please, Mr. Van Daan. Get Father.

Mr. Van Daan. Quiet! Quiet!

(Anne *is shocked into silence.* Mrs. Frank *pulls her closer, holding her protectively in her arms.*)

Mrs. Frank *(softly, praying).* "I lift up mine eyes unto the mountains, from whence cometh my help. My help cometh from the Lord who made heaven and earth. He will not suffer thy foot to be moved . . . He that keepeth thee will not slumber . . . "

(She stops as she hears someone coming. They all watch the door tensely. Mr. Frank comes quietly in. Anne rushes to him, holding him tight.)

Mr. Frank. It was a thief. That noise must have scared him away.

Mrs. Van Daan. Thank goodness.

Mr. Frank. He took the cash box. And the radio. He ran away in such a hurry that he didn't stop to shut the street door. It was swinging wide open. *(A breath of relief sweeps over them.)* I think it would be good to have some light.

Margot. Are you sure it's all right?

Mr. Frank. The danger has passed. *(Margot goes to light the small lamp.)* Don't be so terrified, Anne. We're safe.

Dr. Dussel. Who says the danger has passed? Don't you realize we are in greater danger than ever?

Mr. Frank. Dr. Dussel, will you be still!

(Mr. Frank takes Anne back to the table, making her sit down with him, trying to calm her.)

Dr. Dussel *(pointing to* Peter*).* Thanks to this clumsy fool, there's someone now who knows we're up here! Someone now knows we're up here, hiding!

Mrs. Van Daan *(going to* Dr. Dussel*).* Someone knows we're here, yes. But who is the someone? A thief! A thief! You think a thief is going to go to the Green Police and say . . . I was robbing a place the other night and I heard a noise up over my head? You think a thief is going to do that?

Dr. Dussel. Yes. I think he will.

Mrs. Van Daan *(hysterically).* You're crazy!

(She stumbles back to her seat at the table. Peter *follows protectively, pushing* Dr. Dussel *aside.)*

Dr. Dussel. I think someday he'll be caught and then he'll make a bargain with the Green Police . . . if they'll let him off, he'll tell them where some Jews are hiding!

(He goes off into the bedroom. There is a second of appalled silence.)

Mr. Van Daan. He's right.

Anne. Father, let's get out of here! We can't stay here now . . . Let's go . . .

Mr. Van Daan. Go! Where?

Mrs. Frank *(sinking into her chair at the table).* Yes. Where?

Mr. Frank *(rising, to them all).* Have we lost all faith? All courage? A moment ago we thought that they'd come for us. We were sure it was the end. But it wasn't the end.

Words to Know and Use | **appalled** (ə pôld') *adj.* horrified; shocked **appall** *v.*

We're alive, safe. (Mr. Van Daan *goes to the table and sits.* Mr. Frank *prays.*) "We thank Thee, oh Lord our God, that in Thy infinite mercy Thou hast again seen fit to spare us." (*He blows out the candle, then turns to* Anne.) Come on, Anne. The song! Let's have the song!

(*He starts to sing.* Anne *finally, falteringly, starts to sing, as* Mr. Frank *urges her on. Her voice is hardly audible at first.*)

Anne (*singing*).
"Oh, Hanukkah! Oh, Hanukkah!
The sweet . . . celebration . . . "

(*As she goes on singing, the others gradually join in, their voices still shaking with fear.* Mrs. Van Daan *sobs as she sings.*)

Group.
"Around the feast . . . we . . . gather
In complete . . . jubilation . . .
Happiest of sea . . . sons
Now is here.
Many are the reasons for good cheer."

(Dr. Dussel *comes from the bedroom. He comes over to the table, standing beside* Margot, *listening to them as they sing.*)

"Together
We'll weather
Whatever tomorrow may bring."

(*As they sing on with growing courage, the lights start to dim.*)

"So hear us rejoicing
And merrily voicing
The Hanukkah song that we sing.
Hoy!"

(*The lights are out. The curtain starts slowly to fall.*)

"Hear us rejoicing
And merrily voicing
The Hanukkah song that we sing."

(*They are still singing as the curtain falls.*)

*R*esponding to Reading

1. How would you describe the changes of mood in Scene 5?

2. Scene 5 begins with a prayer and ends with a song. How do the words of the prayer and the song relate to the situation of the people in hiding?

Responding to Reading

First Impressions

1. What thoughts do you have about the events in this play so far? In your journal or on a sheet of paper, jot down your reactions.

Second Thoughts

2. What are your impressions of Anne at this point in the play?

3. Which character do you like the least? Which character do you like the most? Explain.

4. Look back at what you wrote in Write Before You Read. What would you say is the most difficult part of living in hiding?

Broader Connections

5. In extreme situations, many people develop coping mechanisms that help them deal with hardships. For example, one prisoner of war, fearing he'd go mad without mental activity, played chess games in his mind. Describe the coping mechanisms of the main characters in this play. What do you think your coping mechanism would be?

Literary Concept: Diary

Anne Frank's **diary,** like most diaries, contains a personal, day-by-day account of thoughts and experiences. Most diaries are never intended to be shared. Anne's father was very reluctant at first to allow Anne's diary to be published. He was finally persuaded that his daughter's diary deserved a worldwide audience. What do you think of Mr. Frank's decision? Explain.

Writing Options

1. Prepare a holiday **gift list** for your family, as Anne did. Include only items that cost no money. Write an explanation of why each gift is just right for the person receiving it.

2. Choose one character from the play and write a **character analysis.** Describe two of the character's traits. For each trait cite an example from the play that shows the trait.

Vocabulary Practice

Exercise A   On your paper write the letter of the word or phrase that best completes each sentence.

1. The family escaping from the Nazis could not dress **ostentatiously;** so they wore   (a) simple dark clothes   (b) shorts and T-shirts   (c) military uniforms.

2. A **compassionate** response to a family seeking to hide from the Nazis would be,   (a) "That's tough"   (b) "I can't afford to help"   (c) "I will help you."

3. The most **insufferable** part of hiding would be (a) making loud noises   (b) having time to read (c) knowing you might be found and killed.

4. The family worried about how they would get their **sustenance**—   (a) sleep   (b) books   (c) food and water.

5. If a person's behavior was **aggravating,** the person might be given   (a) praise   (b) a scolding   (c) extra food.

6. One girl gave evidence of her **pent-up** emotions by (a) smiling warmly   (b) taking a nap   (c) clenching her fists.

7. Another person was apt to **wallow** in self-pity because he (a) refused to feel sad   (b) felt very sorry for himself   (c) was a little sad.

8. The family was **outraged** that someone in their group would   (a) steal food from them   (b) make presents for them   (c) settle an argument.

9. One illustration of Nazi **oppression** was the existence of   (a) Allied resistance (b) concentration camps   (c) relief flights.

10. When the war ended, the townspeople showed their **jubilation** by (a) dancing in the streets   (b) marching to the cemetery   (c) building a monument.

Exercise B   On your paper write the letter of the word that is most nearly opposite in meaning to the capitalized word.

1. APPALLED: (a) delighted   (b) disgusted   (c) mocked   (d) hated
2. INDIFFERENCE: (a) disinterest   (b) difference   (c) concern   (d) sameness
3. LOATHE: (a) win   (b) love   (c) loaf   (d) hate
4. TYRANNY: (a) freedom   (b) dictatorship   (c) dinosaur   (d) leadership
5. VILE: (a) good   (b) nasty   (c) foul   (d) calm

> *Words to Know and Use*
> ___
> **aggravating**
> **appalled**
> **compassionate**
> **indifference**
> **insufferable**
> **jubilation**
> **loathe**
> **oppression**
> **ostentatiously**
> **outraged**
> **pent-up**
> **sustenance**
> **tyranny**
> **vile**
> **wallow**

Reading On

What will happen next? How might the relationships among the people in hiding change? Also think about the various threats to the group's security.

ACT TWO

Scene 1

In the darkness we hear Anne's *voice, again reading from the diary.*

Anne's Voice. Saturday, the first of January, nineteen forty-four. Another new year has begun, and we find ourselves still in our hiding place. We have been here now for one year, five months, and twenty-five days. It seems that our life is at a standstill.

(The curtain rises on the scene. It is late afternoon. Everyone is bundled up against the cold. In the main room Mrs. Frank *is taking down the laundry which is hung across the back.* Mr. Frank *sits in the chair down left, reading.* Margot *is lying on the couch with a blanket over her and the many-colored knitted scarf around her throat.* Anne *is seated at the center table, writing in her diary.* Peter, Mr. *and* Mrs. Van Daan, *and* Dr. Dussel *are all in their own rooms, reading or lying down.*

As the lights dim on, Anne's *voice continues, without a break.)*

Anne's Voice. We are all a little thinner. The Van Daans' "discussions" are as violent as ever. Mother still does not understand me. But then I don't understand her either. There is one great change, however. A change in myself. I read somewhere that girls of my age don't feel quite certain of themselves. . . .

(We hear the chimes and then a hymn being played on the carillon outside. The buzzer of the door below suddenly sounds. Everyone is startled. Mr. Frank *tiptoes cautiously to the top of the steps and listens. Again the buzzer sounds, in* Miep's *V-for-Victory signal.[1])*

Mr. Frank. It's Miep!

(He goes quickly down the steps to unbolt the door. Mrs. Frank *calls upstairs to the* Van Daans *and then to* Peter.*)*

Mrs. Frank. Wake up, everyone! Miep is here!

(Anne quickly puts her diary away. Margot *sits up, pulling the blanket around her shoulders.* Dr. Dussel *sits on the edge of his bed, listening, disgruntled.* Miep *comes up the steps, followed by* Mr. Kraler. *They bring flowers, books, newspapers, and so forth.* Anne *rushes to* Miep, *throwing her arms affectionately around her.)*

Miep . . . *and* Mr. Kraler . . . What a delightful surprise!

Mr. Kraler. We came to bring you New Year's greetings.

Mrs. Frank. You shouldn't . . . you should have at least one day to yourselves. *(She goes quickly to the stove and brings down teacups and tea for all of them.)*

Anne. Don't say that; it's so wonderful to see them! *(sniffing at* Miep's *coat)* I can smell the wind and the cold on your clothes.

---

1. **V-for-Victory signal:** three short rings and one long one, Morse code for the letter *v*.

Words to Know and Use | **disgruntled** (dis grunt' 'ld) *adj.* displeased and irritated   **disgruntle** *v.*

Miep Gies.

Miep *(giving her the flowers).* There you are. *(then to* Margot, *feeling her forehead)* How are you, Margot? . . . Feeling any better?

Margot. I'm all right.

Anne. We filled her full of every kind of pill so she won't cough and make a noise.

(She runs into her room to put the flowers in water. Mr. and Mrs. Van Daan come from upstairs. Outside there is the sound of a band playing.)

Mrs. Van Daan. Well, hello, Miep. Mr. Kraler.

Mr. Kraler *(giving a bouquet of flowers to* Mrs. Van Daan*).* With my hope for peace in the New Year.

Peter *(anxiously).* Miep, have you seen Mouschi? Have you seen him anywhere around?

Miep. I'm sorry, Peter. I asked everyone in the neighborhood had they seen a gray cat. But they said no.

(Mrs. Frank gives Miep a cup of tea. Mr. Frank comes up the steps carrying a small cake on a plate.)

Mr. Frank. Look what Miep's brought for us!

Mrs. Frank *(taking it).* A cake!

Mr. Van Daan. A cake! *(He pinches Miep's cheeks gaily and hurries up to the cupboard.)* I'll get some plates.

(Dr. Dussel, in his room, hastily puts a coat on and starts out to join the others.)

Mrs. Frank. Thank you, Miepia. You shouldn't have done it. You must have used all of your sugar ration for weeks. *(giving it to* Mrs. Van Daan*)* It's beautiful, isn't it?

Mrs. Van Daan. It's been ages since I even saw a cake. Not since you brought us one last year. *(without looking at the cake, to* Miep*)* Remember? Don't you remember, you gave us one on New Year's Day? Just this time last year? I'll never forget it because you had "Peace in nineteen forty-three" on it. *(She looks at the cake and reads.)* "Peace in nineteen forty-four!"

Miep. Well, it has to come sometime, you know. *(as* Dr. Dussel *comes from his room)* Hello, Dr. Dussel.

Mr. Kraler. How are you?

Mr. Van Daan (*bringing plates and a knife*). Here's the knife, *liefje.* Now, how many of us are there?

Miep. None for me, thank you.

Mr. Frank. Oh, please. You must.

Miep. I couldn't.

Mr. Van Daan. Good! That leaves one . . . two . . . three . . . seven of us.

Dr. Dussel. Eight! Eight! It's the same number as it always is!

Mr. Van Daan. I left Margot out. I take it for granted Margot won't eat any.

Anne. Why wouldn't she!

Mrs. Frank. I think it won't harm her.

Mr. Van Daan. All right! All right! I just didn't want her to start coughing again, that's all.

Dr. Dussel. And please, Mrs. Frank should cut the cake.

┌**Mr. Van Daan.** What's the difference?

Together

│**Mrs. Van Daan.** It's not Mrs. Frank's
└cake, is it, Miep? It's for all of us.

Dr. Dussel. Mrs. Frank divides things better.

┌**Mrs. Van Daan** (*going to* Dr. Dussel). What are you trying to say?

│
Together

│**Mr. Van Daan.** Oh, come on! Stop wast-
└ing time!

Mrs. Van Daan (*to* Dr. Dussel). Don't I always give everybody exactly the same? Don't I?

Mr. Van Daan. Forget it, Kerli.

Mrs. Van Daan. No. I want an answer! Don't I?

Dr. Dussel. Yes. Yes. Everybody gets exactly the same . . . except Mr. Van Daan always gets a little bit more.

(*Van Daan advances on* Dr. Dussel, *the knife still in his hand.*)

Mr. Van Daan. That's a lie!

(*Dr. Dussel retreats before the* onslaught *of the* Van Daans.)

Mr. Frank. Please, please! (*then to* Miep) You see what a little sugar cake does to us? It goes right to our heads!

Mr. Van Daan (*handing* Mrs. Frank *the knife*). Here you are, Mrs. Frank.

Mrs. Frank. Thank you. (*then to* Miep *as she goes to the table to cut the cake*) Are you sure you won't have some?

Miep (*drinking her tea*). No, really, I have to go in a minute.

(*The sound of the band fades out in the distance.*)

Peter (*to* Miep). Maybe Mouschi went back to our house . . . they say that cats . . . Do you ever get over there . . . ? I mean . . . do you suppose you could . . . ?

Miep. I'll try, Peter. The first minute I get, I'll try. But I'm afraid, with him gone a week . . .

Dr. Dussel. Make up your mind, already someone has had a nice big dinner from that cat!

(Peter *is furious,* _inarticulate._ *He starts toward* Dr. Dussel *as if to hit him.* Mr. Frank *stops him.* Mrs. Frank *speaks quickly to ease the situation.*)

Mrs. Frank *(to* Miep*).* This is delicious, Miep!

Mrs. Van Daan *(eating hers).* Delicious!

Mr. Van Daan *(finishing it in one gulp).* Dirk's in luck to get a girl who can bake like this!

Miep *(putting down her empty teacup).* I have to run. Dirk's taking me to a party tonight.

Anne. How heavenly! Remember, now, what everyone is wearing and what you have to eat and everything so you can tell us tomorrow.

Miep. I'll give you a full report! Goodbye, everyone!

Mr. Van Daan *(to* Miep*).* Just a minute. There's something I'd like you to do for me.

(He hurries off up the stairs to his room.)

Mrs. Van Daan *(sharply).* Putti, where are you going? *(She rushes up the stairs after him, calling hysterically.)* What do you want? Putti, what are you going to do?

Miep *(to* Peter*).* What's wrong?

Peter *(sympathetic toward his mother).* Father says he's going to sell her fur coat. She's crazy about that old fur coat.

Dr. Dussel. Is it possible? Is it possible that anyone is so silly as to worry about a fur coat in times like this?

Peter. It's none of your darn business . . . and if you say one more thing . . . I'll, I'll take you and I'll . . . I mean it . . . I'll . . .

(There is a piercing scream from Mrs. Van Daan *above. She grabs at the fur coat as* Mr. Van Daan *is starting downstairs with it.*)

Mrs. Van Daan. No! No! No! Don't you dare take that! You hear? It's mine!

(Downstairs Peter *turns away, embarrassed, miserable.*)

My father gave me that! You didn't give it to me. You have no right. Let go of it . . . you hear?

(Mr. Van Daan *pulls the coat from her hands and hurries downstairs.* Mrs. Van Daan *sinks to the floor, sobbing. As* Mr. Van Daan *comes into the main room, the others look away, embarrassed for him.*)

Mr. Van Daan *(to* Mr. Kraler*).* Just a little—discussion over the advisability of selling this coat. As I have often reminded Mrs. Van Daan, it's very selfish of her to keep it when people outside are in such desperate need of clothing . . . *(He gives the coat to* Miep.) So if you will please to sell it for us? It should fetch a good price. And by

Words to Know and Use | **inarticulate** (in' är tik' yo͞o lit) *adj.* speechless

the way, will you get me cigarettes? I don't care what kind they are . . . get all you can.

Miep. It's terribly difficult to get them, Mr. Van Daan. But I'll try. Goodbye.

(She goes. Mr. Frank *follows her down the steps to bolt the door after her.* Mrs. Frank *gives* Mr. Kraler *a cup of tea.)*

Mrs. Frank. Are you sure you won't have some cake, Mr. Kraler?

Mr. Kraler. I'd better not.

Mr. Van Daan. You're still feeling bad? What does your doctor say?

Mr. Kraler. I haven't been to him.

Mrs. Frank. Now, Mr. Kraler! . . .

Mr. Kraler *(sitting at the table).* Oh, I tried. But you can't get near a doctor these days . . . they're so busy. After weeks I finally managed to get one on the telephone. I told him I'd like an appointment . . . I wasn't feeling very well. You know what he answers . . . over the telephone . . . Stick out your tongue! *(They laugh. He turns to* Mr. Frank *as* Mr. Frank *comes back.)* I have some contracts here . . . I wonder if you'd look over them with me . . .

Mr. Frank *(putting out his hand).* Of course.

Mr. Kraler *(rising).* If we could go downstairs . . . *(*Mr. Frank *starts ahead;* Mr. Kraler *speaks to the others.)* Will you forgive us? I won't keep him but a minute. *(He starts to follow* Mr. Frank *down the steps.)*

Margot *(with sudden foreboding).* What's happened? Something's happened! Hasn't it, Mr. Kraler?

*(*Mr. Kraler *stops and comes back, trying to reassure* Margot *with a pretense of casualness.)*

Mr. Kraler. No, really. I want your father's advice . . .

Margot. Something's gone wrong! I know it!

Mr. Frank *(coming back, to* Mr. Kraler*).* If it's something that concerns us here, it's better that we all hear it.

Mr. Kraler *(turning to him, quietly).* But . . . the children . . . ?

Mr. Frank. What they'd imagine would be worse than any reality.

(As Mr. Kraler *speaks, they all listen with intense* apprehension. *Mrs. Van Daan* comes down the stairs and sits on the bottom step.)*

Mr. Kraler. It's a man in the storeroom . . . I don't know whether or not you remember him . . . Carl, about fifty, heavyset, nearsighted . . . He came with us just before you left.

Mr. Frank. He was from Utrecht?

Mr. Kraler. That's the man. A couple of weeks ago, when I was in the storeroom, he closed the door and asked me . . . how's Mr. Frank? What do you hear from Mr. Frank? I told him I only knew there was a rumor that you were in Switzerland. He said he'd heard that rumor too, but he thought I might know something more. I didn't pay any attention to it . . . but then a thing happened yesterday . . . He'd brought some invoices to the office for me to sign. As I was going through them, I looked up. He was standing staring at the bookcase . . . your bookcase. He said he thought he remembered a door there . . . Wasn't there a door there that used to go up to the loft? Then he told me he wanted more money. Twenty guilders[2] more a week.

Mr. Van Daan. Blackmail!

Mr. Frank. Twenty guilders? Very modest blackmail.

Mr. Van Daan. That's just the beginning.

Dr. Dussel (coming to Mr. Frank). You know what I think? He was the thief who was down there that night. That's how he knows we're here.

Mr. Frank (to Mr. Kraler). How was it left? What did you tell him?

Mr. Kraler. I said I had to think about it. What shall I do? Pay him the money? . . . Take a chance on firing him . . . or what? I don't know.

Dr. Dussel (frantic). Don't fire him! Pay him what he asks . . . keep him here where you can have your eye on him.

Mr. Frank. Is it so much that he's asking? What are they paying nowadays?

Mr. Kraler. He could get it in a war plant. But this isn't a war plant. Mind you, I don't know if he really knows . . . or if he doesn't know.

Mr. Frank. Offer him half. Then we'll soon find out if it's blackmail or not.

Dr. Dussel. And if it is? We've got to pay it, haven't we? Anything he asks we've got to pay!

Mr. Frank. Let's decide that when the time comes.

Mr. Kraler. This may be all my imagination. You get to a point these days where you suspect everyone and everything. Again and again . . . on some simple look or word, I've found myself . . .

(The telephone rings in the office below.)

Mrs. Van Daan (hurrying to Mr. Kraler). There's the telephone! What does that mean, the telephone ringing on a holiday?

Mr. Kraler. That's my wife. I told her I had to go over some papers in my office . . . to call me there when she got out of church. (He starts out) I'll offer him half then. Goodbye . . . we'll hope for the best!

(The group calls their goodbyes halfheartedly. Mr. Frank follows Mr. Kraler, to bolt the door below. During the following scene, Mr. Frank comes back up and stands listening, disturbed.)

Dr. Dussel (to Mr. Van Daan). You can thank your son for this . . . smashing the light! I tell you, it's just a question of time now.

(He goes to the window at the back and stands looking out.)

Margot. Sometimes I wish the end would come . . . whatever it is.

Mrs. Frank (shocked). Margot!

---

2. **guilders** (gil′ dərz): the basic monetary unit of the Netherlands.

(Anne *goes to* Margot, *sitting beside her on the couch with her arms around her.*)

Margot. Then at least we'd know where we were.

Mrs. Frank. You should be ashamed of yourself! Talking that way! Think how lucky we are! Think of the thousands dying in the war every day. Think of the people in concentration camps.

Anne (*interrupting*). What's the good of that? What's the good of thinking of misery when you're already miserable? That's stupid!

Mrs. Frank. Anne!

(*As* Anne *goes on raging at her mother,* Mrs. Frank *tries to break in, in an effort to quiet her.*)

Anne. We're young, Margot and Peter and I! You grown-ups have had your chance! But look at us . . . If we begin thinking of all the horror in the world, we're lost! We're trying to hold on to some kind of ideals . . . when everything . . . ideals, hopes . . . everything, are being destroyed! It isn't our fault that the world is in such a mess! We weren't around when all this started! So don't try to take it out on us! (*She rushes off to her room, slamming the door after her. She picks up a brush from the chest and hurls it to the floor. Then she sits on the settee, trying to control her anger.*)

Mr. Van Daan. She talks as if we started the war! Did we start the war?

(*He spots* Anne's *cake. As he starts to take it,* Peter *anticipates him.*)

Peter. She left her cake.

(*He starts for* Anne's *room with the cake. There is silence in the main room.* Mrs. Van Daan *goes up to her room, followed by* Mr. Van Daan. Dr. Dussel *stays looking out the window.* Mr. Frank *brings* Mrs. Frank *her cake. She eats it slowly, without relish.* Mr. Frank *takes his cake to* Margot *and sits quietly on the sofa beside her.* Peter *stands in the doorway of* Anne's *darkened room, looking at her, then makes a little movement to let her know he is there.* Anne *sits up quickly, trying to hide the signs of her tears.* Peter *holds out the cake to her.*)

You left this.

Anne (*dully*). Thanks.

(Peter *starts to go out, then comes back.*)

Peter. I thought you were fine just now. You know just how to talk to them. You know just how to say it. I'm no good . . . I never can think . . . especially when I'm mad . . . That Dr. Dussel . . . when he said that about Mouschi . . . someone eating him . . . all I could think is . . . I wanted to hit him. I wanted to give him such a . . . a . . . that he'd . . . That's what I used to do when there was an argument at school . . . That's the way I . . . but here . . . And an old man like that . . . it wouldn't be so good.

Anne. You're making a big mistake about me. I do it all wrong. I say too much. I go too far. I hurt people's feelings . . .

(Dr. Dussel *leaves the window, going to his room.*)

Peter. I think you're just fine . . . What I want to say . . . if it wasn't for you around here, I don't know. What I mean . . .

(Peter *is interrupted by* Dr. Dussel's *turning on the light.* Dr. Dussel *stands in the doorway, startled to see* Peter. Peter *advances toward him forbiddingly.* Dr. Dussel *backs out of the room.* Peter *closes the door on him.*)

Anne. Do you mean it, Peter? Do you really mean it?

Peter. I said it, didn't I?

Anne. Thank you, Peter!

(*In the main room* Mr. *and* Mrs. Frank *collect the dishes and take them to the sink, washing them.* Margot *lies down again on the couch.* Dr. Dussel*, lost, wanders into* Peter's *room and takes up a book, starting to read.*)

Peter *(looking at the photographs on the wall)*. You've got quite a collection.

Anne. Wouldn't you like some in your room? I could give you some. Heaven knows you spend enough time in there . . . doing heaven knows what . . .

Peter. It's easier. A fight starts, or an argument . . . I duck in there.

Anne. You're lucky, having a room to go to. His lordship is always here . . . I hardly ever get a minute alone. When they start in on me, I can't duck away. I have to stand there and take it.

Peter. You gave some of it back just now.

Anne. I get so mad. They've formed their opinions . . . about everything . . . but we . . . we're still trying to find out . . . We have problems here that no other people our age have ever had. And just as you think you've solved them, something

comes along and bang! You have to start all over again.

Peter. At least you've got someone you can talk to.

Anne. Not really. Mother . . . I never discuss anything serious with her. She doesn't understand. Father's all right. We can talk about everything . . . everything but one thing. Mother. He simply won't talk about her. I don't think you can be really intimate with anyone if he holds something back, do you?

Peter. I think your father's fine.

Anne. Oh, he is, Peter! He is! He's the only one who's ever given me the feeling that I have any sense. But anyway, nothing can take the place of school and play and friends of your own age . . . or near your age . . . can it?

Peter. I suppose you miss your friends and all.

Anne. It isn't just . . . (*She breaks off, staring up at him for a second.*) Isn't it funny, you and I? Here we've been seeing each other every minute for almost a year and a half, and this is the first time we've ever really talked. It helps a lot to have someone to talk to, don't you think? It helps you to let off steam.

Peter *(going to the door)*. Well, any time you want to let off steam, you can come into my room.

Anne *(following him)*. I can get up an awful lot of steam. You'll have to be careful how you say that.

Peter. It's all right with me.

Anne. Do you mean it?

Peter. I said it, didn't I?

Peter Van Daan.

(*He goes out.* Anne *stands in her doorway looking after him. As* Peter *gets to his door, he stands for a minute looking back at her. Then he goes into his room.* Dr. Dussel *rises as he comes in and quickly passes him, going out.* He starts across for his room. Anne *sees him coming and pulls her door shut.* Dr. Dussel *turns back toward* Peter's *room.* Peter *pulls his door shut.* Dr. Dussel *stands there, bewildered, <u>forlorn</u>.*

The scene slowly dims out. The curtain falls on the scene. Anne's voice comes over in the darkness . . . faintly at first and then with growing strength.)

Anne's Voice. We've had bad news. The people from whom Miep got our ration books have been arrested. So we have had to cut down on our food. Our stomachs are so empty that they rumble and make strange noises, all in different keys. Mr. Van Daan's is deep and low, like a bass fiddle. Mine is high, whistling like a flute. As we all sit around waiting for supper, it's like an orchestra tuning up. It only needs Toscanini[3] to raise his baton, and we'd be off in the Ride of the Valkyries.[4] Monday, the sixth of March, nineteen forty-four. Mr. Kraler is in the hospital. It seems he has ulcers.[5] Pim says we are his ulcers. Miep has to run the business and us too. The Americans have landed on the southern tip of Italy. Father looks for a quick finish to the war. Dr. Dussel is waiting every day for the warehouse man to demand more money. Have I been skipping too much from one subject to another? I can't help it. I feel that spring is coming. I feel it in my whole body and soul. I feel utterly confused. I am longing . . . so longing . . . for everything . . . for friends . . . for someone to talk to . . . someone who understands . . . someone young, who feels as I do . . .

(As these last lines are being said, the curtain rises on the scene. The lights dim on. Anne's voice fades out.)

---

3. **Toscanini** (täs' kə nē' nē): Arturo Toscanini, a famous Italian orchestral conductor.
4. **Ride of the Valkyries** (val kir' ēz): a stirring passage from an opera by Richard Wagner, a German composer.
5. **ulcers**: open sores in the lining of the stomach or intestine.

Responding to Reading

1. In this scene Anne and Peter's relationship turns into friendship. Considering what you know about both of them, do you think they would have become friends if they had not been thrown together by the war?

2. Anne tells Peter, "We have problems here that no other people our age have ever had." What are some problems that people your age have today? Are any of them problems that people your age have never had before?

3. Why do you think difficult situations like the one in this play bring out the best in some people and the worst in others?

4. What parts of this scene foreshadow the possible discovery of the hiding place?

Scene 2

It is evening, after supper. From outside we hear the sound of children playing. The grown-ups, with the exception of Mr. Van Daan, *are all in the main room.* Mrs. Frank *is doing some mending.* Mrs. Van Daan *is reading a fashion magazine.* Mr. Frank *is going over business accounts.* Dr. Dussel, *in his dentist's jacket, is pacing up and down, impatient to get into his bedroom.* Mr. Van Daan *is upstairs, working on a piece of embroidery in an embroidery frame.*

In his room Peter *is sitting before the mirror, smoothing his hair. As the scene goes on, he puts on his tie, brushes his coat, and puts it on, preparing himself meticulously for a visit from* Anne. *On his wall are now hung some of* Anne's *motion picture stars.*

In her room Anne *too is getting dressed. She stands before the mirror in her slip, trying various ways of dressing her hair.* Margot *is seated on the sofa, hemming a skirt for* Anne *to wear.*

In the main room Dr. Dussel *can stand it no longer. He comes over, rapping sharply on the door of his and* Anne's *bedroom.*

Anne *(calling to him).* No, no, Dr. Dussel! I am not dressed yet.

(Dr. Dussel walks away, furious, sitting down and burying his head in his hands. Anne *turns to* Margot.)

How is that? How does that look?

Margot *(glancing at her briefly).* Fine.

Anne. You didn't even look.

Margot. Of course I did. It's fine.

Anne. Margot, tell me, am I terribly ugly?

Margot. Oh, stop fishing.

Anne. No. No. Tell me.

Margot. Of course you're not. You've got nice eyes . . . and a lot of animation, and . . .

Anne. A little vague, aren't you?

(Outside, Mrs. Frank, *feeling sorry for* Dr. Dussel, *comes over, knocking at the girls' door.)*

Mrs. Frank *(outside).* May I come in?

Margot. Come in, Mother.

Mrs. Frank *(shutting the door behind her).* Dr. Dussel's impatient to get in here.

Anne. Heavens, he takes the room for himself the entire day.

Mrs. Frank *(gently).* Anne, dear, you're not going in again tonight to see Peter?

Anne *(dignified).* That is my intention.

Mrs. Frank. But you've already spent a great deal of time in there today.

Anne. I was in there exactly twice. Once to get the dictionary and then three-quarters of an hour before supper.

Mrs. Frank. Aren't you afraid you're disturbing him?

Anne. Mother, I have some <u>intuition</u>.

Mrs. Frank. Then may I ask you this much, Anne. Please don't shut the door when you go in.

Anne. You sound like Mrs. Van Daan! *(She picks up her blouse, putting it on.)*

Words to Know and Use | **intuition** (in′ to̅o̅ ish′ ən) *n.* a knowledge obtained without the conscious use of reasoning

Mrs. Frank. No. No. I don't mean to suggest anything wrong. I only wish that you wouldn't expose yourself to criticism . . . that you wouldn't give Mrs. Van Daan the opportunity to be unpleasant.

Anne. Mrs. Van Daan doesn't need an opportunity to be unpleasant!

Mrs. Frank. Everyone's on edge, worried about Mr. Kraler. This is one more thing . . .

Anne. I'm sorry, Mother. I'm going to Peter's room. I'm not going to let Petronella Van Daan spoil our friendship.

(Mrs. Frank *hesitates for a second, then goes out, closing the door after her. She gets a pack of playing cards and sits at the center table, playing solitaire. In* Anne's *room* Margot *hands the finished skirt to* Anne. *As* Anne *is putting it on,* Margot *takes off her high-heeled shoes and stuffs paper in the toes so that* Anne *can wear them.*)

Margot (to Anne). Why don't you two talk in the main room? It'd save a lot of trouble. It's hard on Mother, having to listen to those remarks from Mrs. Van Daan and not say a word.

Anne. Why doesn't she say a word? I think it's ridiculous to take it and take it.

Margot. You don't understand Mother at all, do you? She can't talk back. She's not like you. It's just not in her nature to fight back.

Anne. Anyway . . . the only one I worry about is you. I feel awfully guilty about you. (*She sits on the stool near* Margot, *putting on* Margot's *high-heeled shoes.*)

Margot. What about?

Anne. I mean, every time I go into Peter's room, I have a feeling I may be hurting you. (Margot *shakes her head.*) I know if it were me, I'd be wild. I'd be desperately jealous, if it were me.

Margot. Well, I'm not.

Anne. You don't feel bad? Really? Truly? You're not jealous?

Margot. Of course I'm jealous . . . jealous that you've got something to get up in the morning for . . . But jealous of you and Peter? No.

(Anne *goes back to the mirror.*)

Anne. Maybe there's nothing to be jealous of. Maybe he doesn't really like me. Maybe I'm just taking the place of his cat . . . (*She picks up a pair of short white gloves, putting them on.*) Wouldn't you like to come in with us?

Margot. I have a book.

(The sound of the children playing outside fades out. In the main room Dr. Dussel can stand it no longer. He jumps up, going to the bedroom door and knocking sharply.)

Dr. Dussel. Will you please let me in my room!

Anne. Just a minute, dear, dear Dr. Dussel. (*She picks up her mother's pink stole and adjusts it elegantly over her shoulders, then gives a last look in the mirror.*) Well, here I go . . . to run the gauntlet.[6]

(She starts out, followed by Margot.)

Dr. Dussel (as she appears—sarcastically). Thank you so much.

---

6. **to run the gauntlet:** to endure a series of troubles or difficulties.

(Dr. Dussel goes into his room. Anne goes toward Peter's room, passing Mrs. Van Daan and her parents at the center table.)

Mrs. Van Daan. My God, look at her!

(Anne pays no attention. She knocks at Peter's door.)

I don't know what good it is to have a son. I never see him. He wouldn't care if I killed myself.

(Peter opens the door and stands aside for Anne to come in.)

Just a minute, Anne. *(She goes to them at the door.)* I'd like to say a few words to my son. Do you mind?

(Peter and Anne stand waiting.)

Peter, I don't want you staying up till all hours tonight. You've got to have your sleep. You're a growing boy. You hear?

Mrs. Frank. Anne won't stay late. She's going to bed promptly at nine. Aren't you, Anne?

Anne. Yes, Mother . . . *(to Mrs. Van Daan).* May we go now?

Mrs. Van Daan. Are you asking me? I didn't know I had anything to say about it.

Mrs. Frank. Listen for the chimes, Anne dear.

(The two young people go off into Peter's room, shutting the door after them.)

Mrs. Van Daan *(to Mrs. Frank).* In my day it was the boys who called on the girls. Not the girls on the boys.

Mrs. Frank. You know how young people like to feel that they have secrets. Peter's room is the only place where they can talk.

Mrs. Van Daan. Talk! That's not what they called it when I was young.

(Mrs. Van Daan goes off to the bathroom. Margot settles down to read her book. Mr. Frank puts his papers away and brings a chess game to the center table. He and Mrs. Frank start to play. In Peter's room Anne speaks to Peter, indignant, humiliated.)

Anne. Aren't they awful? Aren't they impossible? Treating us as if we were still in the nursery.

(She sits on the cot. Peter gets a bottle of pop and two glasses.)

Peter. Don't let it bother you. It doesn't bother me.

Anne. I suppose you can't really blame them . . . they think back to what *they* were like at our age. They don't realize how much more advanced we are . . . When you think what wonderful discussions we've had! . . . Oh, I forgot. I was going to bring you some more pictures.

Peter. Oh, these are fine, thanks.

Anne. Don't you want some more? Miep just brought me some new ones.

Peter. Maybe later. *(He gives her a glass of pop and, taking some for himself, sits down facing her.)*

Anne *(looking up at one of the photographs).* I remember when I got that . . . I won it. I bet Jopie that I could eat five ice-cream cones. We'd all been playing Ping-Pong . . . We used to have heavenly times . . . we'd finish up with ice cream at the Delphi or the Oasis, where Jews were allowed . . . there'd always be a lot of boys . . . we'd laugh and joke . . . I'd like to go back to it for a few days or a week. But after that I know I'd be bored to death. I think more seriously about life now. I want to be a journalist . . . or something. I love to write. What do you want to do?

Peter. I thought I might go off someplace . . . work on a farm or something . . . some job that doesn't take much brains.

Anne. You shouldn't talk that way. You've got the most awful inferiority complex.

Peter. I know I'm not smart.

Anne. That isn't true. You're much better than I am in dozens of things . . . arithmetic and algebra and . . . well, you're a million times better than I am in algebra. *(with sudden directness)* You like Margot, don't you? Right from the start you liked her, liked her much better than me.

Peter *(uncomfortably)*. Oh, I don't know.

(In the main room Mrs. Van Daan comes from the bathroom and goes over to the sink, polishing a coffee pot.)

Anne. It's all right. Everyone feels that way. Margot's so good. She's sweet and bright and beautiful, and I'm not.

Peter. I wouldn't say that.

Anne. Oh, no, I'm not. I know that. I know quite well that I'm not a beauty. I never have been and never shall be.

Peter. I don't agree at all. I think you're pretty.

Anne. That's not true!

Peter. And another thing. You've changed . . . from at first, I mean.

Anne. I have?

Peter. I used to think you were awful noisy.

Anne. And what do you think now, Peter? How have I changed?

Peter. Well . . . er . . . you're . . . quieter.

(In his room Dr. Dussel takes his pajamas and toilet articles and goes into the bathroom to change.)

Anne. I'm glad you don't just hate me.

Peter. I never said that.

Anne. I bet when you get out of here, you'll never think of me again.

Peter. That's crazy.

Anne. When you get back with all of your friends, you're going to say . . . now what did I ever see in that Mrs. Quack Quack.

Peter. I haven't got any friends.

Anne. Oh, Peter, of course you have. Everyone has friends.

Peter. Not me. I don't want any. I get along all right without them.

Anne. Does that mean you can get along without me? I think of myself as your friend.

Peter. No. If they were all like you, it'd be different.

(He takes the glasses and the bottle and puts them away. There is a second's silence, and then Anne speaks, hesitantly, shyly.)

Anne. Peter, did you ever kiss a girl?

Peter. Yes. Once.

Anne *(to cover her feelings)*. That picture's crooked. (Peter goes over, straightening the photograph.) Was she pretty?

Peter. Huh?

Anne. The girl that you kissed.

Peter. I don't know. I was blindfolded. *(He comes back and sits down again.)* It was at a party. One of those kissing games.

Anne *(relieved)*. Oh. I don't suppose that really counts, does it?

Peter. It didn't with me.

Anne. I've been kissed twice. Once, a man I'd never seen before kissed me on the cheek when he picked me up off the ice and I was crying. And the other was Mr. Koophuis, a friend of Father's who kissed my hand. You wouldn't say those counted, would you?

Peter. I wouldn't say so.

Anne. I know almost for certain that Margot would never kiss anyone unless she was engaged to them. And I'm sure, too, that Mother never touched a man before Pim. But I don't know . . . things are so different now . . . What do you think? Do you think a girl shouldn't kiss anyone except if she's engaged or something? It's so hard to try to think what to do when here we are with the whole world falling around our ears and you think . . . well . . . you don't know what's going to happen tomorrow and . . . What do you think?

Peter. I suppose it'd depend on the girl. Some girls, anything they do's wrong. But others . . . well . . . it wouldn't necessarily be wrong with them.

(The carillon starts to strike nine o'clock.)

I've always thought that when two people . . .

Anne. Nine o'clock. I have to go.

Peter. That's right.

Anne *(without moving)*. Good night.

(There is a second's pause; then Peter *gets up and moves toward the door.)*

Peter. You won't let them stop you coming?

Anne. No. *(She rises and starts for the door.)* Sometimes I might bring my diary. There are so many things in it that I want to talk over with you. There's a lot about you.

Peter. What kind of things?

Anne. I wouldn't want you to see some of it. I thought you were a nothing, just the way you thought about me.

Peter. Did you change your mind, the way I changed my mind about you?

Anne. Well . . . You'll see . . .

(For a second, Anne *stands looking up at* Peter, *longing for him to kiss her. As he makes no move, she turns away. Then suddenly* Peter *grabs her awkwardly in his arms, kissing her on the cheek.* Anne *walks out dazed. She stands for a minute, her back to the people in the main room. As she regains her poise, she goes to her mother and father and* Margot, *silently kissing them. They murmur their good nights to her. As she is about to open her bedroom door, she catches sight of* Mrs. Van Daan. *She goes quickly to her, taking her face in her hands and kissing her first on one cheek and then on the other. Then she hurries off into her room.* Mrs. Van Daan *looks after her and then looks over at* Peter's *room. Her suspicions are confirmed.)*

Mrs. Van Daan *(knowingly)*. Ah hah!

(The lights dim out. The curtain falls on the scene. In the darkness Anne's *voice comes*

faintly at first and then with growing strength.)

Anne's Voice. By this time we all know each other so well that if anyone starts to tell a story, the rest can finish it for him. We're having to cut down still further on our meals. What makes it worse, the rats have been at work again. They've carried off some of our precious food. Even Dr. Dussel wishes now that Mouschi was here. Thursday, the twentieth of April, nineteen forty-four. Invasion fever is mounting every day. Miep tells us that people outside talk of nothing else. For myself, life has become much more pleasant. I often go to Peter's room after supper. Oh, don't think I'm in love, because I'm not. But it does make life more bearable to have someone with whom you can exchange views. No more tonight. P.S. . . . I must be honest. I must confess that I actually live for the next meeting. Is there anything lovelier than to sit under the skylight and feel the sun on your cheeks and have a darling boy in your arms? I admit now that I'm glad the Van Daans had a son and not a daughter. I've outgrown another dress. That's the third. I'm having to wear Margot's clothes after all. I'm working hard on my French and am now reading "La Belle-Nivernaise."[7]

(As she is saying the last lines, the curtain rises on the scene. The lights dim on as Anne's voice fades out.)

---

7. **"La Belle-Nivernaise"** (lä bel nē′ vɛr nez′): a story by Alphonse Daudet, a French author.

Responding to Reading

1. Would you rather have Mrs. Frank or Mrs. Van Daan as your mother? Why?

2. Why do you think Anne kisses her family and Mrs. Van Daan after she visits with Peter?

3. In what ways does Anne seem to be changing in this scene?

   Think about
   • her attitude toward her mother
   • her attitude toward Peter
   • her attitude toward Dr. Dussel

Scene 3

It is night, a few weeks later. Everyone is in bed. There is complete quiet. In the Van Daans' room a match flares up for a moment and then is quickly put out. Mr. Van Daan, in bare feet, dressed in underwear and trousers, is dimly seen coming stealthily down the stairs and into the main room, where Mr. and Mrs. Frank and Margot are sleeping. He goes to the food safe and again lights a match. Then he cautiously opens the safe, taking out a half loaf of bread. As he closes the safe, it creaks. He stands rigid. Mrs. Frank sits up in bed. She sees him.)

Mrs. Frank *(screaming)*. Otto! Otto! *Komme schnell!*[8]

(The rest of the people wake, hurriedly getting up.)

Mr. Frank. *Was ist los? Was ist passiert?*[9]

(Dr. Dussel, followed by Anne, comes from his room.)

Mrs. Frank *(as she rushes over to Mr. Van Daan)*. *Er stiehlt das Essen!*[10]

Dr. Dussel *(grabbing Mr. Van Daan)*. You! You! Give me that.

Mrs. Van Daan. *(coming down the stairs).* Putti . . . Putti . . . what is it?

Dr. Dussel *(his hands on Mr. Van Daan's neck)*. You dirty thief . . . stealing food . . . you good-for-nothing . . .

Mr. Frank. Dr. Dussel! Oh! Help me, Peter!

(Peter comes over, trying, with Mr. Frank, to separate the two struggling men.)

Peter. Let him go! Let go!

(Dr. Dussel drops Mr. Van Daan, pushing him away. He shows them the end of a loaf of bread that he has taken from Mr. Van Daan.)

Dr. Dussel. You greedy, selfish . . . !

(Margot turns on the lights.)

Mrs. Van Daan. Putti . . . what is it?

(All of Mrs. Frank's gentleness, her self-control, is gone. She is outraged, in a frenzy of indignation.)

Mrs. Frank. The bread! He was stealing the bread!

Dr. Dussel. It was you, and all the time we thought it was the rats!

Mr. Frank. Mr. Van Daan, how could you!

Mr. Van Daan. I'm hungry.

Mrs. Frank. We're all of us hungry! I see the children getting thinner and thinner. Your own son Peter . . . I've heard him moan in his sleep, he's so hungry. And you come in the night and steal food that should go to them . . . to the children!

Mrs. Van Daan *(going to Mr. Van Daan protectively)*. He needs more food than the

---

8. *Komme schnell!* (kôm′ ə shnel) *German:* Come quickly!
9. *Was ist los? Was ist passiert?* (väs ist lôs väs ist pä sērt′) *German:* What's the matter? What has happened?
10. *Er stiehlt das Essen!* (er shtēlt däs es′ ən) *German:* He is stealing the food!

Words to Know and Use | **stealthily** (stel′ thə lē) *adv.* sneakily; slyly

rest of us. He's used to more. He's a big man.

(Mr. Van Daan *breaks away, going over and sitting on the couch.*)

Mrs. Frank *(turning on* Mrs. Van Daan*).* And you . . . you're worse than he is! You're a mother, and yet you sacrifice your child to this man . . . this . . . this . . .

Mr. Frank. Edith! Edith!

(Margot *picks up the pink woolen stole, putting it over her mother's shoulders.*)

Mrs. Frank *(paying no attention, going on to* Mrs. Van Daan*).* Don't think I haven't seen you! Always saving the choicest bits for him! I've watched you day after day, and I've held my tongue. But not any longer! Not after this! Now I want him to go! I want him to get out of here!

⎡**Mr. Frank.** Edith!

⎢**Mr. Van Daan.** Get out of here?

Together

⎣**Mrs. Van Daan.** What do you mean?

Mrs. Frank. Just that! Take your things and get out!

Mr. Frank *(to* Mrs. Frank*).* You're speaking in anger. You cannot mean what you are saying.

Mrs. Frank. I mean exactly that!

(Mrs. Van Daan *takes a cover from the Franks' bed, pulling it about her.*)

Mr. Frank. For two long years we have lived here, side by side. We have respected each other's rights . . . we have managed to live in peace. Are we now going to throw it all away? I know this will

never happen again, will it, Mr. Van Daan?

Mr. Van Daan. No. No.

Mrs. Frank. He steals once! He'll steal again!

(Mr. Van Daan, *holding his stomach, starts for the bathroom.* Anne *puts her arms around him, helping him up the step.*)

Mr. Frank. Edith, please. Let us be calm. We'll all go to our rooms . . . and afterwards we'll sit down quietly and talk this out . . . we'll find some way . . .

Mrs. Frank. No! No! No more talk! I want them to leave!

Mrs. Van Daan. You'd put us out, on the streets?

Mrs. Frank. There are other hiding places.

Mrs. Van Daan. A cellar . . . a closet. I know. And we have no money left even to pay for that.

Mrs. Frank. I'll give you money. Out of my own pocket I'll give it gladly. *(She gets her purse from a shelf and comes back with it.)*

Mrs. Van Daan. Mr. Frank, you told Putti you'd never forget what he'd done for you when you came to Amsterdam. You said you could never repay him, that you . . .

Mrs. Frank *(counting out money).* If my husband had any obligation to you, he's paid it, over and over.

Mr. Frank. Edith, I've never seen you like this before. I don't know you.

Mrs. Frank. I should have spoken out long ago.

Dr. Dussel. You can't be nice to some people.

Mrs. Van Daan (*turning on* Dr. Dussel). There would have been plenty for all of us if *you* hadn't come in here!

Mr. Frank. We don't need the Nazis to destroy us. We're destroying ourselves.

(*He sits down, with his head in his hands. Mrs. Frank goes to Mrs. Van Daan.*)

Mrs. Frank (*giving* Mrs. Van Daan *some money*). Give this to Miep. She'll find you a place.

Anne. Mother, you're not putting *Peter* out. Peter hasn't done anything.

Mrs. Frank. He'll stay, of course. When I say I must protect the children, I mean Peter too.

(*Peter rises from the steps where he has been sitting.*)

Peter. I'd have to go if Father goes.

(*Mr. Van Daan comes from the bathroom. Mrs. Van Daan hurries to him and takes him to the couch. Then she gets water from the sink to bathe his face.*)

Mrs. Frank (*while this is going on*). He's no father to you . . . that man! He doesn't know what it is to be a father!

Peter (*starting for his room*). I wouldn't feel right. I couldn't stay.

Mrs. Frank. Very well, then. I'm sorry.

Anne (*rushing over to* Peter). No, Peter! No!

(*Peter goes into his room, closing the door after him. Anne turns back to her mother, crying.*)

I don't care about the food. They can have mine! I don't want it! Only don't send them away. It'll be daylight soon. They'll be caught . . .

Margot (*putting her arms comfortingly around* Anne). Please, Mother!

Mrs. Frank. They're not going now. They'll stay here until Miep finds them a place. (*to* Mrs. Van Daan) But one thing I insist on! He must never come down here again! He must never come to this room where the food is stored! We'll divide what we have . . . an equal share for each!

(*Dr. Dussel hurries over to get a sack of potatoes from the food safe. Mrs. Frank goes on, to* Mrs. Van Daan.)

You can cook it here and take it up to him.

(*Dr. Dussel brings the sack of potatoes back to the center table.*)

Margot. Oh, no. No. We haven't sunk so far that we're going to fight over a handful of rotten potatoes.

Dr. Dussel (*dividing the potatoes into piles*). Mrs. Frank, Mr. Frank, Margot, Anne, Peter, Mrs. Van Daan, Mr. Van Daan, myself . . . Mrs. Frank . . .

(*The buzzer sounds in* Miep's *signal.*)

Mr. Frank. It's Miep! (*He hurries over, getting his overcoat and putting it on.*)

Margot. At this hour?

Mrs. Frank. It is trouble.

Mr. Frank (*as he starts down to unbolt the door*). I beg you, don't let her see a thing like this!

Dr. Dussel (*counting without stopping*). . . . Anne, Peter, Mrs. Van Daan, Mr. Van Daan, myself . . .

Margot (*to Dr. Dussel*). Stop it! Stop it!

Dr. Dussel. . . . Mr. Frank, Margot, Anne, Peter, Mrs. Van Daan, Mr. Van Daan, myself, Mrs. Frank . . .

Mrs. Van Daan. You're keeping the big ones for yourself! All the big ones . . . Look at the size of that! . . . And that! . . .

(*Dr. Dussel* continues on with his dividing. Peter, *with his shirt and trousers on, comes from his room.*)

Margot. Stop it! Stop it!

(*We hear* Miep's *excited voice speaking to* Mr. Frank *below.*)

Miep. Mr. Frank . . . the most wonderful news! . . . The invasion has begun!

Mr. Frank. Go on, tell them! Tell them!

(*Miep* comes running up the steps ahead of Mr. Frank. *She has a man's raincoat on over her nightclothes and a bunch of orange-colored flowers in her hand.*)

Miep. Did you hear that, everybody? Did you hear what I said? The invasion has begun! The invasion!

(*They all stare at* Miep, *unable to grasp what she is telling them.* Peter *is the first to recover his wits.*)

Peter. Where?

Mrs. Van Daan. When? When, Miep?

Miep. It began early this morning . . .

(*As she talks on, the realization of what she has said begins to dawn on them. Everyone goes crazy. A wild demonstration takes place.* Mrs. Frank *hugs* Mr. Van Daan.)

Mrs. Frank. Oh, Mr. Van Daan, did you hear that?

(Dr. Dussel *embraces* Mrs. Van Daan. Peter *grabs a frying pan and parades around the room, beating on it, singing the Dutch national anthem.* Anne *and* Margot *follow him, singing, weaving in and out among the excited grown-ups.* Margot *breaks away to take the flowers from* Miep *and distribute them to everyone. While this* pandemonium *is going on,* Mrs. Frank *tries to make herself heard above the excitement.*)

Mrs. Frank (*to* Miep). How do you know?

Miep. The radio . . . The BBC![11] They said they landed on the coast of Normandy![12]

Peter. The British?

Miep. British, Americans, French, Dutch, Poles, Norwegians . . . all of them! More than four thousand ships! Churchill spoke, and General Eisenhower! D-day they call it!

Mr. Frank. Thank God, it's come!

Mrs. Van Daan. At last!

---

11. **BBC:** British Broadcasting Corporation.
12. **Normandy:** a region in northwestern France, on the English Channel.

Words to Know and Use | **pandemonium** (pan′ də mō′ nē əm) *n.* a wild disorder, noise, or confusion

Miep *(starting out).* I'm going to tell Mr. Kraler. This'll be better than any blood transfusion.

Mr. Frank *(stopping her).* In what part of Normandy did they land, did they say?

Miep. Normandy . . . that's all I know now . . . I'll be up the minute I hear some more! *(She goes out hurriedly.)*

Mr. Frank *(to* Mrs. Frank*).* What did I tell you? What did I tell you?

(Mrs. Frank indicates that he has forgotten to bolt the door after Miep. He hurries down the steps. Mr. Van Daan, sitting on the couch, suddenly breaks into a convulsive sob. Everybody looks at him, bewildered.)

Mrs. Van Daan *(hurrying to him).* Putti! Putti! What is it? What happened?

Mr. Van Daan. Please. I'm so ashamed.

(Mr. Frank comes back up the steps.)

Dr. Dussel. Oh!

Mrs. Van Daan. Don't, Putti.

Margot. It doesn't matter now!

Mr. Frank *(going to* Mr. Van Daan*).* Didn't you hear what Miep said? The invasion has come! We're going to be liberated! This is a time to celebrate! *(He embraces* Mrs. Frank *and then hurries to the cupboard and gets the cognac and a glass.)*

Mr. Van Daan. To steal bread from children!

Mrs. Frank. We've all done things that we're ashamed of.

Anne. Look at me, the way I've treated Mother . . . so mean and horrid to her.

Mrs. Frank. No, Anneke, no.

Volunteers search the rubble of Amsterdam after the bombing of the city by the Germans in May 1940.

(Anne runs to her mother, putting her arms around her.)

Anne. Oh, Mother, I was. I was awful.

Mr. Van Daan. Not like me. No one is as bad as me!

Dr. Dussel *(to* Mr. Van Daan*).* Stop it now! Let's be happy!

Mr. Frank *(giving* Mr. Van Daan *a glass of cognac).* Here! Here! Schnapps! *L'chaim!*[13]

(Mr. Van Daan takes the cognac. They all watch him. He gives them a feeble smile. Anne puts up her fingers in a V-for-Victory sign. As Mr. Van Daan gives an answering V-sign, they are startled to hear a loud sob from behind them. It is Mrs. Frank, stricken with remorse. She is sitting on the other side of the room.)

---

13. **Schnapps! L'chaim!** (shnäps lə khä′ yim) *German:* Brandy! To Life!

Mrs. Frank *(through her sobs)*. When I think of the terrible things I said . . .

(Mr. Frank, Anne, and Margot hurry to her, trying to comfort her. Mr. Van Daan brings her his glass of cognac.)

Mr. Van Daan. No! No! You were right!

Mrs. Frank. That I should speak that way to you! . . . Our friends! . . . Our guests! *(She starts to cry again.)*

Dr. Dussel. Stop it, you're spoiling the whole invasion!

(As they are comforting her, the lights dim out. The curtain falls.)

Anne's Voice *(faintly at first and then with growing strength)*. We're all in much better spirits these days. There's still excellent news of the invasion. The best part about it is that I have a feeling that friends are coming. Who knows? Maybe I'll be back in school by fall. Ha, ha! The joke is on us! The warehouse man doesn't know a thing, and we are paying him all that money! . . . Wednesday, the second of July, nineteen forty-four. The invasion seems temporarily to be bogged down. Mr. Kraler has to have an operation, which looks bad. The Gestapo have found the radio that was stolen. Dr. Dussel says they'd trace it back and back to the thief, and then it's just a matter of time till they get to us. Everyone is low. Even poor Pim can't raise their spirits. I have often been downcast myself . . . but never in despair. I can shake off everything if I write. But . . . and that is the great question . . . will I ever be able to write well? I want to so much. I want to go on living even after my death. Another birthday has gone by, so now I am fifteen. Already I know what I want. I have a goal, an opinion.

(As this is being said, the curtain rises on the scene, the lights dim on, and Anne's voice fades out.)

Responding to Reading

1. At fifteen Anne has "a goal, an opinion" about what she wants from life. What are some of your own goals and opinions?

2. Why do you think Mrs. Frank reacts so strongly when Mr. Van Daan is caught stealing food?

3. How do you think the situation might have been resolved if the group had not received the news about the invasion?

Scene 4

It is an afternoon a few weeks later . . . Everyone but Margot *is in the main room. There is a sense of great tension.*

Both Mrs. Frank *and* Mr. Van Daan *are nervously pacing back and forth.* Dr. Dussel *is standing at the window, looking down fixedly at the street below.* Peter *is at the center table, trying to do his lessons.* Anne *sits opposite him, writing in her diary.* Mrs. Van Daan *is seated on the couch, her eyes on* Mr. Frank *as he sits reading.*

The sound of a telephone ringing comes from the office below. They all are rigid, listening tensely. Dr. Dussel *rushes down to* Mr. Frank.

Dr. Dussel. There it goes again, the telephone! Mr. Frank, do you hear?

Mr. Frank *(quietly).* Yes. I hear.

Dr. Dussel *(pleading, insistent).* But this is the third time, Mr. Frank! The third time in quick succession! It's a signal! I tell you it's Miep, trying to get us! For some reason she can't come to us, and she's trying to warn us of something!

Mr. Frank. Please. Please.

Mr. Van Daan *(to* Dr. Dussel*).* You're wasting your breath.

Dr. Dussel. Something has happened, Mr. Frank. For three days now Miep hasn't been to see us! And today not a man has come to work. There hasn't been a sound in the building!

Mrs. Frank. Perhaps it's Sunday. We may have lost track of the days.

Mr. Van Daan *(to* Anne*).* You with the diary there. What day is it?

Dr. Dussel *(going to* Mrs. Frank*).* I don't lose track of the days! I know exactly what day it is! It's Friday, the fourth of August. Friday, and not a man at work. *(He rushes back to* Mr. Frank, *pleading with him, almost in tears.)* I tell you Mr. Kraler's dead. That's the only explanation. He's dead, and they've closed down the building, and Miep's trying to tell us!

Mr. Frank. She'd never telephone us.

Dr. Dussel *(frantic).* Mr. Frank, answer that! I beg you, answer it!

Mr. Frank. No.

Mr. Van Daan. Just pick it up and listen. You don't have to speak. Just listen and see if it's Miep.

Dr. Dussel *(speaking at the same time).* Please . . . I ask you.

Mr. Frank. No. I've told you, no. I'll do nothing that might let anyone know we're in the building.

Peter. Mr. Frank's right.

Mr. Van Daan. There's no need to tell us what side you're on.

Mr. Frank. If we wait patiently, quietly, I believe that help will come.

(There is silence for a minute as they all listen to the telephone ringing.)

Dr. Dussel. I'm going down.

(He rushes down the steps. Mr. Frank *tries ineffectually to hold him.* Dr. Dussel *runs to the lower door, unbolting it. The telephone*

stops ringing. Dr. Dussel *bolts the door and comes slowly back up the steps.)*

Too late.

(Mr. Frank *goes to* Margot *in* Anne's *bedroom.)*

Mr. Van Daan. So we just wait here until we die.

Mrs. Van Daan *(hysterically).* I can't stand it! I'll kill myself! I'll kill myself!

Mr. Van Daan. Stop it!

(In the distance a German military band is heard playing a Viennese waltz.)

Mrs. Van Daan. I think you'd be glad if I did! I think you want me to die!

Mr. Van Daan. Whose fault is it we're here?

(Mrs. Van Daan starts for her room. He follows, talking at her.)

We could've been safe somewhere . . . in America or Switzerland. But no! No! You wouldn't leave when I wanted to. You couldn't leave your things. You couldn't leave your precious furniture.

Mrs. Van Daan. Don't touch me!

(She hurries up the stairs, followed by Mr. Van Daan. Peter, *unable to bear it, goes to his room.* Anne *looks after him, deeply concerned.* Dr. Dussel *returns to his post at the window.* Mr. Frank *comes back into the main room and takes a book, trying to read.* Mrs. Frank *sits near the sink, starting to peel some potatoes.* Anne *quietly goes to* Peter's *room, closing the door after her.* Peter *is lying face down on the cot.* Anne *leans over him, holding him in her arms, trying to bring him out of his despair.)*

Anne. Look, Peter, the sky. *(She looks up through the skylight.)* What a lovely, lovely day! Aren't the clouds beautiful? You know what I do when it seems as if I couldn't stand being cooped up for one more minute? I *think* myself out. I think myself on a walk in the park where I used to go with Pim. Where the jonquils and the crocuses and the violets grow down the slopes. You know the most wonderful part about *thinking* yourself out? You can have it any way you like. You can have roses and violets and chrysanthemums all blooming at the same time . . . It's funny . . . I used to take it all for granted . . . and now I've gone crazy about everything to do with nature. Haven't you?

Peter. I've just gone crazy. I think if something doesn't happen soon . . . if we don't get out of here . . . I can't stand much more of it!

Anne *(softly).* I wish you had a religion, Peter.

Peter. No, thanks! Not me!

Anne. Oh, I don't mean you have to be Orthodox[14] . . . or believe in heaven and hell and purgatory[15] and things . . . I just mean some religion . . . it doesn't matter what. Just to believe in something! When I think of all that's out there . . . the trees . . . and flowers . . . and sea gulls . . . when I think of the dearness of you, Peter . . . and the goodness of the people we know . . . Mr. Kraler, Miep, Dirk, the

---

14. Orthodox (ôr′ thə däks′): strictly conforming to the rites and traditions set forth in Jewish sacred literature.

15. purgatory (pur′ gə tôr′ ē): according to some Christian teaching, a state or place where souls undergo suffering after death in order to be purified for heaven.

vegetable man, all risking their lives for us every day . . . When I think of these good things, I'm not afraid any more . . . I find myself, and God, and I . . .

(Peter *interrupts, getting up and walking away.*)

Peter. That's fine! But when I begin to think, I get mad! Look at us, hiding out for two years. Not able to move! Caught here like . . . waiting for them to come and get us . . . and all for what?

Anne. We're not the only people that've had to suffer. There've always been people that've had to . . . sometimes one race . . . sometimes another . . . and yet . . .

Peter. That doesn't make me feel any better!

Anne *(going to him).* I know it's terrible, trying to have any faith . . . when people are doing such horrible . . . But you know what I sometimes think? I think the world may be going through a phase, the way I was with Mother. It'll pass, maybe not for hundreds of years, but some day . . . I still believe, in spite of everything, that people are really good at heart.

Peter. I want to see something now . . . Not a thousand years from now! *(He goes over, sitting down again on the cot.)*

Anne. But, Peter, if you'd only look at it as part of a great pattern . . . that we're just a little minute in the life . . . *(She breaks off.)* Listen to us, going at each other like a couple of stupid grown-ups! Look at the sky now. Isn't it lovely?

(*She holds out her hand to him.* Peter *takes it and rises, standing with her at the window, looking out, his arms around her.*)

Some day, when we're outside again, I'm going to . . .

(*She breaks off as she hears the sound of a car, its brakes squealing as it comes to a sudden stop. The people in the other rooms also become aware of the sound. They listen tensely. Another car roars up to a screeching stop.* Anne *and* Peter *come from* Peter's *room.* Mr. *and* Mrs. Van Daan *creep down the stairs.* Dr. Dussel *comes out from his room. Everyone is listening, hardly breathing. A doorbell clangs again and again in the building below.* Mr. Frank *starts quietly down the steps to the door.* Dr. Dussel *and* Peter *follow him. The others stand rigid, waiting, terrified.*

In a few seconds Dr. Dussel *comes stumbling back up the steps. He shakes off* Peter's *help and goes to his room.* Mr. Frank *bolts the door below and comes slowly back up the steps. Their eyes are all on him as he stands there for a minute. They realize that what they feared has happened.* Mrs. Van Daan *starts to whimper.* Mr. Van Daan *puts her gently in a chair and then hurries off up the stairs to their room to collect their things.* Peter *goes to comfort his mother. There is a sound of violent pounding on a door below.*)

Mr. Frank *(quietly).* For the past two years we have lived in fear. Now we can live in hope.

(*The pounding below becomes more insistent. There are muffled sounds of voices, shouting commands.*)

Men's Voices. *Auf machen! Da drinnen! Auf machen! Schnell! Schnell! Schnell!*[16]

---

16. *Auf machen! . . . Schnell!* (ouf mäkh′ ən dä drin′ ən ouf mäkh′ ən shnel shnel shnel) *German:* Open up! Inside there! Open up! Quick! Quick! Quick!

Movable bookcase hiding entrance to the secret annex.

(The street door below is forced open. We hear the heavy tread of footsteps coming up. Mr. Frank *gets two school bags from the shelves and gives one to* Anne *and the other to* Margot. *He goes to get a bag for Mrs. Frank. The sound of feet coming up grows louder.* Peter *comes to* Anne, *kissing her goodbye, then goes to his room to collect his things. The buzzer of their door starts to ring.*

Mr. Frank *brings Mrs. Frank a bag. They stand together, waiting. We hear the thud of gun butts on the door, trying to break it down.*

Anne *stands, holding her school satchel, looking over at her father and mother with a soft, reassuring smile. She is no longer a child but a woman with courage to meet whatever lies ahead.*

Close-up view of movable bookcase.

The lights dim out. The curtain falls on the scene. We hear a mighty crash as the door is shattered. After a second, Anne's voice is heard.)

Anne's Voice. And so it seems our stay here is over. They are waiting for us now. They've allowed us five minutes to get our things. We can each take a bag and whatever it will hold of clothing. Nothing else. So, dear Diary, that means I must leave you behind. Goodbye for a while. P.S. Please, please, Miep, or Mr. Kraler, or anyone else. If you should find this diary, will you please keep it safe for me, because someday I hope . . .

(Her voice stops abruptly. There is silence. After a second the curtain rises.)

Scene 5

It is again the afternoon in November 1945. The rooms are as we saw them in the first scene. Mr. Kraler *has joined* Miep *and* Mr. Frank. *There are coffee cups on the table. We see a great change in* Mr. Frank. *He is calm now. His bitterness is gone. He slowly turns a few pages of the diary. They are blank.*

Mr. Frank. No more. *(He closes the diary and puts it down on the couch beside him.)*

Miep. I'd gone to the country to find food. When I got back, the block was surrounded by police . . .

Mr. Kraler. We made it our business to learn how they knew. It was the thief . . . the thief who told them.

(Miep goes up to the gas burner, bringing back a pot of coffee.)

Mr. Frank *(after a pause).* It seems strange to say this, that anyone could be happy in a concentration camp. But Anne was happy in the camp in Holland where they first took us. After two years of being shut up in these rooms, she could be out . . . out in the sunshine and the fresh air that she loved.

Miep *(offering the coffee to* Mr. Frank*).* A little more?

Mr. Frank *(holding out his cup to her).* The news of the war was good. The British and Americans were sweeping through France. We felt sure that they would get to us in time. In September we were told that we were to be shipped to Poland . . .

The men to one camp. The women to another. I was sent to Auschwitz.[17]. They went to Belsen.[18] In January we were freed, the few of us who were left. The war wasn't yet over, so it took us a long time to get home. We'd be sent here and there behind the lines where we'd be safe. Each time our train would stop . . . at a siding or a crossing . . . we'd all get out and go from group to group . . . Where were you? Were you at Belsen? At Buchenwald?[19] At Mauthausen? Is it possible that you knew my wife? Did you ever see my husband? My son? My daughter? That's how I found out about my wife's death . . . of Margot, the Van Daans . . . Dr. Dussel. But Anne . . . I still hoped . . . Yesterday I went to Rotterdam. I'd heard of a woman there . . . She'd been in Belsen with Anne . . . I know now.

(He picks up the diary again and turns the pages back to find a certain passage. As he finds it, we hear Anne's *voice.)*

Anne's Voice. In spite of everything, I still believe that people are really good at heart. (Mr. Frank *slowly closes the diary.)*

Mr. Frank. She puts me to shame.

(They are silent.)

---

17. Auschwitz (oush′ vits): a Nazi concentration camp located in Poland, notorious as an extermination center.
18. Belsen (bel′ zən): a village in Germany, the site of a Nazi concentration camp and extermination center.
19. Buchenwald (boo′ k'n wôld′): a Nazi concentration camp and extermination center in Germany.

Responding to Reading

1. What do you think might have happened if someone had answered the telephone?

2. What is your reaction to Mr. Van Daan's speech that begins "We could've been safe somewhere . . ."? Do you agree or disagree with Mr. Van Daan?

3. What do you think of Anne's advice to Peter to "look at it as part of a great pattern . . . that we're just a little minute in the life . . ."?

Responding to Reading

First Impressions

1. What words come to mind to describe your feelings at the end of this play? Jot them down in your journal or on a sheet of paper.

Second Thoughts

2. Mr. Frank says, "Anne was happy in the camp in Holland where they first took us." Considering what you know about Anne, how do you think she could have been happy in a concentration camp?

3. On page 540 you predicted what you thought would happen in the final act. How do your predictions compare with what actually happens?

4. Anne's diary was published in more than fifty countries. This play, based on the diary, won a Pulitzer Prize and was made into a movie. Why do you think Anne's diary and her story have attracted so much attention?

Broader Connections

5. In 1987, Miep Gies wrote a book called *Anne Frank Remembered*, in which she told how she and others had helped the families remain hidden for two years. Punishment would have been very harsh if Miep and her friends had been caught. What do you think makes people risk their lives to help others survive? Do you think you or your family would be willing to take such a risk? Why or why not?

Literary Concept: Scene

Like the chapters of a book, the **scenes** of a play are the segments into which the play is divided. Usually each scene occurs at a different time or place. In *The Diary of Anne Frank*, the setting remains the same, but each scene takes place at a different time. Why do you think the writers chose to have the first and last scenes of the play take place in the hiding place after the war?

Concept Review: Irony Recall that **irony** is a contrast between what is said and what is actually the case. A writer can inject irony into a play by allowing the audience to become aware of something that the characters do not know. Why do you think it is ironic that the characters worry that rats are eating their food?

Writing Options

1. Some people are trying to stop students from reading *The Diary of Anne Frank.* These people feel that Anne's story is depressing. What is your opinion? Write a **persuasive essay,** arguing for or against the use of the diary.

2. If you were the director of this play, how would you want the characters' appearance and behavior to reflect the fact that the second act takes place 1½ years later than the first act? Write a set of **director's notes.**

3. Take the role of one of the characters other than Anne, and write two **diary entries** by him or her. The entries should reflect the character's thoughts and feelings during the first and second acts. How does this character change over time? What causes the changes?

4. *The Diary of Anne Frank* is filled with strong statements of ideas by the characters. Choose one quote about which you have strong feelings and respond to it in an **essay.**

Vocabulary Practice

Exercise A   On your paper write the word from the list that is most clearly related to the situation conveyed in each item.

1. Although they had no solid information, the Jewish family had a strong feeling that the invasion would allow them to come out of hiding by spring.

2. The family had to keep their hiding place a secret. During the day they kept their shoes off and tiptoed quietly.

3. Some Dutch people felt a growing sense of fear and discouragement as they awaited the invasion. They predicted that it would come too late to save them.

4. Suddenly several Nazi soldiers knocked down the door and strode into the family's hiding place.

5. Although the family tried to resist the soldiers' attack, they were outnumbered and their efforts were useless.

Exercise B   On your paper write the letter of the word that is most nearly opposite in meaning to the capitalized word.

1. APPREHENSION: (a) anxiety   (b) peace   (c) confusion (d) danger

2. DISGRUNTLED: (a) content   (b) hungry   (c) annoyed   (d) immature

3. FORLORN: (a) depressed   (b) crowded   (c) cheerful   (d) naughty

4. INARTICULATE: (a) silent   (b) doubtful   (c) hopeful   (d) talkative

5. PANDEMONIUM: (a) comedy   (b) intelligence   (c) order   (d) chaos

Words to Know and Use

apprehension
disgruntled
foreboding
forlorn
inarticulate
ineffectually
intuition
onslaught
pandemonium
stealthily

E X T E N D

Options for Learning

1 • And Then What Happened? Although this play ends with the capture of the Franks and their companions, their lives and stories continued. Research what happened to Anne and her companions and share your findings.

2 • Acting Out What is your favorite scene in this play? Why is it your favorite? With some of your classmates, choose a scene upon which you all agree and dramatize it for the rest of the class. Afterwards, you may want to share your reasons for choosing that scene.

3 • Now Playing Make a poster that advertises the play. Include an eye-catching graphic, critics' comments, and some basic information for people who may not know what the play is about.

4 • Life After Death Anne Frank has lived on through her diary. The Anne Frank Foundation, a nonprofit organization, aids children in dangerous situations all over the world. Research the foundation and report on it to your class.

 FACT FINDER HISTORY

How and when did Anne Frank die?

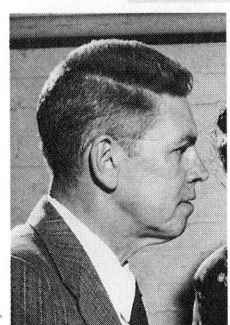

Frances Goodrich and Albert Hackett

1891–1984   1900–

Frances Goodrich and Albert Hackett met in 1927, when they were both actors in a stock acting company in Denver, Colorado. They soon began writing plays and movie scripts together.

Many of the films Goodrich and Hackett scripted became box-office and critical successes, including the "Thin Man" series, *Seven Brides for Seven Brothers, Father of the Bride,* and *It's a Wonderful Life.*

To prepare for the production of *The Diary of Anne Frank,* Goodrich and Hackett went to Amsterdam to meet with Mr. Frank. They visited the attic, studied the neighborhood, listened to the sounds of the canals, and asked Mr. Frank questions to get details and general impressions. In 1959, reflecting back on writing the script, Hackett said, "No one working on the Diary thought about money. We all felt we were working for a cause, not just a play."

Goodrich and Hackett considered *The Diary of Anne Frank,* which they worked on from 1953 to 1955, to be the high point of their careers. They wrote eight drafts of the play before they were convinced they had it right. Their efforts paid off: the play won the New York Drama Critics' Circle Award, the Antoinette Perry Award, and the Pulitzer Prize in 1956.

WRITER'S WORKSHOP

WRITING ABOUT LITERATURE

USE COMPARISON/
CONTRAST FOR
critical reviews
social studies reports
science lab reports
editorials
speeches
literary analyses

The Diary of Anne Frank offers insights about how ordinary people deal with an extreme situation. Why do some characters cope with the situation better than others? What personality clashes disrupt the group? What similarities and differences exist between the characters? In this workshop you will explore these and other questions in a **literary analysis,** an in-depth discussion of a literary work. You will compare and contrast two characters in the play.

Here is one writer's PASSkey to this assignment.

GUIDED ASSIGNMENT: CHARACTERS IN CONTRAST

Write a comparison-contrast essay about two characters in *The Diary of Anne Frank.* Use evidence from the play as support for your ideas.

P URPOSE: To analyze

A UDIENCE: Other readers

S UBJECT: Two characters

S TRUCTURE: A comparison-contrast essay

STUDENT MODEL ▶
Before you write, read how one student responded to a similar assignment about the play *The Kid Nobody Could Handle.*

The writer sets the stage for her comparison-contrast essay with a controlling statement telling what the paper will show about two characters—Bert Quinn and George Helmholtz.

> ### Who Knows the Way?
> ### by Amy Cohen
>
> The play <u>The Kid Nobody Could Handle</u> is about a troubled high school student named Jim Donnini. Bert Quinn and George Helmholtz, the two main adult characters, both try to help Jim straighten out. Bert fails, but George succeeds. A look at the differences in their personalities and attitudes shows why.
>
> Bert and George are both successful. Bert owns a restaurant, and George is a band director. However, their outlooks on life are quite different. Bert is a very negative person. "He has only two moods: one suspicious, the other arrogant." Bert doesn't even like the food at his own restaurant. In

contrast, George is more positive. He loves working with kids and music. George's outlook on life is that "you're better than you think you are!" Both Bert and George have a dream. Bert's dream is to make money from his land. George's dream is to lead "as fine a band as there is on the face of the earth."

Bert and George both try to handle Jim, but in different ways. Bert is Jim's uncle, but he doesn't really like Jim. He says, "Then they [the court] decided to get him clear of Chicago, so they stuck me with him." Bert thinks he's helping Jim by being tough on him. When Bert finds out that Jim has vandalized the school, he wants to send Jim away. George, on the other hand, has a very different way of dealing with Jim. George takes an interest in him and asks him to join the band. Basically, Jim says "no way." When George catches Jim wrecking a science lab, he tries to find a way to get through to Jim. He gives Jim his prized trumpet. When George sees that his sacrifice hasn't changed anything, he smashes the trumpet. Maybe Jim has never had anyone care about him this much, because at this point Jim's eyes "became human."

Bert's negative, tough-guy attitude doesn't work with Jim at all. Basically, it is George's caring that wins over Jim.

Notice how Amy organizes her treatment of the characters in a feature-by-feature pattern. She devotes one paragraph to each feature, discussing the differences (and to a lesser extent the similarities) between the two characters.

◄ Transitions such as *but, in contrast,* and *on the other hand* help to signal differences.

◄ Notice that Amy explains characters' actions and uses quotes from the play to support her points.

◄ In the conclusion Amy recaps what her comparison-contrast essay has shown about the characters.

Now begin your own comparison-contrast essay.

Prewrite and Explore

1 **Select two characters** Which character did you like the most (or the least!) in *The Diary of Anne Frank?* It helps to write about a character you find interesting. Think about whether this character has a conflict with anyone else. Characters in conflict often demonstrate obvious similarities and differences. You should be able to discuss at least two types of similarities or differences in the characters.

TIP
. . . .
Keep in mind that the characters you choose should have something in common. For example, Mrs. Frank and Dr. Dussel have very little to do with each other.

LITERARY MODEL

To help you decide what you want your comparison-contrast essay to show about the two characters, ask yourself some questions about the characters. Amy asked herself, Why was George able to help Jim, when Bert was not? She decided that her essay would answer that question.

STUDENT MODEL

WRITER'S CHOICE

Another way to organize your information is to use a Venn diagram like the one below. Label each circle with a character's name. Then note the similarities between the characters in the overlapping part and the differences in the outer parts.

2 **Write a controlling statement**   Decide whether you will emphasize the differences or the similarities between your characters. Also decide what you want to show through your analysis. Look back at Amy's essay. She wanted to emphasize the differences between Bert and George. By discussing the differences, she hoped to show why George is able to get through to Jim when Bert can't. She expressed this purpose in a **controlling statement,** the focus of her essay. Her controlling statement guided both her note taking and the development of her essay. Write a controlling statement for your paper.

GATHERING INFORMATION

Go through the play and carefully note what each of your characters does and says. Also note what other characters and the stage directions say about your characters. Look specifically for quotes or descriptions that show the differences or similarities between them. To organize your notes, use a **comparison chart** like this one, which Amy made about Bert and George.

Bert	George
Outlook on Life	
-"small, humorless"	-sensitive, affectionate
-"has only two moods: one suspicious, the other arrogant"	-loves kids and music
	-not money minded
-dreams of making money from his land	-dreams of leading "as fine a band as there is on the face of the earth"
-doesn't like food in his restaurant	-"It can be like picking up the keys to a whole new world."
-can't stop working	-"You're better than you think you are!"
-not a well man	
Attitude Toward Jim	
-doesn't like Jim	-takes an interest in Jim
-"Then they decided to get him clear of Chicago, so they stuck me with him."	-asks Jim to join band
	-catches Jim vandalizing, tries to help him
-is going to be tough on Jim	-gives Jim prized trumpet
-wants to send Jim back to Chicago after Jim vandalizes school	-when sacrifice has no effect on Jim, smashes the trumpet
	-Jim's eyes "became human."

574   UNIT FIVE   THE INVINCIBLE SPIRIT

Draft and Discover

1 **Make a strong start**   In the introductory paragraph identify the literary work you are analyzing. State what characters you are discussing. Mention what they have in common. Also, make sure you have your controlling statement in this paragraph.

2 **Organize your evidence**   A common way to organize a comparison-contrast paper is a **feature-by-feature** pattern, in which differences or similarities are discussed. Often one paragraph is devoted to each category or feature, with both characters being discussed in each of these paragraphs.

3 **Support your points**   Begin each middle paragraph with a topic sentence stating that the characters are different or similar in a particular way. Then give evidence that supports this topic sentence. Draw on your notes for actions, statements, descriptions, and quotes that illustrate your point. The better your evidence, the better your paper will be.

Revise Your Writing

1 **Smooth the way**   Look for places where you can use transitional words and phrases. They help to identify similarities and differences.

2 **Exchange papers**   Trade papers with a partner so that you can respond to each other's draft. Use the following questions.

◀ **WRITER'S CHOICE**

An alternative way of organizing your paper is to use a **subject-by-subject** pattern, in which you discuss one character completely and then discuss the second character.

◀ **WORD CHOICE**

Words such as *both, likewise, similarly,* and *also* signal similarities. You can highlight differences with words and phrases like *in contrast, unlike, on the other hand,* and *but.*

COMPUTER TIP

Ask your peer reader if the order of your statements about the characters can be improved. If you need to rearrange the order of any statements, the "move" function on your word processor will help you make the change easily.

Revision Questions	
For You	**For a Peer Reader**
1. Did I clearly state my purpose in a controlling statement?	**1.** Was my essay organized in a logical and clear way?
2. Does my organizational pattern make sense?	**2.** What evidence was the most convincing?
3. Did I use quotes effectively as evidence?	**3.** Are there any places where transitions need to be added?

Proofread

After making revisions to your paper, proofread for errors in punctuation, spelling, and grammar. Pay special attention to how you use adjectives and adverbs to make comparisons.

THE EDITOR'S EYE: MAKING COMPARISONS

Use adjectives and adverbs correctly when making comparisons.

When you use an adjective or adverb to compare two or more things, you must choose the correct form. Use the **comparative** form if you are comparing only two things. Use the **superlative** form to compare more than two things.

| **Problem** | In contrast, George is (more, most) positive. |
| **Correct** | In contrast, George is more positive. |

NEED MORE HELP?

See the Language Workshop that follows (pages 577–579) and pages 794–795 of the Language Handbook.

Publish and Present

Here is a suggestion for sharing your work with others.

Group Discussion Get together with other students who wrote about the pair of characters you chose. Discuss the different approaches taken in comparing and contrasting the two characters. Share with the full class any insights you gain about the writing process or the characters.

Reflect on Your Writing

FOR YOUR PORTFOLIO ▶

Answer the following questions about your essay. Attach your answers to your paper, and put both in your portfolio.

1. Which evidence do you think best supports your controlling statement? Explain.
2. As you wrote this essay, did you learn anything new about the characters in the play? Explain.

LANGUAGE
WORKSHOP

MAKING CORRECT COMPARISONS

> Use **adjectives** and **adverbs** correctly when making comparisons.

As you know, adjectives and adverbs are two kinds of **modifiers.** You use them to modify, or describe, nouns, pronouns, verbs, and other adjectives and adverbs. You can also use modifiers to make comparisons.

Modifiers have three forms, or degrees. The **positive degree** modifies a word but does not make a comparison. **The comparative degree** compares two of anything. The **superlative degree** compares three or more of anything.

Positive	Anne Frank was *young.*
Comparative	Anne Frank was *younger* than Peter Van Daan.
Superlative	Anne Frank was the *youngest* person in the attic.

Forming Comparatives and Superlatives

1. A one-syllable modifier is made comparative or superlative by adding *-er* or *-est* to the positive form.

Positive	**Comparative**	**Superlative**
dark	darker	darkest

2. Most two-syllable modifiers are made comparative or superlative by adding *-er* or *-est*. Sometimes, however, a two-syllable modifier sounds awkward with *-er* and *-est* endings. In such a case, use *more* and *most* to form the comparative and superlative degrees. Also use *more* and *most* with all two-syllable adverbs that end in *-ly.*

Positive	**Comparative**	**Superlative**
simple	simpler	simplest
helpful	more helpful	most helpful
quickly	more quickly	most quickly

3. Modifiers of three or more syllables are made comparative or superlative by using *more* or *most* with the positive form.

Positive	**Comparative**	**Superlative**
satisfying	more satisfying	most satisfying
dangerous	more dangerous	most dangerous
carefully	more carefully	most carefully

◀ SPELLING TIP

When you add *-er* or *-est* to a modifier that ends in *y,* be sure to change the *y* to an *i*: hungry, hungrier, hungriest.

◀ HINT

For most adjectives ending in *-ful* and *-ous,* use *more* to form comparatives: *more hopeful; more curious.* Use *most* to form superlatives: *most hopeful; most curious.*

4. A few modifiers have comparative and superlative forms that are completely different words. Try to become familiar with these exceptions.

Positive	Comparative	Superlative
good	better	best
well	better	best
bad	worse	worst
much	more	most
many	more	most
little	less *or* lesser	least

Exercise 1   Concept Check   Write the correct form of the modifier given in parentheses.

1. Hanukkah is not the (important) of all the Jewish holidays.
2. Jewish families have made it the (festive) one, however, because it falls close to the Christian holiday of Christmas.
3. One of the (popular) Hanukkah songs is "Hanukkah, O Hanukkah."
4. Spinning a dreidel is one of the (old) Hanukkah games.
5. Often, the gifts children get during Hanukkah get (good) on each of the eight nights.
6. Even in the (bad) situation possible, the people in the attic celebrated Hanukkah.
7. Anne's Hanukkah gifts were (creative) than Margot's.
8. Anne's mother said her gift was the (good) she had ever received.
9. Anne made Peter's cat, Mouschi, the (odd) gift of all.
10. The gift Anne gave Peter was (useful) than the one she gave her father.

Avoiding Errors in Comparisons

Use the following rules to avoid making comparison errors.

1. Comparisons are never formed by using both -*er* or -*est* and *more* or *most.* Be sure to avoid such double comparisons.

Problem   Mr. Frank was the *most bravest* of all the captives.
Correct   Mr. Frank was the *bravest* of all the captives.

2. Remember to include the word *other* when you are comparing something with all others of its kind.

Problem   The Franks' hideout was cleaner than any Amsterdam attic. (This sentence says that the hideout was not an Amsterdam attic.)
Correct   The Franks' hideout was cleaner than any *other* Amsterdam attic.

Exercise 2   Concept Check   Find the comparison errors in the following sentences. If a sentence has no errors, write *Correct.*

1. Amsterdam is the capital of the Netherlands and the country's most largest city.
2. Amsterdam's more prosperous time was during the seventeenth century.
3. Amsterdam's canals make the city one of the charmingest cities in Europe.
4. The Amsterdam stock exchange, founded in 1612, is one of the oldest exchanges in the world.
5. Which Dutch industry is larger, diamonds or shipping?
6. One of the most frequentliest visited points of interest is the Rijksmuseum.
7. The museum owns works by some of the most famous Dutch painters.
8. Amsterdam was one of the most earliest cities to fall to German aggression.
9. If I visited Amsterdam, I would be most eager to see Anne Frank's hideout than Van Gogh's paintings.
10. The hideout reminds us that hope may be the stronger instinct of human beings.

Exercise 3   Proofreading   Rewrite the following paragraph. Correct any errors in the modifiers used to make comparisons.

> *The Diary of Anne Frank* is one of the most movingest plays I have ever read. I like it gooder than any other play I've read lately. Anne's words are naturaler and humaner than any history book could ever be. The scene where Anne has a nightmare is the sadder to me. I can't really imagine being most frightened than she must have been that night. Still, her optimistic outlook was more healthier than anyone else's.

Exercise 4   Revising Your Writing   Reread the comparison-contrast essay you wrote for the Writer's Workshop on pages 572–576. Correct any errors you find in the modifiers you used to make comparisons.

LANGUAGE HANDBOOK

For review and practice: Section 6, Using Modifiers, pages 794–795.

SPEAKING AND LISTENING
WORKSHOP

DRAMATIC READING SKILLS

One way to present a play like *The Diary of Anne Frank* is to stage a dramatic reading. The readers sit or stand in front of the audience and read from a book or a script. There are no costumes, props, or sets, so the readers must use their voices and body language to capture the feeling of the play. Consider the following techniques when doing a dramatic reading.

Prepare   Read and reread the material to become familiar with it. Note the dramatic high points. Then practice reading your lines aloud, emphasizing those moments.

Project   Your audience must hear you. Project your voice to the back of the room, but don't shout. Use the volume and tone of your voice to highlight the dramatic moments.

Find a special voice   Experiment with altering your voice to sound more like your character. For example, if you are playing a nervous person, try putting a slight quaver in your voice.

EXCEPTION
Don't pause at the beginning of a character's speech. Doing so makes dialogue sound unnatural. When a character finishes speaking, the next character should usually begin speaking immediately.

Pause   Your goal is to capture your character's natural way of speaking—and thinking. Silences can be very effective. Don't be afraid to pause during a speech, especially when you want to create tension.

Interact   Listen carefully as the other readers speak. When you speak, speak to them. Respond to their tone of voice and body language. If you are presenting a monologue, think about what you are saying.

Use body language   Body language is an important tool in creating a dramatic effect. Don't be afraid to move. Use the gestures and facial expressions that you think your character would use.

Exercise   With a group of classmates, prepare a dramatic reading of one scene from *The Diary of Anne Frank* or another play. Use the steps above to guide your preparation. Do your dramatic reading for the class.

$\mathcal{C}$AUGHT IN CIRCUMSTANCES

Sitting in the middle of its sticky web, the spider waits patiently for its prey. The fly it catches has no means of escape. Still, the captive struggles, but its will to survive ensnares it even further.

When people feel caught in circumstances like a fly entangled in a spider's web, they also struggle to survive. People's struggles, however, may not be merely for physical survival but also for emotional survival.

The main characters in the selections you are about to read all find themselves in circumstances beyond their control. The personalities and experiences of these characters give them the strength and perseverance to survive. Imagine how you would feel and act if you were caught in the same circumstances!

Fiction

Getting the Facts of Life

PAULETTE CHILDRESS WHITE

Examine What You Know

What does it mean to feel like an adult? Have you ever had an experience that made you feel grown-up? In your journal or on a sheet of paper, explore these questions. If you wish, begin with one of the following starter sentences:

- I had an experience that made me feel like an adult.
- I have more responsibilities now than I did a year ago.
- I see my parents differently now than I did a few years ago.

Expand Your Knowledge

Minerva, the main character in this story, gains insights into herself and the adult world when she visits a welfare office with her mother. In the United States, various government welfare programs are designed to help families in need of financial assistance. One such program is Aid to Families with Dependent Children, or AFDC. This program provides financial aid primarily to children and to the parents or other adults taking care of these children. Most families qualifying for AFDC have only one parent in the home, but AFDC also pays benefits to two-parent families as long as both parents are unemployed.

Enrich Your Reading

Characterization   During this story Minerva changes as she gains knowledge about the adult world. When you have finished reading, use a chart like the one below to show how she changes.

	Minerva at Beginning	Minerva at End
Her Feelings About Welfare		
Her Feelings About Her Mother		
Her Feelings About Herself		

■ *Author biography on Extend page*

Getting the Facts of Life

PAULETTE CHILDRESS WHITE

The August morning was ripening into a day that promised to be a burner. By the time we'd walked three blocks, dark patches were showing beneath Momma's arms, and inside tennis shoes thick with white polish, my feet were wet against the cushions. I was beginning to regret how quickly I'd volunteered to go.

"Dog. My feet are getting mushy," I complained.

"You should've wore socks," Momma said, without looking my way or slowing down.

I frowned. In 1961 nobody wore socks with tennis shoes. It was bare legs, Bermuda shorts[1] and a sleeveless blouse. Period.

Momma was chubby, but she could really walk. She walked the same way she washed clothes—up-and-down, up-and-down until she was done. She didn't believe in taking breaks.

This was my first time going to the welfare office[2] with Momma. After breakfast, before we'd had time to scatter, she corralled everyone old enough to consider and announced in her serious-business voice that someone was going to the welfare office with her this morning. Cries went up.

Junior had his papers to do. Stella was going swimming at the high school. Dennis was already pulling the *Free Press*[3] wagon across town every first Wednesday to get the surplus food—like that.

"You want clothes for school, don't you?" That landed. School opened in two weeks.

"I'll go," I said.

"Who's going to baby-sit if Minerva goes?" Momma asked.

Stella smiled and lifted her small golden nose. "I will," she said. "I'd rather baby-sit than do *that*."

Why do you think Stella doesn't want to go to the welfare office?

evaluate

That should have warned me. Anything that would make Stella offer to baby-sit had to be bad.

A small cheer probably went up among my younger brothers in the back rooms,

---

1. **Bermuda shorts:** short pants ending just above the knee.
2. **welfare office:** a government office responsible for providing assistance to needy people.
3. *Free Press:* a daily newspaper published in Detroit, Michigan.

SEVENTH AVENUE BETWEEN 22ND AND 21ST STREETS, NYC   1967   Red Grooms   From the collection of Mr. & Mrs. Elie Hirschfeld.

where I was not too secretly known as "The Witch" because of the criminal licks I'd learned to give on my rise to power. I was twelve, third oldest under Junior and Stella, but I had long established myself as first in command among the kids. I was chief baby sitter, biscuit maker and broom wielder. Unlike Stella, who'd begun her development at ten, I still had my girl's body and wasn't anxious to have that changed. What would it mean but a loss of power? I liked things just the way they were. My interest in bras was even less than my interest in boys, and that was limited to keeping my brothers—who seemed destined for wildness—from taking over completely.

Even before we left, Stella had Little Stevie Wonder turned up on the radio in the living room, and suspicious jumping-bumping sounds were beginning in the back.

They'll tear the house down, I thought, following Momma out the door.

We turned at Salliotte, the street that would take us straight up to Jefferson Avenue where the welfare office was. Momma's face was pinking in the heat, and I was huffing to keep up. From here, it was seven more blocks on the colored side, the railroad tracks, five blocks on the white side and there you were. We'd be cooked.

"Is the welfare office near the Harbor Show?" I asked. I knew the answer; I just wanted some talk.

"Across the street."

"Umm. Glad it's not way down Jefferson somewhere."

Nothing. Momma didn't talk much when she was outside. I knew that the reason she wanted one of us along when she had far to go was not for company but so she wouldn't

have to walk by herself. I could understand that. To me, walking alone was like being naked or deformed—everyone seemed to look at you harder and longer. With Momma, the feeling was probably worse because you knew people were wondering if she were white, Indian maybe or really colored. Having one of us along, brown and clearly hers, probably helped define that. Still, it was like being a little parade, with Momma's pale skin and straight brown hair turning heads like the clang of cymbals. Especially on the colored side.

"Well," I said, "here we come to the bad part."

Momma gave a tiny laugh.

Most of Salliotte was a business street, with Old West-looking storefronts and some office places that never seemed to open. Ecorse, hinged onto southwest Detroit like a clothes closet, didn't seem to take itself seriously. There were lots of empty fields, some of which folks down the residential streets turned into vegetable gardens every summer. And there was this block where the Moonflower Hotel raised itself to three stories over the poolroom and Beaman's drugstore. Here, bad boys and drunks made their noise and did an occasional stabbing. Except for the cars that lined both sides of the block, only one side was busy—the other bordered a field of weeds. We walked on the safe side.

If you were a woman or a girl over twelve, walking this block—even on the safe side—could be painful. They usually hollered at you, and never mind what they said. Today, because it was hot and early, we made it by with only one weak "Hey baby" from a drunk sitting in the poolroom door.

"Hey baby yourself," I said, but not too loudly, pushing my flat chest out and stabbing my eyes in his direction.

"Minerva girl, you better watch your mouth with grown men like that," Momma said, her eyes catching me up in real warning, though I could see that she was holding down a smile.

"Well, he can't do nothing to me when I'm with you, can he?" I asked, striving to match the rise and fall of her black pumps.

She said nothing. She just walked on, churning away under a sun that clearly meant to melt us. From here to the tracks it was mostly gardens. It felt like the Dixie Peach I'd used to help water-wave my hair was sliding down with the sweat on my face, and my throat was tight with thirst. Boy, did I want a pop. I looked at the last little store before we crossed the tracks without bothering to ask.

Across the tracks, there were no stores and no gardens. It was shady, and the grass was June green. Perfect-looking houses sat in unfenced spaces far back from the street. We walked these five blocks without a word. We just looked and hurried to get through it. I was beginning to worry about the welfare office in earnest. A fool could see that in this part of Ecorse, things got serious.

We had been on welfare for almost a year. I didn't have any strong feelings about it—my life went on pretty much the same. It just meant watching the mail for a check instead of Daddy getting paid and occasional visits from a social worker that I'd always managed to miss. For Momma and whoever went with her, it meant this walk to the office and whatever went on there that made everyone hate to go. For Daddy, it seemed to bring the most change. For him, it meant staying away from home more than when he was working and a reason not to answer the phone.

At Jefferson, we turned left and there it was, halfway down the block. The Department of Social Services. I discovered some strong feelings. That fine name meant nothing. This was the welfare. The place for poor people. People who couldn't or wouldn't take care of themselves. Now I was going to face it, and suddenly I thought what I knew the others had thought, *What if I see someone I know?* I wanted to run back all those blocks to home.

I looked at Momma for comfort, but her face was closed and her mouth looked locked.

Inside, the place was gray. There were rows of long benches, like church pews, facing each other across a middle aisle that led to a central desk. Beyond the benches and the desk, four hallways led off to a maze of partitioned offices. In opposite corners, huge fans hung from the ceiling, humming from side to side, blowing the heavy air for a breeze.

How would you feel if you were Minerva?

evaluate

Momma walked to the desk, answered some questions, was given a number and told to take a seat. I followed her through, trying not to see the waiting people—as though that would keep them from seeing me.

Gradually, as we waited, I took them all in. There was no one there that I knew, but

Words to Know and Use

maze (māz) *n.* a confusing network of passageways
partitioned (pär tish' ənd) *adj.* divided by interior walls **partition** *v.*

somehow they all looked familiar. Or maybe I only thought they did, because when your eyes connected with someone's, they didn't quickly look away and they usually smiled. They were mostly women and children, and a few low-looking men. Some of them were white, which surprised me. I hadn't expected to see them in there.

Directly in front of the bench where we sat, a little girl with blond curls was trying to handle a bottle of Coke. Now and then, she'd manage to turn herself and the bottle around and watch me with big gray eyes that seemed to know quite well how badly I wanted a pop. I thought of asking Momma for fifteen cents so I could get one from the machine in the back, but I was afraid she'd still say no, so I just kept planning more and more convincing ways to ask. Besides, there was a water fountain near the door if I could make myself rise and walk to it.

We waited three hours. White ladies dressed like secretaries kept coming out to call numbers, and people on the benches would get up and follow down a hall. Then more people came in to replace them. I drank water from the fountain three times and was ready to put my feet up on the bench before us—the little girl with the Coke and her momma got called—by the time we heard Momma's number.

"You wait here," Momma said as I rose with her.

I sat down with a plop.

The lady with the number looked at me. Her face reminded me of the librarian's at Bunch school. Looked like she never cracked a smile. "Let her come," she said.

"She can wait here," Momma repeated weakly.

"It's OK. She can come in. Come on," the lady insisted at me.

I hesitated, knowing that Momma's face was telling me to sit.

"Come on," the woman said.

Momma said nothing.

*S*ome of them were white, which surprised me.

I got up and followed them into the maze. We came to a small room where there was a desk and three chairs. The woman sat behind the desk, and we before it.

For a while, no one spoke. The woman studied a folder open before her, brows drawn together. On the wall behind her there was a calendar with one heavy black line drawn slantwise through each day of August, up to the twenty-first. That was today.

"Mrs. Blue, I have a notation here that Mr. Blue has not reported to the department on his efforts to obtain employment since the sixteenth of June. Before that, it was the tenth of April. You understand that department regulations require that he report monthly to this office, do you not?" Eyes brown as a wren's belly came up at Momma.

"Yes," Momma answered, sounding as small as I felt.

"Can you explain his failure to do so?"

*Words
to Know
and Use* | **notation** (nō tā′ shən) *n.* a short note added to a document

587

WAITING ROOM
1984 Phoebe Beasley
Collection Mr. and
Mrs. Samuel B. Casey.

Pause. "He's been looking. He says he's been looking."

"That may be. However, his failure to report those efforts here is my only concern."

Silence.

"We cannot continue with your case as it now stands if Mr. Blue refuses to comply with departmental regulations. He is still residing with the family, is he not?"

"Yes, he is. I've been reminding him to come in . . . he said he would."

"Well, he hasn't. Regulations are that any able-bodied man, head-of-household and receiving assistance, who neglects to report to this office any effort to obtain work for a period of sixty days or more is to be cut off for a minimum of three months, at which time he may reapply. As of this date, Mr. Blue is over sixty days delinquent, and officially, I am obliged to close the case and direct you to other sources of aid."

"What is that?"

"Aid to Dependent Children would be the only source available to you. Then, of course, you would not be eligible unless it was verified that Mr. Blue was no longer residing with the family."

Words to Know and Use	**comply** (kəm plī´) *v.* to obey a rule or command **reside** (ri zīd´) *v.* to occupy a home **eligible** (el´ i jə bəl) *adj.* qualified to receive something **verify** (ver´ ə fī´) *v.* to prove or demonstrate

Another silence. I stared into the gray steel front of the desk, everything stopped but my heart.

"Well, can you keep the case open until Monday? If he comes in by Monday?"

There was only my face, which wouldn't disappear.

"According to my records, Mr. Blue failed to come in May, and such an agreement was made then. In all, we allowed him a period of seventy days. You must understand that what happens in such cases as this is not wholly my decision." She sighed and watched Momma with hopeless eyes, tapping the soft end of her pencil on the papers before her. "Mrs. Blue, I will speak to my superiors on your behalf. I can allow you until Monday next . . . that's the"—she swung around to the calendar—"twenty-sixth of August, to get him in here."

"Thank you. He'll be in," Momma breathed. "Will I be able to get the clothing order today?"

Hands and eyes searched in the folder for an answer before she cleared her throat and tilted her face at Momma. "We'll see what we can do," she said finally.

My back touched the chair. Without turning my head, I moved my eyes down to Momma's dusty feet and wondered if she could still feel them; my own were numb. I felt bodyless—there was only my face, which wouldn't disappear, and behind it, one word pinging against another in a buzz that made no sense. At home, we'd have the house cleaned by now, and I'd be waiting for the daily appearance of my best friend, Bernadine, so we could comb each other's hair or talk about stuck-up Evelyn and Brenda. Maybe Bernadine was already there, and Stella was teaching her to dance the bop.

Then I heard our names and ages—all eight of them—being called off like items in a grocery list.

"Clifford, Junior, age fourteen." She waited.

"Yes."

"Born? Give me the month and year."

"October 1946," Momma answered, and I could hear in her voice that she'd been through these questions before.

"Stella, age thirteen."

"Yes."

"Born?"

"November 1947."

"Minerva, age twelve." She looked at me. "This is Minerva?"

"Yes."

No. I thought, no, this is not Minerva. You can write it down if you want to, but Minerva is not here.

"Born?"

"December 1948."

The woman went on down the list, sounding more and more like Momma should be sorry or ashamed, and Momma's answers grew fainter and fainter. So this was welfare. I wondered how many times Momma had had to do this. Once before? Three times? Every time?

More questions. How many in school? Six. Who needs shoes? Everybody.

"Everybody needs shoes? The youngest two?"

"Well, they don't go to school . . . but they walk."

My head came up to look at Momma and the woman. The woman's mouth was left open. Momma didn't blink.

The brown eyes went down. "Our allowances are based on the median costs for moderately priced clothing at Sears, Roebuck." She figured on paper as she spoke. "That will mean thirty-four dollars for children over ten . . . thirty dollars for children under ten. It comes to one hundred ninety-eight dollars. I can allow eight dollars for two additional pairs of shoes."

"Thank you."

"You will present your clothing order to a salesperson at the store, who will be happy to assist you in your selections. Please be practical, as further clothing requests will not be considered for a period of six months. In cases of necessity, however, requests for winter outerwear will be considered beginning November first.

Momma said nothing.

The woman rose and left the room.

For the first time, I shifted in the chair. Momma was looking into the calendar as though she could see through the pages to November first. Everybody needed a coat.

I'm never coming here again, I thought. If I do, I'll stay out front. Not coming back in here. Ever again.

 *review* Why does Minerva have such strong feelings about the welfare office?

She came back and sat behind her desk. "Mrs. Blue, I must make it clear that, regardless of my feelings, I will be forced to close your case if your husband does not report to this office by Monday, the twenty-sixth. Do you understand?"

"Yes. Thank you. He'll come. I'll see to it."

"Very well." She held a paper out to Momma.

We stood. Momma reached over and took the slip of paper. I moved toward the door.

"Excuse me, Mrs. Blue, but are you pregnant?"

"What?"

"I asked if you were expecting another child."

"Oh. No, I'm not," Momma answered, biting down on her lips.

"Well, I'm sure you'll want to be careful about a thing like that in your present situation."

"Yes."

I looked quickly to Momma's loose white blouse. We'd never known when another baby was coming until it was almost there.

"I suppose that eight children are enough for anyone," the woman said, and for the first time her face broke into a smile.

Momma didn't answer that. Somehow, we left the room and found our way out onto the street. We stood for a moment, as though lost. My eyes followed Momma's up to where the sun was burning high. It was still there, blazing white against a cloudless blue. Slowly, Momma put the clothing order into her purse and snapped it shut. She looked around as if uncertain which way to go. I led the way to the corner. We turned. We walked the first five blocks.

Words to Know and Use | **median** (mē′ dē ən) *adj.* being the middle value in a series
moderately (mäd′ ər it lē) *adv.* reasonably; not excessively

I was thinking about how stupid I'd been a year ago, when Daddy lost his job. I'd been happy.

"You-all better be thinking about moving to Indianapolis," he announced one day after work, looking like he didn't think much of it himself. He was a welder with the railroad company. He'd worked there for eleven years. But now, "Company's moving to Indianapolis," he said. "Gonna be gone by November. If I want to keep my job, we've got to move with it."

We didn't. Nobody wanted to move to Indianapolis—not even Daddy. Here, we had uncles, aunts and cousins on both sides. Friends. Everybody and everything we knew. Daddy could get another job. First came unemployment compensation.[4] Then came welfare. Thank goodness for welfare, we said, while we waited and waited for the job that hadn't yet come.

The problem was that Daddy couldn't take it. If something got repossessed or somebody took sick or something was broken or another kid was coming, he'd carry on terribly until things got better—by which time things were always worse. He'd always been that way. So when the railroad left, he began to do everything wrong. Stayed out all hours. Drank and drank some more. When he was home, he was so grouchy we were afraid to squeak. Now when we saw him coming, we got lost. Even our friends ran for cover.

At the railroad tracks, we sped up. The tracks were as far across as a block was long. Silently, I counted the rails by the heat of the steel bars through my thin soles. On the other side, I felt something heavy rise up in my chest, and I knew that I wanted to cry. I wanted to cry or run or kiss the dusty ground. The little houses with their sun-scorched lawns and back-yard gardens were mansions in my eyes. "Ohh, Ma . . . look at those collards!"

"Umm-humm," she agreed, and I knew that she saw it too.

"Wonder how they grew so big?"

"Cow dung, probably. Big Poppa used to put cow dung out to fertilize the vegetable plots, and everything just grew like crazy. We used to get tomatoes this big"—she circled with her hands—"and don't talk about squash or melons."

"I bet y'all ate like rich people. Bet y'all had everything you could want."

"We sure did," she said. "We never wanted for anything when it came to food. And when the cash crops were sold, we could get whatever else that was needed. We never wanted for a thing."

"What about the time you and cousin Emma threw out the supper peas?"

"Oh! Did I tell you about that?" she asked. Then she told it all over again. I didn't listen. I watched her face and guarded her smile with a smile of my own.

We walked together, step for step. The sun was still burning, but we forgot to mind it. We talked about an Alabama girlhood in

---

4. **unemployment compensation:** a regular payment of money for a limited time to people who have lost their jobs.

a time and place I'd never know. We talked about the wringer washer[5] and how it could be fixed, because washing every day on a scrub board was something Alabama could keep. We talked about how to get Daddy to the Department of Social Services.

Then we talked about having babies. She began to tell me things I'd never known, and the idea of womanhood blossomed in my mind like some kind of suffocating rose.

"Momma," I said, "I don't think I can be a woman."

"You can," she laughed, "and if you live, you will be. You gotta be some kind of woman."

"But it's hard," I said. "Sometimes it must be hard."

"Umm-humm," she said, "sometimes it is hard."

When we got to the bad block, we crossed to Beaman's drugstore for two orange crushes. Then we walked right through the groups of men standing in the shadows of the poolroom and the Moonflower Hotel. Not one of them said a word to us. I supposed they could see in the way we walked that we weren't afraid. We'd been to the welfare office and back again. And the facts of life, fixed in our minds like the sun in the sky, were no burning mysteries. ❧

---

5. **wringer washer:** an old-fashioned type of washing machine, having a device that squeezes the water out of wet garments.

I N S I G H T

The Dream Keeper
LANGSTON HUGHES

Bring me all of your dreams,
You dreamers,
Bring me all of your
Heart melodies
That I may wrap them
In a blue cloud-cloth
Away from the too-rough fingers
Of the world.

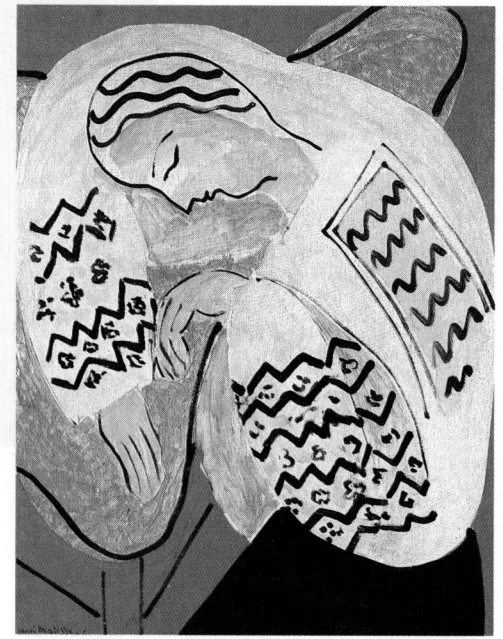

LE REVE (The Dream)   Henri Matisse
© 1992 Succession H. Matisse / ARS, New York.

E X P L A I N

Responding to Reading

First Impressions

1. How did you feel about Minerva's experiences? In your journal or on a sheet of paper, write your feelings.

Second Thoughts

2. Study the chart you made for Enrich Your Reading. Which change in Minerva do you think is the most important? Explain.

3. Why do you think Minerva feels so strongly about never returning to the welfare office?

4. How do you think Minerva feels about becoming an adult?

5. What words or phrases would you use to describe Minerva's mother? Explain.

6. Do you think that Minerva's father will go to the welfare office by the appointed day? Explain your prediction.

7. In what ways does this story reflect the subunit theme, "Caught in Circumstances"?

Broader Connections

8. Supporters of the United States welfare system say that financial assistance is a necessary "safety net" for families who get caught in circumstances and encounter hard times. Critics of the system claim that welfare discourages recipients from seeking employment and that it may, in some cases, undermine families. What are your thoughts about the welfare system?

Literary Concept: Point of View

As an author plans a story, he or she must decide from whose **point of view** the story will be told. Should the story be narrated by a character within the story—that is, from a **first-person point of view**—or should it be told by a person outside the story, from a **third-person point of view?** In "Getting the Facts of Life," Paulette Childress White has Minerva tell the story from the first-person point of view. Why do you think White does this, instead of telling the story from a third-person point of view?

*W*riting Options

1. Write a **character sketch** of one person in the story. Describe three character traits and explain how each is shown in the story.

2. Near the end of the story, Minerva says that she and her mother "talked about how to get Daddy to the Department of Social Services." Write the **conversation** that they might have had.

3. Reread "The Dream Keeper" on page 592. Then write a **poem** from Minerva's point of view. Have her describe her dreams for the future.

4. Imagine that you are the welfare worker that interviewed Minerva's mother. Write a **report** explaining in detail the current situation of the Blue family.

*V*ocabulary Practice

Exercise   Write the word from the list that best completes the meaning of the sentence.

1. In the late 1980s, the poverty line was an income of $12,000 for a family of four people, well below the _?_ family income of $30,000.

2. When a family can no longer pay their bills, a loan company may have to _?_ the family's car or other possessions.

3. Typically, a government welfare center is a large room with many _?_ offices.

4. Welfare workers must keep accurate records on every recipient; one careless _?_ on a report can lead to problems.

5. A welfare worker must ask questions in order to _?_ that the recipient is still unemployed.

6. If a welfare recipient cannot _?_ with the department's rules, the recipient may lose his or her benefits.

7. Critics of the welfare system say it is a _?_ of complex rules, forms, and procedures.

8. Public-housing programs allow needy families to _?_ in low-cost rental apartments.

9. To be _?_ for Supplemental Security Income, or SSI, one must be at least 65 years old, blind, or disabled.

10. Compared with Medicaid, the most expensive welfare program in the United States, AFDC is only _?_ expensive.

> *Words to Know and Use*
>
> **comply**
> **eligible**
> **maze**
> **median**
> **moderately**
> **notation**
> **partitioned**
> **repossess**
> **reside**
> **verify**

EXTEND

Options for Learning

1 • On the Case Call the welfare office in your town and arrange a brief interview with a caseworker. Go to the interview prepared with questions about social work as an occupation. Share the results of this interview with your class.

2 • Artistic Interpretation Draw a picture or find a magazine photograph that shows your feelings about "Getting the Facts of Life." If you prefer, compose or choose a piece of music that accomplishes the same purpose.

3 • Pro and Con Choose a classmate who disagrees with you on a topic related to the welfare system. Research the topic on your own. Then debate the topic with your classmate in front of your class.

4 • Stage It With some of your classmates, stage a Readers Theater presentation of one scene from "Getting the Facts of Life," such as the scene in the welfare office or the scene of Minerva and her mother walking home.

 FACT FINDER SOCIAL STUDIES

Find out how much a family of two unemployed adults and eight children would receive in AFDC payments in your state.

Paulette Childress White
1948–

Like Minerva Blue, the twelve-year-old narrator of the autobiographical story "Getting the Facts of Life," the author grew up in Ecorse, Michigan, a town that was racially divided by the railroad tracks. White currently lives in Detroit, Michigan, with her husband and five children. She teaches at Henry Ford Community College and at Wayne State University.

White has written a collection of poetry entitled *The Watermelon Dress.* She has also contributed to such magazines as *Essence,* *Redbook,* and *Callaloo.* Her short stories are included in the anthologies *Black-Eyed Susans/Midnight Birds* and *Memory of Kin: Stories About Family by Black Writers,* from which "Getting the Facts of Life" was taken.

About her writing the author says, "I write from a sense of irony, because I want to make sense of my experience of life. I am also a painter. I write and paint because I have a need to give substance to my ideas, feelings, and experiences, and because I believe it is good and important work."

Poetry

Moco Limping
DAVID NAVA MONREAL

Pigeon Woman
MAY SWENSON

Examine What You Know

An old saying claims that a dog is "man's best friend." If you have ever loved a pet, you can probably relate to this expression, even though you might need to change the word *dog* to *cat* or *hamster* and the word *man's* to *woman's* or *child's*. Besides providing friendship, how else can animals benefit people? How do people benefit animals? In small groups, make two lists like the ones below.

How Animals Benefit People	How People Benefit Animals
1. Provide friendship 2. Serve as guide dogs	1. Work to protect animals' habitats 2. Work as animal-rights activists

Expand Your Knowledge

Did you know that pets can improve some people's health? Medical studies show that petting an animal can actually lower a person's blood pressure and reduce tension. For this reason, a pet might be prescribed as therapy for someone who is ill or lonely. Animals can also be taught to help people in special situations. Guide dogs, for example, can help the blind travel through traffic and down busy streets. Fox terriers can alert their deaf owners when callers are at the door. Capuchin monkeys and some dogs can be trained to fetch and hold things for owners who cannot use their arms or legs.

Write Before You Read

Think of an animal that is or was your "best friend"—perhaps a pet, an animal at a zoo, a favorite stuffed animal, or even an animal that you read about in a book. In your journal or on a sheet of paper, describe your feelings about that animal.

■ *Author biographies in Reader's Handbook*

Moco Limping

DAVID NAVA MONREAL

My dog hobbles
with a stick
of a leg that
he drags behind
5 him as he moves.
And I was a man
that wanted a
beautiful, noble[1]
animal as a pet.
10 I wanted him
to be strong and
capture all the
attention by
the savage grace
15 of his gait.[2]
I wanted him to
be the first
dog howling in
the pack.
20 The leader,
the brutal hunter
that broke through
the woods with
thunder.

Illustration by Petra Mathers.

---

1. noble: having a grand, impressive appearance.
2. gait (gāt): a way of walking.

25 But, instead he's
this rickety
little canine[3]
that leaves trails
in the dirt
30 with his club foot.[4]
He's the stumbler
that trips while
chasing lethargic[5]
bees and butterflies.
35 It hurts me to
see him so
abnormal,
so clumsy and
stupid.

40 My vain heart weeps
knowing he
is mine.
But then he turns
my way and
45 looks at me with
eyes that cry out
with life.
He jumps at me with
his feeble paws.
50 I feel his warm fur
and his imperfection is
forgotten.

---

3. **canine** (kā′ nīn′): a dog.
4. **club foot:** a deformed foot.
5. **lethargic** (li thär′ jik): moving in a sluggish, weary manner.

*R*esponding to Reading

First Impressions of "Moco Limping"

1. What emotions did you experience at the end of the poem? Write your impressions in your journal or on a sheet of paper.

Second Thoughts on "Moco Limping"

2. How does the speaker's relationship to his pet compare with the one you wrote about before reading?

3. In your opinion, what kind of person is the speaker of this poem?
   Think about
   • the kind of dog he wanted
   • his attitude toward Moco
   • what he concludes is really important

4. Which words or phrases in the poem do you think create the most effective descriptions?

5. What do you think is the theme of this poem?

Pigeon Woman

MAY SWENSON

Slate, or dirty-marble-colored,
or rusty-iron-colored, the pigeons
on the flagstones in front of the
Public Library make a sharp lake

5 into which the pigeon woman wades
at exactly 1:30. She wears a
plastic pink raincoat with a round
collar (looking like a little

girl) and flat gym shoes,
10 her hair square-cut, orange.
Wide-apart feet carefully enter
the spinning, crooning[1] waves

(as if she'd just learned how
to walk, each step conscious,
15 an accomplishment); blue knots[2] in the
calves of her bare legs (uglied marble),

age in angled cords of jaw
and neck, her pimento-colored hair,
hanging in thin tassels, is gray
20 around a balding crown.

The day-old bread drops down
from her veined hand dipping out
of a paper sack. Choppy, shadowy ripples,
the pigeons strike around her legs.

25 Sack empty, she squats and seems to rinse
her hands in them—the rainy greens and
oily purples of their necks. Almost
they let her wet her thirsty fingertips—

but drain away in an untouchable tide.
30 A make-believe trade
she has come to, in her lostness
or illness or age—to treat the motley[3]

city pigeons at 1:30 every day, in all
weathers. It is for them she colors
35 her own feathers. Ruddy-footed
on the lime-stained paving,

purling[4] to meet her when she comes,
they are a lake of love. Retreating
from her hands as soon as empty,
40 they are the flints[5] of love.

---

1. **crooning**: singing in a soft, gentle way.
2. **blue knots**: swollen veins in the legs.
3. **motley** (mät′ lē): many-colored.
4. **purling**: swirling or rippling, like a stream.
5. **flints**: hard stones from which sparks can be struck.

Responding to Reading

First Impressions of "Pigeon Woman"

1. What words or images stayed with you after you read this poem? Write or sketch them in your journal or on a sheet of paper.

Second Thoughts on "Pigeon Woman"

2. What are your impressions of the pigeon woman?

3. What do you think the speaker means by first referring to the pigeons as "a lake of love" and then as "the flints of love"?

Comparing the Poems

4. Compare Moco's owner with the pigeon woman. Who do you think benefits more from his or her relationship with animals? Why?

5. Which poem has a stronger effect on you? Why?

Broader Connections

6. Some animal-rights activists are outraged when doctors transplant animal organs into humans when suitable human organs cannot be found. These activists believe that killing or using animals for the benefit of humans is wrong. What do you think? Think about the ideas you developed in Examine What You Know as well as what you learned from reading the two poems.

Literary Concept: Extended Metaphor

You may recall that a **metaphor** compares two unlike things without the use of the words *like, as, than,* or *resembles.* A metaphor that is developed through an entire piece of writing is called an **extended metaphor.** How does the author of "Pigeon Woman" develop the extended metaphor in this poem?

Writing Options

1. Put yourself "into Moco's paws" and write an **interior monologue** that tells what this dog thinks of his owner.

2. What if pigeons could talk? Write a **conversation** that the pigeons and the woman might have.

Nonfiction

Baseball and the Facts of Life

BOB GREENE

Examine What You Know

What is your favorite extracurricular activity? Do you like to play a sport—such as baseball, tennis, or volleyball—or do you prefer playing in the band, singing in the chorus, or acting with the drama club? Think back to when you became involved in your favorite activity. What were some of your fears and goals? Once you began, did participating in the activity meet your expectations? In small groups, discuss your experiences.

Expand Your Knowledge

Brett, the boy in this selection, plays on a Little League Baseball team. Little League Baseball, founded in 1939 in Williamsport, Pennsylvania, encourages children aged eight to twelve to participate in the sport of baseball regardless of ability. At first, only boys played on Little League teams. In 1974, however, girls were also allowed to join. Today, more than 2.5 million boys and girls compete on 60,000 Little League teams throughout the world.

Write Before You Read

Think back to the discussion you had in Examine What You Know. In your journal or on a sheet of paper, write about a time when you began to participate in a particular club, sport, or activity. What were you feeling before you tried out or joined? Did being involved in the club, sport, or activity meet your initial expectations?

■ *Author biography in Reader's Handbook*

Baseball and the Facts of Life

BOB GREENE

He is nine years old; his name is Brett. For three years he has been asking his parents if he could play in the Little League. This summer they said yes.

He is small for his age, with curly brown hair and bright blue eyes. The girls think he is cute, but he tells his mother he doesn't care about that. When his mother and father said he could play in the league this year, he just about exploded with joy. In other summers, he watched baseball on television; this year he was going to play.

His parents took him to the first practice, and they could see it in his eyes: he idolized the man who was coaching the team. The other boys had played in years before—Little Leaguers start young—but Brett didn't care. At last he was going to be one of them.

After the first few games, he would come home from practice, and his parents could sense that something was wrong. It is best not to pry into the secrets of little boys, but they were concerned. So one night, after dinner, they walked over to see his team play.

They watched as the game started, and their son did not get in. There were fifteen boys on the team, some of them very good.

But most of them were bigger than Brett, and stronger; they were the ones who played the whole game. The coach let Brett in for one inning; when the inning was over, the coach took him out.

At home, after the game, Brett's parents asked him what had been bothering him.

He said that at the beginning of the season, the coach had said that every boy would play. But for Brett, that meant only the bare minimum—one inning each game. The coach was afraid that if Brett stayed in for too long, the team might lose the game. As it was, he was put in right field, the place that boys who are not good enough are traditionally sent.

His mother started going to every game. She would watch as Brett stood on the sidelines, his eyes alive, everything in his face almost begging to get in. And every game, she watched as the coach reluctantly let her son play for one inning, and not a moment more.

At home, Brett would put his uniform on four hours before he was supposed to go to the game. He would walk around the house in it, look at himself in the mirror, check the clock every few minutes; the games were scheduled to start at six P.M., but Brett would get there at quarter to five, just to be sure. Every game was going to be the one when he would really get to play.

And his mother kept going to the games. Even from a distance she could see those eyes lighting up every time it seemed he might get to go in. She would see those eyes, and then she would see the coach not even knowing her son was there. The coach looking at the more skillful boys out on the field, and her son looking at the coach; it made her feel sick to see it.

*E*very game, he would be the first one at the field.

One day, after the game, when no one was looking, she approached the coach. She asked him why.

"I have to keep the best ones in," the coach said. "We're in a league, you know. We're trying to win. I have five boys on the team who only play one inning. Your son is one of them."

At home, Brett would ask his father to practice with him in the driveway. The father is not an athletically inclined man, but of course he said yes; Brett said he was "working on his arm," as if that would help change things at the next game.

And every game, he would get into his uniform early; every game, he would be the first one at the field.

His mother watched one game as he got in. The boys who got to play regularly—the skillful ones—horsed around between innings, did tricks on their bikes and made jokes with each other. Brett, though, looked only at the game. He never even got a drink of water. This night, when he got to bat, he

© Walter Iooss, Jr. / The Image Bank.

kept in mind the coach's admonitions[1] about not backing away from the ball. The pitch came in hard and close, and it hit him hard enough to make him cry. When the inning was over, he stood expectantly on the sidelines, hoping to get back in. But the coach

---

1. admonitions (ad' mə nish' ənz): warnings or scoldings.

only called to the regulars: "Double the limit at the Dairy Queen if you win." Brett did not play again that night.

One evening it happened: for some reason a lot of the boys had other things to do, and there were only nine present when it was time for the game to begin. His mother was there again, and she saw the coach tell Brett that he was going to get to start the game in right field. She saw him begin to smile and then to suppress it; he ran out to right field, part of the starting team.

In the middle of the first inning, one of the regulars rode up on his bike. The coach was clearly glad to see him. When Brett trotted off the field, he saw that the other boy had arrived. The coach took Brett out; his evening was over.

The season is almost finished now. Brett does not put his uniform on four hours early anymore; he does not watch the clock.

He still goes to the games, but he has learned his lesson. He doesn't talk about baseball around the house.

His parents are trying to find a moral in all of this. They know it happens to many boys in thousands of cities around the country every summer. His parents tell themselves that maybe it will turn out to be a good experience; maybe it will teach their son something about life, and about dreams, and about putting too much faith in those dreams.

That's what they tell themselves, but they don't believe it. All they know is that their son, at the age of nine, has been shown that he isn't good enough. We all learn that sometime in this life; some find it out earlier than others. The other night, Brett told his parents that he wasn't going to play baseball next summer. The eyes weren't as bright; that's what hurt his parents the most. The eyes weren't as bright. ❧

*R*esponding to Reading

First Impressions

1. What feelings do you have about Brett at the end of this selection? Record them in your journal or on a sheet of paper.

Second Thoughts

2. How do Brett's eyes reveal his personality throughout this selection?

Think about

- how he looked as he stood on the sidelines
- how he looked when he had the chance to start in a game
- how he looked when he said he wouldn't play next season

3. In what ways do you think Brett is caught in circumstances?

4. Do you think the coach was right in playing Brett and the weaker players less frequently than the stronger players? Why or why not?

5. How do you feel about the way Brett's parents handled this situation?

6. Brett and Minerva, the main character in "Getting the Facts of Life," both learn lessons about life. Compare these lessons.

Broader Connections

7. Like other organized sports for children, Little League has its fans as well as its critics. What do you feel are the advantages and disadvantages of organized sports for children?

*W*riting Options

1. In this selection, Bob Greene focused mainly on the feelings of Brett's parents. What might have been different if Greene had focused on Brett's feelings? Choose a particular scene and write an **interior monologue** that tells what Brett was thinking and feeling during the scene.

2. Imagine that Brett's coach handed out questionnaires at the end of the season to get parents' opinions of their children's Little League experiences. What do you think Brett's parents might have written about their son's experiences? Write the **response** as if you were one of Brett's parents.

Fiction ## *A*ppetizer

ROBERT ABEL

*E*xamine What You Know

You are enjoying your first night of camping in a beautiful forest setting. You are in your tent and just about to fall asleep when you hear a sound. Slowly you peek out and see . . . a huge brown bear glaring at you. Think fast. What should you do?

With a fellow classmate make some notes about the situation.

*E*xpand Your Knowledge

A wildlife agent in Kodiak, Alaska, once described the giant brown bear as "brown dynamite, timed with a very short fuse." The Alaskan brown bear shows little fear of people and is known to be short-tempered and dangerous when annoyed. It is the largest carnivore, or meat eater, on earth. A fully grown male tips the scales at 1,000 to 1,500 pounds. The female is one-half to two-thirds the size of the male. The brown bear travels far in search of food, often wading into streams to catch fish. It has a very acute sense of smell. A Native American saying puts it this way: "A pine needle fell. The eagle saw it. The deer heard it. The bear smelled it."

*E*nrich Your Reading

Prefixes   In this story the author describes an encounter with an Alaskan brown bear. He uses many words that may be unfamiliar to you. One way you can figure out the meaning of an unfamiliar word is to study its parts. If you know a prefix, suffix, base word, or root word within a word, you can often make a good guess as to the word's meaning. For example, knowing the meaning of certain prefixes may help you understand these words from the story: *superabundance, restore, revision,* and *inedible.*

Prefix	Meaning
super-	over, above
re-	back, again
in-	not, in, into

■ *Author biography in Reader's Handbook*

Appetizer

ROBERT ABEL

I'm fishing this beautiful stream in Alaska, catching salmon, char, and steelhead, when this bear lumbers out of the woods and down to the stream bank. He fixes me with this half-amused, half-curious look which says: You are meat.

The bear's eyes are brown, and his shiny golden fur is standing up in spikes, which shows me he has been fishing, too, perhaps where the stream curves behind the peninsula of woods he has just trudged through. He's not making any sound I can hear over the rumble of the water in the softball-sized rocks, but his presence is very loud.

I say "his" presence because temporarily I am not interested in or able to <u>assess</u> the creature's sex. I am looking at a head that is bigger around than my steering wheel, a pair of paws, awash in river bubbles, that could cover half my windshield. I am glad that I am wearing polarized fishing glasses so the bear cannot see the little teardrops of fear that have crept into the corner of my eyes. To assure him/her I am not the least bit intimidated, I make another cast.

Immediately I tie into a fat chinook.[1] The splashing of the fish in the stream engages the bear's attention, but he/she registers this for the moment only by shifting his/her glance. I play the fish smartly, and when it comes gliding in, tired, pink-sided, glittering, and astonished, I pluck it out of the water by inserting a finger in its gill—something I normally wouldn't do in order not to injure the fish before I set it free, and I do exactly what you would do in the same situation—throw it to the bear.

The bear's eyes widen, and she—for I can see now, past her huge shoulder and powerful haunches, that she is a she—turns and pounces on the fish with such speed and nimbleness that I am numbed. There is no chance that I, in my insulated waders,[2] am going to outrun her, dodge her blows, escape her jaws. While she is occupied devouring the fish—I can hear her teeth clacking together—I do what you or anyone else would do and cast again.

God answers my muttered prayer, and I am blessed with the strike of another fat salmon, like the others, on its way to spawning grounds upstream. I would like this fish to survive and release its eggs or sperm to perpetuate the salmon kingdom, but Ms.

---

1. chinook (shə noŏk′): short for "chinook salmon," a large fish of northern Pacific regions.
2. waders: a waterproof combination of trousers and boots, used for walking in water.

Words to Know and Use | **assess** (ə ses′) *v.* to determine or judge

OUT OF THE FOG © 1990 Morten E. Solberg.

Bear has just licked her whiskers clean and has now moved knee-deep into the water and, to my consternation,[3] leans against me rather like a large and friendly dog, although her ears are at the level of my shoulder and her back is broader than that of any horse I have ever seen. Ms. Bear is intensely interested in the progress of the salmon toward us, and her head twists and twitches as the fish circles, darts, takes line away, shakes head, rolls over, leaps.

With a bear at your side, it is not the simplest thing to play a fish[4] properly, but the presence of this huge animal, and especially her long snout, thick as my thigh, wonderfully concentrates the mind. She smells like the forest floor, like crushed moss and damp leaves, and she is as warm as a radiator back in my Massachusetts home, the thought of which floods me with a terrible nostalgia.[5] Now I debate whether I should just drift the salmon in under the bear's nose and let her

take it that way, but I'm afraid she will break off my fly and leader,[6] and right now that fly—a Doctor Wilson number eight—is saving my life. So, with much anxiety, I pretend to take charge and bring the fish in on the side away from the bear, gill and quickly unhook it, turn away from the bear, and toss the fish behind me to the bank.

The bear wheels and clambers upon it at once, leaving a vortex of water pouring into the vacuum of the space she has left, which almost topples me. As her teeth snack away, I quickly and furtively regard my poor Doctor Wilson, which is fish-mauled now, bedraggled, almost unrecognizable. But the present emergency compels me to zing it out

---

3. **consternation** (kän′ stər nā′ shən): confusion; dismay.
4. **play a fish:** to keep a hooked fish on the line until it tires.
5. **nostalgia** (näs tal′ jə): homesickness.
6. **fly and leader:** a fishing lure made to look like an insect and the part of the line to which it is attached.

Words to Know and Use

furtively (fʉr′ tiv lē) *adv.* in a secret or sneaky way
compel (kəm pel′) *v.* to force

once again. I walk a few paces downstream, hoping the bear will remember an appointment or become distracted and I can sneak away.

But a few seconds later she is leaning against me again, raptly watching the stream for any sign of a salmon splash. My luck holds; another fish smacks the withered Wilson, flings sunlight and water in silver jets as it dances its last dance. I implore the salmon's forgiveness: something I had once read revealed that this is the way of all primitive hunters, to take the life reluctantly and to pray for the victim's return. I think my prayer is as urgent as that of any Mashpee or Yoruban, or Tlingit or early Celt,[7] for not only do I want the salmon to <u>thrive</u> forever, but I want a superabundance of them now, right now, to save my neck. I have an idea this hungry bear, bereft of fish, would waste little time in conducting any prayer ceremonies before she turned me into the main course my salmon were just the appetizer for. When I take up this fish, the bear practically rips it from my hand; and the sight of those teeth so close and the truly persuasive power of those muscled, pink-rimmed jaws cause a wave of fear in me so great that I nearly faint.

My vertigo[8] subsides as Ms. Bear munches and destroys the salmon with hearty shakes of her head, and I sneak a few more paces downstream and rapidly also, with trembling fingers, tie on a new Doctor Wilson, observing the utmost care (as you would, too) in making my knots. I cast and stride downstream, wishing I could just plunge into the crystalline water and bowl away like a log. My hope and plan is to wade my way back to the narrow trail a few hundred yards ahead and, when Ms. Bear loses interest or is somehow distracted, make a heroic dash for my camper. I think of the thermos of hot coffee on the front seat, the six-pack of beer in the cooler, the thin rubber mattress with the blue sleeping bag <u>adorning</u> it, warm wool socks in a bag hanging from a window crank, and almost burst into tears; these simple things, given the presence of Ms. Hungry Bear, seem so miraculous, so emblematic of the life I love to live. I promise the gods—American, Indian, African, Oriental—that if I survive, I will never complain again, not even if my teenage children leave the caps off the toothpaste tubes or their bicycles in the driveway at home.

What should the fisherman do?

predict

"Oh, home," I think, and cast again.

Ms. Bear rejoins me. You may or may not believe me, and perhaps after all it was only my imagination worked up by terror, but two things happened which gave me a particle of hope. The first was that Ms. Bear actually belched—quite noisily and unapologetically, too, like a rude uncle at a Christmas dinner. She showed no signs of having committed any impropriety,[9] and yet it was clear to me that a belching bear is

---

7. **Mashpee or Yoruban** (yō′ rōō bən), **or Tlingit** (tliŋ′ git) **or early Celt:** names of early groups of people in Asia, Africa, North America, and Europe.

8. **vertigo** (vʉr′ ti gō′): dizziness.

9. **impropriety** (im′ prō prī′ ə tē): improper behavior.

Words to Know and Use | **thrive** (thrīv) *v.* to grow in strength or numbers; flourish
adorning (ə dôrn′ iŋ) *adj.* decorating; ornamenting **adorn** *v.*

609

probably also a bear with a pretty-full belly. A few more salmon and perhaps Ms. Bear would wander off in search of a berry dessert.

Now the second thing she did, or that I imagined she did, was to begin—well, not *speaking* to me exactly, but *communicating* somehow. I know it sounds foolish, but if you were in my shoes—my waders, to be more precise—you might have learned bear talk pretty quickly, too. It's not as if the bear were speaking to me in complete sentences and English words, such as "Get me another fish, pal, or you're on the menu," but in a much more indirect and subtle way, almost in the way a stream talks through its bubbling and burbling and rattling of rocks and gurgling along.

Get me another fish, pal, or you're on the menu.

Believe me, I listened intently, more with my mind than with my ears, as if the bear were telepathizing; and I know you're not going to believe this, but it's true—I am normally not what you would call an egomaniac with an inflated self-esteem such that I imagine that every bear which walks out of the woods falls in love with me, but I really did truly believe now that this Ms. Bear was expressing feelings of, well, *affection*. Really, I think she kinda liked me. True or not, the feeling made me less afraid. In fact, and I don't mean this in any erotic or perverse kind of way, but I had to admit, once my

fear had passed, my feelings were kinda mutual. Like you might feel for an old pal of a dog. Or a favorite horse. I only wish she weren't such a big eater. I only wish she were not a carnivore,[10] and I, carne.

Now she nudges me with her nose.

"All right, all right," I say. "I'm doing the best I can."

Cast in the glide behind that big boulder, the bear telepathizes me. *There's a couple of whoppers in there.*

I do as I'm told, and wham! The bear is right! Instantly I'm tied into a granddaddy chinook, a really burly fellow who has no intention of lying down on anybody's platter beneath a blanket of lemon slices and scallion shoots, let alone make his last wiggle down a bear's gullet. Even the bear is excited and begins shifting weight from paw to paw, a little motion for her that nevertheless has big consequences for me as her body slams against my hip, then slams again.

Partly because I don't want to lose the fish, but partly also because I want to use the fish as an excuse to move closer to my getaway trail, I stumble downstream. This fish has my rod bent into an upside-down *U*, and I'm hoping my quick-tied knots are also strong enough to take this salmon's lurching and his intelligent, broadside swinging into the river current—a very smart fish! Ordinarily I might take a long time with a fish like this, baby it in, but now I'm putting on as much pressure as I dare. When the

---

10. **carnivore** (kär′ nə vôr′): a meat-eating animal.

Words to Know and Use | **indirect** (in′ də rekt′) *adj.* not straightforward; roundabout
burly (bʉr′ lē) *adj.* big and muscular

salmon flips into a little side pool, the bear takes matters into her own hands, clambers over the rocks, pounces, nabs the salmon smartly behind the head, and lumbers immediately to the bank. My leader snaps at once, and while Ms. Bear attends to the destruction of the fish, I tie on another fly and make some shambling headway downstream. Yes, I worry about the hook still in the fish, but only because I do not want this bear to be irritated by anything. I want her to be replete and smug and doze off in the sun. I try to telepathize as much. Please, Bear, sleep.

Inevitably, the fishing slows down, but Ms. Bear does not seem to mind. Again she belches. Myself, I am getting quite a headache and know that I am fighting exhaustion. On a normal morning of humping along in waders over these slippery, softball-sized rocks, I would be tired in any case. The added emergency is foreclosing on my energy reserves. I even find myself getting a little angry, frustrated at least, and I marvel at the bear's persistence, her inexhaustible doggedness. And appetite. I catch fish; I toss them to her. At supermarket prices, I calculate she has eaten about six hundred dollars worth of fish. The calculating gives me something to think about besides my fear.

At last I am immediately across from the opening to the trail which twines back through the woods to where my camper rests in the dapple shade of mighty pines. Still, five hundred yards separate me from this imagined haven. I entertain the notion perhaps someone else will come along and frighten the bear away, maybe someone with a dog or a gun; but I have already spent many days here without seeing another soul, and in fact have chosen to return here for that very reason. I have told myself for many years that I really do love nature, love being among the animals, am restored by wilderness adventure. Considering that right now I would like nothing better than to be nestled beside my wife in front of a blazing fire, this seems to be a sentiment in need of some revision.

Now, as if in answer to my speculations, the bear turns beside me, her rump pushing me into water deeper than I want to be in, where my footing is shaky, and she stares into the woods, ears forward. She has heard something I cannot hear or smelled something I cannot smell, and while I labor back to shallower water and surer footing, I hope some backpackers or some bear-poaching Indians are about to appear and send Ms. Bear a-galloping away. Automatically, I continue casting, but I also cannot help glancing over my shoulder in hopes of seeing what Ms. Bear sees. And in a moment I do.

It is another bear.

Unconsciously, I release a low moan, but my voice is lost in the guttural warning of Ms. Bear to the trespasser. The new arrival answers with a <u>defiant</u> cough. He—I believe it is a he—can afford to be defiant because he is half again as large as my companion. His fur seems longer and coarser, and though its substance is as golden as that of the bear beside me, the tips are black, and this dark surface ripples and undulates over his massive frame. His nostrils are flared, and he is staring with <u>profound</u> concentration at me.

evaluate   What would you do in a situation like this?

Now I am truly confused and afraid. Would it be better to catch another salmon or not? I surely cannot provide for two of these beasts, and in any case Mister Bear does not seem the type to be distracted by or made friendly by any measly salmon tribute. His whole bearing—pardon the expression—tells me my intrusion into this bear world is a personal affront[11] to his bear honor. Only Ms. Bear stands between us, and after all, whose side is she really on? By bear standards, I am sure a rather <u>regal</u> and handsome fellow has made his appearance. Why should the fur-covered heart of furry Ms. Bear go out to me? How much love can a few hundred dollars worth of salmon buy? Most likely, this couple even have a history, know and have known each other from other seasons, even though for the moment they prefer to pretend to regard each other as total strangers.

How disturbed I am is well illustrated by my next course of action. It is completely <u>irrational</u>, and I cannot account for it or why it saved me—if indeed it did. I cranked in my line and laid my rod across some rocks, then began the arduous process of pulling myself out of my waders while trying to balance myself on those awkward rocks in that fast water. I tipped and swayed as I tugged at my boots, pushed my waders down, my arms in the foaming, frigid water, then the waders also filling, making it even more difficult to pull my feet free.

I emerged like a nymph from a cocoon, wet and trembling. The bears regarded me with clear stupefaction, as if one of them had casually stepped out of his or her fur. I drained what water I could from the waders, then dropped my fly rod into them and held them before me. The rocks were brutal on my feet, but I marched toward the trail opening, lifting and dropping first one, then the other, leg of my waders as if I were operating a giant puppet. The water still in the waders gave each footfall an impressive authority, and I was half thinking that, well, if the big one attacks, maybe he'll be fooled into chomping the waders first and I'll at least now be able to run. I did not relish the idea of pounding down the trail in my nearly bare feet, but it was a better way to argue with the bear than being sucked from my waders like a snail from its shell. Would you have done differently?

Who knows what the bears thought, but I tried to make myself look as much as possible like a camel or some other extreme and inedible form of four-footedness as I plodded along the trail. The bears looked at

---

11. **affront** (e frunt′): an insult.

| *Words to Know and Use* | **defiant** (dē fī′ ənt) *adj.* boldly challenging
profound (prō fōund′) *adj.* deep
regal (rē′ gəl) *adj.* magnificent; kingly
irrational (ir rash′ ə nəl) *adj.* senseless; not thought out carefully |

MIDSTREAM   J. Seward Johnson, Jr.   Photo courtesy of Sculpture Placement, Ltd., Washington, D.C.

each other, then at me as I clomped by, the water in the waders making an odd gurgling sound and me making an odd sound, too, on remembering just then how the Indians would, staring death in the eye, sing their death song. Having no such melody prepared and never having been anything but a bathtub singer, I chanted forth the only song I ever committed to memory: "Jingle Bells."

Yes, "Jingle Bells," I sang, "jingle all the way," and I lifted first one, then the other, wader leg and dropped it, stomping down. "Oh what fun it is to ride in a one-horse open sleigh-ay!"

The exercise was to prove to me just how complicated and various is the nature of the bear. The male reared up, blotting out the sun, bellowed, then twisted on his haunches and crashed off into the woods. The female, head cocked in curiosity, followed at a slight distance, within what still might be called striking distance, whether I was out of my waders or not. Truly, I did not appreciate her persistence. Hauling the waders half full of water before me was trying work, and the superfluous thought struck me: suppose someone sees me now, plumping along like this, singing "Jingle Bells," a bear in attendance? Vanity, obviously, never sleeps. But as long as the bear kept her distance, I saw no reason to change my modus operandi.[12]

My truck was being smothered in bear.

When I came within about one hundred feet of my camper, its white cap gleaming like a remnant of spring snow and beckoning me, I risked everything, dropped the waders and sped for the cab. The bear broke into a trot, too, I was sure, because although I couldn't see her, had my sights locked on the gleaming handle to the pickup door, I sure enough could hear those big feet slapping the ground behind me in a heavy rhythm, a terrible and elemental beat that sang to me of my own frailty, fragile bones, and tender flesh. I plunged on like a madman, grabbed the camper door and hurled myself in.

I lay on the seat panting, curled like a child, shuddered when the bear slammed against the pickup's side. The bear pressed her nose to the window, then, curiously, unceremoniously licked the glass with her tongue. I know (and you know) she could have shattered the glass with a single blow, and I tried to imagine what I should do if

indeed she resorted to this simple expedient. Fisherman that I am, I had nothing in the cab of the truck to defend myself with except a tire iron, and that not readily accessible behind the seat I was cowering on. My best defense, obviously, was to start the pickup and drive away.

Just as I sat up to the steering wheel and inserted the key, however, Ms. Bear slammed her big paws onto the hood and hoisted herself aboard. The pickup shuddered with the weight of her, and suddenly the windshield was full of her golden fur. I beeped the horn loud and long numerous times, but this had about the same effect as my singing, only caused her to shake her huge head, which vibrated the truck terribly. She stomped around on the hood and then lay down, back against the windshield, which now appeared to have been covered by a huge shag rug.

Could I believe my eyes?

No, I could not believe my eyes. My truck was being smothered in bear. In a moment I also could not believe my ears—Ms. Bear had decided the camper hood was the perfect place for a nap, and she was snoring, *snoring* profoundly, her body twitching like a cat's. Finally, she had responded to my advice and desires, but at the most inappropriate time. I was trapped. Blinded by bear body!

My exhaustion had been doubled by my sprint for the camper, and now that I was not in such a desperate panic, I felt the cold

---

12. **modus operandi** (mō dəs ō′ pə rän′ dē): a way of doing something.

Words to Know and Use	**superfluous** (sə pʉr′ fl○○ əs) *adj.* unnecessary; extra
	resort (ri zôrt′) *v.* (followed by *to*) to make use of
	accessible (ak ses′ ə bəl) *adj.* able to be reached

of the water that had soaked my clothes, and I began to tremble. It also crossed my mind that perhaps Mister Bear was still in the vicinity, and if Ms. Bear was not smart enough or cruel enough to smash my window to get at me, he just might be.

Therefore, I started the engine—which disturbed Ms. Bear not a whit—and rolled down the window enough to stick my head out and see down the rocky, limb-strewn trail. I figured a few jolts in those ruts and Ms. Bear would be off like a shot.

This proved a smug assumption. Ms. Bear did indeed awaken and bestir herself to a sitting position, a bit like an overgrown hood ornament, but quickly grew quite adept[13] at balancing herself against the lurching and jolting of my truck, which, in fact, she seemed to enjoy. Just my luck, I growled, to find the first bear in Alaska who wanted a ride into town. I tried some quick braking and sharp-turn maneuvers I thought might send her tumbling off, but her bulk was so massive, her paws so artfully spread, that she was just too <u>stable</u> an entity. She wanted a ride, and there was nothing I could do about it.

When I came out of the woods to the gravel road known locally as the Dawson Artery, I had an inspiration. I didn't drive so fast that if Ms. Bear decided to clamber down, she would be hurt; but I did head for the main road which led to Buckville and the Buckville Cannery. Ms. Bear swayed happily along the whole ten miles to that intersection and seemed not to bat an eye when first one big logging truck, then another, plummeted by. I pulled out onto the highway, and for the safety of both of us—those logging trucks have <u>dubious</u> brakes, and their drivers get paid by the trip—I had to accelerate considerably.

I couldn't see much of Ms. Bear except her back and rump, as I had to concentrate on the road, some of which is pretty curvy in that coastal area, shadowed also by the giant pines. But from the attitude expressed by her posture, I'd say she was having a whale, or should I say a salmon, of a time. I saw a few cars and pickups veering out of the oncoming lane onto the shoulder as we swept by, but I didn't have time, really, to appreciate the astonishment of their drivers. In this way, my head out the window, Ms. Bear perched on the hood, I drove to the Buckville Cannery and turned into the long driveway.

The first bear in Alaska who wanted a ride into town.

Ms. Bear knew right away something good was ahead, for she rose on all fours now and stuck her nose straight out like a bird dog on a pheasant. Her legs quivered with nervous anticipation as we approached, and as soon as I came out of the trees into the parking area, she went over the front of the camper like someone plunging into a pool.

---

13. **adept** (ə dept′): skilled.

Don't tell me you would have done any differently. I stopped right there and watched Ms. Bear march down between the rows of cars and right up the truck ramp into the cannery itself. She was not the least bit intimidated by all the noise of the machines and the grinders and stampers in there, or the shouting of the workers.

Now the Buckville Cannery isn't that big—I imagine about two dozen people work there on any given day—and, since it is so remote, has no hurricane fence around it and no security guard. After all, what's anybody going to steal out of there besides a few cases of canned salmon or some bags of frozen fish parts that will soon become some company's cat food? The main building is up on a little hill, and conveyors run down from there to the docks where the salmon boats pull in—the sea is another half mile away—and unload their catch.

I would say that in about three minutes after Ms. Bear walked into the cannery, twenty of the twenty-four workers were climbing out down the conveyors, dropping from open windows, or charging out the doors. The other four just hadn't got wind of the event yet, but in a little while they came bounding out, too. They all assembled on the semicircular drive before the main office and had a union meeting of some vigor.

Myself, I was too tired to participate and in any case did not want to be held liable for the disturbance at the Buckville Cannery; and so I made a U-turn and drove on into Buckville itself, where I took a room above the Buckville Tavern and had a hot shower and a really nice nap. That night in the Tap and Lounge, I got to hear many an excited story about the she-bear who freeloaded at the cannery for a couple of hours before she was driven off by blowing, ironically enough, the lunch whistle loud and long. I didn't think it was the right time or place to testify to my part in that historical event, and for once I kept my mouth shut. You don't like trouble any more than I do, and I'm sure you would have done about the same. ❧

Words to Know and Use

remote (ri mōt') *adj.* off the beaten track

Responding to Reading

First Impressions

1. What part of this adventure is the most memorable to you? Jot down your thoughts in your journal or on a sheet of paper.

Second Thoughts

2. What do you think of the narrator and his behavior?

   Think about
   - his reactions to "Ms. Bear" during the story
   - his odd escape from the bear
   - his dropping the bear off at the cannery

3. Think about what you wrote in the Examine What You Know activity. What do you think you would have done if you had been caught in the same circumstances as the narrator?

4. Would you recommend this story to other readers? Explain.

Literary Concept: Humor

Much of the **humor** in "Appetizer" is based on **irony of situation.** Things happen that are totally contrary to what one would expect. For a man and a deadly bear to work together to catch fish is an ironic situation. Driving down a road with a huge bear on one's hood is another example. Identify another humorously ironic situation in "Appetizer."

Writing Options

1. In "Appetizer" the narrator imagines what the bear might be thinking. Go one step further and tell this **story** from the bear's point of view.

2. Write a local **news article** about the bear's showing up at the cannery. Remember to answer the questions *who, what, when, where, why,* and *how*. Include some workers' theories about how the bear got to the cannery.

3. After the narrator returns home, his wife will undoubtedly ask him why the hood of the truck is dented. Write the **dialogue** that might take place between the narrator and his wife.

Vocabulary Practice

Exercise A Write the letter of the word pair that expresses the relationship most similar to that expressed by the original pair.

1. ACCESSIBLE : AVAILABLE :: (a) possible : impossible (b) capable : able (c) easy : difficult (d) helpful : harmful

2. INDIRECT : DIRECT :: (a) slender : slim (b) silent : quiet (c) courageous : brave (d) incomplete : complete

3. KING : REGAL :: (a) cat : calico (b) tea : cup (c) lion : peaceful (d) loafer : lazy

4. DISTANCE : REMOTE :: (a) height : lofty (b) flag : red (c) deep : shallow (d) criminal : crime

5. STABLE : STURDY :: (a) disorderly : neat (b) funny : mournful (c) pleasant : nice (d) ungrateful : thankful

Exercise B Write the letter of the word that is most different in meaning from the other words.

1. (a) adorning (b) decorating (c) simplifying (d) ornamenting

2. (a) evaluate (b) judge (c) assist (d) assess

3. (a) slender (b) slim (c) thin (d) burly

4. (a) require (b) compel (c) force (d) repeat

5. (a) timid (b) defiant (c) meek (d) mild

6. (a) laziness (b) determination (c) doggedness (d) stubbornness

7. (a) definite (b) certain (c) dubious (d) sure

8. (a) openly (b) secretly (c) furtively (d) privately

9. (a) logical (b) senseless (c) unreasonable (d) irrational

10. (a) profound (b) shallow (c) deep (d) bottomless

11. (a) resort (b) use (c) surrender (d) utilize

12. (a) self-satisfied (b) conceited (c) smug (d) humble

13. (a) thought (b) speculation (c) wondering (d) action

14. (a) superfluous (b) useful (c) extra (d) unnecessary

15. (a) wither (b) fail (c) thrive (d) decline

Words to Know and Use

accessible
adorning
assess
burly
compel
defiant
doggedness
dubious
furtively
indirect
irrational
profound
regal
remote
resort
smug
speculation
stable
superfluous
thrive

Nonfiction

from Survive the Savage Sea

DOUGAL ROBERTSON

*E*xamine What You Know

Imagine that your sailboat has sunk and you are drifting on a life raft with five other people in the middle of the ocean. You have some supplies that may help you survive. These are listed below. With a small group of classmates, discuss the importance of each item to your survival and rank the items—1 for most important, 16 for least. Compare your rankings with those of other groups.

compass	fishhooks	rope	gun
candy	knife	flares	first-aid kit
jugs of water	lemons	paddles	sunscreen
deck of cards	pencil	matches	flashlight

*E*xpand Your Knowledge

In 1970, Dougal Robertson and his wife sold their farm in England, bought a fifty-year-old sailboat, the *Lucette,* and began a trip around the world with their three sons and a family friend. Two years into their voyage, the unexpected happened. While they were sailing from the Galápagos Islands to the Marquesas Islands, their boat sank. Having few supplies in their crowded life raft, the Robertsons faced a brutal test of survival.

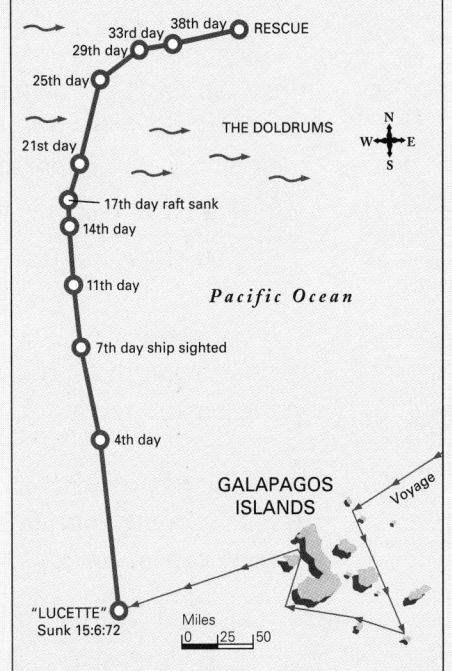

*E*nrich Your Reading

Examining a Word's Context You may encounter some unfamiliar words in Dougal Robertson's diary entries. Often you can figure out the meaning of an unfamiliar word by thinking about the meaning of the passage in which the word appears—that is, the word's **context.** For example, consider this sentence: "We watched the gathering clouds obscure the stars." The word *obscure* may be unfamiliar to you; however, from the context you might guess that the word *obscure* means "to hide." Use this strategy as you read.

■ *Author biography on Extend Page*

from *Survive the Savage Sea*

DOUGAL ROBERTSON

On June 15, 1972, the forty-three-foot schooner Lucette, *sailed by Dougal Robertson, was attacked by killer whales in the Pacific Ocean and sank in sixty seconds. Set adrift in a rubber raft towed by a sail-powered dinghy, Robertson and his crew of five—his wife, Lyn; their eighteen-year-old son, Douglas; their twelve-year-old twin boys, Neil and Sandy; and Robin Williams, a friend of the family—had lost all their maps, compasses, and other instruments. Equipped with only enough emergency rations to last three days, they realized their only chance to survive lay in sailing with the trade winds[1] toward the doldrums,[2] four hundred miles to the north. Through his journal entries, Robertson describes the efforts to "survive the savage sea."*

First day

We sat on the salvaged pieces of flotsam[3] lying on the raft floor, our faces a pale bilious color under the bright yellow canopy, and stared at each other, the shock of the last few minutes gradually seeping through to our consciousness. Neil, his teddy bears gone, sobbed in accompaniment to Sandy's hiccup cry, while Lyn repeated the Lord's Prayer, then, comforting them, sang the hymn "For Those in Peril on the Sea." Douglas and Robin watched at the doors of the canopy to retrieve any useful pieces of debris which might float within reach and gazed with dumb longing at the distant five-gallon water container, bobbing its polystyrene lightness ever further away from us in the steady trade wind. The dinghy *Ednamair* wallowed, swamped, nearby, with a line attached to it from the raft, and our eyes traveled over and beyond to the heaving undulations of the horizon, already searching for a rescue ship even while knowing there would not be one. Our eyes traveled fruitlessly across the limitless waste of sea and sky, then once more ranged over the scattering debris. Of the killer whales which had so recently shattered our very existence, there was no sign. Lyn's sewing basket floated close, and it was brought aboard, followed by a couple of empty boxes, the canvas raft cover, and a plastic cup.

I leaned across to Neil and put my arm round him. "It's all right now, son, we're safe and the whales have gone." He looked at me reproachfully. "We're not crying cos we're frightened," he sobbed. "We're crying

---

1. **trade winds:** steady winds blowing from the southeast toward the equator in the Southern Hemisphere.
2. **doldrums** (dōl′ drəmz): ocean regions near the equator, known for their lack of wind.
3. **flotsam:** floating cargo from a shipwreck.

Words to Know and Use	**debris** (də brē′) *n.* the remains of something destroyed
	undulation (un′ dyo͞o lā′ shən) *n.* a wavelike motion
	reproachfully (ri prōch′ fəl ē) *adv.* in a blaming way

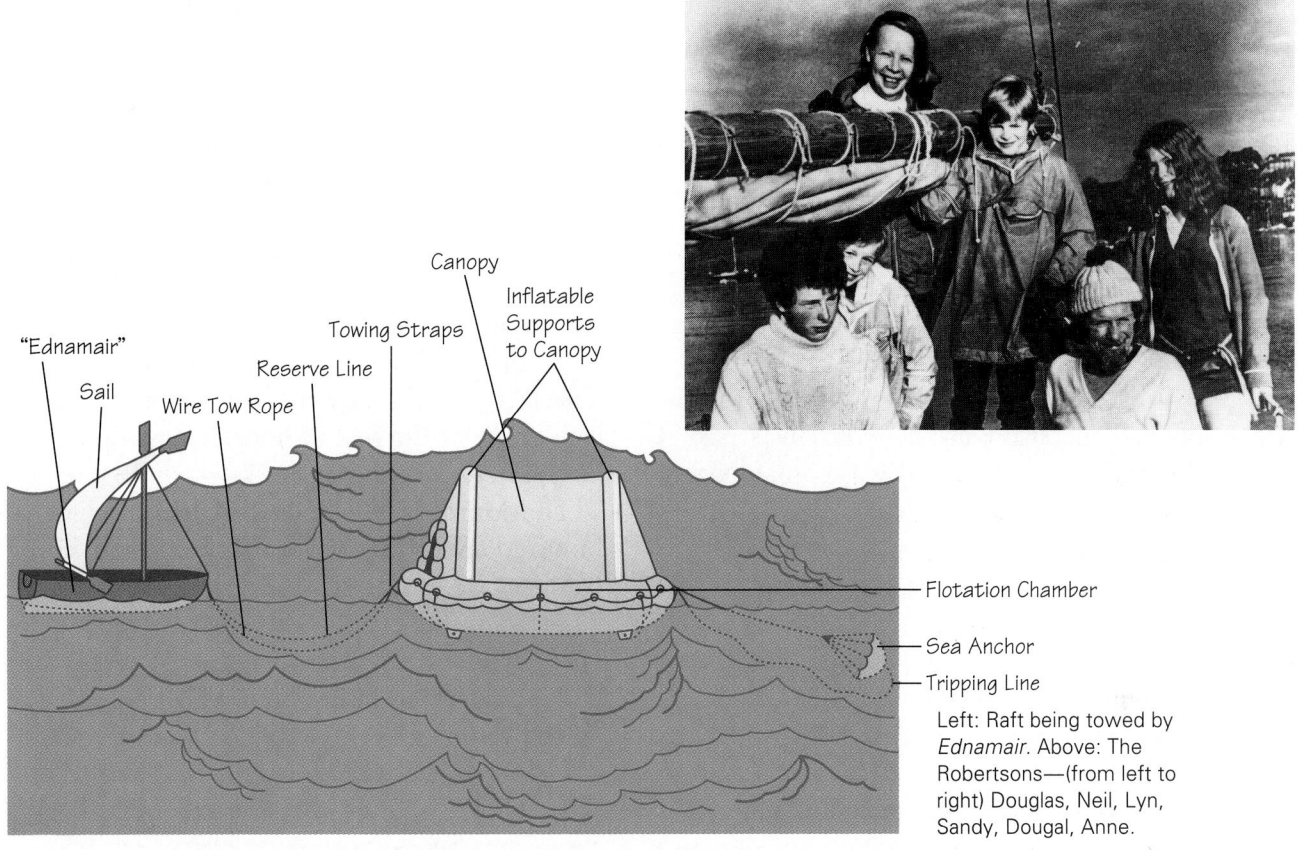

"Ednamair"

Sail

Wire Tow Rope

Reserve Line

Towing Straps

Canopy

Inflatable Supports to Canopy

Flotation Chamber

Sea Anchor

Tripping Line

Left: Raft being towed by *Ednamair*. Above: The Robertsons—(from left to right) Douglas, Neil, Lyn, Sandy, Dougal, Anne.

cos Lucy's[4] gone." Lyn gazed at me over their heads, her eyes filling with tears. "Me too," she said, and after a moment added, "I suppose we'd better find out how we stand."

This was the question I had been dreading; feelings of guilt, that our present predicament was due not only to my unorthodox ideas on educating our children (there had been plenty of critics to object that I was needlessly jeopardizing the children's lives) but also to the fact that I had failed to foresee this type of disaster, now engulfed me; and this, added to the fact that we had lost almost everything we possessed as well as *Lucette*, depressed me to the depths of despair. How could I have been so foolish as to trust our lives to such an old schooner! Then I saw, once again, in my mind's eye that damage under the floorboards of *Lucette*. Not only had the frames withstood

the impact of the blow, but the new garboard strake[5] of inch-and-a-half pitch pine, fitted in Malta at the surveyor's recommendation, had been one of the hull planks which had been smashed inward. Her hull had taken a full minute to sink below the waves, but a modern boat, constructed with less regard to brute strength than *Lucette,* would have sustained much heavier damage and sunk even more quickly, with more terrible results.

I looked at Douglas; he had grown to manhood in our eighteen months at sea together; the twins, previously shy, introspective[6] farm lads, had become interested in the different peoples we had met

---

4. **Lucy's:** a reference to the schooner *Lucette*.
5. **garboard strake:** one of the two bottommost of the horizontal planks forming the hull of a wooden ship.
6. **introspective:** turned inward in thought.

and their various ways of life and were now keen to learn more; I tried to ease my conscience with the thought that they had derived much benefit from their voyage and that our sinking was as unforeseeable as an earthquake, or an airplane crash, or anything to ease my conscience.

We cleared a space on the floor and opened the survival kit, which was part of the raft's equipment and was contained in a three-foot-long polyethylene[7] cylinder; slowly we took stock:

Vitamin-fortified bread and glucose[8] for ten men for two days.

Eighteen pints of water, eight flares (two parachute, six hand).

One bailer, two large fishhooks, two small, one spinner and trace, and a twenty-five-pound breaking-strain fishing line.

A patent knife which would not puncture the raft (or anything else for that matter), a signal mirror, torch, first-aid box, two sea anchors, instruction book, bellows, and three paddles.

In addition to this there was the bag of a dozen onions which I had given to Sandy, to which Lyn had added a one-pound tin of biscuits and a bottle containing about half a pound of glucose sweets, ten oranges, and six lemons. How long would this have to last us? As I looked around our meager stores, my heart sank, and it must have shown on my face, for Lyn put her hand on mine. "We must get these boys to land," she said quietly. "If we do nothing else with our lives, we must get them to land!" I looked at her and nodded. "Of course, we'll make it!" The answer came from my heart, but my head was telling me a different story. We were over two hundred miles downwind and downcurrent from the Galápagos Islands.[9] To try to row the small dinghy into two hundred miles of rough ocean weather was an impossible journey even if it was tried by only two of us in an attempt to seek help for the others left behind in the raft. The fact that the current was against us as well only put the seal of hopelessness on the idea. There was no way back.

The Marquesas Islands[10] lay twenty-eight hundred miles to the west, but we had no compass or means of finding our position; if, by some miraculous feat of endurance, one of us made the distance, the chances of striking an island were remote.

The coast of Central America, more than a thousand miles to the northeast, lay on the other side of the windless doldrums, that dread area of calms and squalls which had inspired Coleridge's

Water, water, everywhere,
And all the boards did shrink;
Water, water, everywhere,
Nor any drop to drink.

I was a Master Mariner, I thought ruefully, not an ancient one, and could count on no ghostly crew[11] to get me out of this dilemma!

---

7. polyethylene (päl′ ē eth′ ə lēn′): a lightweight, flexible plastic.

8. glucose (glo͞o′ kōs): a form of sugar.

9. Galápagos (gə lä′ pə gōs′) **Islands:** an island group belonging to Ecuador, located on the equator in the Pacific Ocean.

10. Marquesas (mär kā′ zəz) **Islands:** an island group in the South Pacific, part of the region known as French Polynesia.

11. Water . . . ghostly crew: reference to "The Rime of the Ancient Mariner," written by the British poet Samuel Taylor Coleridge in 1798.

Words to Know and Use

derive (di rīv′) *v.* to get; obtain
ruefully (ro͞o′ fəl ē) *adv.* with sorrow and embarrassment

What were our chances if we followed the textbook answer, "Stay put and wait for rescue"? In the first place we wouldn't be missed for at least five weeks, and if a search was made, where would they start looking in three thousand miles of ocean? In the second place the chance of seeing a passing vessel in this area was extremely remote and could be discounted completely, for of the two possible shipping routes from Panama to Tahiti and New Zealand, one lay four hundred miles to the south, and the other three hundred miles to the north. Looking at the food, I estimated that six of us might live for ten days; and since we could expect no rain in this area for at least six months, apart from an odd shower, our chances of survival beyond ten days were doubtful indeed.

My struggle to reach a decision, gloomy whichever way I looked at it, showed on my face, and Lyn leaned forward. "Tell us how we stand," she said, looking around. "We want to know the truth." They all nodded. "What chance have we?" I could not tell them I thought they were going to die, so I slowly spelled out the alternatives, and then suddenly I knew there was only one course open to us: we must sail with the trade winds to the doldrums four hundred miles to the north. We stood a thin chance of reaching land, but the only possible shipping route lay in that direction, our only possible chance of rainwater in any quantity lay in that direction even if it was four hundred miles away, and our only possible chance of reaching land lay in that direction, however small that chance might be. We would work

and fight for our lives at least; better than dying in idleness! "We must get these boys to land," Lyn had said. I felt the reality of the decision lifting the hopelessness from my shoulders and looked around; five pairs of eyes watched me as I spoke, Lyn once again with her arms around the twins. "We have no alternative," I said.

During the days that followed, all of the crew wrote farewell letters to their loved ones on pieces of sail. They then placed their letters in a waterproof wrapping and tucked them into a pocket of the raft. By the seventh day, still 150 miles from the doldrums, the Robertsons had only six pints of water left.

Seventh day

The windless night filled our ears with unaccustomed silence, and in the quiet of the calm swell, the phosphorescent gleam of the large dorado,[12] streaking from under the raft and leaping high into the air, to land in bursting showers of green-glowing fire, was a display not often seen by men.

The foul dryness of our mouths aggravated the discomfort of our sleepless bodies as we tried to ease the agony of our thirst, twisting this way and that; then breathlessly we watched the gathering clouds obscure the stars, and as dawn paled the eastern horizon, it began to rain, a heavy shower this time, with a steady downpour. Slowly the water in the pipe from the canopy ran clear, and we filled our empty cans and

---

12. **dorado** (dō rä′ dō): a large saltwater fish.

Words to Know and Use | **alternative** (ôl tʉr′ nə tiv) *n.* an available choice
obscure (əb skyoor′) *v.* to hide from view

623

spare plastic bags, our bellies and our mouths until we could not force down another drop. We lay with our faces turned to the sky and let the pure fresh water cleanse the salt from our beards and hair; suddenly everything had changed from the shadow of the specter of death to the joyful prospect of life, and all by a shower of rain. We would make the doldrums now! We lay uncaring, chewing strips of dorado and reveling in the absence of thirst, talking excitedly of good food and watching the bulging plastic bags swing lazily from the roof of the canopy. We had water!

Douglas, lazily watching the dispersing clouds, suddenly sat up with a start, pointing excitedly. "A ship! A ship! It's a ship!" We all crowded to the door of the raft, staring in the direction of his pointing finger; a cargo vessel of about six thousand tons was approaching us on a course that would bring her within three miles of us. I felt my heart pound against my ribs. "Get out the flares," I said hoarsely, "and pass them to me in the dinghy; they'll see us better from there."

Three miles was a fair distance, but on a dull day like this, against a background of rain, they should see us easily. I clambered into the dinghy, and Douglas passed me the rockets and hand flares; my hands trembled as I ripped open a parachute rocket flare and, with a mute appeal to the thing to fire, struck the igniter on the fuse. It spluttered and hissed, then roared off on a trajectory high above the raft, its pinkish magnesium flare slowly spiraling downward, leaving a trail of smoke in the sky. They couldn't fail to see it. I waited a moment or two, watch-ing for the ship to alter course, then struck a hand flare, holding it high above my head. The blinding red light was hot to hold, and I pointed it away from the wind to ease my hand, the red embers of the flare dropping into the dinghy; as it went out, I struck another, smoke from the first now a rising plume in the sky; surely they must see that. I waited a little, my hands trembling. "This chance might not come again," I said, anxious faces crowding the door of the raft. "I'm going to use our last rocket flare and one more hand flare." We watched tensely as the second rocket flare soared and spiraled its gleaming distress message high above us; desperately I struck the third hand flare and held it high, standing on the thwart[13] and holding on to the mast. "Look, look!" I shouted. "Set fire to the sail!" Lyn's voice. I stuck the flare to the sail, but it only melted. The ship sailed on, slowly disappearing behind a rain shower, and when she reappeared, her hull was half obscured by the horizon, five miles distant and disappearing fast. The time was eleven o'clock. My shoulders drooped. "We daren't use another," I said. "They won't see it now, and we have to keep something for the next one." We had three hand flares left. Lyn smiled cheerfully. "It says in the instruction book that the first one probably wouldn't see us," she said slowly, "and I'd already told the twins not to expect anything." She gathered the twins to her, comfortingly. We stared at the dwindling speck on the horizon and felt so lonely that it hurt.

---

13. **thwart** (thwôrt): a seat in a rowboat.

Words to Know and Use | **dispersing** (di spurs′ iŋ) *adj.* scattering **disperse** *v.*
clamber (klam′ bər) *v.* to climb clumsily
spiraling (spī′ rəl iŋ) *adj.* moving in circles **spiral** *v.*
dwindling (dwin′ dliŋ) *adj.* shrinking **dwindle** *v.*

Each night, the older members of the crew took turns bailing out the leaking raft and blowing air into its flotation chambers. By day, they kept a wary eye on huge sharks that became their constant companions. They managed to catch a large turtle to use for food. Everyone grew increasingly uncomfortable with boils, swellings of the skin caused by the irritation of continuous contact with sea water.

Fourteenth day

The beautiful starlit night shone sparkles of stars on the quiet swells of the now distant trade winds and seemed to mock our feeble struggle for existence in the raft; to become one with the night would be so easy. We blew and bailed the forward section[14] continually, and when Sandy found the hole which leaked into the after section,[15] surrounded by transparently thin fabric, I felt that this was the beginning of the end of the raft. I knew that it was unlikely that I would be able to plug this one, and yet if I left it, it would certainly split open in the next heavy sea. I made a plug and inserted it into the hole, tape ready to bind it if it held. The hole split across, and water flooded into the after compartment[16]; I rammed the plug home in disgust and stopped enough of the water to bail the compartment dry, but the raft would now need constant bailing at both ends. Apart from discomfort, my only real opposition to abandoning the raft was because it would mean abandoning the shelter afforded by the canopy, so I decided to think of a way of fastening the canopy on the dinghy to give us continuing shelter from the sun if we had

to abandon.

We had a sip of water for breakfast, with no dried food to detract from its value, after which I crossed to the dinghy to try for a dorado. The heat of the sun's rays beat on my head like a club, and my mouth, dry like lizard skin, felt full of my tongue; the slightest <u>exertion</u> left me breathless. I picked up the spear; the dorado were all deep down, as if they knew I was looking for them. A bump at the stern of the raft attracted Sandy's attention. "Turtle!" he yelled. This one was much smaller than the first, and with great care it was caught and passed through the raft—with Douglas guarding its beak, and the others its claws, from damaging the fabric—to me on the dinghy, where I lifted it aboard without much trouble. I wrapped a piece of tape around the broken knife blade and made the incision into its throat. "Catch the blood," Lyn called from the raft. "It should be all right to drink a little." I held the plastic cup under the copious flow of blood; the cup filled quickly, and I stuck another under as soon as it was full; then raising the full cup to my lips, I tested it cautiously. It wasn't salty at all! I tilted the cup and drained it. "Good stuff!" I shouted. I felt as if I had just consumed the elixir of life. "Here, take this," and I passed the bailer full of blood, about a pint, into the raft for the others to drink. Lyn said afterward she had imagined that she would have to force it down us, and the sight of me, draining the cup, my mustache dripping blood, was quite

---

14. **forward section:** the front part of a boat.
15. **after section:** the rear part of a boat.
16. **after compartment:** a room or walled area in the rear of a boat.

Words to Know and Use | **exertion** (eg zʉrʹshən) *n.* an effort

625

revolting. I don't know what I looked like, but it certainly tasted good; and as the others followed my example, it seemed they thought so too. I passed another pint across, and though some of this coagulated before it could be drunk, the jelly was cut up, and the released serum collected and used as a gravy with the dried turtle and fish.

I set to cutting my way into the turtle much refreshed and, even with the broken knife, made faster work of it than the first one, both because it was smaller and because, being younger, its shell was not so tough; the fact that I now knew my way around inside a turtle helped a lot too.

The sky was serenely blue that afternoon, and with our position worked out at 500 north, 250 miles west of Espinosa, we had arrived at the official limits of the doldrums. Was this, then, doldrums weather? Was "The Rime of the Ancient Mariner" right with its "Nor any drop to drink?" We had four tins of water left, one of them half sea water, and if any of the other three contained short measure, well, there might come another turtle. I looked around the raft at the remains of Robin and the Robertson family, water-wrinkled skin covered with saltwater boils and raw red patches of rash, lying in the bottom of the raft, unmoving except to bail occasionally, and then only halfheartedly, for the water was cooling in the heat of the day; our bones showed clearly through our scanty flesh; we had become much thinner these last few days, and our condition was deteriorating fast. The raft was killing us with its demands on our energy. Douglas looked across at me. "Do you think it'll rain tonight, Dad?" I looked at him and shrugged, looked at the sky, not a cloud. "I suppose it could do," I said. "Do you think it will?" he insisted. "For heaven's sake, Douglas, I'm not a prophet," I said testily. "We'll just have to wait it out." His eyes looked hopelessly at the blue of the sea from the deep cavities under his brow; how could I comfort him when he knew as well as I that it might not rain for a week and that we'd be dead by then. I said, "Fresh turtle for tea; we can suck something out of that." We could live on turtles, maybe.

We took no water that evening, only a little for the twins. We talked of the dishes we'd like to eat in the gathering twilight, and I chose fresh fruit salad and ice cream; Lyn, a tin of apricots; Robin, strawberries and ice cream with milk; Douglas, the same as me; Neil, chocolate chip ice cream; Sandy, fresh fruit, ice cream, and milk—gallons of ice-cool milk. Later that night, as I took the watch over from Douglas, he described in detail the dish he had dreamed up during his watch. "You take a honeydew melon," he said. "Cut the top off and take out the seeds; that's the dish. Chill it and drop a knob of ice cream in, then pile in strawberries, raspberries, pieces of apple, pear, orange, peach, and grapefruit, the sweet sort, then cherries and grapes until the melon is full; pour a lemon syrup over it and decorate it with chips of chocolate and nuts. Then," he said with a dreamy expression on his face, "you eat it!" "I'll have one too," I said, taking the bailer from his boil-covered hand. I looked at the sky; to the northeast a

Words to Know and Use | **deteriorate** (dē tir′ ē ə rāt′) *v.* to become worse
testily (tes′ tə lē) *adv.* in an irritated way

faint film of cirrostratus cloud[17] dimmed the stars. "You know, I think it might rain by morning." I could feel him relax in the darkness; his voice came slowly. "I'll be all right if it doesn't, Dad," he said.

I started to bail mechanically. We would have to abandon the raft soon, I thought, and that meant ditching all the unnecessary stuff overboard; in the dinghy there was only room for food, water, flares, and us. We'd start to sort things out in the morning.

It rained at dawn, beautiful, gorgeous rain. We saved three and a half gallons and drank our fill besides; the wind, from the south, freshened a little, and as the weather cleared, we lay back and enjoyed the sensation of being without thirst, bailing and blowing unheeded for the moment. We talked of the ship that didn't see us, for that had happened after the last rain, and argued whether it would have seen us better if it had been nighttime. The twins were talking when Douglas, on watch, his voice desperate with dismay, called, "Dad, the dinghy's gone!" I was across the raft in an instant. I looked at the broken end of wire trailing in the water, the broken line beside it. The dinghy was sixty yards away, sailing still, and our lives were sailing away with it; I was the fastest swimmer, no time for goodbyes, the thoughts ran through my head as I was diving through the door, my arms flailing into a racing crawl even as I hit the water. I heard Lyn cry out, but there was no time for talk. Could I swim faster than the dinghy could sail, that was the point; I glanced at it as I lifted my head to breathe;

the sail had collapsed as the dinghy yawed; I moved my arms faster, kicked harder, would the sharks let me, that was another point; my belly crawled as I thought of the sharks, my arms moved faster still; I glanced again, only thirty yards to go, but she was sailing again; I felt no fatigue, no cramped muscles; my body felt like a machine as I thrashed my way through the sea, only one thought now in mind, the dinghy or us. Then I was there; with a quick heave I flipped over the stern of the dinghy to safety, reached up and tore down the sail before my knees buckled, and lay across the thwart trembling and gasping for breath, my heart pounding like a hammer. I lifted my arm and waved to the raft, now two hundred yards away, then slowly untied the paddle from the sail and paddled back to the raft; it took nearly half an hour. The long shapes of two sharks circled curiously twenty feet down; they must have had breakfast.

Lyn had been sitting against the central thwart, trying to rest after her watch, and the following is her account of what happened in the raft after Douglas shouted, "Dad, the dinghy's gone!"

I saw Dougal's body hurtle past me as he dived into the sea. The silence was broken by the cry of "Shark" from Douglas, followed by a despairing shriek from Neil, "Daddy! Daddy!" We all crowded to see past Douglas, blocking the doorway. Dougal was cutting through the water faster than *Ednamair* was sailing and could not have kept up such a speed for more than a few

---

17. cirrostratus cloud (sir′ ō strāt′ əs): a thin layer of cloud in the upper atmosphere.

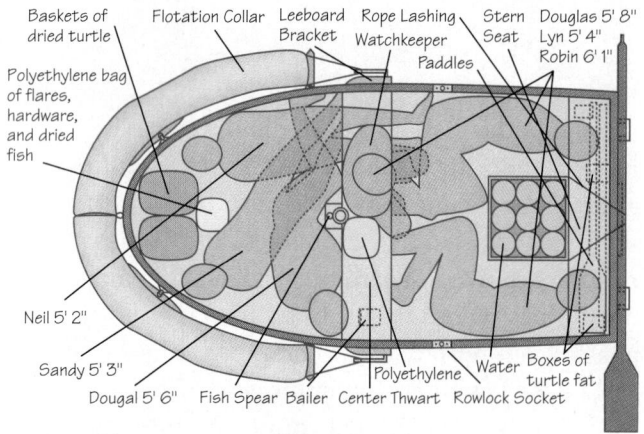

Arrangement of bodies at night in *Ednamair*.

Baskets of dried turtle
Polyethylene bag of flares, hardware, and dried fish
Flotation Collar
Leeboard Bracket
Rope Lashing
Watchkeeper
Paddles
Stern Seat
Douglas 5' 8"
Lyn 5' 4"
Robin 6' 1"
Neil 5' 2"
Sandy 5' 3"
Dougal 5' 6"
Fish Spear
Bailer
Center Thwart
Polyethylene
Rowlock Socket
Water
Boxes of turtle fat

minutes. The shark was close behind him to his right, and his feet were threshing the water in a racing crawl. "I can't see him," I said. "He's gone." The raft had slued around in the swell, and we had lost sight of him. "Don't panic! Don't panic!" Robin shouted. Then Douglas cried, "He's done it! He's made it!" "Good old Dad," this from Sandy. Only Douglas could see him now, and he gave us a running commentary. "He's taking the sail down now, it's down, he's getting the paddle off the sail." Douglas craned his neck to see as the raft slued around more, and we scrambled over the thwart to the aft compartment to look through the back door. There, miraculously, we saw him, the dinghy like a cockleshell on the crest of a wave, with Dougal paddling furiously, first one side, then the other, with such a look of concentration and determination on his haggard face. Relief flooded through me, and I heard myself singing "Somewhere My Love," that wonderful song from *Dr. Zhivago*. It was a long time before he reached us, and as he fell through the doorway into the bottom of the raft, his face gray with exhaustion, I pressed the sipper jar to his lips. He shook his head, but I made him drink, then put a piece of glucose

in his mouth, cradling his head in my arms until his strength returned and shuddering as I thought of how lonely and desperate we had felt, cut off from our only hope for survival, *Ednamair* and my beloved Dougal.

On the seventeenth day, the family finally deserted the sinking raft for the dinghy, where they then had to endure crowded sleeping conditions. On the twenty-ninth day, a fierce battle took place between Dougal and a pesky shark; Dougal won. Celebrating his victory over the shark, Dougal said: "We had turned the tables on our most feared enemy; sharks would not eat Robertsons, Robertsons would eat sharks!"

In quieter moments, the family sang songs and told stories. They also played games and discussed Dougal's Kitchen, a fantasy restaurant where each member imagined a wonderful menu.

Thirty-eighth day

I chopped up some dried turtle meat for tea, and Lyn put it with a little wet fish to soak in meat juice. She spread the dry sheets for the twins under the canopy, then prepared their "little supper" as we started to talk of Dougal's Kitchen and if it should have a wine license. As we pondered the delights of Gaelic coffee, my eye, looking past the sail, caught sight of something that wasn't sea. I stopped talking and stared; the others all looked at me. "A ship," I said. "There's a ship and it's coming toward us!" I could hardly believe it, but it seemed solid enough. "Keep still now!" In the sudden surge of excitement, everyone wanted to see. "Trim her! We mustn't capsize now!" All sank back to their places.

I felt my voice tremble as I told them that I was going to stand on the thwart and hold a flare above the sail. They trimmed the dinghy as I stood on the thwart. "Right, hand me a flare, and remember what happened with the last ship we saw!" They suddenly fell silent in memory of that terrible despondency[18] when our signals had been unnoticed. "O God!" prayed Lyn. "Please let them see us." I could see the ship quite clearly now, a Japanese tuna fisher. Her gray and white paint stood out clearly against the dark cross-swell. "Like a great white bird," Lyn said to the twins, and she would pass within about a mile of us at her nearest approach. I relayed the information as they listened excitedly, the tension of not knowing, of imminent rescue, building like a tangible, touchable, unbearable unreality around me. My eye caught the outlines of two large sharks a hundred yards to starboard. "Watch the trim," I warned. "We have two man-eating sharks waiting if we capsize!" Then, "I'm going to light the flare now; have the torch ready in case it doesn't work."

I ripped the caps off, pulled out the striker, and struck the primer. The flare smoked, then sparked into life, the red glare illuminating *Ednamair* and the sea around us in the twilight. I could feel my index finger roasting under the heat of the flare and waved it to and fro to escape the searing heat radiating outward in the calm air; then, unable to bear the heat any longer, I dropped my arm, nearly scorching Lyn's face, and threw the flare high in the air. It curved in a brilliant arc and dropped into the sea. "Hand me another; I think she's altered course!" My voice was hoarse with pain and excitement, and I filled with apprehension that it might only be the ship cork-screwing in the swell,

The crew of the *Ednamair* (the rescued) with the crew of the *Toka Maru II* (the rescuers).

for she had made no signal that she had seen us. The second flare didn't work. I cursed it in frustrated anguish as the priming substance chipped off instead of lighting. "The torch!" I shouted, but it wasn't needed; she had seen us and was coming toward us.

I flopped down on the thwart. "Our ordeal is over," I said quietly. Lyn and the twins were crying with happiness; Douglas, with tears of joy in his eyes, hugged his mother. Robin laughed and cried at the same time, slapped me on the back, and shouted, "Wonderful! We've done it. Oh! Wonderful!" I put my arms about Lyn, feeling the tears stinging my own eyes. "We'll get these boys to land after all." As we shared our happiness and watched the fishing boat close with us, death could have taken me quite easily just then, for I knew that I would never experience another such pinnacle of contentment. ❧

---

18. despondency (di spän′ dən sē): hopelessness.

*R*esponding to Reading

First Impressions

1. In your opinion, which part of the Robertsons' ordeal is the most memorable? In your journal or on a sheet of paper, write your impressions.

Second Thoughts

2. What factors do you think helped the Robertsons to survive? Explain your ideas.

   Think about
   - the crew members' physical abilities and knowledge
   - their inner strengths (psychological and spiritual)
   - the circumstances beyond their control

3. Do you think Dougal Robertson is a hero or a fool? Explain.

4. If you had gone through this ordeal with the Robertsons, what would have been the worst hardship for you to endure? Explain how you would have tried to cope with it.

5. What do you think was the most important item the Robertsons had with them? Now that you've read about the Robertsons' experience, in what ways might you revise your ranking of items for Examine What You Know?

6. What lasting effects do you think this trip might have had on the twelve-year-old twins?

Broader Connections

7. Dougal and Lyn Robertson believed that sailing around the world would teach their children more than they could learn if they stayed in school. Explain why you agree or disagree with the Robertsons' educational beliefs.

Writing Options

1. Imagine that you are a reporter who has been granted an exclusive interview with the Robertsons after their ordeal. To prepare, write your **pre-interview notes,** including five to ten questions you want to be sure to ask them.

2. After killing a shark, Dougal Robertson creates this motto for his family: "Sharks would not eat Robertsons; Robertsons would eat sharks." Write a **motto,** or slogan, that describes the spirit of your family. Then explain the qualities of your family that make your motto appropriate.

3. Write a **ship's log entry** from the point of view of the captain of the ship that rescued the Robertsons. Describe the rescue, the condition of the people in the life raft, and what they did and said once on board your ship.

4. Imagine that you are in a situation similar to the Robertsons', stranded in a boat in the ocean. You can keep with you one personal possession that is not a necessity. Which possession will you choose? Write an **essay** explaining the special importance of the item you choose.

Vocabulary Practice

Exercise Decide if the words in each pair are synonyms or antonyms. On your paper write *S* for synonyms or *A* for antonyms.

1. alternative—choice
2. debris—wreckage
3. buckle—collapse
4. undulation—flatness
5. exertion—effort
6. obscure—show
7. clamber—scramble
8. testily—gleefully
9. dwindling—increasing
10. derive—obtain
11. dispersing—scattering
12. reproachfully—approvingly
13. ruefully—happily
14. spiraling—circling
15. deteriorate—improve

Words to Know and Use

alternative
buckle
clamber
debris
derive
deteriorate
dispersing
dwindling
exertion
obscure
reproachfully
ruefully
spiraling
testily
undulation

*O*ptions for Learning

1 • Survivors! Research another true survival story. Your local librarian can direct you to books and magazine articles on this topic. Make a chart showing the similarities and the differences between the story you research and the Robertsons' experience. Share what you discover in an oral report to your class.

2 • The Robertsons Speak With several classmates stage a press conference. Imagine that the Robertson family is being interviewed after their rescue. Play the roles of the reporters and the Robertsons. To prepare, read the rest of the book *Survive the Savage Sea.*

3 • Robertson Cruise Company Create a humorous brochure advertising the Robertson Vacation Survival Cruise, a round-the-world trip for hardy travelers. Include captioned pictures and persuasive descriptions.

4 • Survival Game With a classmate create a survival game. You might decide to make this a board game, with various penalties and bonuses on the way to the final rescue. Study a popular board game to get ideas for your game.

 FACT FINDER SCIENCE

How long can a human survive without food? without water?

*D*ougal Robertson
1924–1992

Born in Edinburgh, Scotland, Dougal Robertson served during World War II with the British Merchant Marine. After the war, Robertson worked as a sailor in the Far East, eventually winning a master mariner's certificate.

In Hong Kong, Robertson met and married Lyn, a nurse in the Colonial Nursing Service. Dougal and Lyn Robertson spent the next seventeen years raising their four children on a dairy farm in England.

In 1968, the family was discussing a world yacht race when nine-year-old Neil asked, "Daddy's a sailor—why can't we go round the world?" The idea intrigued the family, and two years later they began their voyage. In 1973, Dougal told the complete story of their ordeal in his book *Survive the Savage Sea.* He wrote, "Survival is the hardest school in life; there are no failures."

INFORMATIVE WRITING

Are there rules governing Little League baseball? How did the welfare system begin, and has it been successful? These are a few of the questions that you might have asked yourself while reading this subunit. One way to find answers to these questions—and to other questions that you might have from your reading—is to research them and present your findings in a research report. A **research report** is a detailed informative report that investigates a particular topic. In a research report, you present and analyze information from a variety of sources.

USE INFORMATIVE
WRITING FOR

feature articles
biographies
instructions
consumer reports
essays
research papers

Here is one writer's PASSkey to this assignment.

GUIDED ASSIGNMENT: RESEARCH REPORT

Write an in-depth research report on a topic related to one of the selections in this book or on another topic of interest to you.

P URPOSE: To inform
A UDIENCE: Readers who are interested in your topic
S UBJECT: A topic that interests you
S TRUCTURE: A research report

Black Contributions to the Whaling Industry
by Andrew Fleming

Before the Civil War, few professions were open to black workers. One business, however, that did accept black people was whaling. People of all races could find work in the whaling industry because poor conditions and wages and long voyages made whaling unpopular work. Several blacks made significant contributions to American whaling. These black workers served as sailors, shipbuilders, and blacksmiths.

. . . .

Another noteworthy black who made a great contribution was Lewis Temple.

◄ **STUDENT MODEL**
Before you write, read how one student responded to the assignment.

◄ The introduction states the topic and lets the reader know what the writer plans to do.

◄ The middle section of Andrew's report is not shown.

Lewis Temple was born in Richmond, Virginia, in 1784. Records do not indicate whether he was a free man or a slave. Later, he moved to New Bedford, Massachusetts, an important whaling seaport during the early 1800s. In 1829, Temple married a free black woman. He worked as a blacksmith until his death in 1854.

This paragraph develops the first main idea. A direct quote from a source is given to provide details. Notice that Andrew introduces the quote by using the words *According to*. This shows the reader where the information comes from.

Lewis Temple's business was making iron tools for the whaling industry. His main duty was making and molding harpoons, an important tool used at that time to capture whales. According to <u>Cobblestone</u> magazine, "Temple was familiar with the fact that many harpoons cut their way out of the whale's flesh." Thus, many whales were able to escape.

In 1848, Lewis Temple designed a new type of harpoon. He hoped this harpoon would help sailors hang on to more of the whales they struck. Instead of a fixed head, the head of Temple's new harpoon was attached to a toggle, a small flexible bolt. In this way, the toggle would allow the barbed head to pivot as the harpooned whale plunged away, thus hooking the harpoon more firmly into the whale's flesh.

The conclusion summarizes the main ideas.

Temple's idea worked, and the new "Temple Toggle" harpoon was soon being used by almost all U.S. whalers. Thus, Lewis Temple made an important contribution to the history of whaling in the United States.

List of Works Cited

Bigg, Michael A. "Whale." <u>The World Book Encyclopedia.</u> 1988 ed.

Ellis, Richard. <u>Men and Whales.</u> New York: Knopf, 1991.

Shebar, Sharon Sigmond. <u>Whaling for Glory.</u> New York: Messner, 1978.

Weston, Beth Turin. "Temple's Toggle." <u>Cobblestone</u> Apr. 1984: 26-27.

Now begin a research report on a topic that interests you.

Prewrite and Explore

1 **Review your reading**   If you need some writing ideas, look through the table of contents for this book. Think about some of the subjects discussed in the selections. Brainstorm a list of topics, then choose the one that interests you most.

2 **Narrow your topic**   Once you've chosen a topic, be sure it will work as the focus of a research report. Can you find enough information? Can you cover it completely in the time and space allowed? To answer these questions, do some preliminary reading in general sources such as an encyclopedia. You may find that you want to slightly refocus your topic. Because there was so much information available about whaling, Andrew narrowed his topic to cover one person's contribution to the whaling industry.

WRITER'S CHOICE
You can also try skimming the *Books in Print* Subject listing for each possible topic. One of the book titles may suggest an approach to or aspect of the topic that interests you.

GATHERING INFORMATION

Make sure the sources you find tell you what you need to know. On separate index cards, write down publication information for each of your sources. Number each card. You will use this number as a reference when you take notes. You also need this information to create a list of sources for the end of your report. Make sure you have the following information on each source card.

```
Book—author, title, city of publication,
   publisher, copyright date
Magazine—author, title of article, name and date
   of magazine, page numbers
Encyclopedia—author, title of article, name of
   encyclopedia, year of edition
```

As you read, take notes on index cards. Use one card for each piece of information. Do not copy information word for word. Summarize the information or jot down phrases as Andrew did.

[Topic]	[Source Number]	[Page Number]
Lewis Temple	3	143

```
--born in Richmond, Virginia, in 1784
--not known whether free person or slave
--was blacksmith on whaling ship
--invented toggle harpoon
```

◀ SOURCES
Check the card catalog or the computer catalog in the library. Use the *Readers' Guide to Periodical Literature* to locate magazine articles. You can also look for articles in encyclopedias and other reference books.

COMPUTER TIP
List your information sources in a computer document rather than on paper. Later you can alphabetize this list and attach it to your finished report.

3 **Say it your way**   When you copy what an author says word for word, you are writing a **direct quote.** You must enclose direct quotes in quotation marks and give credit to the person who wrote the words. If you leave the quotation marks out, you are guilty of **plagiarism** (plā′ jə riz′ əm), or stealing someone else's words. When Andrew included a direct quote from a magazine article, he used quotation marks to make it clear he was using someone else's ideas.

4 **Organize your notes**   Review your notes. Separate your note cards into stacks according to main idea. Then decide on two or three main ideas to include in your report. For example, Andrew separated his notes into stacks for each time period in Lewis Temple's life.

Draft and Discover

1 **Outline your report**   Think about your purpose for writing a research paper. Then review your notes, paying special attention to the headings on your note cards. Sort the cards into groups of related ideas. Then turn each group into a major division of your outline. Write the main ideas as outline headings. Write specific facts from your note cards as subheadings. To see how this works, look at Andrew's outline.

STUDENT MODEL ▶

```
                        Title
      I.  Introduction
     II.  Lewis Temple
          A. Year of birth, place of birth
          B. Free man or slave?
    III.  Contributions
          A. Blacksmith
             1. Made harpoons
             2. Recognized flaws
          B. Inventor
             1. Created "Temple Toggle"
             2. Changed whaling practices
     IV.  Conclusion
```

2 **Begin drafting**   As you write, use your outline as a guide. Refer to your note cards if necessary. Try creating topic sentences from the main ideas in each heading of your outline. Then write sentences that include details to support each topic sentence.

3 **Be flexible**   Be flexible when you write the first draft. As your paper takes shape, you may find that some information is unnecessary or that you need additional facts. Remember, you can always do more research. For now, however, just make a note in your draft to hold a space for that information and then keep writing.

4 **Wind up**   Draft a conclusion that sums up all your ideas. This last paragraph should provide a clear ending without being dull or simply repeating what you've already said.

5 **Cite your sources**   Write your list of sources in alphabetical order according to the authors' last names. If no author was given for a source, list the title of the article or book first.

Revise Your Writing

1 **Make connections**   Smooth out the rough edges. Consider how well your information flows together. Is it in the best sequence? Does each idea connect with the others around it?

2 **Add some punch**   Is your report interesting to read? Does your prose sound lively and engaging? As you revise your draft, consider varying your sentence structure. Focus also on choosing precise and vivid language.

3 **Check with a peer reader**   Ask a friend to review your revised draft. Use the following questions as a guide.

WRITER'S CHOICE
Remember, your outline is only a guide. As you draft, you may decide to reorganize your ideas or even to refocus your paper completely.

NEED HELP?
For more information about how to list sources, see Guidelines for Research and Report Writing in the Writer's Handbook.

NEED MORE HELP?
For help in understanding how sentence structure can be varied, see "Sentence Combining," the Language Workshop on pages 301–303.

Revision Questions

For You	For a Peer Reader
1. Does my introduction tell about the topic?	**1.** Did I clearly state my main ideas? Were my supporting details clear and complete?
2. Is my language descriptive and lively?	**2.** Did you find any part of my report difficult to follow?
3. Have I included enough information to cover my topic?	**3.** Do you fully understand my topic now?

Proofread

After revising your paper, reread it for mistakes in grammar, punctuation, capitalization, and punctuation. Double-check dates, names, and direct quotes. If possible, ask a friend to review your paper too.

NEED MORE HELP?
See the Language Workshop that follows (pages 639–640) and pages 785–788 of the Language Handbook.

THE EDITOR'S EYE: CORRECT VERB TENSES

Use correct verb tenses when showing two or more actions that occur at the same time.

When you write, you must be sure to keep your tenses consistent. Ask yourself when each event takes place.

Incorrect	In 1829, Temple *marries* a free black woman. He *worked* as a blacksmith until his death in 1854.
Correct	In 1829, Temple *married* a free black woman. He *worked* as a blacksmith until his death in 1854.

Publish and Present

Here is a suggestion for sharing your work with others.

Information Booklet   With your classmates, choose several interesting reports on related topics and combine them into an information booklet. Add photographs, charts, or other visuals to highlight each report. As a group, write an introduction to the booklet that explains how each report addresses the overall subject.

Reflect on Your Writing

Consider the questions below. Attach your answers to your paper and place both in your portfolio.

FOR YOUR PORTFOLIO ▶

1. What was your greatest challenge in writing a research paper? Which part of the process did you find the most interesting?
2. Think about the research techniques you used in writing your report. How might you apply these techniques to other classes and other kinds of papers?

LANGUAGE
WORKSHOP

USING VERB TENSES CORRECTLY

Use the correct **verb tense** to show when an action occurs.

Verbs tell you not only what action occurs in a sentence but also *when* the action occurs. By changes in their form, verbs indicate whether an action takes place in the present, the past, or the future. These changes in form are called tenses. Every verb has six **tenses.**

Tenses of the Verb *Drift*		
Present	The raft *drifts.*	Shows an action that occurs now
Past	The raft *drifted.*	Shows an action completed in the past
Future	The raft *will drift.*	Shows an action that will occur in the future
Present Perfect	The raft *has drifted.*	Shows an action completed in the past or that began in the past and continues into the present
Past Perfect	The raft *had drifted.*	Shows an action in the past that occurred before another action in the past
Future Perfect	The raft *will have drifted.*	Shows an action in the future that will occur before another future action or time

PROGRESSIVE FORMS

Each verb tense also has a progressive form, which shows continuous action. To form the progressive, add a form of the verb *be* to the verb's present participle. Example:
The raft *is drifting.*
The raft *was drifting.*
The raft *will be drifting.*
The raft *has been drifting.*
The raft *had been drifting.*
The raft *will have been drifting.*

Making Correct Shifts in Tense

> Use the same tense to show two or more actions that occur at the same time.

In your writing, keep your tenses consistent.

Incorrect	The janitor *vacuums* the rug and *washed* the floors.
Correct	The janitor *vacuums* the rug and *washes* the floors.
Correct	The janitor *vacuumed* the rug and *washed* the floors.

There are times, however, when shifting the verb tense makes your meaning clearer.

> The janitor *will have finished* (future perfect) cleaning the apartment by the time the new tenants *arrive* (present).

Exercise 1　Concept Check　Write the correct verb tenses.

1. In 1845, Alexander Cartwright (started, starts) a club that he later (will call, called) the Knickerbocker Base Ball Club of New York.
2. Cartwright and others (wrote, had written) a set of baseball rules after he (had organized, will organize) the club.
3. The rules (established, will have established) the distance between bases and (provide, provided) for nine players on each team.
4. Later, the club (added, had added) two more rules that (did, does) much to make baseball the game it is today.
5. An 1848 addition (includes, included) the rule of tagging first base to put a batter out on a ground ball; in 1854, the force-out rule (will be added, was added).

PROOFREADING TIP
Whenever you proofread your writing, check for unnecessary changes in verb tense that may confuse your reader.

Exercise 2　Proofreading Skill　Rewrite the following paragraph, correcting any errors in verb tense.

> Pets helped people in many ways. Victims of autism—a disease in which people will live in a world of their own—failed to communicate with others. Autistic children touched pets and began to communicate with adults. Pets also will help fight heart disease. Doctors studied ninety-three heart patients, over half of whom will have owned pets. A year later, one-third of the petless patients had died, and all but three of the pet-owning patients were still alive.

LANGUAGE HANDBOOK
For review and practice: Section 5, Using Verbs, pages 785–788.

Exercise 3　Revising Your Writing　Reread the research report you wrote for the Writer's Workshop on pages 633–638. Circle and correct any errors that you find in verb tense.

READER'S WORKSHOP

ADJUSTING READING RATES

When you read to gather information, you need to vary your reading rate to suit your research goals. When you want to find a specific fact, **scanning,** or sweeping your eyes across each page, allows you to quickly spot what you are looking for.

If you need to understand the main idea of a piece or to get an overview of its contents, **skimming** is more appropriate. To skim, read the title, headlines, any highlighted words or phrases, and the topic sentences. In addition, read any introduction, conclusion, or summary.

When studying, you'll need to read material more slowly and thoroughly. First, skim the piece to get an overview. Next, slow down and carefully read the material, looking for main ideas and supporting details. Notice all the key words, dates, and facts. As you read, take careful notes.

Exercise   Follow these directions step by step. Do not read through all the directions at once.

Step 1   Skim the following article Write one sentence that summarizes the main idea of the article.
Step 2   Scan the article to find two examples of unusual animals found in the Galápagos Islands.
Step 3   Read the article in depth. Write at least three details that support the main idea of the article.

The Galápagos Islands are located in the Pacific Ocean about 600 miles west of Ecuador. They are made up of volcanic peaks and cover an area of 3,029 square miles. There are fifteen islands in all, but the five largest are Isabela, Santa Cruz, San Cristobal, Fernandina, and San Salvador. About 6,000 people live on the islands.

The Galápagos Islands are important because of the many unusual birds and animals that are found there. Among the birds are a cormorant that cannot fly; the penguin, thought by many to live only in the Antarctic region; and a rare type of mockingbird. Other birds include the heron and the booby, a type of sea bird.

Most fantastic of all the animals in the Galápagos are the iguanas. Many of them are four feet long. There are also huge turtles that weigh more than five hundred pounds. The Spanish word for the turtles, *galápagos,* gave the islands their name.

◀ HOW TO SCAN
To practice scanning, try the following steps:
1. Choose a familiar textbook.
2. Place a folded paper or index card over the first line of a page. Then move the paper quickly down the page.
3. Watch for key words or phrases that suggest you are near the information you need.
4. When you spot such clues, slow down and read more carefully.

Reading on Your Own

Suggested Novels for Unit Five

The novels introduced on these pages will allow you to explore the unit theme, "The Will to Survive." The main characters in these novels struggle to overcome great obstacles.

SCORPIONS

WALTER DEAN MYERS ©1988

Many young people in the inner city fear that gang involvement might destroy them. Twelve-year-old Jamal Hicks is no different. He constantly worries about his life in Harlem—especially his connection with the Scorpions, a street gang run by his older brother Randy. When Randy is jailed for holding up a delicatessen, he asks Jamal to run the Scorpions. Jamal's mother and Tito, his best friend, try desperately to reason with him, hoping that he will not take part in the gang's activities. Despite their wishes—and his own hesitancy—Jamal takes over the gang. Unfortunately, his decision leads to tragic results. As you read, try to imagine what life is like for Jamal. Ask yourself . . .

- why Jamal agrees to his brother's request that he lead the Scorpions

- what happens when he makes his decision

- how his involvement in the Scorpions leads to tragic results

WHERE THE LILIES BLOOM
VERA AND BILL CLEAVER ©1969

Imagine that you were suddenly faced with the responsibility of supporting younger brothers and sisters. What would you do? In *Where the Lilies Bloom*, Mary Call Luther, the fourteen-year-old daughter of an Appalachian sharecropper, struggles to support the younger members of her family after the death of their father. Mary Call and her siblings secretly bury their father in hopes that the authorities will not learn of his death. Think about Mary Call's character traits as you read this novel. Consider these questions:

• Why doesn't Mary Call want the authorities to learn of her father's death?

• What gives Mary Call the strength to hold her family together?

• How does Mary Call manage to support her family?

NO HERO FOR THE KAISER
RUDOLF FRANK ©1931, ©1983

Jan Kubitzky will never forget his fourteenth birthday. On that day—September 14, 1914—Jan is caught in the middle of fighting between Russian and German soldiers deep in the Polish woods. The Germans drive the Russians back to the east, and then they destroy Kopchovka, the hamlet that Jan calls home. Sadly, only Jan and his little dog Flox survive. Jan is taken by the Germans, and for over two years he learns everything about war—much more than he wants to know. Read to find out . . .

• what Jan learns about war

• what decision he makes

• whether it is the right decision

Other Recommended Books

Franklin Delano Roosevelt by Russell Freedman (©1990). This fascinating biography describes the life of Franklin Delano Roosevelt, who overcame great obstacles to become the thirty-second president of the United States.

Rice Without Rain by Minfong Ho (©1990). A poor village in Thailand faces the prospect of crop failure. The villagers listen to strangers with revolutionary ideas that could change the little village forever.

Lost in the Barrens by Farley Mowat (©1956). A Woodland Cree boy and a white boy fight for survival in a remote arctic wilderness.

Talking in Whispers by James Watson (©1984). In this political thriller, a young boy is hunted by the security forces of an oppressive military government.

THEMES IN FOLKLORE FROM THE AMERICAS

W e have stories

as old as the great seas

breaking through the chest

flying out the mouth.

Linda Hogan

THE BLIND STORYTELLER
1987 Julio Larraz
Courtesy, Nohra Haime Gallery,
New York.

645

UNIT PREVIEW

The unit you are about to read is set apart from the other units in two ways.

Folklore All the selections in this unit are classified as folklore–traditional literature that was passed along by word of mouth before being written down. You will learn more about such literature in Elements of Folklore on pages 648–649.

Thematic Links to Previous Units The folklore in this unit is divided into five groups. The selections in each group relate to the theme of a previous unit in this book. For example, the first group of folklore selections extends the theme of Unit One, "Personal Codes."

Elements of FOLKLORE

Folklore can be defined as all the traditions, customs, and stories that are passed along by word of mouth in a culture. The stories of folklore have their beginnings in spoken language, not the written word. Because these stories are passed along from teller to teller and from generation to generation, their authorship cannot be traced to any one person. A single story may undergo frequent changes as each storyteller adds his or her special twist. Typically, folklore stories are collected and written down only after they have been told for many years. Most of the stories you will read in this unit were not created by the authors listed but were retold or translated by them.

When storytellers weave their tales, they offer more than entertainment. Their stories **keep the past alive,** introducing young people to the history, beliefs, and religions of their societies. The stories **teach moral lessons** and **illustrate qualities that are valued by the society,** such as kindness or courage. They also **expose negative qualities,** like greed and foolishness.

Very often, the same basic story appears in different cultures. For example, versions of the Cinderella story have been found in Europe, Africa, Asia, and the Americas. The similarities in these stories point to values that many cultures hold in common.

Most American folklore reflects the same characteristics as the folklore of other cultures. Some American folklore, however, takes on a very special flavor. Early American settlers faced the incredible challenge of taming the vast wilderness that stretched from the Atlantic Ocean to the Pacific Ocean. Settlers had two choices—give up or cope. One way of coping was to tell stories about the rugged heroes and heroines who tamed the wilderness and made it safe for all that followed. Stories of folk heroes and heroines, both real and fictional, were soon popping up in every region of the country. John Henry, Davy Crockett, Calamity Jane, Paul Bunyan, Flatboat Annie—these are only a few of the heroes and heroines that have become part of American folklore.

Folklore can be grouped into four major categories: **myths, folk tales, fables,** and **legends.**

*M*yths

Myths were created to answer basic questions about the world and human life. Myths tell about events from the distant past and were considered truthful and often sacred by the societies that told them.

Many myths offer explanations of natural events. You will read a Blackfoot **creation myth** about the origin of death.

*F*olk Tales

Folk tales are told primarily for entertainment; they are not supposed to be truthful or factual.

The characters in folk tales are either ordinary humans or animals that act like humans. Typically, the humans are peasants or other members of the lower class; often, they are portrayed as having better values than the rich and powerful.

These tales are told in a simple style, sometimes with each character representing one human trait (greed, curiosity, or kindness, for example). In many folk tales, magic and enchantment play a key role.

The themes of folk tales are usually simple—the reward of good, the punishment of evil, the exposing of a fool. Some folk tales teach practical lessons. Others illustrate moral truths or offer warnings.

Some folk tales, such as the **trickster tales**, poke fun at human weaknesses. In a trickster tale a smart person or animal outwits or takes advantage of a fool.

Fables

Fables are very short tales that illustrate a clear, often directly stated, **moral**—a principle of right and wrong behavior. The characters are often animals that act like humans. Often these animals have human faults.

Legends

Legends are considered factual by those who tell them, and many have some basis in historical fact. For example, the legends surrounding John Henry and Johnny Appleseed are based upon people who actually existed. These stories tend to be set in the recent past.

Tall tales are humorous legends with exaggerated characters and impossible events. Often the most important characters in American tall tales are heroes and heroines. They are usually strong, thoughtful, and courageous.

A special kind of legend is called the contemporary urban legend. **Contemporary urban legends** are realistic stories that are said to have happened recently. They often have a supernatural element, such as a ghost. Quite often they start out as rumors, but as they grow they begin to be accepted as true.

Strategies for Reading Folklore

1. **Enjoy** the tale. These stories are fun because they are filled with action and adventure. As you read, imagine the stories being repeated through many generations.

2. **Think about the purpose** of the story. Is its purpose to explain a mystery of nature, to teach a lesson, or to poke fun at human weaknesses?

3. **Look for values and customs** of the culture from which the story comes. What does the culture consider to be virtuous behavior, and how is this behavior rewarded? What traits are admired and respected? Which are not?

4. **Decide who holds the power** in the story. Do humans control their own fate, or are the gods or some supernatural power in charge?

5. **Compare the story** to another story that you know about, perhaps from some other culture. What do the stories have in common?

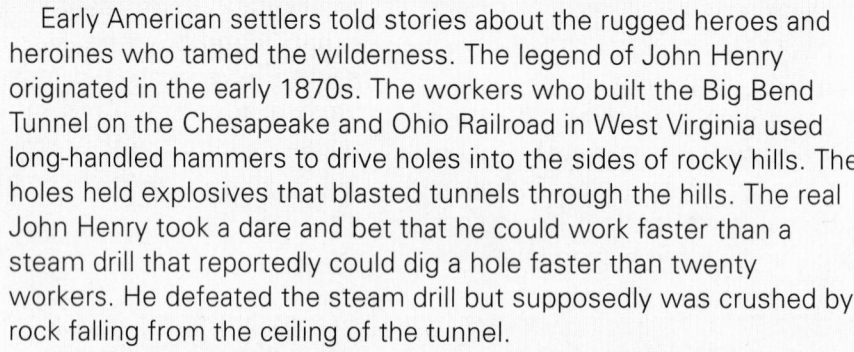

Personal Codes

**Links to
Unit One**

John Henry, the Hammerman ADRIEN STOUTENBURG
Pecos Bill and the Cyclone HAROLD W. FELTON
The Growin' of Paul Bunyan WILLIAM J. BROOKE

*E*xamine What You Know

Superman, known by many as a crime-fighting hero, usually triumphs over evil. In small groups, make a list of other American heroes and heroines, both real and fictional. Next to each name, jot down three important qualities each hero or heroine possesses.

*E*xpand Your Knowledge

Early American settlers told stories about the rugged heroes and heroines who tamed the wilderness. The legend of John Henry originated in the early 1870s. The workers who built the Big Bend Tunnel on the Chesapeake and Ohio Railroad in West Virginia used long-handled hammers to drive holes into the sides of rocky hills. The holes held explosives that blasted tunnels through the hills. The real John Henry took a dare and bet that he could work faster than a steam drill that reportedly could dig a hole faster than twenty workers. He defeated the steam drill but supposedly was crushed by rock falling from the ceiling of the tunnel.

The tall tales of Pecos Bill came from Texas in the 1830s. A hero of the American West, Pecos Bill was the legendary inventor of roping, branding, and many other cowboy skills. In "Pecos Bill and the Cyclone," he battles one of his toughest opponents.

Two legendary heroes—Paul Bunyan and Johnny Appleseed— meet in the third tale in this group. Lumberjacks first told the tales of Paul Bunyan. No task was too huge for this giant, who dug Puget Sound to transport his logs and who cleared forests to make good farmland. Johnny Appleseed was the name given to John Chapman (1774–1845), an American pioneer famous for planting apple trees in Pennsylvania, Ohio, and Indiana.

*W*rite Before You Read

■ *Author biographies
on Extend page*

In your journal, write about your favorite hero or heroine. In your opinion, what is this hero's personal code?

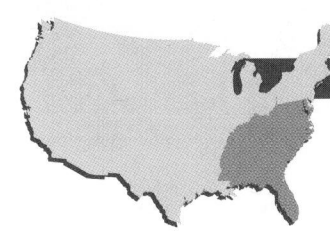

John Henry, the Hammerman

ADRIEN STOUTENBURG

People down South still tell stories about John Henry, how strong he was, and how he could whirl a big sledge so lightning-fast you could hear thunder behind it. They even say he was born with a hammer in his hand. John Henry himself said it, but he probably didn't mean it exactly as it sounded.

The story seems to be that when John Henry was a baby, the first thing he reached out for was a hammer, which was hung nearby on the cabin wall.

John Henry's father put his arm around his wife's shoulder. "He's going to grow up to be a steel-driving man. I can see it plain as rows of cotton running uphill."

As John Henry grew a bit older, he practiced swinging the hammer, not hitting at things, but just enjoying the feel of it whooshing against the air. When he was old enough to talk, he told everyone, "I was born with a hammer in my hand."

John Henry was still a boy when the Civil War started, but he was a big, hard-muscled boy, and he could outwork and outplay all the other boys on the plantation.

"You're going to be a mighty man, John Henry," his father told him.

"A man ain't nothing but a man," young John Henry said. "And I'm a natural man, born to swing a hammer in my hand."

At night, lying on a straw bed on the floor, John Henry listened to a far-off train whistling through the darkness. Railroad tracks had been laid to carry trainloads of Southern soldiers to fight against the armies of the North. The trains had a lonesome, longing sound that made John Henry want to go wherever they were going.

When the war ended, a man from the North came to John Henry where he was working in the field. He said, "The slaves are free now. You can pack up and go wherever you want, young fellow."

"I'm craving to go where the trains go," said John Henry.

I'm a steel-driving man.

The man shook his head. "There are too many young fellows trailing the trains around now. You better settle down to doing what you know, like handling a cotton hook or driving a mule team."

John Henry thought to himself, there's a big hammer waiting for me somewhere, because I know I'm a steel-driving man. All I have to do is hunt 'til I find it.

That night he told his folks about a dream he had had.

"I dreamed I was working on a railroad somewhere," he said, "a big, new railroad called the C. & O., and I had a mighty hammer in my hand. Every time I swung it, it made a whirling flash around my shoulder. And every time my hammer hit a spike, the sky lit up from the sparks."

"I believe it," his father said. "You were born to drive steel."

"That ain't all of the dream," John Henry said. "I dreamed that the railroad was going to be the end of me and I'd die with the hammer in my hand."

question   What was the meaning of John Henry's dream?

The next morning John Henry bundled up some food in a red bandanna handkerchief, told his parents goodbye, and set off into the world. He walked until he heard the clang-clang of hammers in the distance. He followed the sound to a place where gangs of men were building a railroad. John Henry watched the men driving steel spikes down into the crossties to hold the rails in place. Three men would stand around a spike, then each, in turn, would swing a long hammer.

John Henry's heart beat in rhythm with the falling hammers. His fingers ached for the feel of a hammer in his own hands. He walked over to the foreman.

"I'm a natural steel-driving man," he said. "And I'm looking for a job."

"How much steel driving have you done?" the foreman asked.

"I was born knowing how," John Henry said.

The foreman shook his head. "That ain't good enough, boy. I can't take any chances.

Steel driving's dangerous work, and you might hit somebody."

"I wouldn't hit anybody," John Henry said, "because I can drive one of those spikes all by myself."

The foreman said sharply, "The one kind of man I don't need in this outfit is a bragger. Stop wasting my time."

John Henry didn't move. He got a stubborn look around his jaw. "You loan me a hammer, mister, and if somebody will hold the spike for me, I'll prove what I can do."

The three men who had just finished driving in a spike looked toward him and laughed. One of them said, "Anybody who would hold a spike for a greenhorn[1] don't want to live long."

"I'll hold it," a fourth man said.

John Henry saw that the speaker was a small, dark-skinned fellow about his own age.

The foreman asked the small man, "D'you aim to get yourself killed, Li'l Willie?"

Li'l Willie didn't answer. He knelt and set a spike down through the rail on the crosstie. "Come on, big boy," he said.

John Henry picked up one of the sheep-nose hammers[2] lying in the cinders. He hefted it and decided it was too light. He picked up a larger one which weighed twelve pounds. The handle was lean and limber and greased with tallow to make it smooth.

Everyone was quiet, watching, as he stepped over to the spike.

John Henry swung the hammer over his shoulder so far that the hammer head hung

---

1. **greenhorn**: a beginner.
2. **sheep-nose hammers**: long-handled hammers with tapered heads.

down against the back of his knees. He felt a thrill run through his arms and chest.

"Tap it down gentle, first," said Li'l Willie.

But John Henry had already started to swing. He brought the hammer flashing down, banging the spike squarely on the head. Before the other men could draw a breath of surprise, the hammer flashed again, whirring through the air like a giant hummingbird. One more swing, and the spike was down, its steel head smoking from the force of the blow.

The foreman blinked, swallowed, and blinked again. "Man," he told John Henry, "you're hired!"

That's the way John Henry started steel driving. From then on, Li'l Willie was always with him, setting the spikes or placing the drills that John Henry drove with his hammer. There wasn't another steel-driving man in the world who could touch John Henry for speed and power. He could hammer every which way, up or down or sidewise. He could drive for ten hours at a stretch and never miss a stroke.

A MAN AIN'T NOTHING BUT A MAN   Palmer C. Hayden
Museum of African American Art, Palmer C. Hayden Collection,
Gift of Miriam A. Hayden.

review   How did John Henry become a steel-driving man?

After he'd been at the work for a few years, he started using a twenty-pound hammer in each hand. It took six men, working fast, to carry fresh drills to him. People would come for miles around to watch John Henry.

Whenever John Henry worked, he sang. Li'l Willie sang with him, chanting the rhythm of the clanging hammer strokes.

Those were happy days for John Henry. One of the happiest days came when he met a black-eyed, curly-haired girl called Polly Ann. And, on the day that Polly Ann said she would marry him, John Henry almost burst his throat with singing.

Every now and then, John Henry would remember the strange dream he had had years before, about the C. & O. Railroad and dying with a hammer in his hand. One night, he had the dream again. The next morning, when he went to work, the steel gang gathered round him, hopping with excitement.

"The Chesapeake and Ohio Railroad wants men to drive a tunnel through a mountain in West Virginia!" they said.

"The C. & O. wants the best hammermen there are!" they said. "And they'll pay twice as much as anybody else."

Li'l Willie looked at John Henry. "If they want the best, John Henry, they're goin' to need you."

John Henry looked back at his friend. "They're going to need you, too, Li'l Willie. I ain't going without you." He stood a minute, looking at the sky. There was a black thundercloud way off, with sunlight flashing behind it. John Henry felt a small chill between his shoulder blades. He shook himself, put his hammer on his shoulder, and said, "Let's go, Willie!"

When they reached Summers County where the Big Bend Tunnel was to be built, John Henry sized up the mountain standing in the way. It was almost solid rock.

"Looks soft," said John Henry. "Hold a drill up there, Li'l Willie."

Li'l Willie did. John Henry took a seventy-pound hammer and drove the drill in with one mountain-cracking stroke. Then he settled down to working the regular way, pounding in the drills with four or five strokes of a twenty-pound sledge. He worked so fast that his helpers had to keep buckets of water ready to pour on his hammers so they wouldn't catch fire.

Polly Ann, who had come along to West Virginia, sat and watched and cheered him on. She sang along with him, clapping her hands to the rhythm of his hammer, and the sound echoed around the mountains. The songs blended with the rumble of dynamite where the blasting crews were at work. For every time John Henry drilled a hole in the mountain's face, other men poked dynamite

and black powder into the hole and then lighted a fuse to blow the rock apart.

One day the tunnel boss, Cap'n Tommy Walters, was standing watching John Henry when a stranger in city clothes walked up to him.

"Howdy, Cap'n Tommy," said the stranger. "I'd like to talk to you about a steam engine I've got for sale. My engine can drive a drill through rock so fast that not even a crew of your best men can keep up with it."

"I don't need any machine," Cap'n Tommy said proudly. "My man John Henry can out-drill any machine ever built."

"I'll place a bet with you, Cap'n," said the salesman. "You race your man against my machine for a full day. If he wins, I'll give you the steam engine free."

Cap'n Tommy thought it over. "That sounds fair enough, but I'll have to talk to John Henry first." He told John Henry what the stranger had said. "Are you willing to race a steam drill?" Cap'n Tommy asked.

John Henry ran his big hands over the handle of his hammer, feeling the strength in the wood and in his own great muscles.

"A man's a man," he said, "but a machine ain't nothing but a machine. I'll beat that steam drill, or I'll die with my hammer in my hand!"

"All right, then," said Cap'n Tommy. "We'll set a day for the contest."

Polly Ann looked worried when John Henry told her what he had promised to do.

"Don't you worry, honey," John Henry said. It was the end of the workday, with the sunset burning across the mountain and the sky shining like copper. He tapped his chest. "I've got a man's heart in here. All a machine has is a metal engine." He smiled and picked Polly Ann up in his arms, as if she were no heavier than a blade of grass.

On the morning of the contest, the slopes around the tunnel were crowded with people. At one side stood the steam engine, its gears and valves and mechanical drill gleaming. Its operators rushed around, giving it final spurts of grease and oil and shoving fresh pine knots into the fire that fed the steam boiler.

John Henry stood leaning on his hammer, as still as the mountain rock, his shoulders shining like hard coal in the rising sun.

"How do you feel, John Henry?" asked Li'l Willie. Li'l Willie's hands trembled a bit as he held the drill ready.

"I feel like a bird ready to bust out of a nest egg," John Henry said. "I feel like a rooster ready to crow. I feel pride hammering at my heart, and I can hardly wait to get started against that machine." He sucked in the mountain air. "I feel powerful free, Li'l Willie."

Cap'n Tommy held up the starting gun. For a second everything was as silent as the dust in a drill hole. Then the gun barked, making a yelp that bounced against mountain and sky.

John Henry swung his hammer, and it rang against the drill.

At the same time, the steam engine gave a roar and a hiss. Steam whistled through its escape valve. Its drill crashed down, gnawing into the granite.

John Henry paid no attention to anything except his hammer, nor to any sound except the steady pumping of his heart. At the end of an hour, he paused long enough to ask, "How are we doing, Li'l Willie?"

Willie licked his lips. His face was pale with rock dust and with fear. "The machine's ahead, John Henry."

John Henry tossed his smoking hammer aside and called to another helper, "Bring me two hammers! I'm only getting warmed up."

He began swinging a hammer in each hand. Sparks flew so fast and hot they singed his face. The hammers heated up until they glowed like torches.

"How're we doing now, Li'l Willie?" John Henry asked at the end of another hour.

Li'l Willie grinned. "The machine's drill busted. They have to take time to fix up a new one. You're almost even now, John Henry! How're you feeling?"

"I'm feeling like sunrise," John Henry took time to say before he flashed one of his hammers down against the drill. "Clean out the hole, Willie, and we'll drive right down to China."

Above the clash of his hammers, he heard the chug and hiss of the steam engine starting up again and the whine of its rotary drill biting into rock. The sound hurt John Henry's ears.

"Sing me a song, Li'l Willie!" he gasped. "Sing me a natural song for my hammers to sing along with."

Li'l Willie sang, and John Henry kept his hammers going in time. Hour after hour, he kept driving, sweat sliding from his forehead and chest.

The sun rolled past noon and toward the west.

"How're you feeling, John Henry?" Li'l Willie asked.

"I ain't tired yet," said John Henry, and he stood back, gasping, while Willie put a freshly sharpened drill into the rock wall.

HAMMER IN HIS HAND
Palmer C. Hayden
Museum of African American Art,
Palmer C. Hayden Collection,
Gift of Miriam A. Hayden.

"Only, I have a kind of roaring in my ears."

"That's only the steam engine," Li'l Willie said, but he wet his lips again. "You're gaining on it, John Henry. I reckon you're at least two inches ahead."

John Henry coughed and slung his hammer back. "I'll beat it by a mile, before the sun sets."

At the end of another hour, Li'l Willie called out, his eyes sparkling, "You're going to win, John Henry, if you can keep on drivin'!"

John Henry ground his teeth together and tried not to hear the roar in his ears or the racing thunder of his heart. "I'll go until I drop," he gasped. "I'm a steel-driving man and I'm bound to win, because a machine ain't nothing but a machine."

The sun slid lower. The shadows of the crowd grew long and purple.

"John Henry can't keep it up," someone said.

"The machine can't keep it up," another said.

Polly Ann twisted her hands together and waited for Cap'n Tommy to fire the gun to mark the end of the contest.

"Who's winning?" a voice cried.

"Wait and see," another voice answered.

There were only ten minutes left.

"How're you feeling, John Henry?" Li'l Willie whispered, sweat dripping down his own face.

John Henry didn't answer. He just kept slamming his hammers against the drill, his mouth open.

Li'l Willie tried to go on singing. "Flash that hammer—uh! Wham that drill—uh!" he croaked.

Out beside the railroad tracks, Polly beat

her hands together in time, until they were numb.

The sun flared an instant, then died behind the mountain. Cap'n Tommy's gun cracked. The judges ran forward to measure the depth of the holes drilled by the steam engine and by John Henry. At last the judges came walking back and said something to Cap'n Tommy before they turned to announce their findings to the crowd.

Cap'n Tommy walked over to John Henry, who stood leaning against the face of the mountain.

"John Henry," he said, "you beat that steam engine by four feet!" He held out his hand and smiled.

John Henry heard a distant cheering. He held his own hand out, and then he staggered. He fell and lay on his back, staring up at the mountain and the sky, and then he saw Polly Ann and Li'l Willie leaning over him.

"Oh, how do you feel, John Henry?" Polly Ann asked.

"I feel a bit tuckered out," said John Henry.

"Do you want me to sing to you?" Li'l Willie asked.

"I got a song in my own heart, thank you, Li'l Willie," John Henry said. He raised up on his elbow and looked at all the people and the last sunset light gleaming like the edge of a golden trumpet. "I was a steel-driving man," he said and lay back and closed his eyes forever.

Down South, and in the North, too, people still talk about John Henry and how he beat the steam engine at the Big Bend Tunnel. They say if John Henry were alive today, he could beat almost every other kind of machine, too.

Maybe so. At least John Henry would die trying. 🐚

In what way did the ending surprise you?

evaluate

Responding to Reading

1. Do you think John Henry was heroic or foolhardy to try to beat the steam drill? What other words would you use to describe him? Explain your thoughts in your journal or on a sheet of paper.

2. Do you agree that, like John Henry, most people have a destiny to fulfill—one particular thing they are born to do? Explain.

3. Like the steam drill in John Henry's day, modern machines often take jobs away from people. Machines, however, can also make our lives considerably easier. Are there any labor-saving machines today that you would argue against having? Explain.

Pecos Bill
and the Cyclone

HAROLD W. FELTON

One of Pecos Bill's greatest feats, if not the greatest feat of all time, occurred unexpectedly one Fourth of July. He had invented the Fourth of July some years before. It was a great day for Texas cowpunchers. They had taken to it right off like the real Americans they were. But the celebration had always ended on a dismal note. Somehow it seemed to be spoiled by a cyclone.

Bill had never minded the cyclone much. The truth is, he rather liked it. But the other celebrants ran into caves for safety. He invented cyclone cellars for them. He even named the cellars. He called them 'fraid holes. Pecos wouldn't even say the word *afraid*. The cyclone was something like he was. It was big and strong, too. He always stood by, <u>musing</u> pleasantly as he watched it.

The cyclone caused Bill some trouble, though. Usually it would destroy a few hundred miles of fence by blowing the post holes away. But it wasn't much trouble for him to fix it. All he had to do was to go and get the post holes and then take them back and put the fence posts in them. The

holes were rarely blown more than twenty or thirty miles.

It should be said that in those days there was only one cyclone. It was the first and original cyclone, bigger and more terrible by far than the small cyclones of today. It usually stayed by itself up north, around Kansas and Oklahoma, and didn't bother anyone much. But it was attracted by the noise of the Fourth of July celebration in Texas and, without fail, managed to put in an appearance before the close of the day.

On this particular Fourth of July, the celebration had gone off fine. The speeches were loud and long. The contests and games were hard fought. The high point of the day was Bill's exhibition with his horse, Widow Maker.

Widow Maker had put on a good show, bucking as no ordinary horse could ever buck. Then Bill undertook to show the <u>gaits</u> he had taught the palomino. Other mustangs at that time had only two gaits, walking and running. Only Widow Maker could pace. But now Bill had developed and taught him other gaits. Twenty-seven in all. Twenty-four forward and three reverse. He was very proud of the achievement. He

Words to Know and Use	**musing** (myo͞oz′ iŋ) *adj.* thinking in a relaxed, quiet way **muse** *v.* **gait** (gāt) *n.* a foot movement of a horse

showed off the slow gaits, and the crowd was eager for more. He showed the walk, trot, canter, lope, jog, slow rack, fast rack, single-foot, pace, stepping pace, fox trot, and running walk and the others now known.

Then the cyclone came! All of the people except Bill ran into the 'fraid holes. Bill was annoyed. He stopped the performance. The remaining gaits were not shown. From that day to this, horses have used no more than the gaits Widow Maker was able to exhibit that day. It is unfortunate that the really fast gaits were not shown. If they had been, horses might be much faster today than they are.

Bill glanced up at the cyclone, and the quiet smile on his face slowly faded into a frown. He saw that the cyclone was angry. Very, very angry indeed.

The cyclone had always been the center of attention. Everywhere it went, people would look up in wonder, fear, and amazement. It had been the undisputed master of the country. It had observed Bill's rapid climb to fame and had seen the Fourth of July celebration grow. It had been keeping an eye on things all right.

In the beginning the Fourth of July crowd had aroused its curiosity. It liked nothing more than to show its superiority and power by breaking the crowd up sometime during the day. But every year the crowd was larger. This preyed on the cyclone's mind. This year it did not come to watch. It deliberately came to spoil the celebration. Jealous of Bill and of his success, it resolved to do away

with the whole institution of the Fourth of July once and for all. So much havoc and destruction would be wrought that there would never be another Independence Day celebration. On that day in future years, it would circle around the horizon leering and gloating. At least, so it thought.

The cyclone was resolved, also, to do away with this bold fellow who did not hold it in awe and run for the 'fraid hole at its approach. For untold years it had been the most powerful thing in the land. And now here was a mere man who threatened to usurp[1] its position.

When Bill looked at the horizon and saw the cyclone coming, he recognized the anger and rage. While a cyclone does not often smile, Bill had felt from the beginning that it was just a grouchy fellow who never had a pleasant word for anyone. But now, instead of seeing merely an unpleasant character, Bill saw all the viciousness of which an angry cyclone is capable.

Bill knew he must meet the violence of the onslaught.[2] The center of the cyclone was larger than ever before. The fact is, the cyclone had been training for this fight all winter and spring. It was in best form and at top weight. It headed straight for Bill, intent on his destruction. In an instant it was upon him. Bill had sat quietly and silently on the great pacing palomino. But his mind was working rapidly. In the split second between his first sight of the monster and the time

---

1. **usurp** (yo͞o zʉrp′): to take the position or rights of another.
2. **onslaught** (än′ slôt′): a violent attack.

for action, he had made his plans. Pecos Bill was ready! Ready and waiting!

Green clouds were dripping from the cyclone's jaws. Lightning flashed from its eyes as it swept down upon him. Its plan was to envelop Bill in one mighty grasp. Just as it was upon him, Bill turned Widow Maker to its left. This was a clever move, for the cyclone was right-handed, and while it had been training hard to get its left in shape, that was not its best side.

Bill gave rein to his mount. Widow Maker wheeled and turned on a dime which Pecos had, with great foresight and accuracy, thrown to the ground to mark the exact spot for this maneuver. It was the first time that anyone had thought of turning on a dime. Then he urged the great horse forward. The cyclone, filled with surprise, lost its balance and rushed forward at an increased speed. It went so fast that it met itself coming back. This confused the cyclone, but it did not confuse Pecos Bill. He had expected that to happen. Widow Maker went into his twenty-first gait and edged up close to the whirlwind. Soon they were running neck and neck.

At the proper instant Bill grabbed the cyclone's ears, kicked himself free of the stirrups and pulled himself lightly on its back. Bill never used spurs on Widow Maker. Sometimes he wore them for show and because he liked the jingling sound they made. They made a nice accompaniment when he sang his cowboy songs. But he had not been singing, so he had no spurs. He did not have his rattlesnake for a whip. Of course there was no bridle. It was man against monster! There he was—Pecos Bill astride a raging cyclone, slick-heeled and without a saddle!

The cyclone was taken by surprise at this sudden turn of events. But it was undaunted. It was sure of itself. Months of training had given it a conviction that it was invincible. With a mighty heave it twisted to its full height. Then it fell back suddenly, twisting and turning violently, so that before it came back to earth, it had turned around a thousand times. Surely no rider could withstand such an attack. No rider ever had. Little wonder. No one had ever ridden a cyclone before. But Pecos Bill did! He fanned the tornado's ears with his hat and dug his heels into the demon's flanks and yelled, "Yipee-ee!"

The people who had run for shelter began to come out. The audience further enraged the cyclone. It was bad enough to be disgraced by having a man astride it. It was unbearable not to have thrown him. To have all the people see the failure was too much! It got down flat on the ground and rolled over and over.

Bill retained his seat throughout this ruse. Evidence of this desperate but futile stratagem[3] remains today. The great Staked Plain, or as the Mexicans call it, Llano Estacado,[4] is the result. Its small, rugged mountains were covered with trees at the time. The rolling of the cyclone destroyed the mountains, the trees and almost everything else in the area. The destruction was so complete that part of the country is flat and treeless to this day. When the settlers came, there were

---

3. **strategem** (strat′ ə jəm): a trick used to defeat an enemy or accomplish a purpose.
4. **Staked Plain . . . Llano Estacado** (lä′ nō es te kä′ dō): a region of high, level country located in parts of Texas and New Mexico.

Illustration by J.W. Stewart.

no landmarks to guide them across the vast unmarked space, so they drove stakes in the ground to mark the trails. That is the reason it is called the Staked Plain.

It was far more dangerous for the rider when the cyclone shot straight up to the sky. Once there, the twister tried the same thing it had tried on the ground. It rolled on the sky but to no use. Bill could not be unseated. He kept his place, and he didn't have a sky hook with him, either.

Bill was having the time of his life, shouting at the top of his voice, kicking his opponent in the ribs and jabbing his thumb in its flanks. It responded and went on a wild bucking rampage over the entire West. It used all the bucking tricks known to the wildest broncos as well as those known only to cyclones. The wind howled and beat against the fearless rider. The rain poured. The lightning flashed around his ears. The fight went on and on. Bill was enjoying him-

self immensely. In spite of the fury of the elements, he easily kept his place.

The raging cyclone knew then who the victor was. It was twisting far above the Rocky Mountains when the awful truth came to it. In a horrible suicidal heave it disintegrated! Small pieces of cyclone flew in all directions.

Bill still kept his seat on the main central portion until that rained out from under him. Then he jumped to a nearby streak of lightning and slid down it toward earth. But it was raining so hard that the rain put out the lightning. When it fizzled out from under him, Bill dropped the rest of the way. He lit in what is now called Death Valley.[5] He hit quite hard, as is apparent from the fact that he so compressed the place that it is

---

5. **Death Valley:** a desert area of California and Nevada, site of the Western Hemisphere's lowest point.

still 276 feet below sea level. The Grand Canyon[6] was washed out by the rain, though it must be understood that this happened after Paul Bunyan had given it a good start by carelessly dragging his ax behind him when he went west a short time before.

The cyclones and the hurricanes and the tornadoes nowadays are the small pieces that broke off of the big cyclone Pecos Bill rode. In fact, the rainstorms of the present day came into being in the same way. There are always skeptics, but even they will recognize the logic of the proof of this event. They will recall that even now it almost always rains on the Fourth of July. That is because the rainstorms of today still retain some of the characteristics of the giant cyclone that met its comeuppance[7] at the hands of Pecos Bill.

Bill lay where he landed and looked up at the sky, but he could see no sign of the cyclone. Then he laughed softly as he felt the warm sand of Death Valley on his back.

It was a rough ride, though, and Bill had resisted unusual tensions and pressures.

When he got on the cyclone, he had a twenty-dollar gold piece and a bowie knife[8] in his pocket. The tremendous force of the cyclone was such that when he finished the ride, he found that his pocket contained a plugged nickel and a little pearl-handled penknife. His two giant six-shooters were compressed and transformed into a small water pistol and a popgun.

It is a strange circumstance that lesser men have monuments raised in their honor. Death Valley is Bill's monument. Sort of a monument in reverse. Sunk in his honor, you might say. Perhaps that is as it should be. After all, Bill was different. He made his own monument. He made it with his hips, as is evident from the great depth of the valley. That's doing it the hard way. 🐾

---

6. Grand Canyon: a wide, deep gorge in northwestern Arizona, formed by the Colorado River.

7. comeuppance (kum´ up´ əns): a deserved punishment.

8. bowie (bōō´ ē) **knife:** a long knife with a heavy blade.

*R*esponding to Reading

1. What do you think of Pecos Bill? Write your thoughts in your journal or on a sheet of paper.

2. Which parts of the story did you find the most ridiculous or farfetched?

3. Why do you think the tales about Pecos Bill have been so popular and enduring?

Words to Know and Use | **skeptic** (skep´ tik) *n.* a person who questions what is accepted by others

The Growin' of Paul Bunyan

WILLIAM J. BROOKE

This is a story about how Paul Bunyan met up with Johnny Appleseed an' what come about because o' that meetin'. But it all got started because o' the problems Paul had with his boots one mornin'.

The hardest thing for ole Paul about gettin' started in the mornin' was puttin' on his boots. It wasn't so much the lacin' up that got him down (although when your bootlaces are exactly 8,621 feet an' four an' three-quarters inches long, an' each one has to be special ordered from the Suwanee Steamship Cable Company in New York City, an' if because you're strong as ole Paul you tend to snap about two laces a week as a rule, then just tyin' your boots can be a bit of an' irritation, too).

No, the hardest part o' puttin' on his boots was makin' sure he was the only one in 'em. Because, you see, they was so big an' warm that all the critters liked to homestead in 'em. So he'd have to shake 'em for nine or ten minutes just to get out the ordinary rattlesnakes an' polecats. Then he'd reach in an' feel around real careful for mountain lions an' wolf packs an' the occasional caribou[1] migration. Fin'ly he'd wave his hand around real good to see if any hawks or eagles was huntin' game down around the instep. Then he could start the chore o' lacin'.

But ever' now an' then, no matter how careful he was, he'd miss a critter or two an' then he'd just have to put up with it. 'Cause once he had those laces all done up, it just wasn't worth the trouble to untie 'em all again.

So on this partic'lar day ole Paul is out o' sorts because of a moose that's got stuck down betwixt his toes. Paul's appetite is so spoiled he can't get down more than three hunnert pancakes an' about two an' a half hogs worth o' bacon afore he grabs up his ax an' takes off to soothe his ragged nerves in his usual way, by shavin' a forest or two.

Well, the more his toes itch, the faster he chops; an' the faster he chops, the more his toes itch. Fin'ly he can't stand it no more, so he sets down on a medium-size mountain an' undoes all 8,621 feet, four an' three-quarters inches o' his right bootlace an' takes it off an' shakes it out for twenty minutes afore he remembers it was his left foot that was itchin'. So he gives a big sigh an' starts in on the other boot.

---

1. **caribou** (kar′ ə bōō′): a large deer found in the Arctic; a reindeer.

Illustration copyright © 1991 by Michael McCurdy.

Fin'ly both boots is off, an' a slightly bruised moose is shakin' his head an' blinkin' his eyes an' staggerin' off betwixt the stumps. An' Paul has his first chance to take a deep breath an' have a look round. An' he's surprised, 'cause he can't see any trees anywheres, only stumps. So he gets up on a stump an' looks around, an' he still can't see any standin' timber. He'd been so wrought up, he'd cleared all the way to the southern edge o' the big woods without noticin'.

Now this annoys Paul, 'cause he's too far from camp to get back for lunch, an' nothin' upsets him like missin' grub. An' when he's upset, the only thing to soothe him is chop-

pin' trees, an' all the trees is down, so that annoys him even worse.

There he sits, feelin' worse by the minute, with his stomach growlin' like a thunderstorm brewin' in the distance. An' then he notices somethin' way off at the horizon, out in the middle o' them dusty brown plains. All of a sudden there's somethin' green. As he watches, that green starts to spread in a line right across the middle of all that brown.

Now the only thing I ever heard tell of that was bigger than ole Paul hisself was ole Paul's curiosity. It was even bigger than his appetite. So, quick as he can get his boots on, he's off to see what's happenin'. What he sees makes him stop dead in his tracks. 'Cause it's trees, apple trees growin' where nothin' but dirt ever growed before. A whole line of apple trees stretchin' in both directions as far as you can see.

It makes him feel so good he just has to take up his ax an' start choppin'. An' the more he chops, the better he feels. An' as he marches westward through all the flyin' splinters an' leaves an' applesauce, he sees that the trees is gettin' shorter until they're just saplin's, then green shoots, then just bare earth.

Paul stops short then an' leans on his ax handle to study the funny little man who turns around an' looks up at him. He's barefoot an' wears a gunnysack for clothes, with a metal pot on his head for a hat. He looks up at Paul for a second, then reaches in a big bulgy bag hangin' at his side an' takes out somethin' teeny-tiny, which he sticks in the ground. He gathers the dusty brown dirt around it an' pats it down. He stands up, an' out of a canvas water bag he pours a little bit o' water on the spot. Then he just stands an' watches.

For a few seconds nothin' happens; then the tiniest, littlest point o' green pokes out o' the dust an' sort o' twists around like it's lookin' for somethin'. All at once, it just stretches itself toward the sky an' pulls a saplin' up after it. An' it begins to branch an' to fill out, an' its smooth green skin turns rough an' dark an' oozes sap. The branches creak an' groan an' stretch like a sleeper just wakin' up. Buds leaf out an' turn their damp green faces to the sun. An' the apples change from green to red an' swell like balloons full to bustin' with sweet cider.

The funny little man looks up an' smiles an' says, "My name's John Chapman, but folks call me Johnny Appleseed."

"Pleased to meet you," says Paul.

The little man points at his tree. "Mighty pretty sight, don't you think?"

"Sure is," says Paul, an' with a quick-as-a-wink flick o' his ax, he lays the tree out full length on the ground. "My name's Paul Bunyan."

The little man lifts his tin pot an' wipes his bald head while he stares at the tree lyin' there in the dirt. Then he squints up at Paul an' kneels down an' puts another seed in the ground. Paul smiles down at him while the tree grows up, then lays it out by the first. The little man pops three seeds into the ground fast as can be. Paul lets 'em come up, then lops all three with one easy stroke, backhand.

"You sure make 'em come up fast," says Paul, admirin'-like.

"It's a sort o' gift I was born with," says Johnny Appleseed. He looks at the five trees lyin' together. "You sure make 'em come down fast."

"It's a talent," says Paul, real humble. "I have to practice a lot."

They stand quiet awhile, with Paul leanin' easy on his ax an' Johnny lookin' back along the line o' fallen trees to the horizon. He lifts his tin pot again an' rubs even harder at his head. Then he looks up at Paul an' says, "It seems like we got somethin' of a philosophical difference here."

Paul considers that. "We both like trees," he says, real friendly.

"Yep," Johnny nods, "but I like 'em vertical an' you like 'em horizontal."

Paul agrees but says he don't mind a man who holds a differin' opinion from his own, 'cause that's what makes America great. Johnny says, "Course you don't mind, 'cause when my opinion has finished differin' an' the dust settles, the trees is in the position you prefer. Anybody likes a fight that he always wins."

Paul allows he's sorry that Johnny's upset. "But loggin's what I do, an' a man's gotta do what he does. Besides, without my choppin' lumber, you couldn't build houses or stoke fires or pick your teeth."

"I don't live in a house, an' I don't build fires, an' when I want to clean my teeth, I just eat an apple. Tell me, when all the trees are gone, what'll you cut down then?"

Paul laughs. "Why, there'll always be trees. Are you crazy or somethin'?"

"Yep," says Johnny, "crazy to be wastin' time an' lung power on you. I got to be off. I'm headin' for the Pacific Ocean, an' I got a lot o' work to do on the way. So why don't you head north an' I'll head west, an' our paths won't cross till they meet somewheres in China."

Words to Know and Use	**philosophical** (fil' ō säf' ik əl) *adj.* involving general beliefs about the nature of thought and reality

Paul feels a little hurt at this, but he starts off north, then stops to watch as Johnny takes off at a run, tossin' the seed out in front o' him, pressin' it down into the ground with his bare toes, an' tricklin' a little water behind, all without breakin' stride. In a minute he's vanished at the head o' his long line of apple trees.

Now Paul has figured that Johnny hadn't really meant to offend him, but it was more in the nature of a challenge. An' Paul loves any kind of a challenge. So he sets down an' waits three days, figurin' he should give a fair head start to Johnny, who's a couple hunnert feet shorter'n he is. Then at dawn on the fourth day, he stands up an' stretches an' holds his ax out level a foot above the ground. When he starts to run, the trees drop down in a row as neat as the crossties on a railroad line. In fact, when it came time to build the transcontinental railroad, they just laid the iron rails down on that long line o' apple trees an' saved theirselves many thousands o' dollars.

Anyways, Paul runs for two days an' two nights, an' when the sun's settin' on the third day, he sees water up ahead. There's Johnny Appleseed plantin' a last tree, then sittin' on a high, bare bluff lookin' out over the Pacific Ocean. Paul finishes the last o' the trees an' swings the ax over his head with a whoop an' brings it down on the dirt, buryin' its head in the soil an' accident'ly creatin' the San Andreas fault.[2] He mops his brow an' sits down beside Johnny, with his feet danglin' way down into the ocean.

Starin' out at the orange sun, Johnny asks, "Are they all gone?" Paul looks back over his shoulder an' allows as how they are. Paul waits for Johnny to say somethin' else, but he just keeps starin', so Paul says, "It took you six days to plant 'em an' it took me only three days to chop 'em down. Pretty good, huh?"

Johnny looks up an' smiles sadly. "It's always easier to chop somethin' down than to make it grow." Then he goes back to starin'.

Now that rankles Paul. When he beats somebody fair an' square, he expects that someone to admit it like a man. "What's so hard about growin' a tree anyway?" he grumps. "You just stick it in the ground, an' the seed does all the work."

Johnny reaches way down in the bottom o' his bag an' holds out a seed. "It's the last one," he says. "All the rest o' my dreams is so much kindlin' wood, so why don't you take this an' see if it's so easy to make it grow."

Paul hems an' haws, but he sees as how he has to make good on his word. So he takes the little bitty seed an' pushes it down in the ground with the tip o' one fingernail. He pats the soil around it real nice, like he seen Johnny do. Then he sits down to wait as the sun sets.

"I'm not as fast as you at this," Paul says, "but you've had more practice. An' I'm sure my tree will be just as good as any o' yours."

"Not if it dies o' thirst," says Johnny's voice out o' the dark.

Paul hasn't thought about that. So when the moon comes up, he heads back to a stream he passed about two hunnert miles back. But he don't have nothin' to carry

---

2. **San Andreas** (san an drā′ əs) **fault:** a group of cracks in the earth's crust extending about six hundred miles along the California coast.

water in, so he scoops up a double handful an' runs as fast as he can, with the water slippin' betwixt his fingers. When he gets back, he's got about two drops left.

"Guess I'll have to get more water," he says, a mite winded.

"Don't matter," says Johnny's voice, "if the rabbits get the seed."

An' there in the moonlight, Paul sees all the little cottontails hoppin' around an' scratchin' at the ground. Not wishin' to hurt any of 'em, he picks 'em up, one at a time, an' moves 'em away, but they keep hoppin' back. So, seein' as how he still needs water, he grabs 'em all up an' runs back to the stream, sets the rabbits down, grabs up the water, runs back, flicks two more drops on the spot, pushes away the new batch o' rabbits movin' in, an' tries to catch his breath.

"Just a little more water an' a few less rabbits an' it'll be fine," Paul says between gasps.

Out o' the dark comes Johnny's voice. "Don't matter, if the frost gets it."

Paul feels the cold ground, an' he feels the moisture freezin' on his hands. So he gets down on his knees, an' he folds his hands around that little spot o' dirt an', gentle as he can, breathes his warm breath onto that tiny little seed. Time passes, and the rabbits gather round to enjoy the warmth an' scratch their soft little backs up against those big callused hands. As the night wears on, Paul falls into a sleep, but his hands never stop cuppin' that little bit o' life.

Sometime long after moonset, the voice o' Johnny Appleseed comes driftin' soft out o' the dark an' says, "Nothin's enough if you don't care enough."

Paul wakes up with the sun. He sets up an' stretches, an' for a minute he can't

Illustration copyright © 1991 by Michael McCurdy.

remember where he is. Then he looks down, an' he gives a whoop. 'Cause he sees a little tiny bit o' green pokin' up through the grains o' dirt. "Hey, Johnny," he yells, "look at this!" But Johnny Appleseed is gone, slipped away in the night. Paul is upset for a minute, then realizes he don't need to brag to anybody, that that little slip o' green is all the happiness he needs right now.

As the sun rises, he fetches more water an' shoos away the crows an' shields that shoot from the heat o' the sun. It grows taller an' straighter an' puts out buds an' unfurls its leaves. Paul carries in all the animals from the surroundin' countryside, coyotes an' sidewinders an' Gila monsters, an' sets 'em down in a circle to admire his tree growin' tall an' sturdy an' green.

Then Paul notices somethin'. He gets down on his hands an' knees an' looks close. It's a brown leaf. "That's not too serious," he thinks, an' he shades it from the sun. Then he sees another brown leaf, an' he runs back to get more water. When he gets back, the little saplin' is droopin' an' shrivelin'. He gets down an' breathes on it, but as he watches, the leaves drop off an' the twigs snap. "Help me, somebody," he cries out, "help me!" But there's no answer 'cept the rustlin' o' the critters as they slink away from him. An' while he looks down at the only thing he ever give birth to, it curls up an' dies.

For a second he just stands there; then he pounds his fists on the ground an' yells, "Johnny! Johnny! Why didn't you tell me how much it could hurt?"

He sets down an' he stares till the sun begins settin'. Then he jumps up an' says, "Only one thing's gonna make me feel better.

I'm gonna cut me some timber! Maybe a whole forest if I can find one!" He reaches for his ax.

An' that's when he sees it. It stretches right up to the sky, with great green boughs covered with sweet-smellin' needles an' eagles nestin' in its heights. Johnny must have worked some o' his magic afore he left, 'cause when Paul struck it into the ground, it wasn't nothin' but an ax. But now, in the light o' the settin' sun, it shines like a crimson column crowned in evergreen.

"I'll call it a redwood," says Paul, who knew now he'd never want an ax again as long as there was such a tree.

So he waited for the cones with the seeds to form an' drop, an' he planted them all over the great Northwest an' nurtured them an' watched a great woodland spring up in their shelter. An' he never felled a tree again as long as he lived.

For years he worked, an' there are those who say you can still catch a glimpse o' him behind the highest mountains in the deepest woods. An' they say he's always smilin' when you see him.

'Cause Paul learned hisself somethin': A little man who chops somethin' down is still just a little man, but there's nobody bigger than a man who learns to grow. 🍂

Responding to Reading

1. How do you think Paul Bunyan changes during the story?

2. What did you think of Johnny Appleseed's reactions to Paul's chopping down the trees?

3. In your opinion, what did Johnny mean when he said, "Nothin's enough if you don't care enough"?

4. Compare the characters of Paul and Johnny. How are they alike and how are they different?

*R*esponding to Reading

Comparing the Selections

1. Which of these heroes would you like to have as a friend? Explain.

2. In what ways are John Henry, Paul Bunyan, and Pecos Bill alike? In what ways are they different? Think about their backgrounds.

Broader Connections

3. Which of the four heroes in this section would have the best chance of solving the problems the world faces today? Explain.

*L*iterary Concept: Tall Tales

Tall tales are legends in which exaggerated characters perform incredible feats. The heroes and heroines of the tales in the United States display virtues that were needed to settle the frontier— strength, courage, cunning, resourcefulness, and optimism. Why do you think tall tales were so popular in the United States?

*W*riting Options

1. Write an imaginative **tall tale,** about how a geological formation in the United States was created.

2. Write a **ballad** or **rap song** based on one of the tall tales.

*V*ocabulary Practice

Exercise   Decide if the boldfaced words are used correctly in the sentences below. Write *Correct* or *Incorrect.* If a word is incorrect, write a sentence using the word correctly.

1. The mail carrier entered through the **gait** in the front yard.

2. She knew that the baby would find the silly faces **musing.**

3. The political opponents had many **philosophical** differences.

4. "I'm a **skeptic,**" the person said. "I'll believe anything."

5. The earth revolves around the sun. That is an **undisputed** scientific fact.

> *Words
> to Know
> and Use*
>
> ———
>
> gait
> musing
> philosophical
> skeptic
> undisputed

Options for Learning

1 • **Funny Papers** Create a comic strip based on the events of one of the three tales you read. Study other comic strips to decide on a style. Post your comic strip on your classroom bulletin board.

2 • **The Real Story** Research one of the four heroes. Find out about the hero's real or fictional beginnings, his territory, and his adventures. Present the results of your research to your class.

Adrien Stoutenburg   1916–

Adrien Stoutenburg began writing during the 1930s. She has published more than twenty books for children and adults and has had poems published in *The New Yorker* and other magazines.

Stoutenburg says, "Like almost all writers, I was a constant reader. Lacking a college education, I consider the public library my alma mater."

Harold W. Felton   1902–

A long writing career arose out of Harold Felton's early interest in Paul Bunyan. As he read more about this legendary hero, Felton decided to publish his first book, *Legends of Paul Bunyan*. The following year, Felton wrote *Adventures of Pecos Bill*. In addition to books about the heroes of tall tales, Felton has written biographies of famous people, tales that the writer considers to be "no less tall because they were true."

William J. Brooke   1946–

The stories in Brooke's two books—*Untold Tales* and *A Telling of the Tales*—are both humorous and thought-provoking retellings of familiar stories. *Untold Tales* was named a Notable Book by the American Library Association. The author also writes musical revues that have been performed in the United States and Canada. He and his wife are singers and actors who perform primarily in works by Gilbert and Sullivan.

All or Nothing

*Links to
Unit Two*

Raven and the Coming of Daylight GAIL ROBINSON AND DOUGLAS HILL
The Five Eggs FRANK HENIUS
The Souls in Purgatory GUADALUPE BACA-VAUGHN

Examine What You Know

"Gotcha!" Have you ever played a trick on someone—perhaps a sister, a brother, a friend, or a parent—to get something you really wanted? Were you successful? How did you feel afterward? Turning the situation around, can you recall a time when you were the victim of someone else's trick? How did it make you feel? In small groups, discuss your experiences with playing tricks and being tricked.

Expand Your Knowledge

Tricksters are characters who take advantage of the weaknesses of others, often tempting them to play for "all or nothing" stakes. Almost every culture has its own trickster tales. Old Man Coyote, for example, is a trickster in many Native American tales. In West Africa, a spider named Anansi is the trickster.

In each of the tales you are about to read, the trickster wears a different face. In a Haida tale from the Pacific Northwest, "Raven and the Coming of Daylight," the trickster is Raven. An Ecuadorian tale, "The Five Eggs," casts a peasant woman as the trickster. In "The Souls in Purgatory," which is set in Mexico, the tricksters are the souls mentioned in the title.

Write Before You Read

■ *Author biographies
on Extend page*

Consider the discussion you had in Examine What You Know. In your journal or on a sheet of paper, write about a time when you or someone you know or have heard about acted as a trickster.

Raven and the Coming of Daylight

GAIL ROBINSON AND DOUGLAS HILL

When the earth was very young, it was dark and cold like a winter's night through all the year's seasons. Gull was the Custodian of Daylight, and he kept it locked tight in a cedar box beneath his wing. Being Custodian made Gull feel very important, and he was not going to lose his position by letting Daylight out of the box.

"He is too vain!" screeched Owl, at a meeting of the People upon Meeting Hill.

"We can never travel, in this darkness, to our half-homes in the south," cried Robin. Her breast was bleached of color for the lack of light.

"Even the dark mosses wither, and food is scarce," whimpered Rabbit.

"One person is like another because I cannot map his face," shouted Bear. "Enemies pretend to be friends to share my blanket and bowl."

"I cannot see my tail, to clean it of burrs," whined Fox.

So all the People complained of Gull's arrogance and thoughtless self-importance.

Then Squirrel turned to Raven and said, "Gull is your cousin. Perhaps he will listen to you. Perhaps you can tell him of your cold blood and your blunderings in the darkness and make him change his mind."

So it was settled that Raven should meet Gull on Meeting Hill the next day—or the next night, since without Daylight there was no difference between day and night.

Gull agreed to come to the meeting. But it was clear, when he came, that he was not going to change his mind or listen to what Raven said. He had come only because it made him feel even more important to have Raven pleading with him.

"I was made Custodian of Daylight in the beginning of things," said Gull. "I am to keep Daylight safe. And I *will* keep it safe." And he curved his wing tighter around the cedar box.

Raven had run out of words to make Gull see the People's need for light. He thought angrily to himself, "I wish this Gull would step on a large thorn."

No sooner had he shaped this thought than Gull cried out, "Squee! My foot!"

"A thorn, Cousin?" asked Raven innocently. "Let me see—I will take it out for you."

But of course it was so dark that he could not see the thorn to remove it.

"I must have light to take out the thorn," said Raven.

"Light? Never!" said Gull.

"Then the thorn will remain."

Gull complained and hopped on one foot and wept, and he finally opened his cedar box a crack, a crack so narrow that out glanced a shaft of light no brighter than a single star.

Raven put his hand to Gull's foot, then pretended not to see the thorn. Instead, he pushed it in deeper.

"Squee!" cried Gull. "My foot!"

"More light, more light!" shouted Raven.

And the lid of the box rose a further crack, so that light gleamed forth like a winter moon. Then Raven reached again for the thorn and pushed it even further into the soft flesh of Gull's foot.

"More light!" roared Raven.

"Squee, squee, squee!" screamed Gull, and in his pain he flung off the lid of the cedar box.

Like a molten fish the sun slithered from the box, and light and warmth blazed out over the world.

Nor was it ever to be recaptured, no matter how loudly or how sadly Gull called to it to return to its safe hiding place beneath his wing. 🦅

RAVEN OPENED THE BOX OF DAYLIGHT 1970
Dale DeArmond   Anchorage Museum of History and Art.

*R*esponding to Reading

1. What were you thinking and feeling as you finished this tale? Write your thoughts and feelings in your journal or on a sheet of paper.

2. Who do you think was right—Gull, Raven, or neither? Why?

   Think about
   • what might have happened if light had never come out
   • whether it is ever acceptable to do something "wrong" for the "right" reasons
   • whether Raven might have tried another scheme to trick Gull, and if so, what that scheme might have been

3. In animal tales, animals often exhibit human characteristics. Which human characteristics do Gull and Raven exhibit?

The Five Eggs

FRANK HENIUS

In the fields near the city there lived two poor peasants named Juan and Juanica. Since they were very poor, they would sometimes go two or even three days without eating.

Once, after they had had nothing to eat for three days, Juanica asked her husband, "How long are we going to keep on living if we don't eat?"

"Don't worry," he said, "I will go to town today to see if I can manage to find money to buy five eggs for us to boil and eat."

Immediately he set out for town. On arrival, he stood on a corner to wait for a passerby from whom he could ask for alms.[1] When he saw a man coming, he said to him, "Listen, my friend! Would you be good enough to give me four cents to buy an egg?" And the man, who was very charitable, gave him the four cents. That happened five times, and the peasant was fortunate enough not to have one of the five refuse him. When he had enough to buy the five eggs, he went on and bought them. And then he returned home to tell his wife the good news.

When he arrived, he told his wife to boil the eggs at once, for he was so hungry he could eat a burro. When the eggs were all boiled, his wife said to him, "Juan, come eat your two eggs; I shall eat three because I cooked them."

But he immediately said no, that he was the one to have the three eggs and she should have only two. And he kept on by saying, "Three for me and two for you." But his wife was stubborn, maintaining that she was to have three and he two. And that went on and on.

After they had wasted a good deal of time talking, Juanica decided to tell Juan that if he did not give her the three eggs to eat, she would die. But he said to her, very indifferently, "All right, that makes no difference to me. Go ahead and die!"

So she fell to the ground as though dead. Then he began to weep, "Oh, my poor wife, I loved her so. Oh, my poor wife!" And after he had wept until he was tired, he whispered in her ear, "Juanica, don't be so silly. I'll eat three and you two." But she answered, "No, I am going to eat three and you two, or else you can bury me." So he kept on weeping.

After he saw that his wife refused to come to life again, he decided to go and look for his best friends. He had five friends, and when he reached their homes, he told them that he had come to ask them please to bury

---

1. **alms** (ämz): money given to the needy.

SHAKER BERRY BASKET 1986 David Brega
Oil on masonite. Courtesy of the artist.

his wife, who had just died, and that he was counting on them, for he did not have a single cent to buy a casket. So his friends said not to worry, that they would see to that.

On his return home, he found her still playing dead. Then Juan burst into tears again, "Oh, Juanica, do not leave me alone,

please!" And when no one was looking, he slipped near where she lay to whisper in her ear, "I am going to eat three and you two." But she said no, that she was going to eat the three and he two. Then he said to her, "Take care, for we are going to bury you." And she replied, "That's nothing; bury me whenever you like."

After waiting a good while, they put her in the casket to carry her to the cemetery. And on the way, Juan kept on crying, "Oh, my poor wife, don't leave me!" And he made them stop the funeral procession, supposedly to kiss her, but really to tell her that he was going to eat three and she two. But her reply was always the same. When they reached the cemetery, they bore her to the edge of the grave. Then he went up to her and whispered in her ear, "Look, you are on the edge of the grave, and we are about to put you in it." Then, when she realized he was telling the truth, she sat up in the casket and said, "All right, then; you can eat all five of them."

So she got up out of the casket, and they both went home.

But once they arrived there, Juanica set the five eggs on the table—and ate three. ❧

Responding to Reading

1. What are your impressions of Juan and Juanica? Jot them down in your journal or on a sheet of paper.

2. Which character do you think deserved more eggs? Explain.

3. What do you think might have been some better solutions to the problem posed in this tale?

The Souls in Purgatory

GUADALUPE BACA-VAUGHN

Si es verdad, allá va,
Si es mentira, queda urdida.
(If it be true, so it is.
If it be false, so be it.)

There was once an old lady who had raised a niece since she was a tiny baby. She had taught the girl to be good, obedient, and industrious, but the girl was very shy and timid and spent much time praying, especially to the Souls in Purgatory.[1]

As the girl grew older and very beautiful, the old woman began to worry that when she died, her niece would be left all alone in the world, a world which her niece saw only through innocent eyes. The old lady prayed daily to all the saints in heaven for their intercession to Our Lord that he might send some good man who would fall in love with her niece and marry her; then she could die in peace.

As it happened, the old woman did chores for a *comadre*[2] who had a rooming house. Among her tenants there was a seemingly rich merchant who one day said that he would like to get married if he could find a nice quiet girl who knew how to keep house and be a good wife and mother to his children when they came.

The old lady opened her ears and began to smile and scheme in her mind, for she could imagine her niece married to the nice gentleman. She told the merchant that he could find all that he was looking for in her niece, who was a jewel, a piece of gold, and so gifted that she could even catch birds while they were flying!

The gentleman became interested and said that he would like to meet the girl and would go to her house the next day.

The old woman ran home as fast as she could; she appeared to be flying. When she got home all out of breath, she called her niece and told her to straighten up the house and get herself ready for the next day, as there was a gentleman who would be calling. She told her to be sure to wash her hair and brush it until it shone like the sun and to put on her best dress, for in this meeting her future was at stake.

The poor timid girl was dumbfounded. She went to her room and knelt before her favorite *retablo*[3] of the Souls in Purgatory.

---

1. Souls in Purgatory (pʉr′ gə tôr′ ē): spirits of dead people in a place where they undergo temporary suffering to make up for their sins on Earth.
2. comadre (kô mä′ drā) *Spanish:* a female friend.
3. retablo (re tä′ blô) *Spanish:* a wooden panel on which a religious picture is painted or carved.

Words to Know and Use

intercession (in′ tər sesh′ ən) *n.* the asking of a favor on behalf of another
dumbfounded (dum′ found′ id) *adj.* speechless with amazement **dumbfound** *v.*

"Please," she prayed, "don't let my aunt do something rash to embarrass us both."

The next day she obediently prepared herself for the meeting. When the merchant arrived, he asked her if she could spin. "Spin?" answered the old woman, while the poor embarrassed girl stood by with bowed head. "Spin! The hanks[4] disappear so fast you would think she was drinking them like water."

The merchant left three hanks of linen to be spun by the following day. "What have you done, Tía?"[5] the poor girl asked. "You know I can't spin!" "Don't sell yourself short," the old lady replied with twinkling eyes. "Where is your faith in God, the Souls in Purgatory? You pray to them every day. They will help you. Just wait and see!" Sobbing, the girl ran to her room and knelt down beside her bed and began to pray, often raising her head to the *retablo* of the Souls in Purgatory which hung on the wall beside her bed. After she quieted down, she thought she heard a soft sound behind her. She turned and saw three beautiful ghosts dressed in white, smiling at her. "Do not be concerned," they said. "We will help you in gratitude for all the good you have done for us." Saying this, each one took a hank of linen and in a wink spun the linen into thread as fine as hair.

The following day, when the merchant came, he was astonished to see the beautiful linen and was very pleased. "Didn't I tell you, sir?" said the old lady with pride and joy. The gentleman asked the girl if she could sew. Before the surprised girl could answer, the old aunt cried, "Sew? Of course she can sew. Her sewing is like ripe cherries in the mouth of a dragon." The merchant then left a piece of the finest linen to be made into three shirts. The poor girl cried bitterly, but her aunt told her not to worry, that her devotion to the Poor Souls would get her out of this one too, as they had shown how much they loved her on the previous day.

The three ghosts were waiting for the girl beside her bed when she went into her room, crying miserably. "Don't cry, little girl," they said. "We will help you again, for we know your aunt, and she knows what she is doing and why."

The ghosts went to work cutting and snipping and sewing. In a flash they had three beautiful shirts finished, with the finest stitches and the tiniest seams.

The next morning, when the gentleman came to see if the girl had finished the shirts, he could not believe his eyes. "They are lovely; they seem to have been made in heaven," he said.

This time the merchant left a vest of rare satin to be embroidered. He thought he would try this girl for the third and last time. The girl cried desperately and could not even reproach[6] her aunt. She had decided that she would not ask any more favors of the Souls. She went to her room and lay across the bed and cried and cried. When she finally sat up and dried her tears, she saw the three ghosts smiling at her. "We

---

4. hanks: bunches of fibers to be spun into thread or yarn.

5. tía (tē′ ə) *Spanish*: aunt.

6. reproach (ri prōch′): to blame.

THE READING   Helen L. Bellaver   Soft pastel. Courtesy of the artist.

will help you again, but this time we have a condition, and that is that you will invite us to your wedding." "Wedding? Am I going to get married?" she asked in surprise. "Yes," they said, "and very soon."

The next day a very happy gentleman came for his vest, for he was sure that the lovely girl would have it ready for him. But he was not prepared for the beauty of the vest. The colors were <u>vibrant</u> and beautifully matched. The embroidery looked like a painting. It took his breath away. Without hesitation, he asked the old lady for her niece's hand in marriage. "For," he said, "this vest looks as if it were not touched by human hands but by angels!"

The old woman danced with joy and could hardly contain her happiness. She gave her consent at once. The merchant left to arrange for the wedding. Wringing her hands, the poor girl cried, "But Tía, what am I going to do when he finds out that I can't do any of those things?" "Don't worry, my *palomita*,[7] the Blessed Souls[8] will get you out of this trouble too. You wait and see!"

Almost at once the old woman went to her *comadre* to tell her the good news and to ask her to help get ready for the wedding. Soon everything was ready.

The poor girl did not know how to invite the Souls to her wedding. She timidly went and stood beside her bed and asked the *retablo* to come to her wedding.

---

7. *palomita* (pä lô mē′ tä) *Spanish:* little dove.
8. Blessed Souls: the holy spirits of the dead.

Words to Know and Use   **vibrant** (vī′ brənt) *adj.* bright and sparkling

The great day finally arrived. The girl looked beautiful in the gown which the merchant had brought as part of her *donas*.[9] Everyone in the village had been invited to the wedding.

During the fiesta, when everyone was drinking *brindes*[10] to the bride and groom and the music was playing, three ugly hags came to the *sala*[11] and stood waiting for the groom to come and welcome them in. One of the hags had an arm that reached to the floor and dragged; the other arm was short. The second hag was bent almost double and had to turn her head sideways to look up. The third hag had bulging, bloodshot eyes like a lobster. "Jésus María," cried the groom. "Who are those ugly creatures?" "They are aunts of my father, whom I invited to my wedding," answered the bride, knowing quite well who they might be. The groom, being well-bred, went at once to greet the ugly hags. He took them to their seats and brought them refreshments. Very casually, he asked the first hag, "Tell me, señora, why is one of your arms so long and the other one short?" "My son," she answered, "my arms are like that because I spin so much."

The groom went to his wife and said, "Go at once and tell the servants to burn your spinning wheel, and never let me see a spinning wheel in my house; never let me see you spinning, ever!"

The groom went to the second hag and asked her why she was so humped over. "My son," she replied, "I am that way from embroidering on a frame so much." The groom went to his wife and whispered, "Burn your embroidery frame at once, and never let me see you embroider another thing."

Next the groom went to the third hag and asked, "Why are your eyes so bloodshot and bulging?" "My son, it is because I sew so much and bend over while sewing." She had hardly finished speaking when the groom went to his wife and said, "Take your needles and thread and bury them. I never want to see you sewing, never! If I see you sewing, I will divorce you and send you far away, for the wise man learns from others' painful experiences."

Well—so the Souls, in spite of being holy, can also be rascals.

Colorín, colorado, ya mi cuento se ha acabado.
(Scarlet or ruby red, my story has been said.) ❧

---

9. **donas** (dô' näs) *Spanish*: wedding presents a man gives to his bride.
10. **brindes** (brēn' des) *Spanish*: drinks to someone's health or happiness; toasts.
11. **sala** (sä' lä) *Spanish*: a large room for entertaining.

Responding to Reading

1. What do you think of the aunt's scheme to marry off her niece? Write your thoughts in your journal or on a sheet of paper.

2. Do you agree or disagree that the souls were "rascals"? Explain.

3. Will the girl and the merchant have a happy marriage? Explain.

4. What do you think might be a possible moral of this story?

Responding to Reading

Comparing the Selections

1. Which character do you think played the most effective trick? Why do you think so?

2. In the long run, which character do you think will be most pleased with the results of his or her trick? Why?

3. Which tale do you think best shows the unit theme, "All or Nothing"? How does the story you selected show this theme?

Broader Connections

4. What do you think is the lesson of these three tales? How do you think this lesson could be applied to modern situations?

Writing Options

1. Write a **sequel** to "The Five Eggs" that tells what happens right after Juanica eats her three eggs.

2. Write a **toast** to the bride in "The Souls in Purgatory." Write the toast from the perspective of her new husband or one of the "aunts."

3. Rewrite any one of the tales you just read as a **song** or as a **poem.**

Vocabulary Practice

Exercise On your paper, write the word from the list that is most clearly related to the situation conveyed in the sentences.

1. The king had a violent temper. No one wanted to upset him for fear he would do something reckless.

2. When the princess saw who she was supposed to marry, she was shocked and speechless.

3. The princess begged her mother to talk to her father, the king, about the wedding. Only the queen's intervention on her daughter's behalf could stop the king's plans.

4. On her wedding day, the princess looked radiant.

5. After years of marriage, the princess and her husband had grown extremely loyal and affectionate toward each other.

Words to Know and Use

devotion
dumbfounded
intercession
rash
vibrant

EXTEND

Options for Learning

1 • Tales with Tails Make up an animal tale that explains some natural phenomenon in the same sort of way that the Raven story explains daylight. You might, for example, try to explain the weather in your part of the country or why animals or people look a certain way.

2 • Mix and Match What do you think would happen if you put the man from "The Five Eggs" into the plot of "The Souls in Purgatory"? Rewrite one of the stories you have read, inserting a character from a different story. Then share the rewritten story in a class "story hour."

Gail Robinson and Douglas Hill

Gail Robinson and Douglas Hill are noted Canadian poets and folklorists who heard firsthand many of the Native American tales they have recorded. Robinson's poems have been published in various periodicals and read on BBC radio broadcasts. The publication of *Coyote the Trickster,* which includes "Raven and the Coming of Daylight," coincided with the first appearance of her poems in book form. Douglas Hill, who was the Literary Editor of the *Tribune* in London, Ontario, from 1971 to 1984, has published many books, including the first comprehensive history of western Canada.

Guadalupe Baca-Vaughn
1905–

Guadalupe Baca-Vaughn first heard "The Souls in Purgatory" as a child. "It's part of the folklore of New Mexico," Baca-Vaughn says. "I used to have an aunt who told me all these stories. She heard them as a child in Mexico." After retiring from her career as a teacher, Baca-Vaughn received a grant from the Kit Carson Foundation to tell her stories in Spanish and English to children who attended schools near Taos, New Mexico. Baca-Vaughn currently lives in Pojoaque, New Mexico, about eighteen miles from Santa Fe.

Nothing Stays the Same

Links to Unit Three

It Is Better to Die Forever CHEWING BLACKBONES

Aunty Misery JUDITH ORTIZ COFER

The Tale of the Gentle Folk CHARLES J. FINGER

Examine What You Know

"Nothing Gold Can Stay," a poem by Robert Frost, suggests that good things never last. What if you could somehow change this condition? For example, what if people never had to die? Consider some of the advantages and disadvantages of living forever. In small groups, make a list of the pros and cons of living forever.

Expand Your Knowledge

Each culture has myths that attempt to answer life's big questions, such as why death exists. The unique aspects of a culture are often reflected in such mythology. For example, the Blackfoot people lived on the Great Plains of North America, where buffalo hunting and fur trapping were essential to their existence. These essentials are reflected in the myth "It Is Better to Die Forever."

The second tale, "Aunty Misery," comes from Puerto Rico, a Caribbean island. Puerto Rico's folklore combines literary elements from the Orient, Arabia, Spain, and West Africa. The word *misery* refers to the pain and suffering in the world. Note the deal that Aunty Misery strikes with Death—and see if you think the world is better off for her bargain.

"The Tale of the Gentle Folk" is set in the South American country of Argentina. When the Spaniards colonized this region in the 1500s, the native population almost completely died out, killed by the conquering Spaniards and their European diseases. The guanacos (gwä nä' kōz) that are described in the story are related to both camels and llamas. These gentle animals still live on the mountains and plains of South America.

Write Before You Read

■ *Author biographies on Extend page*

Imagine that you are a person who has lived forever. Write your thoughts, telling about the joys and sorrows of never dying.

It Is Better to Die Forever

Retold by CHEWING BLACKBONES

Long, long ago, there were only two persons in the world: Old Man and Old Woman. One time when they were traveling about the earth, Old Woman said to Old Man, "Now let us come to an agreement of some kind. Let us decide how the people shall live when they shall be on the earth."

"Well," replied Old Man, "I am to have the first say in everything."

"I agree with you," said Old Woman. "That is—if I may have the second say."

Then Old Man began his plans. "The women will have the duty of tanning the hides. They will rub animals' brains on the hides to make them soft and scrape them with scraping tools. All this they will do very quickly, for it will not be hard work."

"No," said Old Woman, "I will not agree to this. They must tan hides in the way you say; but it must be very hard work, so that the good workers may be found out."

"Well," said Old Man, "we will let the people have eyes and mouths, straight up and down in their faces."

"No," replied Old Woman, "let us not have them that way. We will have the eyes and mouths in the faces, as you say, but they shall be set crosswise."

"Well," said Old Man, "the people shall have ten fingers on each hand."

"Oh, no!" replied Old Woman. "That will be too many. They will be in the way. There will be four fingers and one thumb on each hand."

So the two went on until they had provided for everything in the lives of the people who were to be.

"What shall we do about life and death?" asked Old Woman. "Should the people live forever, or should they die?"

Old Woman and Old Man had difficulty agreeing about this. Finally Old Man said, "I will tell you what we will do. I will throw a buffalo chip into the water. If it floats, the people will die for four days and then come to life again; if it sinks, they will die forever."

So he threw a buffalo chip into the water, and it floated.

"No," said Old Woman, "we will not decide in that way. I will throw this rock into the water. If it floats, the people will die for four days; if it sinks, they will die forever."

Then Old Woman threw the rock into the water, and it sank to the bottom.

TRIBUTE TO THE DEAD   1912   Roland Reed   Library of Congress.

"There," said she. "It is better for the people to die forever. If they did not, they would not feel sorry for each other, and there would be no sympathy in the world."

"Well," said Old Man, "let it be that way."

After a time, Old Woman had a daughter, who soon became sick and died. The mother was very sorry then that they had agreed that people should die forever. "Let us have our say over again," she said.

"No," replied Old Man. "Let us not change what we have agreed upon."

And so people have died ever since. ❧

*R*esponding to Reading

1. What do you think of the decisions that Old Man and Old Woman make? Jot down your thoughts in your journal or on a sheet of paper.

2. How do your ideas about death compare with the ideas in this myth?

3. If you could change anything about humans, what would it be?

Aunty Misery

JUDITH ORTIZ COFER

This is a story about an old, very old woman who lived alone in her little hut with no other company than a beautiful pear tree that grew at her door. She spent all her time taking care of her pear tree. But the neighborhood children drove the old woman crazy by stealing her fruit. They would climb her tree, shake its delicate limbs, and run away with armloads of golden pears, yelling insults at "Aunty Misery," as they called her.

One day a pilgrim stopped at the old woman's hut and asked her permission to spend the night under her roof. Aunty Misery saw that he had an honest face and bade the traveler come in. She fed him and made a bed for him in front of her hearth. In the morning, while he was getting ready to leave, the stranger told her that he would show his gratitude for her hospitality by granting her one wish.

"There is only one thing that I desire," said Aunty Misery.

"Ask, and it shall be yours," replied the stranger, who was a sorcerer[1] in disguise.

"I wish that anyone who climbs up my pear tree should not be able to come back down until I permit it."

"Your wish is granted," said the stranger, touching the pear tree as he left Aunty Misery's house.

And so it happened that when the children came back to taunt the old woman and to steal her fruit, she stood at her window watching them. Several of them shimmied up the trunk of the pear tree and immediately got stuck to it as if with glue. She let them cry and beg her for a long time before she gave the tree permission to let them go, on the condition that they never again steal her fruit or bother her.

Time passed, and both Aunty Misery and her tree grew bent and gnarled with age. One day another traveler stopped at her door. This one looked suffocated and exhausted, so the old woman asked him what he wanted in her village. He answered her in a voice that was dry and hoarse, as if he had swallowed a desert: "I am Death, and I have come to take you with me."

Thinking fast, Aunty Misery said, "All right, but before I go, I would like to pluck some pears from my beloved pear tree, to remember how much pleasure it brought me

---

1. **sorcerer** (sôr′ sər ər): a person with magical powers; wizard.

Words to Know and Use | **gnarled** (närld) *adj.* twisted and rough

in this life. But, I am a very old woman and cannot climb to the tallest branches where the best fruit is; will you be so kind as to do it for me?"

With a heavy sigh like wind through a catacomb,[2] Death climbed the pear tree. Immediately he became stuck to it as if with glue. And no matter how much he cursed and threatened, Aunty Misery would not give the tree permission to release Death.

Many years passed, and there were no deaths in the world. The people who make their living from death began to protest loudly. The doctors claimed no one bothered to come in for examinations or treatments anymore because they did not fear dying; the pharmacists' business suffered, too, because medicines are, like magic potions, bought to prevent or postpone the inevitable; the priests and undertakers were unhappy with the situation also, for obvious reasons. There were also many old folks tired of life who wanted to pass on to the next world to rest from the miseries of this one.

Aunty Misery realized all this, and not wishing to be unfair, she made a deal with

CASA CON ARBOLES (House with Trees) about 1950
José A. Torres Martino   Instituto de Cultura Puertorriquena.

her prisoner, Death: if he promised not ever to come for her again, she would give him his freedom. He agreed. And that is why so long as the world is the world, Aunty Misery will always live. ❧

---

2. **catacomb** (kat′ ə kōm′): an underground passageway used as a burial place.

*R*esponding to Reading

1. What do you think of the bargain Aunty Misery makes with Death—a bargain that allows both death and misery to remain in the world? Write your thoughts in your journal or on a sheet of paper.

2. Why do you think Misery is portrayed as a woman and Death as a man?

3. What is your explanation for why there is misery-in the world?

The Tale of the Gentle Folk

CHARLES J. FINGER

Let me see. This story begins at the time I climbed down the Andes[1] on the east side and came upon a house by a lake. There were two children living there, one named Juan, the other, his sister, named Juanita, and the boy was seven years old and the girl nine. They had never seen a school, and the nearest house was more than fifty miles away. Still, they had books and knew how to read, and I do not think that they ever found the day long. For one thing the lake was not at all deep, and a little bit off from the shore of it was a small island. That was a kind of playground for them, and often they paddled their boat to it in the early morning and stayed there all day.

There were other things highly interesting. On the second day that I was there, I saw their tame ostrich, a great gray bird that they had had for two years; and now and then Juan would ride it, Delicia, which was the name of the ostrich, spreading his wings like sails and running out in a wide zigzag circle on the pampa,[2] caring no more for the light weight on his back than a chicken would care for a fly. Somehow, the birds of that place were no more afraid of the

children than the cat is afraid of you, and they knew places where they could see the flamingo with its scarlet cloak, the cowbird all glossy violet, the lapwings making a drumming music, gray-and-white scissortails with feathers a foot long, and red ovenbirds. But their great pet was the guanaco,[3] tall and proud looking, all yellow and white, like a camel without a hump, about the size of a donkey. They called him Campeón, and he had been on the place as long as the children could remember. Their father, who owned many sheep, had found him when he was no larger than a fox and brought him to the house, and he had become as tame as a pet lamb. Both Juan and Juanita would roll over on him as he lay in the sun, burying their faces in his gold-colored fur, hugging his long neck, wrestling with him until he got up and walked away to find a quieter place. They would use him as a horse, harnessing him to a little wagon, and all would go well sometimes, but sometimes not so well, for when Campeón took it into his

---

1. **Andes** (an′ dēz′): a mountain range extending along the western side of South America.
2. **pampa** (päm′ pə): a grassy plain in Argentina.
3. **guanaco** (gwä nä′ kō): a wooly, wild llama of the Andes.

head to run, the wagon would upset and the children would roll out on the soft grass, and in a moment Campeón would free himself from the harness, going in great leaps to find a little hill where he would perch himself on the crest and stand like a sentinel.

Now one day the man who was my traveling companion was out with his rifle and, coming upon old Campeón standing on a high rock, took him for a strange and wild animal and, like many thoughtless men with a gun, followed his impulse and shot. Campeón was badly wounded and doubtless astonished to receive such treatment from the hands of a man. Anyway, he limped on three legs to the house. Juan and Juanita grieved sadly, their parents no less, and all was done for Campeón that could be done. As for my friend, seeing what had happened, he was the most sorrowful of us all. For a time it seemed as though Campeón would get better, but one day he was plainly worse. All that day he rested on the sheltered side of the house, refusing food and water, his finely shaped head proudly upright, his eyes turned to the south, and the next morning there was no sign of him. From the hill on which he had stood we could see for miles and miles, and Juanita and I went there, taking a telescope, and we searched the country far and wide. In the afternoon we saddled horses and rode many, many miles until we came to a belt of sandy soil that ran east and west, and there we saw the trail of our Campeón going straight south. So we turned home sadly enough, for we knew that we would see the gentle beast no more.

And this is why: If you have read *The Arabian Nights,*[4] you will remember in the story of Sinbad the Sailor that it is told that he discovered a wonderful valley in which were the bones of hundreds and thousands of elephants. Whether there is any truth or not in that, I do not know, but I do know that in south Patagonia[5] there is a vast valley called the Valley of the Gallegos,[6] and there the guanacos go to lay down their bones when they feel the coming of death. And beautiful Campeón, though he had never seen that valley, somehow felt that he must find it, being so wounded and sick, and, while we slept that moonlight night, had left us. Both Juan and Juanita knew well enough that they would never see Campeón dead, for they had heard the story of the guanaco valley as often as you have heard the story of Cinderella. So had I heard it, and that night, when we fell to talking about Campeón, a gaucho[7] who looked after the horses told us the story again, and this is what he said:

Long, long ago, when there were giants and before there were horses in this land, there lived a gentle people who did not know sickness or pain or anger. They moved about among the animals and the birds as we move about among the flowers in the

---

4. *The Arabian Nights:* a collection of Middle Eastern folk tales.
5. **Patagonia** (pat′ ə gō′ nē ə): the southern part of Argentina.
6. **Gallegos** (gä yā′ gəs): a river in southern Argentina.
7. **gaucho** (gou′ chō): a cowboy of Argentina.

Words to Know and Use

sentinel (sen′ ti nəl) n. a guard
impulse (im′ puls′) n. a sudden urge

Illustration by Cerys Edwards.

garden, and men were much kinder and the maidens more graceful and beautiful than any on the earth today. The colors of the birds were brighter and the scent of the flowers sweeter than now; the sun was never too hot, nor the wind too cold. What was more wonderful, the Gentle People had a strange power by means of which they could change flowers into living things, which turned to bright-colored birds.

Now and then there would be great gatherings, when all the Gentle People would come together before their prince, who sat on a throne decked with precious stones. And the people, who loved him for his wisdom as well as for his goodness, brought to him at such times gold and silver and diamonds and rubies and glittering precious stones, and these he would give to the young people to play with, for in those days people loved things for their beauty alone. The birds and animals, too, would join in the gathering, and the air would be full of song and color and the scent of woods and flowers. On that day each person there

would have his or her wish granted, whatever it was. To be sure, where there was so much that was good, it seemed hard to wish for anything at all.

There was one thing only that was forbidden to the Gentle People, which was to go north until they saw no more the stars of the Southern Cross[8] in the sky, for after many days' journey, they were told, there was a great dark forest, on the other side of which were fierce men who did evil. But one day one of the Gentle People saw a strange bird, more beautiful than anything ever seen, a bird whose breast shone green and blue and gold, with a tail of long feathers white as ivory. Capa it was who saw the bird, and it seemed strange to him that seeing him, the bird flew away. Never before had he seen a bird that he could not touch and hold, and the more the bird avoided him, the more eager he was to take it to the prince. So he followed it as it went from place to place,

---

8. Southern Cross: a group of stars visible only in the Southern Hemisphere.

always thinking that at last the strange bird would allow him to draw near. That it feared him he never knew, for his people knew no fear, nor did the animals or birds that lived among them. At last the bird led him to the edge of the forest, and when he looked into the sky that night, he saw new stars there, at which he wondered. Into the forest he went, always following the bird, and so tall and thick were the trees that the sun did not shine and the stars were blotted out at night.

Then one day he came to a place where he saw men with yellow skins and teeth like a dog, who gathered about him. Never before had he seen such people, who tore animals apart and ate of the flesh, who tore skins from living creatures and wore them on their own bodies. To make matters worse, these yellow-skinned ones seized Capa and took from him his glorious robes of gold-and-silver thread, tore the feathers from his hair, and plucked away the ruby that he wore for its beauty. Then, greatly to his surprise, they fell on one another, fighting for the things that they had taken from Capa, so that the very robe they struggled for was torn and trampled underfoot. At that, Capa turned and fled back through the forest, never stopping day or night, until he came to his own people.

Straight to the prince he went and told his tale, hearing which, the prince was sad at heart.

"You have," he said, "been where there are greed and selfishness and <u>avarice</u>, and it is bad for us. For those of the yellow skin will not rest until they have found us and brought sorrow into our midst."

Then he called all his people together, and they came, as they always did, singing and dancing and bearing flowers, and after them came the birds and animals, skipping and flying, calling. But a great silence fell upon all when they saw their Golden Prince, for his eyes were grave.

So he told the Gentle People all that Capa had seen, and Capa himself stood by the side of his prince and sang a sad song, so that the people knew of the evil on the other side of the dark forest, and the hearts of the Gentle People were as heavy as was the heart of the Golden Prince. And the prince told them that if they chose, he would arm them and lead them so that they could go forth and fight against the yellow-faced men when they came. "But," he went on to say, "having learned to fight and to do hurt and to bring death, then you yourselves will turn on each other, will bring death to your own people. You will turn against the animals, and they will turn against you. You will walk the land alone, and all things will avoid and hide from you. These things of the earth, these bright and shining things which today you take or leave as you wish, you will play with no more but will hide in boxes and under stones so that others may not see them." When he said this last, he picked up a handful of diamonds and rubies, of emeralds and gold dust, and poured them from one hand to another, so that it was as a cascade that fell bright and dazzling in the sunlight.

Words to Know and Use | **avarice** (av′ ə ris) *n.* a great desire for wealth

Fearing that, the Gentle Folk looked at one another, and there was no doubt in their minds. "Far better," said they, "is it that we should change in some manner and flee than that we should do evil to the birds and beasts that are our friends."

Then the Golden Prince called on his people to follow him, and as the yellow men broke through the forest as he had said they would, he led all of them away swiftly, and the <u>multitude</u> of animals and birds followed them. Having arrived at a great valley where there was a river, he told his people that he would change their form so that they would become for a time other creatures, but creatures that would neither bite nor scratch nor spit poison, nor do any kind of harm. So he changed them into guanacos, animals of proud and graceful carriage, and their dress was of red and white like the gold and silver they wore. Then when he saw his people thus, friends of the birds and animals they loved, he changed himself into one also, but greater and more beautiful than any.

But there was a memory of that time, and even to this day, when a herd of guanacos is seen, there also is one standing on a high rock as sentinel, keeping watch for the yellow men. And when at last the prince guanaco died, he died in the valley, seeing which, each of his people also laid down their bones in that place, as you may read in many books. So must it be until each and every guanaco has passed away. Yet remember this: Where dies a guanaco, there springs up a flower blue as the sky, its petals all gold-tipped. And when the day comes on which the last guanaco dies, then the yellow men will be gone. On that day each flower will bend to its neighbor, and at a word there will stand a great host, for the spirit of the guanaco is in the flower that is blue and gold-tipped. Then, for ever and ever, the Gentle People will again have their land, and kindness and gentleness and beauty and joy will be theirs once more. 🐾

*R*esponding to Reading

1. What do you think of the Gentle Folk's decision to become guanacos rather than fight? Write your reaction in your journal or on paper.

2. Reread the information on the Explore page (page 682) about this story. To what extent do you think "The Tale of the Gentle Folk" might reflect the history of the natives of Argentina?

3. How does this story fit the unit theme, "Nothing Stays the Same"?

Words to Know and Use	**multitude** (mul′ tə tōōd′) *n.* a great number; crowd

E X P L A I N

Responding to Reading

Comparing the Selections

1. Compare and contrast the explanations of death in "It Is Better to Die Forever" and "Aunty Misery." Which one better explains death?

2. Which of the three stories do you like the best? Why?

Broader Connections

3. Some scientists feel that people may someday live to be 200 years old. What changes in society might such a long life span cause?

Literary Concept: Pourquoi Tales

Pourquoi (pōōr kwä'), or "why," stories answer questions or offer explanations of why animals, plants, or humans were created. What questions do you think "The Tale of the Gentle Folk" answers?

Writing Options

1. If, like Aunty Misery, you could be granted just one wish, what would your wish be? Write an **explanation** of your choice.

2. For all we know, Old Man and Old Woman are still arguing about the way the world should be. Continue their **conversation** (in a humorous vein if you like) as they discuss their concerns about human beings.

Vocabulary Practice

Exercise   Write the letter of the best answer.

1. A **sentinel** must have   (a) excellent eyesight (b) bright clothes   (c) a light pack.

2. Because a **multitude** of guests came, there were (a) autograph seekers   (b) few people   (c) many crowded rooms.

3. The king showed his **avarice** by   (a) donating to charity (b) flying a kite   (c) raising taxes.

4. Because she had acted on **impulse,** she had   (a) carefully planned her move   (b) acted without thinking   (c) made goals.

5. The **gnarled** tree limbs   (a) were old and twisted (b) pointed straight up   (c) made the tree look young.

Options for Learning

1 • Cultured Research Research one of the three cultures—Blackfoot, Argentine, or Puerto Rican—represented by the selections you have just read. Make a presentation to your class on the land, the flora and fauna, the history, and the folklore of the culture you selected.

2 • A Corner of Paradise Find pictures of beautiful places that convey the spirit of the Valley of the Guanacos. Put the pictures together in a collage. Present the collage to your class and explain your idea of a "perfect place."

Judith Ortiz Cofer   1952–

Born in Hormigueros, Puerto Rico, Judith Ortiz Cofer is the author of two volumes of poetry and a novel, *The Line of the Sun*. She has received fellowships from the National Endowment for the Arts (1989), the Witter Brynner Foundation for Poetry (1988), and the Bread Loaf Writers' Conference (1987).

Cofer has taught in bilingual programs in public schools, as well as in universities. She says, "As a native of Puerto Rico, my first language was Spanish. It was a challenge not only to learn English but to master it well enough to teach it and—the ultimate goal—to write poetry in it."

Charles J. Finger   1869–1941

Born and educated in England, Charles Finger came to the United States in 1887. In his late teens he became a merchant seaman, traveled to South America, then roamed the world for ten years.

Later, Finger traveled to Mexico, Alaska, and Canada, where he was a prospector in the Klondike gold fields. After a successful career in the railroad business, he turned to writing juvenile fiction about his early adventures. "I found myself stuffed with tales," Finger stated, "so full indeed that although I should write for twenty years more at the rate I have written for the five years past I would not have told the half of them." Among Finger's best-loved books are *Tales from Silver Lands* and *Tales Worth Telling*.

Matters of the Heart

Links to
Unit Four

Strawberries   GAYLE ROSS

Owl   DIANE WOLKSTEIN

The First Flute   DOROTHY SHARP CARTER

Examine What You Know

A famous quotation tells us that "love conquers all." Many popular stories seem to agree. "Beauty and the Beast" and "Cinderella," for example, are two tales in which characters overcome great obstacles and love triumphs in the end. In small groups, discuss stories in which characters in love face obstacles. How do the characters attempt to overcome the obstacles? Are they successful?

Expand Your Knowledge

Each of the tales in this section deals with romantic love. "Strawberries" is a Cherokee legend. At one time, most Cherokees lived in the forest-covered mountains of the southeastern United States. The Cherokees were strong and self-reliant, and both men and women could be gentle as well as fierce. "Owl" comes from Haiti, a Caribbean nation. Storytelling in Haiti is a lively oral tradition that combines movement, gestures, and audience participation. "The First Flute" comes from the Mayan civilization, which flourished about A.D. 250 to A.D. 850, in parts of what are now Mexico, Belize, Guatemala, El Salvador, and Honduras. The Mayans were known for their remarkable architecture, art, mathematics, and astronomy, and for the accurate calendar they developed.

Write Before You Read

■ *Author biographies on Extend page*

Think of someone you have read about or heard about who has fought unusual obstacles in the name of love. What difficulties did that person face? How did he or she try to overcome them? Were his or her attempts successful? Write your thoughts about this person in your journal or on a sheet of paper.

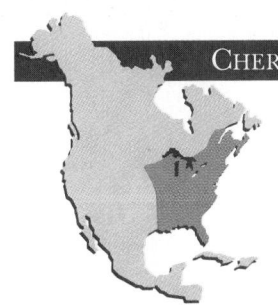

CHEROKEE LEGEND

Strawberries

GAYLE ROSS

Long ago, in the very first days of the world, there lived the first man and the first woman. They lived together as husband and wife, and they loved one another dearly.

But one day they quarreled. Although neither later could remember what the quarrel was about, the pain grew stronger with every word that was spoken, until finally, in anger and in grief, the woman left their home and began walking away—to the east, toward the rising sun.

The man sat alone in his house. But as time went by, he grew lonelier and lonelier. The anger left him, and all that remained was a terrible grief and despair, and he began to cry.

Provider, the creator of all things, heard the man crying and took pity on him. The spirit said, "Man, why do you cry?"

The man said, "My wife has left me."

Provider said, "Why did your woman leave?"

The man just hung his head and said nothing.

The creator asked, "You quarreled with her?"

And the man nodded.

"Would you quarrel with her again?" asked the provider.

The man said, "No." He wanted only to live with his wife as they had lived before—in peace, in happiness, and in love.

"I have seen your woman," the creator said. "She is walking to the east toward the rising sun."

The man followed his wife, but he could not overtake her. Everyone knows an angry woman walks fast.

Finally Provider said, "I'll go ahead and see if I can make her slow her steps." So the spirit found the woman walking, her footsteps fast and angry and her gaze fixed straight ahead. There was pain in her heart.

The creator saw some huckleberry bushes growing along the trail, so with a wave of the hand, the bushes burst into bloom and ripened into fruit. But the woman's gaze remained fixed. She looked neither to the right nor to the left, and she didn't see the berries. Her footsteps didn't slow.

Again Provider waved his hand, and one by one, *all* of the berries growing along the trail burst into bloom and ripened into fruit. But still the woman's gaze remained fixed. She saw nothing but her anger and pain, and her footsteps didn't slow.

And again the creator waved his hand, and one by one, the trees of the forest—the peach, the pear, the apple, the wild cherry—burst into bloom and ripened into fruit. But still the woman's eyes remained fixed, and even still, she saw nothing but her anger and pain. And her footsteps didn't slow.

Then finally Provider thought, "I will create an entirely new fruit—one that grows

LANDSCAPE
WITH PINK SKY
Ivan Rabuzin Courtesy,
Jaro Art Galleries, New York.

very, very close to the ground, so the woman must forget her anger and bend her head for a moment." So the spirit waved his hand, and a thick green carpet began to grow along the trail. Then the carpet became starred with tiny white flowers, and each flower gradually ripened into a berry that was the color and shape of the human heart.

As the woman walked, she crushed the tiny berries, and the delicious aroma came up through her nose. She stopped and looked down, and she saw the berries. She picked one and ate it, and she discovered its taste was as sweet as love itself. So she began walking slowly, picking berries as she went, and as she leaned down to pick a berry, she saw her husband coming behind her.

The anger had gone from her heart, and all that remained was the love she had always known. So she stopped for him, and together they picked and ate the berries. Finally they returned to their home, where they lived out their days in peace, happiness, and love.

And that's how the world's very first strawberries brought peace between men and women in the world and why to this day they are called the berries of love.

*R*esponding to Reading

1. What images stand out in your mind after reading this tale? Write or sketch them in your journal or on a sheet of paper.

2. What do you think might have happened to the man and the woman if Provider had not helped them?

3. How do you think nature helps people forget their problems?

4. Compare and contrast the husband and wife in this tale to the husband and wife in "The Five Eggs" on pages 674–675.

Owl

DIANE WOLKSTEIN

Owl thought he was very ugly. But one evening he met a girl and talked with her, and she liked him. "If it had been day," Owl thought, "and she had seen my face, she never would have liked me." But still she had liked him.

So Owl went to her house the next night. And the next. And the night after that. Every evening he would arrive at the girl's house at seven, and they would sit outside on the porch steps, talking together politely.

Then one evening after Owl had left, the girl's mother said to her, "Why doesn't your fiancé come and visit you during the day?"

"But, Mama, he's explained that to me. He works during the day. Then he must go home and change, and he cannot get here before seven."

"Still, I would like to see his face before the marriage," the mother said. "Let's invite him to our house for a dance this Sunday afternoon. Surely he doesn't work on Sunday."

Owl was very pleased with the invitation: a dance in his honor. But he was also very frightened. He told his cousin, Rooster, about the girl and asked that he accompany him to the dance. But that Sunday afternoon, as Owl and Rooster were riding on their horses to the party, Owl glanced over at Rooster. Rooster held himself with such assurance, he was so elegantly and fashionably dressed, that Owl imagined the girl seeing the two of them and was filled with shame.

"I can't go on," he choked. "You go and tell them I've had an accident and will be there later."

Rooster rode to the dance. "Tsk tsk, poor Owl," he explained. "He has had an accident, and he has asked me to let you know that he will be here later."

When it was quite dark, Owl tied his horse a good distance from the dance and stumbled up to the porch steps.

"Pssst," he whispered to a young man sitting on the steps. "Is Rooster here?"

"Well now, I don't know."

"Go and look. Tell him a friend is waiting for him by the *mapou* tree."[1]

Rooster came out. "Owl!"

"Shhhhhhh–"

"Owl!"

"Shhhh–"

"Owl, what are you wearing over your head–I mean your face?"

---

1. *mapou* (mä poo′) **tree:** a Haitian tree related to the cottonwood.

697

EIGHT HUTS IN HAITI
Roosevelt The Van Hoorick
Collection/Superstock.

"It's a hat. Haven't you ever seen a hat before? Look, tell them anything. Tell them I scratched my eyes on a branch as I was riding here and the light—even the light from a lamp—hurts them. And you must be certain to watch for the day for me and to crow as soon as you see the light, so we can leave."

"Yes, yes," Rooster said. "Come in and I shall introduce you to the girl's relatives."

Rooster introduced Owl to everyone, explaining Owl's predicament. Owl went around shaking hands; his hat hung down, almost completely covering his face. Owl then tried to retreat into a corner, but the girl came over.

"Come into the yard and let's dance," she said.

Dong ga da, Dong ga da, Dong ga da, Dong. Dong ga da, Dong. Eh-ee-oh.

Owl danced. And Owl could dance well. The girl was proud of Owl. Even if he wore his hat strangely and had sensitive eyes, he *could* dance.

Dong ga da, Dong ga da, Dong ga da, Dong. Dong ga da, Dong. Eh-ee-oh.

Rooster was dancing too. When Owl noticed that Rooster was dancing instead of watching for the day, Owl was afraid that Rooster would forget to warn him, and he excused himself to the girl. He ran out of

Words to Know and Use | **predicament** (prĕ dik′ ə mənt) *n.* a troublesome or difficult situation

the yard, past the houses, to a clearing where he could see the horizon. No, it was still night. Owl came back.

Dong ga da, Dong ga da, Dong ga da, Dong. Dong ga da, Dong. Eh-ee-oh.

Owl motioned to Rooster, but Rooster was lost in the dance. Owl excused himself again to the girl, ran to the clearing; no, it was still night. Owl returned.

Dong ga da, Dong ga da, Dong ga da, Dong. Dong ga da, Dong. Eh-ee-oh.

Owl tried to excuse himself again, but the girl held on to him. "Yes, stay with me," she said. And so they danced and danced and danced.

Dong ga da, Dong ga da, Dong ga da, Dong. Dong ga da, Dong. Eh-ee-oh.

The sun moved up in the sky, higher and higher, until it filled the house and the yard with light.

"Now—let us see your fiancé's face!" the mother said.

"*Kokioko!*" Rooster crowed.

And before Owl could hide, she reached out and pulled the hat from his face.

"My eyes!" Owl cried, and covering his face with his hands, he ran for his horse.

"Wait, Owl!" the girl called.

"*Kokioko!*" Rooster crowed.

"Wait, Owl, wait."

And as Owl put his hands down to untie his horse, the girl saw his face. It was <u>striking</u> and fierce, and the girl thought it was the most handsome face she had ever seen.

"Owl—"

But Owl was already on his horse, riding away, farther and farther away.

Owl never came back.

The girl waited. Then she married Rooster. She was happy, except sometimes in the morning when Rooster would crow, "*Kokioko-o-o.*" Then she would think about Owl and wonder where he was. ❧

*R*esponding to Reading

1. What do you think of the girl's decision to marry Rooster? Write your thoughts in your journal or on a sheet of paper.

2. What advice would you give to Owl in this "matter of the heart"?

3. In your opinion, how important a role does appearance play in matters of the heart?

4. What do you think is the moral of this story?

Words to Know and Use	**striking** (strī′ kiŋ) *adj.* impressive; remarkable

The First Flute

DOROTHY SHARP CARTER

During the glory of the Mayan[1] civilization, years before the coming of the Spanish, there lived a *cacique*[2] who had a beautiful daughter, the Princess Nima-Cux, whom he loved dearly.

Not only was Nima-Cux beautiful, but she was possessed of talents. She could plait grass into fine baskets. She could mold little animals out of clay—and you even knew exactly which animals they were supposed to be. The coati[3] had a long ringed tail. The puma[4] had an open mouth showing sharp teeth. The tapir's[5] snout was definitely snoutish. The snake wound round and round and round—and if you unwound him, he reached from Nima-Cux's toes to her ear lobes.

Above all, Nima-Cux could sing like a bird. Her voice tripped up and down the scale as easily as her feet tripped up and down the steps. The cacique sat back and counted his blessings. They all had to do with Nima-Cux, her beauty, her baskets, her clay work, and, especially, her voice.

As princesses should, Nima-Cux had everything she asked for—besides some things she hadn't thought of requesting.

There were finely carved dolls, necklaces of rare shells, a cape of bright parrot feathers, an enormous garden filled with flowers and blossoming trees and singing birds and pet animals. No wonder Nima-Cux was happy.

Thus life flowed along contentedly for everyone in the household until Nima-Cux neared her sixteenth birthday. Suddenly she became sad and melancholy. Nothing made her happy. Then again, nothing made her unhappy. She just *was*, for no reason at all, she said.

What do you think Nima-Cux meant by "just *was*"?   *question*

The cacique was greatly agitated. He strode up and down the garden, wondering, wondering what would please Nima-Cux.

---

1. **Mayan** (mä′ yən): belonging to the Maya, a Native American people of southern Mexico and northern Central America.
2. *cacique* (kə sēk′) *Spanish*: a Native American chieftain.
3. **coati** (kō ät′ ē): a raccoonlike animal of the tropical Americas.
4. **puma** (pyōō′ mə): a mountain lion.
5. **tapir** (tā′ pər): a large, hoglike animal of the tropical Americas.

Words to Know and Use

melancholy (mel′ ən käl′ ē) *adj*. in low spirits; depressed
agitated (aj′ i tāt′ id) *adj*. upset; disturbed

700

Another doll? A bright fish? A golden plate for her breast of pheasant? But to whatever he proposed, Nima-Cux would only murmur politely, "No. But thank you, Papa."

The cook sent boys scampering up the tallest palm trees to bring back heart of palm for Nima-Cux's dinner.

Hunters were ordered into the jungle to capture monkeys. "Mind you, *funny* monkeys to entertain the princess. Not a sad one in the crowd—or off comes your head."

Maidens roamed the royal gardens gathering orchids to ornament the princess's bedchamber.

What happened? Nima-Cux would peer at the rare *palmito*[6] and moan softly, "I am not hungry."

She would stare at the monkeys cavorting[7] on the branches while the royal household screamed in amusement, and she would whisper, "Yes, yes, very comical," and sigh deeply. The household would hush its laughter and echo her sighs.

The orchids went unnoticed until they dropped to the floor with a dry rustle.

Herb doctors came. Witch doctors came. Old hunched crones said to know the secrets of life came. They all said, "But she seems quite well and normal. A bit pale. A trifle listless. Perhaps a good tonic . . ."

Nima-Cux was annoyed enough to argue about the tonic. "That smelly stuff? I won't even taste it."

Finally a sorcerer somewhat wiser than the others spoke to the cacique. "After all, the princess is practically sixteen. Other girls her age are married. Find a good husband for the Princess Nima-Cux—and she will again shine radiant as a star."

The cacique shook his head. A *husband?* How could a mere husband bring her happiness if her own father could not? A poor suggestion. What were sorcerers coming to?

He peeked once more at Nima-Cux's dismal face—and in desperation sent messengers throughout his kingdom. The young man skillful enough to impress the princess and coax a smile to her lips would become her husband. In a week the first tournament would be held.

Not a sad one in the crowd—or off comes your head.

During the next week the roads were worn into holes by the thousands of footsteps. Everyone in the kingdom hurried to

---

6. *palmito* (päl mē′ tô) *Spanish*: a bud of a palm tree, used as a food.

7. **cavorting** (kə vôrt′ iŋ): leaping about.

Words to Know and Use | **dismal** (diz′ məl) *adj.* gloomy; miserable

LA EDAD DE ORO
(The Age of Gold) 1951
Robert Gonzalez Goyri
Courtesy of the artist.

the palace either to take part or to watch the take-parters (or is it takers-part?). Seats were constructed for the nobility. Those not so noble found a patch of thick grass, a loop of vine, or a high branch. The cacique and Nima-Cux sat on a canopied stand. The tournaments began.

The first contestant marched out, proud and arrogant in his gold tunic, attended by a troop of warriors. A handsome youth he was. Maidens fainted with joy at the sight of him. The rest of the contestants growled and trembled.

But Nima-Cux frowned and asked, "What can he *do?* Besides prance and preen, worse than any *quetzal?*"[8]

The cacique sighed and made a sign for the warrior to display his talents—if any. The soldiers stood before the young man and threw ears of corn into the air. With his bow and arrows the warrior shot kernels from the ears in regimental procession. One

---

8. **quetzal** (ket säl'): a Central American bird having brilliant green and red feathers.

Words to Know and Use | **noble** (nō′ bəl) *adj.* of high rank

row, then the next and next until all the kernels were gone.

The spectators cheered and shouted with admiration. Such skill—and such elegance! Ayyyyyyy! The other contestants ground their teeth and sobbed.

Nima-Cux yawned and asked politely, "May we see the second match, Papa? The first has taken up *so* much time."

The cacique sighed again and motioned for the tournament to continue.

The second competitor strode out as confidently and proudly as the first. He walked alone, bearing a large basket. When he set it down, out slithered a tremendous snake of a poisonous variety, its eyes glaring with malevolence.

The spectators gasped with horror. Maidens fainted with fear. The remaining rivals watched with relish.

The youth engaged the angry snake in combat, artfully evading its deadly fangs. The spectators held their breaths.

"How boring!" muttered Nima-Cux, staring into the distance.

"Really? Really, daughter? You don't like it?" asked the cacique with regret. (He was enjoying the contests immensely.)

He motioned for more action. The youth complied by squeezing the life from the snake. Then he bowed to the applause of the crowd. Or most of the crowd. Nima-Cux was already on her way to the palace and her couch with a headache.

For days the tournaments continued. The most handsome and courageous of the Mayan youth competed with each other for the favor of Nima-Cux—favor that was

nowhere to be seen. Certainly not on her lips, which remained clamped in a sulky line. Nor in her eyes, which gazed sadly at the competition without seeing it.

Finally the last contestant appeared, a merry boy wearing the tattered dress of a minstrel. The spectators smiled. The other contestants laughed scornfully. With a quick bow to the princess, the boy began to sing. He sang of the lakes, the forests, the hills of the highlands. He sang of the crystal stars flashing from the dark river of night. He sang of love.

Not bad, not bad, nodded the cacique. Not, of course, to compare with Nima-Cux's singing. He glanced at his daughter. What astonishment! Her eyes resembled the crystal of the song. Her lips were open and curving—upward. She was smiling! The cacique sat back and pondered the puzzle of life and love.

What might the cacique have been thinking about? *question*

"I like him, Papa. We can sing together. I will marry him. Only first, he must learn the song of each bird of the forest. Then he can teach me."

The minstrel was happy to oblige. He had *meant* it when he sang of love. At once he disappeared into the jungle.

Day after day he practiced, imitating this bird, then that one. But Guatemala is home to hundreds, thousands of birds. Some whistle a complicated tune. The minstrel began to despair of his task.

Words to Know and Use | **sulky** (sul' kē) *adj.* irritable and unsociable
minstrel (min' strəl) *n.* a singer or musician

703

The god of the forest, after listening for days to the young minstrel's efforts, took pity on him. Also on the birds and other wild inhabitants of the woods—not to mention himself. He appeared before the minstrel, wearing a kindly smile.

The notes of the birds tumbled out, clear and sweet.

"Perhaps I can help you," he offered. "It is a difficult exercise you are engaged in."

Severing a small limb from a tree, the god removed the pith and cut a series of holes in the tube. "Now attend carefully," he said. And he instructed the young man exactly how to blow into one end while moving his fingers over the holes. The notes of the birds tumbled out, clear and sweet.

With a torrent of thanks, the minstrel flew on his way, carrying the *chirimia,* or flute. Just in time. Nima-Cux, anxious that the chore she had assigned her lover had been impossible, was on the point of another decline. She received the youth with joy. Enchanted she was with the flute and its airs,[9] with the minstrel and his airs.

The two were married and lived long and happily in the palace of the cacique. And today the Indians of Guatemala will point to the *chirimia,* the most typical of native instruments, and tell you this is the way it came about. ❧

---

9. **airs:** melodies.

*R*esponding to Reading

1. What are your impressions of Nima-Cux and the minstrel? Write them in your journal or on a sheet of paper.

2. Why do you think the girl was more impressed with the minstrel than she was with the rest of the competitors?

3. Why do you think Nima-Cux gave the minstrel such a difficult task?

Responding to Reading

Comparing the Selections

1. Which of the three tales was your favorite? Why?

2. Which tale do you think best illustrates the theme of this section?

3. Think back to the discussion you had in Examine What You Know. In which of these three tales do you think the characters were most successful in overcoming obstacles in the name of love?

Literary Concept: Supernatural Helpers

Like Cinderella's fairy godmother, **supernatural helpers** appear in folk tales to help the main characters. Who are the supernatural helpers in "Strawberries" and "The First Flute"? How do they help the main characters?

Concept Review: **Internal conflict** is a conflict that goes on in a character's mind. What is Owl's internal conflict?

Writing Options

1. Write a **critique** of a tale in this section. Explain why you like or dislike it.

2. Owl rode off without ever knowing that the girl he loved found his face handsome. Were you satisfied with that ending? If not, rewrite the tale with a new **ending.**

3. Imagine the origin of another kind of berry or fruit. Write a **myth** similar to "Strawberries" that describes the origin of the fruit.

Vocabulary Practice

Exercise Decide if the following pairs of words are synonyms or antonyms. On your paper, write S for Synonym or A for Antonym.

1. agitated—calm
2. assurance—confidence
3. dismal—hopeful
4. fiancé—fiancée
5. melancholy—delight

6. minstrel—performer
7. noble—aristocratic
8. predicament—trouble
9. striking—ordinary
10. sulky—irritable

Words to Know and Use

agitated
assurance
dismal
fiancé
melancholy
minstrel
noble
predicament
striking
sulky

E X T E N D

Options for Learning

1 • From the Horse's Mouth
Each of these tales was originally passed on orally, not in writing. Choose a tale, practice telling it aloud, and then tell it to another class or to a group of children.

2 • Be My Valentine What do hearts, a bow and arrow, and a picture of Cupid all symbolize? What are some symbols of love in other stories or cultures? Research other symbols of love, and draw or display them for the rest of the class.

Gayle Ross 1951–

Gayle Ross is the great-great-great granddaughter of the famous Cherokee chief John Ross. "I wanted," she says, "to tell the stories I had heard as a child and to honor the legacy of . . . the Cherokees."

Through her storytelling, Ross hopes to give her listeners "a sense of the Native American point of view of our world and the love that the Indians have for our land."

Diane Wolkstein 1942–

When the New York City Parks Department offered Diane Wolkstein a full-time job telling stories, she felt she had finally fulfilled the dream that had been born when she sat, awe-struck, listening to her mother's tales in New Jersey.

Wolkstein's books include *The Magic Orange Tree and Other Haitian Folktales,* from which "Owl" was taken. Wolkstein calls that tale "a story about the importance of trusting in oneself and trusting in another's love of that self."

Dorothy Sharp Carter 1921–

Years of living in Latin America with her husband, a U.S. Foreign Service officer, strengthened Dorothy Sharp Carter's interest in Latin American folklore. The author of three books, *The Enchanted Orchard and Other Folktales of Central*

America, Greedy Mariani and Other Folktales of the Antilles, and *His Majesty, Queen Hatshepsut,* Carter has also contributed short stories to *Travel, Nature, Highlights for Children,* and *Humpty Dumpty* magazines.

The Will to Survive

Examine What You Know

If you were in grave danger, what would you do to stay alive? Some of the most gripping tales ever written tell of people's incredible will to live. In small groups, make a list of the survival stories you have heard or read. Discuss some of the strategies people have used to stay alive.

Expand Your Knowledge

The tales you are about to read are about personal survival. "Brer Possum's Dilemma" is one of a group of animal stories that originated in Africa but are now associated with the Southern United States. "Brer" stories frequently feature a clever, smaller animal that outwits a larger one.

"Spotted Eagle and Black Crow" is an Oglala legend about two warriors who struggle to survive against great odds. The Oglala, a Sioux people, were buffalo hunters known for their bravery and fighting ability. They often called on animal spirits for help in times of need.

"The Girl in the Lavender Dress" is a contemporary urban legend. Over seventy-five versions of this legend exist today. The young girl in the story traveled in a horse-drawn cart in earlier versions, but after the invention of the automobile, the story had her traveling by car.

Write Before You Read

■ *Author biographies on Extend page*

Think back to the discussion you had in Examine What You Know. Choose the most memorable survival story you have ever heard or read. Then, in your journal or on a sheet of paper, describe the ordeal. Explain some of the character traits that the survivor possessed.

Brer Possum's Dilemma

JACKIE TORRENCE

Back in the days when the animals could talk, there lived ol' Brer Possum. He was a fine feller. Why, he never liked to see no critters in trouble. He was always helpin' out, a-doin' somethin' for others.

Ever' night, ol' Brer Possum climbed into a persimmon tree, hung by his tail, and slept all night long. And each mornin', he climbed outa the tree and walked down the road to sun 'imself.

One mornin' as he walked, he come to a big hole in the middle of the road. Now, ol' Brer Possum was kind and gentle, but he was also nosy, so he went over to the hole and looked in. All at once, he stepped back, 'cause layin' in the bottom of that hole was ol' Brer Snake with a brick on his back.

Brer Possum said to 'imself, "I best git on outa here, 'cause ol' Brer Snake is mean and evil and lowdown, and if I git to stayin' around 'im, he jist might git to bitin' me."

So Brer Possum went on down the road.

But Brer Snake had seen Brer Possum, and he commenced to callin' for 'im.

"Help me, Brer Possum."

Brer Possum stopped and turned around. He said to 'imself, "That's ol' Brer Snake a-callin' me. What do you reckon he wants?"

Well, ol' Brer Possum was kindhearted, so he went back down the road to the hole, stood at the edge, and looked down at Brer Snake.

"Was that you a'callin' me? What do you want?"

Brer Snake looked up and said, "I've been down here in this hole for a mighty long time with this brick on my back. Won't you help git it offa me?"

Brer Possum thought.

"Now listen here, Brer Snake. I knows you. You's mean and evil and lowdown, and if'n I was to git down in that hole and git to liftin' that brick offa your back, you wouldn't do nothin' but bite me."

Ol' Brer Snake just hissed.

"Maybe not. Maybe not. Maaaaaaaybe not."

Brer Possum said, "I ain't sure 'bout you at all. I jist don't know. You're a-goin' to have to let me think about it."

So ol' Brer Possum thought—he thought high, and he thought low—and jist as he was thinkin', he looked up into a tree and saw a dead limb a-hangin' down. He climbed into the tree, broke off the limb, and with that ol' stick, pushed that brick offa Brer Snake's back. Then he took off down the road.

Words to Know and Use

commence (kə mens') *v.* to begin

Brer Possum thought he was away from ol' Brer Snake when all at once he heard somethin'.

"Help me, Brer Possum."

Brer Possum said, "Oh, no, that's him agin."

But bein' so kindhearted, Brer Possum turned around, went back to the hole, and stood at the edge.

"Brer Snake, was that you a-callin' me? What do you want now?"

Ol' Brer Snake looked up outa the hole and hissed.

"I've been down here for a mighty long time, and I've gotten a little weak, and the sides of this ol' hole are too slick for me to climb. Do you think you can lift me outa here?"

Brer Possum thought.

"Now, you jist wait a minute. If'n I was to git down into that hole and lift you outa there, you wouldn't do nothin' but bite me."

Brer Snake hissed.

"Maybe not. Maybe not. Maaaaaaaybe not."

Brer Possum said, "I jist don't know. You're a-goin' to have to give me time to think about this."

So ol' Brer Possum thought.

And as he thought, he jist happened to look down there in that hole and see that ol' dead limb. So he pushed the limb underneath ol' Brer Snake, and he lifted 'im outa the hole, way up into the air, and throwed 'im into the high grass.

Brer Possum took off a-runnin' down the road.

Well, he thought he was away from ol' Brer Snake when all at once he heard somethin'.

"Help me, Brer Possum."

Illustration © Barry Moser.

Brer Possum thought, "That's him agin."

But bein' so kindhearted, he turned around, went back to the hole, and stood there a-lookin' for Brer Snake. Brer Snake crawled outa the high grass just as slow as he could, stretched 'imself out across the road, rared up, and looked at ol' Brer Possum.

Then he hissed. "I've been down there in that ol' hole for a mighty long time, and I've gotten a little cold 'cause the sun didn't shine. Do you think you could put me in your pocket and git me warm?"

Brer Possum said, "Now you listen here, Brer Snake. I knows you. You's mean and evil and lowdown, and if'n I put you in my pocket, you wouldn't do nothin' but bite me."

Brer Snake hissed.

"Maybe not. Maybe not. Maaaaaaaybe not."

"No, sireee, Brer Snake. I knows you. I jist ain't a-goin' to do it."

But jist as Brer Possum was talkin' to Brer Snake, he happened to git a real good look at 'im. He was a-layin' there lookin' so pitiful, and Brer Possum's great big heart began to feel sorry for ol' Brer Snake.

"All right," said Brer Possum. "You must be cold. So jist this once I'm a-goin' to put you in my pocket."

So ol' Brer Snake coiled up jist as little as he could, and Brer Possum picked 'im up and put 'im in his pocket.

Brer Snake laid quiet and still—so quiet and still that Brer Possum even forgot that he was a-carryin' 'im around. But all of a sudden, Brer Snake commenced to crawlin' out, and he turned and faced Brer Possum and hissed.

"I'm a-goin' to bite you."

But Brer Possum said, "Now wait a minute. Why are you a-goin' to bite me? I done took that brick offa your back, I got you outa that hole, and I put you in my pocket to git you warm. Why are you a-goin' to bite me?"

Brer Snake hissed.

"You knowed I was a snake before you put me in your pocket."

And when you're mindin' your own business and you spot trouble, don't never trouble trouble 'til trouble troubles you. ❧

*R*esponding to Reading

1. What do you think of Brer Possum and Brer Snake? Write your thoughts in your journal or on a sheet of paper.

2. Do you think Brer Possum deserves to get bitten? Why or why not?

3. This tale ends with a moral: "Never trouble trouble until trouble troubles you." Relate an experience you have had in which you learned this lesson yourself.

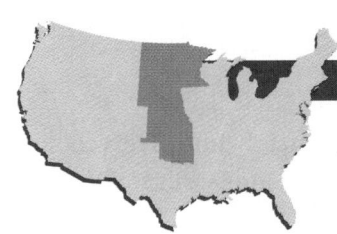

Spotted Eagle and Black Crow

Retold by JENNY LEADING CLOUD

This is a story of two warriors, of jealousy, and of eagles. This legend is supposed to have been a favorite of the great *Mahpiya Luta*—Chief Red Cloud of the Oglalas.[1]

Many lifetimes ago, there lived two brave warriors. One was named *Wanblee Gleska*—Spotted Eagle. The other's name was *Kangi Sapa*—Black Crow. They were friends, but as it happened, they both loved the same girl, *Zintkala Luta Win*—Red Bird. She was beautiful, a fine tanner and quill worker,[2] and she liked Spotted Eagle best, which made Black Crow very jealous.

Black Crow went to his friend and said, "Let us, you and I go on a war party against the Pahani. Let us get ourselves some fine horses and earn eagle feathers."[3] Spotted Eagle thought this a good idea. The two young men purified themselves in a sweat bath. They got out their war medicine[4] and their war shields. They painted their faces. They did all that warriors should do before a raid. Then they went against the Pahani.

Their raid was not a success. The Pahani were watchful. The young warriors got nowhere near the Pahani horse herd. Not only did they capture no ponies, but they even lost their own mounts, because, while they were trying to creep up to their ene-mies' herd, the Pahani found their horses. The two young men had a hard time getting away on foot because their enemies were searching for them everywhere. At one time, they had to hide themselves in a lake, under the water, breathing through long, hollow reeds which were sticking up above the surface. They were so clever at hiding themselves that the Pahani finally gave up searching for them.

The young men had to travel home on foot. It was a long way. Their moccasins were tattered, their feet bleeding. At last they came to a high cliff. "Let us go up there," said Black Crow, "and see whether our enemies are following us." They climbed up. The could see no one following them; but on a ledge far below them, halfway down the cliff, they spied a nest with two young eagles in it. "Let us at least get those eagles," Black Crow proposed.

---

1. **Oglalas** (äg lä′ ləs): members of a Native American group living in what is now western South Dakota.
2. **tanner and quill worker:** a person who prepares leather and who weaves porcupine quills into decorations.
3. **earn eagle feathers:** to perform acts of bravery, for which a warrior was given eagle feathers to wear in his headdress.
4. **war medicine:** herbs, roots, and magical objects believed by Native Americans to protect them in war.

EAGLE DANCER   Oscar Howe   © 1992 Adelheid Howe
Courtesy, The University of South Dakota, Vermillion.

There was no way one could climb down the sheer rock wall, but Black Crow took his rawhide lariat, made a loop in it, put the rope around Spotted Eagle's chest, under his armpits, and lowered him down. When his friend was on the ledge with the nest, Black Crow said to himself, "I will leave him there to die. I will come home alone, and then Red Bird will marry me." And he threw his end of the rawhide thong down and left without looking back and without listening to Spotted Eagle's cries of what had happened to the lariat and Black Crow.

Spotted Eagle cried in vain. He got no answer, only silence. At last it dawned on him that his companion had betrayed him, that he had been left to die. The lariat was much too short for him to lower himself to the ground; there was an abyss of two hundred feet yawning beneath him. He was left with the two young eagles screeching at him, angered that this strange, two-legged creature had invaded their home.

Black Crow came back to his village. "Spotted Eagle died a warrior's death," he told the people. "The Pahani killed him." There was loud wailing throughout the village because everybody had liked Spotted Eagle. Red Bird grieved more than the others. She slashed her arms with a sharp knife and cut her hair to make plain her sorrow to all. But in the end she became Black Crow's wife, because life must go on.

But Spotted Eagle did not die on his lonely ledge. The eagles got used to him. The old eagles brought plenty of food—rabbits, prairie dogs, or sage hens—and Spotted Eagle shared this raw meat with the two chicks. Maybe it was the eagle medicine in his bundle, which he carried on his chest, that made the eagles accept him. Still, he had a very hard time on that ledge. It was so narrow that when he wanted to rest, he had to tie himself with the rawhide thong to a little rock sticking out of the cliff, for fear of falling off the ledge in his sleep. In this way he spent a few very uncomfortable weeks; after all, he was a human being and not a bird to whom such a crack in the rock face is home.

At last the young eagles were big enough to practice flying. "What will become of me now?" thought the young warrior. "Once these fledglings have flown the nest for good, the old birds won't be bringing any more food up here." Then he had an inspiration. "Perhaps I will die. Very likely I will

Words to Know and Use

sheer (shir) *adj.* very steep; vertical
abyss (ə bis') *n.* a deep hole; chasm

die. But I will try it. I will not just sit here and give up." He took his little pipe out of the medicine bundle and lifted it to the sky and prayed, "*Wakan Tanka, onshimala ye. Great Spirit, pity me.* You have created man and his cousin, the eagle. You have given me the eagle's name. I have decided to try to let the eagles carry me to the ground. Let the eagles help me, let me succeed."

He smoked and felt a surge of confidence. He grabbed hold of the legs of the two young eagles. "Brothers," he told them, "you have accepted me as one of your own. Now we will live together or die together. *Hokahay.*" And he jumped off the ledge. He expected to be shattered on the ground below, but with a mighty flapping of wings the two young eagles broke his fall and all landed safely. Spotted Eagle said a prayer of thanks to the Ones Above. He thanked the eagles, telling them that one day he would be back with gifts and have a giveaway in their honor.

Spotted Eagle returned to his village. The excitement was great. He had been dead and had come back to life. Everybody asked him how it happened that he was not dead, but he would not tell them. "I escaped," he said, "and that is all." He saw his love married to his treacherous friend, but he bore it in silence. He was not one to bring enmity to his people, to set one family against the other. Besides, what happened could not be changed. Thus he accepted his fate.

A year or so later, a great war party of Pahani attacked his village. The enemy outnumbered them tenfold, and there was no chance of victory for Spotted Eagle's band.

All the warriors could do was to fight a slow rear-guard action, which would give the women, children, and old folks a chance to escape across the river. Guarding their people this way, the few warriors at hand fought bravely, charging the enemy again and again, making them halt and regroup. Each time, the warriors retreated a little, taking up a new position on a hill or across a gully. In this way they could save their families.

Showing the greatest courage, exposing their bodies freely, were Spotted Eagle and Black Crow. In the end they alone faced the enemy. Then, suddenly, Black Crow's horse was hit by several arrows in succession and collapsed under him. "Brother, forgive me for what I have done," he cried to Spotted Eagle. "Let me jump up on your horse behind you."

Spotted Eagle answered, "You are a Fox. Pin yourself and fight. Then, if you survive, I will forgive you; and if you die, I will forgive you also."

What Spotted Eagle meant was this: Black Crow was a member of the Fox Warrior Society. The braves who belong to it sing this song:

I am a Fox.
If there is anything daring,
If there is anything dangerous to do,
That is a task for me to perform.
Let it be done by me.

Foxes wear a long, trailing sash, decorated with quill work, which reaches all the way to the ground even when the warrior is on horseback. In the midst of battle, a Fox will sometimes defy death by pinning his sash to the earth with a special wooden pin or with a knife or arrow. This means: I will stay here, rooted to this spot, facing my foes, until someone comes to release the pin, or until the enemies flee, or until I die.

Black Crow pinned his sash to the ground. There was no one to release him, and the enemy did not flee. Black Crow sang his death song. He was hit by lances and arrows and died a warrior's death. Many Pahani died with him.

Spotted Eagle had been the only one to see this. He finally joined his people, safe across the river. The Pahani had lost all taste to follow them there. "Your husband died well," Spotted Eagle told Red Bird. After some time had passed, Spotted Eagle married Red Bird. And much, much later he told his parents, and no one else, how Black Crow had betrayed him. "I forgive him now," he said, "because once he was my friend, and because he died like a warrior should, fighting for his people, and also because Red Bird and I are happy now."

After a long winter, when spring came again, Spotted Eagle told his wife, "I must go away for a few days to fulfill a promise. I must go alone." He rode off by himself to that cliff. Again he stood at its foot, below the ledge where the eagles' nest had been. He pointed his sacred pipe to the four directions, down to Grandmother Earth and up to the Grandfather, letting the smoke ascend to the sky, calling out: "*Wanblee, misunkala.* Little eagle brothers, hear me."

High above him in the clouds appeared two black dots, circling. These were the eagles who had saved his life. They came at his call, their huge wings spread majestically, uttering a shrill cry of joy and recognition. Swooping down, they alighted at his feet. He stroked them with a feather fan, and thanked them many times, and fed them choice morsels of buffalo meat, and fastened small medicine bundles around their legs as a sign of friendship, and spread sacred tobacco offerings around the foot of the cliff. Thus he made a pact of friendship and brotherhood between *Wanblee Oyate*—the Eagle Nation—and his own people. After he had done all this, the stately birds soared up again into the sky, circling motionless, carried by the wind, disappearing into the clouds. Spotted Eagle turned his horse's head homeward, going happily back to Red Bird. 🐾

*R*esponding to Reading

1. What were your thoughts at the end of this legend? Write them down in your journal or on a sheet of paper.

2. Do you think Spotted Eagle should have saved Black Crow's life? Why or why not?

3. In your opinion, what character traits do the Oglalas believe are most important? Explain.

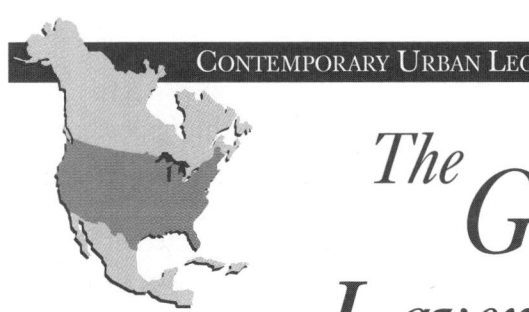

The *Girl in the Lavender Dress*

Retold by MAUREEN SCOTT

My grandmother was, I always believed, a truthful woman. She paid her taxes. She went to church. She considered the Lord's business as her own. When her children told lies, they soon saw the light of truth. They went to bed without any supper, the taste of soap still <u>pungent</u> on their tongues.

That's why the story that follows bothers me so much. It just *can't* be true. Of course, Grandma was ninety-two when she told it to me, and her mind had started to fail. She might have really believed it. Who knows? Maybe you will, too.

I'll try to tell the story just the way she told it to me. She was in a nursing home then. It was late at night, and the two of us were alone in the TV room. Grandma's eyelids hung low over her eyes. She worked her wrinkled jaw a few times and began:

It all happened about '42 or '43 [Grandma said]. It was during World War II. We didn't have much gas in those days. No one did. So whenever Herbert took the car somewhere, I tried to go along for the ride.

We lived in Vermont in those days. This time I'm thinking of, Herbert had some business in Claremont. That's in New Hampshire, just across the river. Well, seems Herbert had saved up the gas to go by car. About twenty-five miles. He said we could leave after work Friday. That night we'd have us a good restaurant meal. Maybe see a movie, too. Then we'd stay in a hotel and drive back the next day.

I don't remember the month, exactly. Sometime in the fall, 'cause it was cool. It was a misty night. I remember Herbert had to keep the wipers going. And it was after dusk when we first saw her. I know it was dark, 'cause I remember first seeing her in the lights ahead.

Neither Herbert nor I spoke. He slowed down, and the girl stopped walking. She just stood there on our side of the road. Not hitching, exactly, but she sure looked like she wanted a ride. It was a lonely road, and there weren't many cars.

First Herbert passed her, going real slow. Then he backed up to where she was. I rolled down my window. She was a pretty little thing, about eighteen or twenty. A round face and big round eyes. Brown hair, cut straight. The mist kind of made her face shine. But the funny thing was what she was wearing: only a thin lavender party dress. In that weather!

Well, I don't remember that anybody did any asking. I just opened the door and leaned forward. She climbed into the back seat, and Herbert started up again. Finally I asked her where she was going.

"Claremont." That was all she said at first. She had a light, breathless voice, like it took a whole lungful of air to say that one word.

"You're lucky," Herbert said. "We're going all the way."

The girl didn't reply. We rode on a little ways. I turned around once or twice, but the girl just smiled, sort of sadly. Anyhow, I didn't want to stare at her. But who was she, and why was she walking on a lonely road at night? I've never been the kind to pry into other people's business. So what I did then was, well, I'd taken off my sweater when the car got warm. I offered it to her, and she put it on.

The mist turned to light rain. Just before we got to the river, Herbert broke the silence. "Where are you going in Claremont, Miss?"

There was no reply.

"It's coming on to rain," Herbert said. "And we got time to deliver you."

"Oh," the girl breathed. "Could you *really?* That would be—that would be *nice.* To my parents' house. Corner of Bond and Mason."

"Claremont must be a nice place to grow up," I said, but again, there was no sound from the back of the car. You couldn't even hear her breathing. I just settled back into my seat and enjoyed the trip. We crossed the bridge and headed into town, and Herbert turned right onto Bond Street.

We rode along, looking at the street signs. Mason was way out. There was only one house on the corner, on the opposite side. Herbert made a U-turn and stopped the car.

There was no one in the rear seat!

I looked at Herbert. He looked at me, his eyes popping. I pulled myself up so I could see the back floor. Nothing. Just a little wetness where her feet had been.

"Where'd she get out?" Herbert asked.

"At a stoplight?" I wondered. But we both knew it couldn't be. It was a two-door car, so we'd know it if a door opened. Both of us looked at the rear windows. They were closed, as they had been. Neither of us had felt a draft.

Yet there had to be some explanation. "Come," Herbert said. We hurried toward the house. It was a big square boxlike building. Lights were on in nearly every room. Splotches of brightness covered the wet lawn.

The door had a name on it: J. R. Bullard. It was opened by a long-faced man about fifty.

"Excuse me," Herbert said, "But there seems to be some mystery. You see, your daughter—"

"Daughter?" said the man. "Why, we don't have any daughter." A small woman, some years younger, now stood at his side.

"Well—" Herbert began.

"We *did* have a daughter," the woman said. "But Carol is deceased, you see. She was buried in Calhoun Cemetery four months ago."

Herbert gripped my arm. We both knew Calhoun Cemetery: it was on the Vermont side of the river. "Then who—?" Herbert wondered aloud. Suddenly he looked embarrassed. "Excuse us," he muttered. "It's all a—a mistake."

"Just a minute," I said. "Would you mind telling us what Carol looked like?"

The couple exchanged glances. If they

were worried, it wasn't about Carol. It was about *us*. "A little on the short side," the woman said, almost to herself. "A round face. Big round eyes. Dark straight hair, cut in bangs."

Herbert's hand was a lobster claw on my elbow. We excused ourselves in a hurry. Back in the car, we sped away through the night. Then we drove around for a long time, looking. Across the bridge. Down every little road. Back into Claremont. Near every stoplight. Along Bond Street.

But we both knew the search was futile. There was only one answer. What we'd had in our car, sitting on the back seat and even talking, was the ghost of Carol Bullard. And the amazing thing was that we had proof. A ghost, you see, cannot cross water. That was why, when we came to the river, the ghost had only one choice: to disappear!

Grandma stopped talking, and I thought that was the end of her incredible story. But no—there was more:

And that isn't all [Grandma went on]. That night—the night that it happened—we were both pretty edgy. Didn't get much sleep, either. Not till the next morning did we think of my sweater. It had disappeared with the ghost.

That was a really good sweater, almost new. You see, we didn't have much money, and it was wartime. Clothes were hard to come by. But once in a while I'd blow a

Illustration © Judy Pederson.

week's pay on something really nice, something that would last for years—like that sweater.

Now listen: it's like this. On the way home, we thought we'd swing around by Calhoun Cemetery. We wanted to find a certain gravestone, the one that would say "Carol Bullard" on it. So we did just that. It took a long time, but finally we found the new graves. And there, at last, was the stone. A small flat stone. Just "Carol Bullard" on it. No dates; nothing more. But next to the stone, neatly folded up, *was my sweater!*

True—or not? You decide. 🍂

Responding to Reading

1. What part of this legend affected you the most?

2. Why do you think the girl was trying to get back home?

3. Do you think this legend could be true? Why or why not?

*R*esponding to Reading

Comparing the Selections

1. Which character do you think had the strongest will to survive? Explain.

2. Which of the tales' themes did you find most meaningful? Why?

Broader Connections

3. People sometimes take extreme measures to survive. Consider your own "ethics of survival." What steps would you take to survive? What would you never do—even if it meant you might lose your life?

*L*iterary Concept: *Urban Legend*

An **urban legend** is a realistic story that is said to have happened recently, often to a relative or to a friend of a friend. Unlike a myth or a folk tale, which is usually obviously fictional, an urban legend often seems as though it actually might have happened. What details make "The Girl in the Lavender Dress" an urban legend?

*W*riting Options

1. What do you think will happen next between Brer Possum and Brer Snake? Write down the **conversation** that might take place as their story continues.

2. Imagine that the girl in the lavender dress left a note in the sweater. What might it have said? Write down the contents of the **note.**

*V*ocabulary Practice

Exercise   On your paper, write the word from the list that best completes the sentence.

1. The _?_ aroma of the campfire drifted toward him.
2. Staring down into the deep _?_, he felt frightened.
3. There was no place to get a foothold on the _?_ rock wall.
4. The _?_ between the Oglalas and the Pahani led to war.
5. The warrior wondered who would cause the battle to _?_.

Words to Know and Use

abyss
commence
enmity
pungent
sheer

*O*ptions for Learning

1 • Terrifying Tales Put together a ghost story-telling contest and feature the winners at a school or community festival. Although this contest would be a natural at Halloween time, ghost stories are popular all year—especially after dark.

2 • Tell Me Another Research one of the types of stories that you particularly liked—"Brer" stories, Native American legends, or urban legends. Share information about your type of tale with the rest of the class.

*J*ackie Torrence   1944–

Jackie Torrence was raised by her grandparents near Salisbury, North Carolina. She delighted in hearing "Brer" stories from her grandfather, the son of an African slave.

A chance incident began Torrence's own storytelling career in 1972. As a reference librarian, Torrence was asked to substitute for a storyteller who had not shown up for work. Four years later, Torrence was telling her stories all over the United States. Since then she has has made seven recordings.

Jackie Torrence first heard "Brer Possum's Dilemma" from her aunt after being bitterly disappointed by the rejection of a high-school friend. Torrence recalls, "When she left, I cried. But Aunt Mildred took me into her arms and said, 'I warned you of her nature.' And she told me this story."

*J*enny Leading Cloud

Jenny Leading Cloud lived in White River, a little town on the Rosebud Sioux Reservation in South Dakota. There she was an outspoken advocate for the rights of Native Americans.

Jenny Leading Cloud never wrote down the stories she heard, but rather told them to her children and her grandchildren. "Spotted Eagle and Black Crow," told and retold for many years, was one of her favorite tales.

WRITER'S WORKSHOP

WRITER'S CHOICE

In this unit you read stories from a variety of cultures, ranging from the Haida people of the Pacific Northwest to the "gentle folk of Argentina." At the same time you encountered several types of folklore—legend, tall tale, myth, and fable. This Writer's Workshop also provides variety. You may choose one of six different writing assignments. The assignments reflect the various types of writing you have done in past Writer's Workshops, and each assignment connects to the folklore in a different way. Which type of writing do you like to do best? Which topic strikes you as the most interesting? It's for you to decide!

A. Descriptive/Narrative Writing: Whopper of the Future

Think of the fabulous exploits of the heroes of tall tales. Pecos Bill and Paul Bunyan fought outlandish battles against the elements of nature and helped tame frontier America. What if a tall tale were set in the future? What would a hero of the future be like and what battles might he, she, or it have to fight? Write a tall tale that is set in the near or distant future. Describe your hero and tell the story of a far-fetched battle somewhere in the universe.

Prewrite and Explore   Think about John Henry, Pecos Bill, and Paul Bunyan. What details make these characters interesting? What battles do they face? What actions make them larger than life? Now imagine your tall-tale hero of the future. Make a list of characteristics you want your hero to have. Take notes about the conflict your character will face.

NEED MORE HELP?

For more about descriptive writing, see the Writer's Workshop on pages 115–119. For more about narrative writing, see the Writer's Workshop on pages 166–170.

Draft and Discover   Using your notes, write the first draft of your story. Describe your hero in vivid detail, then get into the hero's battle. Aim for a clear, fast-paced series of events. Make the actions funny and larger than life.

Revise Your Writing   As you review your draft, consider the checklist questions about character sketches on page 119 and the questions about short stories on page 169. Make any necessary changes and write a final draft.

B. Informative/Narrative Writing: In the Beginning . . .

How did the Rocky Mountains come to be? Why is there rain? Who invented ice cream? Rather than a scientific or historical explanation, can you think of an imaginative, mythical story to explain how one of these things was created? Write a myth that explains the creation of one object in your world.

Prewrite and Explore   Make a list of objects that figure importantly in your life. You might consider such things as the telephone, the bicycle, and the video arcade. You might also add elements of nature to your list. Consider such things as earthquakes, snowstorms, and stars. Choose one subject and freewrite about it for five minutes. Think of an imaginative way for your object to be created. What gods, goddesses, heroes, or heroines could be involved in its creation?

Draft and Discover   Use your freewriting as a guide and write a draft. Tell a simple story that leads up to the creation of the object. Many creation myths begin with a problem (for example, the absence of daylight), and then a hero emerges to solve the problem (the raven sets the daylight free). The object's importance should be made clear, as should your characters' struggle in the creation process.

Revise Your Draft   Work with a partner to review your draft. Use the revision questions on page 169 and page 230 to help you spot ways to improve your paper.

NEED MORE HELP?

For more about narrative and informative writing, see the Writer's Workshops on pages 166–170 and 227–231. For more about myths, see "Elements of Folklore" on pages 648–649.

C. Informative/Persuasive Writing: Now a Word from Our Sponsors

Imagine that a character from this unit is appearing in a TV infomercial to sell a product or service. Picture John Henry selling a spike-driving machine or Owl advertising a self-confidence course. What would their commercials be like? Choose one character from the unit and a product or service that the character could advertise. The possibilities are numerous: Pecos Bill's Storm-Busters Company, Souls in Purgatory Rescue Service, Spotted Eagle's Sky Diving. Write a script for your character's infomercial.

Prewrite and Explore   Review each of the stories in Unit Six and think about the characters. What product could one character have used or what ability could he or she put into a business? Think of an imaginative name for a character's product or service. Take notes, answering the following questions: What is the need for the product? Why is the character an expert on the subject? Why should the viewers buy this particular product?

NEED MORE HELP?

For more about persuasive writing, see the Writer's Workshop on pages 359–363.

Draft and Discover Using your notes, write a draft of the infomercial script. Introduce your character and have him or her give a persuasive testimonial about the product. Include loaded language to appeal to the viewers' emotions. Weave in "facts" about the product. In parentheses describe the scene and the camera movements.

Revise Your Writing Ask a peer to respond to your draft using the revision questions on page 362 as a guide. Consider your classmate's comments as you write your revised draft.

D. Writing About Literature/Persuasion: A Picture of Ourselves

Suppose you are traveling to a world in another galaxy to establish contact with the inhabitants there. Among other things, you can bring one story from Unit Six to give the inhabitants a good idea of human beings. Which story would you bring and why? Write a report for the Space Commission, reviewing the story that you feel will best represent the human race.

Prewrite and Explore Skim through the folklore in the unit. Which story shows the most representative human emotions? Which story has the best moral? Which story displays the finest writing? After you have chosen a story, study it carefully and jot down the reasons why it is the ideal story to represent humankind.

NEED MORE HELP?

For more information on writing a story review, see the Writer's Workshop on pages 479–483.

Draft and Discover Expand your notes into a first draft. At the beginning of your draft, clearly state your opinion of the story. Then specify the reasons why the plot, characters, style, and message reflect humans so well. Include quotes and paraphrased scenes from the story as evidence to support your opinion.

Revise Your Writing Study the revision questions for a critical review on page 482. Make changes based on your answers to these questions.

E. Personal Writing: Family Folklore

Most families have stories of past incidents. Some of these incidents are dramatic—for example, a grandfather's experience in an earthquake. Other incidents are funny—for instance, an aunt's surprise party that went haywire. Such stories are part of a family's culture and are retold and passed along to the children. Write a memorable story that is part of your family's lore.

Prewrite and Explore   Think about the family stories you have heard. Brainstorm with one or more of your family members to recall the most famous stories. Which ones are especially dramatic or funny? Choose one incident and make an outline listing the happenings and the family members involved.

Draft and Discover   Use your outline to write the first draft of your tale. Bring the characters to life with vivid description and realistic dialogue. Build suspense by withholding the resolution until the very end.

Revise Your Writing   Ask someone in your family to read your draft. Have you captured the essence of the story? The revision questions for a memoir on page 59 may be useful.

NEED MORE HELP?

For more information on writing a memoir, see the Writer's Workshop on pages 56–60.

F. Informative Writing: You Could Look It Up

Imagine that a publisher of travel books is creating a series of books called *Cultures of the Americas.* You have been asked to write a report on one culture. The publisher wants information about the people in this culture—their land and lifestyle, their beliefs and traditions, and their pastimes and folklore. Write a research report about one of the cultures represented in Unit Six.

Prewrite and Explore   Review the unit selections, focusing on the region and culture represented in each. Choose one culture you wish to learn more about. Then, consult an encyclopedia and other library sources to find information about the culture. Take detailed notes in four categories: the land, the lifestyle, the beliefs and traditions, and the pastimes and folklore.

Draft and Discover   Refer to your notes as you write the first draft of your report. Organize the report according to the four categories above. Use specifics such as names of places and holidays.

Revise Your Writing   Check your draft against the revision questions on page 637. If possible, ask a classmate to respond to your draft before writing your final report.

NEED MORE HELP?

For more information on writing a research report, see the Writer's Workshop on pages 633–638. See also the Guidelines for Research and Report Writing on pages 758–761 of the Writer's Handbook.

Final Revision

Before you proofread for errors in grammar, spelling, punctuation, and capitalization, check your use of formal or informal language; this topic is explained in the box on the next page.

NEED MORE HELP?

For more information about formal and informal language, see the Language Workshop on pages 726–728.

Publish and Present

Here are some suggestions for sharing your work with others.

Anthology   Collect several futuristic tall tales to put in an anthology. Write an introduction that ties the selections together.

Travel Brochure   Combine the best parts of several research reports on one culture and create a travel brochure about that culture. Include photographs or maps if you wish.

Videotape   Work in a group to stage and videotape one or more infomercials. Make use of props and sound effects.

Reflect on Your Writing

Briefly answer the following questions. Put your answers with your paper and add both to your portfolio.

FOR YOUR PORTFOLIO ▶

1. Which type of writing—descriptive, narrative, informative, persuasive, personal, or literary—do you like best? Explain.
2. How might you use your favorite type of writing in assignments in other classes?

SELF-ASSESSMENT

Portfolio Review

Guided Assignment   Write an essay in which you explain your achievements this year as a writer as well as your goals for future writing.

Prewrite and Explore   Look through your portfolio, taking notes as you go. Also look at your answers to the Reflect on Your Writing questions in the Writer's Workshops. What strengths and weaknesses did you identify in your writing? Has your attitude toward writing changed during the year? Compare papers from early in the year with those you wrote later. You may want to make a chart like the one below.

Strengths	Weaknesses	Ways I Improved	Goals for More Improvement

Draft and Discover   Using your notes and chart, draft your essay. You might begin either with your strengths or with areas you'd like to improve. Use examples from your own work to explain your points. Be sure to include an introduction that will catch readers' attention and a conclusion that includes your goals for future writing.

Revise Your Writing   Create your own Revision Questions that you and a peer can use to review your essay. Be as objective and honest as you can in considering the questions.

Proofread   After completing your revisions, proofread your final draft for errors in spelling, grammar, capitalization, and punctuation.

Publish and Present   Share your essay with your classmates and your teacher. As a group, discuss what you like most—and least—about writing. You might even like to discuss your essay with your parents.

LANGUAGE
WORKSHOP

STANDARD AND NONSTANDARD ENGLISH

When you write, you communicate not only with what you say but also with the way you say it. The way you use language can help you create elements such as character and mood in stories or purpose and tone in informative articles. You can use language differently in various situations as you tailor your writing to your audience and purpose. A knowledge of standard English and nonstandard English can help you vary and enrich your writing. **Standard English** follows accepted standards of grammar, usage, and mechanics. It is used in most professional writing in magazines, books, and newspapers. **Nonstandard English,** on the other hand, does not follow accepted standards of grammar, usage, and mechanics. Expressions like *he don't* and words like *ain't* are nonstandard. Nonstandard English is generally a spoken form of English and usually appears in literature as dialogue.

Formal and Informal English

Standard English can be grouped into two, somewhat overlapping, categories. **Formal English** is suitable for any situation that is serious, dignified, or ceremonial. **Informal English** is suitable for casual situations, such as everyday conversations or class discussions; it is also used in newspapers and magazines.

Both formal and informal English use correct grammar; however, they differ in tone, vocabulary, and organization.

	Formal English	**Informal English**
Tone	Serious, reserved ceremonial	Personal, friendly
Vocabulary	May use long or less common words; avoids contractions and colloquialisms	Uses simple common words; often uses contractions and colloquialisms
Organization	Carefully constructed sentences, many of which are long	Sentences of various lengths; similar to conversation

The examples that follow show situations that range from very informal to very formal. Studying them should help you determine when to use formal English and when to use informal English.

Conversations, friendly letters: I loved that new program about folk tales. You really should see it if you get a chance.

Humorous writing: Once upon a time, there was a magic tree; it grew higher than the eye could see.

Serious essays, news stories: The new musical at the Newberg Theater incorporated a number of well-known folk tales.

Formal speeches, school reports, job applications: Today, I proudly present our Storyteller's Award to Joel King for his work in the preservation of American folklore.

Exercise 1 Concept Check The following sentences were written as part of a school report about folk tales. Rewrite any sentences that are too informal. Mark those sentences that are written at an appropriate level as *Appropriate.*

1. Folk tales get right to the nitty gritty.
2. They paint a picture of people's lives and ideas.
3. Sometimes they give the lowdown on weird stuff in nature that folks can't figure out.
4. For example, "The Growin' of Paul Bunyan" explains how the first redwood tree grew.
5. Paul's redwood tree is really cool.
6. This is why many cultures often have similar tales.
7. Another common theme in folk tales is survival.
8. In those you see these guys turn themselves all inside out to face some big problem without croaking.
9. In "Brer Possum's Dilemma," the snake exhibits friendliness in order to get Brer Possum's help.
10. The snake looked pitiful.

Exercise 2 Revision Skill The following letter is part of an application for a job as a storyteller. Rewrite the letter in more formal English.

Hi Miss Finney,

I was passing by the bulletin board at school the other day and I saw your nifty poster about the storyteller's job. Well, look no further. I'm your gal. Folk tales are my favorite thing to read. They just seem so real. Also, I tell stories every night to my three pesty brothers and sisters. They can tell you how cool my storytelling is. I know lots of great old stuff, and this year in school we read some new tales, so I know those too. I'm free anytime you'd like to talk about the job. I could do this job with my eyes closed. Well, not really, but hire me anyway, OK?

Exercise 3   Revision Skill   Read the following conversation between two friends carefully. Correct any language that is not appropriate to the situation.

> Hi, Gina, it's Theresa. Can you become available for a social engagement on Friday? A bunch of us are going to the dance together. We'd love you to come along. I assure you it won't be a long evening.
>
> Great idea, Theresa. I'll have to ask my mom but I'm sure she'll say it's okay. What would be the correct way to dress?
>
> Wear those neat jeans and a cool top. Then you will certainly be suitably dressed.
>
> Okay. See ya Friday. I shall be prepared to leave at 7:00 in the evening.

Exercise 4   Revising Your Writing

1. Choose the paper your wrote for the Writer's Workshop on pages 720–724 or another paper from your portfolio.
2. Skim your writing for words, phrases, or sentences that are written either too formally or too informally for the assignment.
3. Rewrite the sentences to better fit the situation.
4. Remember to think about how formal your language should be for a given writing assignment.

TRY IT TOGETHER

Informal language is not incorrect—it is simply not suited to some situations. Try the revision exercise with a partner. You may find that you both have different ideas about how formal the language should be.

VOCABULARY
WORKSHOP

IDIOMATIC EXPRESSIONS

There are many ways of making your writing richer and more vivid. One way is by using idioms. An **idiom** is an expression that has a meaning different from the sum of the meanings of the individual words. For example, if you heard someone say that washing a car is "a piece of cake," you would know that the meaning of the expression has nothing to do with cake. Rather, the speaker meant that the task is easy.

You can use idioms appropriately in all informal situations, but you should generally avoid them in formal writing and speaking. Before you use an idiom, ask yourself whether your readers will understand it. Here are some idioms and their meanings.

Idiom	Literal Meaning
in the doghouse	in trouble
catch some z's	sleep
Dutch treat	paying your own way
feather in your cap	honor
a drop in the bucket	very small amount

Exercise   Use context to figure out the meaning of each underlined idiom. Write definitions for the idiomatic expressions. Then, write sentences that show your understanding of the idioms.

1. "Juan, get away from that <u>idiot box</u>. You know you're not supposed to watch it so much!" yelled Rosa.
2. "You're <u>making a mountain out of a molehill</u>, Rosa. I was only watching it for twenty minutes."
3. "Besides, you have to wash dishes," Rosa replied, "and I know you're going to need <u>elbow grease</u> to get them clean."
4. "<u>Cool your heels</u>, Rosa! I'll be there in a minute."
5. "Juan, Mom and Dad just pulled into the driveway," said Rosa, "and I'm going to <u>spill the beans</u>."
6. "<u>You're pulling my leg</u>, aren't you? They're not supposed to be home."
7. "If you think I'm <u>putting you on</u>, look out the front window."
8. "Oh, well! I guess I'm <u>up against a brick wall</u>. I'll wash the dishes, Rosa," said Juan.
9. "One more thing, Rosa, if you <u>button your lip</u> about my TV watching, I'll do your chores for a week."
10. "OK, Juan, you're <u>in business</u>," laughed Rosa.

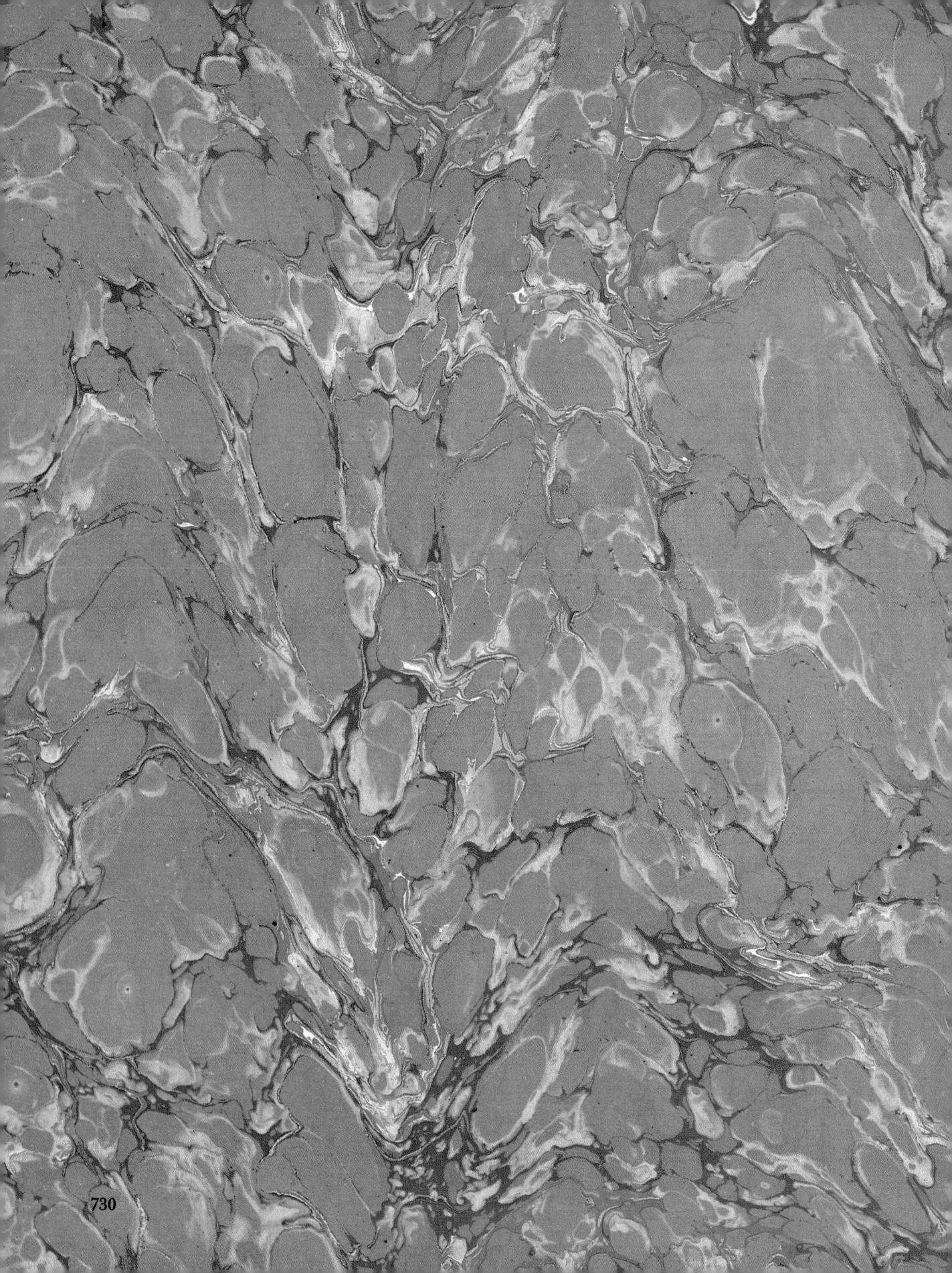

Handbook Contents

READER'S HANDBOOK

GLOSSARY

The **glossary** is an alphabetical listing of words from the selections, with meanings. The glossary gives the following information:

1. The entry word broken into syllables.

2. The pronunciation of each word. The **respelling** is shown in parentheses. The Pronunciation Key below shows the symbols for the sounds of letters and key words that contain those sounds.

A **primary accent** ′ is placed after the syllable that is stressed the most when the word is spoken. A **secondary accent** ′ is placed after a syllable that has a lighter stress.

3. The part of speech of the word. These abbreviations are used:

n. noun *v.* verb *adj.* adjective *adv.* adverb

4. The meaning of the word. The definitions listed in the glossary apply to selected ways a word is used in these selections.

5. Related forms. Words with suffixes such as *-ing, -ed, -ness,* and *-ly* are often listed under the base word.

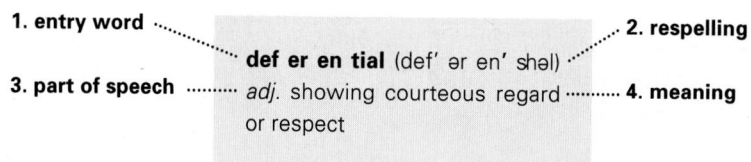

1. entry word ⋯⋯⋯
3. part of speech ⋯⋯⋯

def er en tial (def′ ər en′ shəl)
adj. showing courteous regard or respect

2. respelling
4. meaning

Pronunciation Key

Symbol	Key Words	Symbol	Key Words	Symbol	Key Words	Symbol	Key Words
a	at, gas	o͞o	tool, crew	ə { a	in ago	ch	chin
ā	ape, day	o͝o	look, pull	e	in agent	sh	she
ä	car, lot	yo͞o	use, cute, few	i	in insanity	th	thin
e	elf, ten	yo͝o	cure	o	in comply	th	then
ē	even, me	oi	oil, coin	u	in focus	zh	leisure
i	is, hit	ou	out, sour			ŋ	ring
ī	bite, fire	u	up, cut			′	able (ā′ b'l)
ō	own, go	ʉr	fur, bird				
ô	law, horn	er	perhaps, murder				

Foreign Symbols

à	salle	*n*	mon
ë	coer	ᵭ	abuelos
ö	feu	*r*	gringos
ü	rue		

A

ab surd (ab surd') *adj.* ridiculously false

a byss (ə bis') *n.* a deep hole; chasm

ac ces si ble (ak ses' ə bəl) *adj.* able to be reached

ac com mo da tion (ə käm' ə dā' shən) *n.* a favor or convenience

ac curs ed (ə kur' sid) *adj.* under a curse; enchanted

a cute (ə kyōōt') *adj.* sharp; keen

ad lib (ad' lib') *adv.* by improvising; speaking in one's own words

a dorn ing (ə dôrn' iŋ) *adj.* decorating; ornamenting **adorn** *v.*

ag gra vat ing (ag' rə vāt' iŋ) *adj.* annoying **aggravate** *v.*

a ghast (ə gast') *adj.* horrified

ag ile (aj' əl) *adj.* able to move quickly and easily

ag i tat ed (aj' i tāt' id) *adj.* upset; disturbed

a loof (ə lōōf') *adj.* distant and uninvolved

al ter na tive (ôl tur' nə tiv) *n.* an available choice

am bas sa dor (am bas' ə dər) *n.* a country's chief representative in a foreign land

an ti sep tic (an' tə sep' tik) *adj.* thoroughly clean

anx i e ty (aŋ zī' ə tē) *n.* a feeling of worry, nervousness, and fear

ap palled (ə pôld') *adj.* horrified; shocked **appall** *v.*

ap praise (ə prāz') *v.* to judge the worth or significance of

ap pre hen sion (ap' rē hen' shən) *n.* anxiousness; dread

ar ro gant (ar' ə gənt) *adj.* proud and scornful

as ser tion (ə sur' shən) *n.* a statement

as sess (ə ses') *v.* to determine or judge

as sur ance (ə shōōr' əns) *n.* self-confidence

au dac i ty (ô das' ə tē) *n.* shameless daring or boldness

av a rice (av' ə ris) *n.* a great desire for wealth

B

bel lig er ent ly (bə lij' ər ənt lē) *adv.* in a combative way

ben e fac tor (ben' ə fak' tər) *n.* a person who provides money or help

blurt (blurt) *v.* to say quickly, without thinking

borne (bôrn) *adj.* carried **bear** *v.*

buck le (buk' əl) *v.* to collapse or give way

bur ly (bur' lē) *adj.* big and muscular

C

cap ti vate (kap' tə vāt) *v.* to fascinate or charm

car i ca ture (kar' i kə chər) *v.* to depict features or mannerisms in an exaggerated way

cas cade (kas kād') *n.* a waterfall

cas u al ly (kazh' ōō əl ē) *adv.* in an informal or relaxed way

ca tas tro phe (kə tas' trə fē) *n.* a sudden disaster or calamity

cat call (kat' kôl') *n.* a harsh cry or whistle intended as an insult

cav a lier (kav' ə lir') *adj.* unconcerned; casual

chant (chant) *n.* words repeated in a singsong way

chaste (chāst) *adj.* simple; not fancy

chron i cle (krän' i kəl) *n.* a record of events

clam ber (klam' bər) *v.* to climb clumsily

com mence (kə mens') *v.* to begin

com pas sion ate (kəm pash' ən it) *adj.* sympathizing deeply

com pel (kəm pel') *v.* to force

com pen sate (käm' pən sāt') *v.* to make up for

com pe tent (käm' pə tənt) *adj.* qualified; capable

com plex (käm' pleks') *n.* an exaggerated concern or preoccupation

com ply (kəm plī') *v.* to obey a rule or command

con ceived (kən sēvd') *adj.* thought of **conceive** *v.*

con front (kən frunt') *v.* to face up to; oppose boldly

con se quence (kän' si kwens') *n.* importance

con ser va tive (kən sur' və tiv) *adj.* traditional in style and manner

con sole (kən sōl') *v.* to comfort

con spi ra to ri al (kən spir' ə tôr' ē əl) *adj.* having to do with people secretly plotting together

con tempt (kən tempt') *n.* a feeling of scorn and disgust

con trar y (kän' trer' ē) *n.* the opposite point of view

con vic tion (ken vik' shən) *n.* a firm belief

cor ral (kə ral') *v.* to capture; round up

cow er (kou' ər) *v.* to cringe in fear

crev ice (krev' is) *n.* a crack

cun ning ly (kun' iŋ lē) *adv.* cleverly and slyly

D

dead pan (ded' pan') *adj.* without expression

de bris (də brē') *n.* the remains of something destroyed

de crep it (dē krep′ it) *adj.* broken down; worn out

de fi ant (dē fī′ ənt) *adj.* boldly challenging

del e te ri ous (del′ ə tir′ ē əs) *adj.* harmful

de pre ci ate (dē prē′ shē āt′) *v.* to cause to seem less valuable

de rive (di rīv′) *v.* to get; obtain

de te ri o rate (dē tir′ ē ə rāt′) *v.* to become worse

de test (dē test′) *v.* to hate

dev as tat ing (dev′ əs tāt′ iŋ) *adj.* destructive **devastate** *v.*

de vo tion (di vō′ shən) *n.* a feeling of worship or loyalty

dil i gent (dil′ ə jənt) *adj.* hard-working and careful

dis close (dis klōz′) *v.* to reveal

dis creet (di skrēt′) *adj.* careful and considerate

dis grun tled (dis grunt′ 'ld) *adj.* displeased and irritated **disgruntle** *v.*

di shev eled (di shev′ əld) *adj.* messy; untidy

dis mal (diz′ məl) *adj.* gloomy; miserable

dis pel (di spel′) *v.* to drive away

dis pers ing (di spurs′ iŋ) *adj.* scattering **disperse** *v.*

dis sec tion (di sek′ shən) *n.* a cutting apart for detailed study

dis tinct (di stiŋkt′) *adj.* clear and unmistakable

dog ged ness (dôg′ id nis) *n.* stubbornness

dole ful (dōl′ fəl) *adj.* full of sadness

dom i nate (däm′ ə nāt′) *v.* to rule or control

don (dän) *v.* to put on; dress in

drove (drōv) *n.* a mob or crowd

du bi ous (dōō′ bē əs) *adj.* of questionable value or quality

dumb found ed (dum′ found′ id) *adj.* speechless with amazement **dumbfound** *v.*

dwin dling (dwin′ dliŋ) *adj.* shrinking **dwindle** *v.*

E

ec stat ic (ek stat′ ik) *adj.* overpowered by joy; delighted

e lab o rate (ē lab′ ə rāt′) *v.* to add details to

el i gi ble (el′ i jə bəl) *adj.* qualified to receive something

el o quence (el′ ə kwəns) *n.* ability to speak forcefully and persuasively

en croach (en krōch′) *v.* to intrude in a slow, sneaky way

en gulf (en gulf′) *v.* to flow over; overwhelm

en mi ty (en′ mə tē) *n.* bitter hatred

e vade (ē vād′) *v.* avoid; get away from

ex alt ed (eg zôlt′ id) *adj.* uplifted; elated **exalt** *v.*

ex ca va tion (eks′ kə vā′ shən) *n.* something unearthed by digging

ex er tion (eg zur′ shən) *n.* an effort

F

fath om (fath′ əm) *v.* to understand thoroughly

fe ro cious (fə rō′ shəs) *adj.* wildly cruel; savage

fi an cé (fē′ än sā′) *n.* a man engaged to marry a woman

fix at ed (fiks′ āt′ id) *adj.* having one's attention absorbed; engrossed **fixate** *v.*

fix ed ly (fiks′ id lē) *adv.* in a constant, unmoving way

flour ish (flur′ ish) *v.* to thrive; be successful

flu ent ly (flōō′ ənt lē) *adv.* easily; smoothly

fore bod ing (fôr bōd′ iŋ) *n.* a feeling that something—especially something bad or harmful—is about to happen

for lorn (fôr lôrn′) *adj.* abandoned or deserted

foun der (foun′ dər) *v.* to get stuck; break down

fruit less (frōōt′ lis) *adj.* unsuccessful

fur tive ly (fur′ tiv lē) *adv.* in a secret or sneaky way

fu til i ty (fyōō til′ ə tē) *n.* uselessness

G

gait (gāt) *n.* a foot movement of a horse

gaud y (gôd′ ē) *adj.* showy and tasteless

glade (glād) *n.* an open space in a forest

glib (glib) *adj.* smooth and fluent

gloat (glōt) *v.* to show triumph or delight

gnarled (närld) *adj.* twisted and rough

grim (grim) *adj.* fierce; cruel

gri mace (grim′ əs, or gri mās′) *v.* to make a face

gus to (gus′ tō) *n.* enthusiasm; zest

H

hap haz ard (hap′ haz′ ərd) *adj.* without planning; random

heart en ing (härt′ 'n iŋ) *adj.* cheering **hearten** *v.*

height ened (hīt′ 'nd) *adj.* made stronger or more intense **heighten** *v.*

hid e ous (hid′ ē əs) *adj.* ugly and horrifying

hum ble (hum′ bəl) *adj.* not proud; modest

hur tle (hurt′ 'l) *v.* to dash recklessly

hyp o crit i cal (hip′ ə krit′ i kəl) *adj.* false or deceptive, as of a person who is pretending to be what he or she is not

hy poth e sis (hī päth′ ə sis) *n.* a theory used as the basis for research

I

il lu mi nate (i lōō′ mə nāt′) *v.* to make understandable; explain

im pact (im′ pakt) *n.* a strong effect

im pair (im per′) *v.* to weaken; make worse

im pli ca tion (im′ pli kā′ shən) *n.* a possible meaning or significance

im ply (im plī′) *v.* to suggest indirectly

im pulse (im′ puls′) *n.* a sudden urge

in ar tic u late (in′ är tik′ yōō lit) *adj.* speechless

in cen tive (in sent′ iv) *n.* encouragement to make an effort

in ci sor (in sī′ zər) *n.* a cutting tooth

in com pre hen si ble (in′ käm′ prē hen′ sə bəl) *adj.* not capable of being understood

in con se quen tial (in kän′ si kwen′ shəl) *adj.* of no importance

in cred u lous (in krej′ ōō ləs) *adj.* unbelieving; doubting

in dif fer ence (in dif′ ər əns) *n.* a lack of concern or feeling

in dig nant ly (in dig′ nənt lē) *adv.* in anger at something unfair

in di rect (in′ də rekt′) *adj.* not straightforward; roundabout

in ef fa ble (in ef′ ə bəl) *adj.* not expressible in words

in ef fec tu al ly (in′ e fek′ chōō əl ē) *adv.* without success; uselessly

in ert (in urt′) *adj.* not active; motionless

in her ent ly (in hir′ ənt lē) *adv.* basically; essentially

in sti gate (in′ stə gāt′) *v.* to stir up; provoke

in still (in stil′) *v.* to supply gradually

in stinc tive ly (in stiŋk′ tiv lē) *adv.* in a natural, unlearned way

in suf fer a ble (in suf′ ər ə bəl) *adj.* unbearable

in ten si ty (in ten′ sə tē) *n.* strength or energy

in ter ces sion (in′ tər sesh′ ən) *n.* the asking of a favor on behalf of another

in tim i date (in tim′ ə dāt′) *v.* to frighten with threats

in tu i tion (in′ tōō ish′ ən) *n.* a knowledge obtained without the conscious use of reasoning

ir ra tion al (ir rash′ ə nəl) *adj.* senseless; not thought out carefully

ir ri ta bil i ty (ir′ i tə bil′ ə tē) *n.* state of being easily annoyed

J

jeer (jir) *v.* to make fun of; mock

jos tle (jäs′ əl) *v.* to bump against or push

jo vi al (jō′ vē əl) *adj.* jolly and sociable

ju bi la tion (jōō′ bə lā′ shən) *n.* a happy celebration

ju di cious (jōō dish′ əs) *adj.* careful; showing good judgment

L

la ment (lə ment′) *v.* to express grief

lapse (laps) *v.* to drift or fall

lark (lärk) *n.* a merry adventure

lep rous (lep′ rəs) *adj.* extremely disagreeable

loathe (lōth) *v.* to dislike intensely

lon er (lōn′ ər) *n.* a person who prefers to live, work, or play alone

lu cid (lōō′ sid) *adj.* mentally alert; in one's right mind

M

main stay (mān′ stā′) *n.* a chief member or supporter

maze (māz) *n.* a confusing network of passageways

mea ger (mē′ gər) *adj.* small in quantity

me di an (mē′ dē ən) *adj.* being the middle value in a series

mel an chol y (mel′ ən käl′ ē) *adj.* in low spirits; depressed

merg ing (murj′ iŋ) *adj.* combining; blending **merge** *v.*

me tic u lous ly (mə tik′ yōō ləs lē) *adv.* very carefully

min strel (min′ strəl) *n.* a singer or musician

mod er ate ly (mäd′ ər it lē) *adv.* reasonably; not excessively

mo ti va tion (mōt′ ə vā′ shən) *n.* a driving force; incentive

mul ti tude (mul′ tə tōōd′) *n.* a great number; crowd

mus ing (myōōz′ iŋ) *adj.* thinking in a relaxed, quiet way **muse** *v.*

N

na ïve té (nä ēv tā′) *n.* natural simplemindedness

net tled (net′ əld) *adj.* irritated **nettle** *v.*

no ble (nō′ bəl) *adj.* of high rank

no ta tion (nō tā′ shən) *n.* a short note added to a document

O

ob li ga to ry (əb lig′ ə tôr′ ē) *adj.* required

ob scure (əb skyoor′) *v.* to hide from view

om i nous ly (äm′ ə nəs lē) *adv.* in a threatening way

on slaught (än′ slôt′) *n.* a violent, intense attack

op por tun ist (äp′ ər tōōn′ ist) *n.* a person who takes advantage of any opportunity for self-advancement, even if it means ignoring moral principles

op pres sion (ə presh′ ən) *n.* domination by the cruel use of power

op ti mis tic (äp′ tə mis′ tik) *adj.* hopeful

os ten ta tious ly (äs′ tən tā′ shəs lē) *adv.* with great show

out raged (out′ rājd′) *adj.* angry and insulted **outrage** *v.*

P

pal ate (pal′ ət) *n.* sense of taste

pan de mo ni um (pan′ də mō′ nē əm) *n.* a wild disorder, noise, or confusion

par ti tioned (pär tish′ ənd) *adj.* divided by interior walls **partition** *v.*

pa thet ic (pə thet′ ik) *adj.* pitiful

ped i greed (ped′ i grēd) *adj.* purebred; having recorded ancestors

pent-up (pent′ up′) *adj.* held in check; restrained

per cep tion (pər sep′ shən) *n.* impression; understanding

per ma nence (pur′ mə nəns) *n.* a state of remaining unchanged forever

per se ver ing (pur′ sə vir′ iŋ) *adj.* determined to continue **persevere** *v.*

per sist (pər sist′) *v.* to continue stubbornly

per spec tive (pər spek′ tiv) *n.* a point of view

phil o soph i cal (fil′ ō säf′ ik əl) *adj.* involving general beliefs about the nature of thought and reality

pre car i ous (prē ker′ ē əs) *adj.* not secure; risky

pre dic a ment (prē dik′ ə mənt) *n.* a troublesome or difficult situation

pre dom i nat ing (prē däm′ ə nāt′ iŋ) *adj.* most important or frequent **predominate** *v.*

preen (prēn) *v.* to show pride and self-satisfaction

pre tense (prē tens′) *n.* the act of attempting to fool someone

primp (primp) *v.* to fuss over one's appearance

pro cure (prō kyoor′) *v.* to get; acquire

pro found (prō found′) *adj.* deep

prone (prōn) *adj.* having a tendency; inclined

pro por tion al (prō pôr′ shə nəl) *adj.* having a constant relation in degree or number

pun gent (pun′ jənt) *adj.* sharp and intense odor

Q

quaint (kwānt) *adj.* pleasantly unusual or old-fashioned

qual i fied (kwôl′ i fīd′) *adj.* having met the requirements **qualify** *v.*

quashed (kwäsht) *adj.* ended suddenly **quash** *v.*

quest (kwest) *n.* a search

R

ral ly (ral′ ē) *v.* to come together to provide help

rap port (ra pôr′) *n.* a relationship of understanding and agreement

rash (rash) *adj.* reckless

rav e nous (rav′ ə nəs) *adj.* very hungry

re buke (ri byōōk′) *n.* a sharp criticism

re frain (ri frān′) *v.* to hold oneself back

re gal (rē′ gəl) *adj.* magnificent; kingly

re gres sion (ri gresh′ ən) *n.* the return to a less developed condition

re luc tant (ri luk′ tənt) *adj.* hesitant; unwilling

re luc tant ly (ri luk′ tənt lē) *adv.* unwillingly

re mit (ri mit′) *v.* to send in payment

re morse (ri môrs′) *n.* deep regret for past wrongdoing

re mote (ri mōt′) *adj.* off the beaten track

re pos sess (rē′ pə zes′) *v.* to take back property from a buyer who has not made payment

re pris al (ri prī′ zəl) *n.* an act of revenge

re proach ful ly (ri prōch′ fəl ē) *adv.* in a blaming way

re pul sive (ri pul′ siv) *adj.* disgusting

re side (ri zīd′) *v.* to occupy a home

re solve (ri zälv′) *v.* to make up one's mind

re sort (ri zôrt′) *v.* (followed by *to*) to make use of

re spon sive (ri spän′ siv) *adj.* quick to react to another

re store (ri stôr′) *v.* to bring back to a former condition

rev er ence (rev′ ər əns) *n.* a feeling of deep respect

rev er ie (rev′ ər ē) *n.* a daydream

rue ful ly (rōō′ fəl ē) *adv.* with sorrow and embarrassment

S

sar don i cal ly (sär dän′ ik lē) *adv.* scornfully; in a mocking way

scowl (skoul) *v.* to frown

scru ti nize (skrōōt′ 'n īz′) *v.* to observe carefully

sen sa tion (sen sā′ shən) *n.* something that causes people to become very interested and enthusiastic

sen ti nel (sen′ ti nəl) *n.* a guard

se rene (sə rēn′) *adj.* calm

sheer (shir) *adj.* very steep; vertical

shift less (shift′ ləs) *adj.* lazy; lacking ambition

shrew (shro͞o) *n.* a mean, nagging woman

shrewd ness (shro͞od′ nis) *n.* cleverness

shroud (shroud) *n.* a covering; veil

skep tic (skep′ tik) *n.* a person who questions what is accepted by others

smug (smug) *adj.* self-satisfied

so ci o path ic (sō′ sē ə path′ ik) *adj.* having a mental disorder that causes one to harm others, often violently

so phis ti cat ed (sə fis′ tə kāt′ id) *adj.* mature; stylish

spe cial i za tion (spesh′ əl ə zā′ shən) *n.* focusing on a particular study or activity

spec trum (spek′ trəm) *n.* the complete range of colors

spec u la tion (spek′ yo͞o lā′ shən) *n.* a thought or idea

spi ral ing (spī′ rəl iŋ) *adj.* moving in circles **spiral** *v.*

sta ble (stā′ bəl) *adj.* firm; difficult to move

stalk (stôk) *v.* to pursue or follow in a grim way

sta tis ti cal ly (stə tis′ tik lē) *adv.* in a way that involves numerical facts

stealth i ly (stel′ thə lē) *adv.* sneakily; slyly

steel y (stēl′ ē) *adj.* stern; hard as steel

sti fled (stī′ fəld) *adj.* held back **stifle** *v.*

stout ly (stout′ lē) *adv.* strongly; thickly

strik ing (strī′ kiŋ) *adj.* impressive; remarkable

stunt ed (stunt′ id) *adj.* hindered in growth **stunt** *v.*

sub dued (səb do͞od′) *adj.* calmed down **subdue** *v.*

sub side (səb sīd′) *v.* to lessen in activity or intensity

sub stance (sub′ stəns) *n.* the material from which a thing is made

sulk y (sul′ kē) *adj.* irritable and unsociable

sul len ly (sul′ ən lē) *adv.* in a sulky, resentful way

su per flu ous (sə pʉr′ flo͞o əs) *adj.* unnecessary; extra

sus te nance (sus′ tə nəns) *n.* comfort; nourishment

T

tal on (tal′ən) *n.* an animal's claw

te di ous (tē′ dē əs) *adj.* boring; tiring

ten ta tive ly (ten′ tə tiv lē) *adv.* in an uncertain or hesitant way

tes ti ly (tes′ tə lē) *adv.* in an irritated way

ther a py (ther′ ə pē) *n.* a treatment for mental or physical disorders

thrive (thrīv) *v.* to grow in strength or numbers; flourish

thwart ed (thwôrt′ id) *adj.* frustrated; not satisfied **thwart** *v.*

ti rade (tī′ rād′) *n.* a long, angry speech

to ken (tō′ kən) *n.* a keepsake; souvenir

tor so (tôr′ sō) *n.* the part of the body between the neck and legs, not including the arms

tran quil li ty (tran kwil′ ə tē) *n.* calmness

tyr an ny (tir′ ə nē) *n.* cruel and unjust government

U

un daunt ed (un dônt′ id) *adj.* not discouraged

un dis put ed (un di spyo͞ot′ id) *adj.* not to be doubted; unquestionable

un doubt ed ly (un dout′ id lē) *adv.* definitely

un du la tion (un′ dyo͞o lā′ shən) *n.* a wavelike motion

un nerv ing (un nʉrv′ iŋ) *adj.* causing a loss of courage **unnerve** *v.*

un rul y (un ro͞ol′ ē) *adj.* hard to control; disobedient

un war y (un wer′ ē) *adj.* not cautious or alert

ut ter ly (ut′ ər lē) *adv.* completely

V

vain (vān) *adj.* useless; worthless

ver i fy (ver′ ə fī′) *v.* to prove or demonstrate

vi brant (vī′ brənt) *adj.* bright and sparkling

vig i lant (vij′ ə lənt) *adj.* watchful

vile (vīl) *adj.* disgusting

vi sa (vē′ zə) *n.* an official permission to leave or enter a country

vi va cious (vī vā′ shəs) *adj.* lively

viv id (viv′ id) *adj.* producing clear mental images

vogue (vōg) *n.* style; fashion

W

wal low (wäl′ ō) *v.* to lie relaxed in water

wax (waks) *v.* to grow

wir y (wīr′ ē) *adj.* thin but strong

won der ment (wun′ dər mənt) *n.* a feeling of wonder; amazement

wry ly (rī′ lē) *adv.* in an ironic way; using dry humor

LITERARY AND READING TERMS

Act   An act is a major section of a play. Each act may be further divided into **scenes.** *The Diary of Anne Frank* has two acts.
   See *Drama* and *Scene.*

Alliteration   Alliteration is the repetition of consonant sounds at the beginnings of words. Writers use alliteration to emphasize certain words and to give their writing a musical quality. Note the repetition of the f̲ sound in this line from "Watching Gymnasts":

   They f̲ollow f̲ollow as voices in a f̲ugue.

Allusion   An allusion is a reference to a famous person, place, event, or other work of literature. In "Raymond's Run," Squeaky makes an allusion to Dodge City in the Old West when she meets her competitor on the street.

Analysis   Analysis is the process of breaking something down into its elements and examining each one. For example, to analyze a poem, one would look at such elements as form, rhyme, rhythm, figurative language, imagery, mood, and theme.

Antagonist   The antagonist is the force working against the protagonist, or main character, in a literary work. An antagonist can be another character, a force of nature, society, or even a force within the main character. In "Appetizer," Ms. Bear is the narrator's antagonist.

Author's Purpose   An author's purpose may be to entertain, to explain or inform, to express an opinion, or to persuade readers to do or believe something. The author may combine two or three purposes, but one is usually most important.

Autobiography   An autobiography is a form of nonfiction in which one person tells the story of his or her life. *Once Upon a Time When We Were Colored* is an example of autobiography.
   See *Nonfiction.*

Biography   A biography is the story of a person's life written by another person. The subjects of biographies are often famous people, as in Ann Petry's *Harriet Tubman: Conductor on the Underground Railroad.*
   See *Nonfiction.*

Cast of Characters   In a drama, the cast of characters is usually given at the beginning of the script. It is a list of all the characters in the play, often in order of appearance.
   See *Drama.*

Cause and Effect   Cause and effect describes a relationship between events in literature. One event brings about a second event. The first event in time is the cause; the second event is the effect. These lines from "The Enchanted Raisin" show a cause and an effect: "Little devils . . . if you keep up these stories, you are going to get it. I don't want to hear you mention that raisin again!"

Character   A character is a person, an animal, or an imaginary creature that takes part in the action of a literary work. Generally, a work focuses on one or more **main characters.** Less important characters are called **minor characters.**

Character Change   Characters that grow or change during a story are said to go through character development. A character that changes significantly is called a **dynamic character.** Main characters often develop the most. For example, Connie in "Dancing for Poppa" is a dynamic character. In contrast, characters that change only a little or not at all are said to be **static characters.**

Characterization   Characterization refers to the techniques a writer uses to create and develop a character. There are four basic methods of developing a character: (1) a physical description of the character, (2) the character's thoughts, speech, or actions, (3) the thoughts, speech, and actions of other characters, (4) direct comments on a character's nature.

Chronological Order Chronological order refers to the order in which events happen in time. For example, *Flowers for Algernon* is told in chronological order.

Climax The climax, or turning point, is the high point of interest in the plot of a story or play. At the climax, the conflict is resolved, and the outcome of the plot becomes clear. The climax of "Raymond's Run," for example, occurs when Squeaky wins the race.

    See *Plot.*

Comparison The process of identifying similarities is called comparison. In "Stop the Sun," the writer compares the father's terrified breathing to the panting of "some kind of hurt animal."

Conflict Conflict is a struggle between two opposing forces. In an **external conflict,** such as the battle between Gustus and the hurricane in "The Banana Tree," a character struggles against some outside person or force. **Internal conflict** occurs when the struggle is within a character. In "Checkouts," for example, both the grocery boy and the young girl experience internal conflict about speaking to each other.

    See *Plot.*

Connecting The process of relating the content of a literary work to the reader's own knowledge or experience is called connecting. For example, many readers may connect with the embarrassing moments described by Delia Ephron in "How to Die of Embarrassment."

Context Clues Context clues are the words or phrases before or after an unfamiliar word that help explain its meaning. Context clues may define the word, give a synonym for it, give an example, provide comparisons or contrasts, or enable readers to infer the meaning.

Contrast The pointing out of differences between two or more things is called contrast. In "Dancer" note how Clarissa is contrasted with other children:

Some foster kids come with lots of stuff, but she came with everything she had in a paper bag.

Description Description is a picture, in words, of a scene, a character, or an object. A description might appeal to the reader's senses or provide detailed information about characters or events.

    See *Figurative Language* and *Imagery.*

Dialect Dialect is a form of language as it is spoken in a certain place or among a certain group of people. A dialect has its own pronunciations, spellings, and expressions. Note the rural dialect in this passage from "The Growin' of Paul Bunyan": "So on this partic'lar day ole Paul is out o' sorts because of a moose that's got stuck down betwixt his toes."

Dialogue A conversation between two or more characters is called dialogue. In most literary forms, dialogue is set off by quotation marks. In plays, however, dialogue simply follows the name of the character who is speaking, and it does not require quotation marks.

Diary A diary is a personal, day-to-day account of a writer's experiences, thoughts, and feelings. Diaries are a form of nonfiction since they describe real events. *The Diary of Anne Frank* is a dramatized version of a diary.

Drama A drama, or play, is a form of literature meant to be performed by actors before an audience. In drama, the story is told through the dialogue and the actions of the characters.

    See *Act, Cast of Characters, Dialogue, Scene,* and *Stage Directions.*

Essay A short nonfiction work that deals with one subject is called an essay. A **formal essay** is highly organized, thoroughly researched, and serious in tone. An **informal essay** is lighter in tone and usually reflects the writer's feelings and personality. "Foul Shots" is an example of an informal essay.

    See *Nonfiction.*

Evaluating Evaluating is the process of judging the worth of something or someone. A work of literature or its elements may be evaluated by standards such as entertainment, believability, originality, or emotional power.

Exaggeration An exaggeration is a statement that something is much more than it actually is. An extreme exaggeration made for emphasis or humor is called **hyperbole.** For example, in "White Mice," one student exaggerates the consistency of a bowl of food by asking, "Is this porridge or cement?"

Exposition Exposition is the beginning of a plot in a story or play. It introduces main characters, describes the setting, and often establishes the conflict. For example, the opening paragraphs of "Checkouts" provide the exposition for the story.

Extended Metaphor In an extended metaphor, two different things are compared at some length and in several ways. In "Conversational Ballgames," for example, Nancy Masterson Sakamoto compares sports to the different styles of conversation that exist in different cultures.

External Conflict See *Conflict.*

Eyewitness Report An eyewitness report is writing in which a person tells what he or she saw. In an **objective eyewitness report,** the writer strives to report what happens without adding his or her ideas. In a **subjective eyewitness report,** the writer presents his or her own thoughts and feelings about the event. "Battle by the Breadfruit Tree" is an example of a subjective eyewitness report.

Fable A fable is a brief story that teaches a lesson about human nature. Many fables feature animals that act and speak like humans. Fables often end with a stated moral that summarizes the lesson. "Aunty Misery" is an example of a Puerto Rican fable.
See *Moral.*

Fact and Opinion A fact is a statement that can be proved, such as "There are twelve inches in a foot." In contrast, an opinion is a statement that cannot be proved, such as "A foot is a better unit of measurement than a meter." Opinions usually reflect personal beliefs and are often debatable.

Feature Profile A feature profile is a magazine or newspaper article about an important or noteworthy person. "Tracee" is an example of a feature profile.

Fiction Fiction is prose writing that tells an imaginary story. The term usually refers to novels and short stories. Writers of fiction may invent the entire work, or they may base their story on real people or events.
See *Character, Conflict, Plot, Setting,* and *Theme.*

Figurative Language Figurative language goes beyond dictionary meanings of words to create fresh and original descriptions. For example, in "The Banana Tree" Gustus's shirt is described as "fluttering from his back like a boat sail." The three most common forms of figurative expressions are the simile, the metaphor, and personification.
See *Metaphor, Personification,* and *Simile.*

Flashback In a literary work, a flashback is a scene that interrupts the present action to describe an event that took place at an earlier time. For example, a flashback in "Dancing for Poppa" explains how Connie started dancing.

Folk Tale A folk tale is a simple story that has been handed down by word of mouth from one generation to another. The characters in folk tales may be animals, humans, or superhumans. Folk tales usually occur in the distant past and may involve supernatural events. "The Five Eggs" is a folk tale.

Foreshadowing Foreshadowing refers to a writer's use of hints that suggest events that will occur later in a story. For example, in

"Getting the Facts of Life" Minerva says, "That should have warned me. Anything that would make Stella offer to baby-sit had to be bad." Her comments foreshadow her dislike of the visit to the welfare office.

Form   Form is a term that describes a literary work's structure or organization. In poetry, form describes the physical arrangement of words and lines on a page. Some poems follow a very predictable pattern, such as having the same number of syllables in each line and the same number of lines in each stanza. Other poems, like Barbara B. Robinson's "Foreign Student," have an irregular form.

Formal Essay   See *Essay.*

Frame Story   A frame story is a story that takes place within another story. The larger story serves to introduce the frame story. For example, "The Inn of Lost Time" includes two frame stories.

Free Verse   Poetry with no regular patterns of rhyme, rhythm, or line length is called free verse. Poets use free verse to capture the sounds and rhythms of ordinary language. "Moco Limping" is written in free verse.
     See *Poetry.*

Generalization   A generalization is a broad statement made about a whole group, such as "Whales are larger than salmon." Not all generalizations are true. Some are too broad or not backed by evidence, like the statement "All eighth graders like yogurt."

Genre   The term used to identify the major categories of literature is genre. There are four main literary genres: fiction, nonfiction, poetry, and drama.

Hero   A hero is a character whose actions win great admiration, often for his or her courage or nobility. A hero can be a real person, such as Paul Revere, or a fictional character, such as Paul Bunyan.

Historical Narrative   A historical narrative is a story that tells about something that really happened. Though historical narratives are based on fact, they also include fictional elements such as description and dialogue. "Pompeii" is a historical narrative.

Humor   The quality that makes writing funny or amusing is called humor. Writers create humor through exaggeration, sarcasm, amusing descriptions, irony, or witty and insightful dialogue. For example, "Memories of Dating" contains elements of humor.
     See *Exaggeration* and *Irony.*

Hyperbole   See *Exaggeration.*

Idiom   An idiom is an expression that has a meaning different from the sum of the meanings of the individual words. For example, in "The Moustache," when Mike says that he "must have looked like a nut," he means that he must have looked crazy or silly.

Imagery   Words and phrases that appeal to the reader's senses are known as imagery. Writers use details to help the reader imagine how things look, feel, smell, sound, and taste. Note the imagery in these lines from "The Dream Keeper."

> Bring me all your
> Heart melodies
> That I may wrap them
> In a blue cloud-cloth.

Inference   An inference is a logical guess or conclusion based on evidence. By using information in selections and from their own experience, readers can figure out more than the words say. For example, based on these words from "Baseball and the Facts of Life," you can infer that Brett doesn't take playing baseball for granted: "The boys who got to play regularly—the skillful ones—horsed around between innings, did tricks on their bikes and made jokes with each other. Brett, though, looked only at the game."

Internal Conflict   See *Conflict*.

Interview   An interview is a meeting in which a person is questioned about professional or personal matters. Interviews may be recorded, filmed, or written. Janet Bode's interview of Von was a written interview.

Irony   Irony is a contrast between what is expected and what actually exists or happens. For example, in "On Hope" the thief never expects the diamond necklace to land on a shark and come back to him.

Legend   A legend is a story handed down from the past about a specific person, usually someone of heroic accomplishments. Legends usually have some basis in historical fact. "John Henry, the Hammerman" is an example of a legend.

Lyric Poetry   Lyric poetry is poetry that presents the thoughts and feelings of a single speaker. "Nothing Gold Can Stay" is a lyric poem.
   See *Poetry*.

Main Idea   The main idea is the central idea that a writer expresses in his or her work. Usually, the term is used in discussions of nonfiction. The main idea may refer to the central message of the entire work or of just one paragraph. The main idea is sometimes stated in the topic sentence of a paragraph.

Memoir   A memoir is a first-person recollection of an experience or event. "The Home Front: 1941–1945" is an example of a memoir.
   See *Nonfiction*.

Metaphor   A comparison of two unlike things that have something in common is called a metaphor. A metaphor does not use direct words of comparison such as *like, as,* or *resembles*. A metaphor in "Pigeon Woman" describes a group of pigeons as "a lake of love."
   See *Figurative Language*.

Minor Character   See *Character*.

Mood   The mood, or atmosphere, is the feeling created in the reader by a literary work. In "The Dinner Party," Mona Gardner creates a mood of tension and suspense when the reader learns a snake is loose in the dining room.

Moral   A moral is the lesson taught by a story. Morals are often stated directly.
   See *Fable*.

Motivation   A motivation is a reason that explains why a character acts, feels, or thinks a certain way. Gustus in "The Banana Tree" is motivated by his desire to save his banana tree.

Myth   A myth is a traditional story, usually of unknown authorship, that explains how something came to be or describes the actions of gods and heroes. Myths may explain such things as human nature, the origin of the world, mysteries of nature, or social customs. Most myths were once believed to be true and were tied to a particular society's religious beliefs. "Raven and the Coming of Daylight" is an example of a myth.

Narrative   Any writing that tells a story is called a narrative. The events in a narrative may be real or imagined. Narratives dealing with real events include biographies and autobiographies. Fictional narratives include myths, short stories, novels, and narrative poems.

Narrative Poetry   Poetry that tells a story is called narrative poetry. Like any story, narrative poetry has characters, setting, and plot. Narrative poems may also have other elements of poetry such as rhyme, rhythm, imagery, and figurative language. "Paul Revere's Ride" is an example of narrative poetry.
   See *Poetry*.

Narrator   The narrator is the teller of a story.
   See *Point of View*.

Nonfiction   Writing that tells about real people, places, and events is called nonfiction. Types of nonfiction include biographies, autobiographies, articles, and essays.

Novel   A novel is a work of fiction that is longer and more complex than a short story. The setting, plot, and characters of a novel are developed in detail.

Onomatopoeia   Onomatopoeia is the use of words that imitate their meaning with their sound. *Whack, hiss,* and *sizzle* are examples of onomatopoeia. In "400-Meter Freestyle" the words *crack, tick,* and *snap* are examples of onomatopoeia.

Personification   The giving of human qualities to an animal, object, or idea is called personification. In "The Hurricane" the storm is personified as an "agile dancer" that whirls "on the tip of its toes."

Persuasion   Persuasion is a type of writing that is meant to sway the reader's feelings, beliefs, or actions. Persuasion normally is used to appeal to both the mind and emotions of the reader.

Play   See *Drama.*

Plot   Plot is the sequence of related events that make up a story; it is the action, or what happens in the story. Most plots follow a regular pattern. The **exposition** introduces the characters and the conflict they face. Complications set in as the characters try to resolve the conflict. Eventually, the plot reaches a **climax,** the highest point of interest or suspense. The final stage is the **resolution,** in which loose ends are tied up and the story is brought to a close.

Poetry   Poetry is a type of literature that expresses ideas and feelings in compact, imaginative, and musical language. Poets combine words in patterns to touch the reader's senses, emotions, and mind. Normally, poems are written in lines, which are often grouped in stanzas. Many poems contain a regular rhythm and some use rhyme.

See *Alliteration, Figurative Language, Form, Free Verse, Imagery, Lyric Poetry, Narrative Poetry, Rhyme, Rhythm,* and *Stanza.*

Point of View   The perspective from which a story is told is called its point of view. The most common points of view are first person, third-person omniscient, and third-person limited.

In the **first-person** point of view, the narrator is one of the characters in the story and uses pronouns such as *I, me,* and *we.* "Petty Larceny" uses first-person point of view.

In the **third-person** point of view, the narrator is not in the story and relates the story using pronouns such as *he, she,* and *it.* In the **third-person omniscient,** or all-knowing, point of view, the narrator knows everything about the characters and can see into their minds. "The Souls in Purgatory" is an example of this type of narration.

In the **third-person limited** point of view, the narrator brings us into the mind of only one character. "The Banana Tree" is an example of this type of narration.

Predicting   Using what you know to guess what may happen in the future is called predicting. Good readers gather information as they read and combine that information with prior knowledge to predict the events in a story.

Problem Solving   The process of identifying a problem and considering possible solutions is known as problem solving. First, the problem is defined. Second, the causes of the problem are identified. Third, a list of possible solutions is made and possible outcomes of each of the solutions are considered. Finally, a solution is chosen and applied.

Prose   Prose is the ordinary form of spoken and written language, that is, language that is not poetry.

Protagonist   The protagonist is the main character in a literary work. The protagonist is always involved in the conflict of the story. Stories may have more than one protagonist. For example, Steve and his father are the protagonists in "A Cap for Steve."

Questioning   The process of raising questions while reading is called questioning. Good readers ask themselves questions in an effort to understand characters and events. They look for the answers as they continue to read.

Radio Play   A work of drama written specifically to be heard and not seen is called a radio play. *The Million-Pound Bank Note* is an example of a radio play.

Repetition   Repetition is the repeated use of any element of language—a sound, a word, a phrase, a line, or a grammatical structure. Writers use repetition to stress important ideas and to create memorable sound effects, as in these lines from "If There Be Sorrow."

> If there be sorrow
> let it be
> for things undone
> undreamed
>   unrealized
>   unattained

Resolution   See *Plot.*

Reviewing   Reviewing is the process of pausing while reading to recall previous events and check comprehension. Readers stop to reflect on what they know, to make some inferences about what is happening, and to better understand what they are reading.

Rhyme   Rhyme is the repetition of identical or similar sounds. Two words rhyme when their accented syllables and all the sounds following these syllables sound the same. *Cat* and *bat* are rhymes, as are *whether* and *feather.*

The most common form of rhyme is **end rhyme,** in which the rhyme occurs at the end of the line of poetry. **Internal rhyme** takes place when rhymes occur within lines. Note both the internal and end rhymes found in these lines from "O Captain! My Captain!"

> The ship is anchor'd safe and sound, its
>   voyage closed and done,
> From fearful trip the victor ship comes in
>   with object won.
> See *Poetry.*

Rhythm   The pattern of stressed and unstressed syllables in poetry is called rhythm. When the stressed syllables—the syllables that are emphasized—are arranged in a consistent pattern, the poem has a regular beat. Note the rhythm in this line from "O Captain! My Captain!" The stressed syllables are marked by ⁄ ; the unstressed ones by ◡.

> The port is near, the bells I hear, the people
> all exulting,
> See *Poetry.*

Scanning   In reading, scanning is the process of searching for a particular fact or piece of information. When you scan, your eyes sweep across a page, looking for key words that may lead you to the information you want.

Scene   In a play, a scene is a unit of action that takes place in one setting at one time. For example, *Rip Van Winkle* has three scenes.

Scenery   See *Stage Directions.*

Setting   Setting is the time and place of the action of a story, poem, or play. Sometimes the setting is clear and well-defined; at other times, it is left to the reader's imagination. Setting may include geographic location, the historical period (past, present, or future), season, time of day, and customs and manners of the society.
   See *Fiction.*

Short Story   A work of fiction that can generally be read in one sitting is called a short story. Short stories usually focus on one or two main characters who face a single problem or conflict.
   See *Fiction.*

Simile   A simile is a comparison of two unlike things that have some quality in common. Similes make a direct comparison, using words such as *like, as,* or *resembles.* Note the following simile from "The Moustache": "Her flesh was like a leaf in autumn, crisp and dry."
   See *Figurative Language.*

Skimming Skimming is reading quickly to find the main idea or to get an overview. When you skim, you read only the title, the headings, the words in special type, and the first sentence of each paragraph. You also read charts, graphs, and time lines.

Speaker The speaker in a poem is the voice that talks to the reader. The speaker is comparable to a narrator in a work of fiction. In some poems, the speaker expresses the feelings of the poet, as in "O Captain! My Captain." In other poems, the speaker and poet are not the same.

SQ3R SQ3R is a technique used by readers of nonfiction to help them better understand and remember what they read. The letters stand for the steps in the technique: Survey, Question, Read, Recite, and Review.

Stage Directions Instructions to the actors, director, and stage crew in a play script are called stage directions. These instructions may suggest scenery, lighting, music, sound effects, and how actors should move or speak. In this book, stage directions appear within parentheses in italic type.
See *Drama.*

Stanza A group of lines in poetry is called a stanza. A stanza is like a paragraph in prose. "The Creation," for example, has eleven stanzas.
See *Poetry.*

Stereotype A broad generalization about something or someone that leaves no room for individual differences is called a stereotype. A stereotype is often used to judge people unfairly on the basis of race, ethnic background, or physical appearance.

Style Style is the way in which a piece of literature is written. Style refers to *how* something is said rather than to *what* is said. Many elements contribute to style, including word choice, sentence length, tone, and figurative language. The style of "Memories of Dating," for example, can be described as humorous.

Summarizing To summarize means to tell briefly in your own words the main ideas of a piece of writing, omitting unimportant details.

Surprise Ending An unexpected twist in the plot at the end of a story is called a surprise ending. "White Mice" is an example of a story with a surprise ending.

Suspense The growing tension and excitement felt by a reader is called suspense. Writers create suspense by raising questions in the readers' minds about what might happen in the plot. For example, a suspenseful moment occurs in "Battle by the Breadfruit Tree" as the baboon fights to protect her baby from the leopard.

Symbol A symbol is a person, a place, an object, or an action that stands for something outside itself. A flag, for example, may symbolize a state or country. In "The Banana Tree," the growth of Gustus's tree symbolizes his own growth and power.

Theme A theme is the message about life or human nature communicated by a work of literature. In most cases, the reader must infer the theme. One way of figuring out a theme is to apply the lessons learned by the main characters to all people. For example, the theme of "The Enchanted Raisin" is that children should treat their parents with respect.

Tone A writer's attitude toward his or her subject is called tone. A writer's tone may be angry, sad, humorous, or any number of attitudes. The tone of "How to Die of Embarrassment" is humorous.

Visualizing The process of forming a mental picture from a written description is called visualizing. Good readers use details supplied by the writer to picture characters, settings, and events in their mind.

BIOGRAPHIES OF THE AUTHORS*

ROBERT ABEL

HAZEL SHELTON ABERNETHY

DAVE BARRY

Robert Abel *(1931–1981)* wrote satire to "prove that life is constantly imitating satire." About his writing, Abel said, "Writing is painfully hard work—instant backaches, sudden needs for a cup of tea, et al.—but there are lovely moments when the moon (I, a night person) is right or something, and it all comes out right—and those help—just barely, sometimes, make up for rewrites and late payment and all the other unpleasant business connected with the profession."

Hazel Shelton Abernethy *(1927–   )* teaches history at Stephen F. Austin State Teacher's College in Nacogdoches, Texas. Abernethy recalls, "As teenagers we were certainly influenced by the drama and romance and excitement of wartime. For most of us the war was the defining period of our lives. 'Before the war' and 'after the war' are standard introductions to our remembering."

Julia Alvarez *(1950–   )* was born in the Dominican Republic and emigrated to the United States when she was ten. After receiving undergraduate and graduate degrees in literature and writing, Alvarez spent twelve years teaching poetry. Alvarez's first book of poetry, *Homecoming* (1986), contained the poem "Dusting." Her latest book, *How the Garcia Girls Lost Their Accents* (1991) is a novel about a Hispanic Caribbean family that lives in the Bronx.

Jacqueline Balcells *(1950–   )*, a Chilean journalist, wrote "The Enchanted Raisin" in French for her own children when she lived in Paris. After returning to Chile, Balcells published a Spanish version of the story in 1986. Since then, Balcells has published four other books for children, including co-authoring two science fiction novels, *Adventure in the Stars* and *Alpha Centaur Mission.*

Dave Barry wrote his first humorous pieces in airports and hotel rooms while traveling as a teacher of writing seminars for businesspeople. Today his columns run every week in over 400 newspapers. He has also written thirteen books, including *Homes and Other Black Holes* and *Dave Barry Slept Here.* Barry, who won the Pulitzer Prize for commentary in 1988, says, "What I look forward to is continued immaturity, followed by death."

*These pages provide author biographies for literature lessons that do not already include this information.

James Berry *(1924–   ),*   who was born in Jamaica, says of Jamaicans, "No one has reported our stories, or the way we saw things. It's the function of writers and poets to bring in the left-out side of the human family." Berry says he writes his stories in dialect because "life has given us a rich variety of language. And if we celebrate one language over the many, we are deprived. When people share, they are joyful and enriched."

Janet Bode *(1943–   )*   got the idea for her book *New Kids in Town* from her experiences living in New York City. She says, "Walking by the diner, the stationery store, the market, the restaurant, and the deli, I pass a United Nations of recent immigrants to this country." Bode writes books and articles on a wide range of subjects.

JAMES BERRY

Morley Callaghan *(1903–1990)*   lived most of his life in Toronto, Canada. He wrote several novels, including *The Loved and the Lost,* which won him the Governor General's Literary Award for fiction in 1952. His memoir, *That Summer in Paris,* described how he beat Ernest Hemingway in a fight in 1929. He was usually content to watch other athletes, however, and listed his favorite hobby as "spectator sports."

E. E. Cummings *(1894–1962)*   was a poet, writer, and painter who prized individuality above all other traits. When he spoke at Harvard University in a lecture series, Cummings advised aspiring poets to be themselves and remember that "it's you—nobody else—who determine your destiny and decide your fate."

E.E. CUMMINGS

Emily Dickinson *(1830–1886),*   the author of nearly 1,800 poems, spent most of her adult life on the second floor of her family's home. An introvert, she always dressed in white and kept her work a secret, even to her family. Dickinson's first volume of poetry came out four years after she died, but a complete collection of her poems did not appear until 1955. Today Dickinson's work is widely considered one of the main influences on modern poetry.

Delia Ephron *(1944–   )*   writes screenplays, stories, and essays; she also contributes to many magazines. To write *Teenage Romance: Or How to Die of Embarrassment,* Ephron interviewed seventy-five teens in California and New York. Of teenagers, Ephron said, "They say teens today are more sophisticated, but I believe they're just as nervous and embarrassed as ever."

DELIA EPHRON

ROBERT FRANCIS

NIKKI GIOVANNI

BOB GREENE

Mari Evans began her career in the fourth grade when one of her stories was published in her school paper. Now an editor and writer, Evans has published several poetry collections, novels for adolescents and children, plays, and television scripts. One of her books of poetry, *I Am a Black Woman,* won the Black Academy of Arts and Letters First Annual Poetry Award in 1970. Evans's poetry has been translated into several languages. Her most recent work is *A Dark and Splendid Mass* (1992).

Robert Francis *(1901–1987)* won many awards and honors for his poetry, including the Academy of American Poets Fellowship Award for Distinguished Achievement. In addition to poetry, Francis published a novel, numerous essays, and an autobiography called *The Trouble with Francis.* Francis, who lived most of his life near Amherst, Massachusetts, wrote these words about himself: "His life demonstrates that aloneness need not be loneliness, nor poverty impoverishment."

Mona Gardner *(1900–ָ)* grew up in Seattle, Washington. During her childhood, she frequently visited Japan with her family. There she began a lifelong fascination with the Far East. Gardner began her career as a writer after graduating from Stanford University in 1920. From her home in Japan, she covered the Far East as a correspondent for an American newspaper. One of her three books, *The Menacing Sun,* tells of her travels in Japan, Siam, Malaya, Java, Bali, and India.

Nikki Giovanni *(1943–ָ)*, a popular lecturer and writer, has won many awards and honors, including grants from the Ford Foundation and the National Endowment for the Arts. She says, "I write out of my own experiences—which also happen to be the experiences of my people. Human beings fascinate me. I just keep trying to dissect them poetically to see what's there."

Rogelio R. Gomez *(1950–ָ)* was born in Castano, Coahuila, Mexico, and moved to the United States when he was six years old. Gomez received his B.A. at the University of Texas in San Antonio. A regular contributor of short stories to literary magazines, Gomez is also the fiction editor of the *Cactus Alley Journal.*

Bob Greene *(1947–ָ)*, originally from Ohio and now living in the Chicago area, writes an award-winning column that appears in over two hundred newspapers. Of his writing, Greene said, "If a story is the first thing I would tell my best friend on the phone at the end of the day, then I know it's good to write a column about." In 1977 Greene won the National Headliner Award for the best newspaper column in the United States.

Langston Hughes *(1902–1967),* one of the most important poets in African-American literature, was raised in Lawrence, Kansas. Recalling those days, Hughes said, "Then it was that books began to happen to me, and I began to believe in nothing but books and the wonderful world in books—where if people suffered, they suffered in beautiful language, not in monosyllables, as we did in Kansas. And where almost always the mortgage got paid off, the good knights won, and the Alger boy triumphed."

James Weldon Johnson *(1871–1938)* is best known for his poetry, especially his book *God's Trombones: Seven Negro Sermons in Verse,* which won the Harmon Gold Award. In 1895, Johnson founded the *Daily American,* the first black-oriented daily newspaper in the United States.

Naoshi Koriyama *(1926–)* is a poet and a professor of English. He has published several books of poetry in English, including *Coral Reefs* and *Songs from Sagamihara.*

Maxine W. Kumin *(1925–)* has published ten volumes of poetry, as well as novels, short stories, and essays. Awarded the Pulitzer Prize for poetry in 1973, Kumin says, "Poetry is my life . . . I could no more do without it than breakfast. I try not to write any but 'necessary' poems—the ones that demand my attention." Kumin lives on a farm in New Hampshire where she breeds and trains horses, raises vegetables, and taps maple trees.

Pat MacEnulty *(1955–)* grew up in Jacksonville, Florida, and took ballet lessons as a child. Now a teacher of English and film at Florida State University in Tallahassee, Pat MacEnulty serves as the fiction editor of *Sun Dog: the Southeast Review* and has twice won a Florida screenwriting competition.

Pales Matos *(1898–1959)* grew up in a literary family in Puerto Rico. His father and two of his brothers were also famous poets. Pales Matos published several books, including *Poesia, Obras, Azaleas,* and *Pueblo Negro.* In his poems, Pales Matos celebrated the African rhythms of Puerto Rican blacks.

David Nava Monreal addressed "Moco Limping" to his own dog. In 1975, this poem and several other of Monreal's works appeared in *Sighs and Songs of Aztlan,* a collection of Chicano literature. The same year, Monreal won a nationwide contest sponsored by the Chicano Cultural Center of Bakersfield College. A California native, Monreal has worked on the staff of a public library and as a group supervisor in a county probation department.

LENSEY NAMIOKA

Lensey Namioka *(1929–   ),* born in Beijing, China, began her career as a math instructor. Namioka is the author of travel books and articles, as well as numerous books for young people. Married to a Japanese mathematician and the mother of two daughters, Namioka says, "For my writings I draw heavily on my Chinese cultural heritage and on my husband's Japanese cultural heritage. My involvement with Japan started before my marriage, since my mother spent many years in Japan."

Dorothy Parker *(1893-1967)* wrote criticism, short stories, and poetry for several magazines and collaborated on two plays. Her writing and her lunchtime conversations with other writers at New York's Algonquin Hotel gained Parker a reputation for her sharp, biting wit. Of a new actress in a Broadway play, Parker once wrote that the actress "ran the whole gamut of the emotions from A to B."

DOROTHY PARKER

Francesca Yetunde Pereira *(1933–   )* was born in Lagos, Nigeria, where she returned after graduating from University College in London. As a young woman, Pereira worked as an administrative officer with the Federal Service in Nigeria. One of her early short stories won first prize in a contest sponsored by Nigerian Broadcasting. Pereira is also a popular folk singer.

Richard Rive *(1931–1989)* was a South African professor and author who became known for his writings against apartheid. Rive published two short story collections, *African Songs* and *Advance, Retreat,* as well as two novels and an autobiography entitled *Writing Black.* In 1989 Rive was found beaten and stabbed to death at his home in South Africa.

Barbara B. Robinson *(1921–   )* was born in Honolulu, Hawaii. She began teaching in 1962 and always tested her assignments for her students by doing them herself. As she put it, "I'm learning to write along with my students." Robinson wrote several stories and poems that were published in local and national magazines.

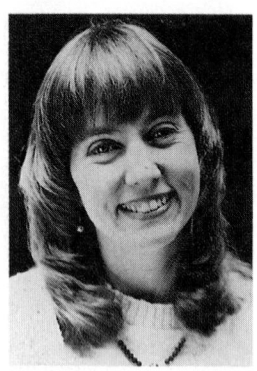

CYNTHIA RYLANT

Cynthia Rylant *(1954–   )* has written *A Kindness, A Blue-Eyed Daisy,* and *A Fine White Dust,* which was a Newbery Honor Book. She has also written *Missing May,* which was awarded the Newbery Medal. Her eight picture books include two Caldecott Honor Books, and she publishes poetry and short stories. She has also written an autobiography, *But I'll Be Back Again.*

Jessica Saiki grew up in Hawaii just before and during World War II. "Petty Larceny" appears in Saiki's first collection of short stories, *Once, A Lotus Garden and Other Stories.* Praising the book, a critic said it was "as delicately crafted as a Japanese wood carving in which the faces of human beings . . . are brought to life with a child's honesty and an adult's humility." Saiki also created the pen-and-ink drawings in her book.

Nancy Masterson Sakamoto *(1931–   )* currently serves as Professor of Intercultural Communications at Shitennoji Gakuen University, Hawaii branch. Her book *Polite Fictions: Why Japanese and Americans Seem Rude to Each Other* is still used as a textbook in Japanese universities. To students who wonder why they can't talk to their parents, Sakamoto says, "Keep in mind that the skills and perceptions acquired in intercultural communication work also for intergenerational communication."

NANCY MASTERSON SAKAMOTO

Gary Soto *(1952–   )*, who writes both prose and poetry, won the American Book Award in 1985 for his memoir *Living Up the Street.* In 1991 Soto published another memoir entitled *A Summer Life.* About his career as a writer, Soto has said, "I like writing. I'm fairly prolific; it's a daily activity for me."

May Swenson *(1919–   )* aims to get her readers to appreciate the content of her poems "eye-wise, ear-wise, taste, touch, and muscle-wise *before* beginning to cerebralize," or think about them. The author of several poetry collections, including *Another Animal, A Cage of Spines,* and *Poems to Solve,* Swenson says, "The analyzing intellect ought to be not the first but the last tool that is applied to a poem." Some of Swenson's poems have been set to music, and she has recorded several others.

GARY SOTO

William Tsuchida   served in the U.S. Army during World War II. While a soldier, he wrote letters home to his family, who spent the war in an internment camp because of their Japanese heritage. Tsuchida's letters were published in 1947 in a book, *Wear It Proudly.*

Theodore Waldeck *(1894–   )* was orphaned as a young child and was raised by his grandfather in Vienna, Austria. At eighteen, Waldeck went on his first African expedition. He later called that safari "the turning point in my life, for I became convinced I wanted to be an explorer." With his wife, writer Jo Besse McElveen Waldeck, he later explored the jungles of Africa and South America and wrote a variety of books for young people, including *On Safari, Lions on the Hunt,* and *The White Panther.*

AL YOUNG

Al Young *(1939–   )* grew up in Detroit. The son of a professional musician, Young began his career as a freelance guitarist and flute player. In addition to novels such as *Sitting Pretty* and *Ask Me Now,* Young has also published several poetry collections and nonfiction books about popular music.

THE WRITING PROCESS

Writing is a process, the steps taken to create a finished product. The process a writer uses is unique to him or her. You need to develop a process that works best for you.

Many writers use stages similar to the ones on these pages to focus their thinking and writing. Feel free to shorten or even skip some stages if you are comfortable doing so.

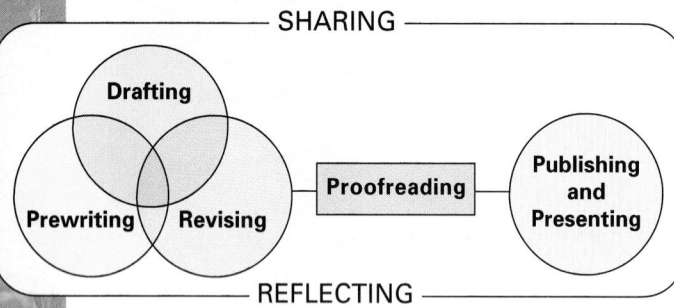

Prewriting and Exploring

Use these steps to help you plan your writing:

1. Clarify the Assignment

When you are given an assignment, make sure you understand what you are being asked to write. To clarify your task, fill out a PASSkey by answering the following questions:

P = Purpose
> Is the purpose stated in the assignment?
> Do I want to inform? to entertain? to analyze? to persuade?

A = Audience
> Who will read my writing?
> How much do my readers know?
> How much more do they need to know?
> What might they find interesting?
> How do I want my audience to respond?

S = Subject
> Has a topic been assigned?
> What topic do I want to explore?
> What topic can I handle well in the length that has been assigned?

S = Structure
> Has a structure or form been assigned?
> What organization would help me accomplish my purpose?
> What should the final product look like?

2. Get Ideas for a Topic

Try some of these ways of finding topics:

Recalling Remember events and scenes from your past. Look through family photo albums, scrapbooks, diaries, or your journal. Talk to family members or old friends.

Brainstorming With a partner or a small group of classmates, think of and jot down as many ideas as possible. One person's ideas will spur another's. Keep the atmosphere positive and don't stop to evaluate. Ideas should be generated, not judged.

Listing Write a topic or category at the top of a page and list every idea you can think of that relates to it. Go in as many different directions as your imagination will allow.

Freewriting Choose a topic you want to explore. For about three minutes, write down everything that comes into your mind. Don't stop to read what you've written. Then stop writing, read what you wrote, and pick out any ideas that you want to explore further.

Webbing Write a central idea in the middle of your page and circle it. Outside the circle write related ideas. Circle each and draw a line connecting it to the central idea. Do the same for each related idea, as in the idea web below.

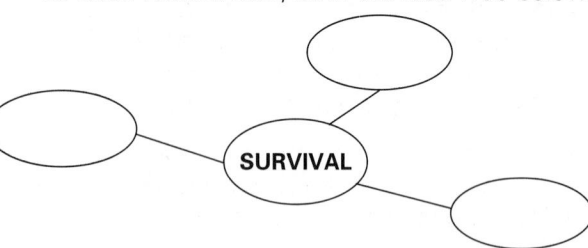

3. Choose and Limit Your Topic

Choose a topic that excites you. Narrow your topic to a size you can deal with. For example, "my family" is too broad a topic to cover in a short composition, but a topic like "my brother's funny habits" could be handled easily.

4. Gather Information

Most writing involves doing some research and/or using your imagination. If you write an informative or persuasive paper, you must do research to get facts and statistics. If you write about your own experience, you will delve into your memory. If you create fiction or drama, you will use your imagination, but you might do research as well. When you write about literature, you study the literary work itself. For whatever type of writing you do, make notes on a piece of paper, index cards, or a computer screen to record your thoughts .

5. Organize Your Ideas

After you have all the information and ideas you need, organize your notes into the order in which you wish to present your ideas. You can organize by outlining, numbering, using graphic devices, arranging index cards, or moving sections of notes on a computer screen.

Draft and Discover

When you draft, you begin to put your ideas on paper, following any notes, graphics, or outlines you have made. Drafting is a time to let ideas flow without concern for spelling and punctuation. Errors can be corrected later.

Revise Your Writing

When you revise, you judge the strengths and weaknesses of your paper. You can do this by yourself or with a peer reader. Try to improve what you said and how you said it.

Ask questions such as the following:

- Are the ideas focused on the topic?
- Is the purpose of the writing clear?
- Do any parts need more details?

- Do the ideas flow in a logical order?
- Is the tone the way I want it?
- Can I add a more exciting beginning?
- Does the piece end in a satisfying way?

Use these proofreading symbols to mark your errors. Then make a clean, corrected copy of your paper.

Proofreading Symbols		
Symbol	**Meaning**	**Example**
∧	insert	leson
=	capitalize	douglass
/	lowercase	History
∼	transpose	veiw
ℓ	take out	lots of a
¶	paragraph	¶The
⊙	add a period	slavery⊙
∧	add a comma	Finally

Publish and Present

Here are a few ways to share your writing:

- Read your writing aloud to classmates.
- Trade papers with a classmate so that you can read each other's work.
- Publish everyone's work in your own magazine.
- Submit your writing to a school newspaper.
- Tape-record a reading of your work.
- Make a videotape of your work.

Reflect on Your Writing

After you have completed your writing, think about it and the process you went through to complete it. What have you discovered about your writing process? Should you change your method the next time around? By learning from what you do each time, you will constantly improve your writing process.

TIPS FOR BETTER PARAGRAPHS

Paragraphs are the building blocks of writing. Whether a paragraph stands by itself or is part of a longer composition, such as an essay or a story, it needs to be solidly constructed.

The following information will help you understand paragraphs and give you tips for constructing better paragraphs.

What Is a Paragraph?

A **paragraph** is a group of related sentences that work together to develop a main idea or accomplish a single purpose. Each paragraph that follows has a single main idea or purpose. In the model below, the first sentence states the main idea.

> That first winter in St. Catharines was a terrible one. Canada was a strange, frozen land, snow everywhere, ice everywhere, and a bone-biting cold the like of which none of them had ever experienced before. Harriet rented a small frame house in the town and set out to work. The fugitives boarded with her. They worked in the forests felling trees, and so did she. Sometimes she took other jobs, cooking or cleaning house for people in the town. She cheered on these newly arrived fugitives, working herself, finding work for them, finding food for them, praying for them, sometimes begging for them.
>
> Ann Petry, "*from* Harriet Tubman. . ."

In the next paragraph, no one sentence states the main idea. All the sentences work together for a single purpose—to describe a fight between a baboon and a leopard.

> The two beasts broke apart, and I saw instantly that the leopard had at last succeeded, managing the stroke he had been trying for since the battle began. He had raked deeply into the abdomen of the baboon. The result may be well imagined. The baboon drew off slowly and looked down at herself. What she saw told her the truth— that even if the leopard turned and ran away this minute, she was done.
>
> Theodore Waldeck,
> "Battle by the Breadfruit Tree"

Unity and Coherence

Well-written paragraphs reflect two characteristics: unity and coherence. A paragraph has **unity** when all the sentences tell about one main idea or serve a single purpose. In this example, which sentence strays from the topic?

> Jeremiah controlled the game from the moment he stepped onto the pitching mound. His first pitch was a fastball, low and inside, that made a loud pop in the catcher's glove. Jeremiah continued to throw fastballs that whizzed by the batters. The aluminum bats, I think, aren't as good as the wooden ones used in the major leagues. With nine pitches, he struck out the side and won the game.

The sentence that begins "The aluminum bats" has nothing to do with the description of Jeremiah's pitching. The sentence breaks the unity of the paragraph and may confuse readers.

A paragraph has **coherence** when the sentences flow smoothly and logically from beginning to end. Compare the following paragraphs. Which has more coherence?

> In recent years arena theaters have become common. An arena theater usually has no raised platform to serve as a stage. The stage is an open space in the middle of the auditorium. The scenery in an arena theater is often changed in full view of the audience. The seats for the audience are set up like bleachers. The performers can be seen from every angle.

> In recent years arena theaters have become common. *In contrast* to traditional theaters, an arena theater usually has no raised platform to serve as a stage. *Instead,* the stage is an open space in the middle of

the auditorium. *Unlike* traditional theaters, which use a curtain to hide scene changes, the scenery in an arena theater is often changed in full view of the audience. The seats for the audience are set up like bleachers *on all sides* of the acting arena. *As a result,* the performers can be seen from every angle.

The second paragraph is more coherent because it makes use of **transitions,** the words in italic type. Transitions are the connecting words that let readers know how the details in a paragraph are related.

When you revise your paragraphs, check to make sure that your sentences are clearly connected to one another. Add transitions to help make the relationships clear.

The chart that follows lists words and phrases commonly used as transitions.

Transition Words and Phrases

Time Order	before	after
	then	meanwhile
	during	first
Spatial Order	above	below
	around	to the left
	inside	outside
Order of Importance	first	strongest
	second	most significant
	third	weakest
Comparison	as	than
	similarly	in the same way
	neither/nor	either/or
Contrast	yet	instead
	unlike	on the contrary
	but	in contrast
Cause and Effect	because	so
	if/then	thus
	as a result	since

Making Your Main Idea Clear

There are two ways of getting across the main idea of your paragraph. One way is to come right out and state your main idea in a **topic sentence.** A topic sentence identifies your topic and tells what you want to say about it. Often, writing that explains or persuades makes use of topic sentences.

The topic sentence may be the first sentence of the paragraph, as in this example.

Modern archaeology began with the discovery of buried Pompeii. Before then, the digging of treasures from the ground had been a haphazard and unscholarly affair. But the excavation of Pompeii was done in a systematic, scientific manner, and so the science of serious archaeology can be said to have begun there. Since the year 1748, generations of skilled Italian workmen have been carefully removing the ashes that buried Pompeii, until today almost four-fifths of the city has been uncovered.

Robert Silverberg, "Pompeii"

A topic sentence may appear elsewhere in a paragraph. Sometimes, the second sentence in a paragraph serves as the topic sentence. At other times, it may be the last sentence.

A good topic sentence does more than state the main idea. It also catches readers' interest. Compare the following topic sentences.

I am going to explain why the student council isn't working very well.

The student council has made many promises about improving the lunchroom, but nothing has changed.

The second sentence is more specific than the first. It tells readers what the paragraph will be about. Use these questions to improve your own topic sentences.

1. Does the sentence tell what the paragraph is about?
2. Is the main idea stated clearly?

3. Is the sentence interesting enough to catch the reader's attention?
4. Is the main idea narrow enough to be developed in one paragraph?
5. Does the sentence cover all the related ideas in the paragraph?

Another way of getting across main ideas is to use an **implied main idea.** Unlike a topic sentence, an implied main idea is not stated directly but is communicated by all the paragraph's sentences working together.

Narrative and descriptive writing often make use of implied main ideas. In the following model, all the sentences work together to describe the narrator's feelings of embarrassment about where she lives.

> Past Donald's house, across the river was where I lived. Home for me was a shabby, paint-peeled house in the rental section of town. With kids who walked the route with me, I exchanged good-byes at the foot of the hill. That way they couldn't see which house was ours. I was afraid they might puncture me with embarrassing questions like "Do you have your own bedroom?" or "Your folks own a radio?" Stuff like that I didn't want to answer.
>
> Jessica Saiki, "Petty Larceny"

Elaboration

A well-constructed paragraph needs details that support its main idea or help to accomplish its purpose. The chart on this page lists some common types of **elaboration,** or ways of adding supporting details, that you might use to develop your paragraphs.

A well-developed paragraph feels complete. It doesn't leave out important information or state ideas without explaining them. Is the following paragraph well developed?

> The Dred Scott Decision of 1857 was one of the most famous Supreme Court cases in our history. The decision, which involved a lawsuit by an African-American slave, brought the country closer to civil war.

This paragraph leaves too many questions unanswered. Who was Dred Scott? What was the Dred Scott Decision about? Why did it prove to be so important? Now read another version of the paragraph, one with more elaboration.

> The Dred Scott Decision of 1857 was one of the most famous Supreme Court cases in our history. Dred Scott was a black slave who sued the federal government. He claimed that since he had once lived in the Wisconsin Territory, where slavery was against the law, he should be given his freedom. However, the court ruled against him. It decided that no black person could claim to be a citizen of the United States. Also, the Court ruled that Congress could not forbid slavery in any U.S. territory. As a result, the country moved closer to civil war.

When you revise your paragraphs, look for places where you need more information or details.

Types of Elaboration

Facts/Statistics
(Statements that can be proved)
> The capital of Spain is Madrid.

Sensory Details
(Words that appeal to the five senses)
> The little dog with the big sad eyes barked loudly.

Reasons
(Logical statements to support an idea)
> Juan deserved to win. He worked very hard and listened to everyone's ideas.

Examples
(Specific cases that illustrate a main idea)
> Picking up garbage is one way to keep parks clean.

Quotations
(Someone's exact words)
> "Pets have a positive effect on humans," said Dr. Terrier.

Paragraphing

When you begin drafting, you often do not know how many paragraphs you will write or what the main idea of each paragraph will be. The following guidelines will help you organize your ideas into effective paragraphs.

Guidelines for Paragraphing

As you draft:

- **Look for related details.**
  Group them together as a paragraph.

- **Look for changes in main ideas.**
  Start a new paragraph with each new idea.

- **Recognize changes in setting or speaker.**
  Whenever the setting or speaker changes, begin a new paragraph.

As you revise:

- **Look for overloaded or overly long paragraphs.**
  Break these down into smaller paragraphs, each focusing on one main idea.

- **Look for strings of short paragraphs.**
  These paragraphs may need to be grouped together or need further elaboration.

- **Make sure each paragraph has a main idea or clear purpose.**
  If you can't tell what the main idea is, how will your reader be able to?

- **Watch out for paragraphs that overlap one another.**
  If two paragraphs cover the same topic, revise one or both of them.

RESEARCH AND REPORT WRITING

This section gives you a brief overview of the steps involved in writing research papers and reports. For further help in this area, consult the Writer's Workshop on Informative Writing on page 633.

Finding a Topic

These tips on finding an idea can make writing easier:

1. Choose a topic that truly interests you. That way you won't get bored and your work will be easier to finish.

2. Check the library. See whether there are enough books and articles available for you to adequately research your subject.

3. Limit your topic. Many topic ideas start out too big. A topic like Native Americans may be too large because there is simply too much to say. Choose a smaller topic, such as cultures of the Southwest or Anasazi Indians. A smaller topic makes a report more manageable.

4. Jot down major points you think you might cover in your report. You may need to look through books to get some general ideas for what you might write about. These general ideas will help you focus your research.

Using the Library

After choosing and focusing your topic, begin your search for information. Like most researchers, you will probably begin with the resources in the library. However, research can also include interviews, TV programs, and many other nonprint sources.

The Card Catalog The card catalog lists all the materials in the library and tells you where to find them. There are three cards for every book: a **title card,** an **author card,** and a **subject card.** Begin by looking up your subject, but don't panic if you can't find what you want right away. You may need to look under a different heading.

Computerized Catalogs Most public libraries now have computerized catalogs. Instructions for using them are usually posted next to the terminals. Generally, you type in your subject; the title of the book; or the last name, then first name, of the author.

Call Numbers Most libraries arrange nonfiction books according to the Dewey Decimal System. The Dewey Decimal System assigns every book a number in one of ten categories. This **call number** is usually printed on the spine of the book. The books are then arranged on the library shelves in numerical order. When you use a card catalog or computer, you are given the call numbers to help you locate the book. Find the area of the library containing those numbers, and search for your book.

Reference Section

The reference section of your library contains all kinds of books that provide facts and statistics, including the different types of materials mentioned below. Ask the librarian for help if you have trouble finding any source.

Readers' Guide to Periodical Literature This journal lists, by subject, articles in current magazines and newspapers. Find the most current *Readers' Guide* and look up the subject of your report. After you find an article that looks promising, write the name and date of the magazine and the page number. Then go to the magazine area and ask the librarian for the issue of the magazine you need.

General Encyclopedias Encyclopedias are often a good place to start your research, since they give a general overview of a subject. Beware of depending on them, however. If you use only an encyclopedia entry, you haven't done any serious research. You need to find more current and detailed information by using other sources as well.

Specialized Dictionaries and Encyclopedias These books focus on a particular area of knowledge. You can find dictionaries for ballet, biographies, and slang, for example, and encyclopedias on science, sports, and so on.

Almanacs and Yearbooks Since these books are published yearly, they have up-to-date facts and statistics. Check the table of contents and the index of the most current almanac to find your subject.

Atlases These books of maps also contain information on other geographical topics, such as population, temperature, and weather.

Parts of a Book

With the help of a card catalog or computer, you will find many nonfiction books on your topic. By scanning the parts of a book, you can decide immediately whether the book will be useful to you or not.

Title Page This gives the full title of a book, the place of publication, and the names of authors, editors, and publishers.

Copyright Page This page has the publication date, so you can decide how current the information in the book is. A 1972 book on Native Americans, for instance, will not discuss the recent election of a Native American to the U.S. Senate.

Foreword, Preface, or Introduction These pages contain important background information, such as the author's purpose for writing or the method used to collect the information.

Table of Contents This is a summary of the contents of the book, arranged in order of appearance. These pages are especially important because they may quickly show you whether the book discusses your topic and whether the coverage is detailed enough for your purposes.

Text This is the body of the book. A quick look can help you decide whether the book is too simple or too technical for your needs.

Glossary This is a dictionary at the back of the book that defines technical terms used in the text.

Index Found at the back of the book, this is an alphabetical list of the subjects in the book, together with the page numbers where they can be found. Check the index to see how many pages are devoted to your topic.

Taking Notes

When you find facts and details you can use, take notes. Using index cards can make note-taking easy for you.

Begin by recording important information about each source you use on a **source card** or **bibliography card**. Include the author or editor, last name first; the title of the book or name of the article (for magazines and encyclopedias); the city and publisher; the year (or date for a magazine) of publication; and the library call number (for nonfiction books). You will use the information on these cards later, when you compile your **bibliography** or list of **works cited**. Notice the example below.

Source Card

```
                                    E99.P9A2313


  Acatos, Sylvio. Pueblos: Prehistoric Indian
     Cultures of the Southwest. New York:
     Facts on File, 1990.
```

Then use one note card for each fact or idea you might want to include in your report. On the first line, write the title of the source. On the second line, write the page numbers. Then write the fact. You will use these cards to organize your outline and write your paper. To see how note cards look, see the example below.

Note Card

The Old Ones	**Title**
105–106	**Pages**
	Information
Around A.D. 700, the Anasazi stopped living in pit houses and began to build simple above-ground houses.	

When to Take a Note   As you read, keep your topic in mind. When you find information that will help you get your ideas across, stop and take a note. Look for the following:

- details about the main ideas you plan to cover in your paper
- important dates and facts
- important people
- interesting events or examples
- conflicting opinions
- special terms or jargon

Summarizing and Quoting   Whenever you can, summarize information in your own words. If you want to include someone else's idea, be sure you say whose idea it is. You might choose to quote someone's exact words because they are clever, famous, or memorable. If so, copy them word for word, and mark the beginning and end with quotation marks.

Remember that **plagiarism** is the use of someone else's words or ideas without giving

that person credit. Plagiarism is against the law. Always give credit to your sources.

If your teacher requires you to credit sources within your report, put the source in parentheses at the end of the passage that contains someone else's words or ideas. Use these guidelines:

Crediting Sources Within Your Paper

- **Work by one author**   At the end of your sentence, put the author's last name and the page number in parentheses.
  (Acatos 81)

- **Work by more than one author**   Put all the last names and the page number in parentheses.
  (Pike and Muench 91)

- **Works with no author**   Put the title or a shortened version of the title and the page number in parentheses.
  ("Ancient Mansions of Chaco Canyon" 74)

- **Nonprint works**   Put the name of the person interviewed, the television program, or other nonprint work in parentheses.
  (Smith)

Outlining

An outline helps you organize your main points and supporting details in logical order. Begin by reviewing your note cards. Group the cards into separate piles, putting together those that are about similar ideas. Then review the groups, thinking about what they have in common. Your groups can help you organize your outline into headings and subheadings.

In a topic outline, use phrases, not complete sentences, in a form similar to that shown on the next page.

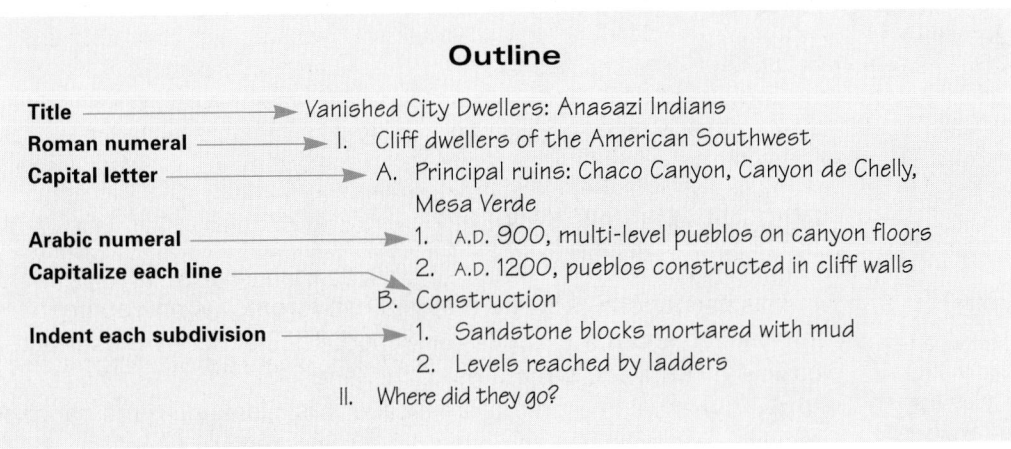

Outline

Title → Vanished City Dwellers: Anasazi Indians

Roman numeral → I. Cliff dwellers of the American Southwest

Capital letter → A. Principal ruins: Chaco Canyon, Canyon de Chelly, Mesa Verde

Arabic numeral → 1. A.D. 900, multi-level pueblos on canyon floors

Capitalize each line → 2. A.D. 1200, pueblos constructed in cliff walls

B. Construction

Indent each subdivision → 1. Sandstone blocks mortared with mud

2. Levels reached by ladders

II. Where did they go?

Guidelines for Listing Works Cited

On a separate sheet of paper at the end of your report, you must list the sources you used while writing. This list is sometimes called a **bibliography.** You can compile the information from your source cards. List sources in alphabetical order by the name of the author. The guidelines and examples below show the correct format and punctuation for several different kinds of sources. Remember to underline any information that appears in italics.

Books Author or editor, last name first; book title; city and publisher; year of publication

Pike, Donald G., and David Muench. *Anasazi: Ancient People of the Rock.* New York: Crown, 1986.

Silverberg, Robert. *The Old Ones: Indians of the American Southwest.* New York: Graphic Society, 1965.

Magazine articles Author, if one is named; article title; name and date of magazine; page numbers

"Ancient Mansions of Chaco Canyon." *Natural History* Mar. 1987: 74–77.

Encyclopedia articles Author, if listed; title of the entry; encyclopedia name; year of publication

Ortiz, Alfonso. "Cliff Dwellers." *The World Book Encyclopedia.* 1988 ed.

Interviews Name of person interviewed; type of interview (personal or telephone); date

Smith, Peter. Personal interview. Oct. 25, 1992.

Television programs Name of program; narrator or other person providing information; name of series; network; local station; date

"A Desert Blooming." Writ. Marshall Riggan. *Living Wild.* PBS. WTTW, Chicago. 29 Apr. 1984.

Recordings Artist; title of work; title of recording; type of recording; manufacturer; catalog number; year

U2. "MLK." *The Unforgettable Fire.* Audiocassette. RCA, 90231-4, 1984.

LANGUAGE HANDBOOK

USING THE LANGUAGE HANDBOOK

This handbook is a guide that you can refer to when you need information about the English language. The handbook presents the basic elements and structures of the language, and it teaches you how to avoid many common grammatical errors. Consulting the handbook regularly will help you improve your writing and speaking.

SECTION 1: PARTS OF SPEECH PREVIEW

All words in our language are classified into eight groups called the *parts of speech.*

Each part of speech has a special function in a sentence. Knowing the parts of speech helps you to analyze and discuss your writing. Below are definitions and examples of the parts of speech.

Noun   A noun is a word that names a person, a place, a thing, or an idea.

> Examples: scientist   Mars   telescope   equality
> The *scientists* studied *Mars* through a *telescope*.

Pronoun   A pronoun is a word used in place of a noun or another pronoun.

> Examples: she   we   yourself   nobody   who   everybody
> "Just be *yourself*," *she* said. "*We* want *you* to feel at home."

Verb   A verb is a word that expresses an action or a state of being. Verb forms usually change to show the time of the action.

> Examples: cook   swoop   dive   is   exist   does
> A pelican *swooped* down and *dove* into the water.

Adjective   An adjective is a word that modifies, or defines by describing, a noun or a pronoun. It tells *which one, how many, what kind,* or *how much.* Often, it comes before the noun it modifies.

> Examples: clean   smart   orange   extraordinary   tricky
> Maria is *smart* and has *extraordinary* energy.

Adverb   An adverb is a word that modifies a verb, an adjective, or another adverb. It tells *where, when, how,* or *to what extent.*

> Examples: suddenly   ordinarily   wonderfully   also
> *Ordinarily,* the band plays *wonderfully.*

Preposition   A preposition is a word that shows how a noun or pronoun is related to some other word in the sentence. Many prepositions indicate direction, position, or relation in time.

> Examples: across   at   of   until   in   about   from   on
> *Across* the creek *at* the edge *of* the field stood a deer.

Conjunction   A conjunction is a word that connects words or groups of words.

> Examples: and   or   but   so   yet   because   if
> Peoples of ancient Egypt, Central America, *and* South America all built pyramids, *but* they developed the pyramid idea independently.

Interjection   An interjection is a word or group of words that shows feeling or sudden emotion. An interjection can stand by itself.

> Examples: wow   hey   my word   oh   well
> *Hey!* That was a shooting star!

Parts of Speech at a Glance

Each word in a sentence is a specific part of speech, as the following graphic shows.

The following exercises will help you to review the parts of speech and prepare for the other sections of this handbook.

Exercise 1   Concept Check

Identifying Parts of Speech   Write the part of speech of each italicized word.

1. How do *you* feel about standing in line at school?
2. *Well,* the custom of standing in line began in Great Britain.

3. Standing in line was a *social* invention, created during times of food rationing during World Wars I and II.
4. From Great Britain, the custom *spread* to the rest of the English-speaking world and to northern Europe.
5. In southern *Europe* and Latin America, the custom did not take hold.
6. In those areas of the world, people *frequently* ignore lines.
7. Perhaps lines are unimportant because the pace *of* life is more relaxed in those regions.
8. In contrast, people in the United States get upset when *someone* cuts ahead of them in line.
9. There are unwritten rules *about* disciplining the person who cuts into line.
10. Someone usually scolds the "cutter" *and* sends him or her to the end of the line.

Exercise 2   Application in Literature

Parts of Speech   Write the part of speech of each italicized word.

LITERARY MODEL
· · · · · · · · · · ·
from "Queue & A: The Long and Short of Standing in Line" by Malcolm Gladwell

In Europe, the most (1) *common* kinds of lines in banks and railway stations (2) *are* what are known as multi-server queues—much like those found in U.S. grocery stores and fast-food restaurants—where each serving station has a separate waiting line. By contrast, over the past decade, U.S. banks, railways, airlines (3) *and* some fast-food restaurants have switched over almost (4) *entirely* to what is known as the "snake" line, where all stations are served (5) *by* one single-file line.

Exercise 3   Drafting Skill

Adding Words   On your paper, write words to complete the following paragraph. Be sure to use the parts of speech indicated on the blanks.

JUST FOR FUN
· · · · · · · · · ·
Read the following sentence, written by the famous language expert Noam Chomsky: *Colorless green ideas sleep furiously.* This sentence is nonsense. See if you can figure out the part of speech of each word in it.

When we (1) __(adverb)__ arrived at the airport in Lima, Peru, the place seemed like a (2) __(adjective)__ madhouse to (3) __(pronoun)__. No one stood in neat lines and waited for his or her turn. (4) "__(Interjection)__!" we said to one another. "This is ridiculous." (5) __(Pronoun)__ didn't understand that people in (6) __(adjective)__ parts of the world (7) __(verb)__ different customs (8) __(conjunction)__ attitudes about standing in line. Travelers to foreign (9) __(noun)__ often find that standing (10) __(preposition)__ line is not an important custom in the local cultures.

SECTION 2: WRITING COMPLETE SENTENCES

A group of words that expresses a complete thought is called a *sentence.* **A sentence begins with a capital letter and ends with a period, a question mark, or an exclamation point.**

Subjects and Predicates

A sentence must have at least one *subject* **and one** *predicate.*

The **subject** is the person or thing that the sentence is about. The **predicate** tells something about the subject.

Subject	Predicate
Bruce Springsteen	sang.
We	were cheering.

Each of the sentences above contains only a **simple subject** and a **simple predicate,** or **verb,** with no modifiers. The sentence below is divided into its **complete subject** and **complete predicate**—which include the simple subject and predicate and their modifiers.

The **complete subject** includes all the words that identify the person, place, thing, or idea that the sentence is about.	The **complete predicate** includes all the words that tell or ask something about the subject.

The **scouts** of Troop 14 **washed** cars in the school parking lot.

The **simple subject** is the key word that tells whom or what the sentence is about. It may be one word or several words, but it does not include modifiers.	The **simple predicate,** or **verb,** tells what the subject does or is. It may be one word or several, but it does not include modifiers.

Sentence Fragments

A *sentence fragment* **is a group of words that does not express a complete thought.**

A sentence fragment may lack a subject, a predicate, or both.

Fragment	Plays guitar in a Mexican restaurant. (no subject)
Sentence	Tomás plays guitar in a Mexican restaurant.
Fragment	Sea otters in the water. (no verb)
Sentence	Sea otters played in the water.
Fragment	By an enormous meteor. (no subject, no verb)
Sentence	Just before the extinction of the dinosaurs, the earth was hit by an enormous meteor.

WRITING TIP

Conversation is full of sentence fragments. When writing dialogue, use sentence fragments to make the dialogue sound realistic. However, avoid sentence fragments in most other writing.

Exercise 1 Concept Check

Identifying Fragments   Write *Sentence* or *Fragment* on your paper for each of the following. Then change all the fragments to complete sentences.

1. Canada is the world's second largest country.
2. Russia, the largest.
3. A long border between Canada and the United States.
4. More than 3,000 miles long.
5. Many big cities, like Toronto, Montreal, and Vancouver.
6. Also has large areas of wilderness.
7. Caribou, moose, otters, and other large mammals in these wilderness areas of Canada.
8. In some parts of Canada, mail is delivered by planes or dog sleds.
9. The United States and Canada are allies.
10. People cross freely from each country to the other.

Run-on Sentences

A *run-on sentence* occurs when two or more sentences are written as one.

Run-ons occur when writers include too many thoughts in a sentence. The end mark may accidentally be left off the end of the first sentence. Sometimes a comma is incorrectly used to separate the sentences, producing what is known as a **comma splice.**

Run-on	Nightjars are common gray or brown birds they are found in many countries around the world.
Corrected	Nightjars are common gray or brown birds. They are found in many countries around the world.
Run-on (comma splice)	Yoshiko is from Japan, she speaks fluent Japanese.
Corrected	Yoshiko is from Japan. She speaks fluent Japanese.

To correct a run-on, use one of the methods that follow.

- Add an end mark to the first sentence and begin the second sentence with a capital letter.
- Add a semicolon after the first complete thought.
- Add a comma after the first complete thought and use a conjunction such as *and, or, nor, for, but, so,* or *yet* to begin the second.

Run-on	Yoshiko is from Japan, she speaks fluent Japanese.
Corrected	Yoshiko is from Japan; she speaks fluent Japanese.
Corrected	Yoshiko is from Japan, and she speaks fluent Japanese.

Exercise 2   Concept Check

Run-ons   Decide if each of the following is a correct sentence or a run-on. If it is correct, write *Correct* on your paper. If it is a run-on, rewrite it correctly.

1. Jim Thorpe was born in what was known as the Indian Territory it is now called Oklahoma.
2. Thorpe was a Native American he was of Sauk and Fox descent.
3. He became one of the greatest all-around athletes in the history of sport.
4. Thorpe showed great ability in many sports basketball, boxing, lacrosse, swimming, and hockey were a few of these sports.
5. In 1911 and 1912 he earned all-American status in college football, in 1912 he won gold medals in the decathlon and the pentathlon in the Olympic Games at Stockholm.
6. The decathlon consists of ten track-and-field events the pentathlon has five events.
7. Shortly after the Olympics Thorpe's medals were taken away Olympic officials disqualified Thorpe because he had played some professional baseball.
8. From 1913 to 1919, Thorpe was an outfielder for several major-league baseball teams.
9. From 1915 to 1930, he played professional football he also became the first president of the American Professional Football Association.
10. The American Professional Football Association later became the National Football League.

Exercise 3   Revision Skill

Correcting Run-ons   Each of the following sentences is a run-on. Correct each sentence in two different ways.

Example	Seven million Native Americans live in the Andes today, their population has returned to what it was when the Spanish arrived.
Separate	Seven million Native Americans live in the Andes today. Their population has returned to what it was when the Spanish arrived.

Combined   Seven million Native Americans live in the Andes today, so their population has returned to what it was when the Spanish arrived.

1. Researchers puzzle over when the first inhabitants of the Americas arrived, they might have come as few as ten thousand or as many as forty thousand years ago.

2. In the 1950s, scientists found an arrowhead in Clovis, New Mexico, the Clovis arrowhead was about ten thousand years old.

3. Most of the remains of the first Americans are no older than that, other evidence points to an earlier arrival.

4. For example, there are about 140 Native American language families, they took a long time to develop.

5. Language experts study the length of time it takes for languages to form, one expert said it would take forty thousand years for the Amerindian languages to develop.

6. She said she knew that no objects that old have been found yet, perhaps there were different tribes that arrived separately.

7. Some Native Americans could have come across the Bering Strait from Mongolia, others could have come by boat across the Pacific.

8. Thor Heyerdahl believed that the natives of Peru traveled from islands in the western Pacific, he tested his theory by taking that journey in a canoe.

9. Scientists study the genes of Native Americans, the scientists try to see how the genes of living peoples differ from the genes found in the cells of ancient bones.

10. Nearly all Native Americans have type O blood I wonder if scientists know why that is true.

Exercise 4   Revision Skill

Sentence Review   Revise the following paragraph by correcting all sentence fragments and run-ons.

(1) Although chocolate candy tastes good. (2) Too much of it can be bad for you. (3) It contains caffeine, the caffeine makes some people uncomfortably nervous. (4) Chocolate can also be found. (5) In ice cream and pastries. (6) Chocolate candy contains sugar and fat, people who eat it can put on unwelcome pounds. (7) It can also contribute to tooth decay.

SECTION 3: USING NOUNS

A *noun* is a word that names a person, a place, a thing, or an idea.

Persons	Janet Jackson, cook, senior, Michelangelo, firefighter
Places	Little Rock, Japan, mall, Atlantic Ocean, island, crater
Things	headphones, tennis racket, flower, Nintendo
Ideas	equality, loyalty, theory, freedom, peace, economy

Types of Nouns

If a noun names a particular person, place, thing, or idea, it is a *proper noun*.

Wilma Rudolph	Smart Museum	Boston
Mario	Buddhism	Zaire

If a noun names a kind of person, place, thing, or idea, it is a *common noun*.

runner	museum	city
man	religion	country

A noun made up of more than one word is called a *compound noun*.

You may have noticed that some nouns, like *Wilma Rudolph, apple pie,* and *Epcot Center* are made up of more than one word.

handball	space shuttle	waterlily
videotape	New Orleans	Lake Michigan

Exercise 1   Application in Literature

Types of Nouns   Write the nouns in the following passage. Label each noun as *Common* or *Proper*. For two nouns, you should add a second label—*Compound*.

> (1) Excitement grew in the Talavera household. (2) If Tracee continued to develop, she might be the darling of the 1980 Olympics. . . .
> (3) "She was the imp," remembers Mulvihill. (4) "The vivacious little teeny-bopper that darted around and really didn't know what was going on but was having a good time."

◀ WHAT'S IN A NAME?

All names are nouns. Many names have interesting origins. Consider, for example, the common Spanish names *Rosa, Dolores,* and *Milagro.* These names are the Spanish words for *rose, sorrows,* and *miracle.* Consult a dictionary to find out about the meanings of other common names.

◀ QUICK TIP

Compound nouns can be spelled as one word, like *handball;* with a hyphen, like *great-grandmother;* or as two words, like *New Orleans.*

◀ LITERARY MODEL

from "Tracee"
by Robert Lipsyte

Exercise 2   Concept Check

Proper Nouns   On your paper write a proper noun that names an example of the person, place, or thing named by each common noun.

> **Example**   river   **Answer**   Mississippi

1. mountain
2. school
3. building
4. ship
5. country
6. desert
7. president
8. organization
9. musician
10. book

Using Nouns

Nouns can be used in sentences in five different ways: as *subjects*, as *direct objects*, as *indirect objects*, as *objects of prepositions*, and as *predicate nouns*.

Uses of Nouns at a Glance

> An **indirect object** tells to whom or for whom something is done or given.

> A **direct object** tells who or what receives the action of the verb.

Dr. Doolittle gave the **lion** some **medicine** in the **evening.**

QUICK TIP
· · · · · · · ·
Prepositions are small words that introduce phrases. Often one of the words that follow a preposition is a noun.
at the *movies*
for *Paula*
in *Detroit*

> A **subject** tells the person, place, thing, or idea that the sentence is about.

> An **object of a preposition** comes after a preposition such as *in, of, at, on, to,* or *for.*

Dr. Doolittle is a **veterinarian** at the **zoo.**

> A **predicate noun** follows a linking verb such as *is, are,* or *seems.* It renames or describes what is named by the subject.

Exercise 3   Drafting Skill

Nouns in Sentences   For each of the following sentences, write a noun that can be used to complete the sentence. Then identify the noun as *Subject, Direct Object, Indirect Object, Object of a Preposition,* or *Predicate Noun.*

> **Example**   _____?_____ is bordered by two nations.
> **Answer**   Kuwait, Subject

1. Kuwait was settled at the beginning of the eighteenth ___?___.
2. This ___?___ became the independent sheikdom of Kuwait in 1756.
3. In 1899, the sheik gave the ___?___ of Great Britain control over Kuwait's foreign affairs.
4. ___?___ formed its own government again on June 19, 1961, when the British government granted it independence.
5. On June 25, 1961, Iraq's government claimed Kuwait; ___?___ argued that Kuwait had always been part of Iraq.
6. The Arab League is a ___?___ of independent Arab nations.
7. The Arab League, which includes Saudi Arabia, accepted Kuwait as one of its member ___?___.
8. When Iraq threatened Kuwait in 1973, the Saudis defended ___?___.
9. In August of 1990, the oil-rich ___?___ was again threatened, and then invaded, by Iraq.
10. In defense of Kuwait, an air war was begun against ___?___ on January 16, 1991.

Using Plural Forms of Nouns

A noun is *singular* if it names one person, place, thing, or idea. A noun is *plural* if it names more than one person, place, thing, or idea.

1. **To form the plurals of most nouns, add -s.**

clown	astronaut	penguin	dancer
clowns	*astronauts*	*penguins*	*dancers*

2. **When a singular noun ends in s, ss, sh, ch, x, or z, add -es.**

glass	beach	dish	fox
glasses	*beaches*	*dishes*	*foxes*

3. **For most singular nouns that end in o, add -s. For some nouns that end in o preceded by a consonant, add -es.**

video	rodeo	tomato	torpedo
videos	*rodeos*	*tomatoes*	*torpedoes*

4. **If a singular noun ends in y preceded by a consonant, change the y to i and add -es. If the noun ends in y preceded by a vowel, add -s to form the plural.**

tragedy	melody	monkey	toy
tragedies	*melodies*	*monkeys*	*toys*

▶ 5. **For some nouns ending in *f* or *fe,* add *-s.* For other nouns ending in *f* or *fe,* change the *f* to *v* and add *-es* or *-s.***

roof	belief	thief	knife
roofs	*beliefs*	*thieves*	*knives*

6. **Some nouns are spelled the same in the singular and in the plural.**

deer	moose	salmon	elk

7. **The plurals of some nouns are formed in ways that are unusual.**

child	ox	mouse	man
children	*oxen*	*mice*	*men*

8. **For a compound noun written as one word, form the plural by changing the last word in the compound to its plural form.**

grandmother	icecap	rainbow	clothesline
grandmothers	*icecaps*	*rainbows*	*clotheslines*

Exercise 4   Concept Check
Plural Nouns   Write the correct plural form of each noun.

1. woman
2. lash
3. snowstorm
4. hero
5. bug
6. puppy
7. fish
8. life
9. mouse
10. fife

Exercise 5   Revision Skill

Plural Nouns   Rewrite the following sentences. Change the italicized singular nouns to their correct plural forms.

1. Reuben has written a new piece for two *soprano.*
2. The performers can be two *boy* or two *woman.*
3. They will be accompanied by two *piano.*
4. The piece consists of a series of related *song.*
5. It contains some elaborate *harmony.*
6. Reuben's *melody* are always quite unusual.
7. In this piece the pianists play only the black *key.*
8. The common thread in the songs is that they all deal with *wish.*
9. One song tells the story of three *stepchild.*
10. The songs are all based on Hungarian *folk tale.*

Using Possessive Forms of Nouns

The *possessive* form of a noun shows ownership or belonging.

1. If a noun is singular, add 's to form the possessive.

Clarissa's pen   the hound's tooth

2. If a noun is plural and already ends in *s,* add an apostrophe.

the teams' captains   five years' growth

3. If a noun is plural and does not end in *s,* add 's.

the children's aunt   the oxen's yoke

WRITING TIP
· · · · · · · · · · · · · ·
For variety, you might try replacing some possessive nouns with prepositional phrases. For example, instead of *the geese's feathers,* you can write *the feathers of the geese.*

Exercise 6   Concept Check

Possessives   On your paper write the possessive forms of these nouns.

1. Patricia
2. classes
3. women
4. rocks
5. book
6. dance
7. cheeses
8. cattle
9. chef
10. chiefs

Exercise 7   Revision Skill

Possessives   Rewrite the following sentences, changing the italicized nouns to their correct possessive forms.

1. Many of the *world* fairy tales and folk tales tell about grateful animals.
2. In the German tale "The White Snake," for example, a young man wins a *princess* hand in marriage as a result of the good deeds he does for animals.
3. The young *man* first good deed is to rescue some fish from the reeds in which they are caught.
4. Then he saves some *ants* lives by turning his horse aside so that the large beast will not step on the tiny insects.
5. Finally, he saves some *ravens* lives by feeding them.
6. After that, the young man learns that in order to win the hand of the *king* daughter, he must perform certain tasks.
7. He is able to perform these tasks because of the *animals* help.
8. For example, the king throws a ring into the *sea* depths and tells the young man to fetch it.
9. Of course, the fish bring the *monarch* ring back to the surface.
10. This is just one of many *children* stories that tell about animals who return favors.

Exercise 8   Revision Skill

Noun Usage Review   Each sentence below has one error in the form of a plural or possessive noun. Find the error and write the word correctly on your paper.

1. One of the most interesting storys I've ever read is "Dream Time," a story about two fishermen who go to northern Ontario.
2. The mens' trip turns out to be quite an education for them.
3. On the night before they are to leave, a snowstorm buries their tent, their cook stove, and their other supplys.
4. One of the men expresses the fear that he will never see his childrens' faces again.
5. The men are reduced to chewing on twiges to combat their hunger.
6. During a long walk out of the wilderness, one of the men collapses and has a strange dream in which he has a fishes body.
7. In the dream he sees himself as a fish in winter, looking up through the water toward the sunlight above the ices surface.
8. He is very hungry, but all around him there are only hookes with bait on them.
9. The dream causes the man to sympathize with animals suffering and to hate fishing and hunting.
10. Eventually, the two men climb a hill and see several bus's in the distance; they emerge from their experience quite changed.

SECTION 4: USING PRONOUNS

A *pronoun* is a word that is used in place of a noun or another pronoun.

Noun   *Jerry* wants a new fishing pole.
Pronoun   *He* wants a new fishing pole.

Personal Pronouns

A *personal pronoun* refers to a particular person, place, thing, or idea.

Because pronouns replace nouns, they can be used exactly as nouns are used. Personal pronouns have three forms: **subject, object,** and **possessive.** The form of a personal pronoun depends on its job in a sentence. The following chart shows all the forms of personal pronouns.

Forms of Personal Pronouns

	Subject	**Object**	**Possessive**
Singular	I	me	my, mine
	you	you	your, yours
	she, he, it	her, him, it	her, hers, his, its
Plural	we	us	our, ours
	you	you	your, yours
	they	them	their, theirs

Exercise 1   Application in Literature

Identifying Pronoun Forms   Write all the personal pronouns in the following passage. Identify the form of each pronoun as *Subject, Object,* or *Possessive.*

(1) I loved the old man. (2) He had never wronged me. (3) He had never given me insult. (4) For his gold I had no desire. (5) I think it was his eye! (6) Yes, it was this! (7) He had the eye of a vulture—a pale blue eye, with a film over it. (8) Whenever it fell upon me, my blood ran cold; and so by degrees—very gradually—I made up my mind to take the life of the old man. . . .

◀ LITERARY MODEL
from "The Tell-Tale Heart" by Edgar Allan Poe

At a Glance: The Uses of Pronouns

A subject pronoun can be used as the **subject** of a sentence.	A subject pronoun can be used as a **predicate pronoun** after a linking verb.

We traveled with my coach.   The coach is **she.**

An object pronoun can be used as an **indirect object.**	An object pronoun can be used as a **direct object.**

Carla gave **us** some apples.   Then **my** family ate **them** with **her.**

Possessive pronouns are used to show ownership.	An object pronoun can be used as the **object of a preposition.**

Using the Subject Form

WHO IS IT?
Sometimes ungrammatical expressions are used so commonly in everyday speech that they become accepted. Although "It's I" is correct, "It's me" has become acceptable in informal situations. However, "It's me" is still considered incorrect in formal writing.

Subject forms of pronouns (*I, you, she, he, it, we, they*) are used as subjects of sentences and as predicate pronouns. Like a predicate noun, a **predicate pronoun** follows a linking verb and renames or describes the subject of a sentence.

Subject	**Predicate Pronoun**
She won the contest.	The winner was *she.*
I was the umpire.	The umpire was *I.*

Using the Object Form

Object forms of pronouns (*me, you, her, him, it, us, them*) are used as direct objects, indirect objects, and objects of prepositions.

Direct Object	Jolene invited *her.*
Indirect Object	The teachers gave *us* a party.
Object of a Preposition	Sharon went swimming with *them.*

Exercise 2   Concept Check

Using Subject and Object Pronouns   Write the correct pronoun.

1. (We, us) know that there are 5.3 billion people on the earth.
2. If you ask (I, me), that's far too many.
3. A recent magazine article, however, tells (I, me) that the future world population will make today's numbers seem small.

4. (I, me) got a chill after seeing this sentence in the article: "At this rate of growth the population would, before 2250, surpass 30 trillion."

5. The writer of the article says that it occurs to (he, him) that there would be over 200 people per acre on the earth.

6. Population experts tell (we, us) that the population of the earth has increased by 2.5 billion in the last forty years.

7. It seems to (I, me) that food production methods have improved in recent years, yet there are many hungry people in the world.

8. We can't adequately feed all of (they, them).

9. Perhaps someday (we, us) will farm the sea.

10. Fish and aquatic plants can provide (we, us) with a lot of nutrition.

Using the Possessive Form

Like possessive nouns, possessive pronouns show ownership or belonging. Unlike possessive nouns, such as *doctor's,* possessive pronouns do not contain apostrophes.

Do not confuse possessive pronouns with contractions that sound similar. If the word you are using takes the place of two words, it is a contraction and needs an apostrophe.

Possessive Pronouns	its	your	their
Contractions	it's	you're	they're

Exercise 3   Revision Skill

Pronouns and Contractions   Rewrite each sentence, correcting errors in the use of possessive pronouns and contractions. If there are no errors, write *Correct.*

1. Mariah said to Angelo, "Its your turn at bat."
2. "Your next after me," said Angelo to Karl.
3. They're team was made up of nine neighborhood kids.
4. The other team was ready when it's turn came up.
5. Their pitcher, known as Piranha, was a very aggressive player.
6. She called out to Angelo, "Your in trouble now, squirt!"
7. "Don't worry. You're the one in trouble," answered Angelo.
8. He smacked the ball over the fence, and its path took it through a school window.
9. "They're really good kids," the baseball coach told the principal.
10. "In fact," said the coach, "I'd like to have you're permission to put Angelo on my first team next year."

Pronouns in Compounds

Sometimes two pronouns, or a pronoun and a noun, are joined by *and, or,* or *nor* to form a compound. Remember, the way a pronoun is used always determines its form. In a compound, use the same form of the pronoun that you would use if the pronoun appeared by itself.

Compound Subject
Nick and *I* baked baklava for the Greek holiday.

Compound Predicate Noun and Pronoun
The team members that day were *Boris* and *I*.

Compound Direct Object
Dad took *Maria* and *me* to the movies.

Compound Indirect Object
Please give *Sheree* and *him* their books.

Compound Object of a Preposition
Yvana is managing the booth for *Martin* and *her*.

Exercise 4   Revision Skill

Pronouns in Compounds   Write the correct pronoun for each sentence. Then identify the form of the pronoun as *Subject* or *Object.*

1. My sister Cara and (I, me) were born in Pisa, Italy.
2. Gina and her brother Aldo were born in Italy too; we're friends with Gina and (he, him).
3. Having spent our childhood in Italy gives Cara and (I, me) certain advantages.
4. For example, when we were young, our relatives and acquaintances taught Cara and (I, me) to speak Italian.
5. When my mother told my father she had found a job in the United States, (he, him) and my grandparents were surprised.
6. (We, Us) and our parents now live in Cambridge, Massachusetts, where my mother is a professor of chemistry.
7. Mama and Papa sent my sister and (I, me) to a school in Cambridge to learn English.
8. (They, Them) and my grandparents are very proud of us.
9. (We, us) and our Italian-American friends have learned English very quickly.
10. We talk about Italy with our American friends and (they, them).

Interrogative Pronouns

Interrogative pronouns are used to ask questions.

The interrogative pronouns *who* and *whom* are often confused. *Who* is a subject pronoun. It is used as a subject or as a predicate pronoun.

Subject	*Who* cooked this fish?
Predicate Pronoun	Our new dance teacher is *who?*

Whom is an object pronoun. It is used as a direct object, an indirect object, or an object of a preposition.

Direct Object	*Whom* did you take to the dance?
Indirect Object	She brought *whom* a present?
Object of a Preposition	About *whom* was that speech made?

◀ *WHOM:* TO USE OR NOT TO USE?
. . . .
To tell whether *who* or *whom* should be used, try answering the question with a statement containing a personal pronoun.
Who is going out? *He* is going out.
Whom did you invite? You did invite *him.*
To *whom* did you speak? You did speak to *her.*

Exercise 5   Revision Skill

Interrogative Pronouns   Write the correct interrogative pronoun.

1. (Who, Whom) has my book on Egyptian mythology?

2. To (who, whom) did you lend the book last?

3. The book's author was (who, whom)?

4. You gave (who, whom) permission to take the book home overnight?

5. (Who, Whom) was doing that report on the Egyptian goddess Isis?

Pronouns and Their Antecedents

Pronouns usually refer back to a noun or another pronoun in the same sentence or paragraph. The noun or pronoun that a pronoun refers to is the pronoun's **antecedent.**

Have you ever visited *Hong Kong? It* is the most densely populated city in the world. (The antecedent of *It* is *Hong Kong.*)

Exercise 6 Concept Check

Pronouns and Their Antecedents Write the pronouns in the following sentences. Then write the antecedent of each pronoun.

Example	Actors wear makeup so that they can create illusions for the audience.
Answer	*they, Actors*

1. Around 550 B.C., an actor named Thespis smeared his face with makeup and stepped onto a stage.
2. Because Thespis had applied white paint and cinnabar, a bright red mineral, he could be seen by 15,000 Greek spectators.
3. Actors like Thespis also wore masks so that they could change character in the middle of a play.
4. Borrowing masks from the Greek theater, the Romans created a group of popular characters with their masks.
5. In sixteenth-century Italy, commedia dell'arte troupes used leather masks as they traveled from town to town.
6. By the nineteenth century, strong light, such as limelight and gaslight, was having its influence on the style of makeup.
7. Carl Baudin combined lard with paint to conceal the edge of a wig, so he is credited with the invention of greasepaint.
8. As the audience has moved closer to the stage, makeup artists have had to improve their techniques.
9. The ancient Greeks would be shocked at makeup budgets for films today—huge compared to their budgets.
10. A million and a half dollars was spent on a group of film actors to transform them into realistic-looking apes!

Indefinite Pronouns

An *indefinite pronoun* is one that does not refer to a particular person or thing.

Singular Indefinite Pronouns

another	either	neither	one
anybody	everybody	nobody	somebody
anyone	everyone	no one	someone
anything	everything	nothing	something
each			

Plural Indefinite Pronouns

both	few	many	several

A possessive pronoun that has an indefinite pronoun as its antecedent must agree in number with the indefinite pronoun.

Singular possessive pronouns (*his, her,* and *its*) should be used with singular indefinite pronouns.

Somebody left *his* backpack in the boys' locker room. (The antecedent of the possessive pronoun is *Somebody,* which is singular. Therefore, the singular form *his* is correct.)

When the person referred to in a sentence could be either male or female, use *his or her,* as in this example:

Someone took a library book without signing *his or her* name.

The plural possessive *their* is used with plural indefinite pronouns.

Both made *their* reservations to fly to New Mexico on Wednesday. (The antecedent of the possessive pronoun is *Both,* which is plural. Therefore, the plural form *their* is correct.)

Depending on how they are used in particular sentences, the indefinite pronouns *all, any, none,* and *some* may be either singular or plural.

Singular *All* of the class has taken *its* Constitution test.
Plural *All* of the students will receive *their* grades on Monday.

◀ NONSEXIST LANGUAGE
· · · · · · · · · · · · · · ·
In the past it was acceptable to use the masculine pronouns *he, him,* and *his* when referring to all people, as in this sentence: *A swimmer must loosen his muscles before every meet.* Now, however, masculine pronouns are often replaced with phrases such as *his or her* and *he or she,* as in this sentence: *A swimmer must loosen his or her muscles before every meet.*

Exercise 7   Revision Skill

Agreement with Indefinite Antecedents   Rewrite the sentences that have agreement problems. If a sentence is correct, write *Correct.*

1. Everybody has their own opinion about whether cross-country skiing or downhill skiing is better.
2. Both have its advantages, but personally I think downhill skiing is rather expensive.
3. Perhaps someone who was willing to spend a lot of their money on downhill skiing would enjoy it more than I would.
4. After big snowfalls some parents take his or her children cross-country skiing at night through quiet streets.
5. For extra protection, each family member wears for its outfit something that glows in the dark.

Pronouns with Nouns

Sometimes the pronouns *we* and *us* appear before nouns. To decide which pronoun is correct, listen to the way the sentence sounds without the noun.

We joggers lost weight. (The subject form *we* is correct. To check, say, "We lost weight.")

Mr. Ramón gave *us* eighth graders a tour of the airport. (The object form *us* is correct. To check, say, "Mr. Ramón gave us a tour of the airport.")

Exercise 8   Concept Check

Pronouns with Nouns   Write the correct pronoun.

1. (We, us) students have been conducting an experiment.
2. Marcy came back from her dentist and told some of (we, us) girls that drinking soda had harmed her teeth.
3. Some of (we, us) soda drinkers didn't believe Marcy's dentist.
4. Marcy gave (we, us) students the tooth that the dentist had pulled.
5. After a few weeks of letting the tooth sit in a glass of soda and observing it decay, (we, us) skeptics are convinced that Marcy's dentist was right!

Exercise 9   Revision Skill

Pronoun Usage   Most of the following sentences contain an error in the use of pronouns or contractions, or in pronoun agreement. Rewrite the sentences that need correction. If a sentence has no error, write *Correct.*

1. The *Columbia Journalism Review* has collected some funny headline errors, and it appear in a book published in 1987.
2. The book, which Bobby and me read, is called *Red Tape Holds Up New Bridge and More Flubs from the Nation's Press.*
3. One of the quotations in that book that really amused Bobby and me was "Services for man who refused to hate Thursday in Atlanta."
4. Another funny part of the book shows a newspaper photo of a French chef whose holding a dog in her arms and standing in front of a table covered with fresh ingredients.
5. The caption says that the chef is displaying the "raw materials" that her uses in her cooking.
6. Of course, us friends know that the caption is not really referring to the dog!
7. A quotation in the book that seemed rather gruesome to Bobby and I was "Workers Accused of Selling Stamps to Be Burned."
8. There was one pronoun error in the collection, in the sentence "Canadian economist feels rates have hit there peak."
9. Us spelling champs found that this error had unfortunately been "corrected" in the second edition.
10. The editor allowed his book to be reprinted with the word *their* misspelled as *thier!*

SECTION 5: USING VERBS

A *verb* is a word that expresses action or state of being.

Jim's father *drives* a truck.   Coal *is* a fossil fuel.

Pedro *won* the talent contest.   Lucy *bought* a piano.

Action verbs are verbs that tell what a subject does.

Raoul *dived* into the water.   Sabrina *stamped* her foot.

Connie *danced* across the floor.   Lee *washed* the car.

A *linking verb* connects the subject to a word that renames or describes the subject.

Ms. Feinstein *is* a senator.   The moon *seems* huge tonight.

Gary Paulsen *is* a writer.   The music *sounds* terrible.

All forms of the verb *be* can be used as linking verbs. These forms include *am, is, are, was, were, be, been,* and *being*. Other common linking verbs are *appear, become, grow, look, seem, smell, sound, taste,* and *feel*.

◀ NOTE

Sometimes verbs that express states of being do not function as linking verbs.
Example: I *am* in the army. (*Am* does not link *I* and *army*.)

Exercise 1   Concept Check

Types of Verbs   Write the verbs in the following sentences. Identify each verb as *Action* or *Linking*.

1. To the ancient Greeks, the earth was a beautiful goddess.
2. They called the earth Ge, the caretaker of all living things.
3. The name Ge is a part of the word *geology,* meaning "the study of the earth."
4. The Greeks also worshiped Demeter, another goddess.
5. This goddess protected the harvest and the fruits of the earth.
6. Hades, the selfish god of the underworld, adored Demeter's lovely daughter, Persephone.
7. Against Demeter's wishes, Hades took Persephone to the underworld.
8. The earth became cold and bare because of Demeter's grief.
9. Eventually, Persephone left Hades for part of each year.
10. According to the Greeks, Persephone's return to Demeter was spring, and her return to Hades, the beginning of winter.

GRAMMAR TIP

A verb that can be replaced by any form of the verb *be* is a linking verb. A verb that can't be replaced by a form of *be* is an action verb. Some verbs, like *grow, look, smell, sound, taste,* and *feel,* can function as linking verbs or as action verbs.
Examples: The air *grew* chilly. ("The air *is* chilly" makes sense, so *grew* is a linking verb.)
Mendel *grew* yellow and green peas. (The *is* test doesn't work; therefore, *grew* is an action verb.)

Verb Phrases

A *verb phrase* consists of a main verb and one or more helping verbs.

Helping Verb(s)	Main Verb
will	take
had been	taking
may have	taken

Some common helping verbs are *can, could, will, would, shall, should, may, might,* and *must.* Other common helping verbs include forms of *be, do,* and *have.*

Forms of *be*	am, is, are, was, were, be, been, being
Forms of *do*	do, does, did
Forms of *have*	have, has, had

Verbs at a Glance

An **action verb** tells what the subject does.

Dr. Mistri **traveled** to Peru. There she **discovered** a previously unknown beetle.

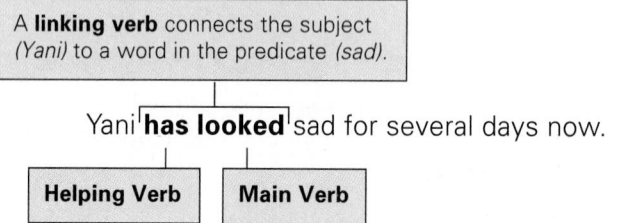

A **linking verb** connects the subject *(Yani)* to a word in the predicate *(sad).*

Yani **has looked** sad for several days now.

| Helping Verb | Main Verb |

Exercise 2   Concept Check

Types of Verbs   Write the verb phrase in each sentence. Underline the helping verb once and the main verb twice. Then identify the verb phrase as *Action* or *Linking.*

1. My family has traveled to San Francisco, California, each spring for the last three years.
2. We will be there again in three weeks.
3. I am amazed by the city's steep hills, giants such as Twin Peaks, Mount Davidson, and Mount Sutro.
4. Nob Hill has become a popular tourist area.
5. Beautiful mansions were built on this hill in the 1870s.

Exercise 3   Drafting Skill

Helping Verbs   Add a helping verb to complete each sentence.

1. If you go to San Francisco, you absolutely __?__ go to Chinatown.
2. Chinatown __?__ said to have the largest urban Chinese population outside of Asia.
3. I __?__ eaten in several great restaurants there.
4. On my vacation I __?__ visit the many colorful shops along Grant Avenue.
5. If I could, I __?__ spend all my time in Chinatown.

Verb Tenses

Every verb has different forms that are used to refer to different times. These forms are called the *tenses* of the verb.

Tenses of Verbs

Present   Shows an action that is happening now or that happens regularly or constantly

Now:	*Take* the bread out of the oven.
Regularly:	The shopkeeper *sweeps* her store every day.
Constantly:	The temperature at the sun's core *is* about 27 million degrees Fahrenheit.

Past   Shows an action that was completed in the past

In A.D. 1066, the English and the Normans *fought* the Battle of Hastings.

Future   Shows an action that will take place in the future

The millennium *will end* in the year A.D. 2000.

Present Perfect   Shows an action that was completed at an indefinite time in the past or that began in the past and continues into the present

The Masai people *have herded* cattle for centuries.

Past Perfect   Shows an action that was completed before a specified time in the past

By the time the 1980s *arrived*, personal computers *had become* commonplace in offices.

Future Perfect   Shows an action that will have been completed by a specified time in the future

By the time the camera crew *arrives*, the sailor *will have finished* her solo trip across the Atlantic Ocean.

Exercise 4 Concept Check

Identifying Tenses Identify the tense of the italicized verb in each sentence.

1. I *like* jeans more than any other type of clothing.
2. I *have learned* that Levi Strauss invented this wonderful article of clothing.
3. Strauss *settled* in San Francisco after the 1849 gold rush.
4. Before going to San Francisco, he *had made* his living by selling canvas for tents and covered wagons.
5. Strauss *discovered* that the tent canvas made a sturdy and useful material for pants.

Exercise 5 Drafting Skill

Using Tenses Complete the following sentences with the verb forms described in parentheses. Write the complete sentences.

1. Before long, Strauss (past of *distribute*) canvas pants to miners.
2. The miners found that Strauss's canvas pants (past of *last*) a long time.
3. By the 1860s, Strauss (past perfect of *discover*) denim.
4. His denim pants, made of a much softer fabric, (past of *become*) even more popular than his canvas pants.
5. Why did Strauss (present of *dye*) jeans blue?
6. Strauss (past perfect of *learn*) that dying his pants was profitable.
7. People (past of *like*) the fact that the dark blue hid stains.
8. I (present perfect of *wonder*) why jeans have become so fashionable in the modern world.
9. I (present perfect of *hear*) that a 1935 issue of *Vogue* magazine featured models in jeans for the first time.
10. From now on, I (future of *remember*) the story of Levi Strauss each morning when I put on my jeans.

Principal Parts of Verbs

Every verb has four *principal parts*. The principal parts are the *present*, the *present participle*, the *past*, and the *past participle*.

For many verbs the past and the past participle are formed by adding -*ed* or -*d* to the present form. These verbs are referred to as **regular verbs.**

The Principal Parts of Regular Verbs

Present	Present Participle	Past	Past Participle
work	(is) working	worked	(has) worked
direct	(is) directing	directed	(has) directed
raise	(is) raising	raised	(has) raised

Irregular verbs have pasts and past participles that are formed in unusual, or irregular, ways. The following are some common irregular verbs.

Irregular Verbs

Present	Past	Past Participle	Present	Past	Past Participle
become	became	(has) become	ride	rode	(has) ridden
begin	began	(has) begun	ring	rang	(has) rung
break	broke	(has) broken	rise	rose	(has) risen
bring	brought	(has) brought	run	ran	(has) run
build	built	(has) built	say	said	(has) said
choose	chose	(has) chosen	see	saw	(has) seen
come	came	(has) come	shake	shook	(has) shaken
do	did	(has) done	shrink	shrank	(has) shrunk
draw	drew	(has) drawn	sing	sang	(has) sung
drink	drank	(has) drunk	sit	sat	(has) sat
drive	drove	(has) driven	sink	sank	(has) sunk
eat	ate	(has) eaten	sleep	slept	(has) slept
fall	fell	(has) fallen	speak	spoke	(has) spoken
fly	flew	(has) flown	spend	spent	(has) spent
freeze	froze	(has) frozen	spring	sprang	(has) sprung
give	gave	(has) given	stand	stood	(has) stood
go	went	(has) gone	steal	stole	(has) stolen
grow	grew	(has) grown	swear	swore	(has) sworn
keep	kept	(has) kept	swim	swam	(has) swum
know	knew	(has) known	take	took	(has) taken
lay	laid	(has) laid	teach	taught	(has) taught
lead	led	(has) led	think	thought	(has) thought
leave	left	(has) left	throw	threw	(has) thrown
lie	lay	(has) lain	wear	wore	(has) worn
meet	met	(has) met	write	wrote	(has) written

NOTE
. . . .
The present participles of both regular and irregular verbs are formed by adding *-ing*.

GRAMMAR TIP
. . . .
Note that the past form of a verb never has a helping verb, but the past participle form always has one.

◄ **ENOUGH SAID**
. . . .
When you write dialogue, you often use the verb *said,* as in *he said* and *she said.* Occasionally, you may want to substitute another word for *said.* Here are some possibilities: *announced, answered, commented, declared, explained, mentioned, observed, remarked, repeated, replied, stated, thought,* and *whispered.*

Exercise 6   Concept Check

Irregular Verbs   Write the correct verb form.

1. Louis Armstrong (grew, grown) up in New Orleans admiring the brass bands that performed in local music halls.
2. Armstrong (took, taken) his interest in music seriously.
3. Before long, he had (began, begun) to play in marching bands and on riverboats.
4. He (threw, thrown) himself into music and eventually traveled from New Orleans to Chicago.
5. From there, Armstrong (sprang, sprung) into national prominence.
6. He (stole, stolen) the shows with terrific solos.
7. In fact, Armstrong (gave, given) the first jazz solos ever.
8. Armstrong also (sang, sung) on occasion and became a band leader, a film star, and a comedian.
9. By the time Armstrong died in 1971, quality jazz music had (rose, risen) in popularity.
10. Many people have (came, come) to realize that Armstrong was a gift to the world of music.

Exercise 7   Revision Skill

Verb Usage Review   Rewrite the following paragraph, correcting any errors in verb usage.

(1) Last night I sit on the couch, watching a special television program about the Amazon River. (2) The river looked like nothing I had ever saw before. (3) The television program teached me that the Amazon is the second longest river in the world and contains one-fifth of the world's river water. (4) The elevation of the river dropped 17,200 feet as it runs from the Andes in Peru eastward to the Brazilian coast. (5) The world's most ferocious fish—piranhas— have always swam in the Amazon. (6) These fish will attack and eaten any creature around them. (7) I have became quite interested in Amazonia, the area around the Amazon. (8) The world's largest rain forest grown in Amazonia. (9) To develop the region, the Brazilian government has build several highways and airports there. (10) I now knew much more about the Amazon from watching this program.

SECTION 6: USING MODIFIERS

An *adjective* is a word that modifies a noun or a pronoun.

foreign soil	*worthwhile* cause	*likely* story
starry night	*infectious* laughter	*glass* figurines

Articles

The three most commonly used adjectives are *a, an,* and *the.* These three adjectives are known as **articles.** *The* refers to specific persons, places, things, or groups. It is known as the **definite article.**

the Arctic	*the* parrot	*the* quilt

A and *an,* which are known as **indefinite articles,** do not refer to specific items. *A* is used before a consonant sound. *An* is used before a vowel sound.

a stingray	*a* unit	*an* economist	*an* hour

Proper and Common Adjectives

Adjectives formed from proper nouns are known as *proper adjectives.*

As you may recall, a **proper noun** names a specific person, place, thing, or idea. Proper nouns often can be turned into proper adjectives.

Proper Noun	Proper Adjective	Example
Kenya	Kenyan	Kenyan folk tale
Spain	Spanish	Spanish literature
Antarctica	Antarctic	Antarctic winter
Cajun	Cajun	Cajun music

Some proper nouns, such as *Cajun,* do not change form when they become proper adjectives. Many proper nouns, like *Kenya* and *Spain,* do change form.

Adjectives that are not articles or proper adjectives are known as **common adjectives.** Here are some examples: *light, clever, squeaky, first, downy, adorable, silly, fat, sneaky,* and *equal.*

OTHER PARTS OF SPEECH USED AS ADJECTIVES

Often pronouns such as *this, these, that, those, his, her, my, our,* and *their* are used as adjectives to modify nouns, as in *this houseplant* or *our slides.* In addition, verb forms that end in *-ing, -ed, -d, -n, -en,* or *-t* are sometimes used as adjectives, as in *the singing sailors, the broken window,* or *burnt toast.* A verb form that is used as an adjective is known as a *participle.*

Exercise 1   Concept Check

Identifying Adjectives   Write the adjectives in the following sentences. Then label each one *P* for proper adjective or *C* for common adjective. Ignore the articles.

1. Francisco Pizarro was the Spanish conquistador who conquered the South American empire of the Incas.
2. A brutal, selfish man, Pizarro came to South America seeking gold and precious gems.
3. The mighty Inca empire had been experiencing internal warfare and a deadly epidemic of smallpox.
4. Pizarro surprised the young, inexperienced Incan ruler Atahualpa.
5. After capturing Atahualpa, the European soldiers told the ruler's loyal subjects to fill a large room with gold and silver treasures as a ransom.
6. The Inca gave in to Pizarro's terrible demands.
7. Nonetheless, the cruel Pizarro had Atahualpa executed.
8. Pizarro himself met a violent death at the hands of one of his own treacherous companions.
9. Today, the body of Pizarro can be viewed in a glass casket in the grand cathedral in Lima, Peru.
10. Pizarro founded the city of Lima, near the dry Peruvian coast, in 1535.

Predicate Adjectives

An adjective may be separated from the noun or pronoun that it modifies by a linking verb. When this happens, the adjective is called a *predicate adjective*.

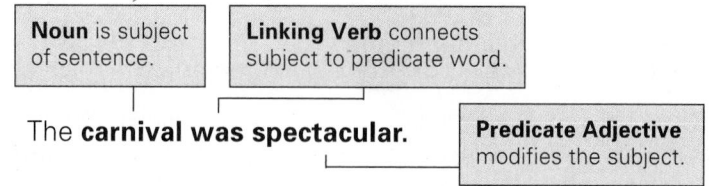

Noun is subject of sentence.　**Linking Verb** connects subject to predicate word.

The **carnival was spectacular.**　**Predicate Adjective** modifies the subject.

Linking verbs, you may recall, include forms of the verb *to be (am, are, be, been, being, is, was,* and *were)* and certain other verbs, such as *become, feel, grow, look, seem, smell,* and *taste.*

Exercise 2   Concept Check

Predicate Adjectives   Write each sentence on your paper. Circle the linking verb. Underline the subject once. Then underline the predicate adjective or adjectives twice.

WRITING TIP

Colorful adjectives will capture a reader's imagination and help him or her clearly see what you're writing about.
EXAMPLE: Rose and Nick's [restaurant] was filled with smoke from *thick* bacon and *burnt* toast. *Heavy white* coffee mugs were planted on *gold-speckled formica* table tops, beneath *groggy* faces. The sound of *sizzling* grease hung in the air.

Kim Leahy,
"Fish Story"

WRITING TIP

Sometimes you can make your writing stronger by combining a sentence that contains a predicate adjective with another sentence. Consider how the first two sentences are combined to form the third sentence:
She arrived in her truck. It was *old.*
She arrived in her *old* truck.

1. Majuro, a coral atoll in the western Pacific Ocean, is small and sandy.
2. With no hills and little greenery, the island appears smooth and silvery from above.
3. The capital of the Marshall Islands, Majuro seems drowsy and informal to most visitors.
4. Chickens near the government buildings aren't uncommon.
5. Their squawks sound funny and sometimes peevish.

Exercise 3 Revision Skill

Sentence Combining Rewrite the sentences, following the directions given in parentheses.

1. Sicily is *unique* and *historic*. It is an island that lies off the southern coast of Italy. (Combine into one sentence. Place the italicized adjectives before the word *Sicily*.)
2. The capital of Sicily, Palermo, lies in an area called "the Golden Coast." This area is *famous*. (Combine into one sentence by moving the italicized word.)
3. Palermo is *ancient*. It is also *fabled*. It has been a thriving seaport since the days of the Phoenicians, who founded the city in the eighth century B.C. (Combine into one sentence. Place the italicized words before the word *Palermo*.)
4. One of Sicily's major exports is its olives. These are *delicious*. (Combine into one sentence by moving the italicized word.)
5. Sicily is also known for its grapes. These grapes are *luscious*. (Combine into one sentence by moving the italicized word.)

Understanding Adverbs

An *adverb* is a word that modifies a verb, an adjective, or another adverb.

Modifies Verb	breaks *easily*, plays *well*, winked *knowingly*
Modifies Adjective	*too* difficult, *moderately* helpful, *somewhat* ridiculous
Modifies Adverb	*so* simply, *quite* often, *most* ably

Many adverbs end with *-ly*. Adverbs tell *how, where, when,* or *to what extent* about the words they modify.

How	called *angrily*	ran *fast*
Where	went *there*	fell *down*
When	begins *soon*	*always* works
To What Extent	*completely* honest	*partially* finished

Exercise 4   Concept Check

Finding Adjectives and Adverbs   Make two columns on your paper. In one column write all the adjectives (except articles) you find in the following paragraph. Write all the adverbs in the second column.

(1) Rachel Carson was a talented writer and biologist. (2) Carson successfully completed a degree in biology at a time when few women graduated from college. (3) She energetically worked to learn about science and the environment. (4) Eventually, Carson decided to work to protect the beauty of nature. (5) She wrote many informative books on the subject. (6) Carson bravely helped stop powerful companies from producing DDT, a dangerous insecticide.

Adjective or Adverb?

As you may recall, an adjective modifies a noun or a pronoun. An adverb modifies a verb, an adjective, or another adverb. Therefore, you can tell an adjective from an adverb by determining what the word is modifying.

Adjective	The frost formed *fantastic* shapes on the windowpanes. *(Fantastic* modifies the noun *shapes.)*
Adverb	Adelita writes *beautifully. (Beautifully* modifies the verb *writes.)*

You should use an adjective after a linking verb such as *is, was, were, looks, feels, grows, sounds, smells, tastes, becomes,* or *seems.* A linking verb connects the adjective to the noun or pronoun it modifies. Do not use an adverb after a linking verb.

Incorrect	You appear *happily.*
Correct	You appear *happy.* (The adjective form follows the linking verb *appear.)*

You should use an adverb, not an adjective, to modify a verb, an adjective, or an adverb.

Incorrect	The band played *bad.*
Correct	The band played *badly.* (The adverb modifies the action verb *played.)*
Incorrect	The clouds passed by *real* slowly.
Correct	The clouds passed by *really* slowly. (The adverb modifies the adverb *slowly.)*

Exercise 5 Concept Check

Choosing the Correct Modifier Write the modifier that is correct.

1. I walked (slow, slowly) down the supermarket aisles, looking for olives.
2. Olives are a (real, really) delicious member of the fruit family.
3. Throughout history, olives have been a (well, good) source of food, medicines, cleansers, and lubricants.
4. Spain, Italy, Greece, and Turkey (regular, regularly) produce many olives.
5. Olive trees are (hearty, heartily), and some can live for more than a thousand years.

Exercise 6 Proofreading Skill

Using Modifiers Correctly Decide whether the italicized modifiers in the following paragraph are used correctly. If the modifier is correct, write *Correct* on your paper. If the modifier needs to be changed, write the correct form on your paper.

(1) Olives grow *good* in places with a hot, dry climate, like California. (2) Olives first came to California in 1769, but they didn't gain popularity *quickly.* (3) Many years went by before the fruit was *real* popular. (4) Today, orchards in California *frequently* produce close to 100,000 tons of olives a year. (5) Olives from California are used most *common* for food rather than for olive oil.

Avoiding Double Negatives

Do not use two negative words together in the same sentence.

Many adverbs, such as *no, not, none, nothing, never, hardly, scarcely,* and contractions that contain *n't*—the shortened form of *not*— are negative expressions. When you wish to express a negative idea, one of these words in a sentence is sufficient. If two of them are used, an error results. That error is called a **double negative.**

Double Negative	He *don't* have *no* common sense.
Correct	He *doesn't* have any common sense.
Correct	He has *no* common sense.

Exercise 7   Proofreading Skill

Correcting Double Negatives   Rewrite the following sentences, correcting all double negatives.

1. There hasn't hardly been another event in U.S. history as difficult as the great Dust Bowl.
2. Back in the 1930s, parts of the Midwest and South didn't see no rain for a very long time.
3. In Oklahoma and in nearby states, topsoil dried up and began blowing away until there wasn't scarcely any of it left.
4. The dust blew so thick that sometimes one couldn't hardly see the sun.
5. Cattle suffocated in the middle of open fields because the animals could not get no clean, fresh air.
6. There wasn't nothing that the farmers of the region could do.
7. Their crops failed, and they didn't have no money to pay the mortgages on their farms.
8. Many of them packed their belongings and headed for California, realizing that they probably wouldn't never return to their homes.
9. The job opportunities many of them found in California weren't no good.
10. Most of them didn't have nothing when they arrived in California, so they went to work as migrant laborers.

Adjectives and Adverbs in Comparisons

When you use a modifier to compare one thing with another, use the *comparative form*.

When you use a modifier to compare one thing with more than one other thing, use the *superlative form*.

Modifier	That runner is *fast*.
Comparative Form	He is *faster* than the top runner on our team.
Superlative Form	He is the *fastest* runner in the whole state.

Most short adjectives and adverbs form the comparative by adding *-er* and the superlative by adding *-est*. Words ending in *n* or *y* may undergo slight spelling changes when *-er* or *-est* are added.

Modifier	Comparative Form	Superlative Form
late	later	latest
true	truer	truest
thin	thinner	thinnest
lively	livelier	liveliest

Longer modifiers form the comparative by adding the word *more,* and they form the superlative by adding the word *most.*

Modifier	Comparative Form	Superlative Form
majestic	more majestic	most majestic
awful	more awful	most awful
bizarre	more bizarre	most bizarre
purposefully	more purposefully	most purposefully
fabulously	more fabulously	most fabulously

Never use *more* and the *-er* ending together, or *most* and the *-est* ending together. This error is called a *double comparison.*

Incorrect	more sooner	most suspensefullest
Correct	sooner	most suspenseful
Incorrect	more quicker	most wonderfullest
Correct	quicker	most wonderful

Exercise 8 Revision Skill

Comparison of Modifiers   Find the errors in adjective and adverb forms in the following sentences. Write the correct forms on your paper.

1. The most unusualest place on the earth is probably the continent of Antarctica.
2. The ice is deepest there than any other place on the globe—two miles thick in some places.
3. In addition, most ice is found there than in any other place—over 90 percent of the frozen water on the earth.
4. The wind blows more colderly there than it does anywhere else.
5. The wind sounds more eerier than the soundtrack in a Hollywood horror movie.
6. Perhaps the more tragic expedition ever undertaken in Antarctica was that of Robert F. Scott.
7. On their return trip from the South Pole, Scott and his men ran into the most cruelest weather they had ever seen, and all of them died.
8. The Norwegian Roald Amundsen was more luckier.
9. More fortunater than Scott, Amundsen was able to lead his party safely to the South Pole and back.
10. Today, Antarctica is the more free of all continents, for it is protected by a treaty and shared by many countries.

Unusual Comparative and Superlative Forms

Some modifiers do not use *-er, -est, more,* or *most* in comparisons. Instead, they change their form completely.

Modifier	Comparative	Superlative
bad	worse	worst
good	better	best
little	less	least
many	more	most
well	better	best

Exercise 9   Concept Check

Unusual Forms   Find the errors in modifier forms in the following sentences. Write the modifiers correctly.

1. Of all the sports, perhaps the better is scuba diving.
2. However, if you don't learn how to dive good, you can be in real danger.
3. The worse part of scuba diving is that there are several ways divers can get injured.
4. A diver who dives down farthest than he or she should can get very sick or even die.
5. However, if one follows the safety rules taught in scuba diving class, the sport can be a lot most fun than swimming.

Using Demonstrative Adjectives

The **demonstrative pronouns** include *this, that, these,* and *those.* They are used to point out a specific person or thing. When used as modifiers, they are known as **demonstrative adjectives.**

Use *this* and *that* to modify singular nouns. Use *these* and *those* to modify plural nouns.

  this candle *these* candles *that* script *those* scripts

The words *kind* and *sort* are singular. Use *kind* and *sort* with *this* and *that.* The words *kinds* and *sorts* are plural. Use *kinds* and *sorts* with *these* and *those.*

  this kind *these* kinds *that* sort *those* sorts

Do not use *here* and *there* with demonstrative adjectives.

Incorrect   *This here* circus needs a high-wire act.
Correct   *This* circus needs a high-wire act.

Exercise 10 Revision Skill

Demonstrative Adjectives   Rewrite the following paragraph, correcting the errors that you find.

(1) This here poet, Robert Frost, says that the idea for his poem "Stopping by Woods on a Snowy Evening" simply came to him one day. (2) These kind of statement bothers me because it suggests that the ability to write just magically comes to people. (3) This here person is visited by a Muse, who inspires great writing. (4) However, that there other person isn't visited by a Muse. (5) I disagree with those sort of view of the writing process because I believe that the ability to write well is gained through hard work.

Exercise 11   Revision Skill

Modifier Review   All of the following sentences contain errors in the use of modifiers. Rewrite the sentences correctly.

1. Do you enjoy those there scary stories that people sometimes tell around campfires?
2. I can't help but not like an evening listening to such stories.
3. I especially enjoy such stories when the storyteller speaks quiet.
4. I like it when the storyteller's voice sounds spookily.
5. Then the night seems to close around the audience, and the story itself seems more scarier.
6. Many campfire tales have been around for a real long time.
7. Others aren't scarcely a few years old.
8. Perhaps the most famousest of all campfire stories, "The Monkey's Paw," was written in this century by W. W. Jacobs.
9. That story is probably told more oftener than any other such tale.
10. Some other campfire tales, like the one about the ghost girl who hitches a ride home from a dance, are very anciently.
11. However, there aren't no stories as good, I think, as the ones that people think up on the spot.
12. Those kind of improvised stories can take amusing twists and turns.
13. It is probable true that people have been telling such stories around campfires since the dawn of time.
14. In fact, such stories, told oral, were the very first literature.
15. There aren't none of the earliest literary works that were not first told aloud, long before they were written down.

SECTION 7: SUBJECT-VERB AGREEMENT

Singular and Plural

A noun that names one person, place, thing, or idea is *singular*.
A noun that names more than one is *plural*.

Singular	Plural
forest	forests
boundary	boundaries

Verbs also have singular and plural forms.

Singular	Plural
I imagine	we imagine
you imagine	you imagine
he, she, or it imagines	they imagine

The verbs that follow have special singular or plural forms.

	Be	Have	Do
Singular Forms	is, am, was	has, had	does, did
Plural Forms	are, were	have, had	do, did

Exercise 1 Concept Check

Identifying Singular and Plural Words   Identify the italicized word in each sentence as *Singular* or *Plural*.

1. The Appalachians *stretch* from the Northeast to the South.
2. These rolling *mountains* contain coal, once a major power source for home heating and for the steel industry.
3. Only twenty years ago, coal mines *were* the biggest employers in Appalachia.
4. Now, coal *is* not as widely used as it once was.
5. The people of Appalachia, however, *work* hard and fearlessly; they make the mines profitable.
6. Most *profit* from the mines goes to owners who live far from the mining towns.
7. Some mine owners use a technique called strip mining; strip mining *lays* bare the coal deposits near the surface.
8. The *splendor* of the mountains is destroyed as heavy machinery damages the top layer of the earth.

9. Nevertheless, the misty hills and hollows of southern Appalachia *bring* visitors throughout the year.

10. Local people *hope* that tourism will bring back some of the jobs that were lost when mining slowed down.

Agreement of Subject and Verb

A verb and its subject must agree in number.

A singular subject takes a singular verb. A plural subject takes a plural verb.

> <u>Jeannette Rankin</u> <u>was</u> the first woman member of the U.S. Congress. (The subject, *Jeannette Rankin,* is singular. Therefore, a singular verb, *was,* is used.)

> <u>Congresspersons</u> <u>are</u> responsible for making the laws under which we live. (The subject, *congresspersons,* is plural. Therefore, a plural verb, *are,* is used.)

Problems with Prepositional Phrases

Sometimes a prepositional phrase appears between a subject and its verb. Remember that a verb never agrees with a word that appears in a prepositional phrase.

> <u>One</u> (of my sisters) <u>sings</u> part time in a band. (The verb *sings* agrees with *one,* the subject of the sentence. It does not agree with *sisters,* which is part of a prepositional phrase.)

> The <u>members</u> (of the band) <u>are</u> college students. (The verb *are* does not agree with *band,* which is part of a prepositional phrase. Instead, it agrees with the plural subject, *members.*)

Exercise 2   Drafting Skill

Making Subjects and Verbs Agree   Write the correct verbs.

1. An astronomer with a ground telescope (measures, measure) the distance to the stars.
2. Special stars called cepheids (is, are) three or four times the size of the sun.
3. The brightness of cepheids varies in regular ways; in other words, sometimes cepheids (is, are) dimmer than at other times.

4. Henrietta S. Leavitt (was, were) the scientist who discovered that the cepheids' behavior was interesting.
5. Leavitt said that cepheids with slower cycles (was, were) brighter.
6. Scientists, by knowing a cepheid's brightness, (determines, determine) its distance from the earth.
7. A distance of 10 million light years (is, are) measured in this way with simple instruments.
8. Scientists on the Hubble Space Telescope team (uses, use) the same technique to measure the distance to the Virgo cluster, 50 million light years away.
9. George Jacoby, along with his colleagues, (uses, use) telescopes to measure distances to galaxies.
10. Astronomers around the world (is, are) unlocking many such secrets about the size and age of the universe.

Agreement with Compound Subjects

A subject made up of two or more parts is known as a *compound subject*.

A compound subject with parts joined by the conjunction *and* is plural and always takes a plural verb.

> Kangaroos and wombats are marsupials—mammals with external pouches in which their young grow after birth.

If the parts of a compound subject are joined by *or* or *nor,* the verb agrees with the part that is closest to the verb.

> Either this dress or those skirts are appropriate for the party. (The plural verb *are* agrees with the nearer noun, *skirts*.)

> Neither Julio nor my other friends have traveled to Mexico. (The plural verb *have traveled* agrees with the nearer noun, *friends*.)

> Neither my other friends nor Julio has traveled to Mexico. (The singular verb *has traveled* agrees with the nearer noun, *Julio*.)

Exercise 3   Drafting Skill

Choosing the Correct Verb   Write the correct verb.

1. Neither jogging nor aerobic exercises (is, are) difficult.
2. Aerobic exercises and jogging (requires, require) little in the way of special equipment.

3. Either jogging or aerobic exercises (requires, require) only decent gym shoes and comfortable clothing.

4. Health clubs and youth centers (is, are) great places to participate in jogging and aerobic exercises.

5. Neither aerobic exercises nor jogging (is, are) for everyone, but both are great ways to stay in shape.

Agreement with Indefinite Pronouns

Singular verbs are used with singular indefinite pronouns.

Plural verbs are used with plural indefinite pronouns.

Singular	<u>Each</u> of these pies <u>tastes</u> good.
Plural	<u>Both</u> of these pies <u>taste</u> good.

These indefinite pronouns are plural in some sentences and singular in others: *all, any, most, none,* and *some.*

Singular	<u>All</u> of the milk <u>is spoiled</u>.
Plural	<u>All</u> of the penguins <u>love</u> to jump into cold water.

Exercise 4   Proofreading Skill

Agreement with Compound Subjects and Indefinite Pronouns
Rewrite the following passage, correcting any agreement errors.

(1) Neither Maika nor her sisters is returning to school this fall. (2) Instead, each of these girls are setting out on an adventure. (3) Maika and her family is going to live for a year in Guatemala. (4) All of the family members is looking forward to the experience, which is coming about because Maika's mother, a diplomat, has been assigned to Guatemala.

(5) Few of the countries in this hemisphere seems as varied and mysterious as Guatemala. (6) Many of the most impressive of the Mayan ruins is found there. (7) Some of the countryside are mountainous, and volcanoes are everywhere. (8) Maika and her sisters is hoping to spend time exploring the Guatemalan countryside. (9) Some of the crafts of Guatemala is among the most beautiful in the entire world. (10) Each of the rugs, hats, scarves, sweaters, bags, and blankets are a masterpiece.

REMEMBER
. . . .
Singular indefinite pronouns:

another	anybody
anyone	anything
each	either
everybody	everyone
everything	neither
nobody	no one
one	somebody
someone	something

Plural indefinite pronouns:

both	few
many	several

Singular or plural indefinite pronouns:

all	any
most	none
some	

GRAMMAR TIP
. . . .
For indefinite pronouns that can be either singular or plural, the number of the noun in an intervening prepositional phrase can give you a clue about whether to use a singular or a plural verb.

Agreement in Inverted Sentences

In most sentences the subject comes before the verb. However, sometimes the subject and the verb are switched around, or **inverted.**

Regular Order   The growl of a tiger came from the jungle.
(The subject, *growl,* comes before the verb, *came.*)

Inverted Order   From the jungle came the growl of a tiger.
(The subject, *growl,* comes after the verb, *came.*)

Subjects and verbs are often inverted in questions.

Is deep space really cold? (The subject is *space.* The verb is *Is.*)

Are the aurora borealis and the northern lights the same thing? (The compound subject is *the aurora borealis and the northern lights.* The verb is *Are.*)

Subjects and verbs are also sometimes inverted after the word *there, where,* or *here.*

Here is a mummy from ancient Ecuador. (The subject is *mummy.* The verb is *is.*)

Where are your mittens? (The subject is *mittens.* The verb is *are.*)

A verb must always agree with its subject, even if the subject and the verb are inverted.

Incorrect   In the sky <u><u>was</u></u> many strange, multicolored <u>lights</u>.
Correct   In the sky <u><u>were</u></u> many strange, multicolored <u>lights</u>.

Exercise 5   Proofreading Skill

Agreement in Inverted Sentences   Rewrite the following paragraph, correcting agreement errors.

(1) Across the sky shoot a tiny speck of light. (2) There, on the horizon, are the place where the light seems to land. (3) Were it simply a trick of the light or of the imagination, or were it something real? (4) In the sky is many strange lights. (5) Is some of them flying saucers? (6) Where there is flying saucers, there is usually overactive imaginations. (7) There is usually more rational explanations. (8) In the sky at night appears many things—such as meteors, satellites, balloons, and weather phenomena—that look like flying saucers but aren't. (9) Is reports of flying saucers always fanciful? (10) There are no one who really knows.

Exercise 6   Drafting Skill

Review of Subject-Verb Agreement   Write the correct verb.

1. (Is, Are) personal computers difficult to use?
2. Computers in school and in the office (has, have) made many jobs much easier than ever before.
3. Neither students nor the average office worker (has, have) anything to fear from these machines.
4. Everyone with any interest in computers (is, are) capable of learning how to use them.
5. Either a computer course or some computer manuals (is, are) helpful in learning how to use a computer.
6. One of the salespeople at a computer store (is, are) likely to know about good introductory computer courses.
7. There (is, are) a good chance that you can find a reasonably priced class at a community college or even at your own school.
8. To these classes (goes, go) the many students, office workers, and others who want to become computer literate.
9. The instructor of one of these classes usually (takes, take) into consideration the different skill levels of the students.
10. Therefore, neither the complete beginner nor experienced computer users (has, have) an advantage.

SECTION 8: CAPITALIZATION

Proper Nouns and Proper Adjectives

Capitalize proper nouns and proper adjectives.

A **common noun** is the name of a whole class of persons, places, things, or ideas. A **proper noun** is the name of a particular person, place, thing, or idea. A **proper adjective** is an adjective made from a proper noun. Proper nouns and proper adjectives are capitalized, but common nouns and common adjectives are not.

Common Noun	**Proper Noun**
president	**J**efferson
nation	**C**anada

Common Adjective	**Proper Adjective**
presidential	**J**effersonian
national	**C**anadian

Names and Titles of People

Capitalize names of persons and initials that stand for names.

Nikki **G**iovanni　　　**D**ave **B**arry　　　**B**arbara **B**. **R**obinson

Capitalize titles and abbreviations of titles when they appear before people's names. Capitalize abbreviations, such as *Jr.*, that appear after a name.

Kurt Vonnegut, **J**r.　　　**M**s. Kumin　　　the **R**ev. Bernice King

Capitalize words such as *mother, father, aunt,* and *uncle* when these words are used as names or when they come just before a name.

Did **U**ncle Peter do the dishes?
Does **M**other Teresa help the poor?

Do not capitalize a word that names a family member when the word is preceded by a possessive such as *your* or *my* or by an article such as *a* or *the.*

My **u**ncle is a pilot.　　　Our **m**other wrote a detective novel.

The Pronoun I

Capitalize the pronoun *I*.

> How **I** loved the poem that Maya Angelou read at President Clinton's inauguration!

Religions, Sacred Beings, and Sacred Writings

Capitalize words that name religions, sacred beings, or religious scriptures. Also capitalize most adjectives formed from these names.

the **K**oran	the **V**edas	the **T**orah	the **B**ible
Siva	**O**siris	the **H**oly **S**pirit	**A**llah
Judaism	**I**slam	**I**slamic	**T**aoism

Races, Ethnic Groups, Languages, and Nationalities

Capitalize the names of races, ethnic groups, languages, and nationalities. Also capitalize most adjectives formed from such names.

Nigerian	**G**uatemalan	**S**wiss watch	**C**hicano
Iraqi culture	**I**roquois	**H**opi mythology	**J**ewish

Exercise 1   Concept Check

Using Capital Letters Write the following sentences, using correct capitalization.

1. Have you heard the story of the french heroine named joan of arc?
2. aunt pat showed my brother and me a painting of joan of arc.
3. France was involved in the Hundred Years' War, and France's ruler, charles VII, was in danger of losing his power.
4. joan of arc, a courageous peasant girl, led the french soldiers to victory over the english soldiers.
5. She claimed that the voices of st. michael, st. catherine, and st. margaret told her to lead the troops to victory.
6. My brother and i were surprised to learn that joan of arc was only seventeen when she showed so much courage in the french city of orléans.
7. Some of the french soldiers were jealous of her, so they allowed the english to capture her and burn her at the stake.

8. Her courage was not forgotten; in 1920, pope benedict XV declared joan a saint.
9. She has been a heroine of the roman catholic church ever since.
10. I told ms. wesley, my teacher, that I would be writing my next research paper on joan of arc and the Hundred Years' War.

Geographical Names

Capitalize each important word in a geographical name. Do not capitalize prepositions, such as *in* and *of,* or the articles *a, an,* and *the.*

Bodies of Water	the Atlantic Ocean, the Amazon River, Lake Erie
Continents	Africa, Asia, North America, Antarctica
Landforms	Nile Delta, Cape Cod, the Sahara, Mount Vesuvius, Baja California
Objects in the Universe	Mars, Neptune, the Milky Way
Political Units	Estonia, the Organization of Petroleum Exporting Countries, Florida, the Seminole Nation, Orange County
Public Monuments	Washington Monument, Monticello, Grant's Tomb, the Lincoln Memorial
Roads, Highways	El Camino Real, Haight Street, Route 128
World Regions	the Near East, the Western Hemisphere, the New World, Polynesia

Directions and Sections

Capitalize names of sections of the United States or the world. Also capitalize adjectives made from these names.

The South and the West grew rapidly during the 1980s.
Our family enjoys Southern cooking, especially biscuits and gravy.

Do not capitalize nouns or adjectives that merely refer to compass directions.

To the west of the Washington Monument is the Lincoln Memorial.

The hurricane struck the southern coast of the United States.

Organizations, Institutions, Buildings, and Structures

Capitalize all important words in the names of organizations, institutions, buildings, and structures.

Organizations and Institutions	the National Organization for Women, the Sierra Club, the House of Representatives, the University of Iowa
Buildings	the Golden Pavilion, the Alhambra, the Dome of the Rock, the Chrysler Building
Structures	the Callahan Tunnel, the Eiffel Tower, the Aswan High Dam, Serpent Mound

Events, Documents, and Periods of Time

Capitalize all important words in the names of historical events, documents, and periods of time.

Events	the Hundred Years' War, the Rose Bowl, the Special Olympics, the American Revolution
Documents	the Bill of Rights, the Panama Canal Treaty, the Constitution of the United States
Periods of Time	the Romantic Era, the Roaring Twenties, the Middle Ages

Months, Days, and Holidays

Capitalize the names of months, days, and holidays, but not the names of seasons.

April   Wednesday   Valentine's Day   spring

Time Abbreviations

Capitalize the abbreviations *B.C., A.D., A.M.,* and *P.M.*

The first recorded Olympic Games were held in 776 **B.C.**
London was founded about **A.D.** 43.
The eclipse will occur at 3:46 **P.M.**

Exercise 2   Concept Check

Using Capital Letters   Write the words and abbreviations in the following sentences that should be capitalized. Capitalize them correctly.

1. Last wednesday I saw an interesting exhibit about the country of panama at the springbook history museum.
2. Panama is located between costa rica and colombia.
3. I enjoyed the part of the exhibit that focused on the panama canal, a project that was started in 1882 by french engineers.
4. Because of construction and health problems, the french offered to turn the project over to the u.s. isthmian canal commission.
5. On august 15, 1914, the canal was opened, and ships could travel more efficiently between the atlantic ocean and the pacific ocean.
6. Before the panama canal was opened, traveling by ship from the northeast to california required going all the way around south america.
7. Now the eastern united states could easily receive products like rubber from indonesia and tin from peru.
8. After world war II, panama and the united states had many disputes over which country would control the canal.
9. In 1977, the panama canal treaty was signed, giving panama the right to take complete control of the canal in the year 2000.
10. If you are interested in learning more, the museum is open monday through saturday, from 10:00 a.m. to 7:00 p.m., and the exhibit will be there until memorial day.

School Subjects and Class Names

Capitalize the titles of specific courses and of courses that are followed by numbers. Always capitalize school subjects that are languages.

> **A**lgebra 101   **E**nglish   **S**panish

Do not capitalize the general names of school subjects.

> **b**iology   **h**istory   **a**rt   **m**athematics

Capitalize a class name only when it is part of the name of a specific group or event or when it is used in direct address.

> The **j**uniors went to an assembly to talk about the **J**unior **P**rom.

Sentences and Poetry

Capitalize the first word of every sentence.

Yollie wanted a new dress for the dance.

Capitalize the first word of every line of poetry.

Listen, my children, and you shall hear
Of the midnight ride of Paul Revere. . .

Quotations

Capitalize the first word of a direct quotation that is a sentence.

The senator said, "A billion here, a billion there—pretty soon you're talking real money."

Do not capitalize the second part of a divided quotation unless the second part starts a new sentence.

"Open your books," said Ms. Harper, "and begin your work."
"I have a question," said John. "What page should we read?"

Parts of a Letter

In the greeting of a letter, capitalize all important words.

Dear Dr. Pearce: Dear Julie,

In the closing of a letter, capitalize only the first word.

Your friend,   Sincerely,

Outlines and Titles

Capitalize the first word of each item in an outline and the letters that introduce major subsections.

I. Bicycles
　A. Racing bikes
　B. Mountain bikes

▶ POETIC LICENSE
. . . .
Poets sometimes choose not to begin each line with a capital letter. This is especially true in contemporary poetry. See, for example, E. E. Cummings's "your little voice" on page 45.

Capitalize the first word, the last word, and all other important words in titles.

Book	*Castle in the Air*
Newspaper	*Chicago Tribune*
Play	*The Diary of Anne Frank*
Television Series	*Northern Exposure*
Short Story	"*Raymond's Run*"
Song	"*We Shall Overcome*"
Work of Art	*Black Iris*

The word *the* at the beginning of a title and the word *magazine* are capitalized only when they are part of a formal name.

Newsweek **m**agazine   *The New York Times **M**agazine*

Exercise 3   Concept Check

Using Capital Letters   Copy the following letter, correcting each error in capitalization.

---

dear aunt Hannah,

(1) I hope you are doing well. (2) I am trying to complete a project for english class about the creative Harlem Renaissance of the 1920s. (3) My class is putting on a play called <u>artists of the harlem renaissance</u>. (4) it's going to be a big show, and I think even the <u>middletown press</u>, our town newspaper, will do a story about it. (5) I told my dad about the project, and he said, "contact Hannah. (6) She did a paper on that when she was a Senior in college." (7) I thought maybe you could give me some interesting facts to include. (8) I'm supposed to be focusing on the writer langston hughes.

(9) Here is the beginning of my outline on hughes:

    I. early life
       a. childhood
           1. parents
           2. Hometown
       B. college life
       c. travels

(10) I'm really becoming interested in this subject. (11) I thought spanish was my favorite class, but now I'm not so sure. (12) Please let me know of any important details that I should include in my project. (13) Thank you.

                           (14)sincerely yours,
                               Hillary

Exercise 4 Proofreading Skill

Using Capital Letters Write the following sentences, using correct capitalization.

1. Since sunday i have been reading various tales from england in the middle ages.
2. On labor day, dad took me to the bennetville history museum.
3. we were able to see a play called *the legend of king arthur.*
4. The play is based on a book called *the sword in the stone.*
5. it tells about a young child, arthur, born to the king of all britain, uther pendragon.
6. A magician named merlin warned that upon uther's death, many would try to hurt arthur and keep him from taking the throne.
7. uther hid arthur with a noble knight, sir ector.
8. When britain needed a new king, merlin placed a large block of marble and an anvil in front of the country's largest christian cathedral.
9. he drove a magic sword through both, and then he inscribed on the stone a short poem:

   whosoever pulls out this sword from this stone and anvil
   is the true-born king of all britain.
10. young arthur pulled out the sword and went on to rule britain from his castle called camelot.

SECTION 9: PUNCTUATION

Can you imagine trying to take a long trip without any signs to guide you? Now imagine trying to read a story or magazine article without any punctuation marks. Punctuation marks, like street signs, help guide you.

End Marks

Punctuation marks that are used to show where sentences end are called **end marks.** There are three different end marks: the period, the question mark, and the exclamation point.

The Period

A period is used in each of the following ways:

- at the end of a **declarative** sentence
- at the end of most **imperative** sentences
- at the end of an **indirect question**
- after an **abbreviation** or an **initial**
- after a **number** or a **letter** that shows a part of an outline or an item in a list

A **declarative sentence** is one that makes a statement.

> Sabrina hopes to be a film animator someday.

An **imperative sentence** is one that gives a command or makes a request.

> Please call Dad when you get home.

An **indirect question** shows that someone has asked a question, but it does not contain the exact words of the question.

> Pedro asked how rocks from the bottom of the ocean could have ended up on top of Mount Everest.

An **abbreviation** is a shortened version of a word or phrase.

Wed. (Wednesday)	Ph.D. (Doctor of Philosophy)
Sen. (Senator)	Inc. (Incorporated)
a.k.a. (also known as)	U.S. (United States)

If an abbreviation comes at the end of a sentence that ends with a period, use one period, not two.

Incorrect   Laura now works for Electric Music Box, Inc..
Correct   Laura now works for Electric Music Box, Inc.

An **initial** is a name's first letter, used by itself.

Maxine W. Kumin   O. Henry   Rogelio R. Gomez

An **outline** or **list** uses periods to mark divisions or items.

I. Types of computers   Ingredients for yogurt dressing:
  A. Mainframe   1. Yogurt
  B. Mini   2. Cucumbers
  C. Personal   3. Garlic
                              4. Onion

Exercise 1   Concept Check

Using Periods Correctly   Copy the following items, adding periods where needed.

1. Radiation is energy emitted as electromagnetic waves or as nuclear particles
2. Think about how important radiation is to us
3. Sunlight, lasers, and X-rays are forms of radiation
4. Radio waves make distant communication possible
5. I   Kinds of radiation

    A Electromagnetic

    B Nuclear

    C Cosmic

6. Major scientists in history of radiation

    1 Sir Isaac Newton

    2 James C Maxwell

    3 Marie and Pierre Curie

    4 Max Planck

    5 Albert Einstein

7. I wonder if Dr Einstein was the most important scientist in recent history
8. In November 1919, the Royal Soc of London proclaimed that his theory of relativity was correct
9. Jim asked the professor whether radiation can be harmful
10. Too much radiation can cause sunburn, radiation sickness, and even death

The Question Mark and the Exclamation Point

Use a question mark at the end of an interrogative sentence.

An **interrogative sentence** asks a question.

> Did you know that the earth is closest to the sun in the winter**?**
> Did you know that a giant asteroid came close to the earth**?**

Remember that a period is used at the end of an indirect question.

> Delores asked if we knew where she lived**.**

Use an exclamation point at the end of an exclamatory sentence.

An **exclamatory sentence** expresses strong feelings.

> I really loved that book by Sandra Cisneros**!**

An exclamation point should be used at the end of an imperative sentence that expresses excitement. Other imperative sentences should be followed by a period.

> Get me out of here**!**　　　Please hand me that eraser**.**

Use an exclamation point at the end of a strong interjection.

> Ugh**!**　　Help**!**　　Wonderful**!**

Exercise 2　Concept Check

Using Question Marks and Exclamation Points　Copy the following sentences and add the proper end marks.

1. Have you read the myth of the twins Romulus and Remus
2. They were sons of the war god Mars and a Latin priestess
3. Can you believe that when they were babies, a jealous uncle tried to drown them
4. They survived and were fed by a female wolf Weird
5. That is why the wolf is the symbol of Rome today
6. Later, a shepherd took them in until they were grown
7. Which brother was it that first had the idea of building a city near the Tiber River
8. Romulus ultimately killed his brother Remus in an argument over who would rule the city Good grief
9. Romulus ruled Rome for many years, but then what do you think happened
10. He disappeared mysteriously in a storm

Commas in Compound Sentences and in Series

Use a comma before the conjunction that joins the parts of a compound sentence.

A **compound sentence** contains two or more parts that could stand alone as complete sentences. The parts are joined together with a coordinating conjunction such as *and, or, nor, for, but, so,* or *yet.*

> The alligator seemed to be sleeping, **so** we crept up for a closer look.

Do not confuse compound sentences with compound sentence parts. In a compound sentence, each main part has both a subject and a verb.

Compound Sentence	Hector ran for class president, **and** he won.
Compound Sentence Parts	Hector ran for class president **and** won.

Use commas to separate items in a series.

A **series** is a group of three or more items listed within a sentence. The commas should appear after each item in the series except the last.

Words in a series	In the ape house were gorillas, chimpanzees, and orangutans.
Phrases in a series	The baby chimpanzee walked to the window, pressed its nose against the glass, and stared at us.
Sentences in a series	We stared back, the chimpanzee chattered, and Mom videotaped the scene.

Use commas between two or more adjectives of equal rank that modify the same noun.

> Mark has a weakness for dreamy, romantic songs.

Exercise 3   Proofreading Skill

Commas in Compound Sentences and Items in a Series   Rewrite the following paragraph, adding commas where needed.

(1) Mercury Venus Earth and Mars are described as terrestrial planets. (2) These planets all have a solid earthy surface but Earth is the only one that has trees grass and flowers. (3) Mercury's nights are much colder than Earth's and the days are much hotter. (4) Mercury is closer to the sun but Mercury has no atmosphere to

NOTE

To determine whether two adjectives are equal in rank, place the word *and* between them. If the *and* sounds natural, and if you can change the order of the adjectives without changing the meaning of the sentence, then use a comma.

hold in the heat. (5) Venus has a very hot dry surface. (6) Metal becomes liquid on the Venusian surface and lightning storms are frequent. (7) Venus is one of the prettiest brightest objects in the night sky. (8) Mars may have once had life but scientists say there are no living things on the planet now. (9) The Martian surface has canyons gorges and volcanoes. (10) The Martian "canals" may be dry riverbeds but some scientists disagree with that theory.

Commas with Introductory Elements

Use a comma to separate an introductory word or phrase from the rest of a sentence.

> Well, have you pitched the tent yet?
> Looking for a snack, several raccoons raided our campsite.

A comma is usually unnecessary after a single introductory prepositional phrase. However, a comma is necessary after two or more introductory prepositional phrases.

> On the table Maria placed a bottle of spring water and some cheese.

> On the table near the flowers, Maria placed a bottle of spring water and some cheese.

Commas with Interrupters

Use a comma before and after a word or group of words that interrupts a sentence.

> This, my friend, is the best story you've ever written.

> Ms. Heilbrun mentioned, by the way, that she is accepting submissions to the school literary magazine.

Use a comma to set off nouns used in direct address.

> Dr. Jarrow, can you explain why the coral reefs are dying?

> Well, Susan, the widespread destruction of the coral reefs is due largely to human interference.

Use a comma after most appositives. An *appositive* is a word or group of words that renames something.

> Van Gogh, my favorite painter, often loaded his brush with more than one color in order to make multicolored brush strokes.

Exercise 4   Concept Check

Using Commas Correctly   Copy the following sentences, adding commas where needed.

1. Mr. Huff tell us about the period before the American Revolutionary War.
2. In a royal proclamation in 1763 the British king the ruler over the American colonies ordered the colonists to stop moving westward.
3. By stopping the westward expansion Britain could govern the colonies more easily and avoid wars with the Native Americans.
4. The colonists however did not want to stop expanding westward.
5. They felt that George III the British king was taking away their rights.
6. Step by step the British king began to make even greater demands.
7. With military obligations around the globe the king needed tax revenue.
8. Well the colonists who were electing their own assemblies stated that they could only be taxed by their own representatives.
9. A favorite saying was this: King George we are not your children.
10. The king and the British Parliament on the other hand did not want to give up their colonies in the New World.

Commas in Quotations

Use a comma to set off a direct quotation from the rest of a sentence.

A **direct quotation** is a quotation that uses the exact words of the speaker. A speaker's tag, such as *she replied* or *Jason said,* may come before, after, or in the middle of the quotation. If the speaker's tag comes first, put the comma immediately after it.

> Sandra Cisneros wrote, "You can never have too much sky."

If the speaker's tag comes last, put the comma inside the quotation marks that end the quotation.

> "You can never have too much sky," wrote Sandra Cisneros.

If the speaker's tag comes in the middle of the quotation, use commas both before (inside the quotation marks) and after the speaker's tag.

> "A man can be destroyed," said Ernest Hemingway, "but not defeated."

Do not use a comma to separate an **indirect quotation,** one that does not use the speaker's exact words.

> Ernest Hemingway said that a man can be destroyed but not defeated.

Commas in Dates, Addresses, and Letters

Use commas to separate the parts of dates and addresses.

When writing dates, use a comma between the day of the month and the year. If the month and year are given alone and no particular day is mentioned, then the comma is not needed.

> Edgar Allan Poe died on October 7, 1849.
> The space probe will reach Alpha Centauri in June 2011.

Use a comma between the name of a city and its state or country.

> I was born in Peru, Indiana.   Reza was born in Tehran, Iran.

When writing addresses, use a comma after the name of the street and after the name of the city. Do not use a comma before the ZIP code.

> Send your inquiries to 85 Eastern Avenue, Gloucester, MA 01966.
> The President lives at 1600 Pennsylvania Avenue, Washington, D.C.

Use a comma after the salutation of a friendly letter. Use a comma after the closing of a friendly letter or a business letter.

> Dear Jan,   Your pal,   Sincerely yours,

NOTE
. . . . . .
Use a colon (:) after the salutation of a business letter.
Dear Madam:
Dear Senator Moseley-Braun:

Exercise 5   Concept Check

Correct Comma Usage   Copy the following sentences, adding commas where needed.

1. Dear Keith
   I received my plane ticket. I will meet you at the camp on August 9 1994.
   See you soon
   Marcus

2. Marcus is going camping near Cody Wyoming next month.

3. He said that he had never seen the mountains and was excited to be going.

4. "Go over the directions to the camp one more time" said Marcus.
5. The last trip Marcus took was to Dallas Texas in July 1992.

Exercise 6 Proofreading Skill

Checking for Comma Errors Write the following paragraph, correcting all errors in comma usage.

(1) Wolves believe it or not can help prevent erosion. (2) Scientists in Arizona were worried that deer were losing their struggle against one of their predators wolves. (3) Consequently the scientists decided to kill off the wolves. (4) Twenty years later no big surprise there were too many deer. (5) The deer had no more mature trees to eat and they began to eat the young trees. (6) Soon there were no trees left and the deer began to starve to death. (7) With the trees gone the soil began to erode. (8) Obviously deer wolves and trees had an important connection in the region's ecology. (9) When scientists broke the food chain all three groups suffered. (10) Living in Phoenix Arizona I am far from the forests but I'm glad the scientists are trying to bring the wolves back now.

Exercise 7 Revision Skill

Using Commas and End Marks Copy the following sentences, adding end marks and commas as needed.

1. "Stop Get out of there" yelled Lana
2. "What's the matter" I asked
3. "There's a polar bear in the back yard" she answered "and it's eating from your garbage cans"
4. Lana a friend of mine from California had never seen a polar bear before
5. Here in Barrow Alaska polar bears are quite common
6. I banged on some pans and the noise soon drove the bear away
7. "Well Alicia" said my friend "I guess I now know what to do when I see polar bears back home in Los Angeles"
8. We both had a long hearty laugh
9. Pulling a note pad out of her bag Lana began to ask me questions about polar bears
10. "I can't wait to get back to tell Dr Garcia my science teacher about seeing a real polar bear" she said

The Semicolon

Use a semicolon (;) to join parts of a compound sentence if no coordinating conjunction is used.

> The photographer dresses his subjects in period costumes; Sandy and I decided to dress as flappers of the 1920s.

Use semicolons between items in a series if the items contain commas.

> Have you ever been to Cairo, Illinois; Rome, Georgia; or Paris, Texas?

The Colon

Use a colon (:) to introduce a list of items.

A sentence containing a word or phrase such as *these, the following,* or *here* is often followed by a colon. A colon is used only after a complete sentence. It never comes directly after a verb.

Incorrect Her favorite singers are: Patti Smyth, Gloria Estefan, and Suzanne Vega.

Correct These are her favorite singers: Patti Smyth, Gloria Estefan, and Suzanne Vega.

Use a colon between the hour and the minute in a time expressed in numerals.

> 1:00 A.M.   3:30 P.M.

Exercise 8   Concept Check

Using Semicolons and Colons   Read each sentence. If the sentence needs a semicolon or a colon, write the sentence, adding the needed punctuation. If no additional punctuation is needed, write *Correct.*

1. Some myths explain natural phenomena the Norse myth of Loki and Balder explains earthquakes.
2. In this myth Balder is loved by all the gods except one the god Loki is jealous of Balder.
3. Balder tells the goddess Frigg about his fear of Loki, and she makes the following request of everyone "Please don't hurt Balder."
4. Because the gods know that Balder can't be hurt, they throw things at him.

5. The gods throw all kinds of things at Loki, including the following sticks, stones, spears, mud, fire, and ice.

6. I wonder if the word *balderdash* comes from this myth I wonder what the word means.

7. Loki learns that Balder has the following weakness mistletoe can hurt him.

8. When Balder is hit with mistletoe, he dies consequently, the gods punish Loki by chaining him in a cave.

9. In the cave a serpent drips poison on him, and when the poison falls, Loki experiences great pain.

10. According to the myth, the reason for earthquakes is this the poison hits Loki, he shudders, and the earth shakes.

The Hyphen

Use a hyphen (-) to show a word break at the end of a line. Make sure to break words between syllables.

> The tourists snapped pictures of the magnifi-
> cent sequoia trees in the Mariposa Grove.

Use a hyphen between the words that make up a compound adjective when the compound is used before a noun.

> *The Diary of Anne Frank* is a well-written play.
> A sonnet is a fourteen-line poem.

Use hyphens in some compound words.

freeze-dry	ring-necked pheasant
labor-intensive	chain-link
shoo-in	double-park

Use hyphens in compound numbers from twenty-one to ninety-nine.

> twenty-three players   ninety-two years

Use a hyphen in a fraction.

> three-fourths   two-sixteenths   one-fifth

Exercise 9   Concept Check

Using Hyphens   Write the words that need hyphens in the following sentences, adding the hyphens that are needed.

1. Multistep word problems are math problems that are similar to real life situations.
2. For example, suppose Matty has twenty nine dollars and he buys two pens at four dollars apiece.
3. To find out how much money Matty has left, you would first multi ply and then subtract.
4. After the pen purchase, Matty has twenty one dollars.
5. Now, suppose that for Sunday dinner your great grandmother makes her famous toad in the hole casserole for five people.
6. She gives one sixth of the casserole to each of your three little cousins.
7. Then she gives one half of the remaining casserole to you.
8. To find out how much the well respected chef has for herself, first multiply, then subtract, then divide.
9. Now you know that your kind relative has one fourth of the casserole left for herself.
10. This is the kind of figuring that people find it neces sary to do outside the classroom.

The Apostrophe

Use an apostrophe (') to make the possessive form of a noun.

Make the possessive of a singular noun by adding an apostrophe and s, even if the noun already ends in s.

> the class**'s**   a boss**'s**   Marcia**'s**

Make the possessive of a plural noun that ends in s by adding just an apostrophe.

> the ponies**'** saddles   the workers**'** hard hats

Make the possessive of a plural noun that does not end in s by adding an apostrophe and s.

> the sheep**'s** heads   the women**'s** careers

Use an apostrophe to show that one or more letters have been left out of a contraction.

> it**'s** (it is)   shouldn**'t** (should not)

Add an apostrophe and *s* to form the plural of a letter or a word referred to as a word.

How many *o*'s are there in the word *cooperate?*
There were too many *you know*'s in that speech.

Exercise 10   Concept Check

Using Apostrophes   Write the words that need apostrophes in the following sentences. Add the needed apostrophes.

1. Im always interested in peoples names and in various names popularity through the years.
2. My friend Claras name means "bright," and her mother claims to have given it to her because of her sparkling brown eyes.
3. Leslie Dunklings book *First Names First* lists names in order of popularity, based on newspaper birth announcements.
4. In the years 1900, 1925, and 1950, there were more announcements for Marys than for girls of any other name.
5. In 1975, however, Jennifers took first place.
6. According to this books lists, Johns ranked first among boys in 1900 and 1950.
7. Ive got a preference for unusual names; I like the name Milagro, which means "miracle" in Spanish.
8. Pacarino is another popular boys name.
9. I wonder what that names meaning is.
10. Shakespeares Juliet asked, "Whats in a name? That which we call a rose / By any other name would smell as sweet."

Exercise 11   Proofreading Skill

Using Punctuation Correctly   Rewrite the following paragraph, adding the additional punctuation that is needed.

(1) Recently, I read Jamaica Kincaids book *Annie John.* (2) The main characters a girl from Antigua. (3) Annie, whos very bright and independent, has frequent run ins with one of her teachers. (4) One day, Annies reading ahead in her textbook in class. (5) She begins to write on Christopher Columbuss picture. (6) Heres what Annie writes "The Great Man Can No Longer Just Get Up and Go." (7) When Miss Edwards Annies teacher sees Annies writing, she is furious. (8) She tells Annie to copy long sections of the poem *Paradise Lost.* (9) Annie goes home, hoping for her mothers comforting words and a nice meal. (10) Instead her mother serves her a much hated meal, breadfruit.

Quotation Marks

Use quotation marks (" ") at the beginning and the end of a direct quotation.

> "This abandoned building is an eyesore and a danger to the community," explained Ms. Neruda.

Capitalize the first word of a quotation that is a sentence. Separate the quotation from explanatory words like *she said* with commas. A comma or a period before a quotation is placed before the quotation marks. A comma or period after a quotation goes inside the quotation marks.

> "Yes," said Sherlock, "I think I see the solution to our mystery."

A question mark or an exclamation point goes inside the quotation marks if it is part of the quotation, outside the quotation marks if it is not part of the quotation.

> Jeremy asked, "What exactly is New Age music, anyway?"
> Did he really say, "I've never heard of it before"?

Use quotation marks around both parts of a divided quotation.

Do not capitalize the first word of the second part unless it begins a new sentence.

> "Go now," said the cowhand. "Take 'em out for a ride."
> "Do you know," he asked, "how to mount up?"

When punctuating dialogue, begin a new paragraph to indicate a new speaker.

> "Have you ever seen a whale?" asked one of the members of the ship's crew.
> "No, I haven't," I replied, "but I sure would like to."
> "Well, that's one right in front of us," she said, pointing to a bit of spray on the horizon.

Exercise 12   Concept Check

Using Quotation Marks and Other Punctuation   Write the following sentences, adding quotation marks and other punctuation as needed.

1. That was quite a storm we had over the weekend exclaimed Sonia
2. I know Mary said The wind split one of our pine trees right in half
3. My mother told me that we haven't had a hurricane that strong in twenty years Sonia said

4. Did you hear the governor say on TV that Dade County will have a ten o'clock curfew she continued

5. Mary asked Ms Patchek, the science teacher What makes a storm a hurricane

6. A hurricane is probably one of the windiest and rainiest of all storms Ms Patchek replied

7. In fact said Ms Patchek for a storm to be a hurricane, its winds must be greater than 73 miles per hour

8. Cant a tornado be just as destructive asked Mary

9. Well Ms Patchek answered tornadoes have winds of 100 to 300 miles per hour but they are much smaller than hurricanes

10. Wow said Sonia No wonder a tornado could carry away a whole house in *The Wizard of Oz*

Exercise 13   Revision Skill

Punctuating Dialogue   Rewrite the following passage using correct paragraphing and punctuation.

(1) I'm out of money and I want a hamburger said Julie. (2) Hey look I see a clown near the ferris wheel said Cassandra. (3) Lets go Maybe hes giving away free food or tickets for rides Julie said. (4) Hi kids the clown said. (5) Are you giving away anything free Julie asked. (6) No the clown answered but I can do tricks. (7) Can you bend balloons into animals Cassandra asked. (8) Yes What kind of animal would you like the clown said. (9) Id like a horse so that I can ride home and get a hamburger Julie answered.

Punctuating Titles

Use quotation marks to set off the titles of short stories, poems, essays, magazine articles, chapters, television episodes, reports, and songs.

Short Story	"The Dinner Party" by Mona Gardner
Poem	"I'm Nobody! Who are you?" by Emily Dickinson
Essay	"Pompeii" by Robert Silverberg
Song	"From a Distance" by Bette Midler
Television Episode	"Big Trouble in Gotham City"

▶ **Underline the titles of books, newspapers, magazines, movies, television series, plays, works of art, and long musical compositions.**

Book	The Diary of a Young Girl
Newspaper	Chicago Sun-Times
Movie	Aladdin
Television Series	The Simpsons
Long Musical Composition	Mozart's Don Giovanni

Underline the names of planes, trains, and ships.

the Queen Elizabeth II   the Orient Express

Exercise 14   Concept Check

Punctuating Titles   Write each title in the following sentences. Underline the title or enclose it in quotation marks.

1. Libraries contain nonfiction books, like Isaac Asimov's Words from the Myths, and fiction books, like Ursula K. LeGuin's A Wizard of Earthsea.

2. One of my favorite library books was a collection of photographs of famous airplanes, like the Spirit of St. Louis and the Enola Gay.

3. According to a magazine article entitled Today's Library, libraries offer much more than just books.

4. At my local library I found magazines like People.

5. I also found videotapes of classic films, like Hard Times, and modern films, like Wayne's World.

6. In the record section of the library, I found an Eric Clapton album containing the song Tears in Heaven.

7. I also found recordings of poems, such as one of Robert Frost reading his poem Mending Wall.

8. The library also had a large collection of recordings of musicals, such as Cats and Les Miserables.

9. For excellent fiction you should look at a book called Great American Short Stories.

10. Among the stories in the book are The Lady or the Tiger? and The Lottery.

Exercise 15   Revision Skill

Using Punctuation Marks Correctly   Write the following sentences, correcting any errors in punctuation.

1. Today, said Ms. Battacherya, we shall begin our unit on reptiles

2. I opened my notebook and at the top of the page I wrote today's date September 23 1993

3. Ms Battacherya then explained that the major groups of reptiles are turtles lizards snakes and crocodilians

4. "Reptiles arent slimy, said Ms. Battacherya. They have hard scales"

5. Ms Battacherya then showed us some pictures of reptiles from a book called The Reader's Digest Living World of Animals

6. She explained that reptiles are cold blooded air breathing animals with backbones and scales

7. Among the largest reptiles include the following the Anaconda, at 30 feet in length, the rock python, at 24.6 feet, the gavial, at 30 feet, and the saltwater crocodile, also at 30 feet

8. Those arent however the largest reptiles that have ever lived

9. Several large plant eating dinosaurs reached lengths of over ninety nine feet and weights of over 200,000 pounds

10. The smallest reptile today is a $1\frac{1}{4}$ inch long species of gecko

11. Ms. Battacherya asked us to read an article in our textbook called What We Know About Dinosaurs

12. The article covered these topics when dinosaurs lived when they became extinct and why they died out

13. On the basis of evidence from around the world scientists have concluded that the dinosaur's probably died out because of a giant meteor that hit the earth

14. The meteors impact sent clouds of dust into the sky this dust blocked out the suns rays

15. Therefore many plants died out and the plant-eating dinosaurs soon died out as well

Index of Skills

Literary Terms

Allusion, 144, 738
Author's purpose, 738
Autobiography, 41, 47, 53, 60, 738, 742
Ballad, 669
Biography, 40, 41, 163, 186, 296, 738, 742
Cast of characters, 207, 738
Character, 25, 31, 37, 87, 168, 420, 720, 721, 722, 738, 745
  antagonist/protagonist, 249, 738, 743
  change in, 103, 738
  dynamic/static, 103, 738
  hero/heroine, 648, 720, 721, 741
  main/minor, 15, 16, 249, 738, 740, 745
Characterization, 37, 53, 167, 582, 738
Climax, 15, 168, 200, 224, 739, 743
Colloquialisms, 724, 726–28
Concrete poetry, 202, 206
Conflict, 15, 154, 166, 168, 200, 443, 451, 720, 739
  external, 25, 113, 154, 739
  internal, 25, 113, 154, 705, 739
Description, 457, 741
Dialect, 146, 739
Dialogue, 31, 167, 207, 208, 318, 726, 739, 741
Diary, 40, 539, 739
Drama, 207–208, 739
  acts, 208, 738
  characters, 207, 208
  costumes, 580
  dialogue, 207, 208
  plot, 207, 208
  radio play, 226, 744
  resolution, 224
  scene, 208, 569, 722, 738, 744
  scenery/props, 207, 580, 744, 745
  script, 207, 580, 721
  set, 494, 580
  setting, 207, 208, 744
  sound effects, 207, 744, 745
  stage directions, 207, 360, 403, 745
  theatrical conventions, 342
Essay, 40, 296, 378, 739, 742
  formal, 378, 739
  informal, 40, 739
Exposition, 15, 740, 743
Eyewitness report, 465, 740
Feature profile, 163, 740
Fiction, 15–16, 740

horror story, 129, 135, 166
myth, 742
novel, 15, 742, 743
short story, 15, 742, 744
Figurative language, 738, 740, 742
  extended metaphor, 380, 600, 740
  metaphor, 90, 257, 740, 742
  personification, 90, 257, 740, 743
  simile, 90, 102, 206, 257, 740, 744
Flashback, 87, 116, 118, 740
Folklore, 646, 648–49, 685–86
  animal tales, 673, 681
  fables, 649, 685–86, 708–10, 740, 742
  folk tales, 648–49, 671, 674, 676–79, 687–91, 697–99, 700–704, 740
  legends, 356, 649, 650, 651–57, 658–62, 663–68, 669, 695–96, 711–14, 715–17, 718, 742
  myths, 648, 672–73, 682, 683–84, 721, 742
  Pourquoi tales, 692
  tall tales, 649, 650, 669
  trickster tales, 649, 671
Foreshadowing, 293, 335, 480, 550, 740–41
Form, 89, 202, 206, 738, 741
Formal English, 723–24
Frame story, 335, 741
Historical narrative, 318, 741
Horror story, 129, 135
Humor, 42, 46, 57, 60, 617, 741
Hyperbole, 42, 46, 57, 59, 740, 741
Idiom, 729, 741
Imagery, 89, 206, 454, 738, 741, 742
Informal English, 723–24, 726–28
Informal language, 299
Interior monologue, 31, 441, 477, 605
Interview, 742
Irony, 135, 440, 569, 741, 742
  situational, 617
Journal, 40
Lyric poetry, 453, 742
Memoir, 40, 56, 60, 266, 742
Mood, 97, 98, 135, 538, 738, 742
Moral, of a fable, 649, 710, 742
Motivation, 420
Narrative, 166, 742
Narrative poetry, 91, 97, 742
Narrator, 37, 403, 742
Nonfiction, 40–41, 378, 742
  article, 742
  autobiography, 40, 41, 47, 53, 56, 60, 742, 742
  biography, 40, 41, 163, 186, 296, 738, 742
  diary, 40, 539, 739

*R*eading and Critical Thinking

*G*rammar, Usage, and Mechanics

Writing Skills, Modes, and Formats

Vocabulary Skills

Research and Study Skills

*S*peaking, Listening, and Viewing

Index of Titles and Authors

Page numbers that appear in italics refer to biographical information.

Acknowledgments

(continued from page iv)

The Dramatic Publishing Company and Donald C. Farber: "The Kid Nobody Could Handle" by Christopher Sergel based upon an episode from *Welcome to the Monkey House* by Kurt Vonnegut, Jr., copyright © 1970. Used by permission of The Dramatic Publishing Company, Publisher, and Donald C. Farber, Attorney for Kurt Vonnegut, Jr.

Mari Evans: "If There Be Sorrow," from *I Am A Black Woman* by Mari Evans, published by William Morrow & Company, copyright © 1970. Used by permission of the author.

Firebrand Books: "Dancer," from *Simple Songs* by Vickie Sears. Published by Firebrand Books, Ithaca, New York. Copyright © 1990 by Vickie Sears. Used by permission of Firebrand Books.

Globe Book Company: "The Girl in the Lavender Dress" retold by Maureen Scott from *The American Anthology,* edited by Robert R. Potter. Published by Globe Book Company, copyright © 1987. Reprinted by permission of Globe Book Company.

Harcourt Brace Jovanovich, Inc.: "The First Flute," from *The Enchanted Orchard and Other Folktales of Central America* by Dorothy Sharp Carter. Copyright © 1973 by Dorothy Sharp Carter. "Mother and Daughter," from *Baseball in April and Other Stories* by Gary Soto. Copyright © 1990 by Gary Soto. Reprinted by permission of Harcourt Brace Jovanovich, Inc.

HarperCollins Publishers, New York: "The Growin' of Paul Bunyan" from *A Telling of the Tales* by William J. Brooke. Copyright © 1990 by William J. Brooke. Reprinted by permission of HarperCollins Publishers, New York.

HarperCollins Publishers, London: Excerpt from *Survive the Savage Sea* by Dougal Robertson. Published by Paul Elek Books Ltd, now part of HarperCollins Publishers. Reprinted by permission of HarperCollins Publishers, London.

Harvard University Press and the Trustees of Amherst College: "I'm Nobody! Who are you?" by Emily Dickinson from *The Poems of Emily Dickinson,* Thomas H. Johnson, editor, Cambridge, Mass.: The Belknap Press of Harvard University Press, copyright 1951, 1955 © 1979, 1983 by the President and Fellows of Harvard College. Reprinted by permission of the publishers and the Trustees of Amherst College.

Spencer Holst: "On Hope," from *The Language of Cats and Other Stories* by Spencer Holst. Copyright © 1971 by Spencer Holst. Reprinted by permission of the author.

Henry Holt and Company, Inc.: "Nothing Gold Can Stay" by Robert Frost from *The Poetry of Robert Frost* edited by Edward Connery Lathem. Copyright 1923, © 1964 by Holt, Rinehart and Winston. Copyright 1951 by Robert Frost. Reprinted by permission of Henry Holt and Company, Inc.

Daniel Keyes: "Flowers for Algernon" by Daniel Keyes. Novel version published by Bantam Books. Copyright © 1959, 1987 by Daniel Keyes. Reprinted by permission of the author.

Naoshi Koriyama: "A Loaf of Poetry" from *Time and Space and Other Poems* by Naoshi Koriyama. Copyright © 1985 by Naoshi Koriyama. Reprinted by permission of the author.

The Lazear Agency and *Boys' Life Magazine:* "Stop the Sun" by Gary Paulsen. First appeared in *Boys' Life Magazine,* January 1986. Reprinted by permission of The Lazear Agency, agent for the author, and *Boys' Life Magazine,* published by the Boy Scouts of America.

Liveright Publishing Corporation: "your little voice," from *Tulips & Chimneys* by E. E. Cummings, edited by George James Firmage. Copyright 1923, 1925 and renewed 1951, 1953 by E. E. Cummings. Copyright © 1973, 1976 by the Trustees for the E. E. Cummings Trust. Copyright © 1973, 1976 by George James Firmage. Reprinted by permission of Liveright Publishing Corporation.

Macmillan Publishing Company: "The Five Eggs," from *Stories from the Americas* by Frank Henius. Copyright 1944 by Charles Scribner's Sons. Copyright renewed © 1972 by Gertrude Henius. Reprinted by permission of Charles Scribner's Sons, an imprint of Macmillan Publishing Company. "Baseball and the Facts of Life," from *American Beat* by Bob Greene. Copyright © 1983 by John Deadline Enterprises. Reprinted by permission of Atheneum Publishers, an imprint of Macmillan Publishing Company.

Rubén Sálaz-Márquez: "White Mice" by Rubén Sálaz-Márquez from *Voces: An Anthology of Nuevo Mexicano Writers,* edited by Rudolfo Anaya. Copyright © 1987 by Rubén Sálaz-Márquez. Reprinted by permission of the author.

Pat MacEnulty: "Dancing for Poppa" by Pat MacEnulty. First appeared in *American Way,* November 1991. Reprinted by permission of the author.

William Morrow & Company, Inc.: "The World Is Not a Pleasant Place to Be," from *My House* by Nikki Giovanni. Copyright © 1972 by Nikki Giovanni. Reprinted by permission of William Morrow & Company, Inc.

National Council of Teachers of English: "Foreign Student" by Barbara Robinson, from *English Journal,* May 1976. Copyright © 1976 by the National Council of Teachers of English. Reprinted with permission.

The New York Times: "Foul Shots" by Rogelio R. Gomez from *The New York Times Magazine,* October 13, 1991. Copyright © 1991 by The New York Times Company. Reprinted by permission.

Orchard Books: "The Banana Tree," from *A Thief in the Village and Other Stories* by James Berry. Copyright © 1988 by James Berry. "Checkouts," from *A Couple of Kooks and Other Stories About Love* by Cynthia Rylant. Copyright © 1990 by Cynthia Rylant. Reprinted with permission of the publisher Orchard Books, New York.

Penguin Books USA, Inc.: "John Henry, the Hammerman," from *American Tall Tales* by Adrien Stoutenburg. Copyright © 1968 by Adrien Stoutenburg. "400-Meter Free Style," from *Our Ground Time Here Will Be Brief* by Maxine Kumin. Copyright © 1959, renewed © 1987 by Maxine Kumin.

"The Creation," from *God's Trombones* by James Weldon Johnson. Copyright 1927 by The Viking Press, Inc., renewed 1955 by Grace Nail Johnson. "How to Die of Embarrassment," from *Teenage Romance: Or How to Die of Embarrassment* by Delia Ephron. Copyright © 1981 by Delia Ephron. "The Choice," from *The Portable Dorothy Parker* by Dorothy Parker, introduction by Brendan Gill. Copyright 1926, renewed 1954 by Dorothy Parker. "Battle by the Breadfruit Tree," from *On Safari* by Theodore J. Waldeck. Copyright 1940 by Theodore J. Waldeck, renewed © 1968 by Jo Besse McElveen Waldeck. Used by permission of Viking Penguin, a division of Penguin Books USA Inc.

Plays, Inc.: "The Million-Pound Bank Note" by Mark Twain from *Radio Plays for Young People* by Walter Hackett. Copyright 1950 by Plays, Inc., Publishers. "Rip Van Winkle" by Washington Irving, adapted by Adele Thane in *Plays from Famous Stories and Fairy Tales.* Copyright © 1967 by Adele Thane. Reprinted by permission of Plays, Inc., 120 Boylston Street, Boston, MA 02116.

Raines & Raines and Robert Lipsyte: "Tracee," from *Assignment: Sports* by Robert Lipsyte. Copyright © 1984 by Robert Lipsyte. Reprinted by permission of Robert Lipsyte and his agents, Raines & Raines, 71 Park Avenue, New York, NY 10016.

Random House, Inc. "Spotted Eagle and Black Crow," from *The Sound of Flutes and Other Indian Legends* by Richard Erdoes. Copyright © 1976 by Richard Erdoes. "The Moustache," from *Eight Plus One* by Robert Cormier. Copyright © 1965, 1966, 1967, 1968, 1969, 1971, 1973, 1975, 1980 by Robert Cormier. Reprinted by permission of Pantheon Books, a division of Random House, Inc. "Raymond's Run," from *Gorilla, My Love* by Toni Cade Bambara. Copyright © 1970 by Toni Cade Bambara. *The Diary of Anne Frank,* a play by Frances Goodrich and Albert Hackett. Copyright 1954, © 1956 by Albert Hackett, Frances Goodrich Hackett and Otto Frank. Reprinted by permission of Random House, Inc. "The Dream Keeper," from *The Dream Keeper and Other Poems* by Langston Hughes. Copyright 1932 and renewed © 1960 by Langston Hughes. "Owl," from *The Magic Orange Tree and Other Haitian Folktales,* collected by Diane Wolkstein. Text copyright © 1978 by Diane Wolkstein. "Pecos Bill and the Cyclone," from *Pecos Bill: Texas Cowpuncher* by Harold W. Felton. Reprinted by permission of Alfred A. Knopf, Inc.

Gayle Ross: "Strawberries," an old Cherokee story as told by Gayle Ross from *Homespun: Tales from America's Favorite Storytellers,* edited by Jimmy Neil Smith. Copyright © 1988 by Jimmy Neil Smith. Reprinted by permission of Gayle Ross.

Russell & Volkening: Excerpt from *Harriet Tubman: Conductor on the Underground Railroad* by Ann Petry, published by Thomas Y. Crowell Company. Copyright 1955, renewed © 1983 by Ann Petry. Reprinted by permission of Russell & Volkening, Inc., as agents for Ann Petry.

Nancy Masterson Sakamoto: "Conversational Ballgames" from *Polite Fictions: Why Japanese and Americans Seem Rude to Each Other* by Nancy M. Sakamoto. Copyright © 1982 by Kin-Seido, Ltd. Reprinted by permission of Nancy Masterson Sakamoto, Professor of Intercultural Communications, Shitennoji Gakuen University, Hawaii Branch.

The Literary Estate of May Swenson: "Pigeon Woman" by May Swenson. Copyright © 1962, renewed © 1990 by May Swenson. First published in *The New Yorker.* Used with permission of The Literary Estate of May Swenson.

The Talman Company: "Petty Larceny," from *Once, A Lotus Garden and Other Stories* by Jessica Saiki. Copyright © 1987 by Jessica Saiki. Published by New Rivers Press and distributed by The Talman Company, Inc. Reprinted by permission of The Talman Company.

Jackie Torrence: "Brer Possum's Dilemma" by Jackie Torrence from *Homespun: Tales from America's Favorite Storytellers,* edited by Jimmy Neil Smith. Copyright © 1988 by Jimmy Neil Smith. Reprinted by permission of Jackie Torrence.

Tribune Media Services: "Memories of Dating" by Dave Barry, from *The Chicago Tribune,* March 22, 1992. Reprinted by permission of Tribune Media Services.

University of California Press: Excerpt from *Wear It Proudly* by William Tsuchida. Copyright 1947 by the Regents of the University of California. Reprinted by permission of the University of California Press.

The University of Georgia Press: "Appetizer," from *Ghost Traps* by Robert H. Abel. Copyright © 1991 by Robert H. Abel. Reprinted by permission of The University of Georgia Press.

The University of Massachusetts Press: "Watching Gymnasts," from *Robert Francis: Collected Poems, 1936-1976* by Robert Francis, Amherst: University of Massachusetts Press, 1976. Copyright © 1961 by Robert Francis. Reprinted by permission of The University of Massachusetts Press.

University of Oklahoma Press: Excerpt from *Indian Legends from the Northern Rockies* by Ella E. Clark. Copyright © 1966 by the University of Oklahoma Press. Reprinted by permission of the University of Oklahoma Press.

Constance Urdang and The Modern Poetry Association: "Pole Vault" by Shiro Murano, translated by Constance Urdang, first appeared in *Poetry,* May 1956. Copyright © 1956 by The Modern Poetry Association. Reprinted by permission of Constance Urdang and the Editor of *Poetry.*

Ralph M. Vicinanza, Ltd.: Excerpt from *Lost Cities and Vanished Civilizations* by Robert Silverberg. Copyright © 1962 by Robert Silverberg. All rights reserved. Reprinted by permission of Ralph M. Vicinanza, Ltd.

Watson, Little Ltd.: "Raven and the Coming of Daylight" retold by Gail Robinson and Douglas Hill from *Coyote the Trickster: Legends of the North American Indians.* First published by Chatto & Windus Ltd., Canada and Crane Russak in the USA. Reprinted by Watson, Little Ltd., Authors' Agents.

Franklin Watts, Inc.: Excerpt from *New Kids on the Block: Oral Histories of Immigrant Teens* by Janet Bode. Copyright © 1989 by Janet Bode. Reprinted with permission of the publisher, Franklin Watts, Inc., New York.

Paulette Childress White: "Getting the Facts of Life" by Paulette Childress White from *Memory of Kin: Stories About Family by Black Writers,* edited by Mary Helen Washington, Doubleday, copyright © 1991. Reprinted by permission of Paulette Childress White.

White Pine Press: "The Enchanted Raisin" by Jacqueline Balcells from *Landscapes of a New Land: Fiction by Latin American Women,* edited by Marjorie Agosin. Copyright © 1989 by White Pine Press. Reprinted by permission of White Pine Press, Marjorie Agosin, Editor.

Al Young: "For Poets" by Al Young. Copyright © 1968 by Al Young. Reprinted by permission of the author.

Illustrations

Jerry Nelson 15, 40, 89, 207, 648. Rich Lo: 95, 96. Ana M. Aguilar-Islas: 279. Maps: Robert Voigts: 66, 93, 146, 306, 321, 342, 493, 619, 651, 658, 663, 672, 674, 676, 683, 685, 687, 695, 697, 700, 708, 711, 715.

Author Photographs

Charles Abel: Robert Abel 746 top. AP/Wide World Photos: Robert Cormier 478; Delia Ephron 747, bottom; Robert Francis 748, top; Francis Goodrich and Albert Hackett 571; Maxine W. Kumin 749, middle; Kurt Vonnegut, Jr. 742. Courtesy, Arté Publico Press: Judith Ortiz Cofer 693. © Nancy Crampton: Nikki Giovanni 748, middle. © 1984 David Madison/Duomo: Tracee Talavera 165, bottom. Courtesy, Richard Erdoes: Jenny Leading Cloud 719. Courtesy, Firebrand Books: Vickie Sears 39. The Granger Collection, New York: Langston Hughes 749, top. Courtesy, HarperCollins Publishers: William J. Brooke 670. Historical Pictures/Stock Montage: O. Henry 442; Henry W. Longfellow 98. By permission of the Houghton Library, Harvard University: e.e. cummings 747, middle. Photo © Jay Kay Klein: Daniel Keyes 295, Robert Silverberg 320. Photo by Richard McNamee: Lensy Namioka 750, top. Photo by Margaret Miller: Cynthia Rylant 750, bottom. Photograph by George Cox, Museum of the City of New York, 57.182.10, gift of Miss Rosamond Gilder and Mrs. Walter W. Palmer: Walt Whitman 341. National Portrait Gallery, Smithsonian Institution, Washington, D.C./Art Resource, New York: Robert Frost 341; Washington Irving 358. Courtesy of The Newberry Library, Chicago: Samuel Clemens 226. Photographs and Prints Division, Schomburg Center for Research in Black Culture, The New York Public Library, Astor, Lenox and Tilden Foundation: Toni Cade Bambara 114. Edgar Allan Poe Museum, Poe Foundation, Richmond Virginia: Edgar Allan Poe 137. News and Publications Service, Stanford University, Stanford, California: Al Young 751, bottom. Courtesy, Tribune Media Services: Dave Barry 746, bottom; Bob Greene 748, bottom. Photo by Rachel C. Zucker: Diane Wolkstein 706.

Miscellaneous Art Credits

viii MORNING TIDE 1983 Ken Danby, Courtesy, Gallery Moos, Toronto. x © 1991 Todd Doney/The Image Bank. xii COTOPAXI 1863 Frederick Church, Founder's Society Purchase with funds from Mr. and Mrs. Richard A. Manoogian, Robert H. Tannahill Foundation Fund, Gibbs-Williams Fund, Dexter M. Ferry, Jr. Fund, Merrill Fund and Beatrice W. Rogers Fund. © 1991 The Detroit Institute of Arts. xiv ADA AND VINCENT IN THE CAR 1972 Alex Katz, Collection, The Hirshhorn Museum and Sculpture Garden, Smithsonian Institution, Washington, D.C. Courtesy, Marlborough Gallery, New York. xvi LIBERATION 1945 Ben Shahn, Tempera on cardboard mounted on composition board, 29 3/4 in. x 40 in. Collection, The Museum of Modern Art, New York, James Thrall Soby Bequest. Photograph © 1992 The Museum of Modern Art, New York. xviii THE BLIND STORYTELLER 1987 Julio Larraz, Courtesy, Nohra Haime Gallery, New York. 3, 129 THE SCREAM Edvard Munch, National Gallery, Oslo, Norway Scala/Art Resource. 4 BIRTHDAY 1914 Marc Chagall, Oil on cardboard, 31 3/4 x 39 1/4 inches. Collection, The Museum of Modern Art, New York, through the Lillie P. Bliss Bequest. Photograph © 1992 The Museum of Modern Art, New York. 5, bottom SUDDEN SHOWER 1917 Ito Shinsui Courtesy, The Trustees of the British Museum, London. 5, top, 701 Kimbell Art Museum, Fort Worth, Texas. Photography by Michael Bodycomb. 14 BASKET OF BEAUTY (detail) Lisa Danielle Private collection. 17 © Eddie Hironaka/ The Image Bank. 28 H. Armstrong Roberts. 32 The Philbrook Museum of Art, Tulsa, Oklahoma. 42 Rebecca Brown. 47 H. Armstrong Roberts. 65 BUILDERS (GREEN AND RED BALL) (detail) 1979 Jacob Lawrence gouache on paper. New Jersey State Museum Collection, Purchase FA 1987.28. 80 © Maria Taglienti/The Image Bank. 91 Shelburne Museum, Shelburne, Vermont. 99, 433 © Carmine Fantasia. 103 © Leo de Wys. 112 LAKES EDGE 1989 James Glover Courtesy, S.P.X. Corp., Muskegon, Michigan. 124 *Johnny Tremain: A Story of Boston in Revolt* by Esther Forbes, © 1943. Reprinted with permission of Houghton Mifflin Company. All rights reserved. 125, left Cover of *The True Confessions of Charlotte Doyle* by Avi. Text copyright © 1990 by Avi. Cover illustration by Ruth E. Murry. Used with permission of the publisher, Orchard Books. 125, right From *The Honorable Prison* by Lyll Becerra de Jenkins, jacket illustration by Judy Pedersen. Copyright © 1988 by Lyll Becerra de Jenkins. Used by permission of Lodestar Books, an affiliate of Dutton Children's Books, a division of Penguin USA, Inc. 128 SPIRITUALISM (detail) 1979 Everald Brown Wadsworth Atheneum, Hartford, Connecticut. Ella Gallup Sumner and Mary Catlin Sumner Collection. 138 UPI/Bettmann. 153 © Naoki Okamoto/Stock Market. 155 Courtesy, U.S. Postal Service. 162 © 1979 J. Zimmerman/FPG. 175 THE UNDERGROUND RAILROAD (detail) 1981 Paul Collins Courtesy of the artist. 176 Photographs and Prints Division, Schomburg Center for Research in Black Culture, The New York Public Library, Astor, Lenox and Tilden Foundations. 189 Focus on Sports. 193 National Baseball Hall of Fame and Museum, Cooperstown, New York. 203 The Mansell Collection. 209 © Christie's Colour Library. 228 © Ruben De Anda/Stockworks. 236 From *The Remarkable Journey of Prince Jen* by Lloyd Alexander, jacket art by Paul O. Zelinsky. Copyright © 1991 by Paul O. Zelinsky. Used

by permission of Dutton Children's Books, a division of
Penguin USA, Inc.   237, left *Carry on, Mr. Bowditch* by Jean
Lee Latham. © 1955. Reprinted with permission of
Houghton Mifflin Company. All rights reserved.   237,
right *Legend Day*s by Jamake Highwater. Copyright © 1984
by Jamake Highwater. Cover reprinted by permission of
HarperCollins Publishers.   240 THE CREATION (detail)
1935 Aaron Douglas Howard University Gallery of Art,
Washington, D.C.   241 Photofest.   251 THE
CREATION OF ADAM (detail: hands) Michelangelo The
Vatican, Sistine Chapel. Scala/Art Resource, New York.
258 © W.S. Nawrocki ASMP.   261 collage (except lower
left UPI/Bettmann and lower right National Archives) H.
Armstrong Roberts.   261, 262 Bettmann Newsphotos.
265 AP/Wide World Photos.   267 RIND 1955 M. C.
Escher Cornelius Van S. Roosevelt Collection, © 1992 The
National Gallery of Art, Washington, D.C.   305
AUTUMN LEAVES, LAKE GEORGE, N. Y. (detail) 1924
Georgia O'Keeffe. Columbus Museum of Art: Museum
Purchase Howald Fund II.   368 *Dicey's Song* by Cynthia
Voigt. © 1983. Published by Atheneum. Cover © James
Shecik.   369, right *Shabanu: Daughter of the Wind* by Suzanne
Fisher Staples. Jacket Illustration by Stephen T. Johnson.
Jacket Illustration copyright © 1989 by Stephen T. Johnson.
Reprinted by permission of Alfred A. Knopf, Inc.   369, left
Cover of *Nothing But the Truth* by Avi. Text © 1991 by Avi.
Cover Illustration by Peter Catalanotto. Used with permis-
sion of the publisher, Orchard Books.   372 TAMALADA
(detail) © 1987 Carmen Lomas Garza Courtesy of the
artist. Photo by Wolfgang Dietze.   373 © Dzielak/The
Image Bank.   380 © 1985 Doug Handell /The Stock
Market.   386 © James Jackson/TSW.   399 H. Armstrong
Roberts/Camerique.   432 EVA'S ALMA MATER (detail)
© 1988 Deidre Scherer.   435 © 1991 Scazzoza/FPG.   443
H. Armstrong Roberts/Camerique.   450 © 1981 by
Edward Koren. From *Teenage Romance: Or How to Die of
Embarrassment* by Delia Ephron. Used by permission of
Viking Penguin, a division of Penguin Books USA, Inc.
457 © 1989 Michael Salas/The Image Bank.   467 I WON
HER IN A FIGHT 1991 Dale Rayburn Collection of Dr.
Ben Forbes.   488 Jacket cover painting by David McCall
Johnston from *The Hero and the Crown* by Robin McKinley.
Illustration copyright © 1984 by David McCall Johnston.
Reprinted by permission of Greenwillow Books, a division
of William Morrow & Company, Inc.   489, left Cover
design from *Taking Sides* by Gary Soto, copyright © 1991
by Gary Soto, reproduced by permission of Harcourt,
Brace, Jovanovich, publisher.   489, right *Louisa May: The
World and Works of Louisa May Alcott* by Norma Johnston.
Cover used by permission of The Louisa May Alcott
Memorial Association.   492, 531 Sid Bernstein/Photo
Researchers.   494 Adapted by Robert Voights from set
design by Mark Millmore/Blackstone Theater/De Paul
University, Chicago.   495 Statue of Anne Frank 1959
Pieter d'Hont © 1992. Copyright COSMOPRESS, Geneva
& Anne FRANK-Fonds.   497, 498, 500, 504, 512, 521, 523,
532, 542, 549, 566, 567 © 1992. Copyright COSMO-
PRESS, Geneva & Anne FRANK-Fonds.   503 Collections
of the U.S. Holocaust Memorial Museum in Washington,
D.C.   506 Springer/Bettmann Film Archive.   527© The
Hulton-Deutsch Collection.   561 UPI/Bettmann.   581
Illustration by Petra Mathers.   582 Stock Boston.   596 B.
Taylor/H. Armstrong Roberts.   601 Richard Fukuhara/H.
Armstrong Roberts.   606 T. Ulrich/H. Armstrong Roberts.
611 *The Wilson* fishing fly by Bill Costello.   619, 621, 628,
629 E.T. Archive.   642 *Scorpion*s by Walter Dean Myers.
Cover reprinted by permission of HarperCollins Publishers.
643, right *No Hero for the Kaiser* by Rudolf Frank. German
Reader's Digest Condensed Books; illustrator: Klaus
Steffens.   643, left *Where the Lilies Bloom* by Bill and Vera
Cleaver. Text copyright © 1969 by Bill and Vera Cleaver.
Cover reprinted by permission of HarperCollins Publishers.
646 bottom, 671 © 1975 Graham McCallum.   646, top,
650 Courtesy, U.S. Postal Service.   647 bottom, 707 Brule
Sioux shield with feather decoration. Museum of the
American Indian, New York.   647 middle, 694 Courtesy,
Editorial Piedra Santa.   647 top, 682 Calavera decorated
with animal and plant forms 1990 Felipe Linares Private
collection. Courtesy, Mexican Fine Arts Center Museum,
Chicago.   664, 667 from *American Tall Tales* by Mary Pope
Osborne, wood engravings by Michael McCurdy.
Reprinted by permission of Alfred A. Knopf, Inc.   674
SHAKER BERRY BASKET (detail) 1986 David Brega Oil
on masonite. Courtesy of the artist.   709 Brer Possum ©
Barry Moser from *Jump Again* by Van Dyke Parks, pub-
lished by Harcourt Brace Jovanovich, with permission of
the artist.

The authors and editors have made every effort to trace the
ownership of all copyrighted selections and images found in
this book and to make full acknowledgment for their use.